THE CRUCIAL ROLE OF THE ENVIRONMENT IN THE WRITINGS OF GEORGE STEWART (1895-1980)

THE CRUCIAL ROLE OF THE ENVIRONMENT IN THE WRITINGS OF GEORGE STEWART (1895-1980)

A Life of America's Literary Ecologist

Fred Waage

The Edwin Mellen Press
Lewiston•Queenston•Lampeter

Library of Congress Cataloging-in-Publication Data

Waage, Fred.
The crucial role of the environment in the writings of George Stewart (1895-1980) : a life of America's literary ecologist / Fred Waage.
p. cm.
Includes bibliographical references (p.) [and index].
ISBN-13: 978-0-7734-5757-7
ISBN-10: 0-7734-5757-7
1. Stewart, George Rippey, 1895- 2. Authors, American--20th century--Biography. 3. Environmental protection in literature. 4. Ecology in literature. 5. Nature in literature. 6. Ecocriticism. I. Title.

PS3537.T48545Z86 2006
813'.52--dc22
[B]

2006042368

hors série.

A CIP catalog record for this book is available from the British Library.

Front cover: A. J. Wells, *California for the Settler; the Natural Advantages of the Golden State for the Present Day Farmer*, San Francisco, 1910
Author photo by Deanna Bryant

The Edwin Mellen Press
Box 450
Lewiston, New York
USA 14092-0450

The Edwin Mellen Press
Box 67
Queenston, Ontario
CANADA L0S 1L0

The Edwin Mellen Press, Ltd.
Lampeter, Ceredigion, Wales
UNITED KINGDOM SA48 8LT

Printed in the United States of America

For

Melissa Rose Waage

Princeton Class of 2001

Table of Contents

Preface

Reflecting back on his long and productive writing career, George R. Stewart points to his classic account of the Donner Party, *Ordeal By Hunger* (1936), as the first of his books clearly to develop an environmental theme. As Stewart explains in "Rereading Notes," *Ordeal*'s conflict "is not man against man, but man against nature. In this book and most of the following one I showed an interest in environment, beginning a whole generation before it became fashionable." Among some thirty books that Stewart wrote, a half dozen stand out as especially innovative works in environmental thinking. His novel *Storm* (1941), for example, features a nonhuman central protagonist, a storm name Maria, whose growth and development propels a cast of mostly unnamed human characters into action. *Fire* (1948) again stars a nonhuman agent whose capricious behavior ignites the novel's plot. A lesser known third novel in what Frederick Waage regards as Stewart's ecofiction trilogy is *Sheep Rock* (1951), dominated by Nevada's austere Black Rock Desert, a place where weary emigrants felt utterly dwarfed by immensity and where a latter-day writer struggles to articulate a multi-layered understanding of the place—its deep time, ecology, and human significance. In these three works, nature itself is the central figure as Stewart explores the complexity of natural systems and the multiple threads tying humans to them and to each other in a particular environment. Although originally published in the 1940s and 50s, these novels have an uncanny continuing relevance as natural disasters recur to humble humanity, reminding us anew that nature is not simply a pool of natural resources for human use, nor merely a victim of human abuse, but is itself a powerful actor in human affairs.

A loyal cadre of environmentalists today cite Stewart's futuristic novel *Earth Abides* (1949) as having transformed their thinking. Containing echoes of Ecclesiastes, *Earth Abides* imagines what would happen if a global pandemic wiped out almost all human life. What would happen to the handful of remaining humans, and what would happen to the earth itself? Stewart imagines a re-wilding of the cities and follows a small group of people in the San Francisco Bay Area as they find one another, form a community, adapt to the breakdown of electricity and running water, and evolve from scavengers to gardeners and hunters, reinventing the bow and arrow. As Waage observes, *Earth Abides* reveals "the real vulnerable condition of humanity on the earth, our connection with non-human nature, and or dependence on technological intermediaries for our survival."

Other notable environmental works include Stewart's highly original study *Names on the Land* (1945), a narrative typology of how people have named places in North America. Naming, along with mapping, is viewed as an act of environmental perception, an instance of nature/culture exchange in which, as Waage states, "culture is naturalized and nature is acculturated." In Stewart's "onomatology," further elaborated in his ambitious work *Names on the Globe* (1975), naming is not taming but is, rather, a means of seeing, of individuation. Stewart's experimental *Man: An Autobiography* (1946) is a narrative exposition of Darwinism, told in the first person by the collective "Man," who offers ecological insights such as "I do not exist apart from the outside world but am linked with it . . .I am myself a natural force." While most of Stewart's books are ecological, one of Stewart's last books, *Not So Rich As You Think* (1968), is overtly environmentalist, an extended expose of the various forms and vast amounts of wasted and pollution created by our modern-day consumer culture.

From the standpoint of what Lawrence Buell has called "the environmental imagination," there is so much of value in Stewart's *oeuvre* that it is mystifying why his name is virtually unknown today, even among scholars of environmental literature. Waage speculates that this critical neglect may be due to the fact that Stewart was neither an environmentalist nor a wilderness advocate. He was what Waage dubs a "literary cultural ecologist," interested in the vast workings of nature and the human links to it, namely, how being embedded in nature has influenced human society and culture, and, conversely, how human adaptations to the environment have affected ecological systems and environmental theory. His was a cool, distanced view—"Gaia-esque," as Waage aptly characterizes it—exhibiting at times even a cosmic perspective. Stewart once described himself as a "chronicler of ecology," a label likely to arouse interest among ecocritics today. However, Stewart's follow-up remark, "and in ecology there isn't any good or bad, really" may represent a point of view too value-free, too politically disengaged, for the predisposition of most socially-conscious literary critics today. To appreciate Stewart requires a kind of dispassionate, "scientific" objectivity that activist-oriented, crisis-motivated ecocritics may feel they cannot afford. Nevertheless, Stewart's works, like those of his contemporary Robinson Jeffers, can teach us to consider a more distanced, philosophical perspective, helping us to take the long view, the truly ecocentric view.

Another reason Waage proposes for Stewart's critical neglect is that his works defy easy categorization. They are often hybrid scholarly-popular works, Stewart himself being a career-long professor of English at the University of California, Berkeley, whose first book was about meter in English poetry, followed by a text on teaching composition. Stewart's stature as a novelist thus may have been tainted by his day job as an academic. Perhaps more importantly, Stewart's works fall outside existing genre conventions, and they draw upon many disciplines, including anthropology, geography, biology, sociology, and meteorology. These very qualities of hybridity, unconventionality, and multi-disciplinarity are precisely who Stewart's work may be poised for renewed critical attention today.

Frederick O. Waage brings the distinguished career of George R. Stewart to light. Waage's critical biography, the first book-length study of Stewart, discusses nearly all of Stewart's books and many of his articles, giving special attention to the environmental thread that runs through them and to those works most explicitly ecological in design. Waage's helpful summaries make his study easy to follow even if one is new to Stewart. He does a good job of tracing early influences on Stewart, of placing Stewart in the context of leading ecologist of his day, such as Eugene Odum, and of charting the influence of Stewart's close colleagues at UC Berkeley—geographer Carl Sauer, and anthropologists Alfred Kroeber and Robert Lowie, as well as the Berkeley-trained anthropologist Julian Steward, founder of cultural ecology. Thus, a strength of Waage's study is its illumination of 1940s and 50s intellectual currents, along with Stewart's contributions to them. Stewart's publications resonated in the historical moment in which they appeared, be it the Great Depression, World War II, or the Atomic Age. Waage ably places reviews of his work in historical context. Despite their mid-century origins, however, Stewart's works address concerns alive today. Climate change. Urban environments. Bioregions. Community. Pollution. Pandemics. Natural disasters. Survival. Technology. Adaptation to change. The complex linkages between nature and culture. These things are still worth pondering. Waage's book will make you want to read Stewart's books, not only for their historical interest, but for their enduring insights about the human condition on earth.

Cheryll Glotfelty, Ph.D.
Professor of English
University of Nevada, Reno

Acknowledgements

I am grateful to my wife, Virginia Renner, for her patience, support, and encouragement; to my daughter, Melissa Waage, Policy Advocate of the Center for Biological Diversity, for professional and personal inspiration, and for renewing my involvement with George R. Stewart through *Earth Abides*, which impelled her own career; and to my son, Frederick R. Waage, West Point class of 2007, for his generosity and exemplary fortitude; Branna, Leif, Faye, Ki, Gamine, and Tam Lin for keeping me awake at the computer.

John Stewart, Don Scott, and John Forester have been generous in their advice and information about Stewart. Dayton O. Hyde, Ernest Callenbach, James Cahalan, and Donald Dewey sent me valuable information.

The curators of Stewart materials at various libraries have gone out of their way to be of assistance. I can't name everyone, but particularly want to acknowledge the assistance of the following: Mane Hakopyan, Shatford Library and Archives, Pasadena City College; Margaret Rich and AnnaLee Pauls, Rare Books and Special Collections, Princeton University Library; Susan Snyder and many others at the Bancroft Library, and Richard Smith and staff of the Regional Oral History Project, University of California, Berkeley; Karen Jania, Bentley Historical Library, University of Michigan; John Hurlburt and Lori Work, East Bay Municipal Utility District, Berkeley, CA; Ray Wright and David Stead, C. S. Forester Society; staff of the Columbia University Library, Houghton Library, Harvard University, Harry Ransom Humanities Research Library, University of Texas, Austin.

I appreciate the opportunity given me by John Rupnow and Mrs. Patricia Schultz of the Edwin Mellen Press to bring to light the work of George R. Stewart.

The following are published with permission of the Princeton University Library; all are located in the Manuscripts Division, Department of Rare Books and Special Collections, Princeton University Library:

From the George R. Stewart Alumni File: references on pages 37, 42, 72; Correspondence: C.M. Gayley to Radcliffe Heermance 4. Mar. 1922; George R. Stewart to Radcliffe Heermance, 14 Feb. 1920, 7 Jan. 1922; Radcliffe Heermance to George R. Stewart 17 Apr. 1922; A. N. Rondith to Radcliffe Heermance, 16 Feb. 1922; Shirley W. Smith to Robert C. Clothier, 23 Sept. 1926; Robert C. Clothier to Thomas Marc Parrott, 20 Sept. 1926; Thomas Marc Parrott to Robert C. Clothier, n.d.

From the Charles Scribner's Sons Papers: George R. Stewart to Robert Scribner's Sons, 13 Jan. 1919; Lloyd Osbourne to Robert Bridges, 15 May, 1920.

From the Henry Holt and Company Papers: George R. Stewart to Richard Thornton, 26 Nov. 1934, 222 Oct. 1936, 29 Dec. 1936, 2 Oct. 1937, 5 Dec. 1938, 5 Dec. 1939; Richard Thornton to George R. Stewart, 9 Apr. 1936, 20 Oct. 1936, 12 Nov., 1936, 30 Sept. 1937; George R. Stewart to Publicity Department, Henry Holt and Company, 6 Feb. 1936; George R. Stewart to William Sloane, 18 Mar. 1935.

From the Christian Gauss Papers: Christian Gauss to George R. Stewart, 25 Aug. 1943, 15 May 1935.

From the Willard Thorp Papers: George R. Stewart to Willard Thorp, 21 Feb. 1942.

From the Saxe Commins Papers: George R. Stewart to Saxe Commins, 29 July, 1956, 7 Oct. 1953, 29 July 1956, 7 Oct. 1956, 11 Jan. 1957, 27 June 1957; Saxe Commins to George R. Stewart, 8 Mar. 1948.

From the Allen Tate Papers: George R. Stewart to Allen Tate, 19 Feb. 1961.

Used by permission of the Regional Oral History Office, Bancroft Library, University of California, Berkeley:

Stewart, George R. *A Little of Myself*. Typescript of an oral history conducted 1971-1972 by Suzanne B. Riess, Regional History Office, The Bancroft Library, University of California, Berkeley, 1972, 319 pp. (Interview IX, pp. 254-298 is a joint interview with George R. Stewart and Charles Camp).

All parenthetical citations to *Little* are from the above volume and are used courtesy of The Bancroft Library.

Used by permission of the Bentley Historical Library, University of Michigan:

Two photographic images, wedding of George R. Stewart and Theodosia Burton, Marion Leroy Burton Collection.

Used by permission of University Archives, Department of Rare Books and Special Collections, Princeton University Library:

Photographic image, Princeton University Class of 1917.

All citations in the text designated by an "R" (see below) in the parenthetical reference are used by permission of the Harry Ransom Humanities Research Center, The University of Texas at Austin.

All undesignated citations from correspondence, and all citations from "Random "Thoughts on Doom," "Autobiography," "Rereading Notes," "American Riots before Watts," "If," "Historical Attitudes Toward the California Environment," "Ecological Eclogues," and "Greek Colonies and the American Colonies" are from the George R. Stewart Collection and are printed by permission of the Bancroft Library, University of California, Berkeley.

All citations with an "N" or an "L" in parentheses are from the John Francis Neylan and Benjamin Lehman Collections, respectively, and are printed by permission of the Bancroft Library, University of California, Berkeley.

Used by permission of the Bancroft Library, University of California, Berkeley:

Photographic image, George R. Stewart with Sheep Rock pitcher.

Citations from Ernest Callenbach's preface to the Heyday Press edition of *Storm* are printed with the permission of Heyday Press.

All citations from books by George R. Stewart for which Dr. John H. Stewart holds the copyright are used by permission of Dr. John H. Stewart.

A Note on Permissions

The copyright status of many works by George R. Stewart is extremely confused. As a result it has been impossible for me to determine whose permission is required for use of material from a number of texts written by Stewart. Therefore, I have had to assume that citations from texts written by Stewart himself are covered by the principle of fair use.

Note on Documentation

All manuscript and unpublished materials cited in the text are, unless otherwise noted, in the George R. Stewart Collections at the Bancroft Library, University of California, Berkeley, CA.

Parenthetically cited correspondence is not also listed in the Bibliography.

The location of parenthetically-cited correspondence not in the Bancroft library is indicated by a backslash and a capital letter within the parentheses following the citation. The other locations are indicated as follows:

/B	East Bay Municipal Utility District, Berkeley, CA
/H	Houghton Library, Harvard University
/L	Benjamin Lehman Collection, Bancroft Library
/N	John Francis Neylan Collection, Bancroft Library
/P	Princeton University Library; Seeley G. Mudd Library, Princeton University
/R	Harry Ransom Humanities Research Library, University of Texas

Stewart's manuscript "Autobiography" is referred to parenthetically as "A" and his manuscript "Rereading Notes" as "Rereading Notes;" materials from his file at the Seeley G. Mudd Historical Library at Princeton are referenced parenthetically "Alumni File."

Introduction

The purpose of this introduction is triple: to provide a personal introduction to the writer who is the subject of this study, George R. Stewart (1895-1980), characterizing him as an environmental writer; to discuss the reasons why his work has received so little attention, given its importance as environmental writing, by ecocriticism; and to locate it in the context of 20th century ecological thought.

*

In 1944, an enthusiastic Penn State undergraduate, "Chick C., " wrote to novelist George R. Stewart, calling his novel *Storm* "the best book I ever read," and saying that because of it he planned to study meteorology.

Thirty-three years later, the same writer sent another letter to Stewart, recalling that "as a teen-age fan of STORM, I bothered you with fan letters," and telling him "how enormously important to my life STORM was." The second letter included an ad for the writer's own novel, *Ecotopia*. The letter-writer was the author of that environmental classic, Ernest Callenbach (Callenbach to Stewart, 11 Aug 1944; 17 Jan 1977). Today, Callenbach remembers this correspondence, and says "I find that [Stewart's novel] *Earth Abides* comes up in conversation at least once a year. The paperback was very popular hereabouts with young people for a while. Talk about cosmic melancholia . . ." (Ernest Callenbach, Email to the author 25 June 2005).

Callenbach's sixty-year engagement with Stewart's work is just one example of the passion that work has aroused in readers. It also exemplifies how unjustifiable is the relative oblivion into which Stewart's *oeuvre* has been cast.

My own testimony is similar to Callenbach's. It was not its "cosmic melancholia" that first drew me, as a teenager in the 1950's, to *Earth Abides*: I wasn't mature enough to entertain the concept. What it revealed to me was the truly vulnerable condition of humanity on the earth, our connection with non-human nature, and our dependence on technological intermediaries for survival.

Obviously, the appeal of *Earth Abides* to my generation was enhanced by the "shadow of the bomb," the shadowless menace of polio, the *demon de midi* of excessive security, although Stewart's vision of humanity decimated by plague in that novel did not seek overtly to evoke any of these. However, in Stewart's realm of concern, ecology, the same type of postwar *angst* was manifesting itself, and perhaps influenced him: "Ecologists experienced fragmentation, revolution, and rebellion, as well as growth in their science" (Barbour 248). The traditional conservation movement was being challenged by a new activism, represented in figures like David Brower. Traditional "climax ecology," as preached by Frederic Clements, was being challenged by new research casting in doubt its equilibristic theories. Evidence of environmental deterioration had brought into question the "gospel of success." As Samuel Ordway said, "Success has led us to believe that the earth is a cornucopia, and the machine a god. It has led us to a false faith in man's omnipotence" (Neimark 171).

But, in counterbalance to this mood, Stewart's tales of human survival, in *Storm* and *Fire,* were inspiring to readers of the 1940's and 1950's. These tales demonstrated the triumphant salvation of humans, through collective action, from uncontrollable environmental menace. In context, all of these fictions, inspirational or desperational, jarred those of us "maturing in complacency," and forced us to look "uncomfortably to the world we [would] inherit. They made us feel that, like their protagonists, we would need to "take the responsibility for encounter and resolution. . .because of our common peril" ("Port Huron"), since "Many of the hallowed systems of the land were in disarray" (Sale 12).

It was easy, nonetheless, to "mature in complacency," as I did in the early 1960's at Stewart's *alma mater*, Princeton University. As a graduate student at the same institution, I did encounter his work again indirectly, through the mythical status of his archetypal grad-student novel, *Doctor's Oral*, and, later, through the presence in the university bookstore of high-profile displays for his environmentalist diatribe, *Not So Rich as You Think*. The latter was published in the year of the Santa Barbara oil spill, the Cuyahoga River in flames, and the creation of the Environmental Protection Agency.

Then came the "decade of the environment" following 1970's Earth Day. The decade's "doomsday chord" (Sale 30) was in harmony with Stewart's "cosmic melancholia," and most of his books, headed by *Earth Abides*, were reissued in paperback at the decade's outset. I still treasure that edition of *Earth Abides*, and it became my environmentalist daughter's favorite book. Little did I know, during my own brief career as a "professional" environmentalist (with David Brower's Friends of the Earth in 1974), that the author of *Earth Abides* was living just a short distance away from the FOE office in San Francisco.

Time and the 1970's passed. Stewart died in 1980, just as the environmental presence was rising in literature, under the name, coined by William Rueckert in 1978, of "ecocriticism." My own anthology *Teaching Environmental Literature* (1985) was an early contribution to the movement. But as the accepted canon of environmental literature, from Thoreau to Edward Abbey (fellow native to Stewart of Indiana, Pennsylvania) expanded, I realized Stewart's work had no place in it. His books were out of print, he was not the subject of any significant critical study, people deeply involved in the environmental literature movement hardly knew his name. And yet Stewart had written an epic survival narrative about the Donner Party, *Ordeal by Hunger*; a classic novel of environmental dystopia, *Earth Abides*; three pioneering ecocentric novels with nonhuman entities as protagonists—*Fire, Storm,* and *Sheep Rock*; and a prescient muckraking text, *Not So Rich As You Think*. I was determined to bring his distinguished career to light, but also sought to understand why it had been so unrecognized.

*

I've come up with a number of responses to the above question. They may say something about, why ecocriticism, however devoted to "breaking boundaries" ecocriticism is, it still has a long way to go.

Stewart as a writer defies easy categorization. Throughout his career he experimented with new forms and multimedia texts. His writing exists outside of any generic comfort zones. Because of its diversity, because it draws on knowledge of so many different disciplines, it is hard to find a critical schema in which to discuss it as a whole.

He was not an environmental*ist,* and didn't consort with them. Only once, to my knowledge, did he participate in any environmental action. Though their contemporary, he was not intimate with any of the prewar circle defined by the Wilderness Society, or the postwar one defined by the Sierra Club. He was too old to associate with 1970's movement figures, and too reserved to cross the academic/activist line as did numerous academic acquaintances such as Wallace Stegner. Despite his many leadership roles in clubs and organizations, and his powerful presence as an opponent of the California Loyalty Oath, he was not clubbable with the writers contemporary ecocritics look up to, such as Carson, Leopold, and Krutch.

Stewart was a professor to his fingertips. Although his literary success allowed him, fairly early in his career, the liberty to teach half-time, he enjoyed living in the groves of academe. Although he wrote lots of articles for mass-circulation media, he enjoyed writing scholarly articles for academic periodicals. As "professor" he became typecast against the grain of his actual literary achievement. Even as "professor" of English, his closest professional associates were not other professors of English who wrote literary texts, but anthropologists, sociologists, ethnologists, and other multidisciplinary scholars.

Most importantly, Stewart was not a "tree-hugger." He was not a wilderness advocate. He didn't own a farm. He didn't go to Washington to lobby for environmental causes. He repeatedly calls himself an "ecologist"—but in the "old sense," not the activist new sense of the environmental decade.

To understand that he could be an "ecologist" without doing the things that it was politically correct for "ecologists" to do, one needs to understand in what "old sense" he was such.

*

This understanding could begin with George Perkins Marsh's question of whether humans are "'of nature or above her,'" and his conclusion that they "were above nature, exerting an influence on nature that was different in character from that of other animals . .humans were free moral agents working independently of nature." In tandem, by virtue of this very freedom, "Humans had to become co-workers with nature in the reconstruction of [its] damaged fabric" (Kingsland 9). Therefore, despite his religious caveats, Marsh was implicitly questioning "the distinction between nature and culture fundamental to humanistic disciplines . . ." (Merchant 143).

"Ecology" (in the U.S.) developed ideological and experiential complexity in the earlier 20th century, a development paralleling the expansion of the human domain. So, while we can accept perhaps Merchant's assertion that "in America the nature-culture dichotomy was basic to the tension between civilization and the frontier in westward expansion and helped to justify the continuing exploitation of nature's resources" (143-144), early 20th century ecological thought tended to undermine this dichotomy. Marsh's question involved—for such founding ecologists as Tansley, Huntington, Clements, Cowles, Malin—"How far could one go in 'biologizing' the study of humans and folding human ecology into the broader study of adaptation and evolution that defined general ecology" (Kingsland 131). Once Arthur Tansley's original concept of "ecosystem" became "the center of ecological study" (Kingsland 189), particularly under the "systems ecology" promoted by Thomas and Eugene Odum, the same question evolved yet further. Were human-dominated systems "foldable into" ecosystems? Could an ecosystem, as well as "a lake, a forest, or a grassland," be "the entire biosphere, or a city, a nuclear power plant and surrounding region, or even a single household [?]" (Kingsland 198-99).

The kernel of concern at the center of all these rephrased questions was this relationship of "nature" to "culture," or, in Kingsland's figure, whether (human) "culture" can be "folded into" "nature." It seems that this simply-phrased, yet perhaps ultimately unanswerable question is and will be fundamental to the premises of most social and ecological sciences. From the 20th century sociologist's point of view, "sociology had to decide whether it was to be a social science or largely an appendage to biological ecology." As a result, through midcentury ". . .human beings were increasingly regarded as exempt from the normal run of naturalistic explanation applied everywhere around them. Any effort to introduce things nonsocial into the equation seemed to threaten the very survival of the sociological enterprise itself" (Gross 596). "Few scientists have perceived people or human societies as being integral parts of their ecosystems" (Worster "Appendix" 297), but one social science has—anthropology. And among anthropologists, particularly those of the "Berkeley School," deriving from Franz Boas at Columbia "No one did more to found the ecological study of culture than Julian Steward" (300), the namer and originator of "cultural ecology."

Steward, born in 1902, was deeply influenced by his secondary school education at Deep Springs Prep in the Owens Valley of eastern California. He spent his freshman college year, and later his graduate school years, at Berkeley, as student of its great anthropologists Alfred Kroeber and Robert Lowie. He got his Ph.D. in anthropology from Berkeley in 1929. Although Steward's professional life was led elsewhere, he was, like Stewart, deeply attached to the vivid 1920's intellectual community in Berkeley, which he always considered his intellectual "home" (Murphy 5). Although his academic career was migratory, Steward was consumed by interest in the Native American culture of the Great Basin desert, based on his Deep Springs experience. According to Murphy, Steward's *Basin-Plateau Aboriginal Social Groups* (1938) is "one of the great classics of descriptive analysis in anthropology" and "required reading for anyone who pretends to having a serious thought about ecology" (5). For

Steward, the desert Shoshoni "became the model of men at the threshold of survival" (6). Their terrain is that of Stewart's most ecocentric novel, *Sheep Rock*, a novel in part about humans on the threshold of survival. Steward's observational conclusions about aboriginal adaptation in the above text apply to Stewart's imaginative work. For example, Steward identified "multiple subsistence" among the Shoshoni, with different alimentary adaptations to different "microenvironments" within the Basin-Plateau region as determined by the "biotic zones" at different altitudes ("Foundations" 371). In *Storm, Fire*, and other Sierran writings, Stewart similarly defines as of crucial importance the effects of differences in biotic zones on animal behavior and on human behavior and human use of technology for survival.

I thus present George R. Stewart as a literary cultural ecologist. This assertion is not to be taken in the sense that he was an explicit follower or member of a "school of Steward." Steward was opposed, in fact, to excessive systematization of his ideas. He "viewed cultural ecology as a research agenda rather than a religious dogma" (Moore 198). In much of the following text I will not recur constantly to Steward's writings as some kind of critical template. Rather, I consider Stewart's view of humanity's place in nature as found in his imaginative writing, to be in close agreement with Steward's definition of cultural ecology, just as is that of his college friend Chauncey Leake, in his medical and philosophical writing: "we are part of a generalized dynamic equilibrium which includes life, and which operates within the circumscribed limits of the physical factors of this world" (19). Given this premise, one cannot fold Stewart's writings into Carolyn Merchant's generalization that "Much of American literature is founded on the underlying assumption of the superiority of culture to nature" (144). Although jargonesque, William Paulson's definition of cultural ecology seems to have the comprehensiveness appropriate to Stewart's work:

> . . .[T]he networks of relations by which human activity is linked to a natural environment that both constraints and is altered by it, and by which specific activities such as critical or intellectual interventions take

place (and must be understood as taking place) in a dynamic, situated relation to socio-cultural contexts. (27)

With reservations, Steward's cultural ecology is conceptually totalistic in the "old sense." Unfortunately, since the encompassment of culture within nature, as conceived by Steward, could lead its proponent in the direction of often ecocritically demonized figures such as William Cronon and Patricia Limerick, Stewart is in danger of being, if considered ecologically relevant at all, constructed as an ally of the Enemy. So one needs to understand that cultural ecology is not at the top of a slippery slope toward justifying environmental destruction.

In the above interest, my introduction here to cultural ecology will initially be taken from a lucid expositor of Steward. "Cultural Ecology studies the interactions of societies with one another and with the natural environment, in order to comprehend those processes of adaptation and transformation that operate to alter social institutions, human behavior, and environment" (English and Mayfield 116). Thus an ecosystem contains an "entire range of social and natural phenomena. . .disposing of the artificial separation of culture and nature." Steward ". . .defines cultural ecology as the study of those processes by which a society adapts to its environment." But he denies that any "universal statement" can be made about the functioning of these processes. One can analyze only particular cases of ". . .the relationships between environment and exploitative technology, those patterns of human behavior involved in environmental exploitation, and the relationships between these behavioral patterns and other elements of culture" (117). This formulation is basic to the continuing argument between Steward and his fellow anthropologist Leslie White, since Steward "found White's belief that all environments could be averaged untenable, for in Steward's experience cultural differences were in part a function of the environment" (Peace 167).

In Steward's own words, "Cultural ecology differs from human and social ecology in seeking to explain the origin of particular cultural features and patterns which characterize different areas rather than to derive general principles applicable to any culture-environment situation" (*Theory* 36). "Although the concept of environmental adaptation underlies all cultural ecology" (39), particular cultural and environmental features of particular cases are the cultural ecologist's concern. Thus, taking an example from Stewart, the successes and failures of the Donner Party's snowbound community at adapting to its environment are based on totally different factors than those governing the Confederate and Union forces' adaptations to the physical environment of the Pickett's Charge battlefield. But what "happens" in each case can be analyzed based on ecosystemic circumstances encompassing the emigrants' society and their nonhuman environment, or the soldiers' society and theirs. Like Steward, Stewart is neither a cultural nor an environmental determinist. "Humans through culture transform the natural landscape; the object of study is the cultural landscape, not culture (Norton 38). For Steward "the ecological approach in anthropology recognized the unity of humans and nature and noted that each was to be defined in terms of the other" (144).

I suppose it would be hard to find any imaginative environmental writing that does not in some sense relate to cultural ecology as defined above. The real question is the one Marsh originally addressed, that of the autonomy of human culture. Stewart's writing explores what humans "do to" nature, for sure, but only as partially a function of what nature "does to" them. Human perpetration is partly the result of nonhuman perpetration upon humans.

Robert Bunting, discussing early Oregon settlement, says "As the systematic ordering of the landscape reduced ecological diversity, and nature was converted into segmented parts, the dissociation between nature's wealth and human wealth became easier. The market economy rather than nature's economy increasingly governed the regional landscape" (431). I suggest that this is the kind of environmental change that allows the agency of human culture, here in the form of "human wealth" and "market economy," to be wrongly perceived as autonomous perpetrator acting somehow "outside of" nature.

Murray Bookchin, promoter of "Social Ecology," can, on such a premise, assert "Nearly all the nonhuman life forms that exist today are, like it or not, to some degree in human custody, and whether they are preserved in their wild lifeways depends largely on human attitudes and behavior" (31). The bent of all Stewart's writing is against this view; he might say that human life forms, as well, are partly in nonhuman custody.

Ecological historians themselves do not adopt the perpetrator mentality. Those I have read are concerned with transforming the nature-culture dichotomy into a "dialogue" (Ingerson 65) and conceiving nature as a "multileveled totality" (Patterson 232). Crossover anthropologists, also, find cultural ecology to have theoretical importance. Hardesty expresses this in terms of "reciprocal causality"—". . .the idea that neither environment nor culture is a 'given,' but that each is defined in terms of the other, and the idea that environment plays an active, not just a limiting or selective, role in human affairs" (8-9). Bennett, who bases his *Ecological Transition* on Steward's work, sees him as seeking to reconceive "the ecology of humans" not as a "separate descriptive discipline" in the mode of his mentor Alfred Kroeber, but as a production of "biological adaptation to environment and how it is affected by this adaptation" (213). Even Patricia Limerick, if her ecological theory is not seen through its environmental justice or wise use lenses, is very much akin to Steward's:

> The landscape . . .has a number of layers, all demanding the scholar's attention: rock and soil; plants and animals; humans as a physical presence, manifested in the accumulated stories of their encounter with a place. Our attention and curiosity here cannot be exclusive. One can glimpse the full power of a place only in the full story of human presence there. ("Disorientation" 1026)

However, it seems to me that in the literary realm, contemporary ecocritical theory, if it is concerned at all with nature-culture issues, leans in Bookchin's direction. Certainly it is hard to find ecocritical reference to cultural ecology, Julian Steward, or theory akin to his. The excellent studies in Steven Rosendale's *The Greening of Literary Scholarship* are presented under the aegis of "Extending Ecocriticism," but this process seems to be defined as "expanding the purview of ecocritical practice by widening the canon of texts for ecocritical investigation and placing environmental criticism in a more productive relation with other, *perhaps suspiciously humanistic* [italics mine], theoretic perspectives and critical practices" (xvii). In Glen Love's significant *Practical Ecocriticism*, the nature-culture concern is to refute "cultural constructionism,' in the form of William Cronon's totalization of the "human domain," which "plays into the hands of the destroyers" (21). Lawrence Buell seems to see the future of ecocriticism involved in different subdisciplines of advocacy. He is certainly correct to say the "environmentality" can be "the property of any text" (25), but to state that "Environmental criticism arises within and against the history of human modification of planetary space . . ." (62) is to privilege and autonomize "culture" ("human modification") with respect to nature, a position antithetical to Stewart and to Steward. In fact, one could argue that to characterize environmental criticism as requiring this culture-dominant backdrop is to move, paradoxically, in the direction of the "poststructural paradigm," "totalizing language and culture" (Carroll 50) while proclaiming the opposite. Dana Phillips, of course, considers this to be a fatal flaw in ecocriticism *and* in the science of ecology itself, whose conceptual framework "rests largely on a number of overstatements made by its popularizers" (45). Paulson acknowledges the difficulty that "humanities professors," "natives or naturalized citizens of print cultures," have in "adapting their bodies and minds" to the "unfamiliar and often disconcerting environments" of "contemporary science and philosophy." But he sees a necessity of doing what Stewart as a writer was about doing his whole career, expressing "at a deep level the ecological situation of our culture . . ." (34).

Karl Kroeber seems to me the only prominent ecocritic who approaches the nature-culture issue in the spirit of Steward. In his view, ecological literary criticism must consider works as "dynamic participants in a constantly self-transforming historical environment . . ," whereas much of it today is "enfeebled by reliance (largely unconscious) upon postromantic but now obsolete scientific ideas" (25). "The ecocriticism I am advocating asks that we examine poetry from a perspective that assumes the imaginative acts of cultural beings proffer valuable insights into how and who cultural and natural phenomena have interrelated and could more advantageously interrelate" (140). For Kroeber, ecological awareness, "essential to preventing the insanity of [human] suicide, whether through weaponry, pollution, or sheer overpopulation," must include consideration of self-destructive cultural practices, the "intricate play of contingent human and natural events . . ." (152-3).

In connection with ecocriticism, it is important to note the absence of Stewart, (not to mention Steward) in almost all studies, even those directly relevant to his literary concerns. While, as we will see, Stewart's work is cartographically rich, and his texts are full of maps, he is mentioned in Rick Van Noy's *Surveying the Interior: Literary Cartography and the Sense of Place* only as a source, through his *Names on the Land*, for the implicit cartography in Wallace Stegner's work—which contains much less explicit mapping (140). Despite all of Stewart's literary involvement with the Sierras, he is not mentioned in Corey Lee Lewis's *Reading the Trail: Exploring the Literary and Natural History of the California Crest.* There is probably good reason however, why Phillips does not mention Stewart in his notorious *The Truth of Ecology*, since one of his main arguments is that nature writing is not revolutionary, but reactionary: "Ecocritics and nature writers need to recognize that there is nothing original, and thus nothing revolutionary, about the hope for a national literature redeemed by its fidelity to nature" (237). As suggested above, Stewart is ignored partly because the revolutionary diversity of his literary forms disconcert the critics.

Even in the "other" culture, ecology itself, Steward and cultural ecology aren't mentioned in the two most recent histories of U.S. ecology, by Sharon Kingsland and Joel Hagen. In a provocative essay on historical geography, Michael Williams does refer to the Berkeley School of geographers as concerned with "how culture and nature were linked by adaptive strategies and how successful adaptations led to cultural success." But he defines cultural ecology as different, in that "it emphasizes cultural processes instead of analyzing the impacts of humans on the environment or visible landscape" (114). (I don't really see this distinction. As literary voice of the Berkeley School, Stewart, in my view, emphasized both, while remaining a cultural ecologist). Williams also sees a threat in the invasion of systems ecology by destabilizing ideologies such as chaos theory. This "new ecology," as anti-system, "calls attention to the instability, disequilibrium and chaotic fluctuations that characterize many environmental systems as it challenges the primordial assumption of systems ecology . . ." (Zimmerer 109).

I wonder if Stewart's ecological fictions might be comprehensive enough to follow both the "old" and these "new" ways at the same time. In *Fire* the firefighters' culture interacts with the fire and the forest in a totalized way, but the fire itself is caused by instability and disequilibrium, even literally. Atmospheric physics may explain lightning, but I doubt any systems analysis can really explain the sequence of events the lightening strike creates in the novel: smouldering pine needles, a single burning twig, an exploding pine cone, creeping smoulder toward another cone resting against a twig, a burning through the twig, a toppling of the cone, its rolling downhill spreading fire as it goes. "If it had been the tiny cone of a Douglas fir, it would have lodged in some little roughness of the ground . . ." (105). But since it is a round Jeffrey Cone, it becomes destabilized, and keeps on rolling.

*

A few caveats about my treatment of Stewart's career on the following pages.

Since his work has become so unfamiliar to many people, I have done more summarizing of his works themselves than would be appropriate in a critical study of a better-known writer.

I have tried to discuss Stewart's work as a "literary ecologist," by bringing into the discussion of his works references and ideas from different ecologically-related disciplines progressively as the discussion proceeds. The reader should not expect a highly-structured topic-driven text. My purpose is both to show Stewart as a "literary ecologist" and as an interesting human being in himself.

The initial chapter covers Stewart's childhood, youth, and young adulthood so that the reader can become familiar with him. It does not try to situate these early phases of his life in an "ecological" context.

I have taken the liberty of referring to myself in the first person, when recounting personal experience that relates to Stewart's work.

Chapter I

Indiana to Berkeley

A future veteran, he was born "at 3 A.M." the day after Veterans' Day, May 31, 1895, in "a brick house on the southwest corner of Grant and Thorne Streets" in Sewickley, Pennsylvania, "a borough of nearly 5000 inhabitants, on the bank of the Ohio River, twelve miles below Pittsburg [sic]" (Ellis 17). Characterized by Stewart as a "western suburb of Pittsburgh" (A), Sewickley was, in fact, a "railroad suburb," "distanced from the city, distinguished by an elite dominant class, semirural in orientation, and mixed socioeconomically". In the era of Stewart's birth, the railroad suburb "stood as a model for success" (K. Jackson 102) despite its large proportion of the working poor, many of whom serviced the needs of the elite families of "affluent businessmen" (101).

Vocal Sewickley when Stewart was born didn't acknowledge its socioeconomic mix. Self-describedly characterized in *Sewickley Valley Society* (1895), as quoted by Hardie (50), it was ". . . a place beyond the admission of trades and the realm of the vast industries that darken the sky above the Iron City [Pittsburgh] and fill its vicinity with the eternal din of a million noises." Hence, Stewart's father could have been seen by Sewickley Society if not by himself, as a "failure" when he moved his family East (Stewart surmises on April 1, 1897), to his wife's more rural home town of Indiana. "[A] primary reason for the move was certainly economy, my father having lost heavily, as had many others, in the recent financial troubles [i.e., the depression of 1893, which struck the railroads particularly hard]" (A). He had "made money in the natural-gas business around Pittsburgh," so, his son says, "his wealth was apparently exaggerated in the popular mind" (A).

Although Stewart apparently had no conscious memories of Sewickley itself, he must have been influenced by awareness of the family's history there. Responding to a letter from Stewart, Robinson Jeffers wrote "What you say about Sewickly [sic] and the nearness of our families there interests me much" (Jeffers to Stewart 24 Oct 1938). Sewickley was (and, apparently still is) seen as the archetypal "rich man's suburb" (Hardie 58), but it was a close-knit grid-based project expanded by successive developers. Therefore, it was not hard for its residents, whatever their assets, to access its stores, clustered in "small town" manner, around the main drag, Beaver Street. Stewart's mother Ella could well have patronized the Sewickley Pharmacy, "Prescription and Family recipes a specialty," Mrs. Jennie Gibb's dressmaking and millinery shop, or Lou Matterer's "unisex" barber shop with its private entrance for ladies (Ellis 311-14).

This doubleness of identity—urban dependency yet iconic autonomy—was replicated in the duality of the "rich man's" secular pursuits and the multiclass Presbyterian fundamentalism which dominated its civic life (as it did in Indiana and much of western Pennsylvania). While sectarian debate flourished over whether running a "church train" on Sunday was unacceptable "worldly employment," or whether organ music should be allowed in church services, Sewickleyites joined the many (secular) clubs that sprang up in the 1880's and 1890's, such as the Sewickley Athletic Association, or the Sewickley Valley Wheelmen (bicyclists), and they turned out *en masse* for the opening of Sewickley's first racetrack, the day before the birth of George Stewart, Jr. (Hardie 66-80). Writing in 1893, Agnes Ellis boasts "We have an opera house now [for the] entertainment of the people in their thirst for pleasure . . .some of the people who once frowned down a dance, and thought it a sin to wear a bow of ribbon on their bonnets being seen within its [the opera house's] walls in holiday attire" (290).

Interestingly, in much of Stewart's fiction and nonfiction, these paired dualities of condition figure strongly: idealized community autonomy is contradicted by (benevolent and malevolent) technological dependency; religious belief is a dynamo (to allude Henry Adams) but is always trumped by the dynamics of human physical needs and pleasures, and the power of an encompassing nature.

Sewickley also figures interestingly in Stewart's penultimate book, *Names on the Globe*. Back in 1893, Ellis wonders (uncritically) at the changes wrought since the community's first settlement: ". . . the tread of many feet on the streets where once the echo of [early settler Henry Ulery's] footsteps sent the timid deer fleeing to a place of safety . . ." (308). But for Stewart, Sewickley existed before Henry Ulery and before "Sewickley:" ". . . place-names enshrine both the history and the poetry of man upon the earth, much of his folk-lore, something of his religion" (*NG* 6-7). "[A] Pennsylvania town began with an Indian tribal name and ended as Sewickley, which seem to consist of three common English place-name elements, though again, no such combination exists as an English place-name" (137). Thus, since the individual author first saw light, and the first human set foot and gave name, the place has existed as an ineradicable presence, however much that name evolved.

*

Stewart begins the first chapter, "Into the World," of his autobiography, with a first memory, which may, he says "well be only the memory of a memory." It is of "looking out of a window." He *remembers* looking out of the window but not what he saw through the window. He *knows* that the window is "a large window on the first floor of a house at the corner of Philadelphia . . . Street and Seventh Street in the small town of Indiana, Pennsylvania"—five blocks south of the home of the other famous Indiana Stewart--the actor James (Jimmy) Stewart, born in 1908, the year the Stewart family left Indiana on its epic journey to California.

The window is recalled by the memoirist, seventy-five years later, both literally and figuratively. He would not have remembered what he saw through it, because there was nothing interesting to see, just "a rather broad, small-town street, perhaps inhabited by such then commonplace sights as a pedestrian or two, a horse-and-buggy, and a two-horse wagon" (A). But it was his first realization (at around 22 months) that windows were for seeing through. More figuratively (and perhaps with a tiny tinge of self-satire): "On that day the one half of my professional life began to take shape, for throughout the years and decades that half has been to look through windows, whether real or figurative." Through these windows he saw, and sees, "the pageant of the world." Sometimes through these windows he has beheld "scenes in space, and (what has held my attention even more) I have seen that these scenes changed detail and shifted toward greater and greater complication in time." However, "Then the other and highly active half of my professional life took over, which has been to grasp the pattern of the confusedly-moved pageantry [sic], and then to write it down for others to read . . ." (A).

That this genesis of the author's creative life is a post-genesis construction of the author's imagination really does not compromise its meaningfulness. In this window of memory Stewart sees many of the (openly acknowledged) attributes of his writing career: his cool, judicious, distanced position of observation and his sense of the created world's complexity; and his drive, not to deny this complexity, but to *understand* it, to comprehend its shape and interconnections, and convey this understanding to the reader. Thus, although he does not say so here, he imagines an original vision of the world as a tangled totality of interactions—what he will later (as we will see) consider an *ecological* vision.

Stewart gives great emphasis to the complexity of his childhood experiences in Indiana from 1897 to 1908, although in many ways the town, viewed as a whole, had a harmonious simplicity at the outset of the 20th century. It is in the low Appalachian foothills, fifty miles east of Pittsburgh, "Far from the tightly clustered urban breeding grounds that nurtured a nation of immigrants and people on the move . . .a quiet, remarkably homogenous [sic]small town . . . . . . It was neat and well ordered with stately Victorian homes and a solid middle-class population, mostly God-fearing Presbyterians of Scotch-Irish descent" (Fishgall 15, 19). Although, in the negative, "habitually gloomy skies have saddled the entire region with a reputation as 'the biggest natural darkroom in the world'" and it has suffered from a "silent problem," a "deep current of racism and anti-Semitism" (Dewey 39, 42). Stewart himself says that "Far from having any anti-Semitism, I did not even know that it existed. . ." (A). He readily admits that in Indiana "the most fortunate situation in the world was to be an American of Scotch-Irish and Presbyterian background" (A). This given, Stewart's memories are of a community more like the one described by another famous semi-native Indiana writer, Edward Abbey, as quoted by Jim Cahalan from Abbey's *Appalachian Wilderness*:

> "There was the town set in the cup of the green hills. In the Alleghenies. A town of trees, two-story houses, red-brick hardware stores, church steeples, the clock tower on the county courthouse, and over all the thin blue haze—partly dust, partly smoke, but mostly moisture—that veils the Appalachian world most of the time. The diaphanous veil that conceals nothing." (Cahalan 5).

Stewart's Indiana is remembered as an "environment" by cultural analogy with biology. He likens himself, as child, to a marine animal "completely surrounded by its environment," a previously used figure recycled "because I feel a close fellowship with that animal" (A).

This Indiana was both a stable environment, as in Abbey's vignette, and being altered by new phenomena. One of the hardware stores to which Abbey alludes might have been the one called 'the big warehouse,' J. M. Stewart and Company, run by Jimmy Stewart's father, Alexander, which had been a going enterprise of the same family since 1853 (Busovicki 26). But the famous clocktowered courthouse faced, from 1906 on, a growing streetcar system that brought Indiana County folk increasingly into the town (Wood and Macgregor 52), and that lifeline of Sewickley, the railroad (in this case the Buffalo, Rochester and Pittsburgh Railroad) had brought its first passenger train to Philadelphia Street station on May 2, 1904 (Wood and Macgregor 53). George

Stewart, Sr. was a prime mover in the "street railway" movement; as a member of the committee designated to solicit subscriptions to finance the railway (a headline in the *Indiana Evening Gazette* for February 20, 1906, enthuses in this regard "Now Come On With Your Street Cars" [1, col. 2]).

The Presbyterian Church followed George Stewart around as a constant power, but it too was changing. In Sewickley, the Stewarts had lived across the street from a Presbyterian church and parsonage. He remembers the corner-stone laying for the Second United Presbyterian Church across the street from his home in Indiana—a church built by the separatist traditionalists opposed to organ music (Wood and Macgregor 17). His parents attended church on Sunday, he memorized the Westminster Catechism, and his family shunned cards, alcohol, and dancing. Yet he asserts that he witnessed ". . .the decline and fall of Protestantism. Rapidly, as a few years passed, the whole system went to pieces. We boys successfully revolted against learning the catechism. Sundays loosened up. Family prayers lapsed. So it went" (A).

Such societal changes correlate with those in his own growing consciousness. In the *Autobiography* he finds cascading events which generate new awarenesses and behaviors: conceiving the world as "objective reality," taking "independent action," understanding foresight, and with it the "insidiousness of things," and becoming "conscious of the play of language." This last consciousness is embodied in popular balladry surrounding the Battle of Manila Bay in the Spanish-American War: "He sent the Span-yards/Back to their tan-yards." "I must remember those words from that actual summer, for I think the song too bad a one to have lingered in the popular repertoire for very long." He must have at this point "become conscious of the fascinating non-logical properties of language, as embodied in such a phenomenon as rhyme" (A).

Having surveyed in depth his ancestry, particularly on his mother's side, he finds in heredity "no indication anywhere" of "my imaginative capacity which has enabled me to write novels. . . Apparently that quality sprang from some new shake-up of the chromosomes and genes, or else developed out of a special environment." His discussion of the effects of school (beginning at age six) on his psyche, coupled with the dominance of his older brother Andrew, suggest a "special environment:" "I really believe that my whole character . . . took form by the time I was six or Eight and that my whole subsequent life has been a working out of the mental and emotional situations then established, some of which might now be classified as neuroses" (A).

As an "isolate," he became an obsessive reader and developed "a tremendous day-dream life." Lacking a close friend, he came to make decisions independently of others, and to hold to them stubbornly. This "inner control" and "determination" he says (although much of his future life seems to the observer to contradict this), led to his stance as a writer: "In my writings I have made the reader come to me. I have rarely written 'for' the reader." This is an interesting comment from a writer as physically migratory as Stewart. His works may not migrate toward the reader in the sense of consciousness, but most of them involve "journeys" in which the reader is invited to go toward a new place *with* the writer.

Stewart and his pre-teen peers were collectively isolated, to an extent, from the larger world. They "traveled much in Indiana," as it were. "The horizon of us boys was chiefly determined by the length of our legs." Even now, a contemporary writer can characterize Indiana as appearing to be "part of a more relaxed era, removed from time by a hundred years" (Robbins 15). Therefore, standing out in Stewart's memory are his two experiences beyond the horizon: a rail trip to Pittsburgh with his father in 1902, the first time he saw a city; and a visit to the eastern shore of Virginia in 1905 with Andrew. From this he remembers how Andrew forced him to retrieve the body of an osprey Andrew had shot, despite George's opposition to "the miscellaneous shooting of inoffensive wild creatures." This trip also forced him to view himself as an outsider, in effect a "foreigner," meaning that he could "never again be wholly a provincial" (A).

Another de-provincializing force during the Indiana years was Stewart's obsession with reading. In a chapter of his autobiography ironically titled "My Deprived Childhood," he astutely interprets the effects that his favorite childhood books had on his growing awareness of "the properties of language." Writing stood out for him as the richest expressive medium in Indiana, despite its new nickelodeons, its three "generations" of architecture, and its sparse civic sculpture (a statue of George Washington stood "unattended and unhonored" in a vacant lot; on seeing it, Stewart's cousin Alfred Barr, future famous art historian and director of the Museum of Modern Art, as well as future Princeton classmate, "even in early childhood concerned with artistic problems," exclaimed 'Why did they throw him away?'" [A]).

His history with respect to the arts, he says, is simple "and provides a perfect reflection of the history of the American people to that time"—producers of "great creators in literature," but few in the other arts. Through literature, Stewart "entered into the larger world," and "that simple childhood beginning led to his current station as "Professor of English, Emeritus, and the author of a surprising (even to me) number of books." He read a surprising number of books as a child, albeit erratically, although Indiana had no public library—perhaps because his parents gave him money to buy them.

The first book he definitely remembers in Alfred H. Miles's *Natural History in Anecdotes* . . ., particularly for the stories of animals, which he eventually read so assiduously that the book fell apart: "With a little more push in that direction I could have ended up as a zoologist." Miles begins his book with a metaphor we have already met: "Illustrations are like windows to the house of knowledge" (v) and a sentiment which Stewart's writing career embodies "The book of nature is full of illustrations which help the understanding of the book of life. . ." (v). Despite its discursive and somewhat far-fetched stories of animal behavior, Miles arranges his information in Linnaean taxonomy, by Class and Order. Throughout, the reader will find him emphasizing positive attributes of animals, without grossly personifying them.

Elephants are sagacious, affectionate, intelligent and capable of great friendship. Among dogs, Miles has special respect for the Newfoundland. "Volumes might be filled with stories of his intelligence and prowess. . .One of the most marked characteristics . . .is his generosity to a fallen foe" (108). The Newfoundland has a sense of right and wrong: a grocer's dog observed a thief stealing money from the till, and dug it up where it was buried (112). Impressionable youths could not but gain respect for the creatures of nature from this granary of anecdotes.He of course read the Bible assiduously, and elsewhere points out how many allusions, citations, and paraphrases from it occur in his novels; "I remember being quite addicted to Nahum, thus being perhaps that minor prophet's only fan since the fall of Nineveh. . ." The "juvenile magazines" like *St. Nicholas* and *The Youth's Companion* were staples in his household (A).

Two "contemporary" writers were particularly influential in Stewart's youthful literary awareness, as they were in the lives of Anglophones of all ages at the time. He particularly credits Kipling, particularly *Just So Stories* (which he read at the age of seven) and *The Jungle Book*. Even a child, he says, could sense that Mowgli's decision to return to the village "had something to do with growing up, and that he himself might have to leave his playthings and suffer the infinite sorrow of becoming a grown-up." In Kipling's writing he professes to have sensed "the great human love for the simple, which seems always, in the end, to be forced to yield, tragically, to the complex." This concern with simplicity's tragic loss to complexity can be found in different forms in many of Stewart's writings, from the growth of 19th century California in *East of the Giants* to human evolution in *Man: An Autobiography*, to the re-creation of "civilization" in *Earth Abides*. It is also an inevitable, "natural" process, as can be seen in the life histories of *Storm* and *Fire*, which start as almost imperceptible environmental disturbances and come to embrace entire (human-inclusive) ecosystems. Looking back, Stewart maintains that it has been "the dominating theme of my own writings" (A).

Another Kipling work, the short story "The Knife and the Naked Chalk" "absolutely enthralled" him. It was his "first imaginative encounter with primitive man" and again portrays the "forced abandonment of simplicity and the triumph of complexity." In the story, the children Puck and Una are vacationing (as "outsiders") in alien terrain—the chalk Downs, near the Channel coast of England. Their father has moved from these windy hills to the treed Weald of Sussex, and his old friend, the shepherd Mr. Dudeney, wonders aloud to the children, exhausted from tramping the hills, why he "went off to live among them messy trees in the Weald" (Kipling, "Knife" 2). The children are couched on wild thyme beside the deep Norton pit. Kipling describes their situation in the kind of sensory ecological evocation Stewart was to learn from and master himself: "The little whisper of the sea by the cliffs joined with the whisper of the wind over the grass, the hum of insect in the thyme, the ruffle and rustle of the flock below, and a thickish mutter deep in the very chalk beneath them" (3).

But the heart of the story is the story within it, told to an inquisitive yet knowing Puck in a "dreamtime" outside of the present, by a prehistoric Briton warrior as he chips arrowheads. It is of how the People of Worked Flint, their sheep ravaged and harassed by the Beast (the collective of wolves) are saved by the speaker's quest into the dangerous world of "messy trees" where the dangerous Children of the Night live. The Children of the Night know how to work metal, and by way of the ritualistic sacrifice of one of his eyes, the speaker, now honorifically Buyer of the Knife, Keeper of the People, obtains the Magic Knife which is used to kill and scatter the wolves. In present time, the children return from the pit with "a little blue flint arrow-head as fresh as though it had been chipped that very day" (10).

One can find here an "origin of civilization" parable, which must have been as fresh in Stewart's mind throughout his career as the blue flint arrowhead. (Artifactual heirs to the arrowhead may be the bullets of *Sheep Rock*). The step from flint to iron is a crucial step toward human security and environmental control ("'I desired to master The Beast. It is not right that The Beast should master man'"), but it will lead to at least as much destruction as it prevents: hence the loss of the eye, and of the ability to see things whole and clearly. Hence the distorted vision of life's processes created by the dependency on, and worship of, technology. Stewart says teasingly "anyone sufficiently interested to make a search will find at least one definite influence of this story in my writings," and to this sufficiently interested reader there is not far to search: the "tools" of Ish in *Earth Abides* (e.g. the iconic hammer), but in particular, the bow-and-arrow he makes as a legacy to his Tribe to enable their slow re-climb out of the pit toward a renewed civilization.

Stewart attributes other literary understandings important to his creative development to other readings of his childhood years. *Treasure Island* gave him his "first conscious realization of novelistic technique." Macaulay's poem "Horatius" from his *Lays of Ancient Rome* "carried him away" "as that poem did with thousands of other boys in the nineteenth century," and clearly inspired the enthusiasm for balladry which was fulfilled not in his own poetry, but in his doctoral dissertation. The prefatory formulae of the poems in *Lays*, "A Lay Made About the Year of the City ....." probably led to the title of Stewart's last novel *Years of the City*. I can testify to the incantatory power of this poem, as it had pride of place in the commonplace book kept by my own mother, of Stewart's generation, and was read to me at bedtime so often that "Porsena of Clusium/Is on the march for Rome" remains fixed in my mind as it was in Stewart's.

But the truly central writer in Stewart's early years was one paradoxically influential on, but virtually unknown to, most 21st century people: G. A. Henty.

Horatio Alger and George Alfred Henty were the most popular "boy's book" (or as we might say now, "young adult") writers of the late Victorian Era. Stewart ascribes to his business-oriented brother favoritism for Alger, whose "grubby. . . economic ideal" did not appeal to him. But he insists on many occasions that Henty's "numerous" (an understatement) books deeply influenced his character. To know about Stewart as a writer, one must be familiar with Henty.

Henty's role is clearly stated by Brooke Allen:

> Quaintly written on the one hand, culturally passé on the other, Henty's books were all but forgotten during the second half of the twentieth century, despite the fact that he had inspired not only generations of future soldiers and administrators but also an array of future intellectuals from Henry Miller to Roy Jenkins, for his research and attention to detail was stunning, his historical and local flavor flawless, his battle accounts impeccably accurate. (20)

Born in 1832, Henty attended Westminster School and Caius College, Cambridge, and more or less drifted into war journalism in 1866, covering the Austro-Italian War (Arnold 7). He began writing fiction, through dictation as his fan George Stewart was to do, in 1868, and continued at a great pace. Henty's novels and stories were set in numerous locales of the past and present British *imperium* around the world, most of which he had visited. Naturally, he was an "imperialist:" Leonard Ashley says that "Fundamentally, Henty was a Tory, a capitalist, an expansionist, a militarist, and imperialist" (xii) but his adolescent male protagonists were generally paragons of virtue, true survivors of horrific events, and Henty does not hesitate to criticize cruelty and incompetence on every side.

Guy Arnold points out the paradoxes that these stances lead to, particularly that his protagonists must be both "heroic and ordinary," must be modest but not too modest to recount their own heroic exploits (31-34). Since except for their adventures, they are fundamentally average, he suggests with jaundice that Henty heroes are "more or less uniformly dull: virtuous and heroic, yet destined to be bores in the long twilight of their lives" (43). Interestingly, Henty was much more popular in the U.S. than in Britain—although only six of his novels have North American settings—partly because the cheapness of paper after the Civil War allowed rampant piracy of texts; about fifty different U.S. publishers pirated his novels in volumes "vilely printed and bound to disintegrate" (Arnold 18-19), as I can personally testify from ones I have handled.

Henty's friend and biographer, G. Manville Fenn, mentions another aspect of Henty's stories: when he began writing, it "speedily dawned upon him that there is nothing a boy likes better than a good description of a fight;" in counterpoise, however he "never made his works sickly by the introduction of what an effeminate writer would term the tender passion" (319-21).

Henty's American stories are worth particular notice. *With Lee in Virginia: A Story of the American Civil War* is prefaced by a letter to "my readers beyond the Atlantic," addressed as usual to "my dear lads," in which he admits writing from the Confederate point of view, but asserts that (as of 1884) the war "left but few traces in the life of your generation" (Preface). His protagonist, young plantation heir Vincent Wingfield, becomes a Confederate soldier and fights throughout the war, and "although a slaveholder, is a humanitarian and comes close to being an abolitionist . . ." (Allen 21). When Vincent sees a slave being brutally beaten by a neighboring planter and henchmen, who then turn on the slave's wife, he violates decorum and, in a good old boy's fight, beats up the beaters. His mother protests his action, considering it may paint him as an Abolitionist, but Vincent replies, "'It is not a question of slavery one way or the other. Anyone has a right to interfere to put a stop to brutality" (Henty, *Lee* 35).

Just as, above, Henty's slaveholder's morality renders irrelevant political divisions, so, in his *True to The Old Flag: A Tale of the American War of Independence*, he fictionalizes a revisionist history of the Revolution, based on "authentic contemporary sources" (iv), from the British point of view. His narrator can declare "In the whole history of the British army there is no record of a more gallant feat than the capture of Bunker's Hill. . ." (88). Yet in almost the same breath, "The battle, however, though won by the English, was a moral triumph for the Americans, and the British Parliament should at once have given up the contest . . . it was little short of madness for the English to continue the contest" (89). Henty's "history lessons" are lessons in "tragic complexity," as Stewart's will be. The gallant madness of Bunker Hill will be repeated on a different battlefield by Stewart in *Pickett's Charge*.

Most of Henty's teenage heroes have to be "outsiders," since they are British boys who have had to travel to the exotic locales where their adventures take place. "We sure aren't in Indiana any more," in effect. Henty's assiduous readers had to be imaginative travelers, vicariously experience culture shock and adaptation to alien lifestyles. In this connection, Henty was most conscious of travel narratives' pedagogical value. For example, he edited a collection of *Famous Travels*, telling his readers, "My dear Lads and Lassies" that he understands that geography is a "very dry subject," but travel narratives convey it in "vivid description" easily remembered (xv). He suggests that reading the excerpts he has selected will "excite among its readers a desire to know more" (xvi), and that they should read his anthology with a good atlas beside them. Even more, he suggests his main goal is to do for geography what he hopes his historical novels achieve:

> My hope has been so far to interest my readers that they will not be content with such partial descriptions, but will turn to the books written by historians of the various epochs and reigns, to obtain a full knowledge of the whole course of events that led to the wars I have described, and to learn the political and social conditions of the time. (xvii)

Tellingly, for Stewart's fate and interests, the title page of *Famous Travels* is faced with an engraving of a covered wagon in mountainous terrain, captioned "On the California and Oregon Trail," and one of its selections is from Washington Irving's *Astoria*, titled "In the Great American Desert," a "vast wilderness" where "no man permanently abides" (64-65). Stewart will cross this vast no longer wilderness in 1908, but he might already have read the story of the fictional English boy Frank Norris, who crosses it with a pioneer caravan in Henty's *Captain Bayley's Heir: A Tale of the Gold Fields of California*. Frank, in trouble at Henty's own Westminster School, takes ship to New Orleans, gets hired as a flatboatman on the Mississippi, and decides for the sake of adventure, to go for the famous goldfields. As Kevin Starr points out, the promiscuous flood of gold rush narratives, in which Henty's floats, manifests a "unified expression" of a "collective return to primal experience." It is a return "en masse to primitive and brutal conditions, to a Homeric world of journeys, shipwreck, labor, treasure, killing, and chieftainship" both in the voyages and the mining experience itself (51). If the idea of making this journey, more humbly than Homerically, was in the air of the Stewart household when George was reading *Captain Bayley's Heir*, well-read as he was, he might well have caught some of this primal and epic sense from the novel, as a template on which to form the real and fictional voyaging of his future.

Some of the matter of Stewart's *Ordeal by Hunger* and *The California Trail* seems anticipated in events of Henty's novel. Frank Norris sets out west from Omaha, whose "floating" population is all focused on California: "whole families , who had sold off farms or businesses in the east in assurance of acquiring a fortune at the gold-diggings. Around the little settlement the plain was dotted with the white tilts of the wagons . . ." (128). Frank joins a company of experienced frontier hunters who say, of these migrants, "they don't know what's afore 'em." Frank's adventures *en route* include Indian attacks, having to lower wagons down cliffs with ropes, encountering entire massacred caravans, and crossing the "Alkali Plains" of Nevada, a favorite Stewart locale and site of his novel *Sheep Rock*. As a precocious student of geography, though, the boy might have been amused by Henty's own lapses in this area, particularly when the caravan reaches "the point where the great plateau of Nevada falls abruptly down to the low lands of California many thousands of feet below" (196). Apparently Henty was ignorant of Stewart's beloved Sierras.

I feel this extensive discussion of Henty is relevant because of the emphasis Stewart always places on Henty's importance to his mental growth from his tenth to twelfth years. He took the novelist's pedagogical agenda to heart: from the knowledge he gained "I have recognized my place in history, and have been enabled to live more intelligently and more comfortably. I suppose that, in modern terms, it has something to do with establishing an identity" (A). He gained "objectivity and a consideration for the other person's point of view, even if I was waging war against him." He learned "humanitarianism." He was able to experience what he intuited through the primal window, the "pageant of history," even though the "non-intellectual" heroes in this history leave school early, and are never portrayed as reading books themselves. Addressing Henty's ghost, Stewart imagines he would say "'You, sir, were living on that yacht from the sales provided by boys who read books, but you never gave such boys a good word in all those volumes.'" But he goes on "Well, I was such a boy, and, when I was, I did not note the anomaly. The master gave me much knowledge of history. He reinforced my moral code and my instilled Anglophilism. He provided me many an obliviously happy hour."

So, to a great extent from his literary voyaging and role modeling, Stewart implies that he did "establish and identity." "I left [Indiana] in the early part of 1908, twelve years old. I have rarely been there since that time, but I left with my character largely shaped" (A).

In 1908 Stewart "experienced my first major and conscious shift of environment" when his family moved to "the Celestial Flowery Kingdom of the Christian World" (Taylor 64), that is, California, to save his father's health. (In the winter of 1906-7 his father had become pneumonic, and, at the time, "that very word was one of terror" since "there was no real treatment and no cure." At the age of 61, George Stewart Sr. acted on his belief in the California "myth of healthfulness and longevity" (Starr 443), which led him and countless thousands of his contemporaries to create, particularly in Southern California, what Starr calls "an infirmary culture" (443). It is important to understand how pervasive this myth was, since our writer's whole life was, in a sense, destined by his father's belief in it.

Of course, the most notable herald of an idealized California was one of its most famous citizens, Hubert Howe Bancroft. Unlike other laureates, his figure is of the classical Golden Age restored. He gives heroic tones to a tradition of California as a land of eternal youth, "as in the early days of Greece, when religion was but a love of the beautiful; when every star was tenanted by a god, and every stream was made to move and sing by some laughter-loving nymph." In his tableau,

> Living thus surrounded by such scenes of natural beauty, amidst olive orchards and vineyards, ever looking forth from sunny slopes on the bright water of bay and sea, living so much in the open air with high exhilaration and healthful exercise, many a young woman glowed in her lustrous beauty, and many a young man unfolded as perfect as Apollo. Even the old were cheerful, strong, and young in spirit (266).

Many writers of the late 19th century had elaborated this paradisial myth of California, including such notables as Charles Dudley Warner: "The new-comer may have certain unpleasant sensations in coming here from different altitudes and conditions, but he will soon be conscious of better being, of increased power in all functions of life, more natural and recuperative sleep, and an accession of vitality and endurance" (56). As a consumptive and would-be fruit grower, his father might have picked up for a dollar Samuel Southworth's pamphlet *California for Fruit-Growers and Consumptives. Health, Profits, and Drawbacks. How Californians make a Profit of $150 per Acre*, full of interviews with, and testimony from, said Californian immigrants. He would have noted Southworth's reservations about the fertility of the Sacramento Valley as opposed to that of Southern California. In the latter, he might have noted Southworth's special attention to "the new town of Ontario," laid out on a "beautifully sloping plateau," where "Ten acres of land . . . will afford as good a living to a family as 160 acres will in [Illinois] . . ." (91), and Anaheim, " . .one of the most successful colonies in the state" (92). Not to mention the testimony from Easterners of all walks of life: "They came here with the ominous hacking cough, or perhaps with slight or severe hemorrhages. They came here for relief, and having secured it did not propose running any chances of a recurrence of the disease, and became permanent residents" (103).

Another text, profusely illustrated, would have greatly interested the Stewarts. Prefaced by a Santa Fe railroad ad, it uses the ubiquitous geographical analogy: *The American Italy: The Scenic Wonderland of Perfect Climate, Golden Sunshine, Ever-blooming Flowers, And Always-ripening Fruits* [:] *Southern California*. The American Italy, like the heroic quester's goal, can be reached only by undergoing topographic trials. "The horrors of the desert interpose to ward off intruders. Heat, thirst, and desolation assail those who would enter the modern Eden, up to the very borders of its beauty and bounty" (Hanson 33). Once in paradise, however, the aspiring agriculturist can create his own little paradise for a song—for example, an orange grove:

> Is there any more beautiful object in nature than an orange tree? It dark, glossy green foliage, its snow-white blossoms, each constructed on a plan of ideal simplicity, and grouped with its neighbors in graceful harmony, and all breathing the most intoxicating aroma . . . the symmetry of the whole perfect combination of color and perfume, each a bouquet of beauty, a vase of perfume and a cornucopia of plenty . . . (90)

And as for a residence, Hanson quotes Kate Sanborn that "'Pasadena is as near Eden as can be found by mortal man'" (200). There is definitely a built-in contradiction in the rationale for California's allure at this time. Wells captures it well on a single page. On the one hand the settler "finds the Old California here as Nature made it. The only change he finds is in the minds of men, and this shows itself in a better appreciation of great natural resources and a disposition to develop them." The change is the rub. "That the California future is promising is shown by the flow of Eastern capital for investment in California lands for irrigation or reclamation and subsequent subdivision and sale" (9). A good deal of Stewart's future writing will circle around this contradiction.

*

Long before the dust bowl exodus, so tragically chronicled by John Steinbeck in *The Grapes of Wrath* ("Maybe we can start again in the new rich land—in California, where the fruit grows" [87]) and comically by W. C. Fields in *It's a Gift* (".…the final scene shows the sign for Harold's prosperous property: 'Bissonnette's Blue Bird Oranges.' A relaxed Harold, wearing a pure white shirt, is on the porch of his new home, in the midst of an orange grove—his California dream has come true"["Gift"]), the myth of California also expressed a commercial vision—an agricultural utopia. The orange grove was the Apple Orchard of the Hesperides. "A man with a counterpane of a farm and six hundred orange trees can sit in the shade and draw a Star-preacher's salary without passing the plate" (Taylor 264).

So Stewart's father liquidated his assets (his son estimates them to be a not inconsequential $15,000) and went in 1907 with Andrew on ahead "in one of those Biblical phrases that came so easily to our tongues in those days, …'to spy out the land.'" As a result, the Stewarts' initial home in the "flowery kingdom" was a house of the "Middle Bungalow Epoch" in the "small and raw" town of Azusa, where, because of its favorable location, "my father had decided to invest in an orange grove" (A).

But what really is most significant about this displacement, with respect to Stewart's future careers, is the 1908 rail trip to California itself, which he describes in his autobiography under the telling rubric "The California Trail." This, in his words, was "a shaping experience, since much of my thought and writing (unconscious though I was of it in 1908) was to be involved with the journey across the plains, mountains, and deserts." More generally, this trip initiated (as he says, unconsciously) a number of broad intellectual concerns: the significance of landscape and human manipulation of or subjection to it; the tension between human 'sense of place' and compulsive mobility; and the ways in which American (and by extension all) civilization are/were determined by these factors. Although Stewart adapted quickly to automobile transport, as his 1919 hitchhiking trip shows (see below), he must have for some time retained nostalgia for it. In 1920 *Life* published his "Ballade of Railroad Folders," bewailing in *neiges d'antan* fashion the replacement by the U.S. Railroad Administration of black and white for colored railroad timetables:

Where is the dark blue *Santa Fe?*

Where the bright yellow *Burlington?*
Where the red keystone? (Who shall say?)
Great Northern's green, surpassed by none?
Where is the *S. P.*'s setting sun?
Since when is color judged a crime,
That we the dye so strictly shun?
Where are the folders of old time?

Taylor says "a California train is a human museum" (61), but also that the California trip "gives a lonely *far-away* feeling it will puzzle you to describe. . ." (63). Laura Ingalls Wilder, traveling a route to San Francisco through Denver and Salt Lake City in 1915, also spent lots of time with the comfort of fellow-travelers, exclaiming at one point "I'm rather tired and I wish I was through with this trip. So far everything out of the car windows has been ugly since I left the Ozarks"(13)—and she was only in Denver. Later on, though, Wilder was less interested in the human museum, and more aware of the potential beauty of exotic landscape, as in the Nevada alkali plains, where the rocks "were purple in the hollows and rose and gold and pink on the higher places. There were yellows and browns and grays and the whole softly blended together. . . Such a desolate dreary country even though beautiful in its way," although she ends this passage of lyrical nature description "Oh, this awful, awful country we have come to now!" (21).

Of future relevance is the trip taken in 1913 from Chicago to Salt Lake City by famous pioneering British ecologist Arthur Tansley. Tansley noticed different things than did Wilder and Stewart. In Illinois he noted that ". . .the woods are mostly passing into a degenerate condition owing to their use as pasture grounds for cattle" (332), and near Lincoln ". . .the natural boundary between forest and prairie entirely destroyed" (334). On the eastern Colorado plains, he noticed the destructive practices of overgrazing and "dry farming" (33-34). Tansley's observations led him to make a discreet yet radical proposal:

> No one but a fanatic, indeed, entirely out of touch with the realities of life, would expect to hamper the economic development of a great country, which necessarily involves the replacement of forest and prairie by corn-fields and factories. But here and there tracts of original

> untouched nature can and should be preserved for the enjoyment and use of our successors, without in any way checking general and inevitable economic development. This is work which ought to be undertaken by the community, and indeed the great national and the smaller State "parks" of the west. . . are a sign that America is awake to her responsibilities to the future in this matter. In the east the work of preserving unspoiled areas is more difficult, and there is less opportunity for it because comparatively little original vegetation is left. All honour, then, to those few who have the insight and the generous spirit to subordinate motives of immediate material profit to higher and deeper considerations. (327-27)

Stewart and his mother took the Santa Fe Scout by way of Albuquerque and Flagstaff, and he was happy that it was a "slow train" so he could see more. His train was the "California Limited," equipped with "drawing-room Pullmans, buffet library car (with barber shop), Harvey dining car, and observation car (with ladies' parlor)" (Holder n. pag.). But Stewart was apparently more interested in the landscape outside. He was delighted to cross the "deep and red chasm" of the Canyon del Diablo, feeling already the "poetry of names." When he entered California, it was not amidst the orange groves he anticipated, but on Cajon Pass, where the train was delayed, and the passengers could stretch their legs. It was clearly a dawn of awareness to see the "desert flora" up close and feel the fascination of them, and to "luxuriat[e] in the balmy morning". "With twelve-year-old agility I leaped rabbit-like among the cactus and yucca. . ." But the train whistle brought this "golden first hour" to a sudden end, although he would recreate this delay in a different season and with a different result in his novel *Storm*. The trail ends as they actually are clattering through orange groves. "Thus I entered California, fifty-eight years too late to join the Society of Pioneers and slightly less than that before the triumph of smog" (A).

*

The transition from the "verdant hills of Pennsylvania" to the scrappy L.A. suburb might be considered disorienting to a twelve-year-old who wasn't Huck Finn. George, reflecting back, describes no discomfort. In fact, neither did the numerous other members of his extended family who followed their railpaths fairly soon thereafter, abandoning Indiana as constituents of "the amazing population-burst that turned southern California into Southern California, launched a thousand millionaires, and eventually inundated the whole area with noxious yellow smog" (A).

In fact, the Azusa where Stewart lived from 1908 to 1910 resembled remarkably, excluding topography, his native town. He describes the population as chiefly "white, Protestant, American," and, as the ethnically diverse coal miners lived outside of Indiana, so the "Mexicans" who worked in the orange groves were "out-liers." There was only one black family, whose two sons were named Andrew and Stonewall. (The autobiographer notes "Years later, on the street in Pasadena, I heard someone calling 'George!' 'George!' and there in a big parked car, beneath the cap of a private chauffeur, was Stonewall Jackson").

It is important to note Stewart's emphasis on living in a California "poised on the brink" of the deadly transition from rail to auto. "These were the times before—but only just before—the automobile had rendered such villages [as Azusa] obsolete." He was witnessing what he would describe so often in his writings—the threshold period of cultural change which, although human-created, expressed itself as inevitability, and transformed humans and non-humans in unanticipateable ways. In 1965 he wrote

> Years ago I lived in near [sic.] Los Angeles, and it was a lovely region. Since then, what has happened along with the influx of millions of people is something that I do not like to contemplate. Now, instead of taking the people to the water and building a city at Oroville, we undertake vast expense to take the water somewhere else and to plant half-a-million new smog-makers in a region already in a critical condition with smog (*This California* 96).

Thus, as a boy, his travel was determined not by the "length of his legs" but by his bicycle, the preferred transport of his peers, and by the Pacific Electric trains ("In a few years the automobile had the electric car by the throat and was throttling it along with the railroad, to the glee of those demons who thrive on smog"). Despite access to Los Angeles, and thereby cultural novelties,

Stewart describes his years in Azusa as "the least eventful three years of human history." He experienced "the stirring of anti-Japanese feeling" in California, and the visit of President Taft, who was quoted as remarking "non-controversially" "'You raise oranges here'." He describes his family as expecting to grow oranges and therefore "we all re-oriented ourselves toward being agricultural," and his father invested in a "ten-acre orange grove in Ontario" (which he soon did sell at a profit).

In terms of intellectual growth, Stewart remembers his years in seventh and eighth grade at Azusa as "colorless," although he did get to know well a chubby classmate, Buddy de Sylva, who turned out to be "the first celebrity that I encountered in this earthly pilgrimage." ". . . He wrote our songs for a generation." Stewart reinitiated his friendship with Bud when they met on the Paramount lot in Hollywood after the company had bought the rights to *Storm* in 1943. However, more to the point, Stewart remembers four "pedantic" "adventures in reading" from the Azusa years: Caesar's *Gallic Wars* (in Latin), Green's *History of the English People* (in four volumes), the *Pickwick Papers,* and most momentously, Frank Norris's *The Octopus.* This last was his first introduction to "naturalism." This was the real thing, for in Henty, "the blood is not really red, and the good guys are never killed, crippled, or forced to beg their bread." (A). Norris's novel "opened to me a whole new outlook upon literature, and therefore upon life" As Kevin Starr says, *The Octopus* created a scenario for an imaginative relationship of Californians and nature. While the ranchers exploit the land as much as the railroad exploits them, the protagonists, Annixter, Presley, and Vanamee, "are healed by submission to the natural process" (200).

I think *The Octopus* played an even greater role in Stewart's literary development than he acknowledges. Presley wants to write "the great poem of the West," while Vanamee is content to *live* it (Norris 34). These seem to me two sides of Stewart as writer of the West. Presley is the stranger, seeking to nativize himself; Vanamee is the native, celebrating there those who are "in touch with the essential things, back again to the starting point of civilization, coarse, vital, real, and sane" (95). Norris is concerned with the relationship of the human consciousness and nature. Annie Derrick "felt vividly that certain uncongeniality which.. . . forever remains between humanity and the earth which supports it. . .the colossal indifference of nature. . ." (127). Although Stewart's own writing contradicts Norris's repeated technological figuration of nature, he could have gotten his lifelong fascination with cartography, and the presence of mapping in his work, from its importance in the farmer-railroad conflict. And from this naturalist in one sense he could have learned the power of naturalistic—in another sense—nature-description:

> The California summer lay blanketwise and smothering over all the land. The hills, bone-dry, were browned and parched. The grasses and wild oats, sere and yellow, snapped like glass filaments underfoot. The roads, the bordering fences, even the lower leaves and branches of the trees, were thick and grey with dust. All color had been burned from the landscape, except in the irrigated patches, that in the waste of brown and dull yellow glowed like oases. (337)

Interestingly, in the autobiography Stewart relates *The Octopus* to his own experience of such natural process, the powerful impact of his new life in California: "We were on the edge of wildness. A mile from our house the Sierra Madre Mountains reared up—steep, rough, uninhabited." By witnessing the raging torrents of the flooded San Gabriel River ripping out the railroad bridge, he appears to have come to an awareness analogous to that wrought by Norris. While *The Octopus* chronicles the destruction of nature by the railroad, as a representative technology created by human culture, the wildness of the river gives ocular proof of how vulnerable that technology is to natural forces beyond human control.

At sixteen, Stewart went on his first camping trip, in the San Bernardino, with some other boys and as "a kind of basic human experience" had his first night "under the open sky." Although nothing of great significance occurred, Stewart's summary of the trip is tendentious: "There is charm—at sixteen and for the first time, especially—to move freely in good mountain-country, to make camp and break it, to see untouched landscape, and to hear running water and the wind moving in pines. Even a sixteen-year-old can know that he thus touches something very ancient." But also, ". . .Once we came to a lake, and there, on location, was a primitive movie-troupe shooting a film. So even in those mountains, at what seems now an early date, we could not escape civilization" (A).

On September 26, 1911, occurred an even more crucial change of environment, though infinitely less in space, than the trip from Pennsylvania. This was the family's move to the much more upscale city of Pasadena, ". . .one of the wealthiest places for its size in the whole world" (Holder 11), which was Stewart's "base" henceforth until his marriage in 1924, and his parents' home until their deaths in 1937. Even in 1885, Pasadena was considered a "model settlement," with "a thousand happy and intelligent inhabitants," for whom "beautifying their homes" is "an honorable and constant desire" (Truman 29). Stewart appears to be amused that his first memory of Pasadena is of walking from their house at 388 South Lake Avenue to Colorado Street, where he bought an ice cream cone; this ice cream cone appears like the *madeleine* of the years of self-empowerment Stewart was to experience in Pasadena.

Stewart's emblem for Pasadena is palms, though he says that "today" it often suggests the image of "stainless steel and concrete." From my residence in Pasadena during the same years Stewart was writing his autobiography, I feel that, at least in the 1970's, the palms were keeping pace with the concrete, and my mind is filled with the rustle and smack of falling palm fronds and dates. But Pasadena was (and is) a locale of elegance—in contrast to Azusa, not so many miles away. Incorporated in 1875, the town was determined to be a "garden" city. "The turn-of-the century California dream had been anti-industrial and agrarian in its most fundamental nature…." and Pasadena was one of the California cities that were "consciously anti-industrial" (Starr 304). But it was equally determined not to be agrarian in the Azusan sense. From 1890 to 1910, its population grew by at least 250%, and was over 30,000 when the Stewarts moved there. These two decades also saw its conscious "culturation:" the future Caltech (1891), the Echo Mountain Incline Railway and its resorts (1893), the Tournament of Roses (1898), opulent hotels and private residences, including that of Adolphus Busch, whose elaborate sunken gardens were opened to the public in 1906 (Heckman 41). The imposing First United Presbyterian Church (one of many in the city) was, of course, just a few blocks down Lake from the Stewart residence. Scanning Colorado Street in 1911, George would have seen elegant set-back houses in "Mexican" and other styles, planned by the many architects who had migrated to Pasadena, fronted by wisteriaed porches and groomed lawns, separated by boxwood hedges, with impeccably clean sidewalks, rows upon rows of palm bordering a wide thoroughfare with trolley tracks in the middle (Heckman 68).

Pasadena's "cultural" milieu is described in a more jaundiced manner by native Paul Fussell, the noted historian, author of *The Great War and Modern Memory*, and son of Stewart's closest Pasadena friend, Paul Fussell, Sr. It was a "dull, safe, trim little city. . . where those who commuted to the tougher Los Angeles eleven miles away returned in the evenings to raise families in gentility and peace" (8-9). In Fussell's characterization, Pasadena is not that different from Stewart's natal Sewickley, in its relation to Pittsburgh. However, it was a "philistine city, and despite its attractiveness, profoundly un-European in its self-satisfied puritanism" (10).

Stewart's Paul Fussell, senior, had much in common with him: his father had moved to Pasadena for the same health reasons Stewart's did, but, unfortunately, fairly soon died anyway. His first home, where Paul, Jr., was raised, was also a Middle Epoch Bungalow. He was to graduate from Boult Hall Law School at Berkeley, and eventually, an Anglophile in the depression build a "costly, luxurious, upper-middle-class house" on the upscale Caltech/Huntington Library side of town (15). It should also be mentioned at this point that unlike his friend, who after college graduation joined the military and trained for the Army Ambulance Corps (see below), Fussell Sr. was selected among the college contingent on Henry Ford's ill-fated Peace Ship, and later defended its mission as "the people's spokesman, acting in place of the diplomats who had tried neither to prevent the war nor to end it" (Kraft 295). So the dull, safe city produced at least two who were willing to be unsafe.

Philistinism aside, Stewart describes the Pasadena of his youth as "a very churchly town with the Methodists being heavily entrenched" and exuding a "quiet prosperity." He does not see it as a "commuter city" (although by the time of Fussell, Jr.'s birth, 1924, the automobile may have rendered it so). He wonders what its residents actually lived on, except for the copious number of retirees who "were maintaining their lawns and having their palm trees trimmed from the proceeds of an Iowa farm or of coal-beds under some forested Pennsylvania ridge" (A).

In recollection, Pasadena High School was the center of Stewart's life, and the site of his coming of age, intellectually and socially. Yet there was one other crucial place for him, although it was not in Pasadena itself. This was "The Grove," so important that he calls it a "character of the story." The Grove was, in the persistent parlance, a "ranch;" on a Princeton University form Stewart was to define his father's profession as "Rancher" (Alumni File). The "ranch" was ten acres of Valencia orange trees "two miles west of a somnolent small town called Anaheim . . ." From the perspective of the 1970's, Stewart says "I shudder to think of what the site of the grove may be now—suburban "development" most likely, with the trees bulldozed out, except for two or three left for "ornamental purposes. I often walked out from town to the grove, on the main road, scarcely meeting a car." Nonetheless "Those ten acres supported my parents in quiet comfort, put two sons through Princeton, partly financed me during my graduate work," and even brought him some money for their sale in the late 1940's. "My own association with the grove was not close," but he remembers fondly "the neat and friendly rows of majestic rounded trees . . ." This memory leads him to another, the search, in 1957, for the family's house at 388 Lake Avenue. He found what he expected, an entire business block, the house vanished. "I felt a sense of brutality. No green thing grew—as if Attila's horses had passed that way" (A).

"Uprooted again, not of the nature quickly to take root," Stewart felt lonely and awkward with his peers except for Fussell, his eventual lifelong friend. One thing he did explore with courage was literature. It was only with his senior year at Pasadena High (1912-13) that he experienced a true personality transformation, such that it became "one of the most remarkable years of my life." He was "unnoted and unknown" at the beginning, and among the "prominent" dozen students at the end. It was certainly during this year that his "old preceptor" and admirer, Princeton Prof. J. Duncan Spaeth ". . .after an address at the Pasadena High School. . . shook hands with an eager young boy who said he was looking forward to going to Princeton" (Spaeth to Stewart 21 June 1945).

The supposedly fortuitous event ("luck") that led to his rise was in effect an *actus literariorum*, and an illustration of Stewart's belief in the power of words. As he describes it, he had to write a poem for English class, and thought about the football team's success, caused particularly by a brilliant receiver named Gibbs. So Stewart wrote out a series of quatrains (presumably in the ballad meter that became his prosodic passion), with the refrain "Gibbs got a forward pass." The English teacher had him read it aloud, "and it got a fine reception." Not only that, but the English teacher told the principal about the Gibbs poem, and the principal had him read it at a pep rally. "The success was so amazing that one can only take refuge in the cliché, 'The crowd went wild'."

Stewart considers that the whole event was almost a work of art; in his philosophy the greatness of a moment does not depend upon its importance. "By reading this inherently worthless bit of verse at that particular moment, I had achieved a union of time and place and theme approaching perfection." "Now I blossomed" (A).

In 1971, at Stewart's request, for his autobiography, Paul Fussell wrote some interesting memories of this time. "My earliest recollection of you is that we were seatmates in Miss Deyo's fourth year Latin class and that you were a considerable help to me." "Even in high school you had skill as a writer especially in the field of light verse," he says, and recalls the Gibbs poem. More personally, he remembers the Lake Avenue house "opposite the area now occupied by Bullocks and Magnins. Even after many years I can see your father, mother and brother—your father so dignified and erect, your mother so generous in playing the piano for us, your brother so skilled in the hurdles" (Fussell to Stewart 11 Nov. 1971).

The Pasadena High School "annual" for 1913 reflects Stewart's high repute and his class's literacy. While his great friend Gladys Knowlton (Irvine) "Reminds herself of sunny smiles. Reminds us of the Faerie Queen," Stewart "Reminds himself of the Divine Comedy. Reminds us of the eighth wonder of the world." There were many activities on the resume of the eighth wonder of the world. After an "exciting" election ("All the political activity that marks the presidential elections is present in the fight going on in the high school" [*Item Annual*]), Stewart was elected "Commissioner of Debating" and Fussell, ironically, "Commissioner of Literary Activities."

Stewart's most prominent role was as a debater; debating in L.A. area high schools at the time was almost an athletic activity, with a league and clubs. A high point of the debating season was the contest with *Hollywood*. "Before the debate, songs and yells were shot back and forth with abundance of spirit. Later the excitement deepened, for the debate was close and hard fought" (*Item*). Pasadena barely won, and Stewart for the only time in his life was "carried out. . . on the shoulder of cheering admirers." The *Annual* tells us he "is undoubtedly the most logical thinker among this year's debaters, and he has a pleasing method of expressing his views" (10). He was also the number two player on the tennis team, and characterized by the school paper as "a sure and heady player. While not at all spectacular, he can usually put up a hard fight and beat his man" (12). A second celebrity encounter in his life occurred when Pasadena played the Thatcher School: "After beating one man, I was eliminated by the second man to come up. . . and his name was Wilder. That was undoubtedly Thornton Wilder, who was at Thatcher School at that time" (*Little* 106).

Another result of "Gibbs got a forward pass" was that "for the first time, I became more interested in my English class than in the others," and published his first work of fiction in the March, 1913 *Item*, a short story titled "Blood Against Water," Kipling-inspired (he says), and based on a charged issue of ethnic conflict. Considering the effective narrative technique of this story, it is surprising that Stewart was leery throughout his career of writing short stories, and considered himself not very talented thereat.

In "Blood Against Water," John Beach, a college student, is relaxing in his room after commencement, when "already the old college town had settled into its annual summer slumber;" another young man "very different from Beach, yet much like him" enters the room. This is Beach's college football teammate Nogi, a "son of Japan" (5). Tendentiously, the narrator says "A stranger may well ask how such a close friendship could arise between an Oriental and an American," the answer being their mutual expertise on the gridiron. Beach notices newspaper headlines suggesting Japan will invade the Phillipines; Nogi angrily says "'Of course not.'" The two decide to have a game of chess, while noticing a fistfight outside between an American kid and a Japanese kid, the victory going to the former. "Beach laughed; but Nogi scowled darkley [sic.]. Unconsciously each had sided with his own blood and had picked his champion" (7). They settle down to their game. Nogi chooses the black chessmen. As they play, the give-and take of the game parallels that described of the boys fighting outside, and each player makes martial comments equating his good moves with an imaginary war between Japan and the U.S. Prophetically, the narrator has Nogi imagining a Japanese attack on Hawaii (and San Francisco).

Clearly the author knows chess well. "[C]hess is a strange game, and the habits of its pieces are even stranger." Nogi, moving his knights more, slowly caves to Beach, who's manipulating his rooks. Their moves, and their outbursts of war-talk grow increasingly frenzied. Finally Nogi is checkmated and Beach cries "'Where is Japan now?'" (8). Enraged, Nogi leaps across the board and at Beach's throat, but the latter throws Nogi against the wall. They are ashamed. They agree they are "fools," "but each kept his distance and neither held out his hand" (8). Nogi leaves; he will be going back to Japan.

> They shook hands, each with an appraising glance that went deeper than muscle. "Perhaps we shall meet again in a game which is neither football nor chess."
> "I hope that game will not be played," said Beach.
> Nogi walked away, calling over his shoulder, "I hope so." (8)

To me, this story by a high school senior is precociously subtle. Obviously reflecting anxiety over an impending war, it conflates four conflicts: two games—football field and chessboard, and two literal fights—outdoors and indoors. It also looks back to a previous use of the game figure—the "great game" of the European powers for economic hegemony in the preceding century. Also in the background of the story is the Russo-Japanese War, and the Immigration Act of 1907, limiting Japanese immigration. On the psychological level there is a theme Stewart will return to in many different forms: the relationship between object (or action) and symbol. How easily symbolic conflict can become actual conflict! Yet how different is a map of a fire's, or a storm's, course, from the actual fire or storm. And, again, how necessary is the map—or the game—to create as structure of order out of a seeming chaos of emotions, or actions of human culture and nature. The conclusion re-separates Beach and Nogi from the artifice of being on the same "team," but the symbolic game is also separated from the war they make it symbolize—it is over, but the war has not yet begun, and its very possible existence remains a suspended question.

There was no question that Stewart would enter college following graduation. "I do not remember the time when I was not going to go to college. . . .Going to college was in some way a good thing in itself, like going to church" (A). Stewart attributes the "love of learning" to the "Lowland Scots" tradition, passed through Ulster, and then to the frontier. In this sense, Stewart's high school experience was "remarkable," and its goal, the college experience, "much less important" (*Little* 6). ". . . My high-school education must be considered a preparation for my literary life." In this regard, it is noteworthy that his favorite high school courses were in botany, physics, and chemistry—not English. "Because of them life has always been different for me, for I saw new light and color." One can see how a fascination with physical processes—organic or inorganic—and with human language could come together in the writer's concern for how humans mediate their fated presence in that world to permit their survival.

*

Donald Dewey points out that Princeton was at the beginning of the 20th century still defined as a sectarian—Presbyterian—university, and the pinnacle of education within the religion. "Indiana at the time (even a good part of that area of Pennsylvania) thought of Princeton as the logical place to go for good Presbyterians with some brains and a little more money. In fact, there was significant tracking (in an educational sense) from high school days" (Donald Dewey, Email to the author, 8 Aug. 2005). This would go for Pasadena too, with its proliferation of Presbyterians and churches. Thus to find both Jimmy and George R. Stewart at Princeton was not as anomalous as it may seem today (My freshman year at Princeton, 1961-62 was the last one to require compulsory [ecumenical] chapel attendance).

Jimmy Stewart wanted to go to Annapolis; visiting Eastern colleges with his father (hardware store owner and Princeton graduate), he was tricked into visiting the Princeton campus by that father, for "nostalgic" reasons, and ended up there despite himself. Before going West in 1908, Stewart's mother had taken him to see Princeton, but he reports the visit was "pleasant, but I cannot call it important, even though my life was later to be tied up to a considerable degree with that town" (A). He often expressed regret that he had not gone with Paul Fussell to Berkeley in 1913; definitely he nowhere expresses any personal religious conviction as a source for his college decision. In fact, we have seen him describing the "death of Protestantism" and attrition of ritual during the Indiana years.

In some ways the decision was for the sake of family harmony, and, particularly, his mother's peace of mind, since Wilsons were enmeshed with the institution. Andrew was at Princeton, and in an alumni document, George lists relatives who have attended Princeton: Harry W. Wilson, R. D. Wilson, S. G.Wilson, A. W. Stewart (Andrew), P. H. Wilson, A. W. Wilson, A. H. Barr (Alfred) and "other cousins and cousins' children" (Alumni File). Stewart himself says that "My parents sent me to Princeton, at much expense and some sacrifice, out of the pride in their hearts for a son who always stood at or near the head of his class. . .In accordance with family tradition they thus unwittingly sent me into an environment where my one then-extent capacity was unappreciated, and where my deficiencies were exposed and even magnified" (A). To this I, from my own personal experience, can only say Amen.

The case of cousin Alfred provides an interesting comparison. His father, a Presbyterian minister, graduated from Princeton in 1889, as did related Wilsons from the Theological Seminary across the street. According to Sybil Kantor, Barr did not transform a Christian evangelism into a Modern Art evangelism; rather, it was the "nonauthoritarian organization of Presbyterianism" which "engendered in the young Barr a questioning attitude and supported a fierce independence—just skirting rebellion—that he ultimately expressed in a modernist aesthetic systematized within the context of traditional art history" (6-7).

There might be seen a similarity between Stewart and his cousin in the Princeton education as a religio/cultural tradition, but one which fostered some level of rebellion against tradition itself. And that rebellion might, for the art historian and the literary artist, involve a re-examination of the very history that engenders tradition. "The model of self-determining independence that [Barr] observed in his father's pastorate would also have made him receptive to the indeterminacy of art history" (Kantor 20). Both Stewart and Barr "analyzed complex material in search of patterns and stylistic order" (22). This analytical re-visioning which Barr became involved in under the tutelage of Charles Morey (my own father's mentor) with respect to untangling the complex web of influence on art history, is very similar to what Stewart ended up doing with the complex and disordered history of the Donner Party, of a storm, or of the battle of Gettysburg.

Actually, Stewart seems, whenever he discusses it, to be fairly negative about the meaning his Princeton experience had for him. He certainly did not share Barr's overweening enthusiasm. ". . .Many people have expressed surprise at first learning that I had attended Princeton. Obviously, I lack the stigmata." True for me forty-five years later, as it was then, "Princeton men of my generation headed for finance and business-management. . . Probably I simply fail to fit into people's image of what a Princeton man should be." In his autobiography, the first Princeton chapter is entitled "And did you once see Scotty plain?," and he sees this image problem behind the "did you know?" any time his membership in the Class of 1917 comes up. He recounts the incident to answer this obnoxious question once and for all: In compulsory gym his freshman year, he was number four on a six-man relay team. The third, whose job was to "touch me off, was a slight and handsome boy. You have guessed it! He was, as the old-fashioned novels used to phrase it, 'not other than Francis Scott Fitzgerald'." Since the latter has "attained a kind of apotheosis, I suppose that I may eventually be known as the man who touched Fitzgerald . . ."

As Stewart says, they were "different people in very different orbits," which shows in the biographies of Fitzgerald. Although Stewart reviewed it, he appears not at all in the granddaddy of them, Arthur Mizener ('30)'s *The Far Side of Paradise*. The only reference I can find to Stewart in a book on Fitzgerald is in Matthew Bruccoli's *Some Sort of Grandeur*, where he lists the (relatively few) other future writers in the class of 1917, which was "not overwhelmingly literary. . . George R. Stewart became a professor of English who wrote scholarly and popular books (*Storm*)" (51).

Mizener, however, describes the Princeton Fitzgerald and Stewart entered in 1913 quite vividly:

> Physically Princeton still centered in the old campus above the transverse line set by McCosh Walk, though some of the new dormitories on the lower campus such as Little, Patton, and Cuyler, had been built. The railroad station still stood at the foot of Blair steps, and the old Casino, where the Triangle Club rehearsed, stood not far off. The rickety but partly eighteenth-century façade of Nassau Street had not yet been replaced by faked Georgian; Nassau Street itself was unpaved. (29-30)

Other attributes of Stewart's Princeton were the ongoing construction of Palmer Stadium, the dying traditions of hazing and the "rush," the "deadly seriousness" (31) of football, and the overwhelming importance of the eating club system. "The function of the Princeton clubs is to provide a system of grading people according to social distinction at the middle of the sophomore year" (33).

In one 1951 review of Mizener's *The Far Side of Paradise,* Stewart is generally praiseworthy, but speaking as a "broken-down biographer," he ventures some "remonstrances." He thinks Mizener is too eager to accept the Fitzgerald "myth" and in general is "too ready to accept the great legend of the Twenties. Personally, I lived through the Twenties. For me it was a decade of hard work at not a very large salary. I did not speculate in the stock market and spend most of my time going to parties. Neither did the people I knew" ("Biography"). This attitude is reflected in his own characterization of Princeton, from fifty years of reflection, which is fairly jaundiced. He emphasizes its smallness, its "somewhat snobbish social standard" and its "impoverished" curriculum. He does admit that the individual student received a lot of attention, the teaching was good, and particularly emphasizes the informal preceptorials held by J. Duncan Spaeth in his home and by Thomas Marc Parrott in the students' own dorms. However, "I've never been a protégé.

I always worked on [my] own, really and professors didn't mean too much to me" (*Little* 16).

His greatest criticism is, however, that Princeton lacked (contrary to what Mizener and others assert) "any wide-spread and serious intellectual ferment. . . Perhaps the faculty seethed with intellectuality, but they did not transmit it." His classmate and fellow writer John Peale Bishop tended to agree.". . .the exceptional boy will not come off . . . happily. If he does not flunk out—which he is more than likely to do through indifference or boredom—he will waste most of his time, unless he discovers a more intimate relation with the faculty than the classroom allows or contemptuously devotes himself to reading outside his courses" (*Collected Essays* 397). In almost humorous contrast, Spaeth wrote to Stewart in 1945 ". . .What a ferment of young writers in your day[:] T. K., Bunny Wilson in '16, Scotty Fitzgerald and you in 1917" (Spaeth to Stewart 21 June 1945). There was no "social responsibility" and "little political awareness." There was also little Presbyterian identity left, as Stewart tells it: "very little spirit of religion." In fact (and I can relate most strongly to this) ". . . the very unity of the University... worked too strongly toward the suppression and possible frustration of the off-beat individual—of whom I was one" (A).

Despite these complaints, Stewart's portrait of his class at its convocation is worth quoting at some length:

> As we assembled in that September of 1913, we were all male, and almost all were between their seventeenth and nineteenth birthdays. Geographically, nearly all were from New York, Pennsylvania, and New Jersey. . .Perhaps even a Pittsburgher was to be though[t] a little wild and woolly. Traditionally, Princeton maintained a Southern tie, but few Southerners were in the class. As for Californians, I remember only one other . . .There were no Orientals. . .We had one Mexican, of an upper-crust and wealthy family. There were no Blacks. . . All sorts of legends were current among us as to how the number of Jews was controlled. . .Actually, Princeton may have been needlessly concerned. Intellectually languid, expensive, lacking professional schools, we offered rather little to the thousands of Jewish boys seeking to advance themselves. (A)

Maybe there is a love-hate relationship here. The inadequacies of Princeton that Stewart in retrospect deplores are compensated in the attributes of his works: social egalitarianism, intellectuality, diversity. Yet he owed much of his intellectual growth and many of the career opportunities that led to his literary achievement to his experience at Princeton and the few but strong personal relationships he developed there. He says the banal cynicism of "'Don't let your courses interfere with your college education,'" characterized his peers' goals, and hierarchized them. "Clear at the bottom scholarship rested. In fact, high grades were even to be held a mark against a man." So, perversely, Stewart distinguished himself, not, as Scotty tried to do, through football, dramatics, and club life, but in the "off-beat" realm of scholarship. His lack of interest in the HIGHER GOALS of the typical undergraduate permitted him eventually to stand out for excelling counterintuitively in the area of least importance.

The social connections Stewart did make at college were very meaningful to him. He began rooming off-campus at 25 Bank Street with Dick Reed, who became his good friend until killed in the war in 1917. Then (with the help of a loan from the university to cover the higher cost) he moved into 22 Blair Hall, on the east side of Blair Arch, close to my own room (in the 1960s) at 31, and even closer to my daughter's (in the 1990s). Although the club scene, that so mesmerized Fitzgerald, in life and in *Paradise*, did not do much for him, he did enter "bicker" (Princeton's version of "rush") and though "not a widely desired piece of merchandize," was initiated into Arch Club, of which he says he eventually became quite fond. He developed a "small group" of likeminded friends, including Carl Arnold, Jim Osmer (his later neighbor in Berkeley) and Curtis Williams, who was his roommate his junior and senior years. Perhaps his strongest lifelong relationship was with the "inimitable Chauncey Leake," notable physician and author, who ended up living and working across the Bay from Stewart. Needless to say, as in the early 1900's, Princeton men (Scotty excluded) were generally on a "starvation regime for girls," and he only managed to restore a close relationship, in the summers in 1915 and 16, in

Pasadena with his high school sidekick Gladys Knowlton. Socially, Stewart sums himself up as remaining immature for his age throughout college ". . .[although] even now [I] feel myself immature for seventy-seven." Perhaps Stewart was less obscure at Princeton than he professes to be. For example, William S. Annan writes to Stewart that he was in the same Thomas Marc Parrott class mentioned above and "I have watched your growing fame with much interest" (Annan to Stewart, n.d.)

As far as scholarship goes, Stewart says he chose to major in English "rather more by drift than by conviction"—a judgment one might have cause to doubt. He was one of four juniors who made Phi Beta Kappa, although one of the others, at his fortieth reunion "told me that he had earned all his grades by sheer memory, and that he was not at all intellectual, having spent most of his life playing bridge." Returning to the window image which begins his autobiography, Stewart credits most of his valuable intellectual experience in college to his elective non-English courses, in geology, biology, organic chemistry, Romanesque and Gothic architecture [perhaps under Charles Morey] and economics. He regrets not having been able to take physics ("which I needed for *Storm*") and modern geography. "Even without such aid, I myself have been almost a geographer, and the topic of ecology shows up in many of my books" (A).

At his graduation (ranked third in his class), it is doubtful Stewart shared the nostalgic sentiments Fitzgerald expressed in his *Nassau Lit* poem "Princeton—The Last Day:"

> . . . Oh sleep that dreams and dream that never tires,
> Press from the petals of the lotus-flower
> Something of this to keep, the essence of an hour! (Bruccoli and Breyer 62)

John Peale Bishop published his first book of verse, *Green* Fruit, in 1917 as by a "First Lieutenant of Infantry, Officers Reserve Corps." Its final poem, "Nassau Street," dated April, 1917, anticipates, rather than reminiscing:

> Laurel—maybe some darker leaf than laurel
> Shall find our brows insensate as the clay—

It matters not. This is the supreme quarrel,
And the end comes. What word is there to say? (45)

In this regard, in contrast to the prolific Fitzgerald, the precocious Bishop, and surprising in view of his future literary career, Stewart published only two poems in that magazine during his four years. These poems are, though, tendentious, because one could say they spiritually anticipate what he would do almost immediately upon graduation. In the same May, 1917 issue of the *Nassau Lit* where Fitzgerald's poem appears, is an untitled "Sonnet" which in its octave evokes a happy, rural Hungarian village, "laughing, gay," and in its sestet its devastation by war:

. . . Seeing the crimson-snowed Carpathian hills,
The rivers of Galacia red as wine
The smoking heaps where once Gorizia stood!

And in 1914, "The Knights at Rhodes," fighting unto death:

The honor of our cloven mail
What scimitar can sever!

Be men to-day for half an hour,
And heroes then—forever.

A note in the *Literary Digest* of June 24, 1916 refers to "A Book of Princeton Verse" by undergraduates, edited by Alfred Noyes, "who has gone back to England to offer his services to his country's fighting forces." The reviewer quotes Noyes: "'It is encouraging to find younger men at an American university developing just those qualities of lucidity, order and proportion which are the first essentials of literature, at the very moment when the older generations, both in Europe and America, seem ripe for chaos in both thought and form.'" (n.p.) It is interesting to hear Noyes tacitly equating the chaos of war and the chaos he attributes to birthing literary modernism, and then to see the *Literary Digest* commentator choosing Stewart's "Knights at Rhodes" to illustrate this point: "From this same interesting volume we take this manly lyric. It has the energy and precision of one of Macaulay's ballads." One can imagine the author smiling wryly at this, since it so accurately pins the source of the poem's form and diction, but also since the author is moving aesthetically (at least in attitude) in the opposite direction.

For after April 6, 1917, when the U.S. declared war on Germany, ". . . the University cancelled the schedules of all competitive sports and within ten days the entire campus was drilling" ("Princeton in World War I"). President Hibben was mightily pro-war and refused a petition from two pacifist students to allow anti-war meetings on campus. Presumably Paul Fussell would, if there, have been among the pacifists. Stewart, unlike some, did not immediately enlist, foregoing graduation, but he and other newly-minted graduates went to Philadelphia and ". . .enlisted in May [May 24, 1917] very hastily with the idea that the whole outfit would be sent to France immediately" (Stewart to Philip Van Doren Stern 8 Nov. 1962). Stewart was assigned as a Private to Section 565 of the Army Ambulance Corps. But they were not so sent and ". . .ambulance troops piled up at the camp in Allentown, Camp Crane, so that it became a kind of permanent base instead of a mere staging center and had more troops than it could hold" (Stewart to Stern 8 Nov. 1962).

Camp Crane was the Allentown Fairgrounds, leased to the U.S. government as of June 9, 1917, and transformed into a military base with the express purpose of training volunteers in the newly-established United States Army Ambulance Corps, with the goal of the swiftest possible deployment to the Front:

> They had come out of the classrooms of many colleges, from automotive shops from small businesses, barber shops, and the farms. Some came with the urge to help the great cause of Freedom. Some came to free themselves from final exams . . . But all wanted to get on with the job and into action as soon as possible. (Smucker)

Initially it was called not "Camp Crane" but the "Concentration Camp,"as enlistees were billeted in the Sheep and Hog exhibit or the Poultry and Pigeons Building, and the possibility of swift action began to fade. The city of Allentown did everything they could think of to mitigate the recruits' frustration and their closeness of confinement: for example, the Mayor organized a group of "Big Brothers," citizens who arranged all sorts of entertainments (Smucker).

Stewart was not one to complain, and he was promoted to Private First Class on July 31, but was stuck in Camp Crane until April, 1918. He wrote an article about the Ambulance Corps for a 1917 issue of Princeton's "alternative" magazine, the *Princeton Pictorial Review*. Much of his text is neutrally descriptive, but, he calls the Allentown encampment of the Corps "distinctive" because its 5,000 men "are drawn from the whole country; not even the Rainbow Division can show a personnel more national" ("Corps" 64-65). Since much of the corps was formed of college men from all over the U.S., they often accidentally call the camp a "campus;" also, because these are the "better type of men," they display a "versatility of genius:" musicians, actors, cartoonists, journalists. To Stern he says Camp Crane was "almost a training school for writers." Using a bit of personification in his article, Stewart says ". . .the real commander of the camp was Dame Rumor. Rumors [of overseas deployment] blossomed and flourished like the grass of the field, and were as ruthlessly plucked up" (65). However, Stewart's section would have to encamp at Allentown for the winter. "We have still the great end before us and in the face of that a few months of waiting shrink to insignificance" ("Corps" 67).

Stewart took advantage of his own personal "Valley Forge" and the literacy of his comrades to gorge himself in reading and self-education. He read *Tom Jones* and a lot of other books, and taught himself "Anglo-Saxon" (Old English) (*Little* 18). A long letter to Gladys Knowlton, written in the Allentown YMCA, reveals some of his life there and shows a witty, informal style. He says he's going to do something very dangerous—describe the men he spends time with at camp—but that she should burn the letter afterwards (obviously, in tune with his humor, Gladys didn't) "because results to me otherwise might be fatal" (Stewart to Gladys Knowlton 1 Nov. 1917). The first man, in his enumeration, is "George Stewart—He is a Pasadena fellow but some way or other went to college in the East—Princeton, I think. He is really an inseparable companion; with me practically all the time except when I am asleep (deep stuff!)."

Another comrade was to belie the prediction Stewart makes:

> Morgan Odell:--I appreciate Morgan a lot and he is a fine fellow [.] Some way or other however, I don't believe we shall ever be really close friends. It may be strange but I seem to have to have some particular attraction to a man before I can enter him as one of my inner circle of friends. And I find very few of that class; I only found two or three at Princeton and you can realize that they mean a lot to me each one.

Of Bill Nye, another who will stay in touch with Stewart afterwards, a "man-after-my-own-heart," he says "Bill and I have undertaken the 'Great Quest' here in Allentown but so far have had no such great success." The object of the Great Quest is pretty obvious; Stewart says most of the guys he knows are engaged. He, Bill, and Sumner Reynolds—a big guy with pink hair—"form a trio in working parties. Sumner supplies the muscle and Bill the entertainment; I enjoy the results of both" (Stewart to Knowlton n.d.)

These characterizations suggest that as well as books, Stewart was also studying character, and was, perhaps for the first time, in the company of "kindred spirits" of his own age and inclinations. But the close quarters at Camp Crane and many other overcrowded bases led to rapid spread of pneumonia, yellow fever, and other afflictions; unfortunately, pulmonary difficulties like his father's emerged during these Army years, and he "was left with a permanent disability" which "has slowed me down greatly." My own grandfather, an Army doctor at Fort Bliss, near El Paso is evidence of this situation: he died in 1919 of a heart attack in his forties after three days without sleep ministering to the great numbers of sick and dying troops.

Fortunately, Stewart was transferred to the less overcrowded Army Medical School (to become Walter Reed hospital) in April, 1918, and to the Yale Army Laboratory School in November. But, apparently ill, and with the Armistice signed (the Ambulance Corps was dissolved in 1919), he was sent to the Base Hospital at Camp Upton on Long Island—future site of the Brookhaven National Laboratory.

Camp Upton, named after Civil War General Emery Upton, was constructed in the summer of 1917, and at least 40,000 soldiers including Sergeant Irving Berlin, passed through its gates. But after November, 1918, it was used only as a demobilization site for returning veterans ("Camp Upton"), so Stewart's two months in hospital there in 1919 must have been a preparation for his regaining enough health to be discharged, which he was on March 26.

Despite disease and nondeployment, Stewart's summation of these two military years was:

> . . . I learned a lot in the Army. But I mean this in more than a conventional sense. Like other educational systems, that of the U.S. Army is about 99 per cent waste, but the other 1 per cent, I think, did build itself into that complicated entity which, always changing, has been my personality, or character, or simply my *me*, throughout the years. (Stone 144)

*

Once he was sprung from the Army, Stewart plunged into an adventure in Hentyan self-reliance which, I feel, profoundly influenced his attitudes and values: he decided to hitchhike from Long Island to the West Coast. This deliberative adventure was for Stewart what Edward Abbey consistently considered his hitching to Seattle in the summer of 1944: "In a great many different places, Abbey cited it as the key formative experience of his life. . ." From this experience, in his own words "'I became a Westerner at the age of 17. . .for me it was love at first sight—a total passion which has never left me'" (Cahalan 4).

Although Stewart is infinitely more reserved about his own trip, his later writings, especially *U.S. 40*, testify to its importance. For one thing, he was reinacting, if not redeeming, his father's own migration in 1907, in the grip of the same malady. Secondly, he was engaging in an epical "homecoming" journey, which would establish California as the definitive "home" he would return to, as Yi Fu Tuan says a place of "psychological security," which also necessitates "the periodic need to go beyond . . .to the space of adventure and danger" (164). The "passage and return" life-theme initiated by Stewart's first rail trip to California was affirmed in this next experience. Also, the average Princetonian, as *soi-disant* intellectual, would move, figuratively or literally East in the postwar years, when the doors of Babbitry closed and those of isolationism, prohibition, depression, and the lot opened. But Stewart set his face and fate West, and although he was fairly soon to return East for convenience, it was never from commitment, but rather for adventure.

Most significantly, for his literary career, the hitchhiking experience was an education in several ways. It placed the American landscape, its concrete topography, on the soles of his feet, gave him a sensory awareness of geography and the physical environment, and the cultural presence of the "road" within it. In his quests for the right route, he enhanced his awareness of and sensitivity to the interplay of nature and the primary artifacts of human civilization: roads, settlements, and, above all, names on the land. The collegiality he apparently gained from his Army experience bore fruit in his enforced ability, and evidently growing pleasure, to encounter and talk with the fabulously diverse individuals he encountered and rode with from small town to small town across mid-America. This ability to engage with anyone was crucial to the field research behind many of his most important books.

Apparently Stewart began his pilgrimage almost immediately upon his release, for he writes "I went through G[ettysburg] again in March, 1919, when I was just out of the army and hickhiking [sic] my way west with the aid of a red chevron" (Stewart to Philip Van Doren Stern 8 Nov. 1962). The red chevron was worn by an honorably discharged soldier, and was clearly an aid in getting rides. By April 11, he had crossed the Indiana line, because his fragmentary diary of his journey, which is one of the first extended pieces of his writing available, begins at that date when he is in Marshall, Illinois, just over the state line.

This notebook covers only a brief period of his trip, but is rich with observed detail. Although he describes it as "worst day of all," in Marshall he "hit road at [circa] 7:30 hoping to make 100 miles or at least 80." He may not have perceived in the Marshall, Illinois of 1919 what he perceived in the early fifties, when his *U.S. 40* photograph of downtown Marshall characterizes its "Benjamin Harrison Era" business district ironically as "in its way an architectural gem, and might well be preserved as a historical monument. Individually the buildings are about as ugly as can well be imagined. . . In a hundred years, if they should be preserved so long, people may be comparing them with the Grande place in Brussels or some of the crescents in Bath" (142). In 1919, being "on the road" was all-important, and he records more the "pageant of life" in the characters who pick him up—a "timid henpecked-appearing man," the County School Superintendent, an old lady who lost her boy last fall to the flu and says he would have "survived just as good overseas."

Outside Casey, Indiana he "picked violets" and was picked up by a man "and rather beautiful woman; the man was "rather suspicious of me (I must be getting to look like a bear). Tried to get in with woman but didn't have time" [!]. Then he was picked up in turn by a soldier learning to drive, a tobacco agent, and by men with a sailor on furlough: "They were going somewhere to get beer, advised me to hit rails." He "started walking to Effingham [IL] to test the country; the country almost called my bluff."

On the twelfth he had a hard time—observed lots of birds, but was passed by lots of drivers, waited at various places (usually on bridges or by culverts) ". . .read a little Plato. Finally cursed Illinois and decided to make rest of trip a walk." Finally a nice couple took him to Greenville, and a hotel where a girl was playing the piano. He had hooked up with a guy named Eddie Joy, who'd had a navy career "about the same as mine in army," and who invited him to his house overnight. Eddie's parents were "very fine people. Old Mr. Joy very interesting with stories of early trip up Mississippi with Mr. Perkins, Col[onel] of R.R. engineers."

On the 14th, he crossed the Missouri with a young family, and lunched in Wentztown (actually Wentzville) on cheese and crackers which he "shared with well-behaved collie". He was driven as far as Columbia by a "very evident Jew." "Terry" drove him all day on the 15th, they ferried the Missouri outside Columbia, and continued to Pleasant Hill, southwest of Kansas City. They thus, apparently, left the course of U.S. 40 which he had heretofore followed, perhaps because of Terry's "hunting for wet towns & fear of losing road. Latter not unjustified." On the road again next day "several miles with jolly farmer. Then to K.C. with ex-tourist conductor—52 round-trips Boston to L.A. Friendly but not very interesting." Kansas City "does not seem hospitable for rides; otherwise I like the city well." Veering southwest on what is now U.S. 50, he traveled a distance in a car with an ex-soldier in an army overcoat, "married before he went to army and now rather at loss." They encountered an overturned Ford in the road, but no injuries. "We tipped it up straight and she ran like a clock." In Edgerton, Kansas, he found a "funny hotel with no landlady. Helped myself to room; dust in washbasin." Such a place would not have seemed unusual to Ish, returning to California in *Earth Abides* on a similar route.

Outside of Edgerton, Stewart became confused at a fork in "trails" (a word he significantly uses often in the diary for roads—in many ways they were as rough as trails)—and with good reason, because here current U.S. 56 heads straight west, and U.S. 50 (now partly Interstate 35) continues southwest. Fortunately a dealer in a Liberty car rescued him and took him all the way to Ottawa. Beyond Ottawa he was picked up by an "old settler." He "has been here about 50 years but does not look over 70; came out with wife. Nurseryman but about to retire on son's army insurance." The old settler "Told about old days . . . deer by Ottawa,---buffalo by Wichita; prairie chickens everywhere. Great hunter; has had a desire to shoot a mountain lion before he dies. Going to Colo. therefore, and then to Calif. Anxious to have me keep with him but I was not so anxious."

From Burrton, Stewart was driven to Hutchinson [KS] with another old settler in the back who said the help sent to Kansas in the old days did much more harm than good. The next day he reports "feeling low." He rode with a real estate man, and then with a "funny looking old man and woman. He was born w[ith] sister in sod house and married in one. Hardly been out of state but no fool." Beyond Hutchinson, he was picked up by a Buick that got a flat, and he "deserted." Then

> On with old buffalo hunter and Indian (?) fighter; interesting on old days no money in country except soldiers pensions, hard time but enough to eat and lots of fun when they were young. Few women in the country—10 mi. to see a new girl. On to G.B [Great Bend] in lady car with man and wife—woman very charming but man not too cordial I thought (they were loaded pretty full.) Woman asked me if I were writing book; she thinks I am some one; I am acting very foolishly and keeping her guessing.

This penultimate page of the diary concludes "I was ready to quit this morning but now will stick a while." The last surviving page is a fragment: west of Great Bend he notes a lot of landscape changes…the country is broadening out; there are fewer houses and more stock. The land is a little rolling, and there are "more western signs—Mexicans and cactus." It is as though his energy has been expended and fulfilled in reaching the invisible border of "the West."

Stewart's diary is a revealing artifact of a "rite of passage." In it he shows his adaptability to change, and persistence in the face of adversity. It also shows his interest in the intersection of time and space: as he moves across the land, he has temporally brief encounters with survivors of an earlier era who plunge him momentarily deep into the world of soddies and Indian fighting.

He became un-"stuck" in Kansas: "I got kind of sick, and I had had that bad pneumonia a year or so before," (*Little 255*) so he took the train at Garden City, Kansas. Actually, Stewart says that he wrote up this trip and tried to publish it, but couldn't find a taker, and "I threw it away eventually" (*Little* 255).

Once in California, despite his exhaustion he "hitchhiked up" from Los Angeles to Berkeley. "I slept out for two nights, and there used to be an oak tree some miles north of San Miguel that I could remember as the one I slept under. Once, when I woke up that night, a coyote that had been watching me near-by yelped and ran away. The oak has gone now, or has changed, so that I cannot recognize it. So has a lot else"(*Department* 1).

It was August, 1919. He spent a night in a hotel to get cleaned up: "The next morning I went to the campus to enter into, so to speak, my kingdom. You might even have noticed a certain resemblance between that young man and the present writer. I am gray-haired now [1968], and considerably weather-beaten, but my weight, I am glad to say, has not changed much" (*Department* 1).

Chapter II

Berkeley to Donner Pass

Stewart often retold the story of his entry into his kingdom, but it is worth retelling again:

> As I walked across the campus, that August morning, I had a cylindrical mailing case under my arm. I found the registration desk, rather charmingly placed, out of doors, near the present bridge across the creek . . .I approached the two girls there, pulled something from the mailing case, and handed it across. As it happened, my credentials from Princeton had not arrived, and I had brought my diploma along. If proof was needed that I was a college graduate, here it was!

The girl looked at it, and found it all in Latin, of which she did not read a word. But she could see the orange-and-black ribbon. She said, "That's a pretty one!" And so I was admitted, without the aid of a computer. (Stone 145)

Postwar Berkeley was not totally pastoral and idyllic. Upton Sinclair was stirring the waters at both of Stewart's universities with his attack on higher education, *The Goose-Step*. Princeton, whose library he had used in writing *The Jungle*, was full of "elegant young gentlemen lounging, garbed with costly simplicity and elaborately studied carelessness. . .Then I would go into the library and work for a couple of hours, and come out late at night, and see these same young leaders of the future come staggering out of their clubhouses to vomit in the gutter" (111). Sinclair's Berkeley, a "medieval fortress," becomes "The University of the Black Hand," run by the plutocracy. Benjamin Ide Wheeler, the President, is "intimate with the German kaiser," has been the "Dean of Imperialism," and is presented as insinuating military training into the curriculum wherever possible. "Needless to say, the university authorities see to it that no modern ideas get access to these young barbarians all at play" (141-42).

By the time Stewart returned to Berkeley as a faculty member, Percy Marks (Berkeley '12), who wrote the Ivy League novel *The Plastic Age* (1924), had written his own critique of American universities, especially of graduate education, as a form of complementary revisionism of Sinclair. He found "indubitable truth" in *The Goose-Step* (5), but considered that Sinclair had "shrieked the catalog of faults" of universities, "so raucously," that instead of appearing real they ". . .simply inflated themselves into grotesque exaggerations, gargoyles that were more amusing than awesome." Nonetheless, Marks, using English Departments as his example, rigorously attacked doctoral programs of study such as the one Stewart successfully began at Berkeley. A representative criticism is their specialization: "Most doctors of philosophy have spent so much time investigating the eye of a needle that they are not only unaware of humanity but even of the needle; in other words, they have 'specialized' so industriously on one small detail that they have lost all recognition of the relation of the detail to the subject of which it is a part, not to mention their blindness to universal knowledge" (85). It is interesting that the course Stewart was to embark on in 1919 would lead him to become one of the *least* specialized English Ph.D.'s of his generation.

Nonetheless, the Berkeley community Stewart entered just after the war was a pretty messy place, at least in the undergraduate world, as it is powerfully recreated in Clarkson Crane's shamefully neglected novel *The Western Shore*, which follows the fates of Berkeley students through the 1919-1920 academic year. Crane's students come from diverse, and not always savory, backgrounds. George Towne is returning to college after working in a Northern California lumber camp and visiting Joe Farley, his best friend, an inmate of Alcatraz. Milton Granger, whose father had been a member of Skull and Bones at Yale, makes friends with a fellow undergraduate, Groshen, who has fought in France beside his own English instructor, Philip Burton, who turns out to be gay. Tom Gresham is an older businessman who decides to return to college partly to be close to the girl he wants to marry, Ph.D. student Ethel Davis. Mabel Durant lives in an apartment at the corner of Durant and Telegraph Avenue; separated from her husband, she entertains a diversity of male undergraduates while Philip Burton tries to seduce at least one of them. These diverse figures mix uneasily, and often combatively, in Berkeley fraternity life. Stewart steered clear of deep involvement in Crane's world, as far as I can tell, but had to have been affected by it; for most of that year he escaped Crane's Berkeley by residing at the Berkeley YMCA with his old buddy from Pasadena, Paul Fussell.

*

The English Department at Berkeley, destined to become Stewart's lifelong professional home, in 1919 "occupied the northeast corner of the fourth floor of Wheeler Hall." In 1919 the faculty consisted of nineteen full-time teachers(five with Ph.D.) and five "Assistants" with only an A. B. (*Department* 2). However among these, and in other departments, were some charismatic teachers (all male). "When I came to Berkeley, things were dammed up inside of me, and ready to break loose" (*Department* 6), and, although Stewart sees that a lot of his development in that year was the result of "things that were happening inside of me," the figures he encountered had a great deal to do with breaking the dam.

Primus inter pares was the famous department chair, and dean, Charles Mills Gayley, "a meteoric figure lighting the sky with sparks more brilliant than the Golden Bear that he celebrated in song" (*Department* 14). Gayley was inspirational, democratic in his dealings with others, extremely liberal, and had "organized a volunteer ambulance company in 1917" (*Department* 15). He was also a precisionist with language. Stewart tells the "whore story," about Gayley's teaching, in a graduate Elizabethan Drama course, Dekker's *Honest Whore*. The person asked to give a report on this story was a teacher at Miss Head's school for girls "with all that implies for the year 1910." Nonetheless, she "manfully (if we may use that word)" gave her report, but continually pronounced the title "as if the *w* still did phonetic duty". Gayley "squirmed uneasily" and finally, "quietly but with rising volume" said "'Whore—*whore*—WHORE! It is pronounced *WHORE*! Why, Miss. . .even your little girls down at the school know how to pronounce *that* word!'" (*Department* 16). Gayley was "at his best, a superb teacher, and I am sorry not to have experienced him thus" (Stone 146). He was, however, very enthusiastic about Stewart, "one of the best prepared, most industrious and most capable graduate students that I have ever had under my charge." Writing in response to Princeton's attempt to woo the ABD Stewart to its faculty in 1922, Gayley praises, among other things, his "native as well as acquired critical taste, "his quiet and illuminating enunciation of underlying principles" [a quality that was to characterize his creative works] and his "dignified and pleasing personality" (Gayley to Radcliffe Heermance 4 March 1922/*P*).

Two other instructors were important to Stewart's career; in terms of art, Chauncey Wells "did much to inspire and to shape my style of writing," and Herbert Bolton's course in American Western History "...opened up a new world for me. Out of that course has sprung about half of all that I have written" (Stone 147). Bolton impressed everyone with his "tremendous vigor" and insatiable scholarship; in his joint interview with longtime friend and colleague, paleontologist Charles Camp, they both talk extensively about Bolton, as much about his pecadillos as about his professionalism. Stewart tells of Bolton accidentally getting locked in the library overnight, and, being "resourceful," finding a cot in the ladies' restroom; so in the morning the custodian found the professor sleeping on a mattress outside the ladies' restroom (*Little* 271).

It was Bolton who told Stewart, casting about for a master's thesis subject, that Robert Louis Stevenson had written an article for a Monterey newspaper, on file in the Bancroft Library. This was the beginning of a lifelong beautiful friendship with the library, and also Stewart's first archival discovery, eventually leading to his "first what you might call serious publication that I did in a professional way" (*Little* 228). The article, titled "San Carlos Day" after the Stevenson piece, was excerpted from his thesis and published in *Scribners* in 1920, with an introduction by Stewart. He had enterprisingly approached the magazine, saying he felt "no doubt of my ability to prove its authorship beyond question," and that the piece "is nowhere noted by any biographer or bibliographer. . . of Stevenson" (Stewart to *Scribner's Magazine* 13 Jan. 1919/*P*). Ultimately, *Scribner's* asked Stevenson's stepson and collaborator Lloyd Osbourne to evaluate "San Carlos Day," and Osbourne affirmed that "The article is unquestionably genuine; and to the ardent Stevensonian is of rare charm and value. I get an immense pleasure from it" (Osbourne to Robert Bridges, 15 May 1920/*P*). Stewart must have gained a lot of confidence from this authoritative endorsement of his scholarship.

Stewart's prefatory comments in *Scribner's* might serve as an introduction to this first sustained literary/historical writing, "Stevenson in California:"

> Tradition dwells grewsomely [sic] on a Stevenson at the point of death, sick, starving, and despondent. It is thus all the more interesting to catch this glimpse of a Stevenson in California more consistent with his usual optimism—bearing himself 'like one who does not fear a bottle and a glass,' laughing to himself at the crudity of a Western celebration, and initiating a movement for the preservation of a Spanish church which stands to-day as Stevenson predicted, one of the treasured relics of California. ("San Carlos Day" 209-210).

"From this work sprang a long number of 'firsts' in my life: writing Western history, experiencing the "fascination of old newspapers," the rewards of field work as opposed to library work, the linking of literary with geographical and anthropological investigation. Most tellingly, it led to "my first bit of scholarly-popular publication [the *Scribner's* piece], thus essaying a difficult genre from which I have never escaped and at which I have never been wholly successful" (Stone 150-51). And, we might add, a genre whose hybrid nature may have led to much of the neglect that Stewart's writings have fallen into today.

". . .Every now and then someone gets ["Stevenson in California"] out and reads it! I have no protection against this invasion of my youthful privacy, and I tremble at the thought of the callowness that must be revealed," Stewart exclaims (Stone 150). Well, I did just that, and found the diametric opposite of callowness. It shows already a comfortable fluency with narrative history, a sensitive exploration of character, a smooth integration of research and storytelling, and, above all, insight into the dynamics of an "encounter" with an alien culture and physical environment. The fascination with this encounter, its challenges to psychic and physical survival, goes back to Stewart's earliest reading, and forward into his future scholarly-popular writing. It is the dramatic realization of "complexity" by the innocent outsider.

Stewart sees the "neglect" by critics of Stevenson's California period as due primarily to the fact that almost all his critics have been Europeans or Easterners, and therefore unable to understand its full significance ("Stevenson" i). For example, the author of *On the Trail with Stevenson* (1895) confesses straightforwardly 'I regret to say that I have never been to California," though he has visited every other site of Stevenson residence. ". . .Like many other natives of New York, I have always found it easier to cross the ocean than to cross the continent, and have studied nearly all the European countries before studying my own" (Hamilton 130). Thus, from the outset, Stewart establishes his western identity as a critic; he is one laborer in the "gigantic" process of "informing the East" about the West ("West" 771), and is in the paradoxical position of doing so by informing the East about what a quintessential, naive Easterner (from a continent to the East) discovers about the West.

Stewart is quite accurate in his characterization of Stevenson critics as neglecting California. He had been dead only 25 years, and with his tempestuous and tragic life, it was his subequatorial exoticism that excited. For example, in *The True Stevenson: A Study in Clarification*, published five years after Stewart's thesis, a book whose title promises revisionism, California comes up only twice. The material covered by Stewart's book becomes a footnote (61-2), and the voluminous quoted correspondence of Stevenson's first wife, from California, does not talk about California. The second is a brief reference to a letter from California. No Stevenson biographers to the present, that I know of, have read Stewart's thesis (maybe his spirit is relieved at this). The 1974 Twayne English Authors Series volume on Stevenson gives California a brief mention and then sets off for the South Seas (although one can perhaps see a source of Stewart's affinity with him in the authors remark that Stevenson's "popularity is often held against him as an indication that his literature is suitable only to the less sophisticated" [Saposnik 18]). David Daiches's 1973 illustrated biography has a few good California photos and reproductions, but refers, of his works, only to *The Silverado Squatters*. Ian Bell's 1992 study covers Stevenson's life in California in six pages and makes the assertion that the editor of the Monterey *Californian* "pretend[ed] to take Stevenson on as a part-time contributor" (Bell 137).

Although there's no evidence he read Stewart either, William Gray gives the most careful attention to the California experience in *Robert Louis Stevenson: A Literary Life* (2004), discussing the ideas in his articles and letters, and defining it as a "transition" between his dependency on his father and responsibility to support his own family (91). None of the citees above, however, approaches Stewart's bold assertion that he will "show that it was under the stress of this Californian period that he laid the foundations for the mental and spiritual qualities of a great artist" ("Stevenson" i). Probably none either did what Stewart did, personally interviewing the remaining acquaintances of Stevenson (obviously, of course, except through ouija, our later biographers could not do this); nor did they "visit . . . personally most of the spots formerly familiar to Stevenson.....to connect as closely as possible the writings with the environment from which they developed" (ii).

Here Stewart's sense of cultural ecology is clearly manifested; he needs to experience the actual physical space in nature invested by his subject to "know," as far as is possible, that subject. By going into the field, Stewart also had the opportunity to apply some of his ideas, based on personal experience and deeply-felt reading, of courage, survival, and environmental dependency: ". . .the whole future course of [Stevenson's] life seemed to turn upon a hair. In California Stevenson for the first time met hard realities of life: he faced death, knew poverty, and felt the threat of failure" (1). He was in California "an essentially untried character thrown suddenly into circumstances in which he was tested at every angle by the grimmest realities of life"—a condition which could apply to the Donner Party, Isherwood Williams, and many of Pickett's soldiers at Gettysburg.

Perhaps thinking of his own experience sleeping under trees when he hitched to Berkeley, the first incident of "grim realities" Stewart elaborates is Stevenson's "quixotic" camping in the mountains south of Monterey. "He had often walked thru the pleasant, well populated mountain districts of Europe, but he had probably no conception of the barren and almost uninhabited Coast Ranges of California" (9). Stewart interviewed Mrs. Culp of Monterey, who as a child ran down with the grownups to see the man lying sick under the tree.

Stewart gives as much detail as is known about Stevenson's rescue, his "adoption" by Simoneau, and his often cheerful days writing—despite sometimes despairing—in Monterey. When he went to San Francisco, though, Stevenson is characterized as having been subject to an opposite environmental stress, "the utter loneliness which is all that the great city can offer to the stranger" (18). His recurrence of pleurisy (one strong connection Stewart may have felt with his subject) is described, and his rescue by, and subsequent marriage to, Mrs. Osbourne. Stewart quotes extensively from his letters, as Stevenson vacillates between resignation and defiance in the face of death. He satirically refers to the "graveyard philosophy" of the Stevenson quotes which find their way into all the anthologies, contending "the real test of a man comes when he faces life. . ." (26). Stewart constantly returns to the "testing and proving" theme (33): Stevenson comes to California, still a "boy," a case of "arrested development" due to his illnesses, and leaves a man. Like "The Grove" in Stewart's own boyhood, "California" almost becomes a character in Stevenson's life, a teacher of "how to live," whose natural discipline allowed Stevenson to "grow beyond" his apprenticeship (36).

However, Stewart ponders deeply why California, if it had this role in Stevenson's identity-formation, did not inspire him to more powerful writing:

"it was a land which we should have thought would stir into action all the vivid imaginative powers of which Stevenson was possessed" (55). He goes on, "Stevenson was in California just thirty years after the year '49. The Argonauts, the men of the mining camps and prairie schooners [,] had sunk into tradition just far enough to be lost to the light of reality, and yet not too far to be plainly discernible [sic.] as individuals" (56).

Tellingly, Stewart attributes this "discrepancy" between "opportunity" and "realization" to his basic human psychology. Although it transformed him, Stevenson's experience was negative, and he could not make himself the hero of "his own serious story." "The basically tragic atmosphere of his Californian adventures closed the field of the mock-heroic, while at the same time the common self-respect of the man prevented treatment in a more serious vein" (59).

The remainder of "Stevenson in California" discusses the works he *did* manage to write in, or about, it. Stewart is very interested in Stevenson's description (in *Across the Plains*) of the deserts of Wyoming and Nevada, which would so impress Laura Ingalls Wilder later, and had so impressed Washington Irving, as excerpted in Henty's travel anthology, before. He considers that Stevenson's *The Old Pacific Capital* has "never been surpassed" (64). He is critical, however of Stevenson's "lugubrious predictions" for the future of California:

> In spite of forest fires California remains a land of promise. In spite of "Jew storekeepers," and the truck system, the economic prosperity has survived. As yet the racial mingling does not seem to have produced any 'monstrous hybrid.' And if the Indians have passed, so too have the sacreligious pistol- shots. (65)

Perhaps Stewart's most notable "literary historical" contribution is his discussion of the shadow role California played in Stevenson's later fiction. As cultural geographer, he claims that since in the 1880's San Francisco "lay upon the edge of the island world, ever present altho [sic] perhaps seldom seen," it is "the background of civilization against which the South Seas projected their barbarism . . ." (82). By comparing the real topography and flora of the Monterey Peninsula with those of *Treasure Island*, he argues that the former is the physical model for the latter, and on similar grounds that Mount Saint Helena, in Sonoma, has become Spy-glass Hill (89-90). Future critics of Stevenson cast a glance at this theory, but tend to find the novel's sources in literature, not in life.

All in all, "Stevenson in California" is pretty remarkable as a 1920 M.A. thesis in an academic world still under the aura (although figures like Gayley were changing it) of German philology. It is an anticipation of the "microhistories" Stewart so enjoyed writing, using detail to expand the seemingly trivial or fleeting into the momentous. It articulately combines literary history, sociological commentary, psychological insight and theory, all under the umbrella of an environmental consciousness. Gayley said "it is one of the best theses I have ever seen among those submitted for the master's degree" (Gayley to Radcliffe Heermance 4 March 1922/*P*). It would have been of interest to Stewart that in 1969 Norman and Charlotte Strouse began to plan "The Silverado Museum," near St. Helena, to be devoted to Stevenson and named after his eponymous California book ("Founding").

Of course, Stewart, to achieve his *summa cum laude*, had to undergo a much more painful ordeal: the 5-part M.A. examinations, written and oral. Their existence, he said later "is an evidence of the immaturity and uncertainty of the department at that time" (Stone 148). Of the first M.A. oral (in "expression")--the memory of which Stewart was to conflate with his Columbia Ph.D. oral in the novel *Doctor's Oral*—he says "I am not quite sure what that one was supposed to prove or test. Perhaps the examination was designed to keep you from getting your degree if you displayed too much of a Siskiyou County accent . . ." (Stone 149).

Princeton was pursuing Stewart even before he got his M.A. He replied to a solicitation from Radcliffe Heermance saying "I expect to get my Doctor's degree, however, before I shall be really in field for a position" (Stewart to

Heermance 14 Feb. 1920/*P*). He applied, rather, to the Ph.D. program at Columbia. By his account, despite the high standing of the program at the time, he found the Columbia program pretty disappointing—but then, he seems to have been disappointed with every educational milieu since high school graduation. He had thought about continuing his M.A. thesis for his dissertation to cover all of Stevenson's American experience, but he really wanted to study American literature, in which there was no course at Princeton (and not many even in the mid-1960's). Carl Van Doren at Columbia got him into a study of American writers in England, but Stewart became very discouraged: ". . .I think, as I look upon it now, he didn't handle me right. He threw me into it, and the thing looked too big to me. . ." So, instead, he got involved with metrics. His advisor on this subject was supposedly Ashley Thorndike, "but not really. I mean he wasn't doing much. He just let me stew around, but I came out all right" (*Little* 21). One can notice the less-than-rave reviews given by the "off-beat" Stewart to two of the most respected academic intellectuals of the time.

And the department was apparently surprised at how quickly Stewart completed his study, *Modern Metrical Technique*, covering two centuries of evolution in ballad meter. Stewart's comments, in this regard, on doctoral dissertations, are well worth reading:

> Of course I looked upon the Ph.D. as a thing you ought to get into and get over with, and I think that's the right attitude toward a Ph.D. So many of these people go at it as if the Ph.D. thesis were going to be their great work in life. Often that's what it amounts to, with people working for years and years, and they grow old before they even get their Ph.D. (*Little* 22)

Of course, as well as completing his dissertation, Stewart had to complete his doctor's oral. At Columbia "morale in the graduate school that spring [1922] was very low. Recording [sic] to general gossip, the last six aspirants to the Ph.D. oral had failed. It may have been true, and, at least, the graduate students believed it" (Rereading). At the outset, Professor Krapp of the German department who "was, I think, pro-Stewart from various contacts I had

had with him" asked (in German) the question about the meaning of *Vierhebungstheorie* which actually does initiate the fictional exam in *Doctor's Oral*. Krapp knew full well that Stewart had studied this, the "four-stress theory" and had done reading in German about it. "At that moment in time. . .I probably knew more about that theory, its origin and development than anyone else in the little room—and perhaps in the world" (Rereading). "I always thought I passed my own doctor's oral in the first half minute," when he responded to Krapp's question (*Little* 131-132).

Stewart has a great story about the "publication" of his *Modern Metrical Technique, As Illustrated by Ballad Meter (1700-1920)*. When he was discharged from the Army in 1919 as "permanently disabled," "I became eligible for certain educational benefits." It was, he says, sort of an informal version of the G. I. Bill after World War II. "They" would "paternalistically furnish me with pencils," and other academic needs, but all his personal needs were his responsibility. In May, 1922, his dissertation was submitted and approved; but there was a rub: ". . .the Ph.D. candidate at Columbia, before being awarded his degree must deposit in the University Library one hundred printed copies of his thesis." Reflecting back on "ridiculous and even insulting requirement. . . I wonder why I ever went to Columbia." It would cost $800 to print a hundred copies. "Then I had a big idea." He went to the Veteran's office and pointed out that without 100 copies he would get no degree. He deposited one printed copy with the V.A. in New York, and headed for California. "Some time that summer I got word that the printed copies were deposited in the Library." So his thesis had been published "at public expense." But the whole experience had "a mad Marx-brotherly quality." The "only justification for scholarship lies in its discovery and dissemination of knowledge," but all hundred copies of his scholarship's discoveries remained, and remain, as he assumes in 1979, locked up and undisseminated (Rereading).

Rereading it, Stewart is slightly satiric about his dissertation: "The paragraphs march steadily and sternly forward, like veteran grenadiers." But he finds some redemption in thinking that it has one quality "that some years later would become characteristic of my writing, that is, the development through time of an abstract or non-human entity. An arrangement of syllables, in its way, looks forward to a storm or a fire."

Compared with "Stevenson in California," *Modern Metrical Technique* is substantially retro. Yet there's more to it than this. As modernism was born after World War One, so some other attributes of the Romantic revolution in literature of more than a century earlier returned in their old roles. One was the populistic literarization of the "common," the "everyday," or, to use a tendentious word, the "folk." This movement toward including the popular *in* the scholarly (or literary) can be illustrated by figures such as Francis Child, John Jacob Niles, and Bertrand Bronson (a friend of Stewart's), the heirs of Bishop Percy as gatherers of orature, particularly "folk ballads." Also a great deal of scholarship was emerging which gave a literary *imprimatur* to the non-"literary" ballad. Gummere's *The Popular Ballad* (1907) provided a great impetus toward recognizing the importance of the ballad as literature, through his detailed typology thereof. However, while recognizing the contributions of anthropology, ethnology, and sociology to the understanding of literature (21) he persisted in affirming "the old theoretical and critical antithesis between popular and artistic verse" (21). While affirming the value of popular balladry in a seemingly radical way ("Social realization in art can by no conception be called common or unclean even now, but must rather be regarded as drawing the individual out of his more sordid self; what is bad in art is really antisocial" [322]), Gummere alludes to Taine in declaring ". . .in the affirmation of modern poetry, is the plain negation of the more primitive ballad" (323). Stewart's own study uses, ironically, the epithet "modern" to undercut this simplistic dichotomy. By reducing "ballad" to "meter," its prosodic essence, he can avoid the whole issue of genesis, evolution, and possible extinction of "ballad" as genre.

In this he is harmonious with Louise Pound, whose fairly pugnacious *Poetic Origins and the Ballad* was published in 1921, just in time for Stewart to absorb its ideas. Pound is out to refute the unsupported "assumptions" of Gummere and his school of ballad critics: "communal" authorship of "primitive poetry;" ballad as earliest and "most universal literary form;" the illiterate as ballad creators; and the "belief that the making of traditional ballads is a 'closed account' (vii). She proceeds to deconstruct the word "ballad," by showing the diversity of verse forms it has been applied to, from medieval times to the present. For example, in Stewart's realm of interest, she evokes and rejects John Lomax's attempt to apply the theory of communal origin to cowboy songs of the southwest. "Even the pieces which may be called genuine cowboy pieces," she says, "are no doubt largely adaptations, echoes of some familiar model, or built on and containing reminiscences of well-known texts or airs" (218). And, as far as the 'closed account' goes, "Unless *style* determines what are genuinely ballads and what are not, the making of ballads, *i.e.*, short verse-narratives of singable form, is not a closed account; and there is no reason why it ever should be such" (232).

Stewart's metrical concerns probably fall into Pound's category of "style," but one of his main points is that, while persisting in its simpler forms, ballad meter was various and complex in medieval poetry, has gained increased complexity in the 200+ years his study covers, and persists in many forms. Without implying "communal" authorship, he considers that "As the great popular measure of traditional songs it gained a place in the hearts of the people, and a song which is really of the people is as likely today as ever to be in ballad meter" (20). While Pound takes to task the school of Gummere for a blurred vision of the ballad, within a "cloud of romanticism" (236), a nostalgia for the Romantic era when literary interest in balladry arose, Stewart sees the period of the later 18th century ballad revival as the time when ballad *meter* was freed from earlier stylization by "the restoration to poetry of spoken word order" (34). Although Stewart does not address the Pound-Gummere controversy directly, he implicitly undermines its dichotomies by evoking the cultural diversity of verse based on variations of ballad meter—from the Percy ballads to Cowper, Burns, Vachel Lindsay, Gilbert and Sullivan, Mother Goose, and even an analysis of "Eenee, Meenee, Meinee, Mo," of which he says "The author can here state as an original authority that the metrical effect was entirely satisfactory" (110). In terms of metrical *practice* he draws the opposite conclusion from Pound: the increase in metrical variety merely heightens the presence of the metrical regularity underlying it: "The metrical development of the last two centuries has thus been not a revolt against classicism by a romanticism careless of form. It has been rather the revolt against a special metrical convention and the replacement of an easy by a difficult technique. The end of this revolt has been really a new classicism" (119).

Of course, in characterizing modern metrical technique as a new classicism, Stewart is being a *provocateur*, and must deal with free verse (which he continues to call *vers libre*) by defining it as "a particular type of rhythmical prose" (118). But in doing so he could also be seen as prefiguring the paradoxes of form in his future novels about the "development through time of a non-human entity." The classicism of his complex structuring in these novels—such as *Storm* and *Fire*-- underlies their "romantic," seemingly spontaneous, irregular movement through time and space. While Stewart's dissertation is about prosody, it is about a cultural form of expression suggested to be universal, "natural," and encompassing; thus it could be seen as analogous to any force in nature possessing these same attributes.

His dissertation was not the final trial of Stewart's academic apprenticeship. He still had to pass his Doctor's Oral, which he did successfully with the help of kindly Dr. Krapp. Then, in the summer of 1921, Stewart spent four months escaping from academia on a cycling tour in Europe, from Sweden to Italy. But, returning to Columbia to work on *Modern Metrical Technique*, he was already looking to obtain a full-time teaching position following his graduation. On January 7, he wrote to Prof. Heermance at Princeton (who, it will be remembered, had contacted him about teaching there in 1920), "I am at present looking for a position to teach college English beginning in the fall of 1922" (Stewart to Heermance 7 Jan. 1922/*P*), and followed it with letters of reference. The "Executive Officer" of English at Columbia wrote in support that "He . . . passed the first oral examination with marked success last spring," and that he "has impressed us all as an unusually able and promising man" (A. N. Rondith to Heermance, 16 Feb. 1922/*P*). Apparently, Stewart had also applied for, and been offered, positions at the University of Colorado and the University of Michigan, and had already received an offer from Princeton, since Heermance wrote him in April "about purely personal affairs." He "hope[s] very much that you will accept the Princeton offer," because the position cannot be held open for long. But then he added some articles of persuasion. He realizes Princeton's offer of $1800 (*per annum*) is "not as good financially" as those of Colorado and Michigan. But "All the Western Universities have to pay higher salaries to instructors to get men to go so far west." He recognizes "that the Michigan opening is an attractive one, but then again the opportunity to teach in one's own college particularly appeals to me." And, anyway, ". . .a position in the Princeton Faculty, even at a somewhat lower salary, would be more desirable even from a practical stand point, than a position in some Middle Western or Western University" (Heermance to Stewart 17 April 1922/*P*).

I can almost see the good professor's sneer as he writes that last phrase. Anyone who knew Stewart well would know of his deep love for the West, and the irritation he surely felt at these condescending remarks. He, however, ended up compromising: at its May meeting of 1922, the University of Michigan Board of Regents approved the appointment for the academic year 1922-23 of George R. Stewart, Jr. to the Department of English at an annual salary of $2,100 (*Proceedings* 483).

*

Stewart's one creative work during his year at Michigan, was not literary. ". . .Being my first teaching year my nose was pretty well to the grindstone. I wasn't doing much experimentation. I was getting engaged" (*Little* 169). As he described it, university president Marion Leroy Burton's wife gave a tea, and for some reason he and another new instructor were invited. "The wife of one of the English professors whom I had met, and who was being nice to me, said, 'I'd like you to meet---'" The person in question had been told by the English faculty wife that "'There's a new instructor in the English Department. I want you to be nice to him.'" Stewart notes "(She has been, for a good many years.)" (*Little* 169).

The person in question was the president's own daughter, Theodosia, who, due to illness, had taken a year off from Vassar to help tend to the presidential household. By the end of the academic year, seemingly as planned as clockwork, George and Theodosia ("Ted") were engaged. But for the next year they were apart; Ted finished her college work at Michigan, and her fiancé made his next cross-country trek, to Berkeley, which he had left three years earlier, thus avoiding the "Revolution of 1920," when, with Gayley nearing retirement, a general purge of the English Department's faculty occurred (*Department* 29).

Although he had been reappointed as Instructor by Michigan for 1923-4 with a hundred dollar raise, $2,200 a year (*Proceedings* 727), Stewart chose to be Instructor with "advanced standing" at Berkeley for the same amount (*Department* 31). One can't help feeling that this true "return" had been his goal all along, a complete spatial refutation of Heermance's *dicta*. However, the University of Michigan Secretary, Shirley Smith, had a different take on his reason for leaving: that, although there was no rule there that relatives could not serve on the faculty or staff, ". . .nevertheless, Stewart had sufficient independence and self reliance to make him feel that he would not run the slightest risk of embarrassing either Dr. Burton or himself by his continuance here under the new family relationship." Smith had ". . .always thought that the manner of his leaving here reflected great credit on his substantial manhood and independent character" (Shirley W. Smith to Robert C. Clothier, 23 Sept. 1926/*P*).

This letter appears to be a document in the paper trail of one last attempt—maybe as a matter of university honor—to lure Stewart back to Princeton. Clothier, who was acting director of Princeton's Bureau of Personnel and Appointments, had written to Stewart's old mentor, Thomas M. Parrott, also, for a recommendation, since "it is probable that during the next few months we shall have occasion to consider him for a position" (Clothier to Parrott 20 Sept. 1926/*P*) and Parrott had replied with high praise "He was one of the best undergraduates I ever taught . . .He would make a good assistant professor in any university" (Parrott to Clothier n.d./*P*). Of course, again, Stewart, now married and a father, may already have been feeling the discontent of nonpromotion at Berkeley that was to lead in the 30's to his "breakout" as an imaginative writer; on a personnel form of 1926 he listed Shirley Smith as a reference, and to the question "In what other countries would you be willing to teach?" replied "For sufficient compensation I would teach in any country except Hell" (Alumni File).

Back to Ann Arbor, May, 1924. George marries Ted, "the boss's daughter," in an opulent ceremony ("a Roman Holiday") at the Clemmons Library, and then they attend their reception in the president's house next door. "They invited practically everybody. Among the celebrities came Henry Ford, out from Detroit. And we had the ceremony in the library. That was very fitting after all, for me" (*Little* 170). Ford had his secretary send them as a wedding present a signed set of Joseph Conrad's works; the newlyweds got one of the bridesmaids to stake out Ford and get him to sign the set too, which he did. "It looked like the signature on the old Model T, exactly" (*Little* 170).

In a good counterbalance of aristocracy and populism (of course one could say Henry Ford embodied that himself) they spent their honeymoon driving to California (the emigrant again), "a wild trip in an old Studebaker . ." They had to detour through Canada to get over the Sierras, and the Studebaker broke down on the Redwood Highway in northern California, where they "had to spend three days camped out near a primitive roadside garage" before finally reaching Berkeley, and then Stewart's parents' house in Pasadena (*Little* 171-72).

*

Like many a new academic couple, such as myself and my wife, the Stewarts traveled a lot in Berkeley in their early years: "a tiny place up on Canyon Road, right up above the stadium," "a little apartment . . .on La Loma," "another place down on Hilgard," each for a year. Then for three years, they shared the house that Ted's widowed mother had bought on Hill Court (*Little* 38). In 1924, President Burton could write to his son-in-law "It's great to be 50. Now I have a right to get gray, bald, and cranky" (Marion Leroy Burton to Stewart 7 Sept. 1924). But by November, President Coolidge was writing to Ted, wishing her father hope during "these trying days of his illness" (Calvin Coolidge to Theodosia Stewart ll Nov. 1924). By 1925 Marion Leroy Burton was dead.

The domiciliary itinerancy of his early career didn't seem to impede Stewart's type of informal and affective teaching. A former student remembers being in his first poetry class in 1925. "You were my favorite professor. . . We met . . .at your little house on the hill, there was a fire in the fireplace and your charming wife served tea" (Marion Lehnert to Stewart 27 Jan. 1942). But as far as his personal and professional life went, Stewart is very eloquent in his memories of the stressful times in the 1920's (memories that may have colored his reaction to Mizener's *Far Side of Paradise*:

> I was in a fairly confused state during those years when my children were little, but I think it's a very trying time in many ways. It's a completely new experience. It's a rather difficult thing. . . .And of course at that stage it looks like forever, but actually it's a very short period, if you have a moderate number of children. They grow up so fast that somehow it isn't your whole life after all, but it seems that way at the time. (*Little* 39-40)

Moreover, "even in those years we were playing the Publish-or-Perish game . . ." (Rereading), so, as well as teaching, Stewart was mining and refining the material from his dissertation, and publishing it in the politically correct journals of the time—for example, "The Iambic-Trochaic Theory in Relation to Musical Notation of Verse" in the *Journal of English and Germanic Philology* and "The Meter of Piers Plowman" in *PMLA*. Even in such rarified realms, Stewart injects skepticism. In the former essay he declares he will "shun the extreme technicality of the experimental method which is usually unintelligible and therefore unconvincing to any except the advanced specialist" ("Theory" 61). In the latter he insists on approaching Langland's versification from the point of view of modern metrics, compares him with Eddie Guest and Walt Mason, and considers that "we have no right to hold to these conclusions [that Langland wrote "a debased form of Old English verse"] merely because by so doing we maintain an orthodox connection with a particular theory of Old English verse—which in itself is humanly derived and therefore possibly incorrect" ("Meter" 128).

Stewart also did write articles for less traditional periodicals, using material that he had gathered in his graduate peregrinations or was contemplating anew. From his original Columbia thesis idea, he wrote a most interesting piece, "Whitman and His Own Country," which, while officially about Whitman's reception in England, also suggests his growing interest in American "ways of life," and the interaction of the nation's nature and culture. "Whitman offered to the Americans naturalism, naivete, and apparent formlessness. These were, however, just the qualities which the Americans . . .feared to be already in their possession in too great abundance" ("Whitman" 218). In the 1850's—a period to which Stewart would constantly return—there was in England a minority avant-garde "in revolt against established conditions" (216); Americans, on the other hand, whose lifestyle was collectively more in harmony with Whitman's aesthetics, (quoting John Addington Symonds), "'when refined are apt to be absurdly overrefined'" (217). The case of "sex" is the perfect example: "At that time a writer hardly dared even to call a spade an agricultural implement—the safer course was not to discuss gardening" (216). When Whitman gained more acceptance later in the century, Stewart observes the paradox: "A poet of democracy rejected by democracy, accepted by feudalism, and by feudalism restored to democracy!" (215). This is Hentyism in reverse.

A similar sense of national paradox, and one which borders on the environmental, can be found in a 1926 article on Bret Harte—about whom Stewart was already gathering ideas and information for his future book. In this case he focuses on Harte's journalism in Northern California, and specifically the events of February 20, 1860 when "the superior race decided to display their superiority" over the Indians ("Frontier" 270), and massacred sixty residents of an Indian village near Eureka. Harte, in Stewart's characterization, "lived on the frontier, but was not of it. The goal of life toward which he had set himself was a Tennysonian excellence. . ." (271). But, in his role as assistant editor of the *Northern Californian*, it was precisely this "high-minded" Anglophilia that allowed him to report in disgust and condemnation the details of the attack, calling the perpetrators "butchers" (272). Within a month Harte had fled south to San Francisco, in Stewart's view probably under the threat of mob retaliation. Clearly Harte's role as an outsider in California ended up in strengthening "his sympathy with Indians and Chinese, the downtrodden races in California" (273).

I wonder how many touches of himself Stewart might have felt in Whitman and Harte—was he still at this time experiencing himself as "in" but not "of", a regionalist yet still a stranger? It is thought-provoking to note that his *Bret Harte: Argonaut and Exile* was written in England and "while we was [sic] holed up in a village of southern France across the bay from Toulon" (Rereading).

One other periodical writing of this period, trivial in itself, is worthy of notice since it suggests the lurking urge toward the non-academic writing on which his literary identity was to be based. In the aura of his two children's birth (Jack and Jill—I've often wondered about this), and the child-naming incumbent thereon, Stewart wrote for *Children—the Magazine for Parents*, a little, cutely illustrated piece "What's in a Name?" about the popularity and choosing of children's names. This is, to my knowledge, as well as being Stewart's first piece for a completely non-academic audience, also his first writing in the academic area where he will become prominent—what he calls onomatology, the study of names. He used the Berkeley catalogues to assemble "a statistical study of American names," drawing numerous astute conclusions, such as that the prevalence of Jeans and Joans after World War I was due to France and Joan of Arc ("What's" 22). He also offers advice to parents on name-choice. Don't choose names just rising in popularity or just falling; with the latter "she will probably have to go through life with a name just old enough to be shoddy, yet not old enough to be quaint" (23). He constructs, albeit casually, a sociology of names—Dinah and Chloe are "colored mammies," Bridget is a cook, Geraldine and Alfreda are "Lady." Conservative families choose conservative names, liberal ones liberal names. And many names carry an unintentional social slur. "Consider the suitcase of the poor girl named Alberta Susan Spear!" (23).

Meanwhile, Stewart had been generalizing and expanding his dissertation, as new assistant professors are wont to do, into a full length study of meter, *Techniques of English Verse*. This was to be, except for certain articles, and his many onomatological writings, his last scholarly tome. "It sprang partly out of my teaching, partly out of desire and hope for an additional income, partly from my life-long feud with blank paper" (Rereading). Despite his ironic admission that "A small volume . . . making a general survey of English meter and the conventional forms was not what the American public had been awaiting with bated breath," and it did not get him the promotion he so fervently desired, even now (1979) he gets word that "someone likes and uses the book" (Rereading)—certainly: for example, in 1960 a John T. French wrote Stewart desperately seeking a copy.

The purpose of *Techniques*, the author says, is to provide "deeper insight into the art of verse, so that as reader or writer, he may appreciate more fully its infinite subtleties" (1-2). The most interesting passages are those in which Stewart suggests larger contexts in which verse functions, than metrics. One is its psychological exploitation of illusion based on the strong "tendency of the environment of words to affect our method of hearing them." Thus ". . . the same words placed in different metrical patterns can easily be read, or heard, in different ways." He gives as an example a kinetic environment of music: "The violin player concluding a pianissimo ending sometimes holds his bow suspended over the strings momentarily, in full knowledge that the listeners, still thinking him playing, will continue to hear the same faint sound that they have just been hearing" (6-7). As noted in *Modern Metrical Technique*, this approach to prosody is analogous to the ecological mode of apprehending the individual organism: it exists only as part of a whole.

Other points in the text evoke a realm that might be considered cultural ecology. In an archetypal Stewartian figure, the poetic line becomes a road, and its stresses become milestones; to define four miles, five stones are needed (42). Although Stewart says "Jo[sephine] Miles thinks I'm a great enemy of poetry, but I'm not really" (*Little* 17), you get the feeling from *Techniques of English Verse* that the author sees prose either encompassing or overshadowing it. His references to prose seem to convey it as the large realm to which verse is a mere duchy. For example, the verse paragraph ". . .in its most highly developed form may . . .be defined as an indefinite number of metrical feet grammatically and logically so closely united that no full stop is possible, and with the minor pauses so arranged as not to fall into regular order." Therefore it "is practically coincident with the sentence" (163). Prose might seem to be primal, and verse created by its distortion (the simple become complex): ". . . nearly any passage which would ordinarily seem prose can by a little facility of the tongue be read in such a way that the stressed syllables space themselves, and what were previously the irregularities of rhythm constituting prose become the variations of meter" (191). In printed form, a text is verse "if it can easily and naturally or with pleasing effect be read as verse; if, however, too great distortion of the natural values of the language is necessary, the passage can more naturally be considered prose" (192). The "natural" references reach their apotheosis in the following figure: "Few people can turn from a volume of French forms to a volume of good prose without a feeling of gracious rest; it is like passing from city to country, from a Rococo interior to forest scenery" (196). And, further, "There is something in the very ductility or fluidity of prose which has, at least by contrast, a charm. The rise and fall of a fine prose sentence is in itself pleasing, to say nothing of the fact that its lack of definite form does not allow us to feel it as a thing apart from its meaning" (196).

In the above we might be able to discern a perhaps already decided-upon direction towards prose, and also the analogous prizing of nature over artifice, the feeling of reading or listening to prose presented as equivalent to observing the curve and flow of a sinuous-even sensuous- landscape.

*

In his review of *The Far Side of Paradise*, Stewart finds unusual similarities between the lives and personalities of Fitzgerald and Bret Harte. In *A Little of Myself*, he finds an important difference between himself and the subject of his first extensive, non-technical, scholarly-popular (prose) book:

> . . .writing about Bret Harte was a good thing for me, as a matter of fact. It showed me what a trap writing can be. He was a prime example of a man who should never have cut loose. He should have taken that job at the University of California when he had the chance. That would have changed his whole life. He probably would have written much better, and had a much better life all the way around. (31)

To deconstruct this contrast, one might say that Stewart sees himself as having wanted more than anything else to be an imaginative writer, but that he has learned the freedom of imaginative writing can best express itself in the secure captivity of institutional structure. Applied back to the environment figure in *Techniques*, this might suggest that the countryside of the imagination can best be conveyed from within the security of the (perhaps not Rococo) interior. As far as his devotion to his university "kingdom" this is certainly true, although when *Bret Harte* didn't get him promotion, he became a restless citizen of the kingdom. Certainly Stewart wandered literally far and wide in creating his later works, but he was always ranging *from* that interior, to which he could return. A great force in the shape of Harte's life and the shape of Stewart's fluid book about that life is the itinerancy, the unfixedness of that life. Harte's life was one of "ductility and fluidity," and I suspect that as Stewart researched for it, roughly at the same time he was writing definitely non-ductile works on poetics, he was wondering about this quality in Harte's career in relation to his own migratory urges.

Stewart wrote *Bret Harte: Argonaut and Exile* during his sabbatical in Europe in 1930-31, so in this sense he had wandered far to write about a writer of his native soil. Of course he was writing about someone who had both in lifelong adult persona, and temporarily in literal fact, adopted California as native soil. Harte had come from the East as a stranger—as Stewart did—and returned eventually from whence he came. Stewart migrated to California, adopted it as a surrogate native soil, and in the sense of adoptive homeland also returned from whence he came.

Actually, Stewart's Harte book was the result of an abortive project for a massive "social-cultural history of the Gold Rush period," which Stewart realized was too grandiose to achieve. Having gotten involved with Harte through the article on the Indian massacre, he decided to "save Bret Harte" out of the larger project. "He was a man who needed doing," and there was a degree of "academic opportunism" in the whole project (*Little* 109), although this was his "first real swing at 'general' writing" (Rereading).

Before the European interlude, Stewart had spent a lot of time interviewing relatives and acquaintances of Harte, as he had for Stevenson—in fact the concreteness of reference and personal empathy in both biographies may be due to this fieldwork. He was able to interview both Harte's sister Ethel, still living in San Francisco, and his literary acquaintance Ina Coolbrith (*Little* 115). Some former acquaintances of Harte refused to cooperate, like Clay Greene, who as a child knew Harte but refused rather strongly to be interviewed (Clay Greene to Stewart 27 Oct. 193?). He corresponded with Harte's grandson,

Geoffrey Bret Harte, who had in 1926 published a "sanitized" collection of Harte's letters (only recently superseded by Gary Scharnhorst's restored collection). In answer to Stewart's query, Geoffrey says "I fear I cannot be of much assistance for your biography of Bret Harte," but then goes on at great length and defensively to discuss his collection's purpose to "clear his name of the slander that had been attached to it in America . . ." "The perusal of these letters that form the most human autobiography clearly dissipates the myth that Mrs. Bret Harte and her four children were left stranded in American under circumstances akin to poverty while her husband led a luxurious idle life abroad." Great detail is given of the financial support Harte gave to his wife, and she is indirectly accused of creating the myth of her own neglect, through her choleric "disposition." "I remember my grandfather very well—an old man with snow white hair who was extremely fond of my brother Richard and myself" (Geoffrey Bret Harte to Stewart, 6 Sept. 1930). Perhaps Stewart's sympathetic yet dispassionate reading of Harte's life found motivation in the obvious partisanship of the grandson, and his fixation on family relationships.

He attributes much of his motivation in telling Harte's story to the great interest in biography at the time (inspired by Lytton Strachey's *Eminent Victorians* and such), and the congruent "loosening up of the language with a vigorous use of the colloquial," under the influence of Mencken and others. The prizing of prose in *Techniques* we can see realized in his fusion of biography and unleashed language, such that in the "Rereading Notes" he pronounces narrative as "the queen of literary forms," and in a crossed-out passage he combines to characterize it two figures we've already encountered. It is queen because "like language itself it is single-tracked and . ..indeed, even sinuous, but always holding to the trail for the end."

The dominant themes of the biography itself are connected with the sinuous trail Harte followed, and the contradictions between his itinerancy and the "bioregionalism" he led his audience to identify with him. The European residency his grandson so ardently defends created a complex dual identity in

Harte, as constructed by others—old world dandy and symbol of new world California.

Stewart was always proud of his opening sentences, and in *Bret Harte* he uses paradoxical bathos to create immediate effect: 'In the annals of mankind the year of our Lord 1836 is not memorable." A little further on, "A drab enough time it was to be born,. . .and a drab enough place, too, 15 Columbia Street, Albany, New York" (3). Stewart chronicles Harte's drab and dysfunctional life in Albany and New York, and its contrast to his rich, imaginative precocity, up to the point of where, through his own East-West passage, imagination and "reality" in a way converge, as the boat he and his sister are on passes through the Golden Gate in 1854. Bored in Oakland, his life scarcely documented, Harte is deduced by Stewart, from topographical references in his works, to have escaped it as both a wanderer and a schoolteacher in the Sierra foothills.

Eventually, in 1857, Harte arrived in Union, California—soon to be named Arcata—on Humboldt Bay. Stewart inserts Harte into a vividly-described natural and cultural place:

> There were the usual unkempt streets, a church or two, a flagpole, stores and saloons, and a long pier running out across the tide-flats. A few tall redwoods stood in the outskirts and some great stumps—ten and twelve feet in diameter—studded the town. To the south were the mud-flats and the Bay. ; On the other sides there was a narrow fringe of cleared land and beyond that one of the most magnificent forests in the world—unbroken miles of giant redwoods" (62).

Expelled from Union (as recounted earlier) after his Indian massacre article, Harte returned to San Francisco; he "descended the gangway, and all unknown came into his kingdom" (94). Stewart has used this term for a centering place for himself, and doing so for Harte, he parallels it to Franklin's similar embarkation at Philadelphia. In a few years, as an employee of the San Francisco Mint, Harte, married and parent, maintained a public identity as Bohemian and a private one as *pater familias*, all the while working toward literary recognition in a bestirring artistic community. But Stewart emphasizes that Harte, the urbanite, moved his family from house to house every year. He could not keep still, resigning his position on his friend C. H. Webb's successful periodical the *Californian*, returning (despite family) to Sierran wanderings.

Stewart details the culture-clash in California of the 1860's, which Harte experienced in 1865 with the publication of his California poetry anthology *Outcroppings*—a pioneering attempt at cultural regionalization widely ridiculed for the low quality of its nature verse, yet envied by jealous legions of poets not included in it. This divide in cultural awareness is emphasized by Stewart with respect to mining culture. The aspiring post-gold rush immigrant writers, "looked upon the miner unsentimentally as a person who in intelligence and social position ranked with the ditch-digger of the city and the farmer's hired hand," but, paradoxically, the original 1849 mining generation was "beginning to appear romantic," and one criticism of *Outcroppings* was that its "sunsets, birds, and flowers" ignored "the real glory of the state . . .its crude but heroic beginning" (150-51).

Increasingly, as his life of Harte progresses, Stewart evokes the problematic identity of California as a cultural and bio-region. A striking example of this is the logo Harte chose for the new (1868) San Francisco magazine he had been persuaded to edit, the *Overland Monthly*. Its name was chosen as suggestive of the new transcontinental railroad reaching fulfillment on the old overland trail. The logo on the title-page, however, carried the emblem of "a bear upon a railway track, snarling at a presumably approaching train" (159). The bear, as totemic state emblem, was, said Mark Twain, a "'good'" bear, but an "'*objectless*'" bear. Harte drew in the rail lines, creating a technological environment for the bear. Twain thought it was a great success "'. . .the ancient symbol of California savagery snarling at the approaching type of high and progressive Civilization . .'" (159). Stewart wonders whether any of the principals really understood the "full ironic significance" of this emblem, and the paradox that the magazine's very name suggested "its own worst enemy:"

> As long as California was isolated, it had a chance for its own cultural development; but once the railroad had made it a suburb of New York City, both the possibility and the need of the *Overland's* survival disappeared. Instead of making the inland country tributary to San Francisco, the railroad made both tributary to New York. . .For [Harte] the bear stood for the churlish crudity of the frontier from which he had revolted; the railroad for the East and Europe which had long been his Eldorado, not of the setting, but of the rising sun." (159-60)

Of course, when he had returned to his Eldorado, Harte became the literary symbol of that very frontier from which he had revolted. And that return took the form of a reverse epic journey. Having rejected Berkeley's offer of the position of Professor of Recent Literature and Curator of the Library and Museum, and received tempting offers from Eastern publishers, he determined to go East. As Stewart describes it:

> On the morning of February 2, 1871, the Overland Express clattered away down the Peninsula toward San Jose. Woe to any crude Western grizzly who shall stand snarling in its way! In one of its new-fangled combination parlor-and-sleeping cars rode Bret Harte, his wife, and the boys. He had become too great for the city in which he had become great . . .(185)

Unfortunately, and again paradoxically, Harte disappointed the Easterners who'd been eager to see him. He had retained too much of his Western consciousness. Stewart embodies this no-win situation in describing Harte's visit with Emerson to Walden Pond late in 1871, and his ridicule of the tameness of Eastern life—for example, Emerson's idea of a "wet night" consisting of one glass of sherry (203). But Harte and Emerson conflicted most on what Harte considered a naïve view of California in Emerson's "Civilization." Stewart considers "Transcendentalism and realism were grappling that day, just as, less concretely, they were grappling at the same time everywhere in American thought and literature" (203).

This declaration relates to Stewart's own upcoming career as an imaginative writer with environmental concerns. His characterization of the railroad in Harte's life has been tinged by the realism of *The Octopus*, as his later writing will be. And, similarly, though Stewart wrote his book in Europe, his overarching concern is with a California viewed as both rugged and, realistically, vulnerable. The bear and the railroad could be two magnetic poles between which Stewart's own charged imagination oscillated; both are, and are not, California.

Harte's older years in Europe are powerfully evoked by Stewart—even Geoffrey Bret Harte liked this part. In England of the *fin-de-siecle*,

> He was fast becoming a ghost. The life with which through his constant writings he was most closely bound, had long ceased to exist. The Stanislaus [River], which he remembered so turbid with slumgullion, was clear now; the ditches were weed-choked; the flumes wrecked; the sluice-boxes long rotten. California was growing wheat and fruit, and setting bait for tourists. 'Wingdam' [archetypal mining town] was dust and forgetfulness, a crying-place for coyotes; Los Angeles was growing great in the land." (301)

Stewart's figure for Harte in his ultimate incarnation is the one he repeated in his autobiography (see Chapter 1): the marine animal. "'A marine animal,' wrote the schoolboy, 'is completely surrounded by its environment.'" As Stewart says, incorporating Harte as a representative of all humanity in this ecology, "Unfortunately, this applies also to all human beings, although with some it is more noticeable than with others." Harte, in these later years, was most like the marine animal in his willingness to write for any venue in order to survive economically; he was an aging Donner Party of one, gaunt in a natty suit. Stewart recalls a meeting between Hamlin Garland and Harte in London: "Suddenly Garland sensed the bitterness of exile beneath the fine English clothes" (320). As exile, Harte was not only the marine animal using its resources to survive in its environment, but also one that has been blown off course into strange seas, of necessity making them its own, but rejecting free passage back to the yearned-for habitat of origin.

In a Class of 1917 *Princeton Alumni Weekly* note, in April 1931, Stewart wrote "I have just finished a biography of Bret Harte which I hope to see published before the end of the year. . .I published a book on versification . . .last year but I don't expect anyone to buy that" ("Class Notes"). And although its unfortunate publication when the Depression was shrinking purses limited its sales, the biography received a lot of notice from those related and unrelated to its subject. Geoffrey Bret Harte was extremely impressed: "The time and patience and thoroughness devoted to research is quite awe-inspiring." But his praise of the California chapters is balanced by pretty devastating responses to the chapters on Harte's later years in the East. "I have not anywhere had so strongly the feeling of an unpleasant, unstable and unlovable personality as that conveyed in your book." He considers this effect to be enhanced by Stewart's "apparent impartiality." He also criticizes a review by Newton Arvin, the noted scholar of 19th century literature, in the *New York Herald Tribune*; according to him, Arvin considers Bret Harte as "a reprobate who has been saved from disgrace and dishonor by your book." Much of the letter's continuing verbosity is to this effect. "Please forgive me if my words offend you . . .," but they seem intended to offend (Geoffrey Bret Harte to Stewart 28 Feb. 1932). Harte's daughter was much more level-headed in her response to it, as "absorbingly interesting and well written." However, she takes exception to him as having been "henpecked" by his wife. Otherwise, "you have been very accurate as far as I know and have made a very interesting and dignified addition to the Bret Harte memoirs" (Ethel Bret Harte to Stewart, 5 Dec. 1931).

Stewart could well say "As a character, Harte was good or bad, depending upon whom you were relying [on] for the opinion" (Rereading). He could take comfort from the positive reviews, such as that by Fred Lewis Pattee in *American Literature*, whose take on the European years is the direct opposite of Geoffrey Bret Harte's: "The man's European years of exile one sees now in a new light, one that does honor to him. Instead of leaving his family to their fate, he worked like a plow-horse to keep them in copious spending money" (224). Pattee says "At last an adequate biography of Bret Harte" (223). E. Douglas

Branch calls it "a volume meticulously and unimaginatively conceived, developed, and written" (132).

However I suspect he was gratified by the personal one of his "old friend" at Princeton, J. Duncan Spaeth. Spaeth was "interested in your admirable skill as a biographer," and compounds it of "exact scholarship, minute documentation, sound critical method, with the novelist's skill in telling a story, the psychologist's subtlety in analysis." He only wishes Stewart would now do a book of literary criticism of Harte (Spaeth to Stewart 24 Nov. 1931 [?]). Spaeth's effusive review of *Bret Harte, Argonaut and Exile*, in the *Princeton Alumni Weekly* repeats some of what he told Stewart privately, but, clearly distinguishing between literary criticism and literary biography, calls it a "literary portrait which is itself a work of art—scholarship flowering into literature. . .". This seems to me the most astute estimation yet of the mode Stewart was groping for, to fuse fact and imagination into new forms.

Perhaps the most amusing response was that of the literary periodical *Contempo*, whose editor asked him to send an "author-review" of the biography. Stewart says he can't "answer" his critics, since they've "been so uniformly generous," so he will limit himself to pointing out the "bad qualities" in his own work. As well as petty inaccuracies, he mentions the subtitle as "inaccurate, silly, and nothing but a cheap bid for sales." He does refer to a positive critic who wishes Stewart had included a "critical appraisal" of Harte's work, "an undertaking . . .which I still consider almost as little connected with biographical art as a recipe for onion soup." He concludes ". . .had you granted me more space, I could have thought of many more and worse things to say about my book" (Stewart to the Editor, *Contempo* 29 Mar 1932/*R*). More recent biographies of Harte don't seem to give Stewart any more credit for his work than he himself does here. He is mentioned only twice in Axel Nisson's 2000 biography, even though Nisson's aesthetics of "narrative biography" could have been taken directly from him. Biography is "Positioned as a discourse between fiction and history," and argues for "a greater awareness of the 'fictional,' constructed nature of all historical discourse" (xx). Gary Scharnhorst's more recent biography does allude to or quote Stewart several times, all approbatively. But Stewart is not mentioned in the most recent (2005) article I have seen on Harte, which is concerned with how the "romance of partnership transforms local history into myth" (Watson 40). I guess Stewart's lack of abstraction is considered simply too old-fashioned today.

*

Back in his departmental kingdom, Stewart experienced what he calls the "bad years." The Chairman was "inadequate," there was poor morale, and "A final trouble was that the whole educational world was in the doldrums, largely because of the Depression" (*Department* 32). "What really saved the situation" was the "pleasant" Berkeley community. "In a sense, even, this pleasantness corrupted us. We were sometimes in danger of selling our intellectual heritage for a mess of good friends and a benign climate." As for Stewart himself, "Though I got my Associate Professorship in 1935, things still stagnated, so that I took to writing novels. I should probably never have done so if the opportunities in the Department had been opening up enough to keep me fully interested" (*Department* 33). Some views of Berkeley in the 1930's were not as glum. Robert Nisbet, who refers repeatedly to Stewart's influence in his memoir *Teachers and Scholars: A Memoir of Berkeley in Depression and War*, found the campus full of excitement: "You could, in an almost literal manner, feel the Berkeley campus pulsate as you walked onto it in the 1930's" (Stone 309). John Kenneth Galbraith, who was a research assistant in 1931, recalled that the graduate students in the 1930's were "uniformly radical" and many were communists (Stone 25). The great physicist Glenn Seaborg, who began graduate work at Berkeley in 1934 recalled its "exciting, glamorous atmosphere" (Stone 53).

In 1934, George R. Stewart, still an assistant professor, was surrounded by colleagues of (academic at least) renown, in his department: Arthur Brodeur, John Tatlock, Thomas Whipple (a Princeton graduate), Willard Farnham,

Merritt Hughes, Bertrand Bronson. He was teaching "First Year Reading and Composition" (as were many of his illustrious colleagues, admittedly) "American Literature: 1860-1912,"under the composition rubric, "Biography" and, on the graduate level, "Reading Course I" ("Reading in limited fields, with a report," and "Readings in Medieval Literature" ("Interpretations of the Text") (*Catalogue* 216-222). He and Ted bought the house on San Luis Road, "a terrible place," initially, but "really a very lucky house. The children grew up there and I became a writer and full professor and everything else" (*Little* 39), but the first two years there (1934-6) were the most "discouraging," for his lack of promotion, Depression effects, "and all that." According to Harvey Swados, "the situation for the serious American writer in the bottom of the depression was in its own way as 'unnatural' as that of the novelist during the fifties and sixties, after the dropping of the bomb and the burgeoning of the so-called mass society." It was "unnatural" because "the financial and moral collapse had called all values into question, and beyond despair lay only a faith that was itself to be called into question before the decade was out" (Swados xxvii).

In these depressing years, however, Stewart, as writer, was not driven to despair, questioning all values—or, indeed, drawn to any faith. However one may choose to judge this course, he continued to write prolifically on many subjects unrelated to his political/cultural surroundings. His "The Moral Chaucer" is akin to his conclusion of new classicism in *Modern Metrical Technique*, in that he proposes the unorthodox position that Chaucer was morally orthodox: ". . .nearly half the *Canterbury Tales* are not only directly didactic, but also sufficiently orthodox to have passed any archdeacon" ("Moral" 96), and contrasts to it Chaucer's *Troilus and Criseyde* as a "reading of life" that "attempts to probe the motivation of human existence," with a "strikingly black" conclusion thereon (104-5). He anticipated the genre-breaking of *Ordeal by Hunger* by publishing an essay on "Color in Science and Poetry" in *The Scientific Monthly*. Here he covers scientific texts, natural history texts, books on fabric dyeing, and advertising jargon to support the claim of a scientifically-driven progressive increase in the detail, qualification, and quantity of color-names.

> To Gilbert White straining his eyes over the dead lark, to the chemist watching the marvelous play of color in his Fehling's test, to the physician searching through his microscope for the tints which distinguish the eosinophile from the polymorphonuclear, to the housewife matching scientifically dyed thread to scientifically dyed fabric, to the rancher's daughter isolated beyond the last filling station nervously ordering a spring dress from Sears Roebuck or Montgomery Ward, to the very tot in school studying the color chart arranged according to the discoveries of physics, the accurate distinction of color is the business of every-day life. ("Color" 77-78)

The conclusion drawn from this lusciously logorrheic observation is that the "very standardization produced by science, considered to have killed poetry, has actually aided it, by enriching its palette". In 1935 he contributed an imaginative and detailed study of frontier theater to a festschrift for Thomas Marc Parrott, tracing the diversity of productions available on the frontier through the detailed records of the short-lived Nevada Theater in Nevada City.

So, returning to the Depression, and viewing Stewart's output in this period, if anything he maintained--and dramatized so fully in *Ordeal by Hunger*--a faith in human survival, including his own. As far as books go, at this time he was writing a somewhat dry, but sometimes witty and enlightening pedagogical text, and also practicing his craft in creating another one of great excitement and intensity, one which would spring him into the realm of wide public consciousness, and of truly environmental writing.

The former book was the two-volume freshman composition text, *English Composition: A Laboratory Course*. I can see it as a product of "First Year Writing and Composition," and planned as a final "obligatory" publication in—at the time of planning—Stewart's still futile attempt to gain promotion and tenure, which, ironically, came to him before the text was published. Stewart says

> The originality of the book lies,. . .in the method and in the details. The study of composition is approached as a series of, as it were, laboratory

> experiments. Each assignment presents a definite problem or series of problems which the student must solve to the best of his ability. . .One of the greatest advantages of this method is that the responsibility for the work to be presented in class and for the class-room discussion is placed where it should be, not upon the instructor, but upon the student. By this method it becomes to a greater extent apparent to the student that his advance depends upon his own labor, not upon the amount of advice directed at him by the instructor. (Stewart to Richard Thornton 26 Nov. 1934/*P*)

Admittedly, there was some novelty in the "laboratory" concept of writing instruction, which was to become a term of art in succeeding decades. But the best passages are more or less humorous asides and examples in volume 1 (volume 2 provides writing exercises and sample texts from the canon). For example, he discusses "morals and manners" in language—in effect, content and conduct. Both, abused, receive social punishment: "The man who stabs another with his knife may be hanged; the man who eats mashed potatoes with his knife will probably receive few invitations to dinner." The immoral person who maintains good manners will go unpunished, "But let a man spit his olive-seeds upon the table-cloth and, though he have the morals of a bishop, he will seldom be seen again in good society" (I.1).

The reader following Stewart's dicta in a foreshadowing of *Ordeal by Hunger* will find him meditating on and reaffirming, often in apparent paradox, the qualities he sought in that book. He says "be effective even at the cost of being correct" (4). He calls time the chief organizing element in everything we call literature, and that "time-segments can be reversed and rearranged" (40-41). He articulates the writer's difficulty reconciling interest and ease of understanding: "difficulty repels most people, and in an arrangement by ease difficulty must come at the end" (46). In reader-response mode, he says "A word means what the person it is addressed to thinks it means," so, for example, a "radical" could be to one reader "someone prepared to vote for moderate changes in social legislation," and to another, "someone ready to throw bombs" (155). Finally, with a glance back at Bret, he asserts (to a presumed Californian audience) that most dictionaries are products of New England and may define word usage in other parts of the country as "regional" but do not recognize that New England usage is itself "regional" (157).

*

In the Harte biography, Stewart notes that in Harte's novel *Gabriel Conroy*, the prologue, ". . .a vivid narrative of an emigrant train snow-bound in the high Sierra, [was] suggested obviously by the story of the Donner Party" (226). This suggestion has been greatly elaborated by Michael Clark, with reference to Stewart's *Ordeal by Hunger*, who says the novel. . ."casts—in quite an unattractive light—the pioneers' arrival in California" (50). However, Clark also shows how many incidents—filled out by Stewart—Harte borrowed directly from an early account of the Donner Party by J. Quinn Thornton, the one who recorded Tamsen Donner's dismay (see below), and who also turned off in time from the Donners' fatal route. In both *Gabriel Conroy* and "The Outcasts of Poker Flat," according to Clark, Harte gave the survivors moral attributes—charity and abstention—and the victims' self-indulgent immoralism as causes of their fate. It is hard to know how much of Harte's Donner reference was known to Stewart but not included in his biography; however, he certainly amoralized the history when he came to tell it. As he says, it is not a pleasant story, but "the merely pleasant is thin and bloodless" (241).

In 1940 Stewart's friend, novelist Norah Lofts, who was later to fictionalize the Donner Party in *Winter Harvest*, wrote praising his *Ordeal by Hunger*: "Some passages are the equal of anything ever written, and I think its justice and tolerance are especially notable." She characterizes it as the "study of a mixed mass of people under stress" (Norah Lofts to Stewart 1 Nov. 1940). British expatriate novelist C.S. Forester, who was to become one of Stewart's closest literary friends, on arriving in Berkeley, had Stewart introduced to him as another author. "'One more professor who thinks he can write and has written an unsaleable book,' thought Cecil when being introduced. It was only later that he realized that Stewart had written *Ordeal by Hunger*, the story of the Donner

Party that we had all admired" (Forester I. 370). These responses from acquaintances were echoed by readers everywhere. In no way is *Ordeal by Hunger* an allegory of survival relating to the Depression; but, although narrating a story whose gruesome elements were common knowledge, it had the inspirational effect in its own world that the exploits of Seabiscuit had in "popular culture." It is also, as Lofts suggests, a cultural study of a group under environmental stress surviving through sheer will, a quality in it that Stewart always emphasized later.

To Stewart, *Ordeal by Hunger* was "very valuable training for writing. . .because that's a very complicated book, many sides to the account. It uses a technique that most historians have not known how to use. . .a kind of novelistic technique" (*Little* 11). Interestingly, this very technique led John Langellier to criticize the narrative's "shortfalls:" "Although Stewart crafted a forceful narrative because of his academic background as an English professor, nonetheless his own presentation often reads more as a piece of fiction than an analytical history" (xiii). Presumably "novelistic" is bad and "analytical" is good. The critic misunderstands the author's viewpoint and intent: in it his "weaving" of story threads fuses the affective and objective, and allows the reader to follow the journey in an environmental context. Also, the "novelistic' elements aesthetically parallel the literal content, which involves "writing about trails," and "wandering"—as in his own earlier life and books—although he later insisted that the central "thread of development" in it is "the environmental statement" (11). In his "Rereading Notes" Stewart elaborated on this latter point: "Ordeal by Hunger is . . .the first of my books clearly to develop the environmental theme. Its conflict is not man against man, but man against nature. In this book and most of the following ones I showed an interest in environment, beginning a whole generation before it became fashionable."

After *Bret Harte* and his failure at promotion, Stewart ". . .got to feeling, well, I've done enough work up there to get my promotion, but they won't promote me, so what's the use of doing a lot more just to get my associate professorship. The Donner Party had always appealed to me as a great story which ought to be written. So I pretty consciously said, "What have I got to lose? I might as well risk something and do this." I had a wonderful time doing it" (*Little* 25). Also, despite the protocol of academic writing, he felt "English departments generally have a sneaking admiration for a writer who is trying to produce something original, and not another treatise on a dead author" (Rereading), although elsewhere he characterizes the book as a "revolt against the University" (*Little* 113). So Stewart took the first of many trips to the Donner Pass area on March 4, 1932, "which was the day the banks closed." On these trips he went over much of the territory on foot, and figured out the geographical background; he also found a couple of the tree trunks the snowed-in party had sawed to the snow line, and persuaded the Donner State Park people to preserve them in the museum (*Little* 116).

Stewart had initially become interested in the Donner Party from reading the first synoptic book on it, C.F. McGlashan's *History of the Donner Party: A Tragedy of the Sierras* (1879), "a good story, but badly told" (*Little* 117), in part because of its moralism *a la* Harte, and timidity in discussing the unpleasant. In compensation, Stewart read every conceivable record of the expedition, many of which emerged only after 1879 (he appended even more to the revised edition of 1960), and actually plotted the story as though it was a novel, given that he had to weave six or seven different story lines together.

It is amazing that McGlashan's account was the only full story of the Donner Party before *Ordeal by Hunger*. McGlashan was himself a pioneer, in bringing together what memoirs, selections of letters, and oral accounts he could into a sequential narrative (not that such narratives were unknown—if we consider Henty). But what a difference between the ways the two writers begin their journeys! McGlashan evokes the pastoral panorama of Truckee (now Donner) Lake, site of the expedition's overwintering: "Three miles from Truckee lies one of the fairest and most picturesque lakes in all the Sierras" (1-2), with the unsubtle irony of juxtaposition. "Yet this same Donner Lake was the scene of one of the most thrilling, heart-rending tragedies ever recorded in California history" (10). Stewart, with the benefit of 50 years' change in language and literary technique, and with the idea of historical narrative using fiction's techniques, begins with an (as he notes) as yet unachievable panorama of the West, viewed from "some hundreds of miles above a spot near the center of the state of Nevada." Stewart's scene is not juxtapository. It is holistic. It emphasizes the human-diminishing topography of the entire physical terrain the emigrant trains set out to traverse:

> Far to his left, westward, the onlooker from the sky just catches the glint of the Pacific Ocean; far to his right, on the eastern horizon, high peaks of the Rockies forming the Continental Divide cut off his view. Between horizons lie thirteen degrees of longitude, a thousand miles from east to west. A sweeping glance reveals a region of high plateau, mountain, and desert, brilliantly alight with a seldom-clouded sun. The far-reaching scene is somewhat lacking in the brighter colors, and in general dull green, drab, and gray possess the land. But here and there, spots of bright blue reveal lakes and a shining dazzle of white shows the location of alkali plains. Little snow appears in the scene, but it is, we remember, midsummer. The land knows snow in its season. (13)

"It is a thirsting land" (14), and the elevated observer can see crossing it, on the divergent courses of the California trail, the emigrant trains, just come into view, "their white wagon-tops agleam." "It is a long road. . . .and the chief opponent is Time" (15). So here we can experience the endeavor in a primal nexus of space and time—and of two geometrical dimensions: the vast nonhuman area woven through by the minuscule human line. "If a map produces a static landscape that can be managed from above," says Rick Van Noy, "the sublime produces an active, resistant space and promotes humility" (34). Here Stewart has sought to create a verbal map of the sublime.

All the intimate, the claustrophobic spaces we will experience later can refer back to this almost visionary expansiveness, the temporal needle weaving through the timeless geological and atmospheric fabric. Immediately we are forced into novelistic engagement with one individual. "Tamsen Donner was gloomy and dispirited as the wagons pulled aside; Mr. Thornton noted it in his diary" (15). Tamsen, wife of the train's namesake, "Uncle George" Donner, weaves the dominant narrative thread of the many in the story, and she, perhaps of all the party, has achieved the most mythical status. The last time we encounter her, the final evacuee from the encampment, the unpleasant German Keseberg supposedly tells his rescuer '"He eat her body and found her flesh the best he ever tasted!"' (215). Tamsen's fate is the culmination of many novelizations of the Donner party, although in them it is not in Keseberg's stomach. In Norah Lofts's *Winter Harvest,* disguised as "Mahitabel," she is killed by another crazed woman, Nancy Juror, in the night before morning breaks and "like ants on a white cloth the small dark forms of the relief party. . .showed against the expanse of snow between the cabin and the Pass" (347). In Vardis Fisher's *The Mothers,* Keseberg awakens and "looked with astonishment at the frail little thing lying on the earth floor. He thought at first it was a child. After a long moment, he moved over and laid a palm on a cold brow. Tamsen Donner was dead" (334).

The immediacy of Stewart's entry into the close life of the party, immediately after a Gaiaesque vision, throws us unprepared, "naked" into this new world, just as the Donner Party itself has literally done. There is no contextual introduction, as in the later *California Trail.* The reader is dropped *in medias res* of the expedition, *ex machina,* and might be deliberately disoriented so as to experience unprepared the text as the party experiences unprepared the terrain.

I would like to discuss *Ordeal by Hunger* in terms of form and of content. For the former, I will show, by juxtaposing Stewart's literal chronology of the Donner itinerary with his sequencing of it in the history, his "novelistic" weaving of threads, seeking in a temporal narrative to evoke the simultaneity of events in time. For the latter, I will present *Ordeal by Hunger* as his first venture into environmental history, based on a principal of cultural ecology.

In the following discussion, the entries in Stewart's chronology (294-97) are presented in roman, the sequencing in the narrative itself, and its pagination, in italics. The chapters are the defining units by which Stewart novelizes his history.

July 19, 1846, Camp at Little Sandy Creek [Wyoming]

Three paragraphs (15-16): departing the camp at the "place of separation," to take the Southerly route to Fort Bridger

July 20-28 Travel from Little Sandy Creek to Fort Bridger

16-19 Hastings' advertising of his route, his character, the Donner members persuaded by his untrustworthy propaganda.

19 A paragraph lyrically setting forth the emigrants' position between a "half-remembered past" and "unknown future."

20-29 "Muster Roll;" this chapter is based on their choice of a leader after leaving Little Sandy (July 2), and is imposed by Stewart on the temporal sequence to individuate and characterize by appearance, place of origin, temperament, ethnicity, motivation, wealth, the individuals in this "microcosm of humanity" (19).

July 28-30 At Fort Bridger

July 31-August 6 Follow Hasting's trail from Fort Bridger. . .to Weber River

August 6 Find Hastings's note at Weber River crossing

29-39 "The Trap Clicks Behind:" travel to Fort Bridger, rumors of route ahead; discouraging note from Hastings found; rhetorical questions: "But what could they do now?" (34).

August 6-11 In camp at the crossing; Reed and others sent ahead

August 12-27 Cross Wahsatch Mountains. . .

34-41 "The Wahsatch:" return of Reed; his story of encountering Hastings and difficult route ahead (34-35); details of following days' difficult struggle; arrival of a new wagon—Graves and Fosdick Families; "by pick and shovel they had beaten the Wahsatch;" "playing . . . against Time" (40).

August 28-September 1 Travel from near [Salt Lake City]. . .to springs in [Skull Valley]

September 2 Rest at springs

September 3-8 Cross Salt Lake Desert to spring at base of [Pilot Peak, Nevada]

41-49 "The Dry Drive;" consumptive Luke Halloran dies; burial; details of suffering in Salt Lake Desert; finally cross it.

September 9-15 In camp resting

September 16-30 Travel. .rejoining Fort Hall road about ten miles south of Elko

September 18 (?) Stanton and McCutcheon sent ahead

50-59 "The Long Pull;" exhaustion in camp; first wagons abandoned; set out again; collective indirect discourse on their predicament; send Stanton and McCutcheon to scout ahead"There must have been something dreamlike in thus following a trail with no map or guide, or any known landmark. . ." (55); reach Humboldt River.

October 1-12. Travel along Humboldt River to its sink

October 5. Snyder killed. . .

56-62 "Knife-Play by the River;" details of travel along Humboldt; Indian raids; "Petty disagreements grew more irking. The company had been together for too long;" October 5: brief quarrel between Snyder and Reed, who kills Snyder; Reed "excluded" from company; compromise arranged; Snyder buried; Reed forced to travel ahead of main group; unconfinable "evil feelings;" "Hatred and inhumanity walked beside the wagons" (62).

October 8. Hardkoop left behind. . .

October 13-14. Cross desert between Humboldt Sink and Truckee River; Wolfinger remains behind

62-69 "The Last Desert;" Keseberg throws elderly traveler Hardkoop out of his wagon; Eddy tries to rescue him; no one will help; have to slaughter oxen and abandon wagons; "Daily the journey seemed to become more of a rout" (67); October 13: "That day was sheer horror. Across the heat-stricken sand of the sink naked mountains of rock, luridly sinister in brown, red, and poisonous green, leered out at the straggling train like devil-haunted hills in a dream" (67); reach Truckee River.

October 15. In camp on Truckee River . . .

October 16-19. Travel up canyon of Truckee River to Truckee Meadows . .

October 19. Stanton. .rejoins

October 20-25. Resting in Truckee Meadows (approximate dates)

October 20. Pike killed

October 25 (?)-30. Travel in three sections .. . to Truckee [Donner] Lake

October 28-29. First heavy snowfall on mountains.

October 31-November 3. Attempt to cross pass with wagons. . .

October 31. Reed and McCutcheon leave Sutter's attempting to bring back food

November 4. The Party returns to Donner Lake and establishes camp there

69-79 "—And Closes in Front;" rest in meadows; food low; Stanton arrives with pack-mules and food from Sutter; Stanton's story of his adventures (71-73): Reed just barely got through to Fort; Stanton's imagined view of Party on rejoining: "the cruel individualism of the westerner had gained the upper hand . . ." (73); Pike's gun explodes: Halloran-Snyder-Pike burial sequence shows "progressing rout of company," (74) with Pike just laid in ground; reach cabin at Lake, one inch of snow already; have to abandon most possessions to continue; go beyond cabin, stuck in snow; Stanton says they can get through if there's no more snow; it starts snowing again; they turn back to the lake: "The trap which had clicked behind them at Fort Bridger had closed in front" (79).

Part II: "The Snow"

80-82 "Foreword;" bird's-eye panorama like the one beginning Part I, this time from above the Truckee Lake—Sutter's Fort trail, early winter, 1846; white-green pattern based on terrain and altitude ". . .shows a pattern almost regular enough to be the plan of some landscape architect . . ." (81). The speaker traces the route one must take through this landscape to get to Sutter's Fort.

83-84 "In California:" quotations from Edwin Bryant's What I Saw in California: meeting Reed at Sutter's, signing up with him and others to join Fremont in fighting the "Californians."

84-90 "Two Fathers;" "Sutter's fort lay steaming in the sun. . ." (84); McCutcheon and Reed set out east with a pack train for rescue; meet increasingly deep snow and a castaway family in a shelter; terrible struggles; blocked just twelve miles from Emigrant Pass summit; turn back.

November 4-11 Storm continues, rain and snow . . .

November 12. First attempt to escape across pass on foot.

November 20. Breen begins his diary

November 21-22. Second attempt to escape across pass on foot.

November 25-December 3. Second storm . . .

90-99"Beyond the Wall;" description of encampment and new-built cabins; "About each cabin was a scene of confusion" (91); location and inhabitants of each; Donner family in lean-to five miles east; food issues—hoarding, absence of game; 13 men and 2 women try to escape November 12, including three fathers leaving their families, but are forced to return at the head of the lake; Eddy's hunting expeditions dramatically described; "Surely there must come a thaw sometime; even the big snow in Illinois had lasted only nine weeks (95); universal despondency; Patrick Breen's first diary entry quoted; description of another breakout attempt on the 21st and quarrel between Eddy, who wants to proceed on foot and others who won't go without mules, so they return; effects of the eight-day storm: all the livestock dead.

December 9-13. Third storm

December 15. First death (Baylis Wiliams) at Truckee Lake

December 16-January 17, 18. Journey of snow-shoers from Truckee Lake to Johnson's ranch

December 23-25. Fourth storm. Show-shoers' fire extinguished

January 2. Reed at Battle of Santa Clara

January 4-8. Mrs Reed, Virginia, and milt Elliott attempt to cross pass on foot

January 9-12. Fifth storm.

99-104 "Death Bids God-Speed;" Breen records the making of snowshoes from ox-bows; discussion of men being less able to deal with conditions than women. "The first one collapsed on the eighth" (100); fourteen pairs of snowshoes made; those in the snowshoe party described: "The constituency of the party as a whole showed the growing desperation" (102) and the growing dominance of women; all details of snowshoers' preparations are from records, which note "only the tangible and material" (103)—speculations on motivation and mood of the party; death of Baylis Williams on night of their departure: "It was Death that bade them God-speed" (104).

104-114 "The Snow-Shoers;" details of each day's struggle through the snow; snow-blindness; by the fifth day they are about where Reed and McCutcheon turned back before; Christmas week; Eddy finds a half-pound of bear meat put in his pack by his 'own dear Eleanor.' Stanton won't leave camp: 'I am coming soon' (107); Patrick Dolan suggests drawing lots "to see who should die to furnish food for the others" (109); different suggestions; decide to struggle on until someone dies; Antonio the Mexican does just before a storm breaks; their extraordinary efforts not to freeze to death detailed; on Christmas Day Patrick Dolan becomes delirious, leaves the group's blanket tent and won't return; "taboos of civilization" break; Eddy won't touch it but the others cut off Patrick Dolan's flesh and eat it "'averting their faces from each other and weeping'" (113).

114-120 "The Hunting of the Deer;" after three days' rest, five dead, flesh dried, survivors set out again; Eddy, failing, finally agrees to eat human flesh; finally they are, at New Year's, in sight of the Sacramento Valley far below; more struggle; sight a buck deer but Eddy is too weak to raise his gun, yet manages to wound it and slit its throat; they drink the warm blood.

120-126 "The Will to Live;" Fosdick, left behind with his wife, dies; she's rescued and his flesh dried along with the deer's; Foster becomes unbalanced, suggests killing one of the others, finally kills an Indian; with him as example, stages in the de-civilization of the group over the 25 days are described; encounter an Indian village and rain rather than snow; the women can't go on, but Eddy persists. At the Ritchies' cabin near Johnson's ranch "An hour before sunset, Harriet [Ritchie], going to the door, was thunder-struck to be confronted by two Indians supporting between them something which might be human" (126). Neighbors go back and rescue the six other survivors.

January 22-27. Sixth storm

January 31. Glover's relief party leaves Sutter's

February 2-6. Seventh storm

February 3. Meeting held at Yerba Buena [San Francisco] for raising of relief funds

127-35 "California Responds;" January 19, Eddy writes to the "alcalde" John Sinclair, about the party's situation; Captain Kern at Sutter's Fort recruits a rescue party; Sinclair sends a boat downriver to Yerba Buena [San Francisco] to try to reach Reed, but all is in martial confusion, he fights ranchers in "Battle of Santa Clara" before getting word in San Jose; Sinclair assembles meeting in Yerba Buena to address "petition" from Reed and others in San Jose to form rescue mission; lots of money raised; volunteers, including aristocratic Selim E. Woodworth, U.S.N.; details of complicated plans for a deliberate military-style rescue.

135-141 "Yuletide at the Lake;" monotony and despair; seen through Patrick Breen's diary: ". . . the thoroughly healthy mind of an average man, numbed by long suffering and privation" (126); boiling hides for food; first report on Donners comes through: some dead, George with deep infection.

141-148 "Provisions Scarce;" state of the camp in first week of January after Eddy has shot deer, and Santa Clara battle; Mrs. Reed and children live for a week on body of their pet dog Cash; Mrs. Reed's state of mind describes; she decides to try an escape; wander in bewilderment three days before turning back, just before fifth storm; conditions in Breens' crowded cabin are described; Virginia Reed reads over and over the life of Daniel Boone; entries from

Breen's diary alternate with accounts of progressive deaths, particularly of children; January 31: Breen's diary has note of despair, but the same day seven-man relief party sets out with food from Sutter's.

February 4-18. Glover's relief party journeys from Johnson's to the Lake

148-59"The Seven Against Death;" muster-roll of the fourteen-man party that leaves Johnson's, parallel to that of the Donner group at the beginning; rescuers marooned in snow; Breen's diary records increasing fear of starvation; rescue party improvises river-crossings; Breen records death of Mrs. Eddy; as the rescuers "struggled ahead, death again outraced them" (154) as recorded by Breen; mutiny among rescuers—3 turn back, seven continue; detailed account of their final ascent up to Emigrant Gap; "At the lake the struggle for life was growing fiercer" (158).

159-164 "'Old Dan Tucker's Come to Town;'" February 18; the rescue party crosses the pass and "clung like flies against the white wall working their way downwards" (160); at sunset they cross snow and see no cabins, call, a woman emerges from a hole "like some kind of animal," and cries "'Are you men from California or do you come from heaven?'" (160); the relief party's activities described, and plans to return, choosing twenty-three.

February 7. Reed, Greenwood, and Woodworth . . leave Yerba Buena

February 22-27 Glover's relief party with refugees journeys from the Lake to Bear Valley

February 22-March 1 Reed's relief party meets Glover's relief party with refugees

March 1. Last entry in Breen's diary

165-173 "The Children Walk;" Glover's party starts out, but the two youngest Reed children can't make it and have to be taken back; they find their food cache plundered; Jeremiah Denton can't make it, so he's left with a fire, wrapped in a blanket, looking 'so comfortable that some of the others almost envied him . . .'" (168); Reed's party meets them and he is reunited with Mrs. Reed and Virginia; Glover's party finally reaches Selim Woodworth's camp, green grass, Woodworth has done nothing; Mrs. Reed suggests "'We had better take care of him, reverse the order of things'" (171); by March 4 they reach Sutter's Fort.

173-179 "Reed Tries Again;" summary of Reed's progress from Yerba Buena to the point where we meet him in the previous chapter; difficult passage into the mountains through soggy snow; details of how Reed & McCutcheon clean and take care of the nearly dying children found in the cabins; hear about the week between the two parties' visits; Breen's last diary entry.

179-183 "Reed Visits the Donners;" the accounts of Cady and Clark, the two members of Reed's party sent to the Donner's campsite; body parts; Reed arrives, finds George near death but Tamsen apparently healthy, although she refuses to leave her husband.

March 3-5. Reed's relief party with refugees journeys from the Lake to [Summit Valley]

March 6-8. Eighth storm. Reed's relief party.. . .storm-bound.

March 8-10. Reed with some of the refugees continues journey to Bear Valley.

183-91 "At the Head of the Yuba;" "The behavior of the refugees during this first evening seemed to indicate that they hardly realized themselves still under the shadow of death" as the party sets out across the lake (185); Patrick Breen plays his violin; Woodworth doesn't appear; they cross Emigrant Pass and storm breaks; description of desperation, strong wind, no fire; Reed sinks into coma; McCutcheon gets fire restarted just in time; close-up of little Patty Reed, almost dead, seeing angels, revived; McCutcheon calls her "an angel on earth" (191).

192-196 "Cady and Stone;" the three men left at the Lake, Cady, Stone and Clark, appear to have taken Tamsen Donner's offered money to get her youngest children out, but end up leaving them in the foul cabin of Keseberg and going back after the 8th storm passes.

March 7-13. Eddy and Foster journey from Johnson's to the Lake

196-204 "Eddy and Foster;" scattered situation of rescuers, refugees, and those remaining; flashback to Eddy and Foster resting for their own onslaught and worried by the effects of the 8th storm; they reach Woodworth's still immobile camp; move on; hear sound at evening, and Reed's entire party arrives; recapitulation of the Reeds' experiences now that "the time of terror was past" (199); Eddy and Foster get five other men, including the giant John Starks, to go with them to the Lake; they find Denton's body where he was left and beside him a poem reminiscing about the "summer fields" of England (202); find site where Reed had left some of refugees six days earlier, in snow fire-pit; They divide, some taking the eleven survivors to safety, Eddy, Miller, Reed and Foster heading on to the Lake.

204-208 "Before the Last Plunge;" the next day the four reach the cabins; the story is available only from the Donner children; Keseberg found surrounded by body parts, has eaten Eddy's own son, but "he realized that much as Keseberg might deserve to die, he could not bring himself to strike down such a defenseless, helpless, and withal pitiable creature" (205); a long passage on Tamsen Donner's choice (once more) to go to safety with her three little children, or stay with her dying sister and husband; she chooses the latter; they cross the Gap with the children: "The day was March 14. Not until another month had gone would anyone cross that pass again, or ask the mountains to reveal more secrets" (208).

March 13-17. Eddy and Foster with refugees journey from the Lake to Bear Valley

March 29. Mrs. Murphy dies at Lake (approximate date)

March 23-28 (?). Another relief expedition sent out from Johnson's but fails to advance beyond Bear Valley

March 26. Tamsen Donner comes to the Lake (approximate date)

March 28-April 3 Ninth storm (approximate dates)

April 12-17 Fallon's party journeys from Johnson's to the Lake.

April 21-22. Fallon's party with Keseberg journeys from the Lake to

Bear Valley

208-212 "Interlude;" "In a sense, it was finished. . .Tragedy had yielded to pathos" (208); Starks's courage in carrying children to safety; another party goes out but returns: "the incentive for rescuing one's life had disappeared" (210); mountaineer Fallon arranges party not to rescue but to find "salvage" as snow retreats.

212-218 "Fallon Le Gros;" at Lake, strange footprints are found near the Donners' camp; discussion of their finds, including Donners' possessions and well- swathed body of George Donner; Keseberg, who made the footprints, found in a cabin "amidst human bones" (214), only authority for last weeks; his account retold: Tamsen Donner came in the night, seemed crazed, he put her to bed and she died in the night; Keseberg confesses to eating her; rescuers doubt story; Fallon's diary account of events reprinted from California Star.

Stewart's story does not end here. Part III, "They Rest," is integral to the experience. However, the implications of his narrative technique are most meaningful when juxtaposed to unadorned chronology.

Initially, the evocation of Hastings's dubious reception pollutes the purity of their existential condition between past and future (19). Throughout the first part of the journey, the company travels with no, or conflicting, points of recognition, a "dream" journey launched by accepting as "true," the orienting structure of Hastings's pamphlet and posting. The muster roll (20-29) interrupts the seemingly smooth plains travel from Little Sandy Creek to Fort Bridger with a similar premonitory suggestion. The halt (like that of Chaucer's pilgrims at "the watring of St. Thomas," to choose straws) is to the narrative as one of the innumerable geographical obstacles the party itself faces. It also allows us to evaluate the complex dynamism within the group, its "metabolism" in ecospeak of the time, which will lead to its progressive disintegration as the trek progresses. The "trap" metaphor gives a shape of fatality (some might say contradicting randomness of the expedition's choices) to the often shapeless passage between Fort Bridger and the snow, while the chapter divisions, with their title and coverage-"The Wahsatch, "The Dry Drive," "The Long Pull," "The Last Desert," in one sense might be said to impose a false "quest" paradigm on the chaos of the actual passage. I myself think that within the structure of these four "trials," the extreme courage, suffering, conflict, and despair, human-to-human and human-to-nature are more emphatically shown. Stewart will develop as a structuring format a temporal sequence in later novels—days in *Storm* and *Fire*, generations in *Years of the City*—but there they are overtly and acknowledgedly artifices for order. Here, they are shaped by the unplanned events and duration of the four stages themselves. This "organic" ordering of a temporal sequence has a long heritage, from the "removes" of Mary Rowlandson's captivity narratives to the erratic journal entries in Rick Bass's *Winter*. The party and the physical environment are co-creators of these forms, which take their "The" identity only after they have been perceived as having some kind of unity.

The one qualitatively different incident that interrupts the sequence is Reed's stabbing of Snyder. It occurs almost without thought, and temporally is just a flash of seconds. But it has the same weight as the spans of days that surround it. It is the human-created equivalent of a precipice or a narrow canyon, dividing the party as by statute and a point of reference for an increasing breakdown in the social ecology of the group (particularly as it is followed by the abandonment of Hartkoop. Then, the final chapter of Part I completes the trap metaphor and establishes the intolerable conditions of a "forced inhabitance." At a time of dissention and dissolution, the party is forced to parody, in a way, the form, but not the content, of a small village or extended family. The intolerable ever-changingness of the terrain they have been crossing is replaced by an equally intolerable stasis in a "place" that, totally made of snow, has almost no physical attributes. The intolerable "dreamlike" emptiness of unlandmarked space is replaced by intolerable imprisonment. Unbearable heat is replaced by unbearable cold.

The second "part" of *Ordeal* really itself has two parts, overlapping but dissimilar, and it is here where the narrative is forced to become complicated. The whole expedition has a three-part structure, as an inverse pyramid of the classical plot. The rising action (figuratively and literally) of travel culminates not in *peripeteia* but in *anomie*, a plateau of inaction. But rising in that plateau is the inverted falling action of the escapes and rescues, which are more truly dramatic than what has happened in the first two-thirds of the story.

This part begins with a second bird's-eye view, equal in scope but differently centered—not with the wagon train entering the picture, but with the unpopulated trail its members cannot follow out of the picture to their imagined destination. The immediate leap to sunny Sutter's fort, and the first rescue attempt, which fails, is ironically placed next to a complex description of the conditions of entrapment under repeated storms. Then, rather than alternating the narrative threads in space and time, four sequential chapters detail the 33-day agony of the snowshoers' escape. The author might well have interrupted this sequence and returned to it for the sake of suspense, but it has its own shape, like a miniature of the approach to the Lake. It also, more vividly than the latter, chronicles the progressive attempts at cultural adaptation of the temporary collective to an environment in which no adaptation will permit survival. The progressive deaths of those unable, mentally or physically, to adapt, have a culminative effect, so the first incident of cannibalism can be experienced as just one more action in a sequence of survival techniques.

This might be the place to indicate Stewart's stance toward what he calls ". . . in the popular mind the chief fact to be remembered about the Donner Party" (238). This he expresses in the chapter "Taboo" which concludes the narrative proper. He doesn't hesitate to mention, for example, though without embellishment, such instances as Mrs. Foster "forced to see her husband's heart broiled over the fire" (121). But he emphasizes, first, that the breaking open of the bodies to eat the inner organs—brain, heart, liver— was no "perversion," but an instinctual act to compensate for dietary deficiencies that the vitamin and mineral contents of flesh itself could not provide. Then, in general, the ". . .horror of cannibalism seems to me disproportionate . . .Personally I should rather admit to cannibalism under necessity than to some of the actions to which members of the Donner Party admitted in order to escape suspicion of that particular act" (239). After giving some examples of the latter, he concludes ". . .when I consider such hypocrisy I feel a longing for the society of an honest cannibal!" (240).

So the snowshoers' narrative continues as though the initial eating of Patrick Dolan was just another event in a downhill trek of desperation and is lost under the thick blankets of comfort where Eddy finally lies. Then, abruptly, we are in Southern California with John Reed, in a situation of social confusion of grander scale, if less desperation, than that of the emigrants, focused among the "new" Californians on the financing of a rescue mission. The two succeeding chapters reattach us to the "numbed" life at the Lake, cotemporal with the snowshoers' trek and the rescue organization, emphasizing the ignorance they have of both acts. Stewart then engineers a conjunction in time and space by describing the Glover party's uphill struggle and arrival at the Lake. We are also with Glover's party downhill to Sutter's fort, but are then recapitulatively with Reed coming from Yerba Buena and getting to the Lake (this section could no doubt have been longer, but its foreshortening emphasizes the accelerating pulsebeat of discovery).

A whole chapter is devoted to, in a sense, a "still moment," when Reed visits the Donner site. This, somewhat like the knife fight chapter earlier, gives weight of significance to an event short in time, emphasizing the centrality of Tamsen Donner despite her separation spatially from the group, and, since they will never meet again, in a sense repairing the breach caused by the Reeds' exile because of the earlier incident. There follow two more sustained traverses: Reed's last trial, in his party's nearly fatal return to the valley, and the travel and return of Eddy's and Foster's party. All in all, these sequential rescues are placed to have a rhythm akin to that provided by descriptions of the environmental changes produced by the warming temperatures. The final rescue, of Keseberg by Fallon, is told briefly, as an afterthought almost, except for the matter of Tamsen Donner; Keseberg is not really human, but just another piece of salvage.

Thus, as shaped by Stewart, the history of the party has an "organic form" that transcends chronology but appears to arise from the events themselves, understood environmentally. The form is emphasized by the sequent lives of the rescuees, scattered and "rapidly absorbed into the population of California" (227). The absence of high events in their lives could be cited, speaking environmentally, as evidence of their successful adaptation to their physical and social situations. (It also resembles the fates of Henty's heroes once the adventures are over). The environmentalism of Stewart's book can also be entered topically. Near the beginning of the narrative we read:

> Like humanity which is borne always one way in time, so the wagons moved on unreversing into the west, and like humanity which lives unescapably in the vivid present, between the half-remembered past and the unknown future, so the emigrants moved overland between the horizon which shut down behind and the horizon which lifted up ahead, half forgetting the traveled road and ignorant of what landscape lay ahead beyond the next rise." (19-20)

Environmentally ignorant, this "microcosm of humanity," so diverse, is also collectively and individually ignorant of what potentialities of heroism or depravity each member will be capable of under the most extreme conditions of survival. A daunting task has been set by the author, if we view him as, for the first time, truly a "literary ecologist" and involve in this role the idea of "place." The humans are a tribe bound by only one commonality—the shared goal of arriving in a place where they can separate and no longer have to live as a tribe. And this goal is a "constructed" place, which exists differently in the consciousness of each member. On the journey to Donner Lake they have to adapt to continually changing ecosystemic conditions, so the adaptive behaviors have to be abandoned immediately for new ones, and lose their usefulness. The social dynamics of the group are also constantly changing as it is affected by the physical environment, and as individuals within it affect the behavior of other individuals as a result, usually, of encounters with the nonhuman environment. At Donner Lake, they are forced to inhabit as though it were a permanent destination an almost literally uninhabitable place, to survive in which they lack the adaptive skills.

*

Ordeal by Hunger was written at exactly the juncture when Arthur Tansley coined and elaborated the concept of "ecosystem" as a qualification—not rejection—of the current state-of-the-art "ecological community" paradigm famously elaborated and defended by Frederic Clements (79). In Stewart's descriptions of mountain forestation one can see the influence of Clements's plant succession theories. But the same mid-1930's period saw a "convergence of ecology and history," a theory in Westward expansion of an "ecology of pioneering" (Worster *Economy* 219), wherein the progression of natural and human communities were considered analogous. Worster sees this as a decade of crisis, in that awareness dawned that of the forces in analogy, the human was well on the way to destroying the nonhuman.

Although Stewart does not mention prominent contemporary ecologists, he was beginning to draw from multidisciplinary Berkeley colleagues a similar sense of communities, in the close involvement of biology, geography, sociology, and anthropology with each other. In 1925 Stewart's great intellectual friend and colleague, Carl Sauer, in his "Morphology of Landscape," had articulated a holistic environmental vision, in terms of geography, of which Stewart's narrative could be an illustration. In summary, this vision is of ". . .contact of man with his changeful home, as expressed through the cultural landscape. . . we deal with the interrelation of group, or cultures, and site, as expressed in the various landscapes of the world" (53). The "intersection of the human and the natural order" (Worster *Ends* 91) since the 30's has increasingly been presented as one leading to conflict rather than incorporation. This text has already discussed the importance of Julian Steward's cultural ecology. But a restoration, if you will, of Sauer's vision can be found canonized in the *International Handbook of Environmental Sociology* (1997). Here is a passage from Barbara Adam's essay "Time and the Environment," from that book which, particularized, would be, in my view, a perfect characterization of Stewart's form and theory in *Ordeal by Hunger*:

> Th[e] multitude of coordinated environmental and internal rhythms give a dynamic structure to our lives that permeates every level of our existence. It constitutes temporal frameworks within which activities are not only organized and planned but also timed and synchronized at varying speeds and intensity, and orchestrated to intricate scores of beginnings, sequences, durations, pauses and ends. All aspects interpenetrate and have a bearing on each other. All coexist and are lived simultaneously. . .A symphony of rhythms and temporalities thus underpins our development as humans and as living organisms. It marks us as creatures of the Earth . . . (171)

It is the "coevolution between social and environmental systems" that concerns Stewart. In *Ordeal by Hunger*, due to its historical time and circumstance, it is the cultural, not the environmental system, whose "fitness" is affected by "deliberate innovations, chance discoveries. . .chance introductions," (Norgaard 161), but these changes are ultimately environment-caused, and their effects rebound from the environment onto the society.

Because *Ordeal by Hunger* has grander ambitions than to strip truth naked, its discrediting by more recent Donner historians is somewhat irrelevant to its importance. As an expansion upon the comments of Langellier, mentioned earlier, for example, Joseph King's history, originally published in 1992, positively bristles with hostility. He exaggerates Stewart's admittedly "Anglo-Saxon Protestant" bias, and mischaracterizes him as consistently negative in his portrayal of Patrick Breen: he "never misses an opportunity to take a shot at one or another of the Breens, often the cheapest of shots" (191); this is due, apparently, to Stewart's supposed anti-Catholicism. The book, again using the genre as a derogation "should be treated as fiction, heavily researched indeed, but a fictional account nonetheless" (195). What Stewart has created is a "myth." Stewart would probably be proud to be considered the creator of a myth, but I'm not sure if he would be angry or amused at the criticism of his research, particularly since, in the new 1960 edition of *Ordeal by Hunger*, he acknowledges, and discusses, his errors of fact and chronology in the original edition. In his fascinating collaborative book on the archaeology of the Donner party, Donald Hardesty acknowledges King's criticism of Stewart while calling *Ordeal by Hunger* "the ultimate history of the Donner party" (3). The only significant criticism of Stewart's account provided is of his assumption of abnormal weather conditions in 1846-7 (115).

Stewart sent Holt a detailed list of potential reviewers and review venues for *Ordeal by Hunger*, including Carey McWilliams, Francis Farquhar, and his mentor at Berkeley, Herbert Bolton. The list reveals his sensitivity to the California media and California attitudes. He refers to local organizations like the "Native Sons of the Golden West," as having the "sentimental hero-worshipping attitude toward the pioneers and would probably not like my book. Of course if they were stirred up to protest or ban the book, the result might be just as good. I don't, however, know just what technique should be followed" (Stewart to Publicity Department, Henry Holt and Company, 6 Feb. 1936/*P*). Fortunately, the 1936 reviewers of the book were apparently credulous or ignorant enough to praise it highly. The (obviously biased!) *Oakland Tribune* said Stewart had lifted the episode "to the plane of a universal human saga of courage, defeat, weakness and heroism." Ansel Adams (surely another biased voice) considered it "a wonderful piece of work," "provocative of much thought on the historic and social factors of western expansion." He was even prescient enough to see its sociological implications: "In the times of greatest stress the spirit of the Clan seemed non-existent . . ." (115). To Florence Kelly in the *New York Times*, ". . .it holds the reader's mind in absorbed fascination from beginning to end" ("Tragic" 11). Norah Lofts, who had inquired previously about using Stewart's material for a novel, in a brief preface to *Winter Harvest*, writes "To that beautiful and incomparable study of human beings in the grip of circumstance I owe, not only the impulse to write this story, but the geographical and other detain which made the writing possible" (preface). Bernard DeVoto wrote to Stewart that "I intend to steal from your Donner book with a lavish disregard for your property rights" in preparing his famous study of the West, *The Year of Decision* (DeVoto to Stewart 25 Nov. 1941). DeVoto and Wallace Stegner were, of course, adherents of Stewart's view of a "middle ground" between "fact and fiction." As John L. Thomas says, they

> . . .had a quarrel with the professionals and academicians who dismissed the popular history written as story as 'something faintly disreputable, the proper playground of lady novelists.' Good history could be assembled from documents, policy statements, memoranda, and position papers,. . . but great history is stories that grip the reader. (95)

Thirty years later, Stewart's loyal reviewer Helen Bevington wrote "I know your books well. As I went through the list of them, I realized what a faithful reader I have been and how admiring. Most recently, on an automobile trip home from California [with my son], I read aloud in the car 'Ordeal by Hunger.' That was after we had had lunch, of all the cannibalistic things to do, in Donner Park" (Bevington to Stewart 30 July 1970).

Maybe the highest (and unrealized) tribute occurred after the new edition in 1960 when producer Stuart Millar in 1964 purchased the film rights and, supposedly, got Horton Foote to write the screenplay. Millar is quoted as saying ". . .we have definite ideas on how to handle this difficult subject in good taste and in fine cinematic terms" (Weiler). Ultimately, the world had to wait for *Alive* to be able to witness cannibalism in the local theater.

Photos by Fred Waage

Inscription, University of California, Berkeley (top)
Berryman Reservoir, capped, below Codornices Road (bottom)

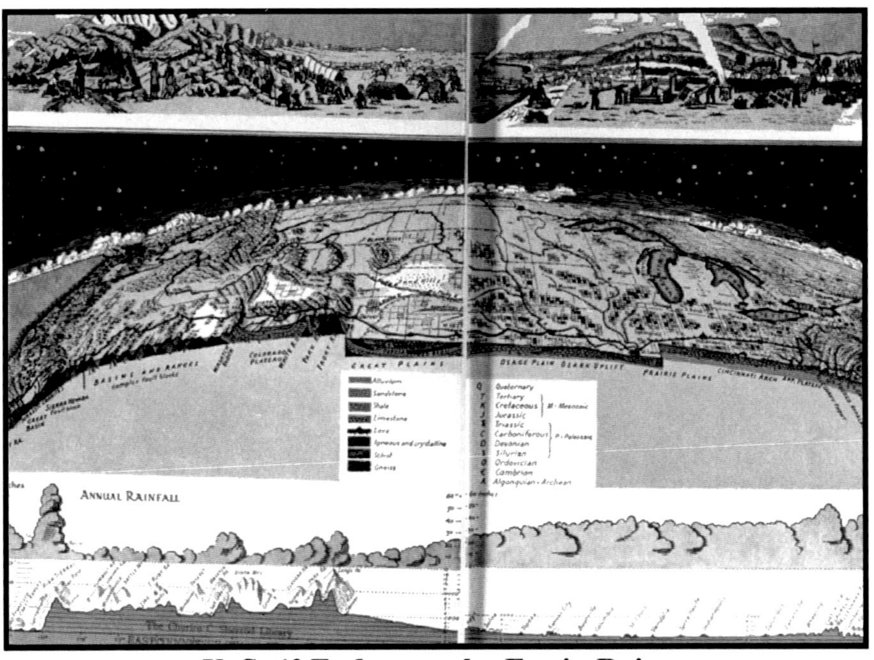

U. S. 40 **Endpapers by Erwin Raisz**

Photos by Fred Waage

Donner Lake from Donner Pass (top)
Playa, Black Rock Desert (bottom)

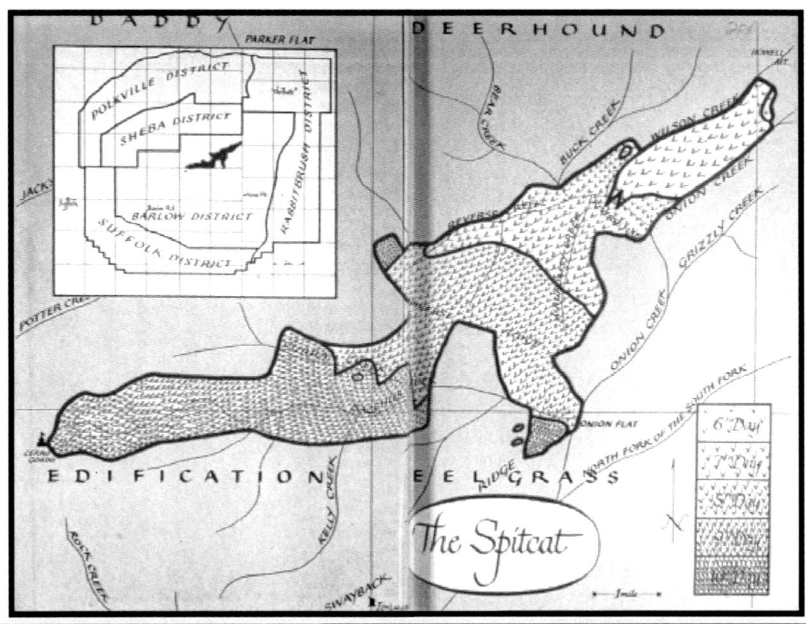

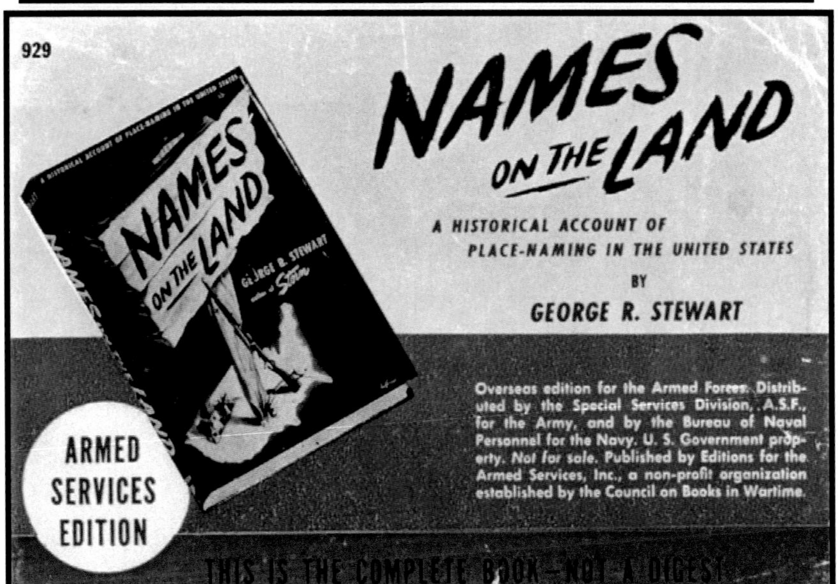

***Fire*, endpaper map (top)**

***Names on the land*, Armed Forces Edition, cover (bottom)**

A. J. Wells
California for the Settler; the Natural Advantages of the Golden State for the Present Day Farmer
San Francisco, 1910

George R. Stewart (l.) and Kenneth Carpenter (r.) with the Sheep Rock pitcher
George R. Stewart Collection, Bancroft Library, University of California, Berkeley
Reproduced courtesy of the Bancroft Library

Samuel Southworth.
California for Fruit-grower and Consumptives: Health, Profits, and Drawbacks
Sacramento, 1883.

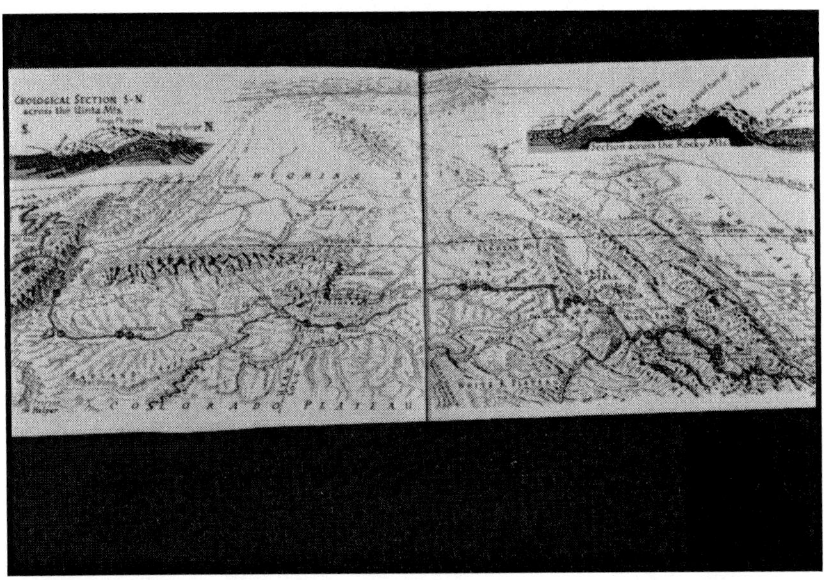

From *U.S. 40*:
Erwin Raisz map, Rockies to the Wasatch (top)
George R. Stewart photograph, Antietam Creek(bottom)

George R. Stewart (top)
George and Theodosia Stewart at The Sequoias (bottom)
Courtesy of the Regional Oral History Office, University of California, Berkeley

Robert Osborn, illustration for *Not So Rich as You Think*

Marriage of George R. Stewart and Theodosia Burton, May, 1924
Marion L. Burton Collection, courtesy of Bentley Historical Library, University of Michigan

"*Life* set out to do a story on C.S. Forester, probably 1945, and (to judge by the daffodils) Spring. We staged a meeting of the Armchair Strategists . . .at Cecil's house, to get a picture. (The article never came off). His house was on Keeler, now owned by Jack Raleigh. Present (left to right): C. D. Brenner; C. S. Forester; GRS; John Forester; Joseph Henry Jackson (deceased); Lewis (deceased), who was friend and neighbor, not a member; Ronald Walpole; Reid Railton; with hands behind head, J. H. Osmer (deceased). The other man we think was a stand-in for *Life*; neither Brenner nor I recognize him. Charlie Camp was a member, but not present." *A Little of Myself.*

Courtesy of the Regional Oral History Office, University of California, Berkeley

From *N.A. 1—Looking North*
George R. Stewart photograph, "Intimate Road"

Class of 1917, Princeton University

Historical Photograph Collection, Seeley G. Mudd Manuscript Library, Princeton University

Reproduced by permission of the Mudd Manuscript Library

Chapter III

The Storm Breaks

In a reference famous among the minuscule number of Stewart *congnoscenti*, he says that the idea of writing a novel first occurred to him "On October 10, 1936, about eleven A. M. driving north on the road to Santa Rosa, U.S. 101, I think somewhere the other side of Petaluma" (Stewart to Vivian Wolfert 16 Feb. 1948). This is tongue-in-cheek accuracy, and in *A Little of Myself* he characterizes the decision more banally: "I had to go up to Santa Rosa, actually, to give a lecture, and on that particular day, I decided I was going to write a novel. My wife was with me in the car there, nobody else, and she thought it was a good idea" (57). The accuracy of his date in the Wolfert letter might be supported by his declaration to T. J. Wilson of Holt "Just how much of the idea is the result of your remark to me may be considered uncertain, but at any rate I have decided to try writing a novel" (Stewart to Wilson 17 Oct. 1936). Actually, the "other job I was doing," on which he was "fed up" at this moment, was published before any novelistic fantasies could reach fruition. This was, to go by its full title, *John Phoenix, Esq. The Veritable Squibob: A Life of Captain George H. Derby, USA*.

Stewart considers writing this biography a "mistake," but he thought since he'd done one biography, why not another? He had always been interested in Derby, who acquired his pseudonyms and local fame as a Twainian satirist in mid 19th century San Francisco, and had been doing research on him since 1923 (*Phoenix* x) . Unfortunately, "Phoenix was not a man of much importance" (*Little* 120), and it is as hard to write about someone unimportant as about someone important; but it was a project hard to resist, since his descendents were enthusiastic about the book and gave him access in 1933 to all his papers and drawings (of which many are reproduced in the volume). He doesn't mention the flap with Holt in which he strenuously objected to Holt's unilateral replacement of his phrase "lapses into insanity," to characterize Derby's father, by "periodical intoxication." His editor, Thornton, defended this editorial decision because "Mrs. George M. Derby is very much opposed to this statement in the text. . .," and because the replacement was hardly a "downright lie" as Stewart said, since Derby Senior was an incorrigible alcoholic anyway (Richard Thornton to Stewart 30 Sept. 1937/*P*). Stewart replied that he had much respect for Mrs. Derby, but "nevertheless this is my book and not hers" (Stewart to Thornton 2 Oct. 1937/*P*).

Rereading *John Phoenix,* Stewart finds it is so far the book he's least happy with, although he concedes "It is tightly constructed, kept to brevity throughout, authoritative, and readable" (Rereading). Initially, Holt was very cool to the manuscript. "It would be extremely hard to convince booksellers that he was an important humorist. Furthermore, it would be difficult to quote many of the humorous passages out of their context" (Richard Thornton to Stewart 20 Oct. 1936/*P*). Stewart replied, "You are probably right about Derby" (Stewart to Thornton 22 Oct. 1936/*P*). It appears they were ultimately swayed to publish it by Stewart's argument that it would be a good lead up to his novel (Richard Thornton to Stewart, Jan. 8 1937/*P*).

John Phoenix is dedicated to the memory of Harold Lawton Bruce, one of Stewart's most admired teachers in the Berkeley English Department—"his counsel meant much to me" (*Department* 5). Derby himself was the "class prankster" (Waugh 528) of the famous West Point class of 1846, whose ranks included Stonewall Jackson, George McClellan, and the subject of a future book by Stewart, George Pickett. At West Point Derby "marched to a drum nobody else seemed to hear" (Waugh 55), but he became a Mexican War hero, and was one of the best draftsmen up to his time to graduate from West Point.

In many ways Stewart's biography is an "orthodox" primary-source based narrative life of "the first Western humorist" (*Bret Harte* 143), without the environmental concerns of *Ordeal by Hunger* or the fluent narrative line of *Bret Harte*. Derby's idyllic childhood in New England, and his parental relationships, are characterized; he was the kid who never studied and always knew the answer (7). Sent to a private school he called the "School for Moral Discipline," he was always in trouble and with his "native relish for sin" (14) he was quickly expelled. Eventually, after itinerancies, ending up at Norwich University, Derby got into West Point ("a struggling experiment without established tradition" [24]) in 1842 through the personal intervention of John Quincy Adams.

Now, while Stewart presents his primary interest as biographer to be in Derby as a California writer, and as an early Western humorist, what I see as his true interest in Derby is his role in the division of the Army he wanted to join, the Corps of Topographical Engineers (33). Also, upon his graduation Derby took the archetypal Stewartian journey to the West. "The life, so long circumscribed by the New England village, suddenly begins to shift scene with kaleidoscopic celerity" (44). The aspiring geographer was introduced to the complex cultural and natural terrain of the country as he and his fellow soldiers travelled by an awkward diversity of conveyances to the far Southwest. Encomiastically, Stewart gives a topographical texture to the fates of these young warriors: "Young and fresh they looked on the day of graduation, but their broken bodies were to lie scattered on battlefields across a continent—on the slopes of Chapultepec, arrow-feathered in western gullies, by the river at Chancellorsville . . ."(39).

In light of Derby's postwar career as surveyor, one might question Wallace Stegner's assertion that previous to the Civil War, ". . .topography and mapping were diversions to occupy the peacetime Army . ." (*Beyond* 117), and not significant in "opening" the West until the ascendancy of John Wesley Powell. Stegner's Powell is a literary scientist and proto-environmentalist: "Powell loomed large in the environmental imagination as offering a needed corrective to the mindless development and exploitation that characterized the mid-twentieth century" (Thomas 110). Stewart's Derby, active in Powell's realm decades earlier, is hardly to be considered in this way, but his surveys and engineering work were to effectuate forms of reconciliation between an inevitably growing population of humans and forces of nature which were too strong to alter, but could be mitigated in their destructive effects through enlightened understanding. Others, of course, do not accept this construction of the surveyors' endeavors: Powell evolved a "control-centered view of nature," "the scientific control of a mechanical nature" which "anticipated the massive technological transformations of the region" in the next century (Bryson 95, 101).

After the war Derby was reassigned to Washington, where he quickly became bored. He was then further reassigned to California, with residence in San Francisco, where he arrived in June, 1849, at the height of gold rush fever. His charge was to survey the Sacramento River, with the goal of finding sites for military posts to protect settlers from Indians (57-61). Here, his "double" personality, serious yet crazy, which Stewart suggests stemmed from his teenage years, reached its true bifurcation and flowering. On the one hand he was mapping and surveying uncharted territory to the north of the Sacramento Valley, and engaging in a dangerous and futile attempt to go up the Colorado River from the Sea of Cortez. On the other, he was providing kinetic and written comedy for the protobohemian culture of San Francisco, centered around Montgomery Street. Stewart says that to the journalists and other "university wits" of this place and time "we owe the tradition which has kept San Francisco from ever being the artistic and intellectual desert which has been the chronic state of many American cities" (76).

In the early 1850's, Derby was transferred to San Diego. At that time ". . .cactus and mixed desert scrub came up to the back doors. . .the streets were mixed sand and horse droppings," and "a few, white-painted square clapboard boxes were the newly-built homes of Americans" (94). Ironically, most of the "Americans" (as distinguished from the "Californians" and the Spanish) were there to "speculate in city lots" (94). Derby was among developers. But his assigned task, although commercially driven, was a true example of restraining ecological degradation: how to prevent the erosive siltation of San Diego harbor (96). In this period, separated from the cultural life he loved, Derby wrote his famous satiric pieces for the *San Diego Herald* under the name "John Phoenix." They were gathered in one volume as *Phoenixiana* and published in 1855, becoming a national best-seller.

Stewart takes the serious/crazy dichotomy into a twist in his characterization of the book and of Derby's writing in general. Although *Phoenixiana* is but "the solidifed ebullition of the writer's own personality" (172), it is also an amoralistic satire of California culture, and an imaginative plunge into the absurd, which questions accepted reality. Thus, "Derby, at 31, five years before the publication of *The Origin of Species*, was farther along in philosophy than most American writers were to be during the rest of the century" (176). As well, by eschewing sentimentality altogether, Derby was in the avant-garde of a realism that would overwhelm "the fine-spun philosophies and brittle culture of the romantic flowering of America" (183).

One might feel that these are hyperbolic pronouncements, particularly when attached to an "unimportant" person. But maybe Derby was important to Stewart at the time, when he was thinking of writing a California novel, and since Derby had many attributes which mirrored Stewart's own aspiration—particularly the combination of verbal dexterity and environmental engagement.

John Phoenix concludes with his tragic, youthful death just as the Civil War began. He is characterized as a total original, "sui generis," and a literary soul-mate, as it were, of James Thurber. Stewart also criticizes a scholar named Partridge, who claims that "John Phoenix" was not Derby, but Mark Twain: "I am unable to understand either Mr. Partridge's logic or his prose; this may indicate that I am insane" (235). Stewart's voluminous correspondent the feckless novelist H.C. Davis, did tell him it was ". . .the best, by a long shot, of all the studies of Western literary men I have read" (Davis to Stewart 26 Dec. 1937).

*

Stewart was flattered that Holt (12 Nov. 1936/*P*) offered him a contract for a novel since it was both unwritten and a genre new to him. In discussing his thoughts about accepting the contract, he revealed a good deal about how he saw his career after the success of *Ordeal by Hunger*:

> I am now planning definitely to leave the more narrowly scholarly fields, and to go on with writings of general interest whether in fiction or non-fiction. I want to have a publisher who will be interested in backing my name over a period of years, and in building up my reputation along with his own profit. My books may never be great money-makers, but I think that those which I do from now on should at least be able to turn in some profit. I am thinking in terms of ten years rather than of the immediate future. (Stewart to Richard Thornton 29 Dec. 1936/*P*).

The publisher that he sought would not be Holt.

"I, like every American," says Stewart, "dreamed of writing the great American novel" in his youth (*Little* 5). " . . .It's a great American ambition. Everybody wants to write a novel, and I did too" (121). He notes the dominance of historical fiction—e.g. *Gone With the Wind* and *Anthony Adverse*, so his first novel, *East of the Giants,* is really a "period piece"—I think both in the sense of its setting and its genre. Its year of publication saw a lot of semi-great fiction—Marjorie Kinnan Rawlings's *The Yearling*, Faulker's *The Unvanquished*, Richard Wright's *Uncle Tom's Children*. There were Western novels galore, May Miller's *First the Blade*, W.R. Burnett's *The Dark Command*, John O'Hara's *Hope of Heaven*. Stewart's fellow novelist and literary correspondent Clyde Brion Davis even wrote a pre-pomo novel called *The Great American Novel*, about a man who wants to write a great American novel (1938).

Much of Stewart's own entry into the Great American Novel sweepstakes was actually written in Mexico, where he went on sabbatical with Ted for 1937-38. That creative period south of the border (where he also actually began his *next* novel, *Doctor's Oral*) is well-characterized by his clever reminiscence of it, "Mexico by Ear." Here, he tells his readers that his most vivid sense-impression of Mexico City is one of "sound," and he thinks this sense, examined, "may make a good beginning toward some interpretation of the Mexican people" (8)—an interpretation which certainly helped him to recreate the Mexican California of *East of the Giants*. "Mexico by Ear" uses sounds to create a vivid cacophony of urban life, where "Upon the broad sidewalks the people found their common ground, much as if they were still living in their villages instead of in a metropolis of over a million people" (8). His scale of Mexican sounds ranges from the raucous garbage men's bell, which signals the end of sleep, to the timeless soft pat-patting of tortillas, which, Stewart presumes, even Montezuma heard. "In spite of its primitiveness, the patting of *tortillas* has a curious effect of restraint and exactitude. It sounds rather like a very genteel and small-handed lady applauding a rendition of *L'Apres-Mide d'un Faune*" (9). For Stewart, animal sounds are as diverse as human (as they will be on the Godoy ranch in *East of the Giants*—particularly pigs and turkeys. "H.L. Davis tells me that these turkeys understand about red and green lights, but I put that down as only another tale out of *Honey in the Horn* [Davis's great novel]" (10). He also has much to say on the sounds of street-vendors and serenaders, although on the latter, "being past the romantic age and loath to rise from my bed at four in the morning out of motives of mere curiosity, he relies on "Theodosian testimony" (25)—Ted is the dedicatee of *East of the Giants*.

In a sidebar, Stewart also tells his Spring, 1938 readers that he and Ted have been in Cuernavaca for the last two months, and *East of the Giants* has just gone to the typists (in March—*Little*, 126). "It is much the longest thing I ever wrote, and like Benet, I feel a little as if I had given birth to a grand piano" (10). He was in correspondence with lots of his north-of-the-border acquaintances during this time. Harvey Fergusson wrote to him in November, 1937 "I was especially delighted to learn that your novel has been pouring off of you like heavy sweat" (Fergusson to Stewart 3 Nov. 1937). In 1938 John Steinbeck replied to a letter, "I hope you had fun down there. I wish I could have been there. This is a mad house. . ." as he works on the first draft of *The Grapes of*

Wrath. "I'll be awfully glad to read your new book. Joe (?) has fine reports of it" (Steinbeck to Stewart, n.d.). In December 1937 Stewart wrote to Richard Thornton that "By the help of God and a second-hand portable typewriter I have now finished the first draft of the novel, and expect to finish it this week" (Stewart to Thornton 5 Dec. 1937/*P*).

Stewart makes several important points about *East of the Giants,* in terms of its form and characters. He readily admits that some of the story is awkward, because he is just learning (by practice) to write novels. But he has a deliberate, and "rebellious," plot strategy: ". . .I took the Western cliche, which is the simple situation of the blonde American man who comes west and falls in love with the dark-haired Spanish beauty, and I reversed that. I had a blonde heroine, a blonde American girl who came out and married a dark man" (*Little* 12).

He also took the totally conventional 3-book structure (heritage of the 19th century 3-decker romance novel), and elaborated the device of "inter-chapters" which he was to use repeatedly, so that it became a "trademark" of his work (*Little* 121). He relates the interchapter technique to the basic issue of scene and summary. "If you can't write good scenes, you can't write a good novel." He calls the evasion of scenes "scene-flinching," and, from his teaching experience, bewails the writer who begins a scene, gets scared of what it demands, and ends up with only a summary. Within *East of the Giants,* the chapters are short, and are, in effect, single scenes, told from alternating narrative points of view. The majority of them are nonetheless told from the point of view of the protagonist, Judith, who is a very enigmatic character, wearing some of the perfume of feminism. In a way, Judith is helpless, "in a historical situation, and as the known history of the period changed, she had to adjust with it" (*Little* 101).

This Judith, and the Judith who is a fire lookout in *Fire,* are the only female protagonists in Stewart's works. He says he doesn't know where she came from, although Ted thinks she's based on his mother (123). Interestingly, the first Judith was imagined as an ancestress of the second one, and the Judith of *Fire* at one point tells her rescuer carrying her off "that this had happened to her ancestress who had been carried away on a horse" (*Little* 165).

Another way of experiencing Judith is as a female avatar of Stewart's archetype, the immigrant, and her movement through temporal history as that of an implicated witness to an evolving, complex relationship between California culture and environment. Like many of his characters, she grows from innocent simplicity through experiential complexity, but unlike many of them, her life is a broken circle, for she dies in the attempt to return to the "innocent" East—an East as might be represented by John Phoenix's New England white frame birthplace.

Judith is clearly, as a character, a counterblast to a semi-racist assumption that the dark-skinned Mexican beauty can be "raised up," even "saved" by the Great White Male. Even in "realistic" *The Octopus*, whose influence can be seen in the lyrical agrarian panoramas of *East of the Giants*, this stylized paradigm is enacted through the relationship between Vanamee and Angele (where, like the wives of Bret Harte, George Derby, and many a fictional female, the white immigrant wife is desperate with alienation and anomie).

Rebellious Gertrude Atherton provides a perfect example in miniature of this motif, summarized by Stewart in his edition of William Henry Thomes's *California Life in 1843* as "the myth of Spanish-Mexican California. Here every lady played the guitar, and every gentleman mounted his horse to cross the street, and nobody cared about money or did any work" (7). Atherton's long short story "The Ears of Many Americans" from her collection *The Splendid Idle Forties*, contemporary in setting and time to Stewart's novel, creates a Mexican Monterey besieged culturally and militarily by the "Americans." Dona Eustaquia hates the Americans, and when Don Fernando predicts that the widow will marry one, she exclaims "'God! I would give every league of my ranchos for a necklace made from the ears of twenty Americans'" (53). Her daughter Benicia, originally shares her mother's hatred, but is allured by a ball the American Consul has arranged to allow the Montereyans to meet the naval officers whose ships are at anchor in Monterey Bay. She professes to want to go only to laugh at the Americans' dancing: "'I love an American? . . . A great, big, yellow-haired bear? . . . No, mamacita, when I love an American thou shalt have his ears for thy necklace'" (60). One of them, Captain Russell, becomes enamored of the coquettish, exotic Benicia. "The Californian beauty was like no other woman he had known, and the victory [in winning her] would be as signal as the capture of Monterey" (77).

He succeeds; eventually a baby is born to him and Benicia, but by this time, from Dona Eustaquia's point of view "Monterey was Monterey no longer" (123), full of Americans, although she professes to forgive Russell for being one. On a typical melodramatic note, however, the curse she originally put on Benicia, to die when she was most happy, comes true when Benicia eats the (poisoned?) orange her mother gives her shortly after the birth. One might not focus on an anti-domestic theme in *The Splendid Idle Forties*—". . .a harsh distinction between the romance of courtship and the drudgery of the marriage (Leider 112)—and more on the "calculated nostalgia for the pre-Yankee past" (111), and, as in the case of Dona Eustaquia, the destructive effects of trying to hold on to it. One also might see in Benicia, in this particular story, a will as strong as that of Judith in *East of the Giants*, but one submerged by submission to the charms of the handsome Yankee. Stewart's Yankee heroine may initially submit to the charms of her dark Californian lover, but she retains an integral identity separate from his.

Another example of the convention Stewart was reversing is Corinne King Wright's *Cold Embers: A Romance of Old California* (1931), set in the ubiquitous 1840's, "When the Adobe Age of the Don is Displaced by the Golden Age of the American Pioneer" (t.p.). Wright's Spanish Californians encounter the American military only in the last quarter of the book. Meanwhile we are treated to a festival of Catholicism and Passion, featuring fiery families, perturbed priests, dashing Dons, and a pair of smashing senorita cousins, Carmela and

Panchita, at the forefront the forbidden love affair between Carmela and the half-Indian Benito. There's a lot of historical detail, but also sentences like "With a single movement, a lightning stroke, she plunged a keen Spanish stiletto into his breast!" (275). The senoritas go ga-ga at the handsome anglo soldiers led by Fremont. In a chapter titled "Nordic vs. Latin," Panchita is introduced by Carmela to the handsome Lieutenant King, who can exclaim only "'You?-You!'" and Carmela leaves them together, "knowing that her cousin had met the mysterious man of her dreams" (303). Stewart's revisionism of such formulae was clearly recognized. The novel's *New York Herald Tribune* reviewer said "For those who are a bit tired of the 'Ramona' view of early California, it is the best novel yet" ("Class Notes" 11 Nov. 1938).

Not all of the California romances Stewart pretends to be revising do follow this formula. In Thomas Grant Springer's *The Californian: A Romance of the Last Frontier,* the gringette Jane Holman ends up with the handsome Romero, outlaw become San Francisco lawyer and civic leader ("She gripped him fiercely, straining him to her breast where her heart seemed to all but leap to meet his [283]). The novel even begins with the "greasers," *bandidos,* blowing up a dam built by imperialistic white ranchers, a scene of which Edward Abbey would be proud. By contrast, *East of the Giants* begins in April, 1837, with the arrival of the merchant ship the *Spanish Belle* (significant name) captained by Peleg [Melvillian] Hingham, from Boston, at Monterey. The *Spanish Belle* is filled with all types of goods, and to an extent becomes a water-borne department store, particularly for the upper-class Mexicans and the "Californians," the Anglo immigrants. On the ship are the captain's daughter Judith, and Mr. Melton, who will sell and purvey his ladies' dress goods inland during the vessel's stay. Melton is the first voice we hear, describing Judith, as "'whiteness and strength'" (1) while the ship breaks through the fog into Monterey Bay. Judith is physically atypical for a White Heroine: she is very tall, not terribly "beautiful," and has "shoulders for a military cadet to be proud of" (2). John Caldwell suggests, perhaps too absolutely, that the arrival of Judith "signaled. . . .the passing of the frontier, the end of a man's world, and the coming of civilization" (24). Melton reflects on her and upon California as a whole: ". . . the long riding from ranch to ranch, the courteous easy-going Californians, and the great open country. It was a hard, primitive land, but not unfriendly. He had his books, and he did not mind the lack of other things which men called civilization. He felt oppressed now when he was back in Boston . . ."(6).

As Judith falls asleep in the harbor, her thoughts reveal for the first time the theme of human linkage with the physical land which will dominate the novel: "Certainly she must explore this new land to which she had come. She wanted to know its smell, its texture, its height and its depth, not merely from the deck to look at it as a flat picture, a panorama as of painted canvas" (9).

Judith is partly defined by her literary education; she maintains a lifeline to the "world of culture" through the books she is sent by her family. In this way she leads a "double life" in a pre-Montgomery Street California, although she will witness the changes in cultural institutions accompanying urbanization (we could reference here Stewart's study on frontier theater discussed above). A telling remark that illustrates this connection is her thought, in indirect discourse, that "She liked dark men. Perhaps they would look like Lord Byron in the engravings" (10). This is a pregnant comment. Byron and all he represents is the East, represented by European romanticism; however, the liking of dark men, in Eastern terms, is "unorthodox" and inverts "acceptable" tastes. It is a form of rebellion against conventional cultural expectations similar to what the fashionable Byronolatry of European youth was to the ideals of neoclassical culture.

Two triggering events in Judith's engagement with California nature and culture become "epiphanic" moments. In the first, she observes vaqueros lasso and cut the throat of a steer on the shore as she watches from the *Spanish Belle*. She faints. The vaqueros are punished not for slaughtering the steer but for doing it "before a lady." Judith sees the event as a "warning." "Her pride of strength had met its fall. . . She had come in past Point Pinos as a conqueror to subdue the land. Had the land subdued her?" (16). The second is her mutual "love at first sight" encounter with Mexican landowner Don Juan Godoy, the "dark man" of her imagination. Don Juan is as disturbed as she by his amative emotions, and goes to consult his Uncle Enrique. Uncle Enrique is more or less the governing sage of the story, whose cultural literacy is as elevated as any easterner's, and who deplores his cousin's lack of interest in education. Uncle Enrique has reservations, not the least of which is Judith's non-Catholicism—to which Don Juan replies "'You may say that I shall become a heretic'" (27). Judith is equally at a loss; there are days of stasis, as it were, between two regional cultures, represented by the lovers. "She had read a good many books which told about love, but the only one which seemed to fit her case was *Romeo and Juliet* and that didn't help" (31).

Ultimately, after she exchanges covert notes with Don Juan, he details a plan to kidnap her from the ship and elope with her. I think this is a plan whose dramatic fulfillment more or less satirizes the "romance" tradition in California novels by fitting in to it so well. She is carried to the shore, put on a horse, and led on a night gallop through an increasingly alien (to her) landscape. Judith knows she has "given herself"—to the person and the land. "She had left her family, she was rushing through wild strange country on a galloping horse at midnight, but still she felt something of the New England village with its prim white-steepled meeting house refusing to die within her" (39).

When she and Juan ride back to Monterey the next afternoon, and a reconciliation with her tolerant father, not only has the tension "gone out of life; they no longer had to strain forward toward some culmination" (42), but she has symbolically made the passage from one environment to another. She made a "leap of faith" from the *Spanish Belle* to the California shore; now she is approaching that shore from the heart of the land, in a sense become a real (though blonde) Spanish belle herself.

The long trek inland, from rancho to rancho, to reach Don Juan's own Rancho Amarillo, is an initiation for Judith into an "environmental consciousness" of place. She is forced to alter her conception of herself and of nature if she is to achieve a condition of inhabitance. For example, she is used to flowers in New England in gardens or speckled in pastures ". . . but here she came to great splashes of color that covered acres—yellow, soft blue, or brilliant orange. The splashes were so lavish and gigantic that they were almost intoxicating. . . .Was such gigantic beauty really beauty at all? . . .Must not real beauty have intimacy?" (46). The natural inhabitants will also have to adjust themselves to her. She is new terrain. Her white hair is to them what the flowers are to her. They stop in the town of San Jose. What seemed like a ball on the top of the village flagpole is actually a human head. She inquires; Don Juan says casually "'Oh yes, that's Ignacio'" (52).

Rancho Amarillo is in a cup-shaped valley 2 miles in diameter. As they descend toward the ranch house, Juan is, in joy, deluged by a "torrent" of "sensations" that to him "are" the place (and which Stewart surely gleaned from his sensory observation of Mexico):

> Smells—the barnyard, decaying meat, hides, woodsmoke, Indian servants. Sight—the squat lines of the house in gray adobe brick, and the hard blue sky above the line of the ridge-pole; two dark naked children capering away but looking back to be sure they missed seeing nothing; the horizontals of the corral bars; the verticals of the porch supports with a contrasting diagonal where a window shutter hung from one hinge. Sounds—dogs, chickens, turkeys, children, two heavy grunts of a hog, and from somewhere faintly the pat-pat of a woman making tortillas. (56)

Aldo Leopold says "The landscape of any farm is the owner's portrait of himself. . .Conservation implies self-expression in that landscape" (*Health* 172). Nothing could better describe the feeling Juan has for Rancho Amarillo, and which Judith will come to share, but slowly. At her introduction, she is intimidated by the rancho's isolation, and Juan's description of the far geography around them. But, in June, she is not intimidated by the ritual slaughter of steers on the "killing-ground." Her unresolved sense of nature is clear in her dialogue with Juan at a time she feels she may be pregnant, ". . .conscious of a new feeling of pressure about her breasts" (64). She has awakened to find the "bright, lively green" of the valley since her arrival has become "darker and duller." In a week all the hills are brown. 'Judith had loathed the change. All her life she had known only a green or white landscape; brown hills seemed a betrayal of nature. It was like death" (64). Juan says it is not dead, "'It's ripe.' Was there any difference. . .Was it death only when something was cut off incomplete? When something went its full cycle, fulfilled its purpose and went to fruition—was that ripeness, an ending not mournful?"

This transformed ecophilosophy—death become ripeness—also affects Judith's view of Juan. He is not poorly educated; he has "strange knowledge" of nature, animals, people. In this way she is able to see him—and potentially herself—speaking in anachronistic but I believe applicable terms, as member of a Leopoldian "biotic community," only a "member of a biotic team." And therefore, much of what is to befall them, the Rancho, and California itself, is produced by "biotic interactions between people and land" (*Almanac* 240-241).

By February 1838, Judith is in her ninth month of pregnancy, Mr. Melton has visited, and she has been wondering how to react to Juan's affair with the servant girl Paquita. On this day, the usual early morning sounds suddenly stop, and then begin in a different way. This collective aural transformation is a sign that someone has entered the valley. It is Juan, in martial array, telling of Indian attacks on neighboring ranchos, which remind Judith of traditional New England stories of King Philip's War. Although the rancheros head out to retaliate, nothing much comes of the episode, but it seems like a prefiguration. By April she has had her baby, and been reconciled to Juan, who spends much of his time patrolling Rancho Amarillo. It is a protected space partly because, unlike other surrounding ranches, it had been granted to his father thirty years earlier when the Missions still controlled the land; and his father in return had to patrol and keep Indians away. This stewardship Juan is continuing without the need for it.

After he has opened up to Judith and explained this, showing how the ranch house Judith has never really liked was designed to become a fort, though never completed, she develops a new sense of purpose, a "dream." She is enlivened by this dream, although it is ambiguous: "Now she knew that they lived at Rancho Amarillo not merely to have beef to eat and horses to ride, but also to maintain the honor of a generation-old promise and to hold the frontier so that civilization might grow up behind them. It gave a meaning to life" (121). This is an ambiguous sense of mission, since, although it creates a center of meaningfulness for the inhabitance of the place, it also implies an instrumentality in enabling the spread of what is, inherently, alien to it.

During this period also, Judith is reading the books her visiting father has left her, one of which is *Gulliver's Travels*, with its satiric map of the world Gulliver has travelled. California is east of Brobdingnag, the land of the giants. "That was where she was living now—east of the giants . . ." (122), as far as you could get from "civilization."

In an interchapter, "Quiet Years (1838-1844)," we are given a wonderful "almanac of the seasons" on the ranch, with all the domestic and wild natural changes that occur and reoccur. For Judith "Year by year, by her own abundant energy, she worked closer to the vision of her dream, and came more to love the lonely valley and the life which centered there" (125). But Stewart emphasizes the nonrepetitive life going on outside the valley. California may not have had much history in this time, but "it had plenty of politics" (129). The ecosystemic harmony on the rancho is contrasted to the polarizations in the public world: between "up-country" and "down-country;" over whether the capital should be at Monterey or Los Angeles; between the clericals and the anti-clericals, the Mexican loyalists and the Californian separatists. "It was all very complicated"(129). Particularly there is the "closing circle" fear: Indians to the west, multinational warships cruising the Pacific. Stewart has Judith happy with the books sent her from the East but experiencing sharp attacks of isolation, and as her children grow, learning of the growing number of immigrants making trails over the Sierra.

At a party in 1844, Judith displays a book by an Englishman (book and Englishman invented by Stewart), *Eight Months on the North-West Coast in the Years 1840-41*, and we are allowed to experience a metanovelistic description, by the imaginary author in the imaginary book, as Judith reads it, of a visit to "Rancho Amarilyo." She herself is described, and summarized: "'In fact, in this most unlikely of all places, I was forced to conclude that my hostess was a veritable Blue Stocking'" (139). There is also a wonderfully derogatory portrait of Juan, who lacks all "civilized traits" and seems to the author most like ". . .some petty Irish landlord in the wildest and furthest removed part of that unfortunate island. There he lives surrounded by his own half-savage bog-trotters, nursing his ignorance against the world. So he of Amarilyo might be considered an epitome of provincials" (139).

This judgmental sophisticated ignorance (one might find it in Professor Heermance of Princeton) is very effective when it encounters the story after we have experienced the flow of rich experience at Rancho Amarillo. It is also played off against the ecological allegory of life that Uncle Enrico subsequently expresses, while drunkenness invades the celebrators: "The life of man, I feel, is like a stream of water" (140); the banks restraining the stream are the world, our surroundings, and the pressure of other people; sometimes the stream flows quietly and peacefully between the banks; sometimes in the hills it breaks into rapids. "The banks press in, and the stream fights back trying to force its will upon them in a fury of foam" (141).

The next morning, jokingly asked how her stream is doing, Judith replies "'I feel . . .as if I were in that little quiet pool just before the stream goes over a waterfall'" (143). Her feeling anticipates the revolutionary chaos of early 1845 between Americans and Californians, in the lead-up to the "Bear Flag Revolt" of the next year. During this period she holds Rancho Amarillo and its residents together by force of will. Afterwards, Judith reflects on being a witness to history and engages in imaginations. She's a hundred years old, in 1916, talking about "those days," with a historian, on her veranda. "Her peach trees would have died and been replanted before that; even her apple and pear trees would be old and gnarled. But the line of the hills would look just the same, and the trees would still grow along the ravines." And she imagines history as a snake, as a rattlesnake she had stumbled upon. ". . .[A]s she sprang back it had struck and missed. History was like that. You seemed to wander along calmly controlling your own steps, and then something you could not control—a war, a revolution, a failure of banks—buzzed and struck, and did not always miss" (155).

At this point the narrative point of view changes, and the reader joins Juan and a ragged multiethnic troop on an expedition to rout the Indians who have been ravaging the ranches. The battle that results is described in genocidal detail. Juan ends up with a life-threatening arrow wound in his arm, but Judith learns of a ship at Yerba Buena with a surgeon. She gives martial orders to her household, and rides off to the coast with gold to get him to treat Juan. "'If she were a Californian', thought Judith, 'she would merely sit by his bed praying to the virgin, and Juan would be dead in a week and it would be the will of God to which wives must be resigned. Possibly that was a better way of life, but it was not her way'" (179).

In another abrupt shift of time and point of view, we overhear the French surgeon, at a later date, telling his brother about his visit to Rancho Amarillo, "a remarkable place. . .Even though the grass was dead, there was a somber beauty to the sweep of the valley and sculpturing of the hills. The house was the best that I saw in California" (189). He explains both that it was Judith's "certain power, a determination to force her will, which emanated from her" that persuaded him to go, and that her journey to Yerba Buena and back while pregnant had caused her to miscarry.

The meditations on history, the effects of changing population on the land, are those of Juan in the following chapter, when he rides off to join the "Bears" against the Americans. What he notices is a "new" kind of American immigrant, unlike the earlier ones, the trappers who mingled with Indians and Hispanics alike. These new Americans are agriculturists and proto-developers, disliked by both Juan and Judith. They are always "assuming that because they were Americans they were close friends," and always talking in terms of "laying out a townsite and selling lots." One had even wanted to do this to Rancho Amarillo, and call it "Godoy City" (195). This reflection is more significant than the military action that follows, ended with the declaration of U.S. war against Mexico. For once the threat to the ranch is not military but economic—a threat to the land itself.

But before this threat becomes immanent, Judith has to face two separate groups of "ugly Americans" set to capture and/or kill Juan. The first group trashes the ranch house. Judith is prepared for the second group, and cons them (with Juan in the house) by dressing up, inviting them in, treating them in an overgentlewomanly manner, learning their names (particularly that of Major Cornelius Baxter and Judge Wingram) giving them tea, getting them drunk, putting them up for the night. This is Judith as she would have been if she had grown up to become a New England wife. She saves her dark husband, whose life has become her own, by inventing an "American" cultural space in which the visitors become comfortable and harmless.

In 1848 gold fever is rising, and we find Mr. Melton, who has bought a lot of property in the new "San Francisco," desperately ill with a real fever acquired in the gold fields, and trying in delirium to ride down to Rancho Amarillo. He has read from his Shakespeare while in the mines, and his delirium mixes the gold-digging memories with characters from the plays; "A lot of men living out in the wilderness just like the Duke in the Forest of Arden" (238). As he reflects, however he thinks that the gold has abolished the "old days," that no one will build a city on the "barren peninsula" of Yerba Buena, and that gold doesn't mean the Forest of Arden, but rather "men and women standing, belligerent, with shotguns" (240). He also remembers his pastoral childhood in the Juniata Valley of Pennsylvania (not far from Indiana). In symbolic mode, he finally discards his money belt, which lightens him enough to reach Rancho Amarillo and faint from his horse into Judith's arms.

"Gold had demoralized the whole countryside" (244), landscape and inhabitants. Judith has to become her own surgeon to cauterize Mr. Melton's wounds, and also become her own husband, as it were, to shoot at and drive off the ranch's odious major-domo, Julio, who has tried to rape her. "It was strange, she thought, how quickly and fiercely the gold had worked though California like some fever in the blood. . . the old settled feudal life suddenly smashed to pieces in a few months. . ." (249). The gold paradoxically estranges the inhabitants from the land they are finding it in. Judith fears she will lose the life of the ranch—". . the valley, the grass, the cattle, the unaltering skyline to the south, the steady rhythm of the change from green to brown and back to green unendingly. In that life a man or woman could feel in touch with things deep, constant, and certain" (249-50).

Juan returns from his own adventures in the mines equally demoralized, although with bags of gold. "When the streams shrank in the fall, I saw bars where the gold lay and glittered like fish scales" (252-3)—an ironic mode of Don Enrique's stream-life metaphor. As Juan plays, childlike, making hills of his nuggets, Judith thinks of that metaphor again. "They had left the old quiet valley behind and were still swirling violently down through the hills; somewhere ahead but still out of sight might lie another valley. Who could survive and reach quiet waters again?" (253).

Representing this time of change, the scene shifts to booming San Francisco at the end of 1849, when Mr. Melton's "worthless" properties have made him so rich he needs a personal bodyguard, Big Mike Shane. Stewart provides a vivid and detailed panorama of San Francisco's topography and ethnicity as Melton meets up, and travels its streets with, all the usual suspects—Juan himself, Judge Wingram, Jerry Graham, of the party hunting Juan that Judith had conned. Here the con is reversed, with the urban developers, on their own turf, seeking to get Juan to sell them the ranch. Here nature is reversed too, with a bull-bear fight staged in the entertainment palace where they are drinking. Juan bets on the bear, and loses, in a bloodily-described scene: Melton finds the fight is a set-up, with the bear's claws clipped flat.

Juan reaches the depth of self-destructiveness when he rides with his brother Miguel and others to drive squatters off a part of his land so that he can sell it. Miguel is killed, and in rage Juan sets fires in his own woodland to burn or drive out for the shooting those who killed him. When Juan returns with Miguel's body, his face is black with soot, and Judith sees "nothing but blackness ahead" (279). This anticipation is realized when Juan is murdered in a gambling fight soon afterwards. Juan had been going out on limbs (Stewart's metaphor for himself) all his life, and this time the limb had broken.

Judith had determined to live self-sufficiently on the ranch, but Mr. Melton offers her all the money she needs to restore it. As they talk, Judith remembers walking with him on the *Spanish Belle*.

> 'It's strange,' she said at last. 'During all those quiet years on the ranch, I looked forward to when civilization would come; and when it came, it brought only trouble and disaster—like this.'
>
> 'Yes,' said Mr. Melton thoughtfully, 'but this isn't civilization. We're still in the turmoil of one way of life changing into another. . .' (284)

The next interchapter, titled "Quiet Years (1850-1856)," summarizes the life of Judith after her marriage to Mr. Melton in 1851. For the first time in her California life she leaves the ranch; Mr. Melton builds a mansion on Stockton Street, and the whole household moves there. The old household staff melts away, and Judith acquires the subordinates of urban wealth—butler, chef, French maid, governess, coachman. Thus she has abandoned, temporarily at least, both the nature and culture of rural California. Her son Luis has changed his name to Lewis, and become a marine insurer. But Judith has come to the realization that she is bored. She " . . .wanted Lupe's beans; she wanted the rough texture of tortillas between her teeth, and the sting of the raw red wine which came from the vineyard on the hill behind the ranch house" (294).

Judith, who has experienced lots of urban chaos, including the reigns of the Committees of Vigilance, of which Stewart will later write in detail, feels nonetheless that "She was too far from where things started. She ate her roast beef without seeing the steer it came from, without seeing the blood flow, often without even seeing the red meat before it was cooked" (295). When she arrives home, a statue is being unpacked, ordered from Boston—an iron bull on a pedestal. Unwrapped, the bull unfortunately "whether from ignorance or accident or prudery . . . was lacking those parts which you might say were really most essential for a bull" (307). Her sense of environmental displacement, of living an un-natural life, is symbolized by the disembodied roast beef and the emasculated bull. "She felt tricked and trapped in civilization" (308).

The artificial dinner party she subsequently hosts surprisingly offers her a way out of the trap, and initiates one of the most interesting and environmentally relevant episodes in the novel. The Meltons' guests include Judge and Mrs. Wingram, Lieutenant Grainger, Sir Robert Tyneman—a visiting English sportsman—and Tony Burke, a "wild Irishman" (291), along with her son Lewis. Mr. Burke and Judge Wingram fall into a discussion of the failures and successes of utopian communities. The Judge cites New Harmony, Brook Farm, and others, as evidence they cannot succeed, while Burke argues that the failure of particular enterprises does not prove the inviability of the principles on which they were based.

Stewart's introduction of this theme is topically accurate; the "contemporary enthusiasm for communities" (312) was strong in pre-Civil War America, and came from many sources, both religious idealism and secular social idealism. Near Santa Rosa, where Stewart was driving when he decided to become a novelist, he could have found the sites of two utopian communities, admittedly of more recent vintage. Fountain Grove, was established by Thomas Lake Harris, a "theological vagabond" and mystic (Hine 12) in 1875 for his Brotherhood of the New Life, devoted to what Harris called "Theo-Socialism" (Hine 28). The manor house named Aestivossa, which was Harris's residence, and the center of the community, was still standing when *East of the Giants* was written, and the community's winery still exists; its final owner and surviving disciple of Harris, Kanaye Nagasawa, had died only in 1934 (Paradise Ridge). Altruria was established by San Franciscans inspired by William Dean Howells's utopian socialist novel *A Traveller from Altruria* (1893), right off of U.S. Route 101 on which Stewart would have been travelling when he supposedly decided to write a novel. Incidentally, the Altrurian traveller is "Mr. Homos," which might make one ponder the influence of Howells's idealism on Stewart's later *Man: An Autobiography*.

Judith, intrigued by Mr. Burke's ardor, tells him "'. . .please go on. Are you a Foo-er-ist?'" (312)—referring, mispronouncedly, to Charles Fourier, whose sociophilosophical writings formed the groundwork for many 19th century utopias, literary and literal. Burke denies being a Fourierist, an Owenite, or an adherent of any movement. He speaks only for himself:

> 'What is the destiny of man? To support himself and make himself happy by cultivating and beautifying this world, by making to bloom its deserts, by draining its noisome morasses, by sowing forests upon its mountains, by regulating and keeping pure its crystal streams. But instead, our present society leads him to fight other men for his existence. To bring men back to their true destiny—toward this, all these new communities strive." (313)

The argument transforms Judith. "An hour before, she had thought of communities . . .as associations of religious fanatics and other queer people, harmless and rather funny. Now she saw them as scattered seedlings, destined to burgeon inevitably and grow and scatter more seeds until they embraced in their growth all society" (314). She has a vision of convergence, of Rancho Amarillo "transfigured." So with the help of her husband and a bottle of cognac, she works out plans to take over Rancho Amarillo again and "establish one of Mr. Burke's co-operative communities upon it" (317-18).

In this enterprise, Stewart approaches again the concept of human association, or community, and its fate as an environmental entity. Stewart's sociologist colleague Robert Lowie defines an association as "a group consolidated by a common end" (74). The snowbound Donner Party as presented by Stewart might be considered an association of necessity, with the short term common end of physical survival. The traditional Californian ranch, like Rancho Amarillo, could then be considered an association of tradition, with the common end of self-perpetuation, and the utopian Rancho—like New Harmony, Altruria, *ad infinitum*, an association of choice, an engineered association, with the end of actualizing an agenda of ideals. Judith's proposed association has serious limitations. It is partly a social "time machine"—an attempt to force a return to the agrarian Arcadia of her memory, an example of what Stewart in his 1960's environmentalist role, would call "restoration." It is also an urban construct: it does not originate, one might say, "where things started," inductively, from the ground up. Its source is in the formal dining room of an urban mansion, and will come into Rancho Amarillo almost like the different invaders of her earlier life there.

In all three of these different incarnations, associations will, for reasons varying with their different ends and organizations, eventually disintegrate. What Lowie says in an anthropological context can be applied: ". . . by the very fact of their existence they have created novel bonds bound to encroach upon the omnipotence of family ties" (108)—if we extend "family ties" to incorporate any priorital relationships between humans or between humans and nature. Mr. Melton has his own slight doubts about Judith's enthusiasm for her utopia; he considers that her passion for it is a "falling in love," such as her passion for

Juan. Perhaps it is even a "transferred" passion for the charismatic Mr. Burke (321).

However, these thoughts don't keep him from accompanying her to do, as it were, fieldwork, to study the organization of the Aurora Community, near Portland. This actual community was founded in 1856 by German immigrant minister William Keil, who ". . .elected to formulate a private theological system representing a mixture of revivalism, millenialism, and communalism" (Friesen and Friesen 161). It was a new outpost for his original Bethel Community in Missouri, established in 1844. Keil and his immense wagon train made a five-month trek to the land, already purchased. His son Willie died just before he left, so they took Willie's body with them. "The first wagon bore Willie's casket, which was filled with alcohol to preserve the body; the journey is sometimes referred to as the longest funeral procession in American history" (Friesen and Friesen 164). Both Aurora (named for Keil's daughter) and Bethel "resembled a common village in a newly-settled country," according to a contemporary (Hinds 334). Hinds characterizes Aurora's beliefs and organization as simple: "Fear God, love one another, and do right in all things; thus they condensed the whole duty of life" (335). However, as Keil dispersed his original ownership of the land among all heads of household without any ill effects, it is clear "how fully grounded the members were in communistic principles and what power those principles possess even under unfavorable circumstances" (336). Keil was a very successful manager, and at its height the Colony had 13,000 acres and 600 members (Old Aurora Colony).

Stewart, however, presents the Aurora visit as not very useful to the couple's plans. They stay only a few hours, and although it is "prosperous after the manner of a frontier village, and the people seemed happy under a benevolent despotism" (324), Keil has the air of a fanatic, and grows cool when he learns their own association will not be faith-based. Judith and her husband are more inspired by reading utopian theory. One utopian "bible" was Etienne Cabet's

Voyage en Icarie, the socialist novel that Cabet sought to make real in a series of communities beset by strife and faction, culminating in a final version, Icaria Speranza (1881-6), in Sonoma County (1881-86). "Organized religion entered but little into the Icarian scheme. Neither atheists nor agnostics, Icarians professed true Christianity, but the forms of religion did not greatly appeal to them" (Hine 72).

An even more influential book for the Meltons is American Fourierist Albert Brisbane's *Social Destiny of Man: or, Association and Reorganization of Industry* (1840), which Stewart quotes through the consciousness of Mr. Melton. Brisbane attributes the evil, misery, and injustice in the world to the "FALSE ORGANISATION OF SOCIETY ALONE" (2), which is causing the decay of civilization (as intuited by Judith herself earlier). The "great object" of Associations is to "increase the product of agriculture . . and to prevent the great accumulation of manufacturing populations in a few cities" (320).

Brisbane-Fourier's vision of dispersed agrarian associations—sort of Jeffersonian, really—is the clincher for a Rancho Amarillo community. Brisbane (or Fourier?) ". . .was like a mad poet. You forgot his madness as you sensed the wild glory of his vision" (*East* 325-26). The couple does find it hard, looking at the ideal community map in Brisbane's frontispiece, ". . .fitting the scheme into the treeless hills of Rancho Amarillo and its nondescript creek bordered by slatternly sycamores" (326). But Mr. Melton will go along with the fantasy, imagining that he and Judith will live in San Francisco and direct their Community from afar.

They cannot be afar, however. At Lewis's request, attending the famous Reverend Doctor Jesson's church in San Francisco, they find their community, and communitarianism in general, attacked as "'Godless, un-Christian, and vicious'" (333). Jesson, who has read his Fourier, Brisbane, and Owen, considers that their environmentalism abolishes all morality, community of property to be unbiblical and destructive of "that sacred institution of the home."

At the Amarillo Community "they might have to expect anything from polygamy, free love, and plain promiscuity to the equal debasement of complete celibacy" (334).

Judith thus is finally drawn to return to the ranch herself, and is very disappointed by its lack of improvement, despite Tony's organizing. Unadaptable crops have been planted, fencing separating grazing and agricultural lands is incomplete, a mill dam is planned on a creek that is dry half the year. More significantly, great numbers of people have come to Amarillo, stayed a while, and left. "It troubled Judith that so many people were quick to be dissatisfied even in Paradise . . ." (343). Tony explains that this was due to the diverse "cranks" with specific communitarian ideas who fought with each other and quit, or urbanites bored "after being a few weeks in a place where they could not see at least the passing of an occasional fire-engine or brewer's dray" (344). There were only a few "who like Tony represented the intellectual reaction against the modern world" (344). Judith thinks that Americans are queer people ". . .with all their running around to subdue the earth without stopping to enjoy it . . ." (345).

We can see the paradox in Judith here. For all her social idealism and environmentalism (in the modern sense), she doesn't recognize the willful individualism of others, using her own will to try to shape an agrarian eco-topia, which to succeed will require the suppression of just such traits in its constituents. Very much like the heroines of Gertrude Atherton's later books, Judith is "adventurous, courageous, combative, and nobody's fool," but unfortunately does not have the "individual will [that] becomes a force in nature, overwhelming every other force" (Leider 327), which Atherton ascribed to herself. She cannot become a Dr. Keil, and compromise the communal ideal with a benevolent despotism. She cannot fight alone against mass violence such as threatened the ranch in the Bear Flag days.

And that is precisely what threatens the Amarillo Community at the time of harvest. It suffers raids, and Judith's son Henry, riding to San Francisco to deliver a letter about the threats to a lawyer, is captured by a "'bunch of good Americans . .'" who've been planning to drive out the "'goddamn Mormons and Com-myun-ists'" (363). The self-described good Americans hang Henry from a tree by his wrists, and he suffers great pain in freeing himself. Before he left the ranch, Judith had been thinking "Probably Daniel was right. The time of violence and gunplay was all over in California. Things were getting civilized. You wrote a letter to a lawyer now, instead of riding out with your men behind you" (36). Henry returns with difficulty to warn of the approaching rural Committee of Vigilance, and Judith decides to place herself in the ritual position where she was so many times in earlier days—at the doorway of the ranch house, seeking to talk down the invaders of Paradise.

Judith's is seemingly successful in pacifying the vigilantes; but in the night they torch the fields and outbuildings, effectively destroying the ranch. Only the older parts of the house remain, in the center of blackness. "The strange thought which struck her was the way in which the cluster of buildings seemed to have reverted to what she had seen when she first came there. Plans and solicitudes and labors of twenty years had flared into that sudden light and vanished" (377). As Stewart defined it later, it was "the breakdown of the primitive paradise" (*Little* 124).

The Meltons return to San Francisco to find newspaper accounts of the Community's destruction and editorials maligning it, including a personal attack on Judith in the *Gazette*: "Neither polygamy nor its reverse can be tolerated, no matter what the color of the skin or the color of the hair . The indignation of the people must be aroused . . . against her of high station who cloaks her actions under the cover of such high-sounding names as Owenism and Fourierism" (386). Melton goes to the office of the editor, Pennington, tells him he lies, and hits him square in the face with a very large, full, inkwell. Realizing what will probably happen, he collaborates with an ex-military friend to send a challenge to Pennington—not that he really wants to duel him, but he knows their offspring will do so if he doesn't.

At the duel site, Mr. Melton thinks of Hotspur before battle, to no effect, because he is killed. When Lewis hears of it, he has complex responses. He wonders if anyone, like Melton's bodyguard, killed Pennington, what good it would do. He is "Just a bit of the system, and you couldn't shoot a system" (410). But he decides it has to be done; with a little help from his friends, he corners Pennington in the Brooklyn Saloon, and is able to induce him to fire first, so when he kills Pennington, it can be considered self-defense.

In May, 1860, Judith goes to Rancho Amarillo for the last time, to show it to the rising young journalist, pen name "Zutano"—clearly modeled by Stewart on Bret Harte. Taking Zutano to the ranch is in a sense a literary act. He's a close friend of Lewis who realizes he has a lot of talent but nothing to write about: "'. . .he's just like a spider, spinning things out of his own insides'' (415). When they arrive, she is irritated when Zutano calls it a "'picturesque old ruin. . .'" "This was no Greek temple or medieval abbey. This was her home" (416). She answers Zitano's questions, knowing from them that he can never be able to understand the ranch as it was, and she more or less "writes" through her answers the kind of story, stereotyping old California, that she knows he can tell skillfully. Exhausted, she goes to sit on the porch. "She was tired and spiritless. The stream of life, she thought again, was still languishing in the morass, not knowing where to issue forth" (419).

In November, 1861, Judith boards the *Magdalena* (presumably this is what the Spanish belle has become) to return to New England by way of Cape Horn. ". . .[S]he had a new faint stirring of interest in life, in the future." She watches the "bold, hard coast" pass by (423), looking little different than when she had first seen it from the *Spanish Belle*. "It was good to get back to the sea" (424). She revisits her inland California experience in a naturalistic way. She thinks of *Gulliver's Travels*: its geography is a fantasy, but a fantasy can be real. "It must mean that somewhere just over the horizon of all human experience lurked an unknown region of gigantic and hovering forces, distorting and misdirecting the projects of the human will . . ." (424).

That night the ship is embayed and driven toward the shore; chaos reigns on board but Judith, daughter of a sea captain, knows exactly how much danger the ship is in. Lifeboats are swamped. She tells her companion, Sir Robert Tyneman of the fatal dinner party, that drowning might be a good way to go: "'My father and any number of Hinghams before him went down in salt water" (432). On shore, finally, with the survivors, the crew brings in the dead and lines them up. They include Judith: "She looked pale and peaceful. The sunlight glinted on her white hair" (434). Spanish horsemen, vaqueros, approach from inland and look at her body with awe: "'Senora . . .blanca'' (434).

It would almost seem as though a personified California has possessed Judith, and would rather have her dead than for her to complete a geographical life-circle alive in the East. Or, in accord with her Swiftian, Hardyesque meditations, some gigantic, hovering forces chose her fate. The geography of her life-course is one of ironic fulfillment, and partakes of bioregional vision. She has come by sea, innocent, to California, is "born" to passionate adulthood when carried to its shores by Don Juan, and, passion spent, dies on those same shores, despite her will to leave. The connection to place, whatever hardships it entailed, seems to triumph over the will to move "elsewhere."

East of the Giants was received with high praise by readers and reviewers. In the *Saturday Review*, it was characterized as revealing a novelist of "major stature:" "The land of California, to which he came as a child, lives in his eyes. The history of California is in his head and heart. He is not a writer of romance, but a realist in the best sense of the word" (5). Maxwell Perkins "wanted to take me over, almost literally," and have him write similar Western novels "at the literary level" (*Little* 111). But Stewart couldn't have that protege-discovery relationship with an editor; I get the feeling that it would have destroyed the autonomy he so much prized.

William Van Wyck, the host of a San Francisco radio program, "Books, Etc." reviewed the novel, saying "I prophesy big things for Stewart if he can overcome his handicap of being a professor. He is too powerfully creative to be ruined by the platitudinous babbitry of a university" (19 Nov. 1938). Stewart says being now a "novelist" didn't really get him much notice, let alone bad press, at Berkeley, since it was so full of writers anyway. Those who praised the novel generally didn't do it in terms of Van Wyck's anti-intellectualism. Fellow novelist Clyde Brion Davis, writing from Carmel, told Stewart "Everyone around here is wildly enthusiastic about *East of the Giants*" (Davis to Stewart 18 Oct. 1938). Perhaps the most authoritative notice came from Robinson Jeffers: "It is spacious, rich, and continuously interesting, and free of the sentimentality that infects so much writing about early California" (Jeffers to Stewart 24 Oct. 1938). By October, it was on the major best-seller lists. One famous person refused to praise it. The novel's British publisher, George Harrap, wanted endorsements from famous U.S. literary figures. One was Margaret Mitchell. She replied "I hope to go on a vacation soon and to have some leisure and I will take Mr. Stewart's book with me. I know I will enjoy it." But she refuses to provide an endorsement. "Because of this frank and understanding attitude on your part, I will be equally frank. I cannot give you an opinion to be used for publicity purposes." Since *Gone With The Wind* was published, her "circumstances have not been ordinary." She's been deluged by such requests, but "Having turned down my friends, I cannot oblige a stranger without giving my friends offense" (Margaret Mitchell Marsh to William Sloane 28 Mar. 1939/*P*).

*

In 1967—year of *The Graduate*—novelist and screenwriter Ken Kolb published a novel entitled *Getting Straight* (later a counterculture film starring Elliot Gould). In it, Harry, a Vietnam Vet, returns to college to get an English

Education M.A. He has a difficult time with the professors, who are mordantly satirized, but he does find a girlfriend, Jan, whose pregnancy he learns of just before he has to undergo his M.A. oral exam. The high point of the novel—and film—is the oral; in this case, Harry, increasingly irritated by the pretensions of the questioners, finally destroys the ritual by responding to the question "'What do you consider the most typical and most enduring form in English poetry?'" (181), by saying it is the limerick, and starts reciting obscene limericks he attributes to great writers. Afterwards, Dr. Kasper, the professor who has been sympathetic to him throughout, asks him why he did it, insisting that literature exists "'in the realm of the intellect.'" Harry replies, in a Van Wyckian mode, "'That's where you Ph.D.'s lose me. I'll go on reading all my life, but I want what I read to make me feel and act and grow. But you scholars think literature is a nicely preserved corpse, and you each have your own little peephole into the coffin. Seems to me like an awful limited kick'" (184). Ken Kolb, according the biography in the text, graduated with Honors in English from Berkeley, but "was fired from his first job there." He was a forest fire lookout, and, at the time of publication, lived in the Sierras (207).

The plot of *Getting Straight* is, with variations, that of Stewart's *Doctor's Oral*. It seems probable to me that Kolb was one of Stewart's students at one time, and was highly aware of the novel. Even if he wasn't, as my own former Princeton professor, Wilbur Samuel Howell, wrote to Stewart "I remember hearing of you first when all the young graduate students of my youth were reading *Doctor's Oral* and identifying themselves with its story and its theme" (Howell to Stewart 19 Mar. 1975). I remember, myself, as a Princeton graduate student in the 1960's, hearing *Doctor's Oral* referred to as an almost mythical book and a brilliant tour-de-force, and my surprise when I learned its author was also the author of *Earth Abides*.

Of course, Kolb, as inferredly one of the students in Howell's formulation, rewrites the novel with a different attitude, particularly on the part of the protagonist, who, unlike Stewart's, and in tune with 1960's culture, learns from his oral that he doesn't want to be an academic, and is happy with his choice. Also, Kolb does not try to perform Stewart's feat of condensing his novel into a single day.

The novel, Stewart says, was begun in Mexico in March, 1938, since he had finished *East of the Giants* by that time, and had two months to go on his sabbatical. He calls it an "in-between" book (*Little* 126). It was also an "in between publishers" book, since his agents, McIntosh and Otis, sold it to Random House, which was to be his publisher for the next decade. "Finally I have signed up with Random House" (Stewart to William Sloane 20 April 1939/*P*). Stewart had told Richard Thornton earlier that he was leaving Holt: "I am loath to enter into a brawl" (Stewart to Richard Thornton 11 Dec. 1938/*P*). In collaboration with Random editor Saxe Commins, Stewart was to publish some of his most impressive work.

In form, *Doctor's Oral* is almost perversely the opposite of its predecessor, as though the writer was indulging in a vice he often refers to, as originating in his childhood, that of "showing off." The scenes of the story are almost entirely indoor ones, and unlike *East of the Giants*, since "the whole thing takes place in about eighteen hours," there is no summary—the entire novel consists of complete scenes (*Little* 126). "You have made a Greek drama," Garland Greever wrote to Stewart, "with unity of time, place, and action out of such an ordeal as still causes some of us to shudder" (Greever to Stewart, ll Sept. 1939). "The story of this one day is as careful, as closely constructed, and . . .as witty as a Restoration comedy" (MacDonald 157). The time is roughly the present, although the author's points of reference seem to have been his M.A. oral at Berkeley, and more extensively, his Ph.D. oral at Columbia (see chapter 1). The setting is urban—basically that of Berkeley itself—and the characters are not involved in extreme experiences. In *Doctor's Oral*, really the first American academic novel specifically concerned with graduate students (I suggest it could play the role of an implicit rebuke to the wild undergraduate capers in his classmate's *This Side of Paradise*), as well as the tight temporal construction, Stewart first used what would become a habitual creative process—mapping the physical space in which the action takes place.

Stewart's novel, it should be mentioned, was preceded by at least two college novels written by his close friends and associates, although I don't see much derivation from them. Stewart greatly admired his colleague, Ben Lehman. "With a touch of genius he learned to draw, for the public good, upon the capacities not only of those who naturally thought as he did, but also of those who might have formed an opposition" (*Department* 33). Lehman's *Wild Marriage* (1925), set at Harvard, tells the story of an undergraduate and Harvard professor's son, Elam Dunster, who gets into many scrapes and whose romance with the seductive and ambiguous Older Woman, Madeleine Colquhom does not end in the wild marriage he is hoping for after all. Irving Stone's *Pageant of Youth* (1933) is set in Berkeley ("Stockley"), and has a lot in common with Crane's *Western Shore*, although it is, if anything, even darker, filled with flagrant politics, flagrant sex, and unsuccessful acquaintance rape. Both novels are more interested, it seems to me, in the private entanglements of their characters than in their characters' roles as university students.

Stewart, while no prude, sees the university as an essential character in his drama. Naturally, he in various places addresses the *roman a clef* issue inevitably raised by its setting and characters. In his "Rereading Notes" Stewart sardonically writes that, from the novel "Around the university, no exact recriminations came to me, but I am sure that there were a few—from some who thought that they were important enough to be cartooned." It was often regarded, though, as an *expose*, despite the author's demurral:

> THE CHARACTERS AND THE UNIVERSITY PICTURED IN THIS NOVEL ARE IMAGINARY. THE DOCTORAL EXAMINATION DESCRIBED IS ALSO IMAGINARY, AND NEED NOT EVEN BE CONSIDERED TYPICAL OF SUCH EXAMINATIONS.

Stewart felt, in the seventies, that those who appreciated *Doctor's Oral* most were people near a university but not of it. "Of course the whole idea of a Ph.D. examination is so fantastic to the ordinary person that he doesn't understand what it's about anyway. A lot of university life is fantastic to people like Governor Reagan, for instance" (*Little* 127).

But the "ordinary people" theme is precisely what Stewart is getting at in the novel. His protagonist, Joe Grantland, is by his own admission an average student, from rural California. His story is bookended between static passages in italics, describing physically and historically, the establishment, on the university library's pediment, of the incised names of Great People representing the different disciplines. Stewart says these passages, like similar ones in other books, are purposely "unrealistic touches" and deliberately "lyrical" (*Little* 5). Yet "The grand theme of the book is the contrast between the great ones whose names appear on the pediment and the everyday people, especially Joe Grantland, whose affairs constitute the story" ("Rereading"). The theme discerned by one skeptical reviewer, more like Kolb's, that "the doctorate in English literature is a vexing thing to obtain and of dubious value once it has been won" (Parker), seems off the mark both in terms of Stewart's intent and his realization. Surely the tone is often satiric, but the protagonist is more an academic *Candide*, trying to get by in a slightly crazy world, than an object of ridicule or denigration.

In fact, if there is any skeptical questioning implied in the story, it is of the meaning of a university itself. The book, like the campus, is confined between walls (of books, since it is the library's facade). The locales outside the walls are, like a serfs' village outside a castle, dependencies of it. To what extent does what goes on in the institutional community, for most of its members supposedly the gaining of knowledge to be applied outside these walls, actually have meaning only within them? Stewart's university community is an interesting counterpart to the Amarillo community in *East of the Giants*. The physical space of that community is meant to be its members' place of permanent residence, but it is beset by itinerancy and invasion. The university community is meant to be a *caravanserai*, but is beset by centripetal forces. Amarillo must work with, and protect itself against, environmental forces. The university is not really subject to the workings of nature (no earthquakes occur), and its issues, even when touching on the former, are more purely cultural: for example, the president (named Flacky!) vetoes, on the library pediment, the name of Darwin to represent biological science because his *"name was anathema to certain state senators of Covenanter and Wesleyan antecedents,"* and, pressed by "academic freedom" issues, finally agrees, as a compromise, to "Huxley" (12). (In 1917, President Flacky is forced to have the sculptor delete the names of Kant [Philosophy] and Goethe [German] because they are—German [14]).

We meet Joe Grantland walking across campus, the morning of his oral, to the 'Latin Quarter," named for its pseudo-Bohemian quality and/or its early residence by a Latin professor, in front of whose former home remains a carved stone with the inscription "This rock shall fly/From its firm base as soon as I." Joe thinks "People didn't settle down to live their lives so solidly these days; even full professors kept thinking about going somewhere else" (34).

Joe arrives at the apartment of his girlfriend and fellow student Julia, who (a lot earlier in the story than Kolb's Jan) tells him she's pregnant. Stewart is amused that this situation upset so many people: ". . . it's funny, but that was considered quite an immoral book by some people. The young couple living in sin" (*Little* 128). Anyway, what to do, with no secure job and a baby and doctorate in progress? Stewart has his couple reference Dreiser's *American Tragedy*. It doesn't have to end tragically, though. "It could be taken care of in a big city like this" (40). Then he starts thinking about Oliver Goldsmith. Throughout the day, the mind-body problems alternate in Joe's thoughts, to very interesting effect. His friend Pat says "'Goldsmith's not a matter of life and death'" (41). Julia's pregnancy is just the most immediate circumstance in a body/nature—mind *pas a deux* that the novel engages.

Julia's thoughts are confused too. She was too emotional in her announcement: "The new Julia raged. That wasn't any kind of code for a modern, sophisticated girl to follow" (43). In the mode of interior monologue expressed through indirect discourse--which the narrator uses throughout the novel--Julia imagines herself satirically as a *magna mater*: ". . .the one who takes men to her bosom as the earth takes the rain and grows fertile of it." She imagines the style of O'Neill and Jeffers:

> I am the earth,
> I am eternal, I am Eve.
> Before Stonehenge or the battlements of Xochicalco,I was, I am;
> You, man, are as incidental as the bee to the flower.
>
> At this, up-state Julia—plump pretty, and full of common sense—rose up to utter two syllables of comment . . . (45).

The "up-state" is important. Julia and Joe (as his last name perhaps suggests) are from rural or semi-rural backgrounds. The novel's references to human sexuality and fertility, its occasional evocations (especially through Joe) of natural space, hover around the world of enclosed spaces—particularly Julia's apartment, the pub and restaurant Le Chat Gris, and ultimately the oral exam's seminar room—like the presences Judith in *East of the Giants* sense just outside her ken. They periodically nudge academia into the ephemeral. John Lyons notes a similar presence in George Weller's Harvard novel *Not to Eat, Not for Love* (1933), where the freshmen are told, Emersonianally, that they will find God at Harvard in "untamed nature" (45).

Pat Roseman, the ubiquitous "oral exam coach" who has designated himself to lead Joe through this difficult day, imagines a Babbittian Joe ten years from now at a small-town junior college, Kiwanis Club, "Works in the garden week-ends, fishes, is a little shocked at the latest novels . . ." (49). Whereas, the literary small-talk and *repartee* at Le Chat Gris are meant to be "the badge and hall-mark that they had left their home towns behind, that they were members now of the University and of *Le Chat Gris*"—presumably counterparts of each other (95). In 1963, incidentally, the UCLA librarian Everett Moore sent Stewart a copy of his library's newsletter, identifying Le Chat Gris as modeled on Drake's Restaurant on Bancroft Way: "The last trace of that affluent corner of University society in Berkeley was demolished by the wrecking crew just a few weeks ago. Its monument is in Mr. Stewart's book" (Moore to Stewart 29 Mar. 1963).

When Joe leaves the pub after lunch, he wants to take a walk in the woods—". . .under the strain he felt that he was reverting to his small-town standards," while his "wet-nurse" friends, Emmet and Pat, were ". . .so urban by instinct that going off to walk in the woods seemed about the same as inviting a horse to dinner" (112-113). But Joe "wanted to be where there weren't people and he couldn't see houses," which is on the undeveloped south side of campus, where there were quail, and likely, therefore, predators like bobcats and foxes. "Joe liked to let his mind play with this idea of foxes and bobcats within sound of the University clock-tower; it seemed so much like America" (116-117). Lying under the trees, he hears the birds: "They might be catching insects or building nests, getting ready to raise their young. *Their young!* My God, Jule and his young! That's what he should be doing, getting ready to—'So comes my fit again!'." (118)

This linkage perfectly epitomizes the rural-urban-literary nexus of the novel. Earlier, at lunch, the students had quailed at the mention that they might be parents one day. Now Joe links non-human nature and his own (presumed) offspring with a famous expostulation from Kyd's *Spanish Tragedy*. In a way, this is literature put to its best use—applied to life itself. But for Joe it is also a mode of evasion of that life; he doesn't seem to see a way to bring the two together, since, unlike Kolb's Harry, he is committed to both. He feels "trapped" between Julia and his exam. In his resentment, at this moment "outside the walls," Joe entertains the temptation of escape: "Below him a breeze had struck the river, and the little waves cast up glints of the sun. A wildness filled him. The stream was high, but he was a good swimmer. And beyond was open country; he could keep going. Out there, would be real things—crops and cows, and men who spat brown and had muscles. He could swim the river and keep going" (120). But he realizes both that the bridge is just three blocks away, and anyway "This was modern times; it wasn't the frontier. This little scrap of woods was just make-believe, stage-money" (121).

To me, Joe's bathetic epiphany in the university woods is a centering moment in the novel, which to some extent plays as a fulcrum of freedom between the student-dominated closed spaces of the Latin Quarter, and the professor-dominated closed space of the examination room. Joe's quandary is a real one. Probably it can be discussed sociologically in terms of the growth of higher-education access by young people from non-academic backgrounds and locales. But I see it more in the mode of Elaine Showalter, who is attracted to academic fiction because of its "seriousness" and "sadness." She sees the satiric mode that dominates academic fiction as a response to "so much pain" in academic life: "Like the suburbs, the campus can be the site of pastoral, or the fantasy of pastoral—the refuge, the ivory tower. But also like the suburbs, it is the site of those perennials of the literary imagination John Updike names as 'discontent, conflict, waste, sorrow, fear'" (2).

It does not discredit Stewart's gentle satire of academia to notice that it is the first and last sections of the novel where the satiric tone reigns; it is in this central passage, one hour in the life "away" (in Emily Bronte's sense), that the underlying discontent and conflict emerge. Showalter has much to say about "academic time"(7-13). The important choice Stewart's protagonist makes is in the shortest stretch of continuous time—the hour before the Faustian clocktower strikes 2:00, the time for the oral to begin.

Walking back to campus, Joe encounters an old, decrepit truck with "MEADSTOWN" on the front license plate. The driver, who "looked just like an ordinary man who would drive a truck" (123) converses with Joe. They're from neighboring counties, the driver, Bob Harris, confesses he's really not from Meadstown—he uses the plate so he'll seem a solid in-state citizen. He's a "cruiser," driving around selling produce he buys elsewhere. He breezes along back roads looking for places to sell it. Joe is suddenly struck with the idea of driving with him, and, putting on his "up-country" accent, offers to go with him as "kind of a pardner" (126). Bob becomes more and more enthusiastic about the "good life" they could have, a very Huck Finn-style life: "Good nights we can lie up along a stream somewhere, do some fishin'. Pretty soon we can get corn and lots o' kinds o' grub outa the fields. . . " (128). The clock has struck two as Bob continues to weave the narrative of his fantasy life—another form of utopian regression-- for them as "pardners." Joe flees. Surely this is no less an "artificial" lifestyle as the one he flirted with rejecting. "He was rejoining the colors; ahead lay duty, respectability, the white collar." "That Bob was nothing but a lousy tramp, scavenging off people who raised things and really did work. . .Bet you he peddles marihuana or something. . .. " (130-31).

In this moment, Joe, unlike Huck, turns back to "civilization" (132), and the speaker's voice again becomes satiric—mainly. But it has to come back to nature in the body. One vehicle for this is the outburst of the one female professor on Joe's committee, Fanny, who is both ridiculed and admired for having "worked her way up in a profession notoriously hostile to women" (138). In the exam, Joe has just mentioned the King of Brobdignag's diatribe against war in *Gulliver's Travels,* and Fanny breaks out in a similar diatribe. In her thoughts, though only the reader is privileged to know them she associates Joe with a younger man on "those spring nights when she had lain beside him" (196). He was her young husband, killed in the Spanish-American war: ". . .her secret was safe. Faculty-wives, secure in their biological function as mothers of two scrawny youngsters, might laugh at the old-maid professor. But Fanny Holtby had loved and been loved, married and widowed before she was eighteen, borne a son and buried him" (197).

This is one of an infinity of potential fates awaiting Julia, as she and her uninhibited friend Gret indulge in girl-talk about her pregnancy, waiting to hear the results of Joe's exam. Gret is amazed and amused that Julia has told Joe about the pregnancy and that he has offered to marry her. To Gret, an abortion is the only path. She imagines a faculty wives' luncheon conversation about the baby: "'My dear, the squalor—absolute squalor—these married graduate students live in! It really makes you want to be a *Communist* or something. Such a pretty little thing too. . .She doesn't look a day over twenty-one, and inexperienced of course. Somebody really ought to tell them something about birth control . ..'" (210).

Julia reflects very seriously on the issue of childbirth and careers—and on women who "protested too much about their careers" (227) as a cover for their regret at childlessness. But that night, after the mandatory celebrations, the decision has been made, and in a slightly satiric way. Julia says "Yes, I guess you're right; getting married is just the simplest way out. And we'd better do it soon. I don't want to be like that poor girl in *A Farewell to Arms*—the one who wouldn't get married because it was too plain he was making an honest woman out of her" (256).

I don't want to scant the center of common interest in the novel—the satire of academicians and the oral itself. John Lyons, in the only critical discussion of *Doctor's Oral* I'm aware of, devotes no space to the issues of place and biology I've suggested above, so, in terms of Stewart's environmentalism, I felt it important to present them. Lyon suggests that "Of all college fiction this work comes closest to making a defense of the process of getting a doctoral degree." But he acknowledges that the author's main concern is, as he sees it "the psychological drama involved in the process. . ." (156-57). Sure, but even the psychological drama is expressed through a mordant view of human motivation, and a perpetual pillorying of professorial egocentrism. Stewart's Princeton classmate and renowned physician Chauncey Leake reacted to this tone, calling the novel ". . .a devastating volume and positively makes me sick to my stomach. I don't ever want to sit on a doctor's examining committee again" (Leake to Stewart 25 Sept. 1939).

Some of the academics do come off better than others. Professor Richard Angle, the linguist, who observes the library facade as he waits for his daughter to pick him up at the end of the day, has emotional intelligence and the type of "deep anthropological" sense of the human condition that Stewart appreciated and sought to bring into his works. Thus, he sees the names on the facade as both ridiculous, and as those of "old friends," kept alive through the "living record" of language (17). Professor Duncan Martiness is, by contrast, a *bete noir* of the narrator's. With reference to him, Stewart says "I took care with the unpleasant characters to have names which probably either did not exist or would be very rare" (Backus 53). He holds forth in Le Chat Gris, surrounded by adoring students, constantly impressed by his own wit. The narrator quotes a campus joke. Someone said '"There sits Martiness. . .like a giant surrounded by pygmies.'" Professor Menzies of Physics responds "'Yes. . . fake giant, real pygmies'" (89). As with his other professors, Stewart hedges on the rumors that Martiness is based on his former colleague Ben Lehman (". . .there may have been some resemblance---the way Ben was in those days. . .[50])."

Professor Edgar Webb, on the other hand, the nervous young assistant professor on the committee, is presented as a straight arrow, but very unsure of himself. He is, says Stewart, more than anyone his own persona in the novel. Webb, like Stewart, is a World War I veteran, and in Le Chat Gris he, like the author in many cases, would rather observe than converse. Thus the reader gets to see the panorama of grad students through his eyes. Although he deplores the lack of preparation of so many students, who come from almost bookless households, looking around he considers them "a very decent-looking lot. He couldn't agree with the tendency among his colleagues to disparage the present run of graduate students" (106), and he is particularly positive about the legs of the female ones. Webb is much more sympathetic than the obnoxious department chair, Professor J. McNair Brice, whose *vita* the narrator recites—an overachiever driven by ambition, whom we first meet "as he left the Faculty Club, after his lunch with a Princeton professor who happened to be passing through . . ." (135). "The whole name, J. MacNair Brice, is an unlikely combination, and also seemed suitable for the character, being a somewhat gadgety name for a somewhat gadgety person" (Backus 54). Also not so pleasantly characterized is the French professor on Joe's committee, Professor Percy R. Kendrick, who falls asleep in the sun after lunch, along with his fat springer spaniel, and is late to the exam.

In a way, the source of humor in the exam itself is the contrast between its ritualization in form and its spontaneity in content. I have already referred (chapter 1) to Angle's first question on the meaning of *volksetymologie* as autobiographical. Joe stumbles but blurts out "Folk-etymology," but has a hard time defining it. Angle asks for an example. Joe says *"'Cockroach!'"* Professor Welland, the representative of another department (Economics) "glanced about to see whether he was to laugh or whether the candidate had gone wholly insane" (168). As the questioning progresses, we get Angle's angles on the candidate and the ritual. "Grantland did not have a great mind, probably, but his sheer lack of knowledge would not be likely to disgrace the University and the Doctorate of Philosophy." To him it is a necessary "ordeal," "a test for fighters" (171). If so, Joe, in its early phases, is well attuned: "His mind seemed to have all the complexity of a campaigning army . . ." (175).

At the break, Stewart presents the humorous situation of Joe and all the male professors urinating in the restroom together. "In fact, at one moment Joe and four of them were standing up side by side, separated only by inch-and-a-half slabs of marble. Here was democracy for you!" (185). Later, after Fanny's outburst, Martiness asks Joe his notorious trick question (which Stewart insists he didn't borrow from anyone) as to what Rossetti's "blessed damozel" is holding in her hand as she looks down from heaven. Joe responds correctly that they are lilies, but Martiness then engages him in an endless dialogue on *how many* lilies there are. Angle becomes increasingly irritated. "By this time Angle himself was not exactly sure how many lilies there were. . .This wasn't an examination in floral arrangement" (199).

As one might suspect, Joe's fate doesn't depend on how he performed on the exam, but on the professorial politics carried on while he is out of the room awaiting the result of the exam. Stewart has beautifully abbreviated and alternated his scenes here, so that we move back and forth between the academic ponderings of the committee and the biological ponderings of Julia over abortion. In the former ones, Holtby votes yes, and Martiness votes no. The French professor, Kendrick, votes to pass Joe because he wants revenge on Chairman Brice who he feels during the exam belittled the French epic *Le Chanson de Roland*. "'I-was-disappointed," said Brice. 'Much-disappointed—in-the-field-of-his-thesis. I-agree-with-Duncan. Fail.' 'On consideration,' said Kendrick abruptly, 'I vote to pass'" (223). The crucial figure is Angle, who, as we have seen, Stewart presents as more enlightened and deeper-visioned than the others. His angle is to reflect not on the candidate's performance, but on the performances of those who are voting on the candidate.

It all comes down to how he feels about Martiness's trick in asking Joe about the number of the damozel's lillies repeatedly, so that he finally agrees with Martiness's number, which is purposely wrong. To Martiness this proves that Joe lacks conviction. To Angle, angered, it shows how oblivious Martiness and the whole lot are to Joe's human situation. He's been trained to consider his professors omniscient, almost "as a private soldier is conditioned that his officers must always be followed. . ." (233). He is naturally nervous and uncertain. It is to be admired that he held his position on the lillies so long. Angle's persuasion is truncated by the author, so that we next, from Joe's point of view as he waits and smokes, see Brice coming towards him, speaking, "with quick vigor,"

"'Passed'" (234). Stewart says that Joe's ". . .virtues are really all in his simplicity . . .He's not brilliant but a very direct and strong person in his way" (*Little* 50). His triumph might be seen as the result of a collaboration between the simplicity of Joe and the complexity of Angle: both in their own ways are in the academy but not ultimately of it.

Doctor's Oral was the first book for which Stewart had an effective agent, and thereby he moved from Holt to Random House, which was his publisher for his mid-career works. That he was not through with the novel imaginatively is shown by a letter to Bennett Cerf proposing a sequel set twelve years later (Stewart to Cerf 25 April 1950). Cerf replied (28 April) that "There hasn't been a novel yet of internal politics on the college campus that has hit popular fancy." Maybe, but Stewart says Jacques Barzun wanted him to have it reprinted; he was a "great admirer" of *Doctor's Oral*, and "thought it was very good for graduate students"*(Little* 131).

One other text published in 1939 deserves mention: *Take Your Bible in One Hand: The Life of William Henry Thomes*, a limited edition biography published by the Colt Press of California. Thomes was a California Henty, a formula fiction writer, whose formula was summed up in a phrase Stewart almost used as his title, according to Joseph Henry Jackson, "gold, blood, and women" ("Between" 20). Stewart acknowledges in his preface, that "the floating redwood-tree and the bullock-killing on the beach" in *East of the Giants* are taken from Thomes (2). The biography is a vehicle for Stewart to make incisive remarks on California culture. Having returned to Boston from a first visit to California in 1843, Thomes heard about the gold in California five years later but was skeptical of the stories at first, "considering that the Government probably wished to incite immigration so that the native Californians should be outnumbered" (30). He quotes Thomes's memory that he and fellow emigrants were considered "pioneers of civilization." His minister told them "'that we were going to a strange wild and immoral country, and that we must take our

Bibles in one hand and our New England civilization in the other and implant our principles upon the soil'" (31).

"They reached the mines, and immediately found that gold-digging was the hardest work imaginable," writes Stewart. At a saloon, Thomes saw a pile of Bibles on the bar, which the publican had taken in exchange for drinks. "From what he saw in the next few months Thomes probably decided that the New England civilization had gone the way of the Bibles" (40-41). "The callousness of the miners often sickened Thomes. Once he saw a half-grown boy shoot and kill an inoffensive Indian, and no one seemed to care" (41-42).

Thomes, however, transmuted all this negative experience into positive fantasy-creation for young males who, Stewart believes, desire, and seldom obtain, three things: riches, beautiful women, and power (49-50). By the 1880's Thomes "found himself a historical figure" (56), and reveled in the attention he gained as a "public benefactor" for, through his novels, luring so many people to move to California.

*

This is how it began. When George and Ted were in Mexico in 1937-38,

> Some of the storms that struck California were reported in the local newspapers. Reading in Spanish about what was happening in my own state, I was doubly impressed with the dramatic values of a California storm. I then definitely, although vaguely, got the idea for a story thus centered. This story, as originally conceived, fell into a familiar enough pattern, that is, the adventures of many unrelated or slightly related people all happening to be affected by the same event. ("Introduction" xii).

When he returned to Berkeley, and started reading about meteorology, Stewart realized that "A storm itself had most of the qualities of a living thing. A storm could be a character, even the protagonist." And in Sir Napier Shaw's monumental *Manual of Meteorology* he read that one meteorologist had felt so personal about storms that he had given them names.

For the next two years, Stewart was a part-time storm chaser—and a chaser of people who had to deal with storms. He spent time at the Weather Bureau in San Francisco. ". . .[W]hen a big storm came up, and we knew it was coming, Ted and I would cut off and go someplace, most often up to Donner Pass to see what was happening there. Gradually, I got more and more idea of the possibilities." He gathered stories—a storm-drowned bull rolled down a mountain and plugged a culvert. He went on the Western Pacific Railroad on a flatcar through Feather River Canyon. The Southern Pacific took him through the snow sheds, and he rode in the engine of a rail snowplow. He went into the mountains on snowshoes with a lineman; a fir tree began to fall on the wires, under its weight of snow, and knocked the lineman off his pole—afraid he'd land on his ski poles sticking in the snow *(Little* 135-36). He traveled with the highway patrol, and drove through the Sacramento Valley in flood ("Introduction" xiii). "I went through two winters, doing that kind of work" (*Little* 135-36).

The second spring, there was nothing left to investigate, so Stewart started drawing maps, and writing from these experiences. In March, 1939 he wrote ". . .I have got a good deal of work done on the storm book" (Stewart to William Sloane 18 Mar. 1939/*P*).

> . . .[I]n *Storm* the dominating character was to be Maria. More than any human character, as much perhaps as all of them put together, she was to be the center of attention. Her birth, growth, adventures, and final death were to be the main vortex of the story, with the various little human beings and their troubles and triumphs isolated here and there around the edges ("Introduction" xii)

Mike Davis quotes from *Storm* wondering "if 'perhaps there was something about the human mind itself that made it feel comfortable to think of a storm as a person, not an equation,'" suggesting the Easter Storm of 1926 could have been named after Professor Moriarty (Davis 161).

In December, 1940, Stewart received a telegram from Bennett Cerf at Random House: "Sat up until two o'clock finishing Storm Book.

Congratulations on a Wonderful Job" (Cerf to Stewart 16 Dec. 1940). In 1941 O. R. Lirsch, Foreman of the Spaulding Power Houses at Emigrant Gap, wrote to Cerf thanking him for the copy of *Storm* sent him at Stewart's request. Lirsch says "I first met Mr. Stewart about three years ago, here at one of the Pacific Gas and Electric Company's Hydro-Electric Plants in the High Sierra," when he had just begun gathering "field-material" for his book. Lirsch goes on,

> And now, after reading STORM, fascinated from the first sentence of the book to the last, I should like to tell you that WE, the MARTLEY'S, and the SUPERINTENDENT'S and the RICK'S and PETERS and SWENSON'S of STORM, owe Mr. Stewart much. Sunshine and Rain and Snow and Ice and the Wild Water and the Tame, are the Fulcrum's of our life and our work, and Mr. Stewart showed us just that . . . .We. . . . the little people of the great Sierra, do not hesitate to say, Mr. Stewart has written a great book that will always have a place of honor on our much to [sic.] meager bookshelfs. (Lirsch to Cerf 28 Sept. 1941)

"When it first appeared in 1941," says Ernest Callenbach, "*Storm* gave readers a frisson similar to what we much later felt on seeing the first photo of Earth from space: a breathless realization that the planet was a working, living whole" ("Foreword" vii). ". . .[T]he text was largely written during those grim and terrible months of Dunkirk and the fall of France" ("Introduction" xiii). Callenbach says ". . .*Storm* showed us, as the world plunged into World War II, a society that made sense—a panorama of lives in touch with vast global realities. . ." ("Foreword" vii).

Storm is indeed a classic of American literature, and one of our most important works of literary ecology. In the sense that Callenbach articulates, it is akin to Rachel Carson's later *The Sea Around Us*. Both provide a vivid sense of how interconnected are the phenomena of global organic and inorganic nature. Both ecological dramas are played out in deliberate contrast to an unmentioned backdrop of human dis-connection: a hot war and a cold war. Stewart, however, is writing as a novelist as well as a natural historian. As such his "synoptic" (Callenbach's word) technique of insinuating human actions and human technology into the temporal flow of one natural phenomenon creates a radically "experimental" literary form, presented as shaped by nature itself, not by an invisible hand. It seeks to reconcile causality (to which the human concept of linear time is a necessity) with a synchronous "manifested" and "manifesting" (Martin 113) spatialization of events which is "nature's time." Martin quotes from a story by Ursula LeGuin—daughter of Stewart's close friend, Alfred Kroeber—on a character who perceives time as a "'landscape in which one may go any number of directions, or nowhere'" (124).

As Stewart more casually expresses it, with reference to his novel, "Most people are not interested in the natural background, at least not most novelists. They want to emphasize the connection of people all the time" (*Little* 141). There are plenty of people connected in *Storm* (and disconnected), but only as particles in an infinitely larger field of forces. They are not the "source" of what happens to them. Most of them are, as Wallace Stegner says, "working parts of larger social entities. . .," "not persons so much as functions" ("Foreword" vii), and their function ("Junior Meteorologist") is their name. The character with a name, and a passionate identity, is the storm, Maria (one must say that here Stegner overmechanizes and oversocializes Stewart's characters. They have personalities and can experience tragedy; for them to be pure functions would compromise the holistic premise of his ecology. But Stewart's hog, coyote, and owl likewise have personalities, and the entity they and their societies are all parts of is nature).

To spatialize the temporal as much as possible in a narrative, which is inherently temporal, Stewart refined and elaborated his "weaving" technique of *Ordeal by Hunger*. "Timed to fit into a tight time schedule" ("Interview" 2), the author used plotted time against itself; so complex is the relation between each causal strand and the others that the reader is forced toward experiencing time as a landscape, and not a line. In fact, this sense is even accentuated by the obsession that the "function" characters have with linear time—like the characters in *Doctor's Oral*--since they, and their technologies, are so dependent on it and have to try to defend its flow against the storm's encompassment. Stewart explains the paradoxical separateness yet tempestocentrism of his narrative threads: "Those different threads could be picked out, you see, rather easily. You couldn't pick out very many of them or you wouldn't have any book left. . .They disentangle very easily. Actually, they weren't connected crosswise. They were connected centrally on the storm theme . . . Each one could come right out" (*Little* 141).

In a similarly paradoxical manner, the ecocentrism of *Storm* might best be appreciated by disentangling some of the threads—as one might compose the totality of an ecosystem by incrementally studying each species endemic to it. Since every word is important in a novel by Stewart, one could begin with the prefatory material. The teasing epigraph is from Shaw's *Manual*: "Every theory of the course of events in nature is necessarily based on some process of simplification of the phenomena and is to some extent therefore a fairy tale." This is both an *apologia* and a theoretical statement. The theory on which the course of events in the novel is based, as well as the course of events itself, is an oversimplification, and therefore the author is off the hook of having to be "truthful." On the other hand, considering the complexity of the story to come, to consider it an oversimplification implies the immense complexity of the actual event. The author also, as conventional, tells us that the characters—including Maria—are imaginary, and the functionaries do not have the personalities of the real "incumbents." Finally, and importantly, "Although the scene is largely California, the story is not a local-color study, and for simplification a few alterations of setting have been introduced." Regionalism does not apply to the novel's events, the author says, but I agree with John Caldwell that, this contradicts his view that all literature is regional, and that it is really about the civilization of the mid-20th century West (30). The text is also dedicated to the entities who helped the author; all these entities are human ones challenged by the storm. The storm herself is not acknowledged.

The first thread, literally, in the novel, is that of a totalistic environmental vision, similar to the initial "bird's eye views" in *Ordeal by Hunger*. These gaia-esque views, as Callenbach says similar to astronauts' earth photos, provide a metahuman plot line and, although descriptions of motion in time, have a lyrical wholeness that defies time. The opening paragraph, the first of these, is worth quoting entirely, particularly since it was one of Stewart's favorite passages in his entire work:

> Enveloped in the gaseous film of the atmosphere, half-covered by a skim of water forming the oceans—the great sphere of the earth spun upon its axis and moved inflexibly in its course around the sun. Continuously, in the succession of day and night, season and season, year and year, the earth had received heat from the sun, and again lost into space that same amount of heat. But this balance of the entire sphere did not hold for its individual parts. The equatorial belt received yearly much more heat than it radiated off, and the polar regions lost much more heat than they received. Nevertheless the one was not growing hotter while the others sank toward absolute zero. Instead, at once tempering cosmic extremes and maintaining equilibrium with the sun, by a gigantic and complex circulation, the poles constantly cooled the tropics and the tropics reciprocally warmed the poles. (3)

In subsequent paragraphs, the omniscient narrator moves spatially ever nearer to the earth, showing the interconnection of increasingly local weather phenomena and this primal reciprocity of earthly temperature. Also, the narrator is speaking in the unexpected past tense, mythologizing by temporal distance the entire world system as though life itself is history. Eventually we reach the area of the Pacific where the storm is born: "As from the union of two opposite germ-cells begins a life, so from the contact of northern and southern air had sprung something which before had not been. As a new life, a focus of activity, begins to develop after its kind and grow by what it feeds on, so in the air that complex of forces began to develop and grow strong. A new storm had been born" (8).

The next wide view of the atmosphere is at the end of the third day, when polar air is about to break southward through the mountains. We partly experience it through the weather-evaluative senses of an anonymous fur-trader in British Columbia whose body knows a storm is coming. Then "Undimmed by day the circling constellations glittered over polar ice and snow; the North Star stood at the zenith. Now and again, above the frozen ocean, the aurora flared bright. Hour by hour the heat radiated off. The temperature fell; the weight of air grew heavier; the pressure rose. And inevitably the hour of the break grew closer" (79).

On the fifth day, the polar air descends on the midwest. "Swifter than Sioux, more terrible than Assiniboine, more pitiless than Arapaho, it swept upon town and farmstead" (120). On the sixth, the south wind blows steadily everywhere. The storm had taken shape "a third of the world away," but "Now, powerful and sedate in maturity, it moved with the steady, sure pace of majesty" (129). By the seventh day the cold air has reached the barrier of the Mexican Cordillera, and is diverted to the Pacific (143-4). On the ninth day, two "wind-torrents" of new polar air reach down into the already raging storm, one over land and one over water, like "identical twins parted soon after birth and reared in different environments" (229).

By the eleventh day, the main storm has moved east, and the warming Chinook winds—their motion described in detail—are melting the snow (292-3). The last paragraph of the novel reads

> Steadily the great sphere of the earth spun upon its axis, and moved in its unvarying course around the sun. From far-off Venus a watcher of the skies (if such we may imagine) viewed it as a more brilliant planet than any to be seen from the earth. It gave no sign that storms or men disturbed its tranquil round. Bright against the black of midnight, or yellow at the dawn, it hung in the sky—unflickering and serene. (349)

Thus, in cosmic terms, the situation is and has been the same as at the beginning.

A second thread of encompassing visions is the chain of effects of the atmospheric conditions on the earth's human and nonhuman nature; these moments are also mingled with the narrator's reflections on how humans have constructed and do construct storms and air in general. The first instance is in the analogy between air and water. "As a crab moves on the ocean-bottom, but is of the water, so man rests his feet upon the earth—but lives in the air" (19) while maintaining the illusion that he/she is a "creature of the land." On the contrary, "As water environs the crab, so air surrounds, permeates, and vivifies the body of man" (19). One human problem in environmental perception is that air is so "bound up with" human life that "only with difficulty can he realize its existence as something in itself" (20). This age-old failure to recognize the atmospheric effect on human societies persists, despite the environmental determination of much of human history—a twentieth-century example is the dust bowl migrations, caused by "a temporary variation in rainfall" (20). Further on, the narrator provides a summary anthropology of humans' attempt to understand—and predict—weather, and the imagination of controlling it (80-82). Elsewhere, a storm is likened to the human organisms who try to understand it. It follows a similar life course to a human's. "The storm, to be sure, develops only in a manner determined by its antecedents and environment—but many philosophers think little also of man's apparent free will." But more closely—and tellingly—a storm is like a community or nation. New storms spawned by old are colonies. "The life-cycle of a storm is like that of a nation which from apparent decadence is sometimes renewed into full vigor," and it also has "an indefinable abstract existence" (104).

Some of Stewart's best passages relating to cultural ecology are those which trace human attempts, not to control the weather, but to control its effects. In these he uses the deep ecological narration that Professor Angle would approve, and that Stewart will bring to fruition in *Sheep Rock.* A good example is that of the Sacramento River, evoked in the cadences of anciency: "Before the melting ice disclosed the Pass, there was the river . . .Elk with branching antlers browsed the willows; huge bears dug among the roots for food" (98-99). The narrator evokes the river's dry season and its wet season when Elk and native humans retreat from its floods. There is an untroubled rhythm to this rise, retreat, fall, and return, until the coming of "men called farmers," who "In disdain and ignorance . . . plowed the rich valley lands, and then cursed when the river rose and destroyed the new crops" (100). They "made no truce with nature" (100), building dikes and levees to protect their land and forcing the river to flood unprotected land. This produced a "peculiar madness" (101) of higher and higher levees, destruction of others' to lower the water level pressing their own. Finally "although the white men hated the very sound of the words, they began to talk more and more of 'the government' and 'regulations.'" Surveyors [like George Derby] were sent, the premise accepted that "Only the Whole People could hope to match the Whole River," and a truce with the river was formulated: highest levees around cities, overflow spaces with none. Nonetheless, ". . .the River frets openly and in secret against the levees, and sometimes still it pours forth over its ancient flood-plain" (102).

Since immediately following this environmental fable the narrative shifts in time—a new day, and in space—a ship in the Pacific, its immediate connection with the storm is not articulated. But it will turn out to be *prolegomena* to the troubles the storm causes one of the main functionaries in the drama—the General in charge of regulating the Sacramento water levels through releasing and impounding water. Linkage of this environmental history to the immediate crisis is provided by the thread of scenes tracing the increasing pressures on the General to make decisions on where the rising waters will be released and where not. On the seventh day we find him, "Czar of the River" (172) remembering a Bret Harte passage on floods while looking at a color-coded map of flood zones and outlet channel. On the ninth day, with the backdrop of farmers driving stock to higher ground, and city folk watching gauge-readings at the river weirs, he gets a call from the delta asparagus growers lobbying him not to open the upriver weirs and flood his crops. On the tenth day he gets an angry visit from a committee of Sacramento businessmen who demand that the cropland by flooded if necessary but not land near the city because that will cause loss of business. "The General reflected a moment, wanting to argue.

Damage to land and crops was real to him, but as a military man he could never quite figure out the meaning of loss of business" (279).

When one of the Committee asks "'. . *say*, you don't by any chance *own stock* in the Delta Asparagus Company?'' (280), he throws them out, and reflects on humans as a "poor lot of mammals" who won't collectively, as in war, fight a common enemy. Through these scenes the peri-mythical environmental history of the river and human manipulation of it are tied to purely economic choices, and on the twelfth day the General has to choose between the livelihoods of two economic constituencies—even though the storm is over—because the Sacramento River's tributary, the American, is rising to overtop the levees protecting Sacramento, and he has to order the opening of the Sacramento Weir, flooding the asparagus fields. After doing so, he remembers a Biblical quotation, sending his literal situation back into the universal past again: "'All the rivers run into the sea; yet the sea is not full; unto the place from whence the rivers come, thither they also return again'" (340).

Other passages are linked by similar reflections on the religious construction and subsequent demystification of storms and waters. In Christianity and in pre-Christian religions water is a multiform symbol "water of purification, water of separation, water of baptism, water of life" (121). "If the waters are freed, then the land shall flourish" (122). All faiths have sky-gods who embody or control storms—Zeus, Thor, Pugulu (139). "Even yet, man seems to carry with him mementoes of some idyllic past" (175). It is theorized that as humans spread beyond tropical lotus lands, they were forced to gain the "power and will to face a harsher world," creating a strange "marriage of civilization and storms" (176-77). Primitive civilizations, like the Southwestern cliff-dwellers, protected themselves from and endured storms, or if land resultantly became uninhabitable, withdrew from it; but 'modern man cannot withdraw. He expects much more of his civilization; he has spread it far and wide until it sprawls; he has given hostages" (257).

Contrasting threads spatialize the temporal by creating causal chains which, on the physical level, link the trivial and the momentous. Synchronously almost imperceptible happenings in the natural world, unnoticed by humans, lead to impact on them individually and collectively. Hence the threaded lives of named and unnamed humans through the twelve days of the storm are permanently altered by events in nature and cannot be separated from them.

On the third night an owl comes to perch on a sixty-foot high spruce electric pole on a forested mountainside. His wing touches a transmission wire, causing a blue-white flash and the fall of the owl's charred body to the snow, where a wildcat finds it and carries it "away from the smell of man which clung to the pole" (51). The Load Dispatcher of the Power-Light company receives word of a momentary short on the system (60). By the seventh day, half-melted snow blowing across the wires and sticking has accumulated ice sheaths six inches in diameter around them, including one already weakened by the incineration of the owl (143). At 9:02 A.M. on that day, the owl-weakened wire breaks. The narrator traces the cascading effects of the break—on power loss and recording instruments—during each fragmentary second of its fall—and the movements of the hands of Power-House operators to increase water-flow to turbines. One operator starts to call for assistance "and the voice stopped talking between two syllables as if someone had suddenly closed fingers around the speaker's throat" (149). When the L. D. has orchestrated the changes necessary to maintain electric flow, a team is sent out to repair the break, which it does with great difficulty, packing in on skis pole to pole.

On the fourth day, two events occur synchronously in time. A two-by-four falls off of a truck on a rough Sacramento Valley road, and lies at the shoulder. The bole of a long-fallen cedar shifts where it rests precariously on a hillside. The original tree first sprouted in 1579, "the year Sir Francis Drake landed on the California coast." A storm toppled it in three pieces in 1789. The top and bottom had rotted away "before the first emigrant train passed close by, letting their wagons down the canyon-side with ropes" (83). Later, below the bole, slowly rotting, railroad, highway, and power lines were built. The bole's rot lightened it, raising its center of gravity, so it with great slowness settles downhill, aided, the previous summer, by a chipmunk digging a hibernation burrow under it.

Later that day we overhear a conversation between a gas station attendant and Mr. Goslin, a flour salesman, who's gassing up in San Francisco for a sales trip to Colusa. On the sixth day, the two-by-four by the road is doused with manure also fallen from a truck. As evening falls, Mr. Goslin is driving in the rain, looking for a shortcut road to Colusa. He misses the shortcut, thinks of going on, turns around, heads down the backroad, sees the two-by-four late, veers right, his car skids, rolls, and vibrates "with a shudder as of a dying animal...." (134). The next morning we hear the radio news report of Mr. Goslin's death—first fatality of the storm.

Friday, before the storm hits, a lineman named Rick meets a cute girl at a dance (97). Next day, we see him happily in his green phone company truck, heading up "to play what he knew was a man's game" (115) in the mountains. He's also happy because he thinks he's in love with the girl. "It was good to be a man, and to work on a job that called on you to do things that were a little dangerous, and to have 'blue eyes in a dark-tanned face' to think about, and to breathe the clean mountain air sweeping in from the pine woods, feeling cooler and snappier the closer you got to the Pass" (116). Later, dispatched to repair a broken wire, Rick skis the fifty feet from the road to the break, "meticulously" repairs it, plants his ski-poles next to the electric pole, climbs it, repairs it (actions described in technical detail by the narrator), and descends. The next day he's sent to fix a break in the transcontinental phone line. As he works, thoughts of the girl distract him; also, as he works, a neighboring lodgepole pine slowly bends toward his pole under its weight of snow. "Voices coursed along the wires in English of a half dozen different intonations, in Dutch, Japanese, German, Spanish, and Greek. An Assistant Secretary of State was talking to the

Minister to Thailand. Teletype circuits were being operated; cable messages were going through in code; a symphony orchestra was playing for a radio network" (189). The tip of the pine touches the pole. Rick doesn't see it. His descending rhythm is broken by the treetop, and he is impaled on his ski poles. Of this, Norah Lofts wrote to Stewart "The episode of the tree bending to the telegraph pole had all the elements of doom and the cool understatement that made *Ordeal by Hunger* so memorable" (Lofts to Stewart 10 July 1942).

Rick is gravely wounded, can't stand up to get in his skis, tries sliding downhill, ends up tangled in a cedar. "It was an extreme pleasure to stop struggling and lie still" (191). "Overhead were passing the strains of the orchestra playing Beethoven's *Third Symphony*. 'This connection is rotten,' said a man in Pocatello angrily to a man in Fresno. A teletype circuit was recording an unsettled market in Chicago caused by nervousness as to the crop effect of the cold wave which was sweeping the wheat belt" (191).

Immediately after Rick's fall we shift to the rocky ledge where the cedar bole is shifting steadily downward. The D. T. S. gets news that a lineman is missing (212). The next morning a rotary plow crew hits Rick's snowcovered truck. They yell "'Hal-*loo*!'" toward the forest twice and both times a "'*Loo-oo*'" comes back, but they decide it's an echo. They suspect it's the truck of the missing lineman but "'You can't without skis, and anyway if he's been in there that long—'" (220).

Later on, a self-important oil magnate in a San Francisco hotel is on the line to his lawyer in New York when the line goes dead, because at that moment the decaying tree bole moves past its point of equilibrium, catapults through the air, and hits the cross-arms of "Pole 1-243-76 of the Transcontinental Lead" and snaps it like a "dry twig" (237). The oil magnate, Thomas Reynoldshurst, is infuriated as he awaits reconnection: "Thirty years earlier, when he was sleeping under a boiler during the Tampico boom, rain used to mean a great deal to young Tom Reynoldhurst; but since he had entered his epoch of limousines and covered entrance-ways with doormen holding umbrellas, Mr. Reynoldhurst had lost his personal feeling for rain" (239). We are told that "Except for two hikers who had sat upon the bole for a few minutes in 1923, no human being had ever known anything about it" (239). For a while no one knew it had fallen. "But the fall affected the lives of many people over a hemisphere" (240). These complex effects resulting from human dependence on phone communication are detailed. The repair crew working on the bole's work learn over their portable phone that Rick's body has been found by a dog team. "They worked hard after that, and nobody talked much" (243). On the eleventh day, with the air warming, the mountain snow becomes rain. The rain wakens some other characters whose threads will be knotted as a result of it—Blue Boy the boar, and Johnny Martley, the damkeeper, but "(Rick, the lineman, did not awake. In the little mountain town where he had been born, he lay quietly in his coffin)" (301). In his film version of *Storm*, it should be mentioned, Walt Disney allowed Rick to be discovered alive, and hauled to safety on a makeshift litter.

I have followed these threads of narrative in such detail in order to emphasize the complex interdependence Stewart has created between humans and nonhuman nature, between "great" and "insignificant" events. There is a prescient ecosystemic sense in the novel: touch one strand and the whole web vibrates. If this can be said, Stewart could be considered to be dramatizing in *Storm* the "systems theory" of time, wherein "each system or structure *generates* its own time and space," and his characters or entities that "stand at the structural couplings of all [his] . . .systems are continuously appearing, participating and disappearing" (Kovel 126-127). Such enlacement, and I have not even touched on the threads of the main "people" in the novel: Stegner's "functionaries."

Stewart has created a roster of abbreviations. If one were to use the old organismic figure for "modern" civilization, these would be the internal organs allowing the whole organism to function. At the center is actually a subsidiary figure, J.M., the Junior Meteorologist, directed by the Chief Meteorologist, of whom he is slightly afraid. There is also the retired Chief Meteorologist, called by one of the weather bureau staff the "Old Master," who keeps visiting the bureau because he likes to look at the maps and reminisce about nineteenth century weather events such as Grant's inauguration. We have already met the General, whose realm is flood control, the Load Dispatcher, who governs the hydroelectric power supply, and the Load Dispatcher, who manages the phone service. The second most significant functionary in the whole story is R. S., the Road Superintendent, whose on-site activity is closest to the storm itself. There is also the C. S. O., the Chief Service Officer of the airport, and the G. M., the General Manager of the Railroad.

Collectively these figures are charged with preserving modern civilization by maintaining the connective tissue that holds it together. This tissue is composed essentially of the technology which permits communication and mobility. In his earlier writings, Stewart had delineated phases in the American past when this technology did not exist, or was in the process of being born. Through the threads of activity they need to perform in order to preserve their mode of technology, we can follow Stewart's thoughts on how this new technology has changed humans' ecological roles. This literary aim is most clearly evidenced by the reflective passage (35-37) on the prehistoric and historic history of the Donner Lake area and the progressive migrants and communication modes passing through it—mountain goats, blacktailed deer, Paiutes and Washoes, white trappers, covered wagon pioneers, stagecoaches, freight-wagons, pony express riders, telegraph poles, and onward. Clearly, Stewart is asking the reader to experience the overlaying of two similar events a century apart, which both involve the same environmental crisis threatening humans:

> So we come, in less than a century, from the death-dogged snowshoers of the Donner Party to the carefree weekend skiers dotting the mountain-sides with bright costumes. Above the place where little Stanton sat to smoke his last pipe, Cisco beacon flashes out to Donner beacon. Where John Denton, plucky Yorkshireman, waited in the snow for death, the streamlined trains slide by. And over that camp where the poor

> emigrants ate the forbidden meat, the pilots of the wide-winged planes follow the whining Reno beam to Blue Canyon, where—turning—they set their last course for the airports of the Bay. (37)

And, we might add, where now you leave the Interstate at the Truckee exit, pass the monuments at Donner Lake State Park, and follow Stewart's now slightly rutty two-lane U.S. 40 past the lake houses, and the pier sunbathers beneath snowy Donner Summit, up to join the touring campers fresh from their Winnebagos at the overlook.

The Road Superintendent's sheds, or their descendents, are still there, just east of the Summit. We can follow his course through the novel to see the interaction between the facilitator of technology and the non-human nature. He is introduced to us directly following the passage quoted above, as he sets off to work on the second day of the storm. ". . .[A]bout the superintendent and his job gathered something of that matter-of-fact heroism which makes the song of Casey Jones the epic of the American working man." We observe as ". . .CALIFORNIA—U.S. 40 stared at him from the neat shield-shaped markers" (37), and as he observes the different out-of-state license plates that pass him. The recitation of state names here is just one example of the epic lists, in the manner of Whitman, that are scattered throughout the novel—lighthouses, mountain peaks, newspaper headlines—and here, again, the names of locales and topographical features all along U.S. 40. The R.S. inspects his plow operators and machines and, to the storm, inwardly voices "*Let 'er come!*" (43).

The R. S. doesn't appear again until the sixth day, when at the Maintenance Station he orders the deployment of plows (134)—the snow needs to become deep enough for to need to exist. But when he next appears, it is after a day of driving back and forth trying to control the passage of the countless cars, trucks, and buses which "converged from dozens of valley roads toward the snow-clogged bottleneck which was the Pass. Just as the roads converged, so did the responsibility . . .As long as he could hold the road . . .then he was master of the situation" (199). While the road is incorporated into the landscape, taken as a given, the drivers of the vehicles on the road, like the Committee that visits the General, are discordant presences, ignorant of their own situation. They have never adapted to their environment, since they have never experienced it except in visual passage, so the R. S. has constantly to deal with their chainless stupidity. While the emigrant parties struggled to adapt to the changing environments they passed through, they were able to survive because they were physically present in them. The drivers the R. S. has to rescue are mainly, he feels, "soft with civilization," except for the few who try to work with him, who show "The blood of the frontiersmen hadn't yet gone altogether thin" (204). Later on, a day after this episode of frenetic action, the R. S. directs the "fight" against a snowslide that has buried a push-plow and its crew and blocked U. S. 40 entirely. He understands the physics of the slide: a "snow-nose" has broken off, and on slippery old snow, accelerating and picking up other new snow as it went. The R. S. views the rescue scene as a microcosmic world:

> Darkness had come on, and the snow was falling as fast as ever. The lights from all the plows and cars that were there were playing on the slide. The men on top looked small and black as ants by contrast with the great white heap. The rotary [plow] was throwing its great arc. And all around, the flying snow reflected back the lights, and shut off the little scene of activity from all the world outside. (284)

The last time we encounter the R. S. is on day eleven, when there is a final blast of snow from the north as Maria is already dying. All of the functionaries are cofunctioning in the most intense spatialization of time in the story. This is when Rick is lying in his coffin. The airplane from Reno is caught in turbulence; the rivers are rising; the "superliner" train is entering Truckee Canyon, the Junior Meteorologist is (for once) in the middle of the weather itself, in high wind on the weather bureau roof; the Old Master is dying in hospital; the boar Blue Boy (whose thread we've followed through most of the story) and Johnny Martley (who will adventurously try to open the French Bar Power House Sluices) are waking up. The C. S. O. is driving to the airport, at the news of bad air over

Reno. And the R. S., with the highway cleared, is looking up because the Reno plane above his head sounds dangerously low.

After this moment, all the functionaries disperse and resolve their charges' difficulties, or disappear altogether—figuratively they "die" just as the storm is more literally dying, their function, as far as the space taken up by the storm system goes, having disappeared. The Chief Meteorologist poetically expresses this congruence:

> 'Everything is always changing, and always it comes back to what it was before. Storms come and go, but there's always weather. I've seen a lot of them—storms and men. Each one is different. There are the big bluffers, and the sneaks, and the honest, dependable ones. . . .Storms and men—they're all different and yet they're all the same. Each little storm starts out hopefully, but until it's all over, you can't say whether it was better than the ones that went before it—or as good' (341-2)

The main thread in the novel is that of the Junior Meteorologist. He is a controlling presence for the reader as the discoverer (figuratively perhaps, creator) of the storm, famously its namer, and—as persona of the author—its biographer in time. The J.M. is also mapper, if not the only mapper, of the storm in space. He is not the only cartographer, or student of cartography, in the cast of functionaries. We have seen the General's flood maps; the L. D. has maps of power demand, the C. S. O. of air traffic routes. Stewart himself (as with many of his other books) drew "complete meteorological maps for every day of the storm. . ." (van Gelder 2). "In a sense when I got that series of maps done, I had written the book" (*Little* 52). The endpapers display two of these maps—the first and seventh days of the storm. But Stewart sees mapping and naming as the most important and basic acts of environmental perception, and the J. M. has the honor of and responsibility for both.

In fact, our first view of the J. M. is of him carefully drawing the day's weather map. ". . .[T]o its maker it was simple, beautiful, and inspiring. Now he was giving it the final revision; with the care of a poet polishing a quatrain, he erased an inch of one line and redrew it with slightly altered curve" (12). From a Pacific ship's barometric readings he induces that a "baby" storm is forming 300 miles southwest of Japan. "As a baby possesses the parts of the adult, so the baby storm displayed as in caricature the features of a mature storm" (16). Mapping its features he reflects that the infant "would live its own life, for good or for bad, just as much as some human child born the same hour," and therefore "He must name the baby" (18). In a famous moment of 20th century literature he comes upon the "homely" name Marie. "And, as if he had been a minister who had just christened a baby, he found himself smiling and benign, inchoately wishing it joy and prosperity. Good luck, Maria!" (18).

We must hold this moment briefly, in order to reflect on the ecology of personification. The J. M. is doing what cultures have done since time immemorial, but in an "officially" secular culture, there is no pantheon which can sport a named god of storms, and, in any case, in the reign of science, naming's purpose is individuation. Stewart's own testimony on the effect of Maria's naming is:

> The book was published just before Pearl Harbor and there was at that time a great expansion in the meteorological program of the Armed Services. Nearly all of the young meteorologists read the novel, some of them as required reading. Some time during the war developed the practice of giving girls' names to storms. I cannot say exactly when because all references to the weather were under very strict security rules at the time. . . .Some meteorologists have told me that the practice originated from the novel, and this has always seemed likely to me because of the circumstances. (Stewart to Editor, *San Francisco Chronicle* 20 Sept. 1954)

When the U. S. Weather Service, presumably, therefore, inspired by *Storm*'s widespread use as an instructional tool for meteorologists, officially adopted female names for storms in 1950, there may or may not have been a personificatory cultural sexism involved—the woman as stormy termagant. Stewart himself was "surprised to find people thinking this constitutes a kind of insult to womanhood. What has become of the famous American sense of humor?" He also says "The man in the book who named her was young and of an age to be interested in girls and it seemed very natural that he would give a girls [sic.] name—thus Maria."(Stewart to Editor, *San Francisco Chronicle* 20 Sept. 1954). When male names were adopted in 1979 to alternate with female ones, this act could be seen as a sidebar to the accomplishments of 1970's feminism. But other than this, storm personification is not homocentric (as opposed to ecocentric). The J. M.'s naming is not taming. He does not endow the storm with physical human attributes. Until near the end of its life the storm is Maria only to him and to the reader. As Stewart will develop the idea more fully in *Names on the Land* and *Names on the Globe*, naming is a tool of environmental perception, like the cartographer's pencil. It creates coherent spatial relationships between nonhuman natural phenomena.

This is shown by the fact that the J. M. names other neighboring storms too: Sylvia, Felicia, Cornelia, Antonia. Individuated thus, their movements on the globe relative to each other can be more clearly understood than if they are neutral clusters of isobar lines. His "paternal discoverer's partiality" (44) does not privilege Maria above his other "girls." By the third day, Maria is "a vigorous and growing young storm" (70). As she grows, interestingly, the J.M. also does, to the reader, inwardly. He becomes a more complex organism. We see his hostility to the "Old Master" who keeps coming in to look at the map and professes to know intuitively that it is going to rain. The J. M. thinks he's "nuts," and pontificates that "'Good forecasting demands good data and good theory. . .'" (72). He sees the other forecasters' appreciation of the Old Master as expressing their jealousy of his better training. But he also questions himself; he may be a good meteorologist, but he can't find companionship. "He was in a strange city and lonely" (74). He dislikes the irony in the others' nickname for him, "Baby Chief" (74).

But the next day, after re-examining the positions of air-masses, of his girls, of ships reporting, he is filled with "childish" enthusiasm for what he's figured. "The great outflow [of cold air] from the north would deflect Maria from the usual course into the Gulf of Alaska; she would come on due east, smash the Pacific High, and let go her rain along the whole length of California" (91). The Chief doesn't buy his prediction: "'Storms are hussies. . .'" he says (91)—unconscious of entering the J. M.'s nomenclature. On the fifth day, the J. M. has not retreated from his assertion; yesterday he said it would rain in 48 hours; today he says in 24. The Chief's interiority is revealed at this point: "As had happened often before, he wished for the moment that he were engaged in some simple line of work such as being a G-man or teaching literature. All very well for the others to predict rain—the one [the Old Master] had his inner light, and the other his textbooks. And neither of them was responsible" (108).

With respect to the Chief Meteorologist, I have the perhaps unproveable suspicion that Stewart based his identity on one of the great figures in American meteorology, Dr. Francis Reicheldorfer. A navy pilot in World War I, his pressure for innovation led to the "new meteorology," employing the many more technological forecasting aids that emerged after World War II. Reicheldorfer became Chief of the U.S. Weather Bureau in 1938 (Williams 105), and remained in that position into the 1960's. An ascerbic and strong-willed figure, ". . .he developed and presided over the most modern and effective national weather service in the world" (Williams 105). Reicheldorfer was interested in Stewart and in *Storm*. After NBC presented a dramatization of the novel on its "Lucky Strike Theater," June 1, 1953, Norman Felton of NBC forwarded a letter from him to the network asking for a print of the film (Felton to Stewart 7 July 1953).

We have witnessed, from the outset, the effects on California's economy of the sustained drought conditions prevailing. The statistician attributes "retail sales resistance" to "deficiency of precipitation. Tehama County farmer Oscar Carlson, at the very time the J. M. has decided Maria will douse California, has received notice of bank foreclosure on his 500 acres. He examines his stricken wheat. "An hour later, in the barn, they found his body hanging" (88-89).

Thus the Chief knows that if he forecasts rain, "Thousands of people would change their plans; hundreds of industries, big and little, would make adjustments. Money would be spent, wisely and foolishly. The very process of adjustment to the single word would mean damaged property and jeopardized lives" (108-09). Here again we see the power of naming. The forecast, a word, not an event, has at the same time an impact on the human community comparable to the actual storm it predicts. The forecast map, as symbol, takes on the power of the thing symbolized, as far as human perception is concerned. After deep consideration, the Chief comes to a decision "and his actions suddenly came to have a continental, almost a god-like sweep" (111). He order storm warnings, and sends rain forecasts to the papers. We have here a chain of causation in human terms analogous to those traced above. The J. M.'s understanding of Maria has persuaded the Chief to predict rain, which affects the behaviors of people in every walk of life; it also affects the actions of the R. S., the C. S. O., and all the other protectors of that "connective tissue" which enables the human community to function, and those actions in rebound also affect the life of the community.

Between the fifth and eleventh days of the storm, the J. M. makes relatively few appearances, though they are significant. He finds a discrepancy on the seventh day between the way Maria is supposed to act in theory, and how she is actually behaving, stuck motionless offshore between two "arms" of polar air, and thereby gaining strength. She has become so "complicated" that "he did not wholly understand her." And "Like a father whose child has suddenly become a powerful and famous person, the J. M. began to feel his affection mingled with awe" (146-7). On the ninth day, the disaffection he felt earlier returns. He has an airline job offer, and feels "unhappy." He feels good only because Maria has had a baby over Utah, undergoing mitotic separation; he thinks of the baby as Little Maria, and thinks "'Why, I've known your mother . . .since she was a little ripple on a cold front north of Titijima!'" (233). But the important thing about this episode is that he lets slip audibly "Little Maria," is horribly embarrassed, and then startled when the Chief replies "'You name them too?. . . I used to do it, but I ran out of names years ago"' (234). Suddenly he feels "at home." "Never before had the Chief and he had anything between them in confidence. He had never suspected the Chief of any hidden imagination" (234). Finally, on the tenth day, he has a scene with the Chief where he "grows warm with a new sense of comradeship" (260). He feels as though he's being addressed as an equal—although it is not said, it is as though in his function he has "grown up," and is no longer "Baby Chief."

It is important to Stewart's environmental construction of the storm that the J. M. be a minor presence from the fifth day to the eleventh day, the period when the storm is at its height. In a sense, he has a lesser role "in" the storm. He assists at Maria's birth, predicts her mature impact, and is witness to her last hours. He frames her life. But he cannot prosper *within* her as a functionary—what he gains during this space of time is emotional and personal. The other functionaries can live, in their functional roles, *only* within her. She feeds their functions. Also, after her prediction, she becomes, first virtually, then actually, a temporally bordered *place* whose size and shape are defined by the "field" of all those human and nonhuman, organic and inorganic entities affected by what she does. The weather bureau is paradoxically at the center of, but not within, this field.

The reader encounters the J. M. only twice more in any case. The first occasion is when the Chief tells him "'Well . . your friend Maria is about done for'" (300). The Chief urges him to go up on the roof and watch the Pacific cold front, following the storm, come in. Buffeted in this elevated space he is able to watch the emergence of sky, the passage "from one world into another. . . Now he could make out, clear across the Bay, the white shaft of the tower on the University campus" (307). And when Maria is "dead," and the Chief gives his homily on men and storms, he revisits sentimentally her whole life course, and scans the charts, hoping to find her successor.

Storm struck at what Stewart at times characterized as a typically unlucky time (like *Bret Harte* in the depression), but in a way this is not true. As Ernest Callenbach says, it conveyed a sense of the earth's, and humans', durability despite disaster, in a "global, indeed cosmic, perspective. . . ". Like Maria, it "changed readers' lives" (viii-ix). It provided a "unique sense of ecological and social connections, but it also appealed directly to a post-depression world. "Stewart writes somewhere that the great storm's rain fell on rich and poor alike: meteorology become morality. We were all in it together, and we had better look out for each other" (xii). Bernard DeVoto called Storm "revolutionary" (De Voto to Stewart 2 Feb. 1942). As the December 1941 Book-of-the-Month Club main selection, its texture was so characterized by Henry Seidel Canby:

> The great storm involves, in some way or another, everyone. The vast equipment for living which we have built up for our civilization is assailed. . .Every [episode] is a short story of its own, bringing in, not only lovers and workers and trippers, but . . the thousands of new kinds of experts that protect our complicated, mechanical civilization . . . (Canby)

Stewart's old friend Buddy de Sylva, executive producer, wrote to him on January 2, 1942 that Paramount had just bought the rights to *Storm* (for $30,000 ["News"]). Unfortunately, shortly thereafter he had to tell the author "how much I enjoyed the book, and how much I regret that it has to be altered for screen presentation . . .We feel it is necessary that we invent a new and more compact story for screen purposes. I can, however assure you that we hope to do it with great dignity" (De Sylva to Stewart 22 Jan. 1942). Softening the "shock" he added "I remember well the days when we sat at adjoining desks at Citrus Union [High School in Azusa]. I think it rather charming that we should be brought together again in this vicarious way." In the summer, he wrote again about the script's progress: "If you are outraged by our new version perhaps we can put a few things in that will help to satisfy your desires" (De Sylva to Stewart, 17 Aug. 1942). By autumn, true pessimism on a filmed *Storm* had set in. "You would never know your child. Now that we have renewed our high-school friendship I hope that the eventual picturization of THE STORM [sic.] will not cause you to stop speaking to me for another twenty five years" (De Sylva to Stewart, 6 Oct. 1942). Ultimately, and perhaps appropriately, the novel proved to be simply unshapeable into cinematic form, despite how often commentators referred to its vignette-scenes as "cinematic." In a way, the very sources of its power, the nonhuman protagonist and the global sychronicity of its events, defeated the attempts to give it a temporal linear plot.

In 1943 the BBC signed a contract for a radio adaptation, and Paramount was still interested enough in the project to have Stewart and Random House sign an agreement on April 5, defining the rights of the two media entities in the matter. The BBC version was not aired until July, 1949. But the novel remained a temptation and a source for (mis)treatment. In 1951, the Lerner and Loewe musical *Paint Your Wagon*, appropriately set in a gold rush mining camp included the by now legendary song, inspired by the book, "They Call the Wind Maria," after which, crediting the Spanish pronunciation Stewart insisted on, the singer Mariah Carey was named (Paint). The book inspired popular culture allusions and cartoons galore, but was not filmed by Paramount. It was, apparently dramatized on June 1, 1963, on NBC's "Lucky Strike Theater" (Norman Felton to Stewart 7 July 1953), and was apparently successfully dramatized on CBS radio's "workshop" series (Wiliam Froug to Stewart 20 Feb. 1956). Ultimately, *Storm* never became a film until in 1960 Walt Disney Studios released a black-and-white dramatized documentary version, titled *A Storm Called Maria*.

The Disney film is pretty faithful to the plot of the novel, although, as mentioned earlier, Rick does not freeze to death. Unfortunately, from 21st century perspective, its episodes are repeatedly interrupted by atmospheric longshots to an accompanying bombastic title song, highly orchestrated, sung by what seems to be a large chorus of male Wagnerian valkyries. The film's narration does not deal with the Junior Meteorologist, and emphasizes the novel's most dramatically conventional elements, not covered in the foregoing discussion (As a Paramount version would have, and as the major studio film of *Fire* was to do later). One of these is the fatal journey in the snow of the couple Jan and Max, who travel from Reno to San Francisco for the weekend, and die in an off-road crash. The other is escape of Johnny Martley from the dam whose sluices he has just opened, a set scene which in *Storm* has the suspenseful power of the cliff-scaling in James Dickey's *Deliverance.* The film tries to get the novel's effect of simultaneity by rapidly sequenced scenes—for example, in one sequence we see cable cars in rain, a suburban woman hysterically taking in laundry, moored boats at Fisherman's pier, kids sailing boats in gutters, rain soaked football game, horse-race, golf course, greyhound bus trapped on flooded road. There are impressive shots of the rotary snowplows working at night (the scene cited above in the novel). We end with a drawn-out scene of happy skiers, juxtaposed to the discovery of Max and Jen's car buried in the snow. The hyperventilating chorus sings eulogistically ". . .her mother was the ocean/her father was the wind . . ." (Maria).

As a text, *Storm* had a much longer life-span and much greater prominence. It was on the best-seller lists along (ironically) with Fitzgerald's *The Last Tycoon*, excerpted in *Liberty Magazine*, and issued in an Armed Services Edition. It was reprinted in a Modern Library edition with an explicatory preface by the author, in 1983 by the University of Nebraska Press with a preface by Wallace Stegner, in 2003, along with an online study guide, by Heyday Books of Berkeley, with an eloquent preface by Ernest Callenbach, who attributed to it the inspiration for *Ecotopia*.

As for Stewart himself, he says frankly "In fact I was very hard up always until *Storm* hit the jackpot there, with the Book of the Month Club. That really put me over the hump financially" (*Little* 38). Beyond the material benefits, the novel's success gave him "much more confidence in myself" (*Little* 142). It also brought him the renewed attention, toward the end of her life, of a famous contemporary, Rachel Carson. Referring to his article in American Heritage's

Book of Natural Wonders (1963), she wrote to Dorothy Freeman: "George Stewart did the section on the Great Basin, which has led me to a rereading of Storm. Now there is much I want to learn about winds, clouds, air movements, and, of course, rain" (Carson *Always* 485).

Chapter IV
World on Fire

Much of Stewart's shorter writing on the eve of World War II was concerned with breaking down generic and disciplinary distinctions as currently applied to literature. Figuratively, this would be through following or breaking new trails. In speaking about his interest in trails and in analogizing the physical trail to the trail of a writer's career, he uses for his own career the "thread" figure which he applies to *Storm*. The "thread of development" he sees in his own work is "the environmental statement" (*Little* 11). For the imaginative writer to make an environmental statement, that writer must strive to give his/her work the inclusiveness of an ecosystem (a word Stewart himself does not use). To approach an understanding and portrayal of an ecosystem one needs inclusive forms, and one needs to draw on the multiple areas of knowledge which can be applied to that understanding—biology, geography, history, anthropology, sociology. I think Stewart would agree with Hubert Zapf that "literature acts like an ecological force *within* the larger cultural system" (86). Literature embodies cultural ecology because it "employs procedures in many ways analogous to ecological principles, restoring complexity, vitality and creativity to the discourses of its cultural world by symbolically reconnecting them with elemental forces and processes of life—in non-human nature, in the collective and individual psyche, in the human body" (93).

Two writings published on the cusp of World War II illustrate Stewart's movement toward this sense of inclusiveness. In 1939 he wrote for the *Saturday Review* an inclusive review of the "Rivers of America" series books so far published . "What should a book about a river really be?" he begins. He examines the series' original prospectus, and finds the subject was meant not mainly to be the rivers themselves, but the "folk inhabiting the drainage basin" thereof, implying the "moralistic purpose" of making people feel good about their country during the depression. But what he really latches on to is its statement that it is to be a *literary* as opposed to a *historical* series. He shows that the first book in the series, Robert P. Tristram Coffin's volume on the Kennebec, is exemplary precisely because it violates these conditions. Coffin "has constantly taken pains to demonstrate a linking between the nature of the region and the nature of its people.. . .the close linking of river and people gives to 'Kennebec' an essential artistic unity." Furthermore, Coffin has struck a "balance between past and present," thereby creating a text which is *both* historical and artistic (12).

Subsequent volumes in the series Stewart considers failures in many ways. Carl Carmer's on the Hudson "fails to bring out clearly the connections between environment and folkways." Julian Dana's Sacramento River volume "fails to make us feel the river intimately." Drawing on his own research on the Sacramento for *Storm*, he criticizes Dana's failure to cover modern developments—particularly the technological manipulation of the river for flood control. ". . .[T]he modern Sacramento with its magnificent system of levees, weirs, and by-passes is really a show-piece among American rivers." The achievements of 20th century river management are ignored, as much as their defects: Dana doesn't discuss the contrast between "the disastrous bottle-necking effects of private levee-building and the excellent results of coordinated Federal planning" (13).

Finally, Stewart gives advice to future writers in the series. "They must study their rivers more intimately and carefully," particularly their geography, and avoid too much emphasis on "frontier exploits, legends, ghost-stories, and good old days." Above all they should not be lured into thinking their writing should be literary and not historical. ". . [W]hen did literature and history become incompatible?" To ask writers not to be historical "is merely to encourage all the natural human tendencies toward carelessness and sloth" (13).

In another, more prominent 1941 article for the same periodical, Stewart deals with an aesthetic equivalent of the disciplinary melding of history and literature. "The Novelists Take Over Poetry" has as a claim that fiction has (justifiably) incorporated techniques previously employed by poetry, and thus enhanced its meaningfulness. Clearly Stewart's own experiences with environmentalizing fiction are sources for this position. His idea, expressed figuratively *via* frontiers, is that non-fiction prose and poetry meet only along a short boundary, whereas non-fiction prose and fiction have a long border, and raid each other across it with impunity. In the last twenty years, "the large-scale warfare has been between the novel and poetry," and "That comparatively new state, the novel, has advanced upon the ancient kingdom of poetry, and reduced it almost to impotence" by appropriating its own weapons (3). His friend Malcolm Cowley objected to this sustained martial metaphor, but agreed with his generic distinction. Only Auden, among contemporary poets, has a "positive message" (Cowley to Stewart 3 June 1941).

Stewart considers the first movement in this direction the development of free verse, which broke down the stylization of typographical form and influenced the shrinkage of the prose paragraph into a "rhythmical unit," which plays into complex patterning and grouping of paragraphs. Overall, the novelist has become "print-conscious" as the poet must be. Secondly, novelists have co-opted the poetic condensation and omission of explicit exposition; "the thread of the narrative" has been broken (4). Summary has atrophied, and sequential scenes been emphasized, giving the novel "much of the intensity formerly called poetic." This tendency ties in with an abandonment of the linear and cumulative progression of plot in favor of the vivid immediacy of the moment, "the vivid use of incident and detail and image," as in what Stewart considers "plotless" novels like *Babbitt*, *The Sun Also Rises*, and *U.S.A.*

Clearly, *Storm* exemplifies, even takes to the extreme, these practices, but the most important aesthetic point made by Stewart in this context is "the complication of the time-element and the complication of the space-element." With the reduction of plot to series of short vivid scenes, the creator can advance multiple narratives simultaneously in time. "Thus develops spatial complexity, for things that happen at the same time naturally must happen in different places. . ."

(18), the same being true for temporal complexity—anti-chronological shifts in time—as Stewart will demonstrate in the future as applied to one of the novels he cites here, *The Sound and the Fury*.

Along with these written promotions of an ecological literature, Stewart was doing the same thing in the field. In 1941 he made one of the first of many trips, in a 1937 Chevrolet, with his great friend, Dr. Charles Camp, to Black Rock, on the emigrant trail in northwestern Nevada. At the time, Black Rock was even more difficult to reach than it is today. The Black Rock desert, the playa, famous for being the flattest area on the surface of the earth, was not host to a Burning Man festival, nor was its surface coursed by ORV's and campers, as I observed it in May, 2005. But the silica surface is still as dangerous with its undetectable mud flats, sand devils, and mirages. The rock, ten miles across the playa from the nearest access now, "used to scare me to death. I suppose that's why it fascinated me so much" (*Little* 190). The playa and the rock continue to fascinate, not necessarily from fear. In his epic, *Mountains and Rivers without End*, Gary Snyder describes repeated visits, like Stewart's

> . . .on the crazed cracked
> flat hard face where
> winter snow spiral, and
> summer sun bakes like a kiln.
> Off nowhere, to be or not be,
>   All equal, far reaches, no bounds. (*Wild* 22)

Stewart and Camp had no tents, but only a pressure cooker. They had no imported water in plastic bottles, but discovered that the terrible-tasting water from the many desert spring, one-third diluted with wine, was "quite palatable" (*Little 276).* Despite their many amusing misadventures on this trip, Stewart found the physical presence of Black Rock just as compelling as Camp, the geologist did. Camp suspects that Stewart was already considering writing a book about it, but it would be another decade before he actually did, in *Sheep Rock* employing the interdisciplinarity and poetic techniques he was experimenting with at the time.

*

Charles Camp was one of a "select group" of colleagues in other disciplines whose disciplinary insights Stewart brought together in his new version of "ecology in the older sense, that is, all the things that go to make up a place" (*Little* 189). Apparently there is not much correspondence between him and these close personal and professional friends; I suspect much of their communication was in conversation. This seems to be as appropriate a place as any to locate them in relation to him, particularly through their own writings.

The last interview in his oral history, *A Little of Myself* is a joint interview with Stewart and Camp. Stewart remembers their meeting around 1934, Camp being surprised that a Princeton graduate would be interested in the Donner Party. He very clearly expresses the discontent that he and others felt with the orthodox dictate to "confine yourself very strictly to your specialty." In fact "It's a good thing to forget that there are boundaries between paleontology, geology, anthropology, and all that. Just forget the boundaries and think of the whole thing as a great sweep of history" (*Little* 256). Camp both formulated and embodied this belief in his *Earth Song: A Prelude to History*, which, he says, the University of California Press initially objected to "because it contained history as well as paleontology, and they didn't think we ought to be mixing the two things up" (*Little 257).*

Published in 1952, *Earth Song* is a most unorthodox scientific text, but perfectly in the Stewartian mode. It is filled both with geophysical charts and graphs, and lyrically epic illustrations of prehistoric life by Margaret M. Colbert. Its affectively chronicled history of the earth and earth's organic and inorganic inhabitants is shaped between italicized "Interludes," lyric evocations of the earth. Its Prelude has the tones of Whitman: "*California! Land thrice-born, cradled between the desert and the sea, hear the Earth Song. . .Child of the rocks and waves, this song is sung for you*" (14). When Camp introduces, under the title "Enigma," the first life on earth, which his subsequent chapter will describe, the narrative voice addresses Life itself: "*Child of the hydrocarbon molecule, you first of Nature's host, destined to spread through sea and land and air in countless ways and forms, what was the meaning of your birth, and what will be your destiny?"* (31). When he reaches the period of human origins, he traces a remarkable litanic "Episode of Folsom Man," in which single descriptive sentences in Roman type: "Wild horses prance on the plain," or "A lion jaguar stalks the herd," alternates with italicized passages which give the intimate details of the summarized action and evoke poetically the sensory texture of each moment in a hunt. This passage is in effect an embodied refutation of disciplinary isolation. The Roman passages link together perfectly in a succinct, emotionless narrative. That is the voice of Discipline. The italicized passages express all that Discipline leaves out.

Camp's last chapter, on California in the present, bewails deforestation and depleted grasslands, the diminished populations of sea mammals, salmon, the introduced diseases of plants and animals. "What a price has been paid for pine blister rust, a deforester that runs a race of destruction with sawmills and fire!" (157).

One other intriguing bit of information about Camp is worth including here. A websearch found a much-forwarded statement from his wife Joanna, which describes, to a religious writer, Camp's deathbed conversion to Christianity. The preface to the letter tells us: "For years a renowned scientist named Charles Camp debated religious leaders on the radio. He advocated the facts of science as opposed to the concepts of Creationism. Over the years he lost faith in God and became known as an outspoken and articulate atheist." The letter from Joanna Camp enhances this summary: "For years he taught medical students. When the subject of near-death experiences would come up in class, Charles would explain that there is no life beyond the grave, that everything ends there, that the body gradually changes to become nourishment for other forms of life" ("Ryan"). This information is significant because, although it does not directly relate to Stewart, it suggests Camp had an ecological rationale for his atheism, and allies him with a group of anthropologists who emphasized "cultural relativism and enculturation"

(Price xii), especially as manifested in environmental causation of cultural attributes.

Of these, the closest to Stewart were two Berkeley anthropologists, both former students of Franz Boas, who was at Columbia when Stewart was studying there—Alfred Kroeber and Robert Lowie. Alfred Kroeber is probably best known for his life-study of Ishi, the Yahi Indian whose life was brilliantly memorialized by his wife, Theodora Kroeber, in the 1961 book *Ishi in Two Worlds*. But he was a central figure in the growth of American anthropology from 1900, when David Starr Jordan named him curator at the California Academy of Sciences, through a long career at Berkeley, until his death in 1957. Julian Steward, in his study of Kroeber, finds his fundamental point of view to be the definition and classification of cultures in a manner "comparable to a natural history procedure," along with "a strong historical sense and a view of cultures as a superorganic phenomenon" (27). Steward sees Kroeber as interested in "culture areas [which]. . .were relativistically defined in terms of their distinguishing characteristics or differences and occurred in different environmental settings" (53). Unlike Camp, Kroeber was not a secular controversialist, but he "did not much believe in ultimates, nor did he find it profitable to look for them. Theodora Kroeber calls him an "untheist" (232).

From a personal point of view, Kroeber's environmental connection is strongest through the 40 wild acres in the Napa Valley that he and Theodora bought in 1930, and named after an imaginary giant, Kishamish. It was the family's summer residence and "To children and adults alike, Kishamish's forty acres were illimitably expandable, becoming for us a complete world," likened, by Theodora Kroeber, to a California Indian's tribal territory, to whom it was "of cosmic variety, complexity, and passionate concern" (141). It was transitorily inhabited by a stream of graduate students, Indians, writers, scholars, and friends—surely including Stewart. Ursula (Kroeber) LeGuin admittedly doesn't remember him there, but she does remember him driving her and his daughter Jill to dance lessons (LeGuin to the author n. d.).

Kishamish might rightly be seen as a physical manifestation of Kroeber's idea of an encompassing environment, whose two components he characterizes as the biological and the sociocultural. The sociocultural element of environment is best examined in terms of the fluid "clustering" of cultural phenomena moving through historical time: ". . .the best understanding we can arrive at, in regard to any cultural phenomenon, is always the complex nexus of the largest historical totality with which the phenomenon can be brought into relation" (20). Cultural patterns move through time in an organic manner—one might say as inhabitants flowed through Kishamish. They have "pulses" and "lulls;" their energy builds into a "florescence" a "climax" of achievement (almost by analogy with Clementsian ecology), they spread and contract "geographically."

Kroeber's views of culture changed and evolved over his many decades of field research and writing, as did his emphases of interest. Like Camp, he brought an archaeological/paleontological fascination to his studies of culture in history—what I would call a "vertical ecology" of temporal entwinements. He came to summarize his professional identity as a "humanist with a sort of natural history slant" (T. Kroeber 227).

In the years before the war, one might be likely to find Stewart, Kroeber, and other luminaries such as Robert Oppenheimer meeting as an informal group which Theodora Kroeber calls the *Stammtich,* at a "shabby" Italian restaurant in Emeryville. The group consisted of a ". . .mixed bag of about twenty people, more or less intimate friends and part of the 'North Berkeley crowd:' artist, professors, poets, intellectuals, living by preference in the hills north of the University campus and locally looked down upon or up to, depending, as a Far West sort of Greenwich Village" [clearly the Latin Quarter of *Doctor's Oral*] (T. Kroeber 235).

Kroeber does not provide a complete *dramatis personae* of the *Stammtich,* but it's hard to believe it didn't include Kroeber's fellow anthropologist of distinction, Robert Lowie. Lowie was critical of Stewart's *Man: An Autobiography* (see below), particularly of the conceit whereby he individualized collective mankind (Lowie to Stewart 8 Oct. 1945), but there was a lot of congruence between their points of view. For example, with reservations, Lowie considers attributes of biological evolution analogous to those of cultural evolution, and uses environmental figures to define the conditions of "permanency" under which true cultural evolution can take place: ". . .organisms put into a new environment sometimes exhibit new features, but promptly lose them when transplanted to their usual habitat. Such alterations . .. are not evolutionary" (*Social* 32).

But probably the colleague who had the most influence on Stewart's thinking was geographer Carl Sauer. Sauer was instrumental in resurrecting the original ecological perspective of George Perkins Marsh, and ". . .'humanizing' ecology by taking humans—especially their actions—into account as much as any other kind of organism" (Kingsland 165). He also sought to bring currency to this belief as articulated by a recent predecessor, ecological entomologist Stephen Forbes. "Forbes believed that an ecological view 'must include the twentieth century man as its *dominant* species—dominant not . . .as simply the most abundant. . .but dominant in the sense of dynamic ecology, as the most influential, the controlling or dominant member of his associate group'" (Croker 124). Unlike many contemporaries, Sauer saw geography and ecology as inseparable, not just meeting in "empirical problem areas" such as economic geography and urban studies (Schnore 215). Sauer, who joined the Berkeley faculty in 1923 "developed a friendship and collaborative relationship with anthropologist Alfred Kroeber. ." (Kingsland 166), which led him toward an integration of the history of human cultures examined via archaeology, and ecology. "Combining his interests in geography and cultural development with his strong historical bent, Sauer discerned that ecological questions concerning the balance of nature and its destruction by modern humans could benefit from a longer historical perspective" (168). Sauer also influenced Aldo Leopold strongly, since he found in Sauer another who was interested in "'putting the sciences together'" (Meine 405).

In a 1938 address, Sauer put one basic aspect of his humanized ecology cogently: "In social science interpreted as culture history, there is a dominant geographic theme which deals with the growing mastery of man over his environment. Antiphonal to this is the revenge of an outraged nature on man. It is possible to sketch the dynamics of human history in terms of this antithesis" (*Land* 145).

Sauer saw in the West a perfect testing ground for such a historical dynamic. In "Historical Geography and the Western Frontier" (1929) he contemplates the "cultural landscapes" in California created by "the transforming hand of man," such that ". . .plant geography today is pretty well a study of plant successions that are taking place under conditions imposed by man" (45). Thus the ecologist must address the history of cultural change. Traditional models of ecology "do not take into account the flux of earth, or natural and cultural history. How organisms have come to live together in any part of the world. . .is an historical problem of large and actual time which may not be explained by schemes of successive stages and climactic climaxes" (183).

At mid-century, in *Agricultural Origins and Dispersals*, Sauer articulated a credo of ecocentrism—including humans. "The history of mankind is a long and diverse series of steps by which he has achieved ecologic dominance" (3).

> Often, however, he overreaches himself, and the new order he has introduced may end in disaster. As man became civilized he has grown more and more inclined to consider the earth as made for him to inherit, himself as the claimant of an anthropocentric order; he has come to believe in an ever-expanding system that places no limits upon himself other than his individual mortality. Often his capacity to know good from evil has been warped by the energy of his activities, his knowledge giving him powers which he has lacked the wisdom to control. Our own time has its prophets of progress unlimited in numerous social and physical scientists who speak of remaking the world. It may be proper, at this time of dizzy cultural change, to regard our past record as modifiers of the organic world. (4)

Although it took place after many of Stewart's works had been written, a crucial event in American environmental history can be considered to represent the above-discussed figures' cultural-ecological interdisciplinarity and also, indirectly, Stewart's own environmental vision. This was the symposium entitled "Man's Role in Changing the Face of the Earth," held at Princeton under Sauer's direction in 1955 (Kingsland 164). Its published proceedings come in at 1,193 pages. Very little notice appears to be given to this conference in the literature of environmental history, yet it involved some of the most significant interdisciplinary scholars dealing with ecological concerns. Dedicated to George Perkins Marsh, the symposium sought to "provide an integrated basis" for understanding "what has happened and is happening to the earth under man's impress" as the "ecological dominant on the planet" (Thomas xxvii). Its approach was basically ecosystemic: " . . .[T]he results of every human interference with nature should be evaluated with relation to the entire variety of environmental conditions, not to one condition only" (Gutkind 3). Its participants accepted, and sought to explore, diverse "culturally conditioned attitudes toward natural resources" (Spoehr 97). The tenor of the whole gathering was to undermine a belief in the autonomy of human agents, as it was trumpeted in this 1920's boosteresque exaltation:

> With advance in civilization man attains relative freedom from environment. . . .Man learns to make nature do his bidding. Where there is dearth of rainfall he supplies rivers of irrigating canals. The water which will not come from the heavens shall be induced to come up through the earth. The wilderness and the desert are made to blossom like the rose; in the dreariest wastes man induces nature to be prodigal of her blessings. As man develops power, as his devices become more ingenious, environment is reinterpreted and remade. (Wallis 708)

In direct contrast to such naive sublimity, at this symposium, for the first time, many diverse disciplinary concerns of humans as environmental *participants*, as a dominant species *within* the environment, were engaged, in presentations and in discussion sessions. For example, Lewis Mumford's paper was on the "natural history of urbanization" (382). Luna Leopold discussed the effects of tillage on soil (with my apologies to feminists): "Putting virgin soil under cultivation initiates a . . .breakdown or degeneration of the soil body . . ."

(651). Marston Bates explored "man as the agent of dispersal of his own parasites," concluding that, compared with other organisms, "the human situation is peculiar: the geography of infectious disease in man is perhaps best understood not in strictly biological terms but in cultural terms" (789). In his concluding remarks, Sauer used a combative analogy:

> Thus are we brought in 1955 to a revised version of Aldous Huxley's "brave new world" of the twenties—to a faceless, mindless, countless multitude managed form the cradle to the grave by a brilliant elite of madmen obsessed with accelerating technologic progress. The original of these fantasies was composed by an Englishman, but the reality is being undertaken especially in this country. The social prospect in growing regimentation, in loss of individual freedom as we have known it, in elimination of unplanned variation, lead to questioning the technologic-economic system that is in the making. (1133)

Not that such outspoken polemic was the byword with Stewart's intellectual companions, but they did share a common concern for the fate of the earth under a technological dispensation.

Two more writer friends of Stewart's must be mentioned here, for the strong connections he had with them as friends and fellow-writers. Wallace Stegner and Stewart were close all their professional lives, even when far apart. Stegner asserts of Stewart that "He was a much more important writer than the general public knew" (*Where* 155), which is one of the premises of this book. Stegner gave him the tribute of imitating his Joe Grantland of *Doctor's Oral* with that of his own Paul Condon, in his own academic novel *Fire and Ice* (1941), although Paul, unlike Joe, is choleric, political, and violent. They guest-taught at each others' classes, corresponded constantly, and worked together on the somewhat subversive *Pacific Spectator* magazine. His son Page and Stewart's son Jack were buddies at Stanford. They shared the same environmental concerns, although their literary approaches to them were quite different.

Another close literary friend was C. S. Forester, who moved to Berkeley in 1940. During the war, Forester, along with Stewart, Joseph Henry Jackson, Arthur Lewis, and others, comprised the "Armchair Strategist's Society," which met once a month to discuss the latest military developments (Forester I. 431). They were met often at social events, and as guests in each others' houses. John Forester tells of Stewart, at his father's house, describing how he tried to authenticate the Jefferson map of the emigrant trail. "This was shortly after WW II. GRS bought a war surplus jeep and set off to follow the trail, according to the diary's account. . .Out in the desert wilderness he found wagon tracks, leaving iron-rust scars, along the diary's route. Where the diary told of a spring, there was a spring" (John Forester, Email to the author 23 June 2005).

In his obituary of Forester, in *Names*, Stewart writes "He was given to dropping in on a Thursday evening, and we would talk about what he was writing, or what I was writing, or just family problems. Sometimes he would tell a story that he was considering, or would read one from manuscript." Unlike the portrait of Forester in his son's biography, Stewart here calls him "a man of immense sympathy and good will" ("In Memoriam" 249-50).

*

It is appropriate to bring up *Names* here, because, although that periodical did not exist at the time, Stewart began his book on names, for which he would gain wide recognition, even before he had finished *Storm*. We may remember that his first "popular" article was on children's names, in the 1920's. Beginning in 1935, first in *American Speech*, and, after its founding in 1950, the American Names Society's *Names*, he wrote many scholarly articles on place names in the United States. A good example of these is "Nomenclature of Stream-Forks on the West Slope of the Sierra Nevada" (1939), in which (quite possibly based on his field research there for *Ordeal by Hunger*) he seeks to define the system of geographically defining branches of streams—e.g. "north" or "south". Here is manifest the writer's interest not only in name-origins *per se*, but in the psychological processes which lead to human naming. Why, for example is one branch defined as the "main" one? " . . . [A] man coming downstream feels unity in the branch which he is following and unless the branches which join his own are definitely larger he will continue to feel that he has been on the main branch all the while. A man advancing upstream, however, feels his unity definitely dividing; he feels loyalty to both the branches which he sees suddenly appear before him" (196).

Another essay on naming, "What is Named?—Towns, Islands, Mountains, Rivers, Capes," is significant because it outlined the "philosophy of naming," he was to expound fully in *Names on the Globe*. It also involves subjectivity, in outlining a spectrum of sources between the naming of persons and the naming of places. The place-naming closest in nature to that of persons is of towns. ". . .[A] town name is rarely if ever a pure place name. In all its three manifestations it has something of the qualities of a personal name" (225). As far as non-human created places go, linguistic custom and the specialized interests of the namer can shape the linguistic existence or nonexistence of places. "On a geological map most islands disappear because to a geologist a film of water is of no importance" (226). Much naming, says Stewart, is based on the human "power of abstraction:" the "what" cannot be defined. When a river is named, what is actually named? The water itself is constantly changes; if it is the bed, then there is no water and no river. He sees a connection between the convenience of abstraction in naming and early animism, wherein a titulary entity bears the physical feature's name.

The subjective sources of names and the act of naming figure strongly in his longer works up to this time: the disorienting namelessness of places in *Ordeal by Hunger*, the transition from Spanish to English place-names in *East of the Giants*, and, of course, Maria herself. Some of the fascination with names goes back to his childhood involvement with atlases and maps.

The book which Stewart decided to write on American place names was ". . .an incredibly hard book to conceive, because it didn't exist, incredibly hard to organize" (*Little* 3). It was to be not a glossary, but a narrative history, and as such, had no generic precedent. Fortunately, Stewart had been offered a fellowship teaching creative writing at Princeton for the 1942-3 academic year, a position held the previous year by Allen Tate, who offered to answer any questions "Mr. Stuart" [sic] had about the position (Tate to Stewart 14 July 1942). Despite war disturbances, Stewart's tenure at Princeton was apparently pleasant. Stegner wrote "I'm glad to hear that Princeton is not a nest of long-hairs in Windsor ties, and that you find [R. P.] Blackmur pleasant. Almost I get a whiff of nostalgia for the old ivy-mantled towers" (Stegner to Stewart 19 Nov. 1942 [?]).

As a result he had a "vacant year" there, and was able to do a lot of work "shaping" a book which had no "model" (*Little* 151). At the same time, ever looking towards the future, he was meditating on the idea of a forest fire book which ". . .might follow up the tradition of STORM which people enjoyed a great deal" (Stewart to Vivian Wolfert 16 Feb. 1948). All his creative activity was, however, devoted to *Names on the Land*, which turned out to be his favorite of all his books, and in the opinion of Wally Stegner, his best: "For *Names on the Land*. . .is provocative in the best sense. It makes a reader look at things he has taken for granted, it stretches the mind with analogies and possibilities, it is made luminous by the learning brought to bear upon a single aspect of our incomparably complex heritage" (*Where* 170).

In *Names on the Land*, Stewart complexly weaves the progressive history of the human presence in North America with the progressive history of ever-multiplying names for places given cultural identity through that naming. Periodically his spacious narrative pauses to allow short narratives of particular events related to particular namings. A lot of his many short chapters are given their own tonal names suggestive of the epic tradition, particularly by beginning with "Of" or "How" ("Of the naming that was before history;" "How the first Spaniards gave names"), which insinuates that the cultural creation of continental identity *is* an epic. The collective naming of places in a defined earthly terrain is really, we are led to feel, a second creation of the terrain itself. Naming of a place is a primal act of reciprocity: culture is naturalized and nature is acculturated at this moment. In another culture/nature exchange, to the extent that a name is derived from sensory attributes of a place, it is an expression of human environmental perception. And once it is named, for any reason, the perception of a place is shaped, in part, by that name. Obviously different names can be given to the same place by different individuals or culture groups, as Stewart elaborately shows. Much of Alfred Kroeber's work with Ishi, as narrated in *Ishi in Two Worlds*, is an exercise in reciprocal translation of names.

The act of naming brings the human cultural presence into a totalized environment, and is a necessary first human step in a sequence of environmental effects created by the human presence. Stewart's story begins with an eloquent evocation of the land before this first step is taken. Horace Reynolds began his review of *Names on the Land* by saying the book's first sentence gave him, a "hardened reviewer" a "thrill" (10). The first paragraph Stewart himself thought one of his best: "Once, from eastern ocean to western ocean, the land stretched away without names. Nameless headlands split the surf; nameless lakes reflected nameless mountains; and nameless rivers flowed through nameless valleys into nameless bays" (3) The endpapers of the first edition cleverly visualize the initial namelessness and the final namefulness: the front papers have a map of the United States with no names, while on the back ones, the names "lie thickly" (3) on the same map. The text then, expresses the flow of time between the two maps.

As this time progresses, the author evolves with it what we might call a "typology of name bestowal," which links geography and group or individual psychology to explain different modes of the naming process. The chronological shape of the history gives this typology an inductive and accretive nature. The ever-thickening layers of names can be seen as equivalent to the ever-multiplying modes of naming, as the cultural presence on the land strengthens. Stewart elaborated a systematics for this typology, which he used in structuring his monumental *Names on the Globe* topically rather than chronologically.

The "naming that was before history" merges an imaginary vignette-narrative of an Indian scout reporting back to a tribe on the features of the new terrain before them, by describing the physical appearance of those features. The phrase describing those features, such as "'stream-where-oak-trees-grow'" (6) becomes the name, once the tribe has become inhabitant of that place. Once inhabitance has taken on some duration and permanence, a place might gain a name from a notable action that occurred there, imaginary or real. As Stewart defines them then, these are the two earliest and most basic types of naming: from description and from action.

Associating actual Native American names with these processes, Stewart then proceeds to characterize the "nameability" (my word) of a place—*what* is named to accompany the *how* of naming. The distinct (from its surroundings) and the useful place is more likely to be named. Thus, Native Americans rarely named mountains but almost always named rivers, "closest of all to the life of primitive man" (9).

The advent of literate Europeans was an absolute and crucial step in the history of American place-naming. Stewart sequences his discussion of the first explorers' and settlers' naming by the approximate arrival period of each linguistic nationality, beginning with the Spanish. He characterizes the most frequent types of European naming as transliteration of Native American names, or names meant to symbolize political control. A typical Stewartian anecdote exemplifies the latter (and many of Stewart's naming stories *are* anecdotal, to be taken with a grain of salt). Raleigh's New World emissaries in 1584 return with the Native American name of the land they explored transliterated to be "Wingandacoa" and its King, "Wingina."

> Then, it may be, that spelling spurred the Queen's thought, and she remembered her own virgin state, which her poets celebrated. Also, that far-off, sweet-smelling land lay untouched and virgin, waiting to be possessed. So while Sir Walter stood by to approve and applaud, the Queen remembered her Latin, and spoke a word of proper form for the name of a province, which was a 'virgin-land.' (22)

In the same vein, Stewart notes the witty names in Gabriel Archer's journal of the Jamestown settlement. On Christopher Newport's expedition to seek the head of the James (previously King's) River: "Poor Cottage, Arahatec's Joy, Powatah's

Tower, Mulberry Shade, Kind Woman's Care, Queen's Bower, and Careless Point." "What man with a beard," our author asks, "could say such fine-spun silken terms without cursing afterward to clear his mouth?" (31). Hence most of Archer's names were stillborn.

Colonial naming is seen by Stewart as reflective of the colonizers' intended roles in their new physical environment. Coining "New England" was a clever move by Captain John Smith, since it was almost a verbal annexation to old England. Charles I domesticated the coastline by naming capes after his mother, sister, and wife—not to mention graciously accepting his own name for one of the southern colonies. The Massachusetts General Court established a precedent of giving names of English towns to frontier settlements—one rationale being to encourage immigration to them by people who might imagine they were mirror-images of their own domesticated towns (46). (Stewart uses a humorous fictional argument in the Court about naming rationale to make this point). By contrast, in the Virginia colony there was much less separation between names and natural features, and more places were named for individuals, since the plantation system was the basis of settlement naming, and plantation grantees had given names to their plantations ungoverned by an ideology of Anglicization.

Another feature of Colonial naming emphasized by Stewart is the effect of conflict between colonizers—the British and Dutch, for example. The premise of ownership by original namers led to name-wars over which name for the same place—the British name or the Dutch one—was the "original" name. When the Dutch were finally driven out of "New Amsterdam," Dutch names were anglicized. Stewart's best example of nationalistic naming and sequential inhabitation is Broadway. "The story of that street and of its name might almost stand for the whole history of the nation" (76). The Dutch had cleared a space north of their fort, on the north-south Indian trail, as a firing range. Named as a street, honorifically "Heeren Straat," Lords' Street, it was called commonly by its physical attribute "Breede Wegh," that is, broad way. As Broadway it was totally English but held within it memory of the Dutch and the Natives.

A different religion-based naming system than that of the New England colonies was that of William Penn. It bears a dual heritage with respect to name-environment correlation. Stewart tells amusingly the (supposedly true) story of Penn proposing "Sylvania" for the name of his land grant, because of its vegetation and because, as a Quaker, he eschewed prioritizing people, including himself, as namesakes. Charles II, of the other persuasion religiously, played a little onomastic joke on Penn by naming, the land "Pennsylvania" in its charter. Penn even tried bribing the King's secretaries to get rid of the "Penn" but he couldn't do it, and was stuck with the indignity of having his own name on his own land. He did succeed in giving his own choice name to his territory's chief city, a name neither sectarian nor environmental, Philadelphia. But he initiated a feature of city planning that was radically to alter the physical environment of the future nation by initiating the grid pattern for urban streets. Those going one direction had neutral numbers as names. Those going the other were named after "'the things that spontaneously grow in the country," from which Stewart quotes the mnemonic verse: "Market, Arch, Race, and Vine,/Chestnut, Walnut, Spruce, and Pine" (105). The long-term success of Penn's geometry and nomenclature eventually eliminated—and still eliminates—places and names from the American land. The ". . . geometrical plans making no allowance for the lay of the land . . ." (248) levelled physical features, overbuilt them, and they and their names were forgotten.

A linchpin chapter in the later Colonial naming period is "How the names became more English and less English." Enumerating and exemplifying the different types of anglicizing non-English names, Stewart also shows how non-English individuals and culture groups infiltrated non-English names on the English colonial landscape, initiating multilingual acculturation of the land—a phenomenon Stewart considers ". . .with its evidence of toleration. . . a chief glory of our heritage" (114). In one county of Pennsylvania (English "Lancaster"), he enumerates township names of Welsh, German, Scotch-Irish, and Dutch. Another deanglicizing force of significance was topographical naming. Names for common topographical features in England (such as moor or heath) became archaisms in America, where these features were uncommon or nonexistent. Plant and animal place-name sources proliferated, but according to Stewart's principle, the rarer the plant or animal in any given locale, the more likely its name would become attached to a place, because its rarity made it stand out (this is a version of the original "distinctive feature" type of naming). "So, according to his imprint upon the folk-imagination, every animal and bird left his mark upon the map" (117)—even those now extinct.

As we pass through these different naming typologies, the author imperceptibly moves us west, so that we, the readers, have, with the explorers and namers, reached the Appalachians. "How they took the names into the mountains" works from William Byrd's 1728 *History of the Dividing Line*. It emphasizes, first, the growing necessity, as settlement moved upland, of giving names to upland physical features—obviously, mountains, but also streams, stream tributaries, passes between mountains. Names also were coined from climatic and seasonal features (and creatures!—the buffalo) which did not exist in northern Europe. Another important quality of surveys and their material products was their status as "metaplaces" (my word). Names might exist, and were more likely to survive in real time, if coined and inscribed on maps before any consistent human intercourse with them. Surveys for establishing boundaries of properties acculturated nature by giving such boundaries the same status, on a map, as physical features. But they naturalized constructed space too, by creating names for physical features to enable the descriptive location of property.

Stewart gives concurrent coverage to the naming of interior places of the continent by explorers, hunters, missionaries, and the like, but another true turning point in naming arroved with the American Revolution. With the political revolution and creation of a new independent nation on the land came a revolution in naming. Names began to spring, as it were, directly from a newly "native" soil. Stewart gives a dramatic abbreviated account of the conflicts at Lexington and Concord. "Lexington! A new name on the land!" (162). He recounts strophically the hearing of the name "Lexington" at different places on the land, and indicates the mimetic naming of places after it—just as would soon happen with Washington. As for Lexington, ". . .now there was a new name in the land, and children learned it with their first words. At last the people had a symbol—not a stupid king across the ocean, but a name red with their own blood" (163).

The most difficult naming act to come from the Revolution was that of the new nation itself. "United States of America" was a politically savvy designation, but after the war it was seen to have no descriptive attributes, and to lack, in effect, *panache*. So a war broke out between "United States" and the oft-used "Columbia." The eventual victory by default of the former is considered by Stewart ". . .the worst misfortune in our whole naming-history" (173). He topicalizes this by suggesting that ". . .the terse Axis is, as a name, much superior to its floundering counterpart, United Nations" (174).

Much naming typology was altered by independence and westward movement. It seems to me that, overall, Stewart considers mid-continent names those furthest removed from environmental relevance, while those in the West recaptured it. As it moved westward, naming became less and less anglocentric, but drew more and more from cultural phenomena. "After the Revolution came a critical period in naming, as in government—a time of new loves and new hatreds, when the brightness of new heroes moved across the land, and new ways of naming must be found" (188). He sees the naming changes more in "governmental units" than in "natural features." Latinate names for towns and cities proliferated during the Classical Revival; males of national prominence and obscurity--landowners, land speculators—were used, as, usually nonsectarianally, was the Bible. Older names in the East were replaced by new ones, for various reasons. Stewart recounts a great story of a renaming battle over a Vermont town. Two prominent citizens were adamant on their different choices for a new name. A public meeting determined the new name should be decided by single combat between the proposers. The combat-ground was a barn, the weapons fists, and the proposer of Barre prevailed (208).

The most random typology of names is that of states and future great cities. With the ". . .new generation. . . of men who had never known what it was to live beneath a king" (226), there was an erratic reversion to Native American and long-surviving names for states and cities, but these native names were verbally reformulated. Eight states admitted to the union before the civil war had "traditional" names, as did thirteen towns "destined to be cities" (232). A major generator of names during this period was a technological phenomenon that radically affected the natural landscape—the railroad. Towns were born and killed by the presence of the railroad lines, despite whatever other nonhuman phenomena were involved. Houses were built in North Georgia around the place where engineer Stephen H. Long had driven a spike to indicate the terminus of Southern railroads. This new town was named "Terminus." An ex-governor renamed it after his daughter, "Marthasville." That name, like Gabriel Archer's seventeenth-century names, seemed effete for an entrepreneurial town. Engineer J. Edgar Thomson was asked to find a new name. His response, as quoted by Stewart: "'Eureka!—Atlanta. . . . Atlantic, masculine; Atlanta, feminine—a coined word. . .'" (257). Thus the place, its generative source, and its ultimate name, were all the products of human construction.

With great enthusiasm, *Names on the Land* turns to California naming, particularly as related to the 49ers, and the births of new towns and cities. Stewart, a persistent critic of Fremont, does credit him with the power of "Golden Gate," mimetic of the Byzantine Chrysoceras, "Golden Horn." His research on Western Sierra stream names comes in handy here, since miners, the destroyers of landscape, had such a vested interest in these physical features and in giving them individual identities. He also discusses the grid-street naming of Sacramento (copied by other California cities), de-naturing Penn's model by designating streets numerically and their cross-streets alphabetically, for the convenience of immigrant orientation. Such a system suggests topographical nihilism, but convenience for the "stranger" seeking swift nativization.

Cultural modes affected mid-century naming as it returned to nature through various sentimental reinterest in Native Americans as their final independent cultures were being annihilated. Stewart tellingly says, "The frontier was not only of the land, but also in the minds of men" (270). This resulted in naming based on Gothicism, and the romance fiction represented by Sir Walter Scott, as well as on the neo-romantic idealization of the Native American. New railway suburbs, such as the one in which Stewart was born, were given "poetic" names suggestive of idealized environmental attributes. His example is "Fair" as a prefix: ". . .it farrowed a numerous litter of Fairview, Fairburn, Fairdale, Fair Haven, and many others" (274). Similarly, it was only after literal threat from Native Americans was extinguished that "The admiration of Indian name as such began with the new love of the strange, mysterious, and primitive" (276). Ironically "While the frontier regions went on disliking Indians and their names, the more settled regions thus began to use them" (276). "The great majority of our present Indian names of towns are . . . not really indigenous" (279).

Another micro-story illustrates the irony of this "rediscovery." California cavalry in 1851, chasing hostile Natives into the Sierras, encounter "the brink of a vast and unprecedented chasm. . ." (280). They follow a Native American trail to the floor of the "chasm" and, progressively more inebriated, argue about a "baptismal name" for this place. A well-educated member of the company suggests that the name should be American, and "Indian." He suggests the name of the tribe the group has been pursuing: "Yo-sem-i-ty." Many reject this; one suggests "Paradise Valley." They decide on a vote and Yo-sem-i-ty (later found to mean "Grizzly Bears") wins (280-82). This is an excellent demonstration of the intersect between culture and nature in naming, and the almost disturbing pre-emption of the latter by the former. I perceive it—Stewart doesn't get into this—as a way of using a name as a weapon. The cultural appropriation of the Native American name by the Whites who are in literal time seeking to kill these same Native Americans is like a cognitive displacement of the natives from their land, by ironically taking on the power to place their name on it.

Stewart tells us the Civil War also had a major impact on American place-naming. As armed conflict approached, the number of localities named "Union" or "Liberty" multiplied. As heroes emerged on both sides, counties and towns took on their names, most prominently, of course, "Lincoln," for mainly small towns. "He was the common man's hero, and in the United States the small town has always been the citadel of the common man" (299). The most environmentally friendly names created by the Civil War were those of battles—Bull Run, Wilderness—possessing ". . .the true flavor of the land" (299). In the immediate postwar decades, 1860's through 1880's, "probably more names were given than in any earlier period of equal length" (314), as the human web spread over the Great Plains and the Rockies, unto the "Great American Desert." There was thereby a great dearth of names, relieved by the Civil War's "fine new crop of heroes" (318) and by the westward migration of eastern names, "transferred names." These were not arbitrary transfers. As with British New England names, they were often transferred to recreate eastern settlers' places of origin. They were also used as a mode of conjuration, as though the naming might magically recreate in the new space the positive attributes—especially commercial—of an eastern place. "Towns named Pittsburgh in western states were founded in the hope of becoming centers of steel-manufacturing or coal-mining" (319). (There is a perfect example of this process in my own city of residence, Johnson City, Tennessee, where toward the end of the 19th century an "industrial district" was laid out in grid pattern and named "Carnegie" with streets named "Iron," "Steel," and the like, in the promoters' unsuccessful hope that Johnson City, as a rail hub near Appalachian mines could become the "Pittsburgh of the South").

Western naming in this period found a dominant source in transportation and communication, particularly the railroad companies and the Post Office Department. New rail routes enabled by the transcontinental railroad created new localities. Where these were in proximity to places already named, by Native Americans or settlers, the rail namers tended to stay close to the land by adopting them. Where there was little prior settlement, and therefore few known preexisting names, figures important in the company, from executives to major stockholders, became sources of names for places they had no connection with and probably had never seen. Likewise, the names devised by Post Office clerks were, in Stewart's word, "rootless." The only principle was that they could not duplicate pre-existing names. One clerk named new post offices for all the "kids and babies" in his neighborhood. As a result, "Oklahoma alone has Amy, Eva, May, Ora, Eda, Fay, Ida, Iva, Ola, and Ona" (327).

Another turning-point in American naming at the end of the century was a "growing self-conscious interest in the whole subject of names" (333). Place-naming and books about place-naming begin to coexist. Stewart does not speculate on the metanominal implications of this coexistence, but it is interesting to speculate on what typology resulted from it. The "first whole book on American names" (333), *Names and Places*, by the notable geologist J. D. Whitney (after whom two of his surveyors named Mount Whitney in California), was published in 1888. In 1890 President Harrison established the first centralized entity charged with establishing what one might call an "official" typology of names, the Board on Geographic Names. "Historians will recognize an aptness in the date; it is the year conventionally set for the closing of the frontier" (341). Many conflicts arose despite the Board's principle of preserving "local usage." In the cases where it changed names by policy, it faced local rebellion. Based on his own region of origin, Stewart traces the conflict over the policy of making all "—burgh" cities into "berg:" ". . . it seemed to Germanize the country overnight, as the old Scottish spelling was wiped out" (343). In the case of Pittsburgh, there was a tough battle between the Board and the city's dominant Scotch-Irish Presbyterian population—Stewart's own tribe. "They are . . . a notoriously stiff-necked and democratic people; if told by self-styled higher authority to do anything, they are very likely to do the opposite" (344), and, through political maneuvering, they ultimately prevailed.

In his chapter "Flavor of California," Stewart says that later California naming is notable for this above-mentioned self-consciousness. The townsite chosen in 1864 for the new University of California was named only after a great deal of self-conscious debate. The university trustees kept looking for the "*mot juste*" (347). Their landscape architect, Frederick Law Olmsted, was into names with "old English" endings, especially those which implied the shelter of high hills. But the trustees ultimately chose the original landowner's name, Peralta, since it could be seen as having an academic Latin homonym, *Per Alta*. Then, in what might be considered a true "metanominal moment" the trustees were walking the site, envisioning its future topographical presence (the "streets" were to be named after American scientists, the cross-streets, "ways," after American men of letters).

> They came to a large outcropping of volcanic rock, and halted there, standing about, or sitting on the ledges. Looking westward, they saw the magnificence of San Francisco Bay and the Golden Gate, beneath a high sun on a clear spring day. . .Again they thought of a name. Mr. Billings was one of the group, and in conjunction with Golden Gate, someone facetiously suggested Billingsgate. But someone else, looking at the out-going ships, quoted, "Westward the course of empire takes its way." At that moment Mr. Billings experienced what he later called "a sort of inspiration." He cried out "Eureka!—Berkeley said that! And that saying fits this location; so, Berkeley would be a good name!" (348)

Twentieth-century naming became more "official," according to Stewart. The preexisting "distinction between naming by official act and by folk-process" (353) tipped toward the official, especially with respect to geographical features. In 1906 the members of the USGS, the Forest Service, and the National Park Service were authorized to name natural features, subject to the approval of the Board on Geographic Names. "Power is a dangerous intoxicant. . ." and with this top-down structure, ". . .the whole process of naming was profoundly affected" (354-55). Despite this, many namers within the above-named entities named by whim, and the Board did not intervene. A. H. Sylvester (appropriate name!) of the Forest Service claimed to have "planted three thousand names." On one expedition he encountered many unnamed lakes; his party began to give them ladies' names. "'The numbers of ladies' lakes grew until practically all the rangers' and other Forest Service men's wives, sisters, sweethearts, mothers, and daughters had lakes named for them.'" Stewart adds "Toward the end, a joke found still another and called it Brigham—'and now Brigham is on the map surrounded by his harem'" (356).

When he comes to summarizing the "heritage" of American naming, Stewart points to certain distinctive qualities. Most prominent is the variety of names, and the relative failure of attempts to standardize them. "Variety. . .sprang from democracy—that stubborn local pride in the local name, and the feeling that I have just as much right to give an deep a name as you have" (382). More important for the environmental implications of American place-naming is ". . .its close connection with both geography and history" (382). Also, "A final value of our names is their poetic quality" (383) as evidenced by their prominence in American literature. Stewart identifies three sources for the "poetry of a name:" the romantic appeal of its sensuous and sonorous qualities, its historical associations, and ". . .the poetic suggestion which springs from the inherent meaning . . ." (384). In his peroration, Stewart frames a contradiction to his initial evocation of "namelessness." He gives names almost a biological existence; they are "strangely permanent." They ". . .cannot be stricken from the map by official decree, because they are not on the map," but in human consciousness. Only the obliteration of the human presence in the physical environment can destroy them.

"The land has been named, and the names are rooted deep." Time-conscious as he is, the author echoes his evocation of the aeons of namelessness with which he began by evoking at the end an undefined future, in which the one seeking to know what America was like can piece together its culture by unearthing its names and parts of names, as he would a physical artifact. "After all else has passed, the names may yet remain" (386).

In October, 1984, the Forest Service officially named a mountain in the Sierras near Donner Pass, Stewart Peak.

It seems to me that the immense appeal *Names on the Land* had, to a much larger national audience than would usually be interested in such a book, was because, like *Storm*, it was perceived in a "patriotic" manner. It could give the wartime reader a sense of pride and confidence in the strength of American civilization and the beauty of the American land. Like *Storm*, it was chosen to be printed by Editions for the Armed Services, in cooperation with Random House, for distribution in an inexpensive paperback edition to soldiers overseas. The armed services editions were printed on very thin, low-grade paper, and shaped to fit in a pocket. It is interesting to see names of some of the other authors represented in the series: Vachel Lindsay, Rex Stout, Clyde Bryon Davis, Ben Hecht, Aldous Huxley, and, interestingly, Mary Shelley, with *Frankenstein*! The anonymous "About the Author" note at the end of this edition is remarkably perceptive about the author's career to this point: "George Stewart has always sought an uncharted course. His early books indicated the independence of his mind. *Storm* showed how he could make even the weather the heroine of one of the most exciting novels of recent years. This book, *Names on the Land*, is on a theme never before attempted on a national scale."

Another evidence of popularity and patriotism attached to *Names on the Land* is the publication of a long, illustrated excerpt from it in the July 2, 1945 issue of *Life* magazine. Befitting the date, the magazine cover flew the Stars and Stripes over a seascape of battleships. It was strangely befitting in another way, since Stewart had, in November 1944, returned from Hawaii, where he had spent much of that year working on undersea mapping for the U. S. Navy's submarine fleet. As the American public celebrated Germany's unconditional surrender, and anticipated (unaware of the bombs of August), a bloody last battle(s) for Japan, they could look at their own country on July 4, through Stewart's prose. The selection is headed by a title photo in American Pastoral mode, of Coon Valley, Wisconsin ". . .named for what seemed most notable about it: raccoons who came to fish in its streams" (47). Stewart appears to have added some material to his abridged text just before that valedictory "After all else has passed, the names may yet remain," obviously as an appeal to *Life*'s readership—names "expressive of modern ideas" from technology and "popular literature" (55). Another, to me awkwardly-chosen excerpt, appeared in *Esquire*, taken from a section devoted to emigration, the railroads, and the 49ers. *Science Digest* also excerpted parts of the book under the title "How Cities Get those Funny Names." Further evidence of the book's popular appeal is a request from Maxwell Nurnberg of the Mutual Broadcasting System for permission to dramatize material from it on his program "What's the Good Word? (Nurnberg to Stewart 29 May 1945). Readers of *Names on the Land* could even be found behind prison walls. The Reverend K. E. Wall, Chaplain of the Ohio Penitentiary wrote "Several men here have requested that I write to you for a copy of your book *Names on the Land*" (Wall to Stewart 30 April 1945).

Lieutenant Victor Moiterot, U.S.N., met Stewart in November, 1944, as they were waiting in Hawaii to return to California. Moiterot, a Berkeley graduate, had for a long time been a great fan of Stewart's, but was amazed to meet him there, particularly having served on the battleship Princeton. He wrote to Stewart the next year from the Naval Academy, praising all his books, having just finished *Names on the Land*. He is "glad to see LIFE give you some of the recognition you deserve." Moiteret understands the doubleness of Stewart's writing. "It is such a scholarly work on the methods and the history of those methods of naming that is so instructive and enlightening to the reader. You write so easily—that's wrong, isn't it—I should say, you can be read so easily, which is far more important!" (Moiteret to Stewart 16 July 1945).

The appreciation came from higher regions too. Dean Gauss of Princeton wrote "You have done a beautiful job. I am amazed at the scholarly mastery of detail that the book shows on every page. But above all I am delighted by the creative imagination you have shown in making the names tell the story of America's history" (Gauss to Stewart 25 May 1945/*P*). H. L. Mencken told Stewart, anent *Names on the Land*, ". . .your plan for it was ingenious and effective, and you executed it with great skill" (Mencken to Stewart 15 May 1945). J. Duncan Spaeth, late of Princeton, now living rustically near Valley Forge, congratulated him on "the excellence with which you have performed your job," while his "philological heart" gently corrected him on some of his assumptions regarding Welsh names in the Philadelphia area (Spaeth to Stewart 21 June 1945). This approval was not shared by everyone with a philological heart. In 1954, the Editor of *Names* undertook to criticize a number of conclusions drawn by Stewart nine years earlier, leading him to an interesting and spirited defense of his book. He considers a true study of names has to deal with the "psychological background" for a name choice, and if, much later in time, this cannot be determined, ". . .our own inability to determine one should not lead us to the assumption that none existed" ("More" 249). He defends his discussion of the name "California" in *Names on the Land* against the charges that he employs "'poetic licence'" and is "'extremely subjective,'" by making a statement that could apply to much of his work. "Because of the readable and sometimes dramatic way in which the material is presented, some scholars merely have assumed that the book cannot also be accurate in details" (250).

*

This is the sort of criticism that followed much of Stewart's career. It was perhaps easier to oppose the "readable" to the "accurate" in the 1940's, because Stewart was amazingly prolific in diverse publishing venues in that decade. For example, he prepared for the California Historical Society a scholarly edition of T. H. Jefferson's *Map of the Emigrant Road*—for which he did the field research in a jeep, as described by John Forester above. Many of Stewart's own characteristics as a writer he finds in Jefferson as a cartographer. "He was accurate, but in a practical rather than a theoretical way. He was resourceful, and meticulous of detail. . . He was independent of judgment. He took hardships as a matter of course" (*Map* iv). One could perhaps consider these to be "subjective" statements, but how would the academic philologist take the pieces he wrote for *Mademoiselle* and *Esquire* in the 1940's?

In the 1942 *Mademoiselle* piece, nestled between ads for "The new short overalls for the useful life," and for deodorants, lingerie, and pancake make-up, we find Stewart's "Gunfire to Westward: The Pacific Coast in Wartime," a beautiful essay, addressed to "you," and evoking the sense of suspended time and ever-present anxiety on the West Coast with the Coral Sea, Midway, and Guadalcanal guns sounding, as it were, just over the horizon. "Always these days it is with you. Perhaps at dinner you catch the sound far off—tump, tump-tump-tump. You look instinctively toward the sunset, knowing it must come from the west. There is that quick hush; even the children know" (37). And yet all that is "there" is an awareness—particularly since only Washington, Oregon, and California have been considered a "war zone," where ". . .we get up and go to bed and sit down to meals under conditions approaching an alert; under immediate threat of air raid and under the clear possibility of an invasion." As he wrote to Willard Thorp at Princeton, "We had a black-out two nights ago, and everyone has learned how to fight incendiary bombs. My station-wagon and I are listed as a 'mobile unit.' But you know as well as I whether anything will happen here" (Stewart to Thorp 21 Feb. 1942/*P*).

The author satirically attacks the Japanese internment. If "they're moving citizens back into the interior, without trial or hearing, waiving constitutional rights for military necessity. Try to laugh at that! Those citizens happen to have straight black hair and moonlike faces and yellowish skin, but they were born under our flag, just the same" (37), and surely they wouldn't be moved unless there was a real threat. Then the brooding "you" goes to sleep, waking to familiar sounds and unfortunately familiar sights—the rope out the window to haul up the hose in case of fire, the warship-profiles in the harbor.

"There is. . . a fine line between being complaisant on the one hand and hysterical on the other" (80), but in general "we," that is, residents of the Pacific coast, "are taking the world more seriously" (82). The speaker evokes blackout precautions, and the block parties where "You invite your neighbors, talk with them, and speculate just how they will respond when the test comes" (82). You speculate on whether the convoy in the harbor is coming in or leaving for war. It's gone, "But you like to think of it as somewhere out there in the sunset." Likewise, "At sunset the wind blows in from the ocean, cold. You go inside, trusting you'll do what is expected of a good civilian, keeping one ear cocked a little for gunfire to westward" (82).

In 1943 Stewart wrote a piece with similar import for the *New York Times Magazine*, based on the cross-country trip back to California from his fellowship year at Princeton. "Report on the Nation" is subtitled in part ". . .a traveler finds tell-tale signs of war amid scenes of the deepest peace." It presents the spaciousness and diversity of the landscape, and the search within that landscape "for the marks of the war," so as to respond to the question "'How has the war changed the land in the view of the cross-country traveler?'" In a way the pastoral farmlands and small towns are "landscapes of the deepest peace," but within this peace "we moved always close to the war." Military vehicles constantly pass, a farm tractor is driven by a girl betrayed by her long hair. "Yes, even in the farthest town, you look in vain for the young men" whose going "has left an emptiness not only on the streets but also in the hearts of the people." What the author seems to want to emphasize is the presence of absence, symbolized by the empty billboards by the highway and their ironic replacement, the plaques in the town squares full of the names of the dead (25).

The landscape is described in temporal contrast: "Driving across the country in 1928 you saw it in boom time: a few years later you saw smokeless factory chimneys and men standing at street corners. Today you see, under the stress of wartime, a curious mingling. Gas stations, restaurants, even stores, are out of business. A roadside diner bears the boldly lettered placard, "Closed. No cooks." (27) Arriving in California ". . .suddenly the war moved in upon us."
In an echo of "Gunfire to the Westward," the piece ends with the hush at sunset: "Suddenly out of the West comes the mutter of engines. There it is—dark against the sunset—four motors, heavy body, slim and wide-spreading wing, double fin. Then, clear against the dimming sky, the great bomber passes, eastward, toward the sound of the guns" [on, presumably, the European front] (28).

Dean Christian Gauss of Princeton, remarking on this article, noted "Things seem to grow more and more hugger-mugger on our poor campus. We are emptying out three more civilian dormitories for occupancy by the Army and our poor civilian students are beginning to feel that they are being kicked around" (Gauss to Stewart 25 August 1943/*P*).

The postwar *Esquire* stories are really the only conventional "short stories" Stewart ever published. He did write for *Esquire* also a nonfiction piece, "Melodrama in the Forties," based on the naming by 1840's emigrants of sites after important people. But I would like to know where these stories "came from," guessing only that they relate, respectively, to his pedagogical and Sierra experiences.

"Time's Petty Pace" is focused around causality and coincidence involving two families, the Irish Donovans and the Scotch Burneses (Stewart's little joke on his own ancestry). It comes across as a riff on themes in a novel like *Storm*, where history is generated seemingly by undirected chance. The story itself is actually a form of untheological parable about why things happen, as expounded by a paradoxical professor. On a September 1945 Sunday, the professor tells us, each family, totally unknown to the other and living twenty miles apart, sets out on a journey on separate roads which intersect at a traffic circle in a town named X. Although their paths will have to cross spatially, the different distances they have to travel, and timings of that travel, make it extremely unlikely that their two cars will be in the traffic circle at the same time.

The professor wants to convey the idea that nothing occurs by accident; accident is that which "seems to thrust in from outside our known universe of so-called cause and effect" ("Pace" 106). If we expand this universe, we perceive the cause and effect and the illusion of accident disappears. The various circumstances causing delays or accelerations in the families' progress toward the traffic circle are narrated. The Donovans, though starting closer to the circle, have Irish bad luck; they're pulled over by a cop and get a flat tire. They call it an accident, but the professor tells us "The disintegration of that tire was part of a great world picture." Its puncture at that particular place and time can be explained by a detailed cause-and-effect sequence. If it was an accident, "so was the presence of the Donovans on highway number one that morning, so was the highway itself, and so is the existence of the world" (107).

The relevance of this story to Stewart's larger themes becomes evident when the professor refers to our "Godlike point of observation," and in mock-heroic style suggests these "two good American families" are being "borne inexorably toward some inevitable, but to them unknown, event" in the manner of a Greek tragedy. But "we might ask: Why should fate work only toward tragedy? Is not comedy equally inevitable?" One realizes that we are being set up as the readers of *Ordeal by Hunger* are, with an aerial view of a group far below moving across the face of the earth toward a fatal destination. But the professor is also creating a miniature postmodern parody of that epic. The two cars negotiate complexly the streets of X, but crash into each other, as inexorably as "the collisions of empires or of planets." The collision "was conceived, we must conclude, in the womb of time." Two alternative outcomes of the collision are suggested: deaths and injuries, riders flying through windows; or, the reasonable negotiations of the Scot and the Mick, with the youths, Jean Burns and Patrick Donovan, making eyes at each other. A conspiracy, as it were, of time and space, can "to put it vulgarly—make things happen" (108). The professor does not suggest what causation would make for a tragic, as opposed to a comic, happening.

The other story, is also, less obliquely, related to the Donner Party. Stewart imagines some California old-timer, in the image of the immortal Jim Smiley, telling an outsider who is writing a book about Californians, the story of McGinnity's Rock. Old Man McGinnity is hiking up to the Gap, hoping to beat an oncoming snowstorm. Night and snow come, but since as a logger he knows the country like a book, he persists in his journey, using his wilderness knowledge, such as identifying trees by the texture of their bark, to direct his course. Stewart provides a vivid picture of a human moving through a known environment, oriented by his tactile senses alone. Ultimately, though, where his route becomes treeless, he loses his way. Finally he runs into a great rock. He feels his way around it, and realizing that he can't be more lost than he is at present, and will freeze to death if he stops moving, continues walking around the rock, counting the circuits as he goes. Dawn finally breaks, and he stumbles down the trail, having circumnavigated the rock more than five hundred times. "Well, lady, that's your story. . .I hope you put McGinnity's Rock in the book. I guess sometimes the little names have got more story behind them than the big ones . . ." ("Rock" 103).

Stewart made another excursion into nonacademic terrain with a reuse of his meteorological background in an article for, of all things, the U.S. Chamber of Commerce's magazine *Nation's Business*. Needless to say, his title says it all: "It Pays to Watch the Sky." The article takes account of technology that doesn't appear in *Storm*, such as radar and airplane scouting, to emphasize what surely the nation's businessmen knew already, that weather can affect commerce. Perhaps the author's real motivation, as well as any profit he may have gained from selling the article, was to give a boost to meteorologists in the eyes of the business community.

Finally, two articles Stewart wrote for the *New York Times Magazine* in 1944 are worth mention, for in them one finds overtly the ecology which is at most a covert presence in the ones previously discussed. They are more or less companion pieces: "The Bad Old Summer Time" was published in June, and "The All-American Season" in September. Both connect climatic conditions with human psychology and natural phenomena. In the first, an (apparent) paradox is the premise: that "No detail of our climate is more melodramatic than the violence of our summers" (20). The violence is atmospheric, in terms of the intense interactions of warm and cold air. It is also wrought upon humans. "The heat wave . . .is the most important agent of summer violence, the one which does the most damage and most severely affects our people, both physically and psychologically" (21) He discusses the midwest heat wave of 1934, the fear it produced, and the damage to animals and crops. "Every large city is a kind of camp fire sheltered among its tall buildings" (22), magnifying the effects of atmospheric heat. He also gives a small roster of summer idealizers, from Shakespeare to Lowell, deconstructing their use of summer as a figure for perfection by pointing out the climatic limitations of their experience.

By contrast, he argues that fall has always meant more to American than any other season. The very word is an Americanism, condensing the fall of the leaves. It provides "to some people almost a rebirth into physical and mental energy" (18). He revisits the chromatic environmentalism of his "Color in Science and Poetry" in describing the "pageantry" of fall colors in different areas of the country, from the yellow valleys of rabbit brush to the red "strings of peppers hanging on an adobe hut" (18). In contrast to summer, the meteorology of fall is in monotonous contrast to its drama on the land, with the exception of "Indian summer" as an "idyllic interlude" created by temporarily northward-flowing tropical air. "The All-American Season" was evocative enough to lure one reader into poetry, as "the beautiful exciting thing that breaks forth from the dried shell of summer" (Gilmore).

It may have been difficult to place Stewart as a writer, but from the 1940's on, as a result of his visibility, all sorts of people wanted him to write books for them. Erskine Caldwell wanted him to do an American Folkways series book on Northern California (Caldwell to Stewart 26 Oct. 1942). Carl Carmer wanted him to do a book on California in a series of 100,000-word regional histories "by distinguished men of letters" (Carmer to Stewart 3 Mar. 1956). Joseph Wood Krutch wanted him to do a book in a nature series for Prentice-Hall (Krutch to Stewart 26 Oct. 1963). The science editor at Harper and Row, following the publication of *Not So Rich As You Think*, asked him to write a 50,000 word book on waste for their new series Man and Environment (Andrew Sinauer to Stewart 6 Sept. 1968). Even the *National Enquirer* was after him to serialize his *Names on the Globe* (Pat Golin to Stewart 1 July 1975), a request which he indignantly refused (Stewart to Golin 20 Aug. 1975).

But Stewart kept his own counsel and followed his own agenda. His personal journal for 1945-46, reproduced in *A Little of Myself*, indicates prolific activity and writing involving larger projects. It took him but two months (February 16-April 26, 1945) to write the first draft of *Man: An Autobiography*. In April *Names on the Land* was published. From June through September he attended fire lookout school in Plumas National Forest, was a temporary lookout, and researched Oregon and California forest fire sites—all as research for his book-after-next, *Fire* (*Little* 57a-b). A reply to a correspondent says "Your letter catches me when I am just back in town for a few days between stretches of investigating forest-fires. . ." (Stewart to Stanley Williams 19 Aug. 1945).

This active period bore fruit of another kind. On January 6, 1945 Stewart received the offer of a professorship at Columbia. On January 28 he wrote to President Sproul to tell him of the $7,500 offer, and setting down some bargaining conditions (Stewart to Sproul 28 Jan. 1946). Sproul replied with an offer of a raise in salary (Sproul to Stewart 11 Feb 1946). Stewart stayed. This is the last time, to my knowledge, that he actively sought or entertained the idea of seeking, a teaching job elsewhere. It is my feeling that he would not have gone anyway. Unlike the Kroebers, George and Ted liked to be professionally and domestically rooted (Ted had a full-time job at the Oakland Family Services Bureau anyway). They loved to travel—later that year they would drive to the east again on what Stewart called his *Earth Abides* trip—but did not want to move.

*

In *The Year of the Oath* (1950) Stewart argues that lack of academic freedom can hamper the education of the student, as a result of the restrictions it puts on the educator. He cites an anecdotal example:

> A writer, having published a popular exposition of Darwinism, received a bewildered letter. "You seem,' his correspondent wrote, "to be presenting something about the origin of animals that is different from Genesis. This is very interesting. Is there another theory?" The apparently intelligent and open-minded writer of this letter might have been educated in an institution which restricted Academic Freedom. Not only had he been kept from forming an opinion as to whether Darwinism was true or false, but he did not even know that it existed. (15-16)

Needless to say, the author was Stewart himself, and the "popular exposition of Darwinism" his controversial book *Man: An Autobiography*. "I've got the most letters of any book on Man, largely because it irritated a lot of religious people, and they wrote letters" (*Little* 42). Ronald S. Cleland, Superintendent of the Children's Home Society of West Virginia, wrote "If our past is in accordance with Mr. Stewart's theory, it doesn't make so much difference if we be the victims of a great atomic war." Stewart scrawled in the margin of this letter "does to me!" (Cleland to Stewart 28 June 1947). One Miss M. J. Corl wrote ". . .evolution *is* a doctrine, it is a *religion* and completely opposed to Christianity . . ." (Corl to Stewart 17 July 1947). Wanda L. Fix, a freshman at Bowling Green State University, had been assigned to read *Man* in freshman English. She growled on paper at him "What are you trying to establish in the minds of us as young Americans? This country was founded on Christianity and your book is helping to tear it down" (Fix to Stewart 31 Mar 1952). By contrast, Clyde Brion Davis praised the book: "The fact that the literate portion of the public is gradually coming to recognize your stature is gratifying" (Davis to Stewart 5 May 1948).

This very topical chorus of indignant expostulations is interesting to read, particularly since the very conservative *Readers' Digest* had condensed *Man* in its July 1947 issue. As Stewart says, "that took it to a group of people that would be stirred up about a problem like that" (*Little* 72). We remember that Robert Lowie disliked Stewart's personification of "Man." Lowie held the same evolutionary views, but, as far as I know, he didn't receive indignant letters about his scholarly texts. Stewart had the gift for attracting public attention to issues, and thereby educating a populace far beyond the ivory tower, even if this education created negative feedback. On the other hand, Stewart wished that *Man* had been more widely adopted as a college text; he saw it as a good pedagogical tool for teaching evolution. Ms. Fix's response to it probably represents why this adoption didn't occur—particularly in the early 1950's when college faculty were being burned for heresy already. Interestingly, while *Man* wasn't considered suitable for college, it was fine for prison: Warden Johnston of Alcatraz said it "was recommended reading to lift the morale of the inmates" (Mavity).

It should be recognized that anti-Darwinism was—and is—respectable in intellectual circles as well. Donald Worster well points out that Darwin himself recognized, and struggled with, the dual directions of his theory: ". . .organicism could not be reconciled with his observations of conflict and violence". In his major books, Darwin ". . .peristently ignored the implications of his principle of ecological divergence and his organismic tree of life," convinced throughout his life of "the universality of violence in man and nature" (Worster, *Economy* 164-5). Worster considers the "struggle for existence" obsession of Darwin as a construction resulting from the social organization of his own culture. While Lowie seems to accept the social analogy to "organicist" evolution in his studies of social organization, Kroeber, writing in 1944, considered that Darwin's scientific hypotheses, "of which natural selection was the most important," have never been confirmed or disproved by science, and " . . .one may suspect that they are unprovable" (Kroeber, *Configurations* 151). In fact, he is skeptical of Lowie's acceptance of social groups' transformations as "universal stages of culture," becoming a "slip into evolutionism" (Kroeber, *History* 103), since he sees "evolution" as merely the reduction of the particularity of temporal history to "the generalization of formula." More violently, Lewis Mumford (1944) whose work Stewart could hardly have avoided reading, emphasizes the "struggle" side of Darwinian evolution.

> Thus Darwin came to confuse the fact of survival, which rests on many other circumstances besides individual ability and capacity, with the fact of biological development; he confused fitness with betterment, and adaptation with physical prowess. In short, he justified man's contemporary inhumanity to man by pinning the whole process on nature (*Condition* 349).

Mumford, speaking as a social ethicist, pins all the evils of industrialism and imperialism on Darwin. Thus we see secular objections to Darwin on the grounds that his theories are unproveable, that they are unhistorical, and that they are immoral.

Stewart says that he had wanted to have his name left off of *Man*, since, actually, it is based on the fictional device of collective Man as the first-person writer. But one might wonder if the critiques of evolutionary theory from both sides had something to do with this desire, although a few years later he had the courage to put his name on the inflammatory *Year of the Oath.* But I think on the whole Stewart didn't take the whole matter as seriously as did his anthropological and sociological contemporaries. He considers *Man* the most "tour de force" thing he ever wrote, although he doesn't really understand what "tour de force" means; he suggests it implies the "superficial or artificial." He considers it to have been his "greatest example of simplification" to the point of "oversimplification." "People didn't like the thing being made so easy" (*Little* 156). Maybe so, but Stewart's Man is a fairly complex, and a definitely skeptical, species.

Man dedicates his autobiography "To Canis, my oldest friend." He is tired of all the histories of him written by others, just "an immense piling-up of gossipy detail" (3). He also admits to his own fallibility. "I shall doubtless make some mistakes and misjudgments about myself. Being a rather stupid and lazy fellow, I do not read as many thick books as I should. I have realized also for a long time that I am not wholly accurate by nature" (4).

Man, despite these encumbrances, considers that his life is as "plain as an old-fashioned novel" (5), and is determined to tell it in simple chronology. As he sees it, he was originally an arboreal creature, considering his decisive migration to the ground a result of simple overpopulation due to reproductive success. To use ecospeak, Man has, as William Vogt says in his important contemporary book on overpopulation, encountered "environmental resistance" limiting his "biotic potential," and, fortunately, can spread to new habitat (21-22). Nonetheless, this was "a time of supreme crisis," a "crisis of descent," in which Man's ancestors and other hominids had to undergo physical adaptation to dwelling on the land.

Hypothesizing about how he developed "civilization," Man considers that he had, in a "world overrun by sticks, stones, and bones" (30), plenty of tools to create his works, but he needed to gain, in a large part through language, the mental capacity to use them. "I like to think," he says, "that the mothers may first have made and practiced language, and that for some generations the fathers still sat around merely grunting while the mothers chattered happily" (33). He coins the saying "'Women invented language, but men invented grammar.'"

Beyond language, the use of tools and fire transformed Man from vegetarian to omnivore, since cookery could soften meat his weak jaws had heretofore been unable to chew. Since meat was concentrated and easily digested "I needed to spend less time eating and lying around stupidly afterward," and could spend more on thought and play (40). Man sees in this time the opportunity to create more complex, and therefore more survival-assuring, tools, based on the primal act of combining two things to achieve a more efficient third thing. He exemplifies this process in the slow development of the spear, a simple object, yet one which "I, Man, still regard . . .with wonder. . . .In making it, I grasped the essence of fabrication and assembly-line production" (49). Man, who is proud of what he has accomplished over the millennia, sees nothing ominous in this foreshadowing, even though one of the first things it leads to is group hunting, conflict between hunting groups, and effectual war. But he does show some topical reservations. Now parents can tell their offspring "'. . .keep the spear ready, and be quick to strike, or they strike first.' For thus the way of thought is, among hunters. (And so it has been the same story ever since—ho-hum!—but also alas! alas!)'"—and so we are thrown into the Cold War.

By the time Man has reached 100,000 B. C. in his autobiography, he asserts he has reached, physically, a stage equivalent to the present. One important point about this time is that "my greatest difference from the animals came to be that they had to adapt themselves to fit the world around them, but I was able, within limits of course, to change the world to fit myself" (68). In this assertion we can see some of the environmental implications of Man's story, and partly why he chose to tell it. Stewart's previous major works had in different ways explored the human place in an encompassing nature, and the conditions of human survival. Here he is exploring, whimsically to be sure, the "vertical ecology" of that changing position. He wants to present the sort of "big picture" of causation the professor expounds in "Time's Petty Pace," but in a deliberately nonscientific way, so that this reflection can reach out to Man's individuals and be active "in" the world, unlike, with all due respect, the kind of discipline-specialized texts discussed above. Also, I see Man's story as a dress rehearsal for a book already under contemplation, the novel *Earth Abides*, wherein the representative man is forced to recreate Man's story, as told here—at least the part beginning in 100,000 B.C.

In fact, the first invention of this period, which causes Man to "really become lost in admiration of myself . . ." (74), is the enabling technology for the humans of *Earth Abides*: the bow. But Man, in his admiration, also has reservations about the bow. As a weapon of skill, not sheer power, it levelled the playing field, and was "a disturbing challenge to the ancient dictatorship of brute force." But it also, ultimately, made the hunting and foraging life it was created for impossible. "It was perhaps too efficient, and threw off the balance" (78) by decimating species faster than they could reproduce. Thus, to survive, "I had to run faster and faster not because I wanted to, but just to avoid falling on my face."

The "chief adventure" of Man, following the invention of the bow, was the domestication of *canis*, an oft-described process that Man presents vividly. "We thought much the same about various matters, and had really much in common" (81). Of all the advantages Man gains from the dog, he considers the greatest one to be "pleasure." "He at last gave proof of what I must often already have asserted: that I was lord over the animals" (84). A companion process Man spends some time describing is the domestication of sheep, as it results from the awareness of species depletion through indiscriminate predation, and consequent periods of famine. By maintaining a controlled herd, and selectively harvesting them, Man could insure a constant food supply. But more important cognitively than this is that, once confined, "the sheep" become "our sheep," and, although Stewart doesn't say it this way, economy is born. Man even imagines the proverbial wisdom of early herders: "'Dead ewes breed no lambs!;' 'A lamb today is a ram next summer!'" (99). By taming food-animals and growing grain, Man feels, he has learned to work "along with earth and sun and rain to *produce* food" (104). We might imagine, though that this ecosystemic collaboration could itself suffer breakdown from overpredation and depletion.

Man takes as his symbol, for the ever-increasing complexity of his life, fences. Fences always fascinated Stewart, as did any space-defining entities, physical or verbal. The fence launches the constructive and destructive concept of property. I think it embodies that theme we saw him earlier applying to his whole work—the drowning of simplicity in complexity. Earlier, Man had talked about his hunting-foraging prehistoric culture as not "nasty, brutish, and short," but actually idyllic. It was filled with believed certainties, and life was so short that the pains of age were not suffered. It is not that Man is illusorily nostalgic; rather it is a realization of the breaking-off of "culture" from "nature," a basic e-strangement codified by the dividing line of the fence.

When humans begin to live in permanent settlements, villages, this estrangement increases. With them comes the concept of work for compensation, and a diminution of self-sufficiency. Along with work, thinks Man, comes leisure, and, as he has said before, with leisure comes invention. But he sees early village life as still unspecialized enough to be conflictful, and eloquently describes its imagined individuals:

> They . . .must have been remarkably like any people you would meet today. Some were tender-hearted and some were cruel—or, to put it better, each had a vein of tender-heartedness mingled with a vein of cruelty. Some were fat and talkative, and some were thin with dreams in their eyes. And even one may have been thin and talkative and another fat with dreams in his eyes. They had their amusements and their pains, their ecstasies and their frustrations. In fact, for various reasons, they may have been much more like modern people than many who came in the centuries later. (123)

When Man comes to the traditional "cradle of civilization," he becomes somewhat of an environmental determinist. He describes in topographical detail the terrain between the Nile and Indus Rivers, and its most favorable feature, ". . .its variety of hot dry plains and cool well-watered mountains."

> In some mountain valley I would look for the beginnings of my great discoveries. Even yet that is the kind of country which I hold beautiful, and I gladly return to it. From plain and city. I notice also that for the simple life a various country is better. When the Americans were going west, they often settled on poorer land in the mountains or at the edge of prairies because there they found wood, water, and game; but later they took up the lands of richer soil but more lacking in other supplies. There is also another detail of evidence—that the people in many of the early cities of the river-plains raised artificial hills for their temples, thus showing probably that in their past they had lived among real hills. (130)

Eventually, Man says, he no longer attained his "greatest complexity of life" in the village, but in the district of many villages, of which certain ones became larger and more complex themselves—they became towns, and villagers became people of lower standing. A class system was developing. Soon you have the city—walled for defense, as aggregations of people had not been before. Man takes us on a walking tour of an early city—a device that will be used by Stewart later in *Years of the City*—with new social phenomena: professional diversity, a priesthood, a military, multiethnicity, the poor and the criminals. In the city center you find the two edifices which hold this congeries together—the palace and the temple. We have reached around 4000 B.C.

The imaginary philosopher of 4000 B.C. conjured up by Man suggests that great innovations will occur as a result of citification. But the philosopher is wrong. The innovations are only in the realm of social control—slavery and conquest. "Slavery was to be the basis of civilization for 5000 years. . .some people would say that it dominates even yet" (164). Man's tendency toward cynicism about himself increases as he leads us through his city period. He suggests slavery should really be called *"Further Domestication"* (164). He goes on to say that "If I were writing as a social reformer, I might of course grow very indignant over this reduction of the freeman to the status of a belabored domestic animal. But being what I am, I get somewhat confused about it all" (165).

Here again, in meditating about slavery, Man hooks up with William Vogt. Vogt tells his readers in 1948 that "By excessive breeding and abuse of the land mankind has backed itself into an ecological trap" (284). Man, speaking of overpopulation in the millennia B.C. imagines that "there may have come a time when the number of mouths began to exceed the food to fill them" (165) and suggests two outcomes. First, everyone could share equally, and get along well in the good years but die by thousands in times of poor crops. Thereby everyone surviving "would all live like slaves, and they would really be slaves—not to any human master, but to earth and sun and rain." The other outcome, which actually prevailed, was that "most of the people became slaves . . .But a few people lived well all the time, and developed what is called civilization. The practical choice may thus have been whether *most* people became slaves or *all* people became slaves" (166).

A short excursus is necessary here. William Vogt had been chief of the Conservation Section of the Pan-American Union in Latin America during the war, and had witnessed vividly there the conditions he and Man describe above. He had been a close associate of Aldo Leopold for years, and had worked with Leopold's son Starker for the Pan-American Union. Starker joined the staff of the Museum of Vertebrate Zoology at Berkeley in 1946, the year of *Man: An Autobiography* (Meine 477-78), and was to become a one of Stewart's admired interdisciplinary colleagues, even going with him on one of the excursions to Black Rock Desert. I have a feeling that this reconnection of nature and human culture in the age of the city, as characterized by Man, draws on the connections made by Leopold and Vogt between population growth, environmental destruction, and human enslavement. Man, of course, is writing his own story, and nature's only when it impinges on it (which may be a telling point in itself), so he doesn't carry the discussion further, as Starker Leopold would, for example: "As the world population spirals upward, there is a corollary increase in the value and importance of every natural resource" (Leopold 172).

Rather, Man proceeds to talk about the genesis and effects of conquest, particularly its three R's: religion, race-prejudice, and revenge. Man is still sardonic, though. He characterizes conquest as the "true sport of kings," as the first Big Business, speculative yet profitable (170). Conquest is also an "ideology," like that of submission to authority. "And an ideology, continuing through centuries, may shape the life of a people or a class of people almost as much as if their actual minds and bodies had changed" (174). Ideology thus drives tradition and resistance to change. Man has some very interesting things to say about tradition. He sees it as a "two-edged tool." It allows the absorption of everything the prior culture has produced, but it "gives little guidance as to how thing may be done better in the future, as to how new problems are to be solved" (179). I see Stewart in the shadows behind Man here, acutely aware of the changed world of 1946, and skeptical of humans' ability to cope with it, since most people are conservative, and therefore traditionalists. Stability breeds stability as change breeds change. Tradition's balance may be tipped only by, for example, some startling technical innovation, like the bow, or an outside force "such as a shift of climate" (180).

Man considers the invention of writing not to be one of these changes. It was a change in quantity, not in quality, but it did do one thing—it created self-conscious history, and therefore the "drama of the particular, and the emergence of the event and the individual" (190). However, the entropy of the city wasn't broken by this discovery. Man is very interested in the incursions of "barbarian" tribes on the urbanized Mediterranean world, as a perfect illustration of this phenomenon; barbarians were absorbed into city (or imperial) life, ceased to be barbarians, and thereby ceased to be creative (197). Man's negative view of his cities is similar to his view of the Bible—which may explain some of Stewart's poison-pen mail. The Bible is the product of a tribe-city struggle, and preserves social artifacts like slave-kingdoms and warrior-bands. Its stories are not important for happening, but for being recorded in a book held sacred by many people. Of course, in places is also justifies "slavery and polygamy, witch-hunting, the divine right of kings, and annihilation of your enemies by fire and sword" (207).

Carrying this de-spiritualized sense of the Bible further, Man declares "I, Man, have never had a religion" (222) at the beginning of his chapter "'Of Heaven or Hell I have no power to sing.'" "Therefore I fittingly concern myself only with This World, not with the Other-world." In Man's history of his religions, Christianity is one of the few that arose from a downtrodden, or slave culture. But its creators could not conceive of any other except the city slave-culture. "Christ accepted the slave-kingdom as natural and inevitable" (233)—"render unto Caesar . . ." At the end of the chapter Man regrets that the makers of his religions were handicapped by their lack of knowledge of his own history: ". . .they accepted the traditions of my sudden creation; they looked back across centuries of a static civilization" (234).

Whipping through the centuries, Man seems very eager to get to the present, which he really wants to talk about. In so doing, he makes a statement which might serve as a credo for Stewart as environmental writer. He has enumerated four basic "modern" changes: his power-relation with the world; his ability to manipulate the primal materials of the world, like the elements; his new ideas about life itself—especially evolution, and finally:

> The fourth of the new ideas of change is that I, Man, am myself involved in change. Naturally I must discuss this matter, not in connection with control of the outside world, but along with social change. Nevertheless some of the change itself is tied up with the knowledge that I do not exist apart from the outside world but am linked with it. I can no longer talk of "man and nature," for I am part of nature. I need not think of "man under the control of natural forces," for I am myself a natural force. I am weaker than some natural forces; stronger than others. A river may rise in flood and devastate my cities; also I may raise levees to control the river, or restrain it with dams. (270).

Another important contemporary issue for Man, unusual for Stewart to write about, is politics. He sees a battle between conservatives and progressives; the conservatives "possess a satisfactory mental state which they do not wish to see overthrown" (275), while the progressives are more complicated, including the restless who will later become conservatives, and the idealists who "themselves living the good life, wish others to share it." Similarly disabused is Man's view of Democracy, which grew up coevally with "the new modern control of the outside world," and may yet establish a new slavery. Man jokes that Democracy since 1800 can be scripted like a medieval morality play: Democracy is an imperiled maiden, frequently assailed by the old villain, Monarchy. Slavery keeps following her. "Capitalism and Big Business—sinister but plausible fellows—insinuated themselves into her company. Imperialism got here drunk on power."

> Demagogy fooled her again and again. Monarchy even, exchanging crown for colored shirt, moved into her house as Dictatorship. Nor can it be argued that Democracy, like a proper heroine, always kept her virtue. No, she played the hussy with all of them. What is more, she has often been particularly odious for her hypocrisy, frequently bragging of her virtue when she least should. She has even lent her clothes around, so that there are always some masqueraders who are no more Democracy than I am Gorilla. (277)

Stewart shows his true political colors when Man defines democracy as "a system in which every individual counts for something," characterized by "joint responsibility" not accepted, in the United States, until 1932 (279-80). And, ultimately "as surely as I came down from a tree, sooner or later [joint responsibility] means some control over population" (280).

Vogt says "If the number of any native species tends to increase disproportionately, some force will arise to control it" (89), unless some untimely intervention—like all the postwar medical aid given to Europe (210)--disempowers this force. Man is unhappy that there are too many of his individuals. "Modern science and democratic government have tampered with natural forces chiefly by preventing individuals from dying, by fighting famines and plagues . . . If all mouths are to be fed, democracy must protect itself against too many mouths" (281), but not, as in the old city-states, through slavery and starvation.

At the conclusion of his autobiography, Man speaks of the dangers to his individuals, and realizes that his story may not, in the end, have been as plain as an old-fashioned novel. People ask him, he says, what his theory of history is. He has to admit he does have one. He produces history "by making adjustments within a set framework" of two parts: all the phenomena of nature, controlled by "natural laws" and "the dead hand of the past which passes on to every generation a body, a mind, and some habits" (291). As far as the future goes, Man is struck that his manuscript was on the way to the publisher when the first atomic bomb landed (294). He thinks he will probably endure for a while; no natural or human disaster can totally eliminate him. Civilization will not be destroyed by war. The future is involved with heredity and environment—future heredity through "conscious control of population." However "The environment will be, as always, a chief concern of civilization as a whole" (301-02).

*

If Stewart, through his protagonist Man, can accurately be characterized as stepping down a bit from his mid-air view of the environment and becoming more partisan, his subsequent novel only continues this descent. By writing *Fire*, he was, whether by choice or chance, inserting his presence into a debate over forest management that centered the energies of governmental entities like the Forest Service, and NGO's like the Wilderness Society; it's a debate that is live and well today.

In the 1940's and 1950's the concerns of forestry and forest preservation advocates were both similar to and different from those of the present. In 2002, "Ten times as many homes are now in areas prone to wildfire as there were 25 years ago" ("Era" 3), and now the fire line is often the "urban-wildland interface." Human causation and victimization, while significant, were not the centers of attention that they are today. The novel's character of Forest Supervisor in the novel probably embodies the dominant forest value of the mid-century: prevention to insure productivity.

It is interesting to examine the authoritative documents relating to forestry and forest fire prevention in the period surrounding mid-century. The conclusions drawn by the California Forestry Study Committee, in its report to the legislature, entitled *The Forest Situation in California* (1947) are in many ways enlightened even in 21st century perspective: acquisition of new state forest lands, forestry courses in primary and secondary schools. The Committee recommended that the diameter limit for harvestable trees be increased due to the accelerated cutting, caused by high demand and prices, down to the 18 inch limit currently in force. "The whole future of the forest resources of the State is at stake and immediate action is necessary to preserve the young trees now if we hope to have any lumber in the future. We must not sacrifice future well-being for immediate profits." Also, completion of the Forest Products Laboratory at Berkeley was urged, because of rapid forest depletion and the current utilization of only 40% of a harvested tree. Finally, the Committee urged the codification of a "Forestry and Fire Control Code at an early date" (*Forest Situation* 35).

Given these recommendations, the entire report envisages forests as first and foremost sources of raw materials. At the Fourth American Forest Congress in 1953, the "trend toward expanded multiple use and services of our forest land . . ." is considered as much of a resource as product materials are, but a "product" nonetheless (*Proceedings* 88). The California Forest Protective Association spokesperson at the Congress supported a balanced multiple use " . . .through a practical approach rather than through a socialistic and hysterical approach," and implied that too little forest land in the state was privately owned and logging-accessible. The director of the California Department of Natural Resources declared "Fire is the greatest single threat to the adequate production of forest products, the protection of watersheds and other reproducible wild-land resources. . ." (89), but spent much time discussing "mass fire" produced by "enemy action," which seems more about cold war atomic fears than about practical approaches. The influential U.S. government-sponsored report *The Nation Looks at Its Resources* (1953)—incidentally, parodied in Allen Ginsberg's poem "America"—

doesn't look very long at its forest resources, and not at all that I can see at fire. The dominant question addressed by the panelists on National Forest issues was "Why aren't the national forests harvesting as much timber as they can grow?" (91), and the dominant answer was what the Stewart's Superintendent argues for to aid fire prevention—the building of more access roads.

Commercial and governmental views of fire prevention thus saw fires as a threat to "sustainable yield" of timber (despite lip service to "watersheds"). The national policy in the late 1940's, "to put small fires out—every single one of them—before they become big fires" (Little 90) to forestall this threat, seems to be taken for granted by the narrator and the Superintendent in *Fire,* although this was by no means universally consensual. Hawley and Stickel, writing in 1937, denounced the idea of the "complete exclusion" of fire (149). Reforestation was championed for commercial reasons: "We must make more timber grow. Otherwise we are watching the death of a great national resource" (Case 14). William Greeley, whose career as chief U.S. Forester and head of the National Lumber Association bridged two worlds, also seems to support this position. "There is a constant spread, in acres and in effectiveness, of organized protection from forest fires" (229) he says in 1950, praising the increased yield produced by the selective cutting of old and downed fireprone trees (230), a rationale for National Forest logging argued by Stewart's Superintendent in the novel. "Timber is no longer a *wild land* crop" (234), and the "long funeral dirge over our virgin woods" (240) is pointless. This opinion was held paradoxically in concert with the Forest Service's "total-suppression fire policy" (Sellars 82) until the first fire research on "prescribed burning" in 1951 led, albeit slowly, to actual experiments in "simulat[ing] natural conditions" (163).

The latter "sentimentalists," however, having achieved a common voice through the establishment of the Wilderness Society in 1936, were gaining strength. Their oracle was Robert Marshall, a co-founder of the Wilderness Society. It is coincidence that Stewart's article "Color in Science and Poetry" in the January, 1930 *Scientific Monthly* was followed in the February issue by

Marshall's classic essay "The Problem of the Wilderness." There, he expounded on the multiple benefits gained from wilderness that "preserves as nearly as possible the primitive environment" (141), and the contrasting disadvantages thereof. One is "the immoderate danger that a wilderness without developments for fire protection will sooner or later go up in smoke and down in ashes."

Also there is "direct economic loss." "By locking up wilderness areas we as much as remove from the earth all the lumber, minerals, range land, water-power and agricultural possibilities which they contain" (145). However there is no "funeral dirge" from Marshall, no "fatalistic attitude . . . in regard to the ultimate disappearance of all unmolested localities," arguing for limited but necessary infringement on undeveloped areas, particularly facilities for the elimination of fire hazard (146).

Nearer to the time of *Fire*, the environmental community voiced mixed variations on Marshall's argument. "Socialistic" and "hysterical" William Vogt writes that ". . .free enterprise must bear a large share of the responsibility for devastated forests, vanishing wildlife, crippled ranges, a gullied continent, and roaring flood crests" (133). He contends that "Until a realization of the relationship between man and his environment has become part of our education and a principal basis of its orientation, a long-range improvement of land use is improbable" (143). Focusing less on systemic economic change, Ira Gabrielson assumes that we all feel wildlife is valuable, and that fire is its "deadly enemy." "Forest conservation and wildlife conservation are closely interwoven. A forest is a biotic community made up of the total population of living things, both plant and animal" (82), so any management policy, such as fire control, directed toward one, will probably affect the others. Aldo Leopold would probably side with the Superintendent's "sentimental" opposite number, Bart. "One of the penalties of an ecological education," he famously said, "is that one lives alone in a world of wounds" (197). One wound, of course, is to the National Forest, especially in the mountain states; as a result of forest management for production there, he notes,

"There is perennial pressure for extension of roads for forest-fire control, and these, by slow degrees, become public highways" (267).

Into this national debate on forest management policy, Stewart introduced a "test case," in a sense: that of a "natural" phenomenon that challenges, and in a way renders irrelevant at the same time, ideological management debates about how to take care of forests. In researching his book, Stewart had the advantage of the presence, since 1928, at Hilgard Hall on the Berkeley campus, of the Park Service's and Forest Service's joint Forest Protection Board devoted to "cooperative fire suppression," and the California Forest and Range Experiment Station, resulting in a concentration of foresters which Sellars considers "surely encouraged an even stronger commitment to strict fire suppression. . ." (83). But as we have seen, and as he describes himself, his real research was in the field: working with fire rangers, witnessing sites of significant past fires, interviewing witnesses to and firefighters of, them—and fighting fires himself. This was true immersion research, and his accounts of it are almost equivalent in interest to the novel it created.

As we have seen, in the summer of 1945, Stewart visited the sites of three significant 1930's forest fires. The second week in July, the Forest Service let him witness a live fire near the site of the Tillamook Burn, one of the most destructive forest fires in American history (actually, "Tillamook Burn" is usually applied to a sequence of fires in the same area, including the 1945 one), in northwestern Oregon. The fires started on August 14, 1933 and reached their "climax" on the 26th. "Low relative humidities, fresh to strong easterly winds, and high temperatures were responsible for this huge fire which started from a tiny spark cause by the friction of one log being dragged across another on an active logging operation at a time when weather conditions were just right for a blow-up" (Dague 227). Stewart took the infinitesimality of the source, but not the unintentional human causation, of the Tillamook fire for his own in the novel. In early August he visited the site of the 1934 "Antelope" (now Dorris, after the town) fire in far north California, where numerous houses were burned, as well as timber. Finally, September 18-21, it was the actual Kimshew fire in Butte County, near Paradise. The Forestry Study Committee's report mentions this fire: it was caused by a campfire left unattended by deer hunters, destroyed $500,000 worth of timber, cost $130,000 to extinguish, but, says the Committee with presumed irony, cost the hunters only $300 each in fines (*Forest Situation*). That Stewart could create a credible composite fire from these separate instances is evidenced by assumptions that one or another of them was the model for his own. Historian Stewart Holbrook, whom Stewart visited in Portland in 1944, assumed the Tillamook Fire was his model (Holbrook to Stewart 23 Feb. 1962). Robert E. Colby, editor of the history periodical *Tales of the Paradise Ridge*, tells us explicitly that "George Stewart based his 1948 novel *Fire* on this [the Kimshew] fire" (Foster and Betts 15).

Similar assumptions were made about the National Forest where Stewart's fire occurs. Stewart's time in the Plumas and Tahoe National Forests and his fire visits were arranged by the Forest Service. In a letter to the USFS in 1945 he sought (presumably renewal of) permission to be a "collaborator" in Forest Service Region 5, proposing that he ". . .will observe at first hand the recruitment, training. . . of fire fighters . . .during the 1945 fires season for the purpose of gathering back ground information in the preparation of a book describing Fire Service firefighting methods and emphasizing the need for forest fire prevention" (Stewart to USFS 20 June 1945). On July 26 (USFS to Stewart) he was granted the role as "collaborator," ". . .although the name has had bad connotations for several years" (Stewart to Vivian Wolfert 16 Feb. 1948). But for his novel, he created an imaginary Ponderosa National Forest, wedged between the Plumas and the Tahoe. He says a Plumas ranger's wife told him people came to see her husband all the time looking for the Ponderosa. They couldn't find the signs for it (*Little* 164).

As "collaborator" he was able to secure his temporary lookout position at the Sierra Buttes lookout with his son Jack. Sierra Buttes is one of the highest and most spectacular fire towers in California, but by virtue of its elevation, not a very "critical point." However, "I learned a lot up there. . . I made my reports and laid out my distances and my angles on smokes, and talked to the other lookouts occasionally" (*Little* 162). I can testify to the height and isolation of Sierra Buttes, having tried to drive the (much improved since 1945) road up to the Buttes from Sierra City in late May, 2005, and finding them so locked in by snow that I couldn't get close enough to see them clearly. (Stewart recounts that it was as he was being driven back from his "collaborative" stay there, that his truck driver said "'Say, did you know we dropped an atomic bomb on the Japanese!'. . . I think I was about the last man in the world to hear about the atomic bomb" (*Little* 162).

He also followed fires in the summer of 1946, one of which he describes vividly in a *Holiday* feature article of that year. "We breasted the trail, twenty men in single file, each armed with a tool, like a band of primitive warriors with their weapons" (66). After hours of toil, "While we had worked, the fire had swung around behind us. Fifty man-hours of good work gone for nothing" (67). That evening, "with the chill and dampness of night, the fury had gone out of the fire," but this was deceptive, because it was "holding its own through the night, making ready for another outbreak with morning" (69). The crew next day were "'pick-ups'—known generally in California as 'winos' from their drinking habits, and for some unknown reason called 'pogies' by the Forest Service men.'"(Stewart learned the etymology of "pogies" later from B. J. McGraw, who traced it to "pokey," British for "poorhouse" and by extension, "jail" [McGraw to Stewart 3 Dec. 1947]). The "pogies" were picked up on a sweep through a "near-by railroad town," having been offered "the blunt choice between going to jail or going to the fire" (69). The pogies play a large role in *Fire*. Whatever their composition, "As we became fewer, we grew stronger. The crew, which had at first been a mere mass of unshaved humanity, began to stand out as personalities" (130). This social evolution also is fully dramatized in the novel. Like the novel's fire, the Spitcat, this fire "will go into the records. . ." in its case as the "Smith Creek Fire (1946), Plumas National Forest, Region 5. It will be set down as a small fire; it burned over something more than a square mile. . ." But it nonetheless occurred at "an unassessable sentimental and esthetic cost" (131). This kind of work "was often hard and dirty and sometimes dangerous. It was also, however, generally stimulating and interesting and I always enjoyed my contacts with the Forest Service men, who are an unusually fine set of individuals" (Stewart to Vivian Wolfert 16 Feb 1948).

It may have been in this fire that Stewart was almost killed. He was walking under a dangerous "very dry old snag." There was a muddy stream below it, he was tired, tried to jump the stream, and fell forward on his face. "And right then I heard the tree go over. . .The tree hit just about fifteen feet ahead of me. . . . If I hadn't fallen, I might have been just about where the tree hit!" (*Little* 162-3). So here in the fire Stewart experienced a confirmation of his belief in cause and effect, again a dynamic of the story he will shape from this experience.

"When I finished writing [*Fire*] I felt terrible," says Stewart. "I was, of course, therefore, all the more pleased when other people, I believe I can say universally, so far, have been so very much pleased with it." It is also *a propos* to *Fire* that Stewart makes one of his most definitive statements about his literary environmentalism—one which may suggest the difference between his primary interest and that of the other great American fire narrative, Norman Maclean's *Young Men and Fire*:

> I consider the main theme of this book, as with STORM, to be the problem of the relationship of man to his environments. I really think of myself, in most of my books, as what might be called an ecologist. I feel that there are a tremendous number of writers who are dealing with the relationship of human being to each other and the study of the individual minds of human beings. That in fact, has been the great and grand theme of literature almost since the beginning of things. I certainly have no quarrel with those writers, but that is not exactly the theme which I am trying to develop. I am trying to develop particularly, the relationship of man to the non-human environment. At time I may get more interested in the environment than I do in man, but I don't care about that either. STORM and FIRE are, of course, the books that I am talking about chiefly in this connection, but that quality of being interested in the environment also shows in nearly all of my other books to some extent. (Stewart to Vivian Wolfert 16 Feb 1948)

Of the novel itself, it is constructed in the same diurnal sequence as *Storm*. Each chapter in it is defined by one day in the short life of the fire. Because the Forest Service requires, for identification, each fire to have a unique name, Stewart's fire, once it has developed into visibility, is called the Spitcat. This name, like those of other fires in the Ponderosa NF, is taken ironically from that of a nearby abandoned mine—like most, probably leeching its chemicals into the watersheds. Once named, and after it has become a tangible threat, the fire has a personificatory identity, which allows its human combatants to experience and speak of it coherently as an "enemy;" the name, like "Maria," is also a psychological enabler of collective solidarity and cooperation among the firefighters and allayer of inward anxiety at encountering an alien "other."

Aiding this process is the Spitcat's *virtual* existence on the Forest Service headquarters map, which the narrator describes being updated every day, as more terrain is burned over. It is a daily shifting shape moving on the map, and this temporal layering of the fire is spatially rendered on the endpapers of the novel, with each day's spatial coverage of the fire coded by lines and symbols. The spatialization of the fire creates an illusion of control over an environmental phenomenon that humans can't control until their actions have suppressed it and given it its final spatial form. The readers may reflect on whether a truly "environmental" attitude (and policy) would find nothing alien in the fire and therefore no need to destroy it, since it is a recurrent "natural" phenomenon.

The Spitcat's temporal and spatial shape also relates to the "triggering" human character in the novel, its only significant female, Judith Godoy. Judith, the Cerro Gordo (read Sierra Buttes) lookout, is stationed at the highest elevation in the forest. Like the male protagonist of Stewart's later environmental novel *Sheep Rock*, Judith (a college student recovering from a relationship that like fire went out of control) uses distinctly human strategies of control to mold her experience of the fire into a form of familiarity. One strategy is to create the illusion of distance from it through calculated displacement—repeatedly thinking of herself in the third person. Another is to place her experience in a universe of words, talking to herself using literary diction and allusions derived from her English classes (taught, according to the author, by a professor modeled on a friend of his [*Little* 165]).

Judith is both the main focus of interest of the forest fire itself (as we will see) and also of the novel's readers. She has to deal with her separation in sexual identity from almost all the other human actors in this drama, since the only other women characters are minor figures—the lumbermen's wives at the Idylhurst lumber camp, the Forest Service telephone operator, the chief ranger's totally anonymous wife.

Speaking historically, Judith is part of the postwar social transformation in Forest Service staffing. During the war, with men gone, the Forest Service, with "great reluctance," hired woman replacements, but then found that they often made better lookouts than men because they were less restive in the 14 X 14 foot cubicle atop a lookout tower (Neuberger). Ella Clark, a college student like Judith, spent three summers as a lookout, and, like her, had to find a way of aesthetically shaping the "chaos of snowfields and sharp ugly rocks" (85) below her—doing so by finding or inventing a principle of composition in the chaos, as one would in a painting.

Speaking literarily, Judith is a very passive character compared with her ancestress. Only at the end of the novel, and briefly, is she in physical jeopardy. On the other hand, she is similarly a stranger—both to her role and her environment, and her sense of its strangeness can be played off against the familiarity of the firefighters on the ground and the analogous, class-differentiated alienation of the "pogies" from the towns. It is interesting that in *A Little of Myself* Stewart's interviewer mentions that in its *Ladies' Home Journal* condensation, Judith's role is highlighted and in the *Readers' Digest* she is left out entirely. Stewart comments "Well, she could be left out" (*Little* 73) which I find disconcerting.

After all, there's a level of *bildungsroman* in her role. In the course of her summer Judith, who gains male respect and personal skill as a lookout, learns to orient herself both to the physical topography she oversees, and to the topography of masculine attitudes among her colleagues. Her position, as woman and lookout, is intriguingly ambiguous. She is both at the center of, and at a great distance from, the holocaust—which, being a cat, is often personified as female in male conversation. She is also, reversing its sexual identity, to be seen as the object of the Spitcat's desire. During its ten-day life, it steadily approaches her tower with a seemingly willful intent, and her position becomes increasingly in jeopardy until the fire is quelled at the very top of Cerro Gordo. So, as female firewatcher on human-created edifice, seeing all and feeling little of the fire until the last day, she and her tower are ultimately engulfed in the fire's final rage, and she is at the center of the action. She is the maiden saved from the questing dragon, from the inquisitional fire.

As reader, looking down on the fire from an even higher point than Judith's, one experiences the author's complexly layered narration. His initial account of the birth of the Spitcat from a lightning strike is, like many of the "insignificant" causal events in *Storm*, brilliantly detailed. The lightning hits a Jeffrey pine on Howell Mountain:

> Fortunately for the tree, the stroke for the tree, the stroke followed the long spiral of a sap-channel, making three circuits of the trunk but keeping just under the bark. Along this narrow channel, however, the intense heat vaporized not only the sap but also the wood itself. . . a long spiral weal rose from tip to root, pieces of bark were blown out and flew through the air . . .

igniting pine needles on the forest floor (11-12). On the third day, still unseen by the lookouts, the smouldering of the needles reaches a five-inch-long twig, burns along its length, and encounters a pin cone which bursts into flame (44-5). Eventually the fire spreads through the duff to a "half-decayed tree butt," home to a colony of carpenter ants: "Already in the last few days the fire had destroyed many of their foragers, but the colony was adjusted to a considerable and continual wastage of ant-power, and if its queen and bureaucracy were not disturbed, the large loss of individuals was of no importance" (84).

The narrator has already described in detail the fire's ecological effects on wildlife—squirrel, rabbit, owl, and hawk. Now several pages describe its invasion and incineration of the ant colony: "Now at last, as when Pyrrhus and the dire Ulysses raged in the streets of Troy, the fall of the city was near" (86). This fall foresees the fall of Phrax in *The Years of the City*.

In the early days of the fire, the reader encounters two more realms of narrative, interwoven with the narrative of the fire's progress. Description of the ant-city immediately precedes that of the dispatcher, Arnold Sorensen, scurrying about to find a previously unused name for the fire. Implicitly, the ant-world and the human world are of equal significance. Here and elsewhere, by juxtaposing human and nonhuman realms directly, the narrator gives them equal standing. A third realm is a Stewart trademark, the universal narrative of natural and human history necessary to understand the environmental meaning of this individual fire. This narrative is recounted in the epic tone used in *Storm* passages, one which both elevates and diminishes the worlds of human and non-human nature in the present. For example, here is the course of forest growth in the Sierras:

> As the ponderosa pines held the frontier of the forest against the drought, so the red first held it against the snow. But as the digger-pines flung themselves as a forlorn hope against the drought, so a few twisted hemlocks, lodge-poles, and white-barks struggled for their hard-held outposts in the country of the snow. And above those outposts, on the wind-swept heights, naked beneath the sky, was only the clean and deathly beauty of snow and ice and granite. (78)

Immediately after this passage, the Fifth Day begins with a similar narrative of the human immigrants' movement across the continent: "During three hundred years the American went west with the smell of smoke in his nostrils" (79)—through the Peshtigo fire of 1871, the Idaho fires of 1910, to the present: "By [now] economists were predicting a timber-famine, and historians were pointing to deforested mountains to explain the fall of Rome" (81).

In the Fourth Day chapter (75), the narrated has mentioned , but not followed the fate of, another pine cone on the slope near the fire, supported by a twig. But at 5:53 P. M., on the Sixth Day, the fire reaches this cone, which blazes up; the twig topples, and because it is a nearly circular Jeffrey pine cone, rather than one from a sugar-pine or Douglas fir, it goes "rolling and bouncing and leaping erratically downward" (105). This spreads widely the fire which, before 5:53, could have been contained by "a single active man with a shovel." At the same time, increasing smoke has at last been able to "attract the attention of creatures whose racial experience, unlike that of the ants, included a familiarity with fire. Men did not merely stand and wave their arms; instead, they came swarming out with a set purpose and weapons of offense." "Men" are just another species in the natural world, with specific behavioral characteristics, who have had till now no knowledge of, or power over, the ecosystemic effects of the young fire at pine-cone level.

It is only at this point, when the fire's life is half over, that the human species finally encounters the Spitcat directly, with the arrival of the first firefighting crew. The whole narrative sequence leading up to this encounter suggests an ecocentric perspective on the autonomy of the fire as a natural phenomenon ruled by causes and effects beyond human control and prediction. On this day also, another environmental force begins to emerge, in two manifestations.

The newly-arrived Forest Service meteorologist, Dave Halliday, begins tracking an Arctic storm forming hundreds of miles away, one which will ultimately preempt the humans' attempts to extinguish the Spitcat. At the same time, the movement of deep attraction between Judith and Dave is about to commence. I don't contend that meteorology and sexuality are meant to be figures for each other. Rather, they are forces entangled in the same environment. This ecology encompassing human emotions is suggested by Judith's perverse love of the fire, as though it were her child: "In spite of herself she kept half wishing that the fire—her fire—would not be crushed out so young but might grow and amount to something" (112). We can recall the J. M.'s feeling for Maria here. On a contrary note, a boy on the first firefighting squad exclaims "'God! She's outsmarted us!'" The narrator wryly comments: "He was no poet, and he had never heard of *pathetic fallacy*, but quite naturally he personified the fire and attributed to it a malignant intelligence" (115).

The final environmental dimensions of the novel I will consider are two continuing developments that have relevance to the difference between ecocentric and anthropocentric constructions of nature.

In the first case, as the fire grows, and breaks through successive fire lines, its "ripple effect" on the human ant community spreads, mimetically, too. First, firefighters and rangers from other divisions of the forest, and from neighboring national forests, are called to the Spitcat (at the Plumas Smith Creek fire, Stewart worked with a troop from Inyo NF). Then, as commonly done, recruiters are sent to Sacramento and other urban centers to bus the winos and pogies in as temporary firefighters: "From the thick-forested ridges of the Klamath where men look out toward Oregon, from the brush-covered peaks of the Cleveland which meet the mountains of Mexico, from Los Padres canyons where the ocean-mist eddies around redwoods, from arid Inyo sloes where the last pines go out to meet the desert—from them all the men were coming" (168).

The professionally, geographically, and ethnically diverse fire camp is similar to any other one, or to a gold rush camp, or a gathering place at any temporary work site. But in context of the way the fire has been characterized by Stewart, the camp becomes a distorted human mirror of the nonhuman event that created it. As in *Storm*, the fire of cultural awareness of the fire spreads far beyond its literal boundaries. One could say that the fire, too remote from humanity to be detected early, as it grows becomes a temporary urbanizer of the wilderness. It involves transportation, temporary inhabitance, and technological invention. If this phenomenon is extended to the U.S. as a whole—and I believe Stewart, with his historical interludes on emigration, tempts us to do this—we could see the continent, perceived by Europeans as wilderness, self-destructively seducing them to destroy it by its possession of what they will destroy it to obtain. As a satiric take on American immigration, settlement, and westward expansion, this communal impact of the Spitcat undercuts a human-nonhuman separation. The narrator emphasizes this by describing the firefighters' diversity:

> Among the pogies there was a good scattering of Negroes, two Filipinos, and a slant-eyed fellow who must be half-Chinese. Among the loggers, three dark and short Indians, remnants of a slaughtered local tribe, walked beside the tall, blond-haired Scandinavians. The brown-faced Mexicans talked musically in a language the others could not even understand. (214)

Here we have a rainbow colonization of the unpopulated wilderness.

The other environmentally important development in *Fire* is the transformation wrought in the veteran Barlow District ranger John Bartley ("Bart") as the fire progresses. Bart and the new Park Supervisor (referred to above) have opposed views of the purpose for which public lands exist. In an early conversation the Supervisor wants Bart to go with him to visit a particular area where a lot of the timber is "over-ripe," and "there's a chance that we might do something with it" (24). Bart understands his meaning and replies ". . .that's an awful pretty country up through there, some of the nicest mature forest in California" (25). Later, on their visit, the two covertly duel over whether the tract should be considered a "'fine logging chance.'" To the Superintendent "'that's what we are for,'" whereas Bart counters "'Why couldn't we just keep it for people to look at?'" The Superintendent lectures him: "'That's National Park stuff, Bart. You know that! We're a working concern. That stuff down there is crying out to be built into houses. As it stands, it's fire-bait. Think of all the down-timber in there. . .'" (50).

The scenes with Bart and the Super engage the forest policy controversies discussed earlier, over dwindling supplies of forest product raw materials, the relation between use and preservation, and the logging status of public versus private land, National Forest versus National Park land. Connected with all of these, as we have seen, is fire management policy. Bart's wilderness ethic, and the Super's wise use, are at odds. They collaborate to fight the Spitcat, but to Bart the Superintendent's policy is as destructive as a forest fire.

The problem with Bart's wilderness ethic is that he goes to an opposite extreme. He loves "his" forest too much (we might compare Judith's "love" of "her" fire). As Stewart says, the trouble with Bart is that he ". . .got emotional about it. . . He tried to save the wrong things" (*Little* 69). Bart's ecological awareness perversely separates him from seeing the forest "holistically." He doesn't like the Super, who Stewart says "came to represent my attitude more than anybody else.. . .He saw it in the larger pattern" (*Little* 69). Bart's sleepless desperation to save "her," and especially his own edenic "place of beauty" in it, "The Glen," leads him to interiorize himself too much, hallucinate, and become ineffective in outward leadership. Of "The Glen" he thinks "This at least. . .was secure" (224). Yet ". . .his heart was sick for the burning trees . . ." (227). To the Superintendent, "Sentiment never was good for fighting fires; the fire itself never showed sentiment. . .Why be sentimental about a tree? It was just a lot of lath, and siding, and two-by-fours, that still happened to have roots on one end and needles on the other" (229). I'm not sure Stewart was remembering speeches like this when, twenty-five years later, he endorsed his Superintendent's vision. His idea in *A Little of Myself* is that cutting down trees is not in itself bad. "It's part of the cycle. . .Just preserving all these forest doesn't strike me as so important, so long as you don't wreck things by bad cutting of the trees and destroying the land . . ." (69).

The debate between Bart and the Superintendent is current as I write. In an eloquent article David Strohmeier debates with himself the credibility of preserving, or restoring, treasured places like "The Glen." He evokes Aldo Leopold dying to fight the fire on his Wisconsin land, arguing that in so doing, Leopold was thinking like a man, not like a mountain. On the other hand,

> Some things are worth protecting from fire simply because they're important to us—even a part of us—and not necessarily because they're resources on their way to becoming beef, venison, or two-by-fours. . .I fear that we've become so transfixed by the power of ecological sounding arguments. . .that we either fail to recognize how values permeate our

> ecology or we downplay the legitimacy of preserving parts of nature for other than strictly ecological or economic reasons. (32-33)

In the novel, finally, a mutinous stampede of pogies, among whom fear has spread like wildfire, abandons the fire line yet one more time, and the fire leaps over it. The Superintendent decides to replace Bart as Fire-boss, and Bart has a hallucinatory vision: ". . .Bart had a horrible vision—as if what had once been a beautiful young girl was stripped and ravished, horribly mutilated and fouled with dirt and black blood, and left thus to lie open to the gaze of all who passed by" (260). This is an ultimate in personification, where it becomes "more real" than that which it personifies. At home, Bart has this vision again at the moment when, on the slope of Cerro Gordo, the fire is destroying "The Glen."

Toward the end of the novel, Bart and the Supervisor go in search of, and find, that first pine tree which was struck by lightning: ". . .even so, it would live and even grow, perhaps for a century still" (331). It seems to me that we might see this pine and Judith's metal lookout tower as poles of an ellipse, not as opposites, at a distance but attached, two forces embraced by the same orbit of fire. Thus, a "larger pattern" includes nature and human construction. The Superintendent thinks of a simpler reconciliation, an ideal of moderation. He professes to believe that ". . .the forest was not a mine, as the old-fashioned lumberman thought, to be plundered once and for all, and also. . .it was not, as Bart like to think, a perpetual primeval park. As man had tamed the apple-tree, so also he would tame the pine-tree, until it grew for his service" (331). Stewart is ambivalent about taming. Fire and Storm will never ultimately be tamed. He says "I got into a little bit of psychological difficulty there," since "this fire was bad," even though ".. .fire <u>is</u> a natural force. The landscape, the forests, and everything else in the world have been formed against the background of fire. . ." (*Little* 69). In this, he was partaking of, not pretending to resolve, the persisting countercurrents of his time.

Fire received at least as much praise as *Storm*, perhaps even more. It was widely excerpted, and was a Book-of-the-Month Club co-choice, which rendered

Saxe Commins, his editor at Random ". . .quivering with excitement and happiness" (Commins to Stewart [?] 1948). Stewart's acquaintances and admirers were deeply impressed. Corliss Lamont wired him from Columbia ". . I have just finished your fire one of the great memorable books I have read[. I]t is better than Storm and so unique as to constitute a landmark in literature[. I] am a stranger but the magic of your writing has stirred me to this message .. ." (Lamont to Stewart n.d.). Josephine Miles said that the novel made "a terrific impact of outward and inward pressures for the reader to sustain" (Miles to Stewart 8 June 1948).

In many cases the novel has been praised more in terms of executive and management issues than of ecological. The organization of firefighting strategy and constant need for readaptation of it to new situations impressed them Frank C. Newman, Dean of the Berkeley Law School, thought it was an impressive book about administration ". . .precisely because of the complexity of the inter-relationships which it encompasses" (Newman to Stewart 17 Sept. 1959).

On a less elevated note, Stewart's agents were able to sell the novel to Paramount, which finally released the film of that "tingling tome" (T., H. H. 9) in 1952 totally rewritten by Art Cohn and Harry Kleiner as *Red Skies of Montana* (originally entitled *Smoke Jumpers*). The film pits smoke jumping crew chief Richard Widmark against a rebellious crew member, Jeffrey Hunter. Despite its "flabby middle," and its greater interest in human conflict than in human-nature conflict, forest historian Stephen Pyne considers it "probably our best fire film" (37). "H.H.T.," the original reviewer was merciless in his derogation of *Smoke Jumpers.* The characters all "stand around and watch and a few random fires smolder, for the most part, in the distance (beyond the budget, we suspect)" (9). A contemporary viewer, by contrast, says "The film is utterly believable. The fire scenes are awesome" (IMDb). It is also almost utterly unavailable. Unbelievably, *Fire* is the only novel by Stewart to have been made—or unmade—into a feature film.

Chapter V

Earth and Oath

> In earlier versions of Western history, the doings of white people, especially white men, controlled center stage. With attention fixed on the westward movement of white Americans, the older Western history could only recognize Indian people as obstacles or barriers to the big process of frontier expansion . . .White Americans were the leading men (and, much more rarely, women) of Western history. (Limerick 19).

Patricia Limerick's New Western History, with its emphasis on conquest and "moral complexity" (21) has, I believe, a lot of relevance to Stewart's perceptions of the West, particularly in his mid-20th century writings. It is surprising how many intellectuals of 55 years ago already held negative views of human "conquest" (in any realm, with an emphasis on technology), with an implicit or explicit belief that it was rooted in a "separation from nature." If applied to the West of the U.S., such beliefs would undercut the "historiographic orthodoxy" (32) of white domination.

For example, Horace Kallen tells us that ". . .faith in Progress created the progress it was faith in" (29). The "institutions of civilization" are basically tools for human defense against the powers of nonhuman nature, and the basic human legend "tells of wilds remade into natural resources, wastes remade into wealth, scarcity into abundance" (13). Ashley Montagu sees the doom of civilization in the false neoDarwinian valuing of "rugged individualism" [inherent to the white myth of the West]. "Our world at the present time is largely directed by criminally irresponsible adventurers and cynical and complacent men who have grown old in the ways of self-interest and ultranationalism" (102). Limerick would say, however, that "rugged individualism" is characteristic of great environmentalists, such as Edward Abbey (180). However, even a 1950 textbook on "Human Ecology" emphasizes repeatedly the mythical status of human autonomy. "Modern man can, within limits, free himself from certain restrictions of <u>local</u> environment, but in the long run he depends as heavily on the external world as did his simplest preliterate ancestor" (Barnes and Ruedi 26).

Such comments on the anthropocentric ideology that "won the West" reflect back interestingly to Stewart's *Man*, are implicitly opposed and supported in some of his shorter writings of the same period, and culminate in his destruction of the anthropocentric West in his greatest novel, *Earth Abides*.

*

In 1945, Wallace Stegner wrote to Stewart with wry humor about the loss of his "bright wits," partly because he had been "front-footed into" writing a section of Robert Spiller's, Willard Thorp's, *et. al.*'s monumental *Literary History of the United States*. " . . . .I sit cowering with volumes of Bret Harte under my arms to protect them from the rain of tears and wonder how in hell I get through what I said I'd get through. I gather that you are also a Literary Historian of the United States and . . . I have been hornswoggled into doing a section that you should have done . . ." (Stegner to Stewart 18 April 1945). Stewart's essay in this massive tome (1948), which I remember only too well, is "The West as Seen From the East." To me it illustrates an unorthodox literary historiography tied in to the New Western History and the envirocentric critique of civilization. In fact, in an early "New Western History" article, Patricia Limerick uses the phrase "verbal activity" to characterize what Stewart was analyzing a half-century earlier. In criticizing Henry Nash Smith for constructing an imaginary West out of words, Limerick, however, lays the ultimate blame not on Smith's *Virgin Land*, but on the "treachery of words" of earlier writers, and particularly historians of the West who "adopted the terms, the point of view, and the assumptions of the people they studied" (Limerick "Making" 168).

In a similar vein, Stewart undertakes to chronicle "The process of informing the East. . ." about the West (771) in the period before the idea of a "closing of the frontier," (in Limerick's view), threw everything out of joint. But Stewart is as much concerned with the *misinforming* of the East about the

West. He focuses on important early literary figures in order to create "an interpretation both of the West and of the men themselves" (771).

He considers Cooper's *The Prairie* (1827) to be ". . .one of the most important single documents in producing a picture of the West in the American mind" (772). But in many ways, he believes, this was a false picture. Cooper used very few sources. He reworked his formula of good Indians "on our side" and bad Indians against us. In *The Prairie* the Pawnees are the former, and the Sioux are the latter, although in reality the tribes were very similar (he also points out that Washington Irving made the Pawnees his villains). Basically, Cooper is guilty of "traducing" the Sioux, particularly by attributing captive torture to them. "Torture," he says, "thrives among more sophisticated peoples who have learned artistic restraint, such as the Iroquois or the Italians of the Renaissance" (772). "*The Prairie* spread misinformation broadcast" (773). Stewart has much more respect for Irving's *Tour of the Prairies* (of course his acquaintance with it may go back to its excerpt in Henty's travel narrative anthology), but he criticizes the Eastern romantic and transcendentalist writers for either ignoring the West or describing it ignorantly. Never a fan of Thoreau, he has contempt for Thoreau's opinion of Westerners, and attributes it partly to jealousy: "The trappers were gloriously shooting the rapids of a hundred uncharted rivers while he floated upon the placid Concord; they made Homeric revelry and battle at Pierre's Hole, but he raised beans within the sound of the home-town dinner horn" (775).

Ultimately, as I understand him, Stewart finds a Romantic West triumphant after all. "People had begun to love deep romantic chasms and forests decaying but never decayed more than well trimmed sylvan parks and enameled meads" (777). He attributes a combination of rapture and advertising to a sense of Western "strangeness" which was translated into a beauty which persists "as dream and partially as reality."

In a clever little piece with a very long title, "Truth Crushed to Earth at Gravelly Ford, Nevada," Stewart uses a detail from his own work on the West,

Ordeal by Hunger, to illustrate how easily falsehood can be passed as truth, as Cooper grandly did, without the primary evidence of observation. Taking as his text Bryant's line "Truth, crushed to earth, shall rise again . . ." while falsehood shall die, he tells of how he learned that even in matters of pure fact, the discovery of truth won't necessarily kill falsehood. The case in point has to do with the location of the Reed-Snyder fight, supposedly at Gravelly Ford on the Humboldt River. Having charted the Donner Party's itinerary, he found they could not have been at the designated site at the time of the fight. Despite the evidence he gave for this discrepancy in *Ordeal by Hunger*, he says later books still make Gravelly Ford the site, and there is even a grave marker for Snyder there. ". . .Error frequently has all the lives of a cat and fight viciously for existence." It has allies: "The very name—Gravelly Ford—is a good one. It is of the earth. It suggests just the kind of place where covered wagons should be passing and where men might well be killed. Moreover, the very fact of a local habitation is an aid to Error" (47). In fact, a tracer of the Emigrant Road has discovered that Stewart's "truth" was actually error too: the Snyder killing took place even further from Gravelly Ford than Stewart had said it did.

Similarly, in another *Pacific Spectator* piece in the same series as the above, "Tradition and the Skeptic," Stewart deconstructs a "very beautiful and revered American legend" of the West: that of the circled wagon train besieged by Indians. He provides the mythical scenario: the men shoot outward between the spokes of the wagons within whose circle the women, children, and domestic animals are sheltered. The Indians gallop around the circle, shooting arrows from the shelter of their horses' necks. "Was ever a wagon train thus attacked by Indians?" The author has never found an account of such an attack in the myriad of diaries he's read, but even if he had read every migrant journal he could still not absolutely disprove that it had occurred (320). Trains were usually circled at night. What Indians would be foolish enough to attack at night? They were often (like the Donner Party's) strung out over a great distance during the day, unable to reunite and make a circle quickly. Why weren't they attacked then, when most vulnerable?

He then considers Remington's famous painting "The Emigrants," which portrays just such an attack on a disunited train, and is supposedly based on an actual occurrence. The Indians have to have galloped across an open plain to have staged such an attack, but not a single rifle is raised among the settlers; there is no rush for shelter. "Were all those people deaf . . .?"(321). He adds that during the period of heavy migration, 1842-1860, most Plains tribes were not in hostilities with the whites. Stewart writes as a "reluctant skeptic" (322). He sees the myth possibly originating in unsourced place-names like "Massacre Lake," again the result of localization.

So, from these three very different pieces, we could come to a sense that Stewart is contemplating both the how error and misrepresentation are constructed as truth, and the power of "localization," concrete experience of specific place, to compound or combat them. These themes bring us to what I consider one of Stewart's most important statements of literary belief, his essay on "The Regional Approach to Literature." *Post mortem*, Stegner said of him "His interests were essentially regional, and his books reflected his interests, and so his readers and his reputation tended to be regional also. He hit only a few of the jackpots by which writers become famous or notorious" (155). I can see Stegner's point, without wholly sharing his opinion. But I suspect Stewart would not himself have objected to it, while pointing out that *all* writers are "essentially regional."

That is the basic message of Stewart's essay. He starts with a "loose" definition of a regional work of art as one "which has as its background some particular region or seems to spring intimately from the background." But this definition is inadequate. Clearly referring to *Earth Abides*, which he is writing at the time, he says "A novel, for instance, may be located in San Francisco and yet deal with problems of human life which are essentially universal, so that the location in San Francisco becomes only incidental" (370). Speaking more precisely, then, a regional work must not only be located in a region but also "derive actual substance from that location" in two ways, from "the natural background—the climate, topography, flora, fauna, etc.—as it affects human life in the region," and from "the particular modes of human society which happen to have been established in the region and to have made it distinctive" (371).

Glancing back to where this chapter began, one might hazard that such a view implies that real knowledge of nature and society (thus, maybe, "human ecology") of any place is necessary to get as close as possible to the truth about that place. In terms of new Western history, this could mean both seeking continuously to approach the (uncomfortable) truth behind the orthodoxy, and seeking the truth about the status of your own perception of the truth, as Stewart does in "Gravelly Ford." (It is such a double truth-search that allows Limerick to ally herself with William Cronon, arch-promoter of ". . .the social and cultural construction of nature" [Limerick 180]. Perhaps Stewart would not accept the idea that his own thinking allies him with Cronon).

A second glance would ally Stewart's regionalism with the belief that human life cannot function unaffected by nonhuman nature. Under this premise ". . .we can actually say that all writers have necessarily been regionalists and that most works of literature show at least some regional tone. . . [O]ur approach to the study of almost any author has to be in part regional" (371). Reciprocally, the regional identity of the perceiver of the work of art co-creates its meaning. Stewart's example is a quote from Edward Fitzgerald's translation of *The Rubaiyat of Omar Khayyam*: "'. . .some strip of herbiage strown/Which just divides the desert from the sown.'"

> One could do a whole dissertation on the word "desert" in its shifting meanings and suggestions. Here I can only point out that to an easterner the passage is merely literary in its reference but that any country boy in California or Arizona is sharply alive to the idea and image of crossing 'the line of the ditch' and passing in three steps from green, cultivated acres into full desert. (372)

". . .[A]ll literature is likely to demand a regional approach in its study. This is because no one—not even though he takes for himself the study of all mankind—can always and wholly deny the influence of that place in which he lives" (372).

Another example in the same vein is taken from Chaucer's praise of May, in *Troilus and Criseyde*, as mother of glad months, quickening the fresh flowers. "The passage means something directly to me because I happen to have spent my boyhood in a region where May was not wholly unlike the May of Chaucer's England" (373). But it is almost impossible to convey May as "mother of months" to California students. As Judith the New Englander in *East of the Giants* perceived it, May is ". . .the time of the death of the year when the hills turn brown, cracks begin to gape in the adobe soil, first forest fires blaze up, and all creatures brace themselves for the long drought which may not be broken" (373).

Stewart makes three cases for teaching regional literature. For students in the region, there are fewer barriers to understanding it, there are more emotional connections, and finally and provocatively, it permits ". . .a cultivation of an intelligent provincialism."

> I am aware, of course, that the chief argument against such courses is that they lead to the glorification of provincialism. But, after all, the great majority of people are destined to be, in some sense, provincials—and so why not try to make them good provincials, not provincials by prejudice, but knowing something about their own province for good or for bad, and, therefore, better able to function also as citizens of the world? (374)

I feel that Stewart's ideas about regionalism, especially as applied to the West, and particularly to California, tie in very closely to those of contemporary scholars of the Western environment. Donald Worster admires Patricia Limerick's work because she focuses on the West's ". . .inner cultural history, as well as an outer ecological one. . ." (*Skies* 231). Worster finds ". . .expressed in western fictional writing. . .first, a strong sense of the embeddedness of human life in the cycles and patterns of nature and, second, a fascination with the distinctive psychological content of western landscapes" (236). Stewart's Western regionalism, fictional and nonfictional, has these attributes.

One could characterize the cultural and social sides of Stewart's regionalism with reference to two other writings of 1949-50, both of which deal, in different ways, with the automobile as inevitable environmental presence. Although these are slight pieces, they do center on the cross-country travel experience which links Stewart's hitchhiking diary of 1919 and his two big road-trip books of the 1950's.

For the *Ford Times* he described an October road trip from San Francisco toward Denver in—what else—a "Ford coupe." The essay is illustrated with maps based on *A Map of the Landforms of the United States* by Erwin Raisz, the future cartographer of *U.S. 40* and *N.A. 1*. We also are allowed to observe Stewart observing scenic natural spots with his plump coupe on prominent display—no doubt Ted and a camera had come along. This is a car's-eye view of the American West, carefully detailed in its description of the topography and autumn vegetation the driver would observe crossing the Sierras, the Great Basin, and the Rockies. The tree zones at different elevations in the Sierra are carefully distinguished. There is a "rhythm to the road" (34) and a chromatic sequence of vegetation color depending on the terrain. Here we are traveling east again, but we are left crossing the last pass in the Rockies. "I see ahead the smoke from the first of the cities of the great plain, and I know that eastward, ahead of me, I would have to drive a thousand miles before seeing more mountains" (36). The smoky "cities of the plain" reference has the tone of a speaker wishing to return to the "clean beauty of shining Sierran granite" (36).

The same year (1949) Stewart gave a speech to the Northern California Section of the Society of American Foresters which appeared in the *Journal of Forestry* as "A Proposal for Forestry Demonstration Areas Along Highways." This proposal has connections with *Fire* and with the two road books mentioned above. It is interesting for if I may coin a word, its Limerickian acceptance of technology. You can see the influence of *Fire*'s Superintendent—and obviously of Stewart's audience's interests—in the introduction to his proposal. He cites forestry's problem of ". . .combatting a curious kind of traditional hostility against the cutting down of trees, which exists among our more intelligent and altruistic people," who are not interested in "intelligent forestry" but are "imbued with the romantic love of the primeval forest" (356), like his character Bart in *Fire.*

This kind of language might be considered automatically to disqualify Stewart's ecological pretensions, but for others it might be considered environmental realism, in kind with Limerick's acceptance of the "commodification of nature," and exhortation to use the vehicles of this commodification precisely to convey ecological messages.

And that is what Stewart is after, although it might be better characterized as naturalizing commodity. ". . .[E]very tree is a natural billboard" (356), not that billboards should be placed upon them, or even that ecotonic strips be preserved to disguise development. Rather, ". . .the forest itself, as made accessible by the highways, should be used to educate the public,

> . . .first, as to what a forest is and as to what different types of forest may exist naturally; second, as to the relationship of man to the forest; that is, how he may work to its betterment or its ruin, and conversely how the forest may work for man's good or man's harm. I am thinking not of the forest primeval, but of the working forest; not of the forest as God made it, but as the forest as man has remade it, and sometimes unmade it . . . (356)

Stewart proposes his "demonstration forests" with these purposes on two routes—California 89 and U.S. 40. The former has the advantage of passing through ". . . .the usual large areas of cut-over and burned-over country;" the latter, particularly between Roseville and Reno, of traversing all the tree zones of the Sierra, allowing one to view ". . .all stages of devastation and regrowth."

In these demonstration areas Stewart proposes not just labels on trees identifying them ("There is nothing duller in the world. . ."), but information on ". . .when the tree first sprouted from a seed, what its average growth has been, when it will be ready to be harvested, what will be the probable use of its wood." The visitor can also be told about the "dynamic and dramatic" features of the forest as a whole, and the history of such phenomena as a grown-over forest fire scar (357).

Another feature of the Western Sierra that he suggests for such demonstration areas is the enduring devastation produced by hydraulic gold-mining and other exploitive technology, and the partial "unaided reforestation" that has occurred since mining, lumbering, and milling ended in that area. He suggests the whole history of the area "with respect to man" could be vividly presented with the surviving sawdust pile near Baxter as a "text." He suggests demonstration areas of "old-fashioned" strip-logging beside contemporary ones, selectively logged. Above all, and in tune with a main literary theme, such a series of demonstration areas should revise its information regularly, so that a recurrent visitor can experience the effects of time on forest change. "Forestry, like most other subjects, can be presented to the public best. . . not by books and articles, not by lectures, not by motion-pictures, but by concrete reality, in this case, the forest itself" (359).

Here we have "reading the landscape" with a vengeance. As usual Stewart's regionalist proposal of place as text was prophetic, and various realizations of his proposal are widespread—although ironically, you most usually have to exit the Interstate to experience them, for example the "Cradle of Forestry" in Pisgah National Forest near my residence. Since he clearly distinguishes between National Forests and National Parks (at present there are many trying to blur this distinction), Stewart is not arguing for a "commodification" of the Pristine, but public awareness of what I guess we would have to call "wise" (versus unwise) "use."

The opposition of place and book he makes above connects to a final essay of this period, equally prophetic, equally accepting of technology, and widely noticed. Anyone familiar with the plans for googlization of research libraries today might be struck by Stewart's 1949 prophecy of "The Twilight of the Printed Book." Here, he foresees (100% seriously?) the supercession of the printed book by "microfilm, miniprint, and audible recordings" (32). He accuses book publishers of being unaware their product is being superseded, ". . .like old-time railroad men who refused to take the automobile seriously." He defends his case by refuting those who would consider his title a "scare tactic." One defense is, of course, historical precedent, as with the railroad-men: many common products of technology in use "now" were inconceivable not too long ago (as, he says, the bow and arrow probably was inconceivable before its invention). Another is that microfilm and other projectible modes of accessing print are difficult and cumbersome. He gives examples of miniaturization, suggesting that the large encyclopedia is the "entering wedge," in that a projector and film equivalent of such a physically large text is actually more portable and takes up less space.

Before he died, Stewart, I am sure, was aware of the dawn of the personal computer. But it is interesting to see his comments in 1949 suggesting the attributes of a new technology of which he, then, could not conceive, although he almost does--not in form but in function. He imagines a "remote-control lever" triggering a device which sequentially displays groups of words on a flat surface, adjustable to the natural reading rhythm of the operator ". . .[T] he eyes no longer have to go to the words, but the words come to the eyes" (35). He also suggests an electronically-run "facsimile machine" (39).

From the point of view of literature, he imagines a progressive regression—the audio book (although he doesn't use that neologism). With the audio book poetry can return to its natural mode of orature, "oral transmission," after aeons of suffering from the invention of writing and of printing, '. . .two body blows from which it never recovered" (37).

To skeptics, Stewart argues that his suggestions are not radical, but actually conservative, since he does not foresee the death of periodical print. In history, technique replacements are never complete. But he toys with the idea of the Sunday newspaper not being thrown against your door; instead it will be softly delivered on one single four by five card—". . .to the great ease of the newsboy and the wholesale conservation of spruce forests" (39).

At least one erudite reader did not pick up on the tone of "Twilight." Albert Guerard of Stanford, assuming, I take it, that Stewart was bewailing the end of books and libraries, exuded fellow-feeling: "We professors of English are suspected of inveterate toryism . ." (Guerard to Stewart 22 Jan 1949).

The fact is that Stewart's writerly collaborations with technology at mid-century were occurring in the time when he was involved in two very different projects that gave the lie to both technological control and its counterpart in social control. Both of these projects involved crises in the life of human communities, threatening their cohesion and even their existence. One was an imagined crisis, caused by environmental factors beyond human control. The other was a real crisis, caused directly by the actions of humans. The first involved the entire human species as its community, whereas the second affected a microcosmic community—the university. Interestingly, the "printed book" is at risk in both—in one case, its survival, in the other, its freedom of access.

The first project is, of course, his novel *Earth Abides*. The second is the arc of active response to the California Board of Regents's imposition of a loyalty oath on university employees, resulting in Stewart's courageous history and manifesto, *The Year of the Oath*. The former was chosen, the latter was thrust upon him, although he chose to be the face of the opposition. Although the California Oath Controversy has no inherently "environmental" components, I hope the reader will find, from Stewart's earlier views of human culture's embedment in nature, that threats to cultural cohesion, even when not environmental in causation, can still be construed as threats to the environment conceived holistically: ". . .the student of culture can call for aid upon each and all of the other branches of learning" (Lowie *Culture* 18).

*

On December 15, 1945, Stewart wrote to his literary agents in New York, "For some time I have been thinking over a book, the idea of which I might pass on to you now.

> This will be a novel—as usual with me, of a rather fantastic type. Perhaps I shall call it WORLD WITHOUT END, unless that has been used before. It will be a novel of the future, and the title may seem ironic at the opening. The story will begin with the death of practically everyone in the civilized world by a plague, very suddenly. In the United States on[ly] a few hundred people are left, scattered and isolated. The theme from then on will be double---what happens to the country after man has gone, and the gradual re-establishment of man at a simpler level.

"I have a lot of ideas for it already," he says, and requests ". . .don't say anything about it at present" (Stewart to Mrs. Mary Squire Abbott 15 Dec. 1945). In *A Little of Myself*, he says "I don't know when the idea first came to me. I suppose it was probably five or ten years in my mind" (69). In his *Fire* letter to Vivian Wolfert, Stewart tells her:

> I am about one-third of the way through with the first draft of a new novel. . .This novel is tentatively titled Earth Abides. It deals with the possible near ext[inct]ion of the human race and what will happen to all the world after the human race has thus nearly been wiped out by some kind of disease which does not affect anything else. We have the struggle between the various plants and animals, and so forth, and then in the later stages of the book, we go on to see the way in which a new human society may re-establish itself. (Stewart to Wolfert, 16 Feb. 1948)

He must have written the last two-thirds fast, for the next month his editor Saxe Commins told him jubilantly: "Once again I am overwhelmed! EARTH ABIDES is magnificent and I can only marvel at your originality, ingenuity, and above all else your ability to make the most complicated scientific phenomena crystal clear." He adds: ". . .I see the novel as the finest piece of science-fiction I have ever encountered" (Commins to Stewart, 8 March 1948).

These various comments on the genesis of *Earth Abides* are significant because it has been defined in two generic ways which have caused tremendous misconstruction of Stewart's purpose and his achievement: that it is generically "science fiction," and that, subgenerically, its plague is figurative for nuclear war.

The December, 1945 letter places his thinking about the novel after the bombing of Hiroshima. "Five to ten" years of thought before its publication places its genesis before the "hell bomb" was dropped. "Nuclear fear" was alive and well in the late 1940's, but for much of the decade the public was in a "collective trance about the nuclear utopia" (Boyer 115). Unfortunately, plenty of critics take it for granted that Stewart's novel is part of the "literature of nuclear disaster." While calling it an "ecological parable," David Dowling derogates it as yet one more reworking of "post-nuclear" cliches, with humans reduced to primitivism ". . .salvaging what [they] can of a technological age," and quotes a Frederick Pohl review of it: '"There is nothing to be said in this story that has not been said in a hundred of stories before'"(90). Paul Boyer places it as a "post-Hiroshima apocalyptic novel," and does concede that it is ". . .not explicitly about nuclear holocaust, bit . . .is clearly a product of, and comment upon, the pervasive fears of the early atomic era" (262).

There are many different tonalities of nuclear awareness suggested here. The real outpouring of nuclear war (*pre-*, *cum-*, and *post-*) occurred after President Truman announced on January 31, 1950, the development of a hydrogen bomb. It would be hard for a reader not to associate Stewart's novel with the nuclear fears generated in the fifties, and the geometrical replication of fear-generating material in every conceivable medium. "For the generation coming of age with the atom, the messages emanating from atomic narratives formed an integral part of its socialization," says Michael Sheibach in his outstanding *Atomic Narratives and American Youth* (10). As one of that generation, I'm sure that the electrifying effect *Earth Abides* had on me was enhanced, as it must have been for countless of my contemporaries, by the atmosphere in which it was read, independent of Stewart's actual intent.

Because Stewart's intent was not to write a post-nuclear narrative. *Earth Abides* was "conceived before the time of the atomic bomb. In a way it's curious people were interested as much in it as they were, because they were thinking so much in terms of the atomic bomb—as they still are" (*Little* 82). As Stewart says, his whole plan was based on *only humans* being decimated, because he wanted to dramatize their survival. In a way, the purpose of this premise is to deflate the idea that only humans have the power, through their technology, to destroy themselves. W. Warren Wagar comes much closer to Stewart's meaning when he places *Earth Abides* in the tradition of the "biological disaster" novel, more or less originating in English in Mary Shelley's *The Last Man* (161-63), which was itself inspired by Jean-Baptiste Cousin de Grainville's *Le Dernier Homme* (Davis 283). In fact, a much closer source of Stewart's scenario is not in his nuclear present, but in his micro-organismic past, namely the influenza pandemic of 1918-19, of which Stewart himself was a victim.

> The interweaving of the war and pandemic make what from a distance of a half-century seems to be a pattern of complete insanity. On September 11 Washington officials disclosed to reporters their fear that Spanish influenza had arrived, and on the next day thirteen million men of precisely the ages most liable to die of Spanish influenza. . .lined up all over the United States. . .to register for the draft. (Crosby 46)

In *Earth Abides,* Ish's physical isolation from news of the plague replicates the World War I public's intellectual isolation from awareness of its immanence. "Until Spanish influenza attained the status of a national catastrophe in autumn 1918, few American paid much attention to it" (Crosby 17). Partly, this was due to its initial presence among the military, at close quarters in mainland reservations, and isolated from the general population, as Stewart was, or in transit on shipboard, spreading and carrying it to U.S. ports. San Francisco was devastated, and all citizens were required to wear masks. Crosby describes the frenetic celebrations there of the armistice: "The scene of tens of thousands of deliriously happy, dancing, singing, masked celebrants was one that could only be described by a word not to enter the language until the next decade: surrealistic" (105). The world scale of the Spanish Influenza pandemic is that of

Stewart's plague. Collier quotes a Dutch doctor: "'Why did I become a doctor? I can do nothing to help, and soon there won't be any more people'" (183).

The recent news that the Spanish Influenza virus has been regenerated from preserved tissue is strangely intertwined with the hypothetical source-event of Stewart's novel proposed here. One of the three people whose body tissue was "miraculously" preserved along with the virus was Private James Downs, encamped in September, 1918 along with 33,000 other soldiers at Camp Upton, where Stewart was hospitalized four months later. In September, one of every ten men in the camp was hospitalized (literally, that translates to 3,300), where Private Downs died on September 26 (Kolata 30). To a soldier confined in this situation, it would have been a microcosm of death, of the plague-ridden world Kolata characterizes:

> Children were orphaned, families destroyed. Some who lived through it said it was so horrible that they would not even talk about it. . .It came when the world was weary of war. It swept the globe in months, ending when the war did. It went away as mysteriously as it appeared. And when it was over, humanity had been struck by a disease that killed more people in a few months' time than any other illness in the history of the world. (5)

Another source that should not be discounted is the periodic bubonic plague outbreaks in the Bay Area, originating in Chinatown in 1900, and re-emerging in Oakland in 1908, the year of the Stewarts' arrival in Southern California. No one in the state could have avoided reading the dramatic Hearstian "apocalyptic headlines and qotations from Daniel Defoe's *Journal of the Plague Year*" (Davis 252). "The American Medical Association's official journal, *American Medicine*, warning of a potential continental epidemic with 'an appalling number of deaths,' attacked San Francisco authorities for the 'crime' of letting the plague escape" (Davis 254).

So I see *Earth Abides* in a "back to the future" manner, presenting its triggering catastrophe as something that has happened before, and will happen in the future, whatever else humanity may do to itself. It could almost be seen as a quiet rebuke to nuclear catastrophists. Greg Garrard astutely defines a tradition of apocalypsism as an environmentalist tool, from Malthus to Ehrlich (the latter seen as considering humans themselves, through overpopulation, a disease). But *Earth Abides*, dramatizing an organically-caused apocalypse, sort of defies Garrard's definition. Ultimately its "apocalyptic rhetoric" is not "tragic," and it does not evoke apocalypse in an attempt "to avert it by persuasive means" (Garrard 95, 99), since no persuasion can avert it.

There are linkages here of course that could lead *Earth Abides* more directly into the realm of its present. One of the "nuclear fear" books which did appear before Stewart's novel was David Bradley's notorious description of the 1946 Bikini Atoll bomb tests, *No Place to Hide*. Bradley's frightening juxtaposition of annihilative explosions and idyllic tropical nature leaves the reader shaken. The "land enchanted" of the coral reef is next door to a shoreline coated by an oil slick ". . heavily impregnated with fission products" (85, 105). The question, says Bradley, ". . .is not political so much as biological. It is not the security of the political system but the survival of the race that is at stake" (165). And all this watched over by a corps of marine biologists, oceanographers, Fish and Wildlife Service scientists. One of these was Roger Revelle, director of the Scripps Institute of Oceanography, who in 1952 invited Rachel Carson to join him as historian for a group of government biologists and botanists studying the biological effects of radiation at Bikini and elsewhere; Carson, despite a strong desire to go, had too many commitments to do so (Lear 237-8). Revelle, an acquaintance of Stewart's and a fellow graduate of Pasadena High School, wrote him from the Scripps Institution ". . .pure unadulterated fan mail" about *Earth Abides*. His whole family thinks the book is wonderful, and has a jingle: "'Stewart helps more than Toynbee can, to understand the ways of man'" (Revelle to Stewart 5 Jan. 1950). If Revelle's reports on Bikini, the Fish and Wildlife Service's reports (Lear 237), or any other such information, had reached Stewart, it might have affected his novel. A contact from the other side would have been Robert Oppenheimer, who, along with Ernest Lawrence and other Livermore Laboratory folk was pretty close to

Stewart's friend Charles Camp. Stewart and Camp were both members of the Cosmos Club, a faculty-centered group frequented by many Los Alamos figures. In fact, Camp has an anecdote about Lawrence at the club toward the start of the war mentioning "a lump of this stuff" which "might blow up the whole East Bay." Camp wasn't sure what he meant then, but "it was the beginning of atomic fission" (*Little* 287).

Inextricable from the nuclear connection, as can be seen from Commins's letter above, is the idea that *Earth Abides* is a work of "science fiction." As winner of the first International Fantasy Award in 1951, as one of *Locus Magazine*'s All Time Best Science Fiction Novels (1987), and a Prometheus Hall of Fame finalist in 1990 (Shade) it must bear that *cachet*. Where it receives popular esteem today, it is usually through the lens of that category. To the extent that any "post-apocalyptic" fiction is "science" fiction, the category applies.

But I don't think Stewart thought of himself as writing "science fiction." If any generic category applies to *Earth Abides* today, it is the underused one created by John Stadler in 1971, "eco-fiction." But it is useful to trace the impotence of human science's material creations in the novel, as it is to see the potency of natural forces in the absence of humans and progressive disfunctioning of their technological creations. Stewart has created a post-apocalyptic novel about the *failure* of "science," particularly in its primal, etymological sense from the Latin *scio*—to "know"—to understand conceptually the workings of the world. *Earth Abides,* for all its beautifully realized characters, is a conceptually-shaped novel about deconceptualization. Its elegaic mood derives from the loss not just of a "known world" but of an ability to know in the world; its suggestion of redemption is based on the possibility of a slow re-evolution (Stewart calls it "rehabilitation" [*Little* 181]) toward that knowledge, symbolized in the creation of technology that plays such an important role in *Man*—the bow and arrow.

If we consider these two themes of concern in *Earth Abides*, ecological processes and science in the way I have defined it, Stewart has a third, and maybe dominant one which is intimately involved in the first two—we might "label" it under the terms behavioral psychology and social anthropology. He wants us to experience the effects of the first two forces on the human species individually and collectively. In so doing, he draws richly on the work of Robert Lowie, Alfred Kroeber, Carl Sauer (who is, in the book, one of Ish's deceased Berkeley professors), and other interdisciplinary humanistic scholars. He tells us he interviewed many scholars and engineers—as on the durability of the Golden Gate Bridge—about what might happen under the conditions he creates (*Little* 180-181). As for Carl Sauer, Stewart's son John says "Earth Abides was influenced greatly by talks with Carl Sauer, a leading anthropologist of the time. I remember going with my Dad to one meeting with Carl. My Dad indicated that Carl was of great help to him, and was very impressed by him" (Email to the author 2 Nov. 2001).

I would like to share a "reading" of *Earth Abides* under the three heads discussed above, but first I think it is important to recognize that however skeptical one might be of the "science fiction" pigeonhole, those contemporary readers most appreciative and understanding of the novel read or have read it as a member of this genre, and on the basis, in one sense, of shared experience. The most insightful discussions of *Earth Abides* today cannot be found in the *MLA Bibliography*, but rather in the proliferation of online science fiction websites. Marian Powell, on "Strange Horizons" speaks for many when she says that "*Earth Abides* is probably more relevant now [2004] than when it was written." She also speaks for many when she says that she first read it "decades ago." It is noticeable that lots of the appreciative commentary I am referring to takes the form of testimony, and that the writers refer to their first reading of *Earth Abides* as teenagers. John Shade, on his "Lost Books" website, uses it as the representative lost book—the unacknowledged classic. One of his correspondents says "I first read the paperback in about 1965 and have never forgotten the story." Another: "I read a battered paperback copy of "Earth Abides" when I was 14 which is more years ago than I'll comfortably admit). It has influenced my life ever since." (One of Stewart's own correspondents remarks that her 16-year-old daughter read the novel and said "'It's a lot better than all the books the kids are reading—*Catcher in the Rye*, *Lord of the Flies*—it's a darn good book'" [Mary W. Cutting to Stewart 14 Nov. 1962]).

As far as I can figure, I first read *Earth Abides* around 1957, when I too was 14 years old. It has influenced my life deeply ever since, and hopefully, my environmental advocate daughter's. "Every time I read it, I'm profoundly affected. . .," as James Sallis says. It possesses he says, quoting Adam-Troy Castro on the "Classic Sci-Fi" website, "'. . .a great, dark beauty'" (Sallis).

I think the key to this testimonial reverence can be found in Michael Scheibach's comments on the "nuclear" generation, referring to the sources of Tom Hayden (*et. al.*)'s 1962 Port Huron Statement (previously cited). "The themes that underscored youthful protests during the Turbulent Decade [the 1960's] were a continuation of those themes accessible *to* youth, directed *toward* youth, and expressed *by* youth between 1945 and the late 1950's" (16-17). He applies Norman Ryder's conception of a "cohort" to this group of youth—a coeval group subjected to the same forces. For Ryder ". . .cohort differentiation . .may be the result of 'traumatic episodes like war and revolution [that] become the foci of crystallization of the mentality of a cohort'" (17). It is interesting how well the cohort concept applies to the "tribe" in Stewart's novel, but it could also be said to differentiate the cohort of *Earth Abides* readers of the 1960's generation, including me and my illustrious contemporary Stephen King, who drew (almost plagiaristically, according to my daughter) on it for his own *The Stand*, from the—perhaps encompassing—cohort of youth affected by the presence of nuclear fear.

Considering the "cohort" idea, and *Earth Abides* as a possible contributary to 60's generation consciousness, it is intriguing to find Stewart and Charles Camp as signatories of a Berkeley Fellows document pleading with rioting student demonstrators of May, 1969, to cease their disturbances, for the sake of the university. This is of course the year after Stewart's environmentalist tract, *Not So Rich as You Think* was published. *Earth Abides* mourns the death of the university and the intellect it fostered. The Fellows' statement says the university is "'. . .man's greatest weapon in winning the battle of the intellect over the environment'" ("Alumni").

Whatever irony may be drawn from the above, Stewart's novel goes, as I said, deeper than technology, to evoke ecological fears based on human vulnerability as part of nature, and thus could tap profound adolescent anxieties during the years of identity-formation. When I cried at 14 over *Earth Abides* I was in the world of Margaret, to misquote a famous ecological poem by Gerard Manley Hopkins ". .It is the fate that man was born for / It was myself I mourned for."

One initial issue of the novel must be discussed and dismissed right away. That is the contention over the name of the protagonist, Isherwood Williams. "'It was my mother's maiden name and so she stuck it on me. Bad, wasn't it?'" he tells Em. George T. Dodds, as do many, sees its inspiration in Alfred Kroeber's Ishi, who, like Isherwood, was the last of his tribe, the Yahi, and whose self-given public name, "Ishi" means "man" in Yahi. "Like Ishi," says Dodds, "Ish emerges from the mountains to a new and incomprehensibly different world, the one going from the stone age to the modern industrialized age, the other doing the converse" (Dodds). Stewart told his student and collaborator Joe Backus that he used "Isherwood" so he could have a name from which "Ish" could be derived, as it means "man" in Hebrew. The Hebrew for "woman" is "ishah" (Stewart notes ". . .which is, incidentally, now the trade name of a widely advertised perfume"). He couldn't have an "Ish" meeting an "Ishah," so he used "Em," Hebrew for "mother." Hence, the association is with the Book of Genesis. He also chose Ezra, as Hebrew for "helper" ("Interview" 55).

The recent exhaustive anthology on Ishi by Karl and Clifton Kroeber, inspired by the great debate over the reburial of his remains following the discovery of his brain at the Smithsonian, adds a certain depth to this naming question. Obviously, as a fairly close friend of Alfred Kroeber, Stewart would have known a good deal about Ishi, even during the period before Theodora Kroeber's *Ishi in Two Worlds* (1961), when he had been to a great extent publicly forgotten. But Ishi was brought to San Francisco in 1911, and his discovery generated "fantastic newspaper accounts, eager crowds, and a deluge of requests to exhibit Ishi on vaudeville and in traveling shows . . ." (Adams 28). As a 16-year-old, Stewart must have been exposed to this publicity. Perhaps he was, as a newly-minted Californian, somewhat sympathetic to Ishi's position. When he came to conceive and write *Earth Abides,* Stewart had already written *Names on the Land,* and reflected deeply on the philosophy of naming. As Gary Strankman eloquently puts it, Ishi was thrice de-humanized by white namers: as "Indian," as "wild," and as "Ishi;" with the last name, "The tribal man, holding the power of his name to himself, becomes Ishi—one of the people, a people of one, a tribe of one, all others having been destroyed by the namers." "The artificial name of the nameless one eclipses the real names of the namers. His authenticity overwhelms the artificial title, and he does become a unique man. The generic "man" becomes the individual: Ishi" (361).

In *A Little of Myself* Stewart somewhat evades the "man" question: "Well, I really explained that pretty well in the book, the fact that we had to have an observer, and Ish was the observer, with that curious intellect, and Em is the figure of courage that holds them all together" (182), which is a response about roles, not about the meaning of names. If we think of Ish in the shadow of Ishi, we can more meaningfully see him as someone like Ishi, deprived of identity by annihilation of his culture, creating an identity in exile from meaning, as did Albert Camus (Vizenor 365-8). Of course, on a more trivial level, in the late 1940's you'd just have to go a bit down the California coast to find a real Isherwood, Christopher, that is, living the fairly decadent life described in the posthumous *Lost Years.* I can't think of anyone more removed in character from the fictional Isherwood than the real one, but the name may have been present in Stewart's mind. He may even have met the man, through his Hollywood connections, when he visited the Walt Disney studios in 1945. The whole discussion of the names seems digressive to me. Why can't a writer create characters whose names have multiple references—for example Hebrew and Native American? After all, there was/is a belief that the latter were descendents of the former.

Earth Abides is dedicated to Stewart's daughter Jill. Its major epigraph is from Ecclesiastes 1.4, "Men go and come, but earth abides," and the novel is pervaded by the allusive presence of that secular and lyrical Old Testament book. In it, the author has used his customary division into sections (3) divided by summary interchapters, "quick years." The first section uses the original working title for the entire novel, "World Without End," and has its own epigraph from a source in violent contrast to Ecclesiastes, *Chemical and Engineering News,* concerning speculations on the possible deaths of millions from a viral mutation (as this text is being written in October, 2005, such speculations are rife, with relation to Avian Flu).

The novel begins with the italicized transcription of a radio broadcast, another beginning Stewart was proud of ". . .*and the government of the United States of America is hereby suspended* . . ." (3). This radio-broadcast motif was borrowed by many future catastrophists, such as Robert Colborn in *The Future Like a Bride*, Pat Frank in *Alas, Babylon,* and, more recently, the film *The Day After*. In our case, it is in the air, but not heard by, Isherwood Williams, who is in the process of being bitten by a rattlesnake in the Sierras. Thus, the reader is thrust immediately into a situation of potential collective and individual mortality, initiating, among other things, a repeated questioning of the relationship of the individual and the collective. Racing back to his cabin after being bitten, Ish drops his prospecting hammer. "It fell, handle up, on its heavy head, rocked back and forth for a moment, and then stood still, handle in the air"

(4). Out of such lucid close-ups is the immediacy of the novel composed. And for all the symbolic heaviness the hammer will accrue, it is also, and definitely, here, just a hammer, decades away from becoming a priestly icon and emblem of office.

Despite his snakebite, Ish has no "premonitions of death" (4) thinking at this time only of an individual crisis. He is, as an individual, in the mountains to do the kind of field study Stewart did for *Ordeal by Hunger*, only the graduate thesis Ish is researching is titled *The Ecology of the Black Creek Area.* "He had to investigate the relationships, past and present, of men and plants and animals in this region" (4-5). Thus Ish's thesis is a microcosmic nonfiction version of what the novel in which he exists will in part become, with the difference that Stewart's fictional thesis includes, despite his desire to remain an observer, the scientist as an element in the ecosystem. Of course, the decimation of humanity will, in due course, remove humans from the ecology of most of the world's places, and the whole earth will become more like the Black Creek area.

Ish has not seen another human in two weeks; he has been "out of touch with things entirely." Thus, feverishly sleeping, he is startled by the intrusion of two men in city clothes. In a first touch of grim humor he exclaims "'I'm sick!'" and the men rush out frantically to their car. We, the readers can see herein how differently the same words can be understood by two different parties, a reality of which the novel is acutely conscious. Our hero has to suffer through another day and night of delirium, where the precariously balanced single-jack hammer he's found discarded by a long-ago miner, fills his consciousness. At this point, again with irony, the hammer is an ". . .actual link with the past" (7). At this point in time Ish has no way of knowing that what he thinks of as his present, in contrast to that past, is already the past with respect to the "real" present with which he is out of touch.

As Ish falls asleep again, the reader encounters one of the italicized reflective passages which are one of the "dark beauties" of *Earth Abides* and which repeatedly ecologize the immediate dramatic situation. In all of these passages we are really reading the words of a voice addressing from on high the total situation of which the limitedly omniscient narrator of Ish's own story can recount for us only a tiny fragment. I have chosen to designate the speaker of these passages as the "Universal Narrator." Here, the Universal Narrator reflects on the false assumption that if something has never happened, it can never happen. This is perhaps a fallacy of the inductive reasoning that underlies so much human "knowledge." It undercuts what might be considered a false but necessary sense of security in human civilization, by contrast to the cyclical gains and depletions in their numbers stoically accepted by other species. It affirms a "biological" law of permanent species fluctuation, the higher the species on the food chain and slower its breeding rate, the longer the highs and lows of its fluctuation. "As for man, there is little reason to think that he can in the long run escape the fate of other creatures. . .Biologically, man has for too long a time been rolling an uninterrupted run of sevens" (8).

As with other cases, the universal narrator is here playing an uncomfortable game with the reader. He is applying what an ecologist might call "stochastic" variation (Chesson 241) to the human species—that is population variation caused by non-recurrent phenomena. Of course, "flux and reflux" is a different idea, but in either case the narrator is not referring to the food availability causation of population fluctuations. Rather, you could imagine he is responding with a "what if?" question to a Sauerian assertion, that "The history of human population is a succession of higher and higher levels, each rise to a new level being brought about by discovery of more food . . ." (173). But "what if" this concept is based on an inductive illusion and is interrupted by an unanticipated stochastic variation? The narrator here is also speaking universally in that this reflection is not addressed only to the situation in the novel but to the human condition anywhere and any time, even the moment when the reader is reading the words. By this narrative strategy, the reader's world is rendered as vulnerable as Ish's, and the reader is asked to contemplate the stability of his/her own ecological niche.

As Ish, recovered, drives down to the first ranch, Johnson's, where there is a gas pump, he feels a sense of strangeness; it is a weekday but no one is there. The reader familiar with Stewart's work will feel a slight jolt perhaps, at an abandoned Johnson's ranch, since the first ranch at the foot of the Sierras, described in *Ordeal by Hunger*, is Johnson's ranch also, and it is there that the snowshoe party survivor arrive to rescue, warmth, and food. The Donner typology is descent to population and security. Ish's descent is to depopulation and insecurity, and the Johnson ranch is the first stage in the literal discovery, and psychological realization, of this fact.

"Now the road wound down restfully between open groves of pine trees along a little rushing stream. By the time he came to Black Creek Power-house, he felt normal in his mind again also," as he hears the comforting whir of the generators (9). The Power-house, reminiscent of the Power-house in *Storm,* is the first representative of the technology of "civilization" we encounter, and it will play an important role in the novel. Stewart says he re-interviewed for *Earth Abides* the same PG & E engineers he did for *Storm*, and by contrasting the power-house roles in the two novels one can see a change in his views, or a widening of them. Ultimately in *Storm* human ingenuity maintains electric power; here, the only effect of this ingenuity is to allow the technology to continue functioning for some time without the presence of humans. Eventually, without human masters, it dies of thirst like the dogs and cats locked in untended kennels.

As Ish approaches the first town, Hutsonville, on the road to the valley, the Universal Narrator breaks in again with the case of "Captain Maclear's rat" on Christmas Island. First observed flourishing in 1887, the rats were hit by an unknown new disease in 1903, and in spite of their great numbers and abundant food, they were soon extinct. This new parable-within-a-parable, if you will, immediately precedes Ish's first gruesome discovery, in Hutsonville: a dead, fully-clothed man with ants crawling over his faced (10-11). Both real rats and real ants will reappear later in the novel, in flux and reflux based on food supply, but here we are more or less being asked to equate the representative dead human with the Christmas Island rat, where we might normally equate the rat with the ants on the face. It is suggested, perhaps, that predation is affectively neutral.

At Hutsonville a number of things happen which bring Ish to an understanding of his historical condition. Although he sees normal domestic animals, dogs and chicken, they cannot conceal the absence of humans. He sees through the pool-room window newspaper headlines: "CRISIS ACUTE." A battle of will and "civilization" goes on within him: he wants to break in to read the newspapers but "restraints of habit" at first prevent him. Then, "With a wild feeling of burning his bridges, of leaving civilization behind, he swung the heavy hammer-head with all his force against the door-lock" (13) and breaks in. For the first time the primal tool has been used as a weapon against one of the artifacts of the civilization that created it. But also, by being "uncivilized," Ish has accepted before his mind understands it, that civilization as he has known it, is no longer operant. He has liberated himself into the locked room of knowledge of his own de-civilized world. Many other locks will be smashed, windows broken, in the future, as humans for the sake of survival (and pleasure) collaborate with nonhuman nature in the destruction of their civilized heritage.

Once inside, he can read in the emaciated *San Francisco Chronicle* a sequence of headlines and news stories, and understand the progress of the unknown disease, which ". . .aided by airplane travel [read AIDS; or by ship, for the Spanish Influenza], it had sprung up almost simultaneously in ever center of civilization, outrunning all attempts at quarantine"(13). His civilized taboos broken, feeling "an overwhelming sense of solitude" (14), Ish goes to the "best house in town" and hammers his way in. "'There's nobody!'he decided. Then the grim suggestion of the word itself struck him: *Nobody—no body!*" (15).

He deploys for the first time one of his trauma-control mechanisms: as a scientist, he can at least be the "observer" of an interesting event. He contrasts the disease, in which ". . .actually mankind seemed merely to have been removed rather neatly, with a minimum of disturbance," to the nuclear fears rampant just beforehand, in a clear authorial attempt to co-opt that interpretation of his own story: "Mankind had been trembling about destruction through war, and had been having bad dreams of cities blown to pieces along with their inhabitants, of animals killed too, and of the very vegetation blighted off the face of the earth." Waking next morning, he decides that "Before he shed any tears over the destruction of civilization and the death of man, he should discover whether civilization was destroyed and whether man was dead" (17), so he takes food from the still-functioning refrigerator for breakfast, realizes there is no need to do the dishes, and heads toward his parents' house on San Lupo Drive (modeled on the San Luis Road house where Stewart was actually living while writing the novel).

On route, details of useless habit and new habitation stand out: he stops unnecessarily at red lights, sees a coyote running beside the road: "Strange how soon it had known that the world had changed, and that it could take new freedoms!" (19). He passes a fine emblem—a neon horse still galloping atop a restaurant's sign. "The horse, suddenly he thought, was like that civilization of which man had been so proud, galloping so hard and yet never arriving anywhere; and sometime destined, when once the power failed, to grow still forever . . ." (20). The horse is also, one might think, the domesticated and commercialized West. So, although in one sense it is representative of doomed civilization, in another it could be seen as suggesting nature unbridled from human yokes as it was before the frontier closed.

Returning to an abandoned family home is another experience in traumatic deculturation for Ish, but not as intense as one might immediately think. It is worth considering how Ish's family home relates to senses of place in a situation where place-defining attributes are about to disappear. Although San Luis Road and North Berkeley in general, were developed too early to be true, in Hayden's term, "sitcom suburbs," nevertheless, as a "street of eminent respectability," San Lupo Drive has a lot of sitcom attributes as an "overly controlled place." Hayden considers the "sitcom suburb"'s attributes to include ". . neo-Colonial clapboard houses, neat lawns framed by picket fences, moms in high heels and dresses making dinner, and racial exclusion." The house is an "emblem of belonging and upward mobility" (10-11).

Stewart's real house on San Luis Road was bought in 1934 and remodeled soon thereafter. Although he calls it a "terrible place," it was "really a very lucky house" in terms of his family's life there (*Little* 39). It may or may not have been new when bought—the implication is probably not—the remodeling puts it in Kenneth Jackson's category of the "model home," stylizedly full of technological gadgetry (187). Revealing, though casually expressed, is Stewart's distinction between "place" and "house." Ish's place is no longer a "lucky house" when he gets there. The only sounds are technological—the clock and the refrigerator. It has "the pathos of any dwelling-place left without people" (22). In this sense, it could stand for every dwelling-place, even Earth. "Yes, it was a simple house—what you would expect of a man who had taught history in high school and liked books, and of a woman who had made it into a home for him and served on the Y.W.C.A" (22). Ish realizes that he is suffering from shock, as he sits on the porch in the evening and observes the bay below him, with all the city lights still burning.

As he ends up living in this house for the rest of his life, we need to pay attention to his ability to submerge his feelings to the degree that he has at this point. Permanent displacement may not be more traumatic than placed abandonment. (Eventually, Ish will establish a new locus of inhabitance centered on this same house, one which, despite its relative disorder, appears to involve more close interaction than did San Lupo Road before the plague). That he can either evade temporarily or recover from his shock is illustrated by his response, as he sits on the porch, to the half-concealed commercial sign below him, repeatedly flashing "Drink—" He tries drinking his father's brandy, but gets no buzz from it; he considers the idea of drinking himself to death, but rejects it. Finally he decides, for the second time, with a new "will to live" that he can be an observer of a unique period in time. However, this is just one pause of relief in a "flux and reflux" of reconciliation and despair. Ultimately "He let the fog and the darkness wrap him round and conceal him" (26).

Mike Davis identifies a psychic landscape which is a creative force in human shaping of the physical landscape in his study of Los Angeles, *The Ecology of Fear*. I would consider Stewart's novel to be an analogous study, with the creative force moving the other direction in an ecology of *abandonment.* The abandoned landscape creates an abandoned psychic landscape, in which some creatures abandon themselves, and others, with more resources, seek to reinhabit their old identities, or recreate new ones. Stewart's imagination of the ecology of abandonment is powerful, and, moreover, non-speciesist. The emotional limbo of concealment where Ish spends his first night at "home" is followed by one of the Universal Narrator's passages, in which the abandoned inner landscape of dogs and cats is explored. The "world of twenty-thousand years" of domesticated *canis,* humanity's oldest friend, is overthrown. The unconfined abandoned animals are disoriented, "And gradually the pangs of hunger breaking down the long centuries of civilization, they drew closer to where the unburied corpses lay" (27). Stewart gives local name and place to *canis,* in limbo between two worlds, breaking the lock of domestication as Ish did, or abandoning themselves to despair: "Bridget, the red setter, shivered and trembled, and now and then howled faintly, with a howl that was scarcely more than a moan; her gentle spirit found no will to live in a world without master or mistress to love" (27).

In the same spirit, but with greater resolve, Ish determines to "find someone, anyone" (27). But the first person he finds is a man in the last stages of alcoholism, like Bridget become the prey of despair at abandonment. "Those eyes had seen too much. There was a fear in them and a horror that could never be told" (29). The drunk, Mr. Barlow, is behind the wheel of a car; Ish sits beside him. The car, in this case displaying a tableau pairing of the emotional victim and potential survivor, is an essential technological product in *Earth*

Abides. Like the power plant, it can outlive its creators, but is eventually doomed. Stewart, however, attributes to the automobile a special place in the pantheon of doomed human artifacts, so much so that in his final moments of life, Ish's companion will be a symbolic abandoned car on the Bay Bridge. Here and elsewhere, characters use cars as symbols of empowerment, or at least of security. Even more than refrigerators or other fixed domestic appliances, they seem able to conjure back, temporarily, the lost world.

One must mention another non-human survivor Ish encounters in his initial survey of his neighborhood, one that becomes a rich symbol in the novel. This is the neighborhood park where he played as a boy, and particularly the "cave" therein, formed by slanted rocks, ". ..a natural primitive refuge-place." The rocks have on them small holes where Indians had once pounded stone pestles. The world of the Indians has passed away, as has the world of young Ish. When the tribe is established, each year's number will be incised on the stones, and near death Ish will, among primitives again, hide from fire in the cave. This space is the titular Earth condensed—providing a "vertical ecology" of human presence in nature like that experienced by Stewart and Charles Camp at Black Rock.

Ish encounters other humans, all displaying in different behaviors different psychological traumae of abandonment: a dangerously hostile couple, a fleet, bewildered teenage girl, a seemingly old man, stealing goods and hoarding them, filled with a "mania of possession." Ish sees him as "essentially dead," and "close to insanity." The man asks "'Why did it happen?'" (34). Ish talks about "natural immunity." The other, shivering, says "*He* may be saving me for something special" (34).

The bridge to San Francisco is really a metasymbol—for us it represents what it symbolizes to Ish, who seeks "communion" with it, "unity and security" (34-35). It can therefore also symbolize, for us, the yearning for what no longer exists, as felt by Ish. Stewart might have experienced Hart Crane's great poem—his is a bridge to the glories of the American past but also an emblem of the technological glories of the American present. Stewart's bridge, with the one little abandoned green coupe, belonging to an average, anonymous citizen of Oakland, on it, is a bridge figuratively to nowhere. Bridge and car have been abandoned to their fates by humans.

During the day that Ish explores his neighborhood, Berkeley, and the bridge, the Universal Narrator intervenes with a mock-prophetic passage: will the creatures of nature exult now that human power has been humbled, and humans are weak as they? No, although ironically the book of Isaiah will disintegrate unread, but I think the Narrator means that the book of nature will be all that need be read: ". . .the spike-buck will graze farther from the thicket without knowing why, and the fox-cubs play beside the dry fountain in the square, and the quail hatch her eggs in the tall grass by the sundial" (36). This is as to say that time will have no human meaning, or, if any, it can be read only by observing the sun, something Ish and Em will actually do. In a later passage, the Universal Narrator also reflects on the tall grass, in this case the hybrid grasses and non-native ornamental plants of the suburban lawn, which are being replaced by drought-enduring natives like the wild cucumber: ". . .the fierce weeds pressed in to destroy the pampered nurslings of man" (43).

These environmentally positive, and humanistically negative excursions are enhanced by Ish's reflections on the idea of a "Secondary Kill." The plague survivors will be subject to "some trouble from which civilization had previously protected them" (37) be it psychological, or biological. He ends the day wondering if human population will reach the "critical point" at which extinction will be inevitable. Hence, he wonders if he is really still sane, and experiences polarized moods, from imagining he will be divinized for saving humanity from extinction through his intellect to intolerable fear of the "Secondary Kill" and "a wild desire for flight and escape" (39).

The desire to escape, with the goal of finding some other coherent human group, leads to one of the most celebrated episodes in the novel: Ish's trip from California to New York City, we might say today, "in search of

America." The trip allows Stewart to show us the geography of abandonment, and in this he must have gained a lot of inspiration from Carl Sauer. It is a trip rehearsed in his "Earth Abides" trip in 1946, when he took the same route. It recapitulates to a great extent his hitchhiking route from New York to Los Angeles in 1919. Although he is part of no wagon train, it has a lot in common with the Donner party's trek in the other direction, in that he must pass through rough lands practically devoid of habitation, on which the orientation points of civilization—names, boundaries—have lost their meaning, or are *reverting* to a time when there were no names on the land.

Mike Davis has provided an excellent survey of literary West Coast urban apocalypsism (276-355), including Upton Sinclair's *The Millenium* (1924) and Ward Moore's *Greener Than You Think* (1947), which chronicles the rebellion of suburban lawns. But he doesn't explicitly address the journey across devastated landscapes—often to the Devastated Megalopolis—a fundamental motif of post-apocalyptic fiction. Robert Lewis Taylor had already created such a journey in his *noir* suburban comedy *Adrift in a Boneyard* (1947), and many another such journey would occur in 1950's fiction and be resurrected in the 1980's in such notable works as *Riddley Walker*, *War Day*, and the *Mad Max* films. In Neville Shute's classic *On the Beach*, the journey is underwater. The quest is often for a "city of hope," and the city reached is often a city of abandonment and despair, as in the New York of Riley Hughes's *The Hills Were Liars* (1955) or the London of Margot Bennett's *The Long Way Back* (1955). Robert Shafer's *The Conquered Place* has a radiated partitioned half of America, and dead cities where "the elderberry had crept in from where the suburbs had been and snakes nested in piles of broken masonry in the streets and muskrats romped through the ruptured sewers" (12). Taylor reversed the quest, and his Robinson family travels from a devastated New York to a Mediterranean Garden of Eden. In Alfred Coppel's *Dark December* (1960), the tables are turned on Stewart, and Coppel's hero, Major Gavin, travels south into a nuked Northern California. The most Stewartian post-apocalyptic quest I've read is in

Wilson Tucker's *The Long Loud Silence* (1952), whose rich topographical detail seems very close to Stewart's, and connects the obligatory nuclear destruction with fears of plague and resultant quarantines. In fact, Tucker's hero ventures to the Indiana University Library to read about biological warfare which "can be a weapon as deadly and as devastating as an atomic bomb" (56).

Ish is thus in the vanguard of such road warriors. He does have a companion, a beaglesque dog who has the wits to reestablish *canis* relationship with him. The dog's seductive antics allow Ish to adopt him, although he initially builds " . . .a wall against more attachments which must only end with death" (41). With his dog, a station wagon, and full supplies, he drives South on California 99 to Bakersfield, and east over Tehachapi Pass. Ish is conscious that his quest is actually a ". . .temporary escaping from the necessity of decision" (43), and when he stops for the night at an abandoned motel he is again gripped by intolerable fear. As he travels, the fear seems to transmute into a manic attachment to the dog, and anxiety when the dog goes off on scents every time he stops. It is as though dog, car, and man have formed a cultural trinity in his mind; he is travelling through, but deliberately detached from, the physical environment around him. When once he's about to abandon the dog and it returns happily, expecting a handout, he suddenly laughs and ". . .something broke inside of him," he feels ". . .infinite relief," and resolves ". . .that if he was to live at all he would live without fear." He calls the dog, ironically, "Princess," and realizes that he has given her a name (48). Naming is an act of hope. It implies the ability to imagine something can endure. Naming banishes the fear of attachment. Ish is able to drive east through the desert into Arizona and free his "trained geographer's mind" to focus "upon that drama of man's passing" (49).

Thus, much of Ish's subsequent journey is not self-focused, but rather, through his eyes, focused on the environmental changes produced by human abandonment. But before noting some of these, it might be good to look down at Ish from above and observe what he is doing, not physically, but conceptually with his "geographer's mind." I'd argue that as Stewart's persona, Ish is doing revisionist environmental history. There could be several elements in this revision. We could again imagine Stewart asking Carl Sauer, who wrote in "The Morphology of Landscape" that ". . .geography is based on the reality of the union of physical and cultural elements of the landscape" (325), what a decultured landscape, or a landscape in the process of deculturation, would look like. One could imagine him testing the Turnerian hypothesis which in 1950 his future Berkeley colleague, Henry Nash Smith (referred to earlier from Limerick's viewpoint), in *Virgin Land* would call into question. Smith brought out the contradiction between Turner's idea that free land was the basis of American democracy, and his view that "the westward advance of civilization across the continent had caused free land to disappear. What then was to become of democracy?" (257). But what of eastward movement through a continent where basically all the land has been suddenly "freed," and there is no civilization, or, equally, not enough surviving humans to establish a political system of any kind? Or, thirdly, we could move him forward in time and imagine him traveling "from the Pacific Coast to the Atlantic Coast, from southern California to southern New England" (187) with Limerick, rediscovering the newly virginated American landscape, from the West.

So this part of Ish's trek reverses in time and space the experience of his friend Robert Frost's "land vaguely realizing westward," now, again, "unstoried, artless, unenhanced," such as she was before the land was "ours."

As ecogeographer, Ish notices the undisturbed-seeming herds of cattle, envisages their population increasing for a time until, through overgrazing and predation, they will reach "some unconscious balance" (50). The Universal Narrator predicts the swift demise of overly human-dependent hoofed animals—the penned dairy cattle and thoroughbred horses. Unconfined range cattle, horses, and asses survive in different flatland terrain, the asses in the desert uplands along with the mountain sheep, the horses on the dry grassed plains with the pronghorns. "The cattle seek the greener lands and the forests" (51) where their rivals for food are the expanding herds of bison, which eventually drive the cattle toward more wooded areas. Sheep, on the other hand, since "Thousands of years ago they accepted the protection of the shepherd and lost their agility and sense of independence," are doomed (54). This is an ironic situation; years earlier, writing about the confusion of American names for the mountain sheep, he had said "The encroachment of domestic sheep upon the former ranges of its wild cousin has increased the need for distinction. Since civilized destruction has almost annihilated the species, however, the question of a name has practically ceased to be of any popular significance" ("Popular" 287). Later on he encounters a pair of sheep dogs still guarding their herd, by long habit. Unlike the cattle, roadways cannot be self-maintained: a plugged culvert over Siltgreaves Pass has allowed eroded sand to cover the roadway. No highway crew exists to remove the plug.

In the desolated landscape beyond Kingman, Ish imagines different scenarios. Although there are few abandoned human artifacts, overgrazing has depleted the ground cover. He imagines complete topographical change as result, the gullying of the plains. Or perhaps the grazers would be reduced by hoof-and-mouth disease from Mexico. One certain thing he does notice increasingly is the overwhelming silence, and he christens "Man" the "'noise-producing animal'" (53).

A loaded cultural encounter then occurs, when he turns off at Walnut Canyon National Monument, where with "grim amusement" he tours the ruins of the Cliff Dwellers, another extinguished population. He spends the night in the park superintendent's house, already invaded by waterflow from above. He imagines that over time this house will fall into ruins, " . . .and be not much different from those old houses sheltering along the cliffs. Here the ruin of one civilization would pile up on the ruin of another" (54).

Route 66 toward Chicago, "that famous road!" is blocked by a single fallen poplar, so Ish has to detour, and ends up going straight east; he imagines that perhaps the fallen tree has therefore changed the whole course of human history. As he goes through Oklahoma and Arkansas, he notices barriers being broken. "The full heat of summer was upon him now, and was breaking down more of his remnants of civilization," such as grooming himself. Similarly, humidity is increasing, and the sharp line between highway and country is being overgrown; in places blackberry shoots have reached the white line in the middle of the pavement, a symbolic breach.

Here, also, he meets his first social group: a man, woman, and young boy, all African-Americans. Ish realizes they are not a family but a "chance association of survivors." They are suffering both from the shock of their new situation, and from the survival of cultural taboos—exaggerated deference towards him as a white man (58). But they are tending a flourishing garden, and as Ish drives on, he realizes that he is living as a "scavenger upon what was left of civilization; they, at least, were still living creatively, close to the land and in a stable situation, still raising most of what they needed" (59). At this point the Universal Narrator chimes in, unavoidably but not explicitly likening Ish to a biological parasite. The Narrator says the only insects directly affected by human extinction are the three species of human body lice. Presumably we can imagine Ish surviving off the remnants of human production, which will eventually run out, unrenewed by their creators, and thus, in a way, being in the position of a louse--at one degree of separation. The Narrator, in a short fit of humor, suggests that at the funeral of *Homo Sapiens, Canis familiaris* may let out a few howls but the former can be happy there will be "three wholly sincere mourners"—the aforesaid species of lice (59).

Perhaps to be seen as misconstruing the "scavenger" lesson, Ish, as the result of his encounter with the black agriculturists, determines to hunt his own food. However, this turns out to be, first, a cow and her calf, shot at "butcher's distance" (61), and later on, pigs, partridges, and turkeys. He feels that he is moving "one step away from a mere scavenging existence," and one step toward the life of self-sufficiency. If such movement is credited as the truth by the reader, then it is consistent with Ish's trip as an eastward advance of de-civilization, and it is consistent with the increasing impact of humanity's disappearance on him as he enters more highly populated, previously "civilized" areas. However, the whole novel's movement does not lead to progressive human adaptation. Pointedly, once he is back in the west, the tribe that accretes around Ish is essentially a tribe of scavengers, adapting only by sheer necessity as civilization's amenities progressively fail. In pointed contrast to the black trinity of Arkansas, the tribe's attempts at agriculture are more of an afterthought, unmaintained and only marginally successful.

Ish is in a bind which is inherent to the role he has constructed for himself to cope with trauma: as the observer he can analyze and debate with himself about the changes he observes, but his participation in creating survival mechanisms for the changed environment is limited and inadequate. He himself is controlled by the power of cultural custom. This can put him at odds with the broader viewpoint of the Universal Narrator. A perfect example is that he feels his hunting is an act of destruction which is an act of creation—of a new self-sufficient lifestyle. But the cow and calf he shoots are still in a fenced field, and will not be available when the fence, as human construct, goes down, thereby "deconstructing" the structures of order humans have placed on the land, reducing or terminating what Carl Sauer called its "habitat value" (*Land* 325), anthropocentrically defined.

The Universal Narrator's commentary on fences is worth quoting *in toto*:

> A fence was a fact, and a fence was also a symbol. Between the herds and the crops, the fence stood as a fact, but between the rye and the oats, it was only a symbol, for the rye and the oats did not mingle of themselves. Because of fences the land was cut into chunks and blocks. The pasture changed to the plowed land sharply at the fence, and on the other side of the plowed land, at the line of the fence, went the highway, and beyond the highway was the orchard, and then another fence with the lawns and the house beyond it, and again at a fence, the barnyard. Once the fences are broken both in fact and in symbol, then there are no more blocks and chunks of land and sharp changes, but all is hazy and wavy, and fades from one into the other, as it was in the beginning. (63)

From Ish's viewpoint, the end of fences, as fact and symbol, means the end of human habitat. From the viewpoint of contemporary environmentalism, the proliferation of fences means the end of non-human habitat. Texas naturalist Roy Bedichek, writing in 1950, says "Free and unlimited fencing has interfered wit the healthy circulation of natural life, congested and confined it in pockets, restricted its channels, and developed conditions analogous to varices and hardened arteries in the human circulatory system" (3). Fencing destroys species diversity and creates ". . .a fundamental, permanent, irremediable impoverishment, differing from the devastation of war, which, being wrought mainly upon the works of man, is by man quickly repaired" (4). To a mid-century reader of both Stewart and Bedichek an intriguing (though perhaps falsely absolute) question might arise: are the human habitat values and the nonhuman habitat values mutually exclusive?

Ish's encounter with New York City is more nuanced than those in other post-apocalyptic urban destinations. There is no "ruins of Rome" iconography, although he thinks "'Falls Rome, falls the world'"(66). There are no piles of decomposing bodies (pointed out as a narrative flaw by some), but their stench is present. The emotion Ish feels on seeing the uninhabited skyscrapers provides a very 9/11 moment (similar to the one of the zoom to the skyscraper storyteller in *Mad Max Under Thunderdome* as borrowed from Russell Hoban's *Riddley Walker*). The Universal Narrator tells us that "the city will last for a long time," but that it will be like a desert (not in Melville's sense): all the tree cover will die; only flying creatures will dwell there.

Ish visits the Cathedral of St. John the Divine, still unfinished, as do the characters in *The Hills Were Liars*. Unlike them, he feels that what has happened "did not inspire one to think that God was particularly interested in the human race, or in its individuals" (69). Like Yank in *The Hairy Ape*, but obviously under different circumstances, he experiences surrealistically the mannequins in the Fifth Avenue windows. The Universal Narrator also describes one other important symbolic space—Central Park, since that is one place in the city where nonhuman nature can flourish. In twenty years, second growth will be well established, ". . .the hardy natives, fast-growing ash and maple, crowding out the soft exotics. . . ." (69). In a hundred years, it will be a full-grown forest.

After a parodically touristic visit to all the major sites in New York—Grand Central, Wall Street, etc.--he reaches Riverside Drive, and there he finds a second cultural enclave, violently in contrast to that of the blacks of Arkansas: an apartment-dweller, Milt Abrams, and his companion Ann. They are living the life of conventional well-to-do urbanites, as though nothing has changed, and invite him to a dinner of cold canned corned beef served with Chateau Margaux wine. They drink liqueurs and play bridge by candlelight.

This would be the moment to examine the subdued multiethnicity of Stewart's survivors. I think it is a key to one aspect of what he is trying to accomplish in presenting human culture as embedded in ecology. "Milt Abrams" is a Jewish-evocative name. The Arkansas agriculturists were black, and, as we will see, Em is understatedly black also. Shade makes much of this, tying *Earth Abides* in to "racial unrest." He considers that Stewart was "taking quite a risk" when he has Ish choose "a strong willed, able, out-spoken African American woman to be his mate" (Shade). Stewart's editor was not happy with this multiethnicity. He referred to Stewart's reason for making Em a "Negress," seeing, at the point the manuscript has reached that "it seems a contrivance by which you will ultimately deal with a racial problem, and I must confess that at this point it seems dragged in," although he admits he may change his mind on reading further. "To a lesser degree, I don't see why Milt Abrams. . .has to be a Jew. Your point is just as effective if he would have been a Unitarian, a Swedenborgian or anything. . .I don't want it thought that this is a social phenomenon that is especially Jewish" (Saxe Commins to Stewart 8 Mar. 1948/*P*).

Actually, the extant text of *Earth Abides* gives racial identities only indirectly to these characters (except for the agriculturists). But the references in the latter episode to submissive behavior make clear that the author is acutely conscious of racial prejudice. I think that both historically and ecologically there are good explanations, *pace* Commins, for Stewart's multiracialism. In the first place, Stewart is writing his novel in an atmosphere of high publicity for efforts to end segregation of blacks in the military, and an equivalent resistance to ending exclusion of antisemitic selection processes for Ivy League schools. These are two types of national institutions in which Stewart took a strong interest. Starting in 1946, when President Truman established his Committee on Civil Rights, and culminating on July 26, 1948, when he issued executive order 9981 outlawing segregation in the military, the visibility of discrimination—at least in this realm of society—was very evident. Everything suggests that Stewart was sympathetic to Truman's initiative, made more generally applicable by the fight over the 1948 Democratic platform's inclusion of a strong or a watered-down plank opposing racial discrimination (the victory of the former led to Thurmond's Dixiecratic initiative). Stewart was highly conscious when at Princeton of its minimal Jewish representation in the student body. Berkeley professor Jerome Karabel, in *The Chosen: The Hidden History of Admission and Exclusion at Harvard, Yale, and Princeton Universities* (2005) has shown that even a 5% Jewish presence in the Princeton student body in the 1920's was regarded as excessive.

"The senators and the judges and the governors are all dead and rotten,, and the Jew-baiters and the Negro-baiters along with them," Ish tells Em. David H. Price describes how the booklet *The Races of Mankind*, by Ruth Benedict and Gene Weltfish (1943), which ". . .presented qualitative and quantitative data demonstrating that differences between American racial groups were due to cultural rather than biological differences" ignited continuing FBI investigations of the co-authors, resulting in its removal from all USO libraries (Price 113-4). Similar investigations were carried out of Ashley Montagu, based on his openly argued beliefs that "cultural" differences, such as race, were misinterpreted as "natural" differences. "The prejudices of a class have often been mistaken for the laws of nature. . ." Montagu wrote in *On Being Human* (1950) [18]. Gene Weltfish was investigated for her public statements that miscegenation had no "deleterious effects on populations" (Price 117).

Stewart skirts quite closely this dangerous terrain, where opposition to racism is equated with sympathy for communism. Julian Steward himself admitted privately that his concept of cultural ecology was influenced by Marxism. At Columbia, he told Marvin Harris, in the 1930's, "curiously, many adopted [Marxist] epolitical and economic orientations yet remained thoroughgoing relativists in their anthropological work" (Peace 179). Peace suggests that Stewart purposely muted material that might be perceived as Marxist-friendly in his academic publications, due to the "culturally prejudiced mentality toward Marxist scholarship" (180). Thus, one can see why Commins was uncomfortable with this issue in *Earth Abides*, particularly with the idea that, if in the interest of cultural relativism, we accept Em's blackness as a reality, the foundation of the new world order created by Ish's "tribe" is miscegenation. Gary Wolfe assumes, in his commentary on the book, that Em is black and that "The nature and values of [their] future community are strongly hinted at by the interracial marriage which begins it" (17).

Also, I suspect that Stewart may have been influenced by the book Wallace Stegner published with *Look* magazine in 1945, *One Nation*, which presented an outspoken text and searing pictures of racial exclusion, covering almost all "minorities" with a significant presence in the U.S. at the end of the war. Stegner makes a case for a failure to "make a place" for all races in the U.S. as "a blow disastrous to the hope for peace in the world." He considers that solving the "problem of the populations of America. . . is the absolutely essential first step of a process which is historically inevitable. . ." (15). The photos from *Look* are at least as daring, for the time, as is Stewart's idea of human annihilation. One can even see a lynched black man with "This Nigger Voted" in blood on his shirt and the legend (misquoted from the song) ". . .hanging Southern trees and poles with a 'strange and bitter crop'" (219). Seven years after *Earth Abides* was published, Stewart wondered aloud to Saxe Commins why there had been no paperback edition of the novel. "The only reason I can think of is that there is a wee bit of miscegenation in the story. Maybe that is taboo for cheap editions despite of all the to-do they are making about racial equality these days" (Stewart to Commins 29 July 1956/*P*).

I do not in any way suggest that there is, speaking historically, a "racial message" in *Earth Abides*. But that is precisely the point. Stewart creates a world in which, as it were, the only criterion for admission is to be alive. It represents somewhat of a negative version of Stegner's argument: permitting survival of the *human* race, reduced to its lowest common denominator, requires the absence from consideration of any attributes which are not in themselves threats to that survival (as is the relationship of Charlie and Evie later in the novel). Stewart's intellectual tradition supports the non-inherency of racism. Lowie says, referring to American colonization, "White colonists who encroach on the territory of aborigines inevitably attach great importance to racial distinctions since *survival* [my italics] may hinge on being aware of them . . . But there is no inborn hostility on the sole ground of racial differences" (18). Julian Steward based one aspect of cultural ecology on the idea that "the transformation from primitive to civilized communities entails some conflict between the egalitarian principles of the former and the differentiation of status and role of the latter," and one "role" can be defined as racial identity (78). Stewart will develop this connection between social role and racial identity in a complexifying culture in his *Years of the City*.

If you posit, then, as even Kroeber (despite his disagreements with the former) does, the potential for coevolution or devolution of "culture growths" and "organic history" (*Nature* 57), the release of nature from human cultural construction is accompanied by the diminishment in complexity of human culture itself. Stewart's reduction of human society to a "primitive" level, particularly as the nonsustainable cultural amenities run out, is in some ways a liberation from the abuses produced by a complex civilization—such as racial discrimination and environmental pollution. In this way Stewart joins, as a fiction writer, the ranks of the "applied anthropologists" of mid-century, who accepted as a given ". . .the inherent equality of all people," and that "race was a social construction" (Price 347). Though he was no social activist, this connection allies *Earth Abides* with *Year of the Oath* in that they both propagated ideas that could be considered by entities such as the FBI to be sympathetic to communism.

Milt and Ann are, however, not potential survivors themselves. They have lasted so long by living only in the present—as upscale scavengers. "There was a great vacantness somewhere. From shock they were walking in a kind of haze. They were people without hope" (74). Ish thinks they will die with the city. "They would pay the penalty which in the history of the world, he knew, had always been inflicted upon organisms which specialized too highly"(75).

Driving west again, "home," Ish's experiences are dominated by the "Secondary Kill." Despite Stewart's nod to the "rich farmlands" of his own Pennsylvania, his protagonist is made constantly aware of people in tiny groups, "clinging to some little spot," physically alive but emotionally dead. "Destroy the culture-pattern in which people lived, and often the shock was to great for the individuals. . .life became a living death" (77). The "Secondary Kill" is psychological in nature. Lewis Mumford states as an absolute that "Fear and grief have their outlets in flight, withdrawal, cowering," ecologically equating refuge behavior in animals and religious claustration in humans (*Condition* 89). Ruth Benedict says "The desire to run away from grief, to leave it behind at all costs, does not foster psychotic behaviour where . . .it is mapped out by institutions and supported by every attitude of the group" (238). Stewart imagines a society so fragmented that there is literally no way to run away from grief, no place or people to run to, no supportive institution to normalize grieving behavior, and, in fact, as with Milt and Ann, an actual self-disguised embrace of grief. This despair-clustering could be characterized under Roszak's (R.D. Laing-derived) "collusive madness" (53-56), in which the opposite of a "survival instinct" is manifest. "Common vision is . . .possible because common fate is ensured" (Winter 282). It could be argued that Ish, as migrant observer of collective despair, is actually in unaware training to be able to re-establish a micro-community of humans based on a psychology of hope for survival. The varied topography of his westward journey is a topography of human response as well as of physical geography. He is educating himself about the reality of his condition in both human and non-human terms.

The fruits of this education are not evident right away. Back in his parents' home, he has to practice living for survival—as opposed to waiting for death—in a "little spot," and without social reinforcement. In some senses he reverts to scavenging, since he lives on surviving prepared food from grocery stores, and the still-functioning electricity and water systems. "His chief interest remained the careful observation of what was happening to the world after the removal of man's controls" (83). He is particularly interested in canine behavior. The surviving dogs in the city seem to be terrier breeds, who live in the waterfront areas where their main prey, rats, are most prevalent, and who have thereby "marked the establishment of some new cycle of life" (83). These dogs exude "vigor and self-confidence" as though aware that they have "solved the problem of life" (84). In the country, he and Princess encounter a different group, a mixed-breed hunting pack, and have carefully to negotiate their way back to his car, wondering if any of their "long-ingrained respect for mankind" has still survived (85). Safe in his car, looking out at the dogs, Ish's fear changes to pity, as he imagines "they might merely have been seeking the companionship of a man because of what they remembered long ago—of food laid out in dishes, of crackling logs in the fireplace, of a patting hand and a soothing voice" (86). Here, maintaining the Freudian impulse, one might wonder if Ish isn't projecting on the dogs his own nostalgia.

In this period of stasis, Ish observes several other environmental phenomena of interest. Ants invade every house and yard, and then vanish, becoming as seemingly extinct as humans. Electric power fails, and he stays awake with his fading lamps "as if he were sitting up by the deathbed of his most treasured and oldest friend" (90). The Universal Narrator explains in detail the self-correcting systems engineered by Power-and-Light which allowed the electricity to flow so long. Ish, however, experiences the loss of light symbolically, and therefore with despair. "The Dark Ages were closing in" (93).

The end of the light initiates a period of transformation for Ish. His long-view response is not despair but a need for change, and particularly, for another person. It is at this point that he turns to Ecclesiastes, whose author, he feels, has sensed one of the most enduring issues of humanity, "the problem of the individual against the universe" (95).

In *Man, An Autobiography*, Stewart had addressed the issue of when self-conscious individualization occurred in human evolution. His Man considers that for the initial foragers, "Life as they lived it allowed little chance to be individual" (23). Perhaps, Ish thinks, the "balance" of the individual and the universe only comes with death (96). Unlike Stephen Crane's universe, Ish's *does* have an obligation to him, as he to it. Any change in him affects, howsoever minutely, some element of the universe, and a change in the universe affects him. Ish's "universe," I suspect is, as it is in Ecclesiastes, the *organic* universe. The Universal Narrator tells us that the "almost complete removal of mankind" (97) had not in the slightest affected the heavenly and earthly bodies that control the weather.

But the change to autumn coolness and rain alters Ish's entropic condition, in a crucial way: he, like any animal, seeks warmth, and that warmth in the form of human companionship. So when he sees a wisp of smoke rising from a house, the "balance" has changed. He knows it involves a human presence, but "Did Crusoe really want to be rescued from his desert island where he was lord of all he surveyed?" (98). Surmising that he fears "human entanglements," Ish drives away from the smoke, but, as though it is a "temptress," he is drawn back to it.

This is a moment of power in the story. It is a post-apocalyptic suburban "encounter narrative," as Ish, with Princess, approaches the door of the house from which the smoke is rising, sees a shadow through a window, is fixed by a flashlight, and hears totally unexpectedly the Other exclaim "'That's a beautiful dog!'" (100). Princess rushes into the house madly, and its inhabitant, a woman laughs: ". . .the sound of laughter was like something remembered from Paradise long ago" (100). One of the suggested racial details of the woman, who is Em, is immediate, with "the flash of white teeth in the dark face" (101). My daughter, recalling how she first read *Earth Abides* at about the age of twelve, remembers immediately being aware that Em was creole or black, and checking the publication date of the novel, being astonished at how prophetic it was (Melissa Waage, interview with the author 24 Dec. 2005).

Without belaboring the issue, the "bonding" of Ish and Em—the handshake, the ritual sharing of food, the sexual union—is an example of the environmental causation of cultural phenomena implied in Ish's reflection on the individual and the universe. The indifferent natural forces which create cold weather drive Ish to Em, despite the defensive psychological barriers he has erected. And thereby, a new human "cycle of life" is created just as it was between the terriers and rats by the Bay.

It is at this moment that the "restoration" Stewart considers the center of his novel begins. Ish and Em break through the dark and cold to create their own light. "They shall call thee blessed, because in a dark time thy look was toward the light," the Universal Narrator intones (110). They set out to recreate a lost domesticity. Here again we see Em's body: "He saw again, more clearly by morning light, the wide-set black eyes in the dark face, the full ripe lips, the swelling curve of the breasts beneath a light-green smock" (105). Initially, after Em has moved to live with him at San Lupo Drive, they are involved with scavenging. Their car "dies," and they find a "new" one in an automobile showroom. As with the ants before, they are beset by a population explosion of rats. Consoled by population ecology, as the rats get fewer, thinner, and more aggressive, Ish is also alarmed by the thought that they are carriers of bubonic plague. He sprays DDT everywhere. The rats begin preying upon themselves. He starts to observe the rat decimation as a "study in ecology," and realizes that the rats ". . .were not actually destroying the species for their own individual preservation; they were really saving the species" (116). If they'd been "sentimental," deciding to die rather than cannibalize, they might become extinct; but as "realists," their "racial future" seems secure. I wonder how much allusion to the Donner Party's cannibalism is implied here.

The rats' solution to overpopulation plays against Ish and Em's solution to underpopulation: having children. Their and the rats' situations both relate to the question of humans' exceptional position in the world ecosystem. In *Earth Song* Charles Camp connects the "penalties of overpopulation" in human spaces with insufficient resources and the potential penalties of environmental overmodification in privileged human communities.

> Man would like to control his destiny. He attempts this by defying and modifying his environment in countless ways not usual among other living things. He has set himself above the rest of life, and uses life for his own purposes.. . . Nature whispers to him saying, 'Take heed or you shall perish.' This warning is not easily heard; and if heard, it is not often heeded. (146)

Ish and Em, at least in theory, are given the opportunity to recommence human civilization with the rats as Nature's voice in their ears. In effect, Em's pregnancy can lead to another long-term study in ecology: how biologically "hard-wired" into the human species are the traits denounced by Camp? Is human "civilization" inevitably as self-destructive as rat civilization, which, dependent on parasitizing the products of human environmental modification, becomes self-destructive when these products run out?

A symbolism akin to that of the hammer, and the car on the bridge, is introduced into the novel when Ish drives to the University library, and has to break in to it, in his search for obstetrical texts. His entrancement with the library's books is a basic crux of the novel, for he sees in the possible use of the books' knowledge a renewal of civilization at the point of development where it was destroyed. I think one thing we are asked to consider in Ish's fixation on the library is that it serves more as a symbol to him as well, as a surviving Monument of a lost past, not as an actual resource for knowledge leading to concrete action in the world. Ish's experience could be related to Roszak's distinction between organic and computer memory. What Ish sees the library preserving is the memory of "mechanical systems" created by humans. He cannot restore that cognitive realm of the remembered past. As symbol, for Ish, the library represents organic memory, ". . .a record of *experience*, an intricate, highly selective blending of emotion, sensuous stimulation, existential crisis" (Roszak 170).

Ish imagines the ecological instrumentality enabled by the knowledge in the library; he thinks about "Seeds, for instance. He must see to it that the more important domestic plants did not vanish from the earth," whereas Em, at his effusions about restoring civilization, defines it as "airplanes going higher and higher and faster and faster . . .mystery-stories and those funny Negro jazz bands that always made my ears hurt" (120). One might consider Em's disabused irony about the achievements of civilization to be more realistic that Ish's sentimentality.

Connected with the impending childbirth and the library is the couple's decision to mark a new calendar on the rocks of his childhood playground park: "Year One" in the "unfolding drama of a new society, reconstructing itself, moving on" (124).

With Year One, the author begins the "interchapter" called "Quick Years." The summarized future history in the interchapter is dominated by the growth in population, not only of Ish and Em's offspring, but of the group brought to San Lupo Drive by Ezra, in his car—Molly, Jean, the carpenter George, and his wife Maurine. During this period of cultural integration the group becomes the "tribe," but in a non-formalized way. There is no tribal totem, and the immigrants are "average" people with few specific skills or intellectual attainments. Their community, although non-nomadic, is as much a community of "convenience" (*Ordeal* 18) as the Donner Party was. The cohesion of the "tribe" is provided by the creation of offspring, the naming of each year for a collective experience, and the sort of mutuality praised by Montagu as an essential attribute of humanity.

Events occur during the "Swift Years," that tend both to unite and to divide the tribe. The first marriage of the second generation, that of Ish and Em's daughter Mary and Molly's son Ralph, creates for the first time a kinship tie between the two component groups of the community. Speaking in cultural ecology terms, this first union creates the "biological" basis that will support a "superfamilial band" developed "in response to cooperative needs" defined by ecological circumstances (Steward *Evolution* 37). It is with the growing biological base of the tribe, and the first mention of Ish's favorite son Joey, the hope of civilization, that the first interchapter comes to an end.

The second section of the novel, titled "The Year 22," is headed by an epigraph from Crevecoeur that characterizes the social bond of Americans as "singular and captivating." There is some irony in this, because although the Tribe is held together by a strong social bond, Ish is dissatisfied with the lack of intellectuality in its members. For example, Ezra's genius is "the genius of living on easy and friendly terms with people, and not the creative drive that leads toward new civilizations" (148). Ish's wish to educate the young of the Tribe, and his unofficial anointing of the precocious and creative Joey as the one who can restore the remembered mechanical past, also bring into question the issue he debated with himself at the beginning of the "Dark Ages:" the role of the individual. Despite his historic position in the Tribe and his hammer of office, Ish's authority is limited, and his dicta are often ridiculed. The Tribe doesn't conform very well to the anthropological models purveyed by Kroeber, Lowie, Steward, *et. al.* There may be some element of *de facto* caste organization, based on the collective perception of individuals' abilities, but the

Tribe seems to resemble in its organization and governance more a New England town meeting than a Western Indian tribe.

Thus when Ish's epiphanic "'Joey! He is the one!'" (152) occurs, he is in a sense predictively usurping the cultural system that has developed in interaction with its environment. Joey becomes the "Child of the Blessing" (152) in Ecclesiastes only to Ish. Ish has avoided bringing religious practice into the tribe because of his own skepticism, his sense of its irrelevance, and its divisive potential. But he has established in his own consciousness a sort of "Church of Joey," whose holy book is pre-holocaust human knowledge. In this case he *is* responding to Kroeber, who denies that "individual superiority" can cause "cultural superiority," and who believes in the "clustering of genius" (*Configurations* 16) as a source of civilization. Em also believes in this, telling her mate that "things would be different if you had a lot of people who were like you, that thought about things a long way off. But all you have is the usual people like Ezra and George and me" (160)

Ish's response to his enlightenment about Joey, however, is to give a speech denouncing the scavenging among relics as opposed to "creating or doing anything for ourselves" (153). He urges the Tribe to get domestic animals, grow more food plants, teach the children to read and write.

Continuing his "sermon," Ish cites his idea of civilization. "Civilization wasn't just only gadgets and how to make them and run them. . ." but all sorts of social organization, rules, laws, government: ". . .we aren't a democracy, or a monarchy, or a dictatorship, or anything" (155). George greets this speech by saying "'I was kind of glad we live in a place where we don't have no laws,'" and Ezra offers a mock-toast to "Law and Order" (156). Ish is between a rock and a hard place, since he has no way of effectuating the changes he wants in the face of social inertia, and no vehicle (or even, in general, desire) for imposing his will on the group, precisely because there exists no "governmental" channel to authorize it. In *The Origins of the State*, if I read it right, Lowie sees "sovereignty" as, if not the necessary, the most important factor in the development from "tribe" to "state." "A coercive force . . . .seems the short cut to intensifying and bringing into consciousness. . ." the feelings of interrelation necessary to an organized society, which may then become the sources of a state "glorified as loyalty to a sovereign king or to a national flag" (116-117). If one accepts this premise, then under it Ish has no power of coercion, and wants to leap directly from "anarchic community" to allegiance to state, not embodied in a flag but in a library.

So, Ish asks himself, how does a society change? Are his fellow tribesmen still suffering from shock as the anthropologists say the plains Indians did, unable to adjust, even losing the will to live? "He was facing a basic question of the dynamics of society," faced by his own group, "a society reduced in size until it had attained the simplicity of a laboratory experiment" (163). Then he reverses the idea. The Tribe isn't "a philosopher's neat microcosm," but a group of individuals. To change the individuals he needs to change the society. What if instead of George he had ". . .one of those high-powered minds that he remembered from his university years—Professor Sauer, perhaps[!]"(164). Maybe Ish didn't remember many of Professor Sauer's ideas, since the Professor, parallelling cultural and biological evolution, says that in the history of man, "independent. . .invention" is "the exception," as opposed to "cultural diffusion" from a limited number of "creative cultural hearths" (*Origins* 3).

At this point in time, as though to confirm Ish's statement about scavenging and dependency, the Universal Narrator, in a manner reminiscent of *Storm*, tells us how the erosion-caused breakage of a single pipe in the until now self-perpetuating aqueduct system will lead to the end of a technology-enabled water supply. As the electric lights died long ago, so now the water pressure weakens. "It had been a gift from the past, as free as air, like the cans of beans and bottles of catsup that could be had just by walking into a store and taking them from the shelves" (171).

Fortunately (a situation Stewart will repeat early in *The Years of the City),* the adventurous children have found out where springs are located. Since lack of population has reduced pollution risks, albeit with some work, fresh water again becomes available. A gathering (more social than parliamentary) is held, and digging a well or an impoundment basin for spring water is desultorily discussed. This eventually leads to enough enthusiasm for the Tribe to dig a well, almost as a game. They are "unable to distinguish between work and play." The Universal Narrator reflects on this, posing the Tribe at the beginning of civilization when "work and play mingled always," whereas, as civilization advanced, "always work became more laborious and odious and play grew more artificial and febrile" (188-189).

At a gathering, Ezra suddenly throws out the idea of sending an expedition east. Ish thinks "'Lewis-and-Clark in reverse!'" (179), making him wonder about his afternoon dream in which a truck labelled "U.S. Government" had rolled up. "How did they really know that the Government of the United States had actually failed?"(180).

The idea of an expedition brings all sorts of Past Times reflections to Ish---the scents of the city, the Bay Bridge. The Universal Narrator describes the persistence of the bridge, its evolution, as it were, into a complex ecosystem of birds, rodents, crabs. "In the enduring structure of the bridge, long-dead civilization still defied the attacks of all the powers of air and sea" (186). The Tribe uses its dog-teams and carts to go to the city, and Ish—as he has long before—uses his hammer to break the locks of auto showrooms, looking for a salvageable vehicle to make the expedition. With great struggle, since they have no mechanical skills, they manage to get a jeep to start.

At this time, in a significant scene, Ish takes Joey to the library. Joey is intrigued by books, and asks many questions. He asks what the "shiny white balls" on the ceilings are. Ish tells him about electric lights. Joey: "'If I read the books, could I make them make light again?'" (197). Ish is both exultant about and frightened by this precocity. He fears Joey will move too fast and warp his personality.

Planning the route the boys will take on the expedition, having gotten yellowed road maps, Ish seems to be reliving his Primal Pilgrimage 22 years earlier. He has to tell them what the words on road signs mean, and the names of geographical entities which have no more reason to exist. The Universal Narrator reflects on the ephemerality of boundaries. Their only physical substance is represented by human construction—e.g., road surfaces, police uniforms.

When the expedition has left, there is another period of stasis, marked by Ish's unsuccessful attempts to bring "culture" to the children of the Tribe. Except for Joey, they aren't interested in music, in literacy, in arithmetic. He fails "to maintain for the Tribe some hold on the basic skills of civilization" (210) as they lose interest in each pedagogical initiative he takes. Significantly, there is no cultural need for these skills, and therefore no interest in developing them. Stewart is being a bit of a cultural primitivist here; this lack of curiosity is not necessarily valid with respect to children, but he needs to illustrate the primacy of survival as motivating force. Only their value for survival would make any of these skills in demand. The children are only mildly interested in anthropology, "the growth of man, that struggling creature" (213).

The artifact that truly arouses the children's interest is Ish's hammer. They are afraid to touch it. It has something "strange and mystical" relating to the far past. "The children had come to think it an implement of power, dangerous for any of them to touch" (215). Stewart uses this awe of the hammer to evoke the dangers to a society without any traditions, its vulnerability to superstition and demagoguery. They need a collective religion and he imagines the different origin myths he could tell them and which they would believe—from Genesis to Coyote, but none of them would be "honest" since he himself didn't believe in them. ". . .[H]e treasured the honesty of his own skepticism" (218). He enumerates the already existing "taboos" in the culture—infidelity, sexual intimacy with the retarded Evie, the hammer itself. This is an intense moment: he considers throwing the hammer into the bay. Then he thinks of its advantages as a cultural symbol—permanence, strength, phallic suggestiveness. He realizes that to an extent Joey has also developed the power of a cultural symbol. Certain members of a tribe are believed to have a special power, according to anthropologists—called *Mana*. And this is true of Joey. "Joey held the hope for the future, Only by the power of intelligence, Ish believed firmly, had mankind ever risen to civilization. . ." and Joey has "intelligence and maybe that other power of *Mana*". Thus Ish moves toward a governance model of future civilization, which he has rejected earlier, projecting Joey as humanity's leader.

The Universal Narrator, however, foresees the collapse of this dream, evoking the "lost leader" syndrome, a sort of Arthurian model. "'If the young king had not fallen ill. . . . .If the prince had lived . .. If the president had not overworked . . ." [the latter, surely, a Rooseveltian reference]. "Between the plan and the fulfillment stands always the frail barrier of a human life" (225). This prophecy is tied to the cycle of nature, it is a time of drought and "Now the god lies dying."

There is a momentous interlude before the prophecy is fulfilled. The boys return from their expedition with something good—news of the world outside California, and something bad—a guy with "boar's eyes" named Charlie who Ish immediately feels is "dirty inside". For once a truly ritual space is created. At a great bonfire, Dick and Bob tell about their expedition—they reached Chicago, which was an abandoned wasteland, but further east the roads became so impassible that they had to turn back. They had encountered human communities near Los Angeles and Albuquerque. The bonfire antics become "bacchanalian;" Charlie joins in, but the suspicion of him still lingers. So although he is welcomed as a good addition to the community, he is still considered by Ish as having something dirty and mean "clear to the middle of him" (241).

At this point, despite outward signs, Ish feels that he is pitted against Charlie in a conflict for the allegiance of the Tribe, that a "struggle of factions" will be inevitable (243). This feeling tacitly acknowledges some kind of structure of governance in the Tribe—in effect, the condition of a nascent State. The presence of Charlie creates an indefinable coldness, particularly around the ashes of the bonfire the next morning. This is a coldness of diverse qualities. It contains fear, both physical and metaphysical, the atmosphere exuded by Charlie, the actually growing change of temperature, and the incipience of disease. Against this fear and apprehension Ish, giving in to the totemism he himself has rejected, takes his hammer to the fire-site where Charlie is seen in close intimacy with the retarded Evie. Verbally confronting Charlie about this, Ish finds himself arguing (like an intellectual) rather than ordering, and begins to feel Charlie has usurped leadership.

When a further gathering occurs, Ish realizes a collective decision has to be made about what to do with Charlie, which means some structure of decision-making must be created. He realizes that "What he was facing was almost like the organization of a new state" (251). After deliberations, Ezra reveals that in talk the previous night with a drunken Charlie he discovered a literalization of Ish's intuition about "dirt," that Charlie has "'Cupid's diseases'" (252).

The discussion then becomes how to get rid of Charlie. Banishment is suggested. There is no cultural precedent for punishment or tribal exclusion. There's a powerful debate between Em and the men about executing Charlie. "'It's against the law.'" But there is no law. Em sees no reason to justify not executing someone who hasn't done anything punishable yet, if it is certain that he will. Ish inwardly agrees with her. "She is the mother; she thinks close to all the basic things of life". Finally Em decides, for them, that they should vote for either banishment or death.

This is the first, and really the last, act of the Tribe as an organized State: a beautifully ironic sentence of death to a bearer of disease. The reader will see the similarity in act, although difference in circumstance, between this vote and the decision of the snowshoe party in *Ordeal by Hunger*. There, a similar community of disaster survivors chooses not to choose, although choice is urged by Patrick Dolan. Here, the disembodied Universal Narrator, in apocalyptic cadence, neither expressing Ish's thoughts nor not expressing them, evokes circumstances under which individuals are sentenced to death. "Knot the rope; whet the ax; pour the poison; pile the faggots" (255). Ish is torn between voting "B" or "D." He finally decides "To be effective, punishment should not be a retribution so much as a prevention" (256). This rationale could arouse a lot of commentary, particularly, say, in the atmosphere of rampant McCarthyism.

The next chapter begins: "They shoveled the dirt back into the grave beneath the oak tree" (257). In an echo of the novel's earliest stages, Ish thinks "Now it would never be the same again" (257). He thinks about his primal act in Hutsonville of smashing the poolhall lock. That was an act of lawlessness, but the actor was not, although he didn't know this, really breaking the law since no law existed any more. Here, there is more the Oppenheimer tone of "we have known sin." As far as the "originating function" of the State goes, it is sort of a declaration of independence for the erstwhile tribe to create a victim rather than to experience itself as collective victims. Constructing the execution of Charlie as an expulsion from Eden is only one way of understanding it. The previous 21 years were not really Edenic as much as anarchic. And there is no primal cause or "spring of action" (259). Losing water led to the expedition which brought Charlie and brought his death.

Ish consoles himself with the idea of planting the corn whose kernels the boys had brought back. In an act of whimsey, he and Joey make popcorn over the stove. The Universal Narrator speaks in a mode that has not been taken up for some time—the deep ecological look at the fate of domesticated species. In this case, wheat and corn are described as sheep have been earlier. They have been domesticated and hybridized so extensively that only in isolated environments can they survive without human cultivation. "For if man cannot prosper without the wheat and the corn, still less can they prosper without man" (261).

Along with Charlie and the corn, we discover, the boys have brought back disease, and members of the community become progressively sick. "Now, just as man lacked the all-embracing power of a nation around him, so also he felt himself bare and exposed and helpless for lack of that age-old tradition of medical skill" (265). This is the fulfillment of the Universal Narrator's prophecy. The epidemic spreads, and fear with it. Ish lies for days in unconsciousness and delirium. One day he wakes to Em beside him, as she has been for days, weary unto death. And she whispers "'Joey'" to him.

"Joey was gone, and Charlie's shadow lay over them, and the all-necessary State had arisen, with death in its hands" (271). The author invites lots of interpretation here. Reading the novel at age fourteen, I was devastated by the death of Joey. It did not occur to me, in the 1950's, that, in the first place, the death of Joey may have been necessary for the survival of the Tribe. He avoided what has been suggested would have been a total failure to educate his people, and they avoided what might, theoretically, have become, a priestly autocracy. I think Stewart is pretty skeptical of the benefits of the State, or at least feels that if the State is to re-emerge, it must re-emerge through an organic process of growth from a more primitive condition, not simply be turned on like an electric light. As with the blacks in Arkansas, the author has emphasized the survival value of being forced into the role of primary producers. Unless the Tribe can resume from that fallen condition, its chance for eventually developing a more complex civilization (which may, in itself, not be desirable), is small.

Hence Em deters Ish from the heretical (to a skeptic) idea that Joey's death was some kind of retribution for the killing of Charlie, and Ish begins to think "Perhaps there were too many people, too many old ways of thinking, too many books. Perhaps the ruts of thinking had grown too deep and the refuse of the past lay too heavy around us, like piles of garbage and old clothes" (275).

After the burial of the dead, Ish pays a somewhat elegiac visit to the University campus, observing the effect on it of "the pageant of the years" (280). Seeing a rattlesnake, and remembering the bite that "saved" him, but feeling no enmity to the "tribe of rattlesnakes," he reflects on the second generation's views of their place in nature: "In the times of civilization men had really felt themselves as the masters of creation. Everything had been good or bad in relation to man. So you killed rattlesnakes. But now nature had become so overwhelming that any attempt at its control was merely outside anyone's circle of thought. You lived as part of it, not as its dominating power" (281). This scene must have carried continuing resonance; in 1964 Defenders of Wildlife requested permission to reprint the rattlesnake encounter in their news bulletin (Mary Hazell Harris to Stewart 6 Jan. 1964).

Ish carries to the library his feeling that nature has benefited from human depletion, where he thinks of the paradoxes in the destroyed civilization it represents. This civilization had grown so complex that humans (Thoreau, Gauguin) fled it to find the natural simplicity which now has been forced upon them. Did not civilization complexify itself through "Forces and Pressures," not human desires, to the point that it was "like Frankenstein's vast monster[?] They had not willed it, but it ruled them all, and they sought to escape it. How, then, could it ever be restored except by "renewed Forces and Pressures" over which the individual human would have no control? (285). He finds in the stacks, as though to contribute to these thoughts, the last book he himself had checked out of the library before the plague, Charles E. P. Brooks's *Climate Through the Ages: A Study of the Climatic Factors and Their Variations* (1926—interestingly, reissued in 1949). Brooks emphasizes that climate is ever-changing and the changes result from forces of which we have little certainty and over which we have no control: "The atmosphere, like the sea, is in a state of perpetual oscillation. . .the result being highly complex changes in the distribution of pressure from day to day, month to month, and year to year" (373-4).

In his meditations, Ish is driven back to what might be the basic question governing cultural ecology. If ". . . humans have been the major ecological force in Nature" (Bennett 17), "How much did man strike outward to affect all his surroundings and how much did the surroundings press against him? Did the Napoleonic age produce Napoleon or did *he* produce it?" (286). Through this question, Ish comes to realize that "even if Joey had lived, things would probably have continued to move the way they already seemed to be moving" (286) since humans seen as *in* nature are subject to too many circumstantial forces for one individual to direct a whole society. "The Tribe was not going to restore civilization. It did not want civilization" (286).

This awareness leads Ish to reenact a primal human act of enabling invention, to provide, given the above conclusion, the greatest chance for human survival when there is nothing left to scavenge. This is the new invention that causes Stewart's Man to become "lost in admiration at myself—at my own ingenuity in discovering something so much more effective than anything before it . .." (*Man* 74)—the bow.

In great detail the narrator describes how Ish fashions a bow from a lemon shoot and braided rawhide, and an arrow from a pine branch. He presents his new invention (considering the play-as-work formulation earlier) as part of a new game, and is thrilled by its success, as the children and youths organize competitions. Even when the children become bored with them after a while, the bows will still be there for use under future necessity. "It was the greatest weapon that primitive man had ever known and the most difficult to invent" (294). So, rather than Joey's "impossible dream" of making the light bulbs glow again, Ish has accepted cultural devolution and chosen to intervene—being the only one left who can—at an earlier stage. It is interesting to compare him, as representative Man, with what his collective Man thought about the bow in the earlier book. That Man thought that ultimately the bow made hunting-and-foraging life impossible. "It was perhaps too efficient, and threw off the balance," by allowing humans to kill animals faster than they could reproduce in nature—which, in turn, led to the necessary act of domestication (*Man* 78).

In the last "Quick Years" interchapter, we experience the deaths of the members of The Tribe's founding generation: George, Maurine, Evie. Another, smaller group of humans is discovered across the bay, and despite the fear of disease from them, Em persuades the Tribe to admit them as a "clan," "The Others:" "' Life is not lived by denying life'" (299). Finally Em's health fails, "And, as it was in the beginning, since love first and sorrow with it came to the world, he sat with his dead" (301). "'We are going, we are going,'" Ish thinks. "'We Americans are old, and are dropping like last spring's leaves'" (301). Ezra urges Ish to take another wife, and although he does not want to, he does take one from "The Others," as comfort and childbearer. In year 43, she ceases bearing children, and with Ish's permission, espouses a younger man. Also, Ish and Ezra, the only survivors now, cease to carve the year number in the stones.

Stewart was proud of his portrayal of Ish and Ezra as old men. He had reservations about the success of the middle of the book, but "I've always liked doing old people" (*Little* 220). He feels that old age is "shunned" as a topic for discussion; ". . I think you ought to be able to play old age as you can play any other part of life" (*Little* 220), and he has Ish and Ezra play it well as they "sit on the hillside in the sun" (302) in a sort of timeless discussion and contemplation of the past and the future. Ezra thinks of a tribe as a child: you can show it the way to grow up, but it will eventually choose its own way regardless. "Almost while they sat there, it seemed to Ish, a fast-growing tree sprang up on the hillside below them, and grew until it cut off the view across the Bay, where the rust-red towers of the great bridge still stood high. And then after a while the tree seemed to sicken and die and fall" (303). After Ezra dies and is no longer beside him, he realizes he has "lost hold of time itself" (305).

The third and final section of *Earth Abides* is titled "The Last American," and has, as its ironic epigraph, "'Tis merry, 'tis merry in good greenwood.'" It opens with one of the best scenes in the book, when in his haze of age Ish finds before him a young man who calls himself Jack. Ish feels he is being made fun of, because Jack, his oldest son (a tribute to Stewart's own son?), looks in no way like this young man. The young man replies "'You are talking, Ish, of my grandfather, as indeed you yourself well know'" (309). This Jack is bearing a bow and arrow, since rifles are good only as "playthings," and has made his own, very efficient arrows, with heads made of hammered coins (although Jack calls them "little round things"). Stewart tells in *A Little of Myself* about a recent visit from a Stanford student. When he asks the student what his favorite part of *Earth Abides* is, he says it is this scene with Jack, and Stewart speculates that the student was "reflecting his own relationship with his father" (71). There is certainly a wonderful mixture of generational distance and emotional closeness between Ish and his great-grandson, but when he comes out of a reverie, Jack is gone and ". . . Ish would have been unable to say surely whether the young man named Jack had been there that same day, or whether this was now some other day, or perhaps even another summer" (315).

Stewart uses a natural phenomenon he knows well to create the closure scenes in *Earth Abides.* The fire that has at different times since the plague struck different parts of the Bay has finally come to the houses of the tribe, and as the Universal Narrator evokes the speed of destruction of different kinds of fire, Ish is awakened by Jack, and helped out of the house. "He had known always that this must happen some time" (318) since year after year of dried grass and foliage had accumulated. He is embarrassed at doing so, but he sends Jack back into the burning house for his hammer. With nowhere to escape the flames, Ish, Jack and other young men take refuge in the cave between the rocks where he played as a child. Ish recognizes that "this little world, my second world, is going" (321). The fire that warms also destroys. "'They used to say that because of the bombs we would go back and live in caves. Well, here is a cave—but we have not marched by the road that anyone imagined" (321).

As he hovers with the young men, Ish focuses increasingly on Jack. He remembers he once asked Jack if he was happy, and Jack had replied "'Yes, I am happy. Things are as they are, and I am part of them'" (325). After the great fire has passed, the young men build a cooking fire and offer Ish the breast of a quail. He has had a sudden period of lucidity, and asks himself "'Why should I consider dying? . . .Life is still good, and I am the last American'" (330).

Although this is a profoundly elegaic episode, Stewart brings almost playfully into these last hours of Ish's life things which he has been deeply involved with before and will be again. As the young men carry him towards the unburned land of lakes where the Tribe has decided to resituate, he realizes he is being carried along the East Shore Highway—U.S. 40—toward the Bay Bridge. As they cross the bridge, Ish can see the waters below. The Universal Narrator:

> This is the road that no man finishes traveling. This is the river so long that no voyager finds the sea. This is the path winding among the hills, and still winding, This is the bridge that no man crosses wholly—lucky is he who through the mists and rain clouds sees, or even believes he dimly sees, the farther shore.(333-34)

He is set down, and knows that he is dying on this allegorical and real bridge, right near the little abandoned car that has been parked their since the plague. It is settling downwards. In a way he is its companion, a dying survivor of the same civilization. Stewart has said that he feels Ish has lived a good life (in the sense of his own later book *Good Lives*), and the mood of this feeling pervades Ish's last thoughts, and his last earthly sight—of the Berkeley hills across the bay, with its hills shaped as woman's breasts. He looks at the young men and thinks "'They will commit me to the earth . . .Yet I also commit them to the earth. There is nothing else by which men live. *Men go and come, but earth abides*" (337).

I have more or less let the last part of the novel speak for itself, since it is so perceptive, lyrical, and moving, and so little known to the world at large. If one were to coin a phrase to characterize it, it could be "lyrical naturalism." The author has created a fear-fraught scenario which ends with a resigned optimism, without improbable narrative manipulations.

Earth Abides did create certain image problems for Stewart as a writer, which in later years sort of amused him. He recalls a bad review by a woman who asked "'Where are all those wonderful engineers and men that went out and fought the storm?' Well, obviously, they were dead, that's what they were!" (*Little* 183-4). David Dempsey of the *New York Times* asked him "Please wire over two hundred words why after scourging land with storm, fire, you unleased [sic] last pestilence in earth abides" (Dempsey to Stewart 7 Oct. 1949). In his oral history, Stewart, much later, contended that, though he's often been called a "chronicler of catastrophe, "That's not altogether true, because after all I'm a chronicler of the ecology, and in ecology there isn't any good or bad, really" (*Little* 145). Replying to Dempsey, he said almost the same like *Storm* and *Fire*, *Earth Abides* ". . deals with an emergency in the relationship of man and his environment." The plague there is just a preface to ". . .a slow but successful reestablishment of mankind to a stable and happy society" (Stewart to Dempsey, draft, n.d.). Some reviewers were a lot less bemused, but they were more interested in literary technique than in theme. Orville Prescott was positively grouchy about the "Universal Narrator" passages, misconstruing their affective intent. He called them "dull and pretentious interludes of semi-poetic prose," and finds on almost every page "a feeling of mechanical contrivance." The novel "bristles with intelligent ideas, but sags woefully because of its literary crudities" ("Books" 29). Also in the *Times*, Granville Hicks, praises the credibility of his situation, but considers that Ish "knows more and cares more about natural processes than he knows or cares about what goes on in people's minds" ("Civilization" 4).

This reader would disagree on both counts, and almost suspect (although you wouldn't think it from Granville Hicks) that the reviewers were retreating from apocalyptic fears of their own into the safe arbor of practical criticism. The view from distance is more enlightened, as in Gary Wolfe's praise of the novel's complexity and regret that it has not received ". . .the attention it deserves among students of science fiction . . ." because it breaks down generic barriers (16)—precisely the source, in my view, of its power.

One tribute to *Earth Abides*, although it never made it to film, was its presentation on the (now classic) radio mystery series *Escape* in November, 1950. This tribute is somewhat dubious, though, in that the radio script, partly of necessity, made a hash of the later parts of the novel. As narrated for most of its length by Ish himself, in the voice of John Zehner, the story starts out initially close to the novel, although the radio Ish doesn't smash open the lock in Hutsonville. It makes the effort to include some of the Universal Narrator passages, such as the Christmas Island rats. San Lupo Drive is in San Francisco, a "naked forest of cement" ("Earth"), not in a fictional Berkeley. Ish does drive East on route 66, where, in a scriptwriters' incident, he encounters no neon horse but a bar jukebox automatically repeating the same cheerful song, and smashes it with his hammer, the sound slowly spiralling down. He meets, in Guthrie, Oklahoma, only one "Negro," who points a gun at him and orders him off the land. The New York couple are not West Side Jews but a presumably WASP couple in a small house in the Bronx. When the radio Ish returns to California, he does link up with Em, but there is no clue that she is black. The greatest plot changes occur in the second half-hour episode. The way the tribe grows varies greatly from the novel. The university library does not appear, and Joey ultimately survives diptheria to attend his aging father's death on the bridge. Most radically, the tribe is driven out of San Francisco by fire and Ish's constantly repeated desire to get "back to the earth," settling in a fertile area (the Central Valley?): "this will be our Eden." The execution of Charlie is caused not because he has venereal disease, but because he wants to control the now greatly-expanded (45 members) tribe, and shoots George. The vote for execution is well detailed: "the power of the new state was born" (Science Fiction Creators).

Despite contemporary cavils, *Earth Abides* has remained almost continuously in print, and had a very diverse influence. Jerry Gross of Ace

Books, arranging a 1962 paperback reprint (Gross remembers none of this [Jerry Gross, Email to the author n.d.]) sent Stewart a blurb from Carl Sandburg: "If I should be naming 5 novels out of the last 10 years most worthwhile, and most worth reading, I would certainly include a book titled Earth Abides by George R. Stewart. It reads as a good story and it has profound meanings. I thank brother Stewart for writing it" (Gross to Stewart 10 May 1962). Brigadier General Bradford Chynoweth, responded to the novel: "Following your logic, I suggest the poison oak for State Flower, the Rattlesnake for our flag, and then turn the sewage plant into the reservoir. That will serve to remind us of our weaknesses" (Chynoweth to Stewart 18 May 1953). More contemporarily, in 1949 Robert Frost's Christmas card to Stewart featured a poem "On a Tree Fallen Across the Road" (alluding to the poplar tree on Route 66), and a note: "All three of your feats of literature have fascinated me. You have found a new kind of things [sic.] to write" (Frost to Stewart, 1949).

Particularly in the time of environmental resurgence, people recurred to *Earth Abides* (reprinted, with many of his other books, after Earth Day in 1970). Willard B. Moore, a former student, wanted to talk with him about *Earth Abides*, "ahead of its time," forerunner of the "ethnographic novel" (Moore to Stewart 10 May 1975). Denis Charlton, artist, of Hampshire England, decided to do a large canvas based on the novel and using its title (Charlton to Stewart 16 May 1968). Nancy Braun wrote a fan letter to Stewart about *Earth Abides*. She "particularly cherishes" it. "Its imagery exposes man's loneliness and alienation and his need for his fellow man. I can hear the shutter banging and the silence" (Braun to Stewart 18 Apr. 1977). Harry Frank, professor at the University of Michigan in Flint read it at fifteen and now teaches it in an interdisciplinary course, Environment and Behavior (Frank to Stewart 21 Nov. 1971).

Most striking to me is a letter to Stewart from Frank Eldridge, professor of music at Ithaca College, and a friend of my parents. "Has anyone ever told you what an impact this book has made on him?. . . It is a book to disturb one's soul." Eldridge says central events in his life were tied to it. In 1957 his family bought 90 acres of land near Ithaca, have been nurturing its natural life, and plan to give it under what we would now call a "conservation easement," to the Nature Conservancy. "Prior to EARTH ABIDES such ideals were not in our thinking. "[S]o much of the focus of your story is on the forces of Nature, and it is all so plausible. The works of naturalist has [sic] suddenly become a passion for me, and I find the natural world around me exceedingly fascinating" (Eldridge to Stewart 19 Dec. 1961).

There was discontent on the author's side. Stewart was in no way nonchalant about making money from his novels, and was also, in late 1949, agitated by the California Loyalty Oath controversy, in which he was becoming deeply involved. By that time he was so committed to opposing the Oath that he may well have been worrying about his financial condition if fired from the University. He protested vehemently to Bennett Cerf about the poor sales of *Earth Abides*, and Random House's failure, as he saw it, to promote the book adequately. Cerf was in defensive mode, especially since Stewart was hinting about moving to Houghton Mifflin. In one reply he says Jim Russell, Random's west coast representative, is "fully aware of your importance as an author in general, and as a headliner of the Random House list in particular." He excuses what Stewart calls his "bad planning" in publishing *Earth Abides* in the same time frame as Herb Caen's collection of columns about San Francisco, *Bagdad on the Bay*. He concludes "We'll be looking forward to receiving the first draft of SHEEP ROCK" (Cerf to Stewart 25 Nov. 1949). Again, the next month, Cerf is "nonplussed" by the failure of *Earth Abides* to sell well in California. He notes the similar sales failure of Aldous Huxley's apocalyptic *Ape and Essence*, suggesting that "The only explanation we can get around New York is that people simply will not go for fanciful stories about possible catastrophes in the future." In general "it has been a terrible season for fiction" (Cerf to Stewart 7 Dec. 1949).

*

Stewart would not give up on Random yet though. They would be publishing *Sheep Rock*, but in the more immediate present, they were offered another, somewhat inflammatory, project (Stewart to Cerf 25 April 1950), which Cerf rejected, even while expressing shock that it had been accepted by Doubleday (Cerf to Stewart 26 May 1950).

Mrs. Stewart explained it in a letter to Cerf which she was writing because her husband was too busy. He was working on a project with nearly fifty other faculty members. "Our house has become what the movies lead me to believe must be like a big city room of a newspaper." After discussing whose names may be affixed to the finished project since "Most of those working on it cannot be allowed to risk signing, and I know these men realize they all may lose their jobs if they do. . .," she admits that "We have also this week given up trying to keep the project a secret." Fairly cleverly, she suggests that with "spy trials, un-American investigations, and McCarthyism in every edition of every newspaper, the universities cannot escape. Universities make headlines too, now." And therefore, the book being created by the project, will be sure to sell (Theodosia Stewart to Bennett Cerf, carbon, 5 May 1950).

The project Mrs. Stewart was talking about was the book to which Stewart eventually had the courage (his most cherished attribute) to affix his name alone, *The Year of the Oath*, a personal, witty, angry, and verbally powerful attack on the California Board of Regents' loyalty oath, demanded of all state higher education employees.

"McCarthyism," says Ellen Schrecker,"was amazingly effective. It produced one of the most severe episodes of political repression the United States ever experienced. It was a peculiarly American style of repression—nonviolent and consensual Only two people were killed; only a few hundred went to jail. Its mildness may well have contributed to its efficacy" (9).

Before Joseph McCarthy entered the national scene, the U.S. Congress passed, on June 29, 1940, the Alien Registration Act, making it illegal to advocate or teach the desirability of overthrowing the government. The House of Representatives Un-American Activities Committee, established in 1939, was empowered to discover individuals in violation of the Act. On June 12, 1942, the governing body of the University of California, the Board of Regents, adopted a resolution that all University employees sign the (already instituted) California loyalty oath, to wit: "I do solemnly swear (or affirm) that I will support the Constitution of the United States and the Constitution of the State of California, and that I will faithfully discharge the duties of my office according to the best of my ability" ("University Loyalty Oath").

In 1947 the Un-American Activities Committee (HUAC) began to investigate the film industry in search of such activities. At the end of 1948, Alger Hiss was indicted for perjury relating to information passed to Whittaker Chambers. Between July 1948 and January 1949, University of Washington tenured faculty were investigated for suspected communist party membership. On January 22, 1949, three tenured faculty members were fired (Schrecker 94-103).

Early in 1949 California's own Un-American Activities Committee introduced legislation, known as the "Tenney bills" after State Senator Jack B. Tenney, aimed at unearthing and removing from positions of authority, any subversive individuals. Moved by this proposed legislation, and by the invitation to debate or speak at UCLA of well-known radical figures, including British economist Harold Laski, the Board of Regents on March 25, 1949, approved Berkeley president Robert Sproul's motion to substitute for the 1942 one a more stipulatory oath, that the employee affirms not to "believe in," "be a member of," or "support . . .any party or organization that believes in, advocates, or teaches the overthrow of the United States Government, by force or by any illegal or unconstitutional methods" (Gardiner 25-26). We must keep in touch with Stewart here, noting that in this same month he was sending to Saxe Commins a good part of his *Earth Abides* manuscript, and it can only be speculated whether, as he was completing it, the thought of the oath as a political version of a biological plague, and a university as a little "world" entered his mind.

A national analogue to this situation is that of Owen Lattimore, a highly respected academic Orientalist, who was accused by McCarthy in March of being a Soviet agent. ". . .[I]f I could be intimidated," Lattimore writes, "or if people could be frightened out of having anything to do with me, it would be a long step toward successful intimation of all university research and teaching. . ." (17). Lattimore's story of his subsequent trial by hearings, *Ordeal by Slander*, is similar in immediacy and content to *Year of the Oath*, and I wonder if he got his title from Stewart's Donner book. Noting the almost simultaneous publication of the two texts, Joseph Henry Jackson said of Lattimore's book, "Oddly, the title is reminiscent of Stewart's narrative of the Donner party some years ago, 'Ordeal by Hunger'" ("Notes" 8). Lattimore describes a collegial support system very similar to that of the Oath opponents: "If you have respected your work, by showing self-respect in your career, other people will respect you for it and stand by you; and if the people who know you and your work believe in you, then other people of the same kind will believe in you" (203).

A major argument for the Regents' action was that it was meant to pre-empt even more restrictive oaths that the Tenney bills might legislate. The immediate cause of faculty outrage at the new oath was not what happened on March 25 itself, but the inclusion of the results of the action in a Faculty Bulletin mailed on May 9, with the information that the signed oath would be required in letters of acceptance of reappointment to the university to be mailed to individual faculty members. The actual text of the oath was not included in this notice (Gardiner 30). In reaction to this mailing the northern and southern branches of the University Faculty Senate met in June, and voted to ask the Regents to revise or remove the oath; they sent committees to President Sproul to that effect. Ironically, on June 24, the State Assembly voted down the Tenney bills, and the Regents adopted a revised oath which in part required the respondent to swear "I am not a member of the Communist Party. . ." (Gardiner 45). On the 27th, sixty prominent members of the Berkeley faculty met at the Faculty Club to discuss this revised oath, which they felt required a relinquishment of academic freedom.

A few days later, President Sproul agreed, based on discussions with Benjamin Lehman and other representatives of the Faculty Senate, to the mailing of faculty checks for July and August without reference to the Oath, but he insisted that new contracts and copies of the new version of the oath be sent, and signed, as separate documents. The Oath text was mailed to University faculty and administration in July. It was to be signed, notarized, and returned by October 1. No reference was made to the decision that reappointment to the faculty would be made contingent on the above actions (Gardiner 51-53).

On July 10, John Caughey, professor of American History at UCLA, sent a long letter to Sproul from Boulder, Colorado, where he was vacationing and teaching at the University of Colorado. Most of it consists of a written statement, which Sproul is invited to share with any other members of the university community. Caughey's points in this letter are worth abstracting here, since they will all recur in *Year of the Oath*. He was also a leading figure among the non-signers of the Oath, and the next April he was chosen among others to speak to the Regents in the presence of Governor Earl Warren, a Regent totally opposed to the oath.

Caughey's first point is that ". . .no explanation of reasons was offered, but instead the oath was to be circulated at contract time with the virtual ultimatum 'Sign or be fired.'. . .As presented, the oath has something of this flavor, 'Will you stop being disloyal?'." His second point is that, although many see oaths as meaningless, this is not the case with "so sensitive a group" as a university faculty. It will impel some patriotic member of the faculty "to take the road to martyrdom." The faculty are loyal not just to this University, but to the University in general as an institution "vital to the welfare of the United States and of mankind in general." Therefore it is likely that "some man of conscience" will feel it demonstrates his loyalty best "to refuse to subscribe to the regents' oath because it undermines the effectiveness of the University as an institution dedicated to the pursuit and the dissemination of knowledge." A broader effect of the Oath will be "an intimidation of the faculty. . . The regents in effect are asking that research and teaching be regimented to endorse the political philosophy of the United States as it now is and to minimize the chances for any change therein. It is in the spirit of an unquestioning preservation of the status quo."

A fourth point Caughey makes is that swearing to support the California Constitution is not as simple as it seems. Writing as a deconstructionist historian, he points out that it was ratified by an extremely narrow margin in the 1870's, and that it is an "outmoded, wondrously complex document, a classic example of what a state constitution ought not to be." Writing as a historian, he says that "the body of principles that we label Americanism" is the product of "growth and gradual change," and that as good Americans we should both conserve what is valuable from the past but "extend and improve upon this heritage." If we don't, we are only "half-patriots." Finally, and in a terrific touch of indirection, he suggests that "Attempts to prevent change . . .are apt to produce revolution." "Change is inexorable, and our option is merely whether it shall be gradual or cataclysmic, orderly or revolutionary." He says he is not talking about a "faculty rebellion," but—with remarkable prescience—"about the inevitable restiveness of the oncoming generation if there is insistence that all wisdom—governmental, social, etc.—has been revealed and that current institutions are perfect for all time to come." Universities are not charged to search only for as much of the truth as is "comfortable," but "must give us the whole truth even if it hurts" (Caughey to Sproul, carbon 10 July 1949). Despite his adamancy, Caughey later wrote to Stewart basically with the wish that he hadn't included as chapter 13 in *Year of the Oath* "To the Dissident Minority: A Letter," a collective snide attack on the pro-oath Regents by the "non-signers." Caughey considered it "overstated" (Caughey to Stewart 22 Sept. 1950).

On October 21, Sproul wrote to Stewart asking why he had not returned his signed copy of the Oath, due October 1, and relaying the reaffirmation made by the Academic Senate and the Regents in concert on September 30, that university policy was to exclude ". . .members of the communist party from employment and communist teaching and influence from the campuses of the University . . " He concluded "It is hope that we shall hear from you soon, in order that errors in recording the responses of faculty embers, or the absence thereof, may not be made" (Sproul to Stewart 21 Oct 1949). Sproul here does not include the nuance that the above reaffirmation was of a policy; from the point of view of the Senate it was *not* an endorsement of an oath requirement based on the policy. It was, David Gardiner says, meant as a "point of departure for further negotiations" (74), since the Regents had agreed to mail reappointment letters even to those who had refused to sign, pending further action against them. Nationally, on this same date eleven U.S. communist leaders were sentenced after conviction for conspiracy to overthrow the government.

It should be noted that on September 27 national danger was approaching, as HUAC opened notorious inquiries into communism at the Radiation Laboratory at Berkeley. During the course of the inquiries, David Fox, a researcher at the laboratory, had refused to answer questions before HUAC. This refusal was to loom large in upcoming months, as an ominous link between national and state investigations. This linkage between national and state or local anti-communist oaths for educators and researchers was a highly visible phenomenon in the fall of 1949. Jean Begeman reported in that month that as schools opened, teachers in 26 states were being required to take "an oath of allegiance or otherwise satisfy the employing agencies that they are loyal to the Government of the United States. This extension of anti-Communist agitation into the sphere of education has caused deep concern to many, who fear that such measures, by threatening to impair the tradition of academic freedom, entail greater risks than those they are intended to meet" (15). As oath requirements were multiplying, so were the educators who questioned their purpose. "Is there any suggestion in any of the forms of oaths that teachers will have to take as to the meaning of loyalty?" The oaths seem totally negative—simply affirmations that you are not disloyal. In analogy, "Teachers. . .are expected to teach pupils and students how to swim, but must themselves not go near the water" (K., I. L. 283).

Stewart clearly was agonizing over the choice of signing the oath—joining the majority of signers, who were nonetheless overwhelmingly opposed to it, or the minority (31) of non-signers such as Caughey, psychologist Edward Tolman, and geologist James Gilluly, who were risking their reputations and careers. Frederick Carpenter resigned as "Research Associate in the Department of English" "in protest against the recent action of the Regents in dismissing those members of the faculty who refused to sign the non-communist contract." Carpenter considered the Regents' appeal "to the principle of arbitrary authority" by definition "Fascism" (Carpenter to ?Robert Sproul, n.d.).

Stewart recognized that for many such colleagues it was "a highly charged, emotional issue, and it became more and more so," but he professes not to have been as deeply involved emotionally as others were. "I finally decided that it wasn't my bag, as they would say these days, that I was really not enough committed on the matter to hang out as a non-signer. . . .Then I decided I would do my part. I would do this book" (*Little* 185).

Looking back, Stewart does not believe people had been thinking much about academic freedom before the Oath controversy. "[I]n a sense you don't have academic freedom when you start thinking about it. You've got to be in a state of innocence, so to speak, to have it. . .," because when you start thinking you have to save it, by definition you have it no longer" (*Little* 186). He propagated the slogan "'Sign, stay, and fight,'" on the premise that if all the people who opposed the oath were on principle to leave the university, "you would have had a dead, conservative University left" (*Little* 187). Again, I speculate whether this stance could be made slightly analogous to that of Ish, who accepts the Tribe's abnegation of civilization, but who stays to provide them a tool to survive. *Year of the Oath* was Stewart's bow and arrow.

With the new year came the period of crisis and violent polarization in the Oath controversy, and on the national stage two other crises that increased national tension and fear. In the latter case, not long after Alger Hiss was convicted of perjury (January 21), Joseph McCarthy (February 9) made his famous speech in Wheeling, West Virginia, charging that he had a list of 57 State Department employees who were known members of the Communist Party. In California, the Regents met on January 4 to discuss how to implement the policy reaffirmed on the preceding September 30. From this meeting, and its aftermaths, emerged prominent players in the war between the faculty and the Regents. On the latter side, Governor Warren became fully involved as an oath opponent, and the role of its promoter fell to San Francisco attorney John Francis Neylan, whose rabidity in the matter appears to an outsider almost insane. Another outspoken Oath supporter was Bank of America president Mario Giannini.

The diverse negotiations of early 1950 chronicled by David Gardiner resulted in a steady movement of President Sproul away from the pro-oath position, and a progressive hardening of that position among a slight majority of the Regents. When, on February 24, the Regents accepted a proposal from Neylan that non-signers be fired with or without tenure, if they had not signed by April 30, the die was cast. Gardiner states, in italics "It was a violation of the principle of tenure that provoked the faculty and finally galvanized it into action" (116). "Paradoxically, faculty unity which the Senate committees had for months sought unsuccessfully, was achieved by the Regents in a single stroke" (117). It was decided by the Senate committees to get a clear reading of the University employees' views through a ballot, distributed in March, which revealed overwhelming opposition to the oath. This did not deter Neylan, and resulted in a sort of compromise, where non-signers were allowed a hearing before the Faculty Senate's Committee on Privilege and Tenure. ". . .[M]ost moderates believed that [the hearing] restored to the faculty control over the employment of its members. They also believed that the tenure committees would save the jobs of most non-signers" (Schrecker 120).

On April 4, President Sproul proposed that the Regents change their resolution to state that "Failure to file the oath or affirmation will not be regarded as ipso facto evidence of membership in the Communist Party and no non-signer will therefore be dismissed" (Gardiner 147). On that same day, Stewart and his gang of fifty (or seventy) began the sixty-day research and writing of *Year of the Oath* as described in the letter from Theodosia Stewart cited above. This was a very difficult task, since the authors were, in a way, writing history as it was happening, and it was hard to find a fixed temporal point from which to record that history. Stewart saw it as a "therapeutic project," as much for the benefit of the participants as for the end product, although he got "sore" at Random House for refusing it. "It was an unsatisfactory book in many ways, because it had to be done right in the middle of things. We couldn't really write an ending to it. The controversy was still going on" (*Little* 177).

As the writing proceeded, the Stewart residence became a sort of command central for the oath's opponents. Academics from other universities wrote (despite its supposed secrecy) inquiring about progress or offering donations. President Robert Hutchins of the University of Chicago, a strong opponent of oath promoters in his own state, wrote for information (Hutchins to Stewart 22 April 1950), and ". . .on behalf of his faculty offered a voluntary 2-per-cent deduction from salaries to support California professors in exile" (Wecter 52). This quote is from Dixon Wecter's "Commissars of Loyalty," a sort of "trial balloon" in the *Saturday Review* by one of the anonymous writers of *Year of the Oath*, in which Wecter astutely connects the larger attack on U.S. institutions being carried out under the flag of McCarthy—particularly that on Owen Lattimore, ". . .a gentleman who is both a college professor and occasional adviser to the State Department and thus labors under a dual burden of guilt by association"—to the history of the California controversy up to May (49).

Citing Stewart's judgment, future Chancellor Clark Kerr says "The whole oath episode was unnecessary and took the inevitable course of a Greek tragedy once set into motion" (2.42). To the participants in Stewart's workshop, tragic it might be, but inevitable it was not. Kerr begins his (short) discussion of the controversy with this quote from the first page of *The Year of the Oath: The Fight for Academic Freedom at the University of California*, by "George R. Stewart in collaboration with other professors of the University of California."

> In that year we went to oath meetings, and talked oath, and thought oath. We woke up, and there was the oath with us in the delusive bright cheeriness of the morning. 'Oath' read the headline in the newspaper, and it put a bitter taste into the breakfast coffee. We discussed the oath during lunch at the Faculty Cub. And what else was there for subject matter at the dinner table? Then we went to bed, and the oath hovered over us in the darkness, settling down as a nightmare of wakefulness. (9)

In this evocation of obsession and distress there is no little tonal echo of Isherwood Williams's first day and night in his parents' house. There is also in the book constant unsonamed reference to what Ish calls "Secondary Kill." The oath is more important as a weapon of psychological destruction than as an instrument of political indoctrination.

The Year of the Oath has an organic, personal shape, disguised by the trappings of a tight structure. There are five parts: "Introduction and History," "Results," "Larger Aspects," "The Regential System," and "Conclusion." There are also an updating postscript and two appendices.

In the Introduction, the author says "Many of us aged more than one year during that time" (10). The month-to-month strain wore "us" down. "We were trying to hold the lines, plug a gap here, and stop a hole there. We had not of that high exhilaration that comes with the advance toward victory. Out of this feeling sprang the idea of this book" (11)

The text says the book's purposes are three: to present the facts, to interpret them, and to make proposals for the future. It requires the understanding of two concepts. The first, Academic Freedom means ". . .*the freedom within an educational institution, to teach and be taught the truth*" (14). It keeps a teacher "from losing his job if he teaches an unpopular truth" (15). Similarly, tenure is defined as ". . .*the right of a teacher, after he has amply demonstrated his competence and character, to hold his job, unless proved unfit"* (16). Teachers insist the burden of "proof" is on those pressing the charge of unfitness; unfitness can be defined as having committed a felony or of acts "considered debasing to the profession." "He should not, for instance, appear even slightly alcoholic very often, and he should not take his clothes off in the public square even once" (17).

Having established the principles at stake, the text goes on to define the issues, and (presumably) Stewart says the whole controversy arose over a thirty-four word codicil to the Constitutional oath. "This is an interesting example of the power over human lives which may be exerted by 'mere words,' as they are sometimes called . . ." (20). Showing the influence of Caughey's position, Stewart reduces the arguments against signing the Oath to eight. The first (not applicable to the Oath's revision as explicitly referring to communism) is ambiguity—what are we asking to swear to? Secondly, since the Communist party is a legal party in California, the oath was seen as "a political test for membership in the faculty," and therefore probably unconstitutional. Many thought it involved "guilt by association;" again, this factor was lessened with the revision of the oath, but, ironically in retrospect, "If the issue of the oath had been taken to the courts, these arguments would undoubtedly have been again of primary importance." The irony here is that the oath was rescinded only after Tolman and other non-signers won their case before the California Supreme Court on October 17, 1952, and the Regents decided not to appeal (23).

Very importantly for Stewart's own position, he considers under the rubric of "Personal" the most important arguments against the oath: the emotional effects of an unstated assumption of guilt, the discrimination in requiring only one group of state employees to take such an oath. The other three major arguments Stewart summarizes are more in the realm of policy: the oath is not a strong communist preventive (quoting Warren's famous *mot* "'Any Communist would take the oath and laugh'. . ."); university welfare, in that the Regents were using the oath as a way to gain direct control of the university; that the oath was a frontal attack on tenure itself; and, finally, parallelling tenure, academic freedom, "setting up a field within which thought was no longer free. Having signed the oath, a professor might still think about Communism, but he necessarily had always to come out with the answer that Communism was bad (22-25). The issue of freedom applies to the student as well. The psychology is suggested whereat the procommunist student agitator will argue to the potential convert that since professors have been forced to abjure it, you can't trust them on it and there must be something in it (26).

This text has already covered the chronology of the controversy, so that section of *The Year of the Oath* need not be covered in great detail. But remembering that the text is retrospective from June, 1950, it is interesting to see how Stewart defines the four stages in it up to that point. The "Prelude," January-May, 1949: Sproul proposes the oath and it is mailed in the Faculty Bulletin. "The Faculty Advances, June 7, 1949—January 4, 1950: from when the press gets the oath text to the compromise resolution of January 4. "The Faculty Retreats," January 4-March 31, 1950: To the Regents 10-10 tie on rescinding the oath, which lets it stand. "The Climax," March 31-April 21, 1950: comprising more subjective developments, such as a splintering of faculty views, a "Sign, stay, and fight," movement, the beginning of the book itself, the April 21 Regents meeting to rescind the oath but place it within the body of the annual teaching contract.

The next chapter has a level of humor to it: "The T.A. and the Piano Player," referring to the only two university employees ultimately fired. The T.A. has been referred to before—Irving Fox, the researcher at the Radiation Laboratory. Stewart spends a good deal of time on his case (Sproul had fired Fox in December), with a good sense of history, since he was an *avant-courer* of the wave of nuclear scientist persecutions that were to follow, heightened, to a certain degree, by the arrest for espionage of Klaus Fuchs in England in January, 1950. Fox was ". . .one of a handful of relatively young and unknown physicists who were to tangle with HUAC during the course of that committee's extensive [and unsuccessful] search for spies in the atomic bomb project" (Schrecker 130). He discusses the Regents' apparent unease with their Fox decision, and their conjuring up of new rationales for their action. "If the regents have this power to create new requirements while judging individual cases, is there any guarantee of protection to the faculty?" (45).

The piano player was Miriam Brooks Sherman, a pianist in the Womens' Phys. Ed. Program at UCLA. She was identified by Senator Tenney as a communist. Fortunately for the Regents, her sister was also on the faculty, and she could therefore be thrown out under nepotism, not political, guise. Stewart narrates the expulsion with wry amusement.

> On this day [April 20, 1950], therefore, at eleven forty-five, Mrs . Sherman was called from the middle of a 'Rhythms' class and was informed that since her employment was in violation of the regulation she was dismissed, effective immediately, with pay for the remainder of the contract year. . .There is, of course, something comically pusillanimous in this sudden bundling of her off the campus in the middle of a class, while all the girls on the gymnasium floor, we are left to imagine, stood poised on one toe, waiting for the concluding chords that never came. (47-48)

This novelistic, or, at least, storytelling urge, in Stewart, keeps bubbling toward the surface in his text. Sometimes he suppresses it, sometimes it emerges slightly, sometimes it comes fully forth. It creates the personalization which made the document so compelling to some and so uncompelling to others. For example, he seems arbitrarily to throw in a list of newspaper headlines (like the ones in *Storm*) about communism that appeared in the *San Francisco Chronicle* on June 14, 1949, when the Academic Senate first met to consider the oath (55-56). But this is not solely a lark. It has a psychological message which my own text has been trying to work on through bringing in extra-California happenings relating to communism. "Every headline of *Communist,*" he says, ". . .meant that a state of mind was induced and then transferred to the next headline, which read, *U.C. Oath Controversy.*" Thus, the emotional identity of the controversy is generated as much by "non-events," news "about" events as by events themselves.

One use of fiction in *The Year of the Oath* comes in the chapter of Part 2 titled "The Damage." To try to concretize the somewhat intangible extralegal damage he's addressing, Stewart creates an imaginary dialogue between Professor Doe of the Department of Xology, and an interviewer. Although the professor is described "facetiously," his department is real and "There is no real fiction in what he tells us" (59). The interviewer asks what would have happened in Xology if the freestanding oath had not been rescinded. Doe replies that momentum might have led to the resignation of half the department. He says that in this atmosphere it would be hard to recruit new tenure-track and summer school faculty. Stewart also brings his *Earth Abides* anthropology onto the real campus he dramatizes so extensively in that fiction. "Where a tribe of professors now inhabits the Faculty Club on the Berkeley campus there was once the camp site of a tribe of Costanoans. Under the northeast corner of the present building, anthropologists have discovered graves and skeletons of the former inhabitants" (65). He imagines a dramatic encounter of the tribe (in their sweat lodge, not so different from the Faculty Club), and invading Spaniards, shifting allegiances, a general "disintegration" of culture. "Such a fate also threatened the tribe of professors" (66).

The tribal analogy leads to its opposite, the importance of recognizing the damage done to individual members of the faculty. Over Stewart's signature, he and his collaborators on May 8 sent out 302 questionnaires to affected individuals, with the information that they would be used in the book. One was returned as 'too dangerous' to be involved with. Stewart goes over the answers to the questionnaires, and could be accused of rhetorically skewing some of the results, although, for example, 87 per cent of the respondents felt that some time during the year the University was "endangered" (69).

Complementing the questionnaires, forty-two interviews were held with a diverse population of university personnel, and seven are synopsized in the book as "case studies." Most of the respondents feel angry, gloomy, desperate, depressed. In fact, depression impelled a number of people to collaborate on the book. Some, but not all, "recovered immediately with the opportunity for purposive work. . .They expressed a new interest in life and showed great psychological improvement" (74). Again in light of *Earth Abides* it is worth noting the degree to which this project was an experiment in observation and therapy for those traumatized by a profoundly stressful event. Its originality lies in its existence as a "living" document actively participating in the situation which it is recording.

When he turns to "Larger Aspects" of the case, Stewart and his team give a capsule history of people terminated from faculty positions for loyalty oath reasons, beginning with the famous case of future radical activist and environmentalist Scott Nearing, denied reappointment at Penn in 1915. The conclusion from the cases discussed is that Academic Freedom is most often violated when the professors are less conservative than the Regents. "If the boards were composed chiefly of members of the Society for Classical Music, we should suspect that cases might arise about professors of music who included works of Stravinsky in the programs of university orchestras or were suspected of being secret admirers of Hindemith" (89).

The text cites a speech given at Berkeley by a German scholar on June 14. His theme was "This is the way it begins" (90). This speech is cited in reference to a famous statement by Regent Giannini on April 21: "'I want to organize 20th Century vigilantes, who will unearth Communists and Communism in all their sordid aspects. . .'" (94). Since he was present, Stewart testifies to Giannini's seriousness, the shock felt by the auditors around him, and the seeming unruffledness of his fellow Regents. He also noticed at the meeting several Regents discussing the rights of minorities. This is the time when Giannini was threatening to resign, and he was asked not to because he was a "minority." Stewart thought "'There seems to be a difference between a minority composed of many scores of professors [the non-signers] and a minority composed of the president of the Bank of America'" (96-7).

Stewart's furthest leap into fiction is his account of the "slapstick shenanigans of Professor Elmer Bopp and Regent Ben Calef." It is presented, he says because people tell him his account of the oath controversy "needs a little lightening" (101). The story, as told by Professor Bopp, is that Regent Calef has written to President Sproul asking him to get Professor Bopp to "'come and talk to the Society of Bird and Lizard Watchers on the nesting habits of the white-footed titmouse . . .Regent Calef is president of the society'" (102). Professor Bopp tells Sproul's secretary that he really doesn't have time for the 500 mile trip involved. "At that moment I had an image of Bop [sic.] Sproul as the keeper of a livery stable and of all the professors as livery horses and of Regent Calef ordering out a horse for his own purposes." Two hours later, Bopp gets an ingratiating call from Sproul repeating his request, is about to give in, but thinks of the livery stable and tells him he objects to "'being ordered out like a livery-stable horse by means of a letter that a regent writes to the president'" (103). Sproul calls again, saying it would be a "University service." Bopp suggests that Calef write him a request for the talk himself, but Sproul doesn't approve of this idea. Ultimately Bopp is asked by Calef and goes ahead with the talk. Clearly, from his commentary, this actually happened to Stewart. He resents Calef billing the University for his expenses, wasting the President's time, and feeling that its faculty are at his command.

"What should we do about it?" is the book's final question. The answer is drawn from a gathering of opinions across the university spectrum. One, the most radical, is simply to eliminate the Regents. Why do they exist? Is it just because they're a hangover from a time when professors were considered "impractical?" More practically, a Board of Regents should be smaller, limit the number of *ex officio* members, be more representative of the people of the state, involve the university in Regential appointment.

In the postscript, taking the story to July 23, it is told that at the Regents' June 23 meeting, they were informed that 157 people were no longer "with the university," but not whether this was because they were Communists or for other reasons. "On June 25 the Korean war began" (139). On July 22 the Regents voted to retain 39 non-signers; 6 employees were dismissed.

On July 20, Regent Neylan wrote a hostile letter to Stewart. He's aware that Doubleday is advertising "a book to be written by you and entitled 'The Year of the Oath'." He asserts that "Incontrovertible contemporaneous records have been distorted in many instances and in other instances have been suppressed or falsified to establish the opposite of the truth." He portrays himself as having been forced to take the position he did, and to doing it as a "thankless task," and offers to make all the Regents' documents available to him (Neylan to Stewart 20 July 1950).

The Year of the Oath provoked a fury of response. Stewart's great friend and colleague, Professor of Chemistry Joel Hildebrand, wrote him lengthily in criticism, not of his viewpoint *per se*, but of its omissions and practical ineffectuality. For one thing, the book emphasizes the "emotional reactions of professors but you do not analyze the emotions of regents as aroused by statements and activities of various members of the faculty. Hildebrand considers that it will be ineffectual in "either pursuading [sic.] or forcing unfriendly regents to change their position, or of inducing the public to reform the Board by a constitutional amendment along the lines you suggest" (Hildebrand to Stewart 7 Nov. 1950). At the other end of the continent, distinguished philosopher Sidney Hook, while declaring his own antipathy to loyalty oaths, was fairly condescending to Stewart. Stewart does not understand that "the request for an oath is per se [not] a violation of academic freedom," says Hook in *The New York Times Book Review*. "Mr. Stewart gives a rather misleading picture of the campus situation." Actually, "a wise democracy should tolerate such harmless intransigence [sic.] about relatively unessential matters if only to protect the expression of diversity and individuality threatened by conditions of modern mass culture" ("University" 21). Ultimately, Hook thought the book was a "useful handbook of information" but "seriously marred by a failure to do justice" to the overwhelming majority of the faculty who signed the oath. Carey McWilliams deplored the *Book Review*'s use of Hook as a "hatchet-man" on the book (McWilliams to Stewart 5 Oct. 1950).

In a subsequent reply to letters opposing him, Hook tried to clarify his position, insisting that he was opposed to loyalty oaths as "unnecessary and foolish." Neylan, having read this reply, wrote to Hook, declaring that ". . .neither the Board of Regents nor any member thereof had anything to do with initiating the Loyalty Oath," that is was suggested by President Sproul, "presumably after consultation with his academic advisers." He added, at the end:

> Mr. Stewart did not want the facts.
>
> As one distinguished member of the Faculty stated, Mr. Stewart preferred to write fiction and picture the great Faculty of the University of California as composed mostly of neurotic and intellectual snobs.
>
> I can assure you Mr. Stewart's book was a contemptible libel. (Neylan to Hook, 28 Nov. 1950)

However, clearly Prof. Hook had somewhat the same opinion of Neylan. He says since the Faculty Senate repudiated the Oath, and the Regents insisted thereafter on imposing it, it's hardly germane that where the Oath originated. He cites his own numerous articles on the subject, concluding that "the only way the present situation can be adequately met is . . .to abolish the special loyalty oath for the member of the University." No only this but, "I feel so strongly about this that I should like the privilege of appearing before the Board of Regents to plead in behalf of these recommendations" (Hook to Neylan 8 Dec. 1950).

So Neylan had single-handedly converted Hook from a skeptic of Stewart's book to a volunteer anti-oath testifier before the Board of Regents. It seems that every effort Neylan made to persecute *The Year of the Oath* rebounded on his head. On August 1, President Sproul had sent Neylan a letter Stewart had written to him explaining "his reasons for declining to enter into communication with you" about *The Year of the Oath* (Sproul to Neylan 1 Aug. 1950). On the eighth Neylan wrote back to Sproul, attacking Stewart for not using the Regents records. "During this whole year I have often wondered if some members of the Academic Senate 'searched for the truth' with homicidal intent." He concluded "I have nor further interest in Mr. Stewart or his book" (Neylan to Sproul 8 Aug 1950).

But Neylan kept at it. He wrote to all the Regents on August 9, attacking Stewart and the book. He implicitly threatened legal action against Doubleday in a letter to its editor (Neylan to Ken McCormick 10 Aug. 1950). Howard Cady wrote to Stewart (who was on the road in Topeka, see below), that he wasn't going to "do a damn thing" about Neylan's correspondence. Cady facetiously suggested that Neylan be given the false impression the publication had been delayed indefinitely. Then "The first thing he will know, the book will be on sale, reviews will be appearing in all the papers, and he will have wasted all this time that he could have devoted to writing nasty letters to Doubleday executives" (Cady to Stewart 18 Aug. 1950). On the 28th Cady wrote that if Neylan would copy the complete official records of the Board of Regents and deliver them to his office, he would be happy to examine them (Cady to Neylan 28 Aug. 1950). The last we hear of this final gasp of intimidation is another letter from Neylan: "The suggestion that I should go to the expense of having this voluminous record copied and delivered to you is so absurd I would not debate it. . .It is now quite obvious that you people are determined on a particular course regardless of what the official records might disclose" (Neylan to Cady 6 Sept 1950).

Amid all this, Stewart was long gone. The book complete, he set off on August 10 to travel U.S. Route 40 to Atlantic City to gather the information and photographs for his next road book, *U.S. 40*, and didn't return to California until September 20. On September 8 he stopped to talk with a group of Princeton professors who were sympathetic to the non-signers (Willard Thorp to Howard Cady 18 Sept. 1950). As a result of this, Princeton faculty sent a telegram of support for the non-signers (Gordon Craig to Stewart 18 Sept 1950). Meanwhile, Irving Stone had written a much-noticed, laudatory review of *Year of the Oath*, titled "Twisted Arms Among the Ivy." The *Oakland Tribune* review was also favorable, and Nancy Rogers sent Stewart a letter from the paper's own editor, (future Senator) J. W. Knowland, "a black-hearted Republican" criticizing his own paper's review for not mentioning how widespread loyalty oaths were in the U.S. (Rogers to Stewart Sept 1950). Stone himself called *Year of the Oath* "a brilliant and searing study which in microcosm is the story of our contemporary democracy striving to keep itself from being enslaved by enemies from within" ("Twisted" 11). "Mr. Stewart and the University of California faculty deserve our heartiest thanks. If we survive, it will be because we have idealists and fighters of their caliber to match our men on the battlefields." Chauncey Leake wrote to Stewart, having read the review, praising the book and deploring the "dangers of authoritarianism" (Leake to Stewart 3 Oct 1950).

The *Saturday Review* received mixed responses to Stone. "Letz B . Phaer" (a fairly idiotic pseudonym) of San Francisco says Stone presented it as "an unbiased account, made by a man with extreme bias," and lists all sorts of points in favor of the Regents position. It also printed a detailed refutation by Stone of all "Phaer"'s points. Lewis Terman, the instigator of the ultimately successful suit against the oath, sent a satiric "slippery slope" argument that the "next logical step" would be to require oaths of all students, then all of their parents, then of all marriage-licence applicants that the will swear to guard their children from Communism.

And neither David Gardiner, in his "definitive" history, *The California Loyalty Oath Controversy* (1967), nor Ellen Schrecker, in *No Ivory Tower: McCarthyism and the Universities* (1986) mentions *The Year of the Oath* even once.

Chapter VI

Rock, Road, City

If you drive north from Reno, NV on State Route 446, you will round the south shore of Pyramid Lake, with its pyramidal island in the middle, and turn north on SR 447 at the Native American community of Nixon, and find yourself on a rod-straight two lane highway bounded by eerily colored mountain ranges, sagebrush, and tumbling tumbleweeds. After more than fifty miles you will see on your left signs pointing to the village of Empire, and beyond the houses oddly clustered under deciduous trees, the works and buildings of the U. S. Gypsum Company, whose town Empire is. Directly to your left will be the Empire Store, fronted by gas pumps. A large caricatural statue of the Cat in the Hat stands in front. Local desert dwellers, all who know each other and drive trucks with very large tires, congregate at the gas pumps. Inside you can, if you are a tourist, buy a white t-shirt proclaiming Empire as "Nowhere" or a black one with a burning man on the front, for you are approaching the site of the world-famous annual Burning Man festival.

Not too many miles up the road, you will finally curve west, and encounter a bizarre spectacle: you'll traverse dangerously efficient-looking railroad rails, and then pass over, on an elevated causeway, the very lip of what appears to be a horizonless sheet of white, a "tessellated pavement of cream-colored marble'" (Lillard 105), appearing to reach down as though to wash over you and over the tiny town you are entering, named Gerlach, scattered haphazardly on the edge of the sand, and centered on a few commercial establishments—bar, gas station, motel—all apparently owned by someone named Bruno.

What you will have reached is the playa, the surface of the Black Rock Desert, which stretches north and east between the Calico and Black Rock mountain ranges, and which is the flattest landform in the world. The Black Rock Desert is known to the "outside world" if at all, as a site for vehicle speed testing and the amazingly expanding Burning Man phenomenon. "In 20 years, Burning Man has grown from one man's personal bonfire on a nude beach in San Francisco to a fiery bacchanal that attracts nearly 40,000 artists, intellectuals and nonconformists to Nevada every Labor Day week" (Fulbright and May A1).

However, much of it became, in 2003, by act of Congress, the "Black Rock Desert-High Rock Canyon Emigrant Trails National Conservation Area," encompassing much of the newly-established "Applegate-Lassen National Historic Trail." Former Nevada Senator Richard Bryan says "My goal was to preserve the viewscape, the trail, and the wonderful chronicle of the journey of the first emigrants. . . in short, to create an emigrant experience for twenty-first century Americans to enjoy and relive" (93). Chuck Dodd says "I know of no other accessible area that has retained its primitive character. I know of no other accessible are in which we can really gain the feeling of what is was like in the American West of the 1840s, so we can capture something of the spirit of those who 'settled' the west and of those who lived here before it was settled" (1). On the historic trail "a visitor today views the same terrain as did thousands of emigrants en route to California and Oregon a century and a half ago" (B. Stewart, "Desert" 1, 8).

Standing alone, just beyond the end of the Black Rock Mountain chain is the Black Rock itself. It "served as a pilot point for emigrants who traveled with covered wagons into southern Oregon's Willamette Valley or into northern California along the Applegate Trail" (Dodd 10). About a tenth of a mile south of the rock is "Black Rock Springs," made up of two overlapping pools. Black Rock Springs is a sacred space for the Paiute Indians, and the springs were much frequented by whites attempting to raise livestock. "A cabin once stood west of the springs, and the bed of a Basque sheepherder's wagons [sic] remains south of the springs" (Dodd 11).

George Stewart would be happy, I'm sure, at the preservation of the desert, the rock, and the emigrant trail. In fact, shortly before his death he wrote endorsing the efforts of the Committee for the Emigrant Trail National Monument, to be sited in the Black Rock desert, because, according to the Committee's California coordinator, the desert section is the only remaining part of the trail that "maintain[s] its historical and scenic integrity. He said, though, that "even that desert area needs diligence to protect it (Thomas Hunt to Stewart, 16 Oct 1979; Stewart to Hunt [dictated to Mrs. Stewart] n.d). He would perhaps smile to know that the cabin is still remembered, and that the wagon bed still exists, because the protagonist of his novel *Sheep Rock*, lives in, and burns down, the cabin, and the wagon figures prominently in the novel.

The reader can certainly remember the accident-fraught visit that Stewart and Charles Camp made to Black Rock in 1941 (see chapter 3). From that visit came his inspiration for *Sheep Rock*. "I think I got the idea of a book almost immediately, while I was there." But "I never lived there for more than a few days at a time. . . You're isolated. If you had any accident, you'd never get out" (*Little* 190). After the war, Stewart visited the site several times. John Stewart remembers accompanying him there with A. Starker Leopold, geologist Parker Trask, Carl Sauer, and several graduate students (John Stewart, Email to the author 2 Nov. 2001). He wrote to the FDA in Nevada to inquire about water quality at Black Rock Springs (Stewart to Wayne B. Adams 11 Oct. 1949), probably with respect to the credibility of his novel's characters drinking it.

Stewart wrote his biographer John Caldwell "I am especially fond of *Sheep Rock*; I believe that it is one of the novels that will be 'rediscovered' one day and take its rightful place in American letters" (Stewart to Caldwell 19 Oct. 1978). To him it was a very important work in his literary career. He considered it his "most poetic" book (*Little* 155). It is the one novel, he says, where he "stepped out from behind the mask" and wrote his own identity into his story (*Little* 166). It is the "end point" in a series of "ecological novels" (*Little* 192). In this respect, I feel that it forms a trilogy with *Storm* and *Fire*. Stewart implied as much himself: it is "another 'place' novel" as a companion to *Storm* and *Fire* ("Class Notes" 8 July 1949). In all three a natural phenomenon that humans have only limited ability to affect is the protagonist. Viewing Stewart simply as "catastrophist" ignores this fact. Sheep Rock is just as impermeable as storm and fire, and in many ways, in its towering passivity, just as destructive to humans who through history encounter it.

It is also the end of a "terrific run." "I always had [novels] sort of stacked up waiting to get into production . . .And then, about at *Sheep Rock*, I came to a sort of end. It wasn't the same after that. . .Also in *Sheep Rock* just a little, and then in *Years of the City*, I had a certain sense of a flagging imagination . . .Things didn't come as richly as they had at times before" (*Little* 202). One might wonder if the stress effect of writing the former at the very time the loyalty oath crisis was going on played a part in this feeling.

But, for me, the most important thing Stewart has to say about *Sheep Rock* is that it has "the theme of ecology—I mean ecology in the older sense, that is, all the things that go to make up a place." And Geoffrey, the protagonist, is "a man trying to understand" that ecology (*Little* 189). The "older sense," has been referred to before, but requires more comment here. We have seen that the basic question asked by George Perkins Marsh in *The Earth as Modified by Human Action*, was whether man is "'of nature or above her,'" concluding the latter. But he insisted that "Humans had to become co-workers with nature in the reconstruction of the damaged fabric" (Kingsland 9). This was a constantly recurring question among the ecologists active in Stewart's younger years. Quoting again Kingsland's question, "How far could one go in 'biologizing' the study of humans and folding human ecology into the broader study of adaptation and evolution that defined general ecology?"(131). I suggest that Stewart's "older sense" is the one he shared with Carl Sauer, the (pardon the word) "holistic" sense of "putting people back into the story of the history of the environment. . ." (169-70). Thus *Sheep Rock* is a fictionalized ecological history—past through present--of a distinct bioregion incorporating the human and nonhuman in a single system. This incorporation is akin to what the Odums were attempting to do in "systematizing" regional ecology, and what Julian Steward was doing in biologizing anthropology as cultural ecology. Eugene Odom's and Harry Moore's study of regionalism is very apposite to Stewart's novel. No longer can a region be defined by either natural or social attributes alone. They quote from Sauer's "Morphology of Landscape": "'. . .the cultural landscape is fashioned out of a natural landscape by a culture group; culture is the agent, the natural area the medium, the cultural landscape the result'" (332). "[T]he ecologist is interested in the whole, in synthesis rather than in analysis, and in relationships and connections within that whole as an integrated unit rather than in a study of the parts of the organization" (334-5). Geoffrey in *Sheep Rock* tries to understand the "whole" of the rock-spring region, from primeval origin to present, including his own immediate presence, the interactions of nonhuman nature, and the historical artifacts denoting human presence in the past. His failure does not discredit his conception, but rather his own arrogance in imagining he can grasp it wholly, particularly in the medium of verse.

Sheep Rock is, like Stewart's other "ecological" novels, a time-staged narrative with a frame. The source of the rock's name may be revealed in the future: "(Was Shiprock once Sheep Rock? It looks, indeed, very little like a ship. Perhaps it will be Sheep Rock again)" ("Basin" 311). The italicized framing narratives consist of pre-war and postwar visits to Sheep Rock by two men, modeled on Stewart (tall) and Charles Camp (short). Two other "remembrance" pieces in the same mode are placed between the three Parts which are framed: "The Spring and the Rock" (originally what Saxe Commins wanted for the whole book's title), "The Beaches and the Flat," and "The Mountains and the Sky." Within the Parts are other sections, passages of narrative and prose writing, often in the form of letters from the protagonist Geoffrey Archer back to a scientific colleague at his eastern university. Each of these sections is followed by a flashback narrative, in effect a short story, of how one particular human artifact got to become part of the Sheep Rock environment. And each of these is followed by a third section in which a voice like that of the Universal Narrator in *Earth Abides* evokes the primal geological history of the rock.

This complex "neoclassical" sequencing of prose segments, experienced as a whole, creates a sense of human construction in direct contradiction to the organic, unshaped natural world it describes, and certainly contrary to the ungeometric mass of Black Rock itself. It therefore emphasizes "holistically" the contrast inside the main narrative between Geoffrey Archer's strained attempts to force his experience of place into verse, and the flowing lyricism of his prose in his letters. This might lead us back to the distinction between prose and verse made much earlier in Stewart's *Technique of English Verse*. ". . [If] carefully fitted into the expected pattern by the poet, the most unlikely material becomes verse." To repeat an earlier quoted passage: "Few people can turn from a volume of French forms to a volume of good prose without a feeling of gracious rest; it is like passing from city to country, from a Rococo interior to forest scenery." Prose has "ductility and fluidity" (*Technique* 195-196). If we figure prose as the nonhuman and verse as the human, prose is more the voice of nonhuman nature; but since Stewart holds that nature enfolds culture, then we can hardly exclude either the stanzaic ordering of the novel, or Geoffrey's failed attempts to versify nature, from the ecology, in the "old sense," of his place.

This is a standing paradox of the novel, and one that is, in my view, not meant to be resolved. Geoffrey Archer is an Eastern academic who, on the basis of a published book of poetry, has gained a writing fellowship and chooses to spend its time with his family in a purposely isolated Western place. His goal is to write poetry about the place. It is bad poetry. It is meant by the author to be perceived as bad poetry. Only when the poet stops writing poetry and writes informal, ductile and fluid, prose to his friend does the poetry of his language come out and we get a meaningful sense of his place. Saxe Commins (and a number of reviewers) complained about Geoffrey's poetry; it doesn't live up to the identity he has been given (Commins to Stewart 12 Dec. 1950). Of course it doesn't. We could go further and say that, as an Easterner, Commins couldn't grasp Stewart's Western bias. Geoffrey's poetry is Sheep Rock seen through the uncomprehending Eastern consciousness; his prose is, like Harte's, born of the West itself.

One of Geoffrey's very self-conscious concerns is the general inadequacy of words—prose or verse—to convey the true nature of a place. In his *Names on the*

Globe, Stewart defines a place as ". . .any area which an observing consciousness, whether human or animal, distinguishes and separates, by whatever means, from other areas" (2-3). The place does not need words to establish its separate identity. Does not the act of citing that place in a "world of words" compromise its primal identity? But how can there *not* be compromise in verbal communication between humans about a place? The riddle of word and place fills the minds of the *Sheep Rock*'s author and of the author who is its main character.

A little coda begins the novel: a mountain-ram comes down the mountain to drink at drying Lake Lahontan, (the prehistoric lake whose bottom consists of the playa). ". . .suddenly and silently, like an apparition, bright in the edge of the sunlight along the redness of the ridge . . ." (2). The ram will recur throughout; we are always at that moment when it emerges and descends to drink. It is the totem of Sheep Rock.

In the first frame, the two (unnamed) men have almost blown their radiator crossing the playa to Sheep Rock. They are so close that the mirages are gone (Chuck Dodd says that he orients himself by mirages when crossing the Playa; the same illusions appear in the same places at the same time). After drinking from their canteens, the heavier one (Camp) looks up and reads an 1847 account of Sheep Rock from an emigrant's diary. As they gaze about, features of the environment stand out: the centering twenty-foot circular hot spring, the remains of the sheepherder's wagon, the skull of a mountain-sheep, countless flakes and shards from Indian chipping work, porcelain from an old pitcher. They find the ravaged cabin, "a scene of disorder and desolation" (9), and the name of its former inhabitant, Jeff Matthews. In his sleeping bag, the taller man (Stewart) cannot sleep:

> 'It's the place!' he thought. 'People came, and passed by, and even lived here, and they left mementos of themselves—chips of obsidian, or tin cans, or an ancient wagon, or even a whole house with most of what it had ever contained. And yet they passed on. And the place, that is, the spring and the meadow and the hummocks and the black rock that looms above—the place remained. They could not change it. It was too strong for them.' (11).

As they leave, the taller one determines that he will write a story about it, beginning with the two of them arriving. His friend says you can't make a story about just a bubbling spring. "'But the red mountains and the black rock and the spring, and the flat—what are their stories? How did all of them, one by one, all the parts that make the whole—how did they come to be as we see them here this morning, making all together what we call "a place?"' (13). So we leave, with the taller man's determination to make a story that will encompass the wholeness of the place.

Geoffrey Archer enters the story as he is feeling frustrated at his feeble poetry ("My words could not encompass what I felt, although, for a moment I thought so"[18]), and begins his first letter to his friend back east. He describes arriving with his wife Kathy after driving through the tiny settlement, Harlan (Stewart's name for Gerlach), driving across the playa to the spring. As well, he says his plans have changed. He got his fellowship with a proposal to write a poem about the Italian Renaissance. Instead he will write about this place, ". . .not about this place in the literal sense, but rather about this place as expressing in itself all other places too" (22). Unfortunately, Geoffrey's vapid working title, "Of Time and Space," can clue the reader in to the inherent fallacy of abstraction involved in writing poetry about "all other places too." Fortunately, by writing in prose about what he will write about in poetry, Geoffrey succeeds. The whole paragraph in which he outlines the history of Sheep Rock in deep time and space is worth quoting, since this is Stewart's own perspective on place as first expressed in the bird's-eye passages of *Ordeal by Hunger*:

> 'The vista of time is like the vista of space, for as in a view we see first close to us all the little details and even the leaves of the tree and the insect hovering over it and farther away we see merely the tree and to the leaves, and still farther merely the hill and not the trees, and then only the range of the mountains and not the little hills composing it, and farther still not even the mountains themselves but only the haze and grayness and softness of distance stretching off to a star which is a superworld in itself . . .so also in *time*—in time that takes survey of all the world—in time, also, we feel closest to us, and therefore largest, all the hourly little things that come and

> go, but a little farther back we remember and know only the greater events, which are history, and beyond history we know only that here or there strange men killed bison with obsidian-tipped spears, and farther back all becomes vaguer and vaguer, until at last, we only know that once a river ran here, and that beyond it once stood a mountain, but still farther off we know not even so much, until in the end we know only that there was a great redness and a brilliant whiteness—and still beyond that in the outer darkness, we believe, there is *time*.'

Immediately after writing this passage, Geoffrey and Kathy watch a storm forming far off in space, over a distant mountain range, and their daughter finds an arrowhead, a corroded brass cartridge, a spoon: small objects compared to the storm, human-created at different distances in time from when they are now. This moment looks back to Stewart's memory of Kipling's "The Knife and the Naked Chalk."

Geoffrey ponders "'What is a place?'" and wonders how it can possibly be boundaried. His is centered at the spring and the rock, the "inner place.' Then the meadow is nourished by the spring, and the playa borders, the "ancient beach," until ". . .this little place eventually runs outward to include all space" (33). He seeks to establish a boundary through the artifacts found there (although they would collectively create only a cultural identity for it). One is a silver bullet the children have found. Another is fragments of a pitcher. He tells his addressee that most of the relics found seem to express human aggression, although that should not be a surprise. "Man is a killer," and he (presumably in World War I), member of a gun crew, probably killed men too far off for him even to know they were dead. He critiques Thoreau, frankly admitting he is not pretending to live a life of deprivation. His fellowship money "'. . . was made, I believe, by the exploitation of certain natural resources'" (37).

Another one of Stewart's "Universal Narrators" intercedes, telling of the first expedition through the desert, led by "Lieutenant Camp of the Topographical Engineers" (a nice tip of the hat to his friend, and perhaps allusive to John Phoenix, and the real first expediter, Fremont). After meeting a tribe of Paiutes there, the Lieutenant wrote ". . . these miserable creatures may be considered the nearest approach to the animals. As Thibault put it, in his crude fashion, 'These—lowest people; next them--baboons'"(40). In subsequent pages the Universal Narrator evokes the successive, nameless, tribal groups whose relics can still be found on the "beaches" of the former lake. In so doing, the narrative of *Man* is encapsulated and repeated. By making the despised "Diggers'" ancestors representatives of humanity as a whole, the narrator is expressing Stewart's hatred of racism, first evidenced literarily in his views of Bret Harte's sympathies with Native Americans.

When the reader returns to Geoffrey Archer, he is writing the first poetry we are allowed to read:

> There are places, soft and lush and yielding,
> Places easy to be taken,
> Like pliant and ready women.
> Men come and live there, and possess them. (48)

More lines are in a similar cliched and mysogynistic vein. I hope the reader gets the idea.

Even lines germane to the novel itself reek of self-evidence:

> They have come and gone, and now I walk here—
> A rotting house,
> Some blue-on-white shards of a shattered pitcher,
> A silver bullet, a blue-corroded cartridge.

Geoffrey thinks he is possessing the place through words, but he, in his verse, and in his own over-analysis of it ("'Also beware stepping across the line from art to artifice. I note now the concealed rhyme *same-came*'' [51]), is possessing only the words. As is said of him later, he is verbally paralyzed, as it were, "caught between the tines of his desire to express and his desire to express perfectly . . . ."(101).

The first cultural history of one of the artifacts Geoffrey has enumerated above is of the silver bullet. We understand that Geoffrey does not, and can never, know the history with which the narrator is about to privilege us. Therefore, in learning the history of how the silver bullet ended up at Sheep Rock we are learning the impossibility of totally knowing a "place." The protagonist of the bullet's story is Ewald Broomley, M.D., a prominent physician in Civil War San Francisco, who becomes the victim of a con. He is approached by a man who says his buddy is sick to death in a rooming house by the docks, as a result of their work in the mines. This is a situation similar to the Jerry Graham one in *East of the Giants*, but with a mordant twist. Dr. Broomley plays the stock market big time, and "Like most of his fellow San Franciscans. . .had become infected with the virus of the speculation in silver mines, and cherished dreams of being wealthy after the fashion of some of his more flamboyant stockbroker patients" (56). After several visits to the intangibly sick man, Mr. Rogers, his companion, Mr. Melton (a name we might remember from *East of the Giants)*, tells him he's shipping out and can't pay the fee, but offers him a little bag of silver bullets.

Then Melton tells a strange story of how he and Rogers, coming west in 1849, got lost in the desert and encountered a metallic mass, parts of which they were able to melt and mold into the bullets they needed for defense against the Indians. They left, having broken an axe detaching the silver, never to return, but calling the site the Broken Ax Mine. The doctor is in a frenzy of enthusiasm about relocating this mine—said to be near a hot spring and a big black rock—and claiming it as his own. He has the bullets assayed, gets the name of the site, but Melrose is horrified that other people know. He has Broomley persuade him not to take ship but to accompany him to the mine, and leverages a situation where he, and a seemingly totally-recovered Rogers, are given money by Broomley, supposedly to buy horses and equipment to make the "dry drive" to Sheep Rock.

Our next view is of Dr. Broomley at the hot spring. "His clothes were travel-stained and dusty. A scraggly week-old beard covered his cheeks and chin. From heat and dryness his lips were cracked and bleeding. Eyelids were swollen; eyes, bloodshot" (68). Ravens are tearing at the carcass of one of his horses. "At that moment he stood there in the desert, solitary as the last man on earth . . .Gulled and cozened, caught like a stupid fish on the hook of his own avarice. . ." (69). He throws the bullets on the soil and in the spring. Later of course, he will make himself heroic in tales of how he almost found the Broken Ax Mine, and Melrose and Rogers will make many more bullets and gull many more victims.

Stewart has fun with this story. Of the three artifacts historicized, the most martial-seeming, the silver bullet, has actually the most benign history. It does however serve to link Sheep Rock, as Geoffrey experiences it, with the mining culture so influential in the Black Rock area, evidenced by the ghost towns surrounding it.

There is another "ghost" character in the novel, Jeff Matthews, the previous resident in the Archers' temporary house. Geoffrey finds quantities of domestic artifacts from his residency, doing a sort of archaeological dig into Depression-era misery. Razor blades evidence a man, a cheap compact a woman, broken dolls a little girl, thumbed passages in a baby book, a baby boy. He figures out that Jeff built the house—of railroad ties, chinked, with a corrugated iron roof-- and when he did. Among other things, he figures out from Jeff's bank book that he came in 1932 and left in 1940. Geoffrey figures that for Jeff, "This was a refuge during the depression," and surmises that "in the end, for all his industry and ingenuity, the place broke him" (77). There is a likeness here, for at one time Geoffrey suspects his real reason for his own coming was to escape "from the fear of atomic bombs" (51). He then tells his own speculative story of how Jeff came to leave so quickly, and thinks he could probably find out the truth in Harlan. "But I don't care too much to know the literal truth. At least I know the essential truth that the place was too strong for him" (79).

The drama of Jeff's history is laid beside the drama of a permanent resident—the meadow. "'The meadow is only the spring's larger self'" (79). The drama of the meadow's life begins with the desiccation of Lake Lahontan, although we don't know the whole plot, ". . .for even a meadow has its prologue and its rising action, its climax and catastrophe, whether quick or lingering." A seed is blown to the mucky soil around the spring, other seeds come and plants spread, killing off the forerunners, another plant's roots shelter bacteria which make the earth suitable for a subsequent one. At present certain particular ones hold the stage: bulrushes, wire-grass, nitrophilia, salt-grass—each in minute geographical succession away from the spring itself. And certainly at some time the meadow, like Jeff, will leave, perhaps when the lake begins to fill and rise again.

The drama of the rock is compared with that of the spring. Volcanic cinders spew from the earth, slowly forming a cone, thick lava is forced up and plugs the cone forming a mountainous mass of black rock several hundred feet below the ground. Over millenia the ground is eroded away, earthquakes raise a ridge of land and with it "the great black mass deep within the earth" (91) until its black tip is exposed. Eventually it towers seven hundred feet above the spring that burst out with the earthquakes. And this is even before the lake was formed, flourished, and began drying up. "Then again we come to that morning when the mountain-ram walked down from the red ridge. . ." (93).

Writing to his colleague "Harry," in the present, Geoffrey describes a shorter arc of time, and the Sheep Rock environment at the autumn equinox. With colder weather mosquitoes, dragonflies, and horseflies have vanished. The family celebrates the equinox by walking out over old wheel-tracks which Geoffrey believes are remnants of the emigrant trail, overtopped after a while by obviously recent jeep-tracks. In his mind he imagines the "canvas wagon-tops rising and falling. . ." "Now all the oxen are dead and all the people, and all the wagons burned to ashes or fallen to pieces and rotted. . .But the mere track of their passing, which is like an abstraction, still remains for us to see, and right beside it runs the track of a jeep, just as the tin cans lie beside the arrowheads'" (100).

Just before the end of Part I, the framing narration emerges with the taller man unable to return to Sheep Rock because "a madness fell upon the nations," while he keeps, in different places, imagining a return, with the goal "to learn more about the place than any man has ever known about a place before" (102-3).

Part II begins with the drama of Lake Lahontan, 250 miles long, but existing "only by the sufferance of greater forces" (110). Mountains have risen to the west, the great ice sheet is descending from the north; for millenia it holds its own, its waves cutting the notches in the rock still visible today. The ice sheet falls back, the storm patterns change, the lake dries to a shallow film of saline water.

Then the ice advances again, "as if Nature were a scant-witted jester, telling the same tale twice" (111) and as the millennia "rush" by, the lake rises until it has risen higher than it had the first time.

> Then, when the lake was last in its glory, if you had taken your stand on the tip of the black rock that was then an island and if you had looked level across the blue water, you would have seen, instead of desert grayness, the dark green of pines. And, you would have known, there in the glade among the pines was the winter-range of deer. There also, in the forest, the black bears dug for roots, and hunted for berries, and there the gray squirrels chattered from the branches, and the wood-rats built their nests, and the white-footed mice bred in their millions. (112)

Hence the reader is given a dual forest succession. On the one hand, he/she scans upward, forest species and inhabitants one after the other, until "just below the glitter of the glacier, there were no trees at all. . .." But also, imagined as standing at the tip of Sheep Rock, if "the decades had become as seconds," the reader can witness the slow retreat of all the tree species' belts moving upward as the glacier retreats, the rain no longer falls, and the lake dries up. All the forest-dependent animals retreat upward too, to extinction in that area. Simultaneously, the bared slope below starts to sprout pinyon pines, juniper, sagebrush, and with them come pronghorn antelope, jackrabbits, and mountain sheep. The Universal Narrator likens this progression to a "great death-march—upward, into the sky," for as the soil dries even more, the "deep-soil-loving sagebrush" and its companions vanish. In turn, the bare slopes are invaded by "the ultimate rear-guard of the trees and shrubs," those which can endure almost any heat and drought. "Let us hail them--," the speaker exclaims, "—those last desperate fighters against barrenness—greasewood and seep weed and shad scale, pepperweed, bunch-grass, spiny-sage, and molly" (114).

Of course, as the vegetation dies upward, the lake does so downward, and as it does, the hot springs are uncovered. But the Narrator questions the phrasing "death-march." ". . .[W]hy should we call it a death-march rather than a life-march?" (116). Pronghorns browse where trout spawned, kangaroo-rats dig where otters dove. "The ravens that once had squawked and gorged on the dead trout that drifted to the beach, now squawked and gorged on the coyotes' leavings of the antelope fawns" (116). "And now if we come again to that morning when the ram walked down to drink at the spring, we should no longer think of him as merely a ram traversing a dry mountainside," but of him walking where all the preceding biota lived and throve.

Where, in any mid-century novel, could a reader gain such a lyrically conveyed ecological education? The ram initiates the narrative on a mainly blank landscape. As the ecology of the landscape is progressively enriched, so the ram becomes enniched in an environmental history of increasing complexity. The reader is also made aware, as in the artifact stories, of how little the protagonist of the novel itself can actually "know" about the place. And the protagonist himself gains some knowledge of his ignorance, for his own verses immediately following are fragmentary and almost meaningless in contrast to the rich swaths of time which have just been revealed to us in prose. He lacks the knowledge of cyclic progression, and his verses read "Thus the land died./And beauty and graciousness departed from it. . ." After writing this he throws down his pen in revulsion, exclaiming "'No, that is wrong!. . .Beauty and graciousness are in the human mind and not in any thing or any place . . ." (118). He writes a self-consolatory letter to his Eastern correspondent, which ends "'I must escape from words'" (120). The letter is filled with what is in his mind: "I am beginning to realize that this place here is a place of death, even of annihilation. Fearful and awful things must have happened" (118). The sense of being lost in his own mind is symbolized for him by the mirages of his family, looking to him like alien beings as he drives to the rock. And even in trying to describe them, ". .. for my images I fly to the *Arabian Nights* and Browning's poetry" (120). These mirage images are taken from the Stewart's real experience. Later he was to write: "Driving across the salt flat of the Black Rock Desert, I once saw an approaching car that seemed to be coming at me through the air like a low-flying airplane" (*Basin* 309).

Aware of his imprisonment in solipsism, Geoffrey does not seem to be aware that it is itself part of the place "of death," if you will. Despairing at his psychic separation from the place, he cannot see that the place encompasses his very feeling of separation from it. You can never be "nowhere" if you are alive, because wherever you are is a place. There is no no-place on the earth. Geoffrey's constant mental disharmony could be considered an internalized version of the "twilight zone of haptic confusion," as William L. Fox calls the disorientation in space produced by the playa's featurelessness, "where we're unable to form a sense of how our body connects to the space around it . . ." (58).

Geoffrey's agonies are followed by a long narrative section in which the human cultural elements of the environment are evoked—the first white emigrants who named the rock, the first who mapped it, and their encounters with the indigenous peoples, the "Numu," called "Diggers" by the emigrants. Their cultural ways are described, particularly their subsistence living ". . .stoically, almost as strangers, in a hard country of bitter winters, suffering and going hungry often, and not thinking that anything except suffering and going hungry often was to be expected of life" (128). The speaker gives great detail to the culture of the "lowest" of the Diggers, the Kotisdoka, or Rat-eaters, who live by the rhythm of the year, and quotes derogatory comments about them recorded in emigrant diaries. They were considered "cowards" in comparison with the warlike Sioux or Cheyenne. But they ". . .had no luxuries, could not afford war, which is the greatest luxury of all. Still, they were not cowards, when pushed too hard, they fought bravely and shrewdly" (133).

The Diggers are main players in the second flashback story, "Of the blue cartridge." It involves their conflict with a troop of U.S. Cavalry, and features, among its soldiers, a Brit, Private Smithson—one might say the ultimate Easterner, a fairly degenerate representative of the culture whose tradition Geoffrey Archer, as poet, has internalized. He and Sergeant Burke (Irish?) are approaching the Sheep Rock range, and the can see the line of the emigrant road and in the distance the rock itself. They've been hunting a deserter, Jerry Johnson, and find the skeleton of his horse with a bullet hole it its skull; clearly it broke a leg, the deserter shot it, and Jerry proceeded on foot. By the spring they find his boot-heel marks and an abandoned Kotisdoka camp. Curiously, there are no boot marks heading away from the spring. Then Smithson points out something in the spring itself. "The sergeant looked. Vaguely, through the ruffled surface he saw a white object about the size and shape of a man's head . . ." (146).

We then flash back to Jerry Johnson entering the Kotisdoka camp. He knows them as "miserable and unwarlike creatures. Moreover, female virtue was held in no high regard among them, and a wandering soldier could probably get himself a squaw" (147). Jerry approaches them and says "'How!'"

> He had learned from dime-novel reading when a boy that this was the way in which you addressed Indians. Fortunately for him, the Kotisdoka had already been in contact with many white men who had read dime-novels when boys, and had learned that 'How!' was something which white men said when circumstances dictated their being friendly. The four bowmen relaxed a little. (148)

Stewart's humor has more than one point here. Jerry is a degraded version of Geoffrey Archer—as Geoffrey is an innocent at Sheep Rock, imprisoned in words and the verbal culture of the Great British Poets, Jerry is likewise, but his version of the Great British Poets is the language of dime-novels. The author is also being sardonic about cultural appropriation. "How" is not Indian, but a white construction of Indian; the Indians see it as a white word since so many whites have used it thinking it is Indian. In this verbal environment, hostile cultures are mutually entangled.

Jerry shows "white man's power" by taking one Indian's bow and splintering it with a shot. Satisfied that he has impressed them, he gets involved in another verbal problem by demanding a "common article of trade, a woman." He mangles the Spanish for "woman" by calling out for "'Mahaly!'" There is no response, and "Jerry realized that the Kotisdoka had not been much exposed to the benefits of contact with the civilized white man" (151), so he begins making obscene gestures to get his point across. He displays the spur with which he will pay his way. Finally a line of squaws stand across the fire from him and he is reminded of "a parade of girls that he had once seen in a Baltimore sporting-house"

(152). He picks the best-looking one and retreats with her to some bushes away from the fire. Later "As the stars circled overhead, Jerry Johnson slept heavily. He would perhaps have slept less soundly, had he known that he was on trial for his life" (152).

The narrator makes very clear that none of the moral values of prosperous "romantically minded society" have anything to do with the issue of executing Jerry. The Kotisdoka see him purely on physical grounds (as he saw the squaw, as Ish's tribe sees Charlie). He is a threat to their survival over the winter; he has eaten an entire rabbit, strewn their carefully gathered seeds, and destroyed one of their vital tools, a bow (the bow and the debate over executing the outsider both allude back to *Earth Abides*). So one of the tribe is chosen as executioner. When Jerry rises, he's shot through the chest. The Kotisdoka fear white retribution. They realize the best place to hide the body is the hot spring. So when Smithson and Burke come upon the skeleton in the spring, they initially think it is one of the Indians; the giveaway is that no Indian has a gold tooth.

They recover the skull and take it back to Cavalry Troop C headquarters. The troopers, most of whom are themselves guilty of venal acts, are indignant at Jerry's fate. The narrator points out that the members of the troop are a rainbow of "Americans:" Irish, Germans, Argentinians. Thus they become symbols to us of the collective American culture, and Jerry becomes a symbol to them. "By the killing of Private Jerry Johnson, the white race had been both diminished and insulted" (158). When they learn the Kotisdoka are again encamped at Sheep Rock, they descend upon them and carry out a massacre very similar to the one described and condemned by Bret Harte.

Fortunately, the massacre didn't come to "the notice of any of the meddlesome humanitarians who were interested in Indian affairs," but in the area it was "heartily approved," especially because it would "open up a large are to prospectors" (162). Even in the present, Sessions Wheeler can say "The lack of attention writers have given to this dramatic conflict and the confusion regarding some of the events is amazing." Stewart may have gotten his own information about the original of the massacre from the Thompson and West *History of Nevada* (1881). According to Wheeler, in 1865 and 1866, after the establishment of a military post at Smoke Creek, the Black Rock desert region " . . .became the principal battle ground for a conflict which, in respect to its ferocity, probably had no equal in Nevada history" (60). Although there were many separate attacks on and by Paiutes and Washoes, including one massacre of the latter, two incidents closely resembling Stewart's massacre, in outcome if not cause, occurred in September 1865 and January 1966 near the Quinn River sink, south of Black Rock, in both of which women and children were killed by the victorious "men in blue" (Wheeler 80-92). In his novel *Dust Devils*, Robert Laxalt recreates this period, using the historical Indian leader "Black Rock Tom" as one of his main characters, and using as his plot center the conflict between a rancher who hates Indians and his son who realizes they are the true "owners" of the land: "Like the chiefs who had led their bands there before him, Black Rock Tom believed that the first people rose from the bubbling depths [of Black Rock Springs] millennia ago. So it was holy ground, and the return to it was pilgrimage" (15).

In creating this history of indiscriminate massacre, Stewart has politicized Sheep Rock at a time when Laxalt's pro-Indian stance was much less politically correct than it is now. Basically, Stewart imagines genocide, not only in itself, but as an act of environmental destruction, since all the Diggers are considered in the novel to be as indigenous to the desert as is the bighorn sheep. He also adds a tribute to Alfred Kroeber, by having one boy survive the massacre and the winter. Like Ishi, "He was the last of his tribe" (162). And Stewart uses him as a way of suggesting the contemporaneity of white violence, since the boy lives to see, as an old man, "a great bird [airplane] pass through the sky above him. . ." The blue cartridge is, of course, one of those fired by the soldiers which did not become embedded below the ground.

Geoffrey returns to his alter-ego, Jeff. He is fascinated by him, as one would be by a dark double, and keeps trying to discover more about him, full of satisfaction that he has learned so much. Perhaps Jeff, for all his failure, had succeeded where Geoffrey has not, in becoming a true "inhabitant" of the place. When, in his letters, he writes about Jeff, he seems able to partake of some of that authentic consciousness. For example, having found the remains of a coyote in a rusted trap of Jeff's, he describes to his correspondent in hideous detail the slow dying of the coyote, the emergence of the maggots on its corpse. But he has to question himself. Is he "a sentimentalist and anthropocentric"? "What I am imagining is what I myself might have suffered, had I been caught in the trap" (167). With this thought, Geoffrey in part renounces his "anthropomorphic" construction of Sheep Rock as a "place of death."

> . . .[Y]es, it is cruel, and it has seen deeds of blood, but still it is strong and it is honest. In some lush woodland or along the well-ordered boulevard of any city, is there perhaps not just as much cruelty and suffering? Only there everything is veiled behind the forms of civilization and the softness of plant growth. Here the bare bones of the ancient beaches lie exposed upon the mountainsides and the dead volcano towers up above them, and nowhere are they covered by any deceptive and soft and life-promising mantle of greenery. (168)

One could of course feel this dichotomy between honesty and deception to be no less anthropomorphic than the "beauty and graciousness" that Geoffrey has earlier rejected for the very same reason. Can any place be experienced in itself if it is covered by the illusion that it has a moral identity?

Following the reflections on Jeff come sections that alternate between scenes in which Geoffrey is the protagonist, and those in which the protagonist is the place itself. The narrator gives, as Stewart might call it, a micro-ecohistory of the dominant plant in the place, the greasewood, and its minor coinhabitants, the seepweeds. Geoffrey is watching three ducks circle the spring, when suddenly one plummets straight into it, to its death in the boiling-hot water. He is moved, typically, "more by the symbolism of the event than by the mere death of a duck," and writes some of his most insipid lines of poetry: "A land strange and strong,/Inhospitable and hostile, threatening and treacherous." It is not the day or the mood; he realizes he has not been in the mood for many days. ". . .[H]e sensed the mechanics of [the verses'] construction and of the echo of the sounds in pairs, and he feared that he wrote too much from his brain" (173).

As he so often does, then, Geoffrey soothes himself by writing to his friend in prose. He gives a census of the animal life in the place. In winter there are one coyote, one fox, and one badger, "so that each of them holds his own niche" (174). "'From one of your books,'" he gathers that the fox is a kit-fox. (From the clue in this phrase one might wonder if Geoffrey's correspondent was imagined by Stewart as Starker Leopold. In Leopold's *The Desert* [1962], we can see a picture of the kit fox as Geoffrey describes it, with "enormous upstanding ears," as Leopold says, "well equipped for hunting at night in the desert, it listens with huge ears for the scampering of desert rodents" [85].) He smells the aroma of badger, he observes "two large black ravens" that haunt the tip of Black Rock. Missing in winter are the jackrabbits, but Geoffrey surmises the coyote has reduced "the rabbit population to a minimal breeding-stock" (177). He also observes another ecological strand; right after their dog has excreted, one of the ravens swoops down alights, and begins "to scoop up greedily the still steaming pellets" (179).

Again, the narrator evokes the drying of the lake and the "far-off morning, when the mountain-ram came down to drink" (184). Then he returns to Geoffrey, this time writing on March 1 to the chair of his (presumably English) department, declaring his intention to return to his post as a lecturer for the next academic year. But in telling his friend about this decision, he in effect renounces not just the poem he came to Sheep Rock to write, but poetry in general. His words are worth noting, since they come ultimately from the pen of an academic writer of imaginative literature. Geoffrey writes "'At the moment I can only think of "artist" as some obscene term.'" He declares "'The place is too much for me. It has conquered! I felt for a while the stimulation of its mystery. I tried to deceive it by writing words,'" but he failed. "'Poets should stay indoors, or should remain in towns or at least in quiet green country places such as their kind have known.'" Here, however, "'The old beaches leered at me, and the black rock laughed, and the red mountains sneered, and they all seemed to be saying "Who is this one who is come here to write a poem about us?". . .'I have given up the poem'" (188).

The second italicized "interchapter" tells us of the tall man and the shorter man discussing many things, and describes them aging physically. The former imagines saying, when the war is over "'Let us go there again—now there is gasoline, now we can get tires. We are not the same as we were then. We have gray hairs, and our breath comes shorter, and we dip down the long hill. The world has changed. . .But there we shall find no change, or little!'" (189).

In Part III, we read Geoffrey's description of actually climbing the rock ("a precipitous and crumbling mass of sedimentary and volcanic fragments" [Fox 29]), minutely describing the texture of its surface. The ravens notice him and fly off.

> And now it is as if I were the first man on earth—or perhaps the last man. I rest in utter solitude. At my feet the rock breaks away and falls sheer for two hundred feet, and beyond and below that abyss I see the spring. It is very prominent for so small a thing, because it reflects the light of the sky. I think again of how well the Spaniards call a spring *ojo*—an eye. (194)

Writing as though from this point, he summarizes the failure and success of his attempt to know the place in martial language (we will remember, he is a war veteran). Artillery of words and tanks of emotion can't do it. It requires spadework, and "not only emotion but also knowledge and wisdom." He describes the changing attributes he imposed on the place—beauty and grandeur, then ugliness and fierceness, now "a kind of resignation, or stoicism, or neutrality." The sentimentalist might call this an "ecological epiphany:" "Now I am trying to see the place not as to what my relation is to it, and not as to what the relation of mankind is to it, but rather as to what the place itself may be" (196). It seems to me that there could be no more succinct description of the movement from anthropocentrism to ecocentrism than this.

Geoffrey enhances this ecocentric turn by acting on his "new resolution not to interpret this place in my own terms." He decides to experience it as a ground-squirrel would—is this credible or possible? Is it any different from his verbalized experience of the trapped and dying coyote, to which he attributed anthropomorphism? Maybe so, since in the former case the speaker was describing the coyote as an outside observer. Here the speaker *is* the ground squirrel:

> 'Suddenly the whole country had a new aspect. No longer was it a desert, barren of growth, mercilessly beaten by the sun. Instead, it was like beautiful parkland, generously spotted with magnificent shade-trees. Some of the little bushes, in fact, looked much like miniature oaks. . .To a man, these bushes fail to reach his knee, and so the desert is hideously without shade. But to a ground-squirrel or a lizard or even to a rabbit, this desert is a beneficent checkerboard of sun and shade'

Or, again

> 'If you could penetrate a burrow and talk with an intelligent kangaroo-rat, you would undoubtedly find him highly sceptical of your story of the sun. "I have lived here all my life, and my father before me," he might say, "and I have never seen this thing you call the sun, and never heard tell of it. I am inclined to think, begging your pardon, that your story is pure moonshine".' (198)

After a passage in which the narrator recounts the earliest geological upheavals that formed the region's topography, we return to the "present," and Geoffrey recounting the visit from "a true Paphlygonian man" (Thoreau), a local named Jim Hooper. In an allusion to the 1941 trip with Charles Camp, Geoffrey brings out to his visitor the "half-and-half" he and Kathy drink: half cheap red wine, half cooled spring water.

Jim tells what he knows about Jeff Matthews, and then brings up a subject which connects the issue of *pollution* to Sheep Rock in a strange way. Jim says that Jeff was unsuccessful raising cattle because of two things "'Ar'r-grass and floorhine!'" (209). Geoffrey is mystified, but then learns that both are toxic to cattle. Jim says that he's told fluorine is five parts to a million in this spring, and it is fine for human teeth but too much for cattle. "You pasture them here on this meaduh and they drink the floo-rhine, and after while their teeth gets brittle and breaks off and when they ain't got no teeth they can't eat, and what good's a calf that can't eat?'" (210).

Now Stewart rarely engages as an environmental*ist*, but here he's inserting himself in a vital environmental controversy of the time, one that I myself remember well. On Hallowe'en weekend, 1948, intense smog collected over the industrial town of Donora, PA, near Pittsburgh, in Stewart's sphere of origin. This resulted in the first significant, and first significantly protested, environmental disaster of the postwar era. Twenty people died, and "half the town's population—7,000 people—were hospitalized over the next five days with difficulty breathing" (McCabe). One may remember from Chapter 1, the suburban escapees from Pittsburgh, city of smoke. Supposedly "The investigation of this incident by state and federal health officials resulted in the first meaningful federal and state laws to control air pollution and marked the beginning of modern efforts to assess and deal with the health threats from air pollution" (McCabe).

What does this have to do with the fluoride in Sheep Rock springs? That is the other side of the story. The main source of the Donora Smog was a local zinc mill. The zinc mill had been under scrutiny for a long time by the United Steelworkers "for fluoride and sulphur-gas pollution" (Bryson 124). Scientist Philip Sadtler, who had been active in a number of fluoride pollution cases had, for example, "measured fluoride content in vegetation along the industrialized Delaware Valley and found damage endemic and widespread" (120). Called in to the Donora case, whose casualties had caused anger nationwide, he issued a report blaming them on a sudden burst of fluoride from the zinc plant, and speculated that it might have been cause by secret military work in the plant and other mills—being used not to refine zinc, but to drive off the fluorine from uranium tetrafluoride to purify the uranium (Bryson 129). In a foreshadowing of *Silent Spring*'s effects, the chemical industry was, according to Bryson, outraged by Sadtler's report, and worked underground to discredit it, including manipulation of the official Public Health Service inquiry report into concluding fluoride was not a major agent in the smog.

An aggressive attempt was then undertaken by the relevant industries to make fluoride a "user-friendly" chemical, since, as a 1950 commission on "strategic and critical" materials concluded, it is "'as vital to our national life as a spark plug to a motor car'" (Bryson 148). The industry created documentation that fluoride would prevent tooth decay, and on June 1, 1950, the Public Health Service approved its addition to public water supplies. The attempts to introduce fluoride caused widespread "citizen protest" in many communities, including my own, in the early 1950's. A pamphlet war raged. The ADA was in favor of fluoridation, and published a pamphlet in 1952, *How to Obtain Fluoridation for Your Community Through a Citizens' Committee* (Bryson 167). Although it was well known that fluoride contributed to osteoporosis, and to precisely the bone degeneration described by Jim in cattle, the goal of the chemical industry was to create "an unassailable medical orthodoxy that would block scientists from serving as effective expert witnesses in future court cases" challenging fluoridation (Bryson 185).

So we have in 1951's *Sheep Rock* the voice of scientific ignorance, in the person of dim-witted Jim, assuring us that fluoride is safe for humans although it destroys the teeth of cattle. And when Geoffrey presses Jim about this discrepancy, he purposely evades the question, starting to wander on about his dentistry experiences. Flush with money, he wanted set of new false teeth, but his dentist discovered ". . .that there floo-rhine had gone and *cee*-mented that there tooth right clear into that jaw so's the only way he could get it out was to saw a piece right outta that jaw" (210). Geoffrey reflects on how the place, "in protecting its own inviolability, even its chemistry laid traps for the encroachers, so that its ar'r-grass poisoned the cattle, and the floo-rhine of its water broke their teeth" (211).

Surely, this digression is a subtle dig at the fluoridation proponents; Stewart probably knew very well from his colleague, distinguished chemist and environmentalist Joel Hildebrand, the actual effects of fluoride. That it occurs in "nature" as well as being a by-product of technological processes merely enhances the linkage between human actions and nonhuman nature.

When Jim has left, after giving his own version of the Broken Ax Mine, Geoffrey reflects on how well he has adapted himself to the country, almost as well as an Indian. But his comments on arrow-grass and fluorine make Geoffrey think of "'how much the whole world and mankind with it, lives by sufferance of unknown forces.'"

> 'So, to make this into a parable—a bad habit of mine, I'm afraid—perhaps by some material pouring out from factory-chimneys, or by the action of some cosmic rays, our atmosphere may be changing so that the human race will gradually dwindle and die, or else—equally possible—will evolve into some grander species. And all this may be happening while we, the lords of creation, remain in fatuous ignorance' (215)

The "factory-chimneys" tie back to the Donora episode, and the evocation of "unknown forces" to the world of *Earth Abides*.

The episode with Jim is followed by a transcribed letter from a teenage emigrant back to his mother in the east, describing his experience of the desert, and then by another letter from Geoffrey, focusing attention on the third and final artifact, the broken pitcher, for each new piece of which his kids find, he gives them a penny. He also describes the wagon (see Dodd, above) of the Basque shepherd, which he does not enter, but which is as cluttered with artifacts as Jeff's house was. Then we come to the final flashback story "Of the broken pitcher."

This story is clearly based the emigrant experiences as recounted in the journals Stewart used for *Ordeal by Hunger*. Perhaps he was also inspired—as in the preceding "letter home" from the teenager—by the reminiscences of Moses Schallenberger as recorded by H. H. Bancroft and edited as *The Opening of the California Trail* by Stewart two years later. Schallenberger's is "one of the great human-interest stories of the early West" (1). Stewart's own human-interest story deals with Gideon Barkley, the evangelical, imperious leader of an emigrant train commonly called "Gideon's Band." He is tyrannical, yet efficient. His right hand man is his lieutenant, Joe Utter, considered by some a "son of Belial" but tolerated by Gideon as a "vessel to be used for the Lord's will" (233). His name is not immune from interpretation, since the utterance of words has been central in this novel. Stewart uses his King James fully in this story. Gideon's only remaining of nine children is his daughter Keturah, named after Abraham's second wife—or concubine (the narrator provides chapter and verse). The word means, literally, "fragrance," and at sixteen, Keturah seems already surrounded by a sort of fragrance. We follow the trek of the Band on the emigrant trail as it moves toward the desert, and as Gideon becomes increasingly angry at Keturah, for seemingly no reason. Joe is sent off when he gives Keturah a friendly slap on the shoulder. The members of the Band are strict Christians. "Nevertheless, as natural men and women, not one of them doubted the power of the loins" (240), and in effect, all the men are beginning to feel turned on by Keturah.

Near Rabbit Springs, south of Sheep Rock, Gideon's wagon is tipped over. Much of the quality wash-stand set is smashed, but not the pitcher, which Keturah loves and wishes to keep. She "pleads for" the pitcher. Watching her holding it, Gideon is deeply stirred, and feels both a sensuous and Biblical analogy between the girl and the pitcher. ". .[H]e saw the curves of the pitcher like the soft curves of his daughter's body. . .And the full-flare of the pitcher's mouth was to him suddenly like the fullness of his daughter's lips. . ." (242). Gideon flushes, and turns his rage on Joe Utter. In this scene we can see Stewart's critique of religious hypocrisy, as in the cartridge episode his critique of violence and racism. Gideon's guilt and anger at his own incestuous craving drive him toward insanity as the wagons make the dry drive from Rabbit Springs to Sheep Rock. As Gideon loses control, Joe Utter takes on more and more of his duties. They camp on the playa, and Joe takes the initiative to scout ahead for a campsite at Sheep Rock. Before leaving he, "on a whim," puts out his hand and caresses the pitcher. Gideon rises up and grabs its handle. They struggle for it, but Joe lets go. Katurah, cursed by her father as a "bitch," gallops after Joe who has ridden ahead. He waits for her, and far enough ahead they fall against a hummock together but Joe understands that "though he might take her then, he could not possess her and that she would only be, with him, taking revenge upon her father," (248), so they drive on. In the train behind, Gideon caresses the pitcher, fearing somewhere a crack has opened in it.

At the springs, where it is not as dry as in the desert, Joe throws down his cloak and on it "she received him as a woman receives a man, and in love more than in hate gave to him the perfection of a virgin body that once broken is never to be mended" (250). When Gideon arrives, and sees the dampness on Joe's cloak that Katurah is wearing he realizes that "he had been right and that he had felt a crack in [the pitcher's] perfection," raises it, and "with a strange loud wail, like the sounding of a horn" smashes it on the hub of the wagon (251). None of the Band knows, ultimately, why Gideon really smashed the pitcher, since the whole incident is such a perfect type of Judges 7:19, "'they blew the trumpets, and brake the pitchers that were in their hands'" (253).

Perhaps Stewart gets a little too cute here, but he certainly fulfills a mission to insert cultural history into his physical environment. Geoffrey has commented on his own excessive tendency toward parable. By shaping his cultural history around three parables—of robbery, murder, and lust—the author has in a way created universalized human experience as the equivalent of the universalized nonhuman experience in his passages on the spring, the lake, the rock, and other fundamental physical components of the place.

Writing again to his friend, Geoffrey reflects on his nominal and emotional kinship with Jeff Morrow, imagining him as a representative of an "ancient former race," and that leaving Sheep Rock he will himself have become, with respect to the place, a member of a later "former race" (255). He writes that he has "'learned where I fit in. I too have become part of the place, which itself is part of the earth, and of the whole'" (257). He sends his friend an imaginary letter written to the Directors of the Foundation on whose grant he has lived at Sheep Rock. The best parts of the letter are the postscripts, in which he tells the Directors what he has *not* learned about the place. He knows nothing about the lichens on the rock or the bacteria in the soil. All he knows about is the fluorine in the soil. But he defends his ignorance "'Who has ever penetrated very far into the secrets of any place?''(262). In fact, it seems that the most valuable thing he has learned is his own ignorance—and that of everyone else. As before, he uses the analogy of the broken pitcher.

> Some of the pieces are missing, and even all the pieces that I have found I have not been able to fit in. As with the pitcher, but more so—so with this place, or even with the world, and life. Instead of the quiz with a billion

> questions, we may imagine it all as a pitcher broken into a billion pieces. We have found a few hundred, and have fitted together some dozens, but we cannot even imagine what the whole will be like. (263-4)

The final view of the place as a whole is with respect to the sky above the rock; of all the elements of the place it is the most changeable to the eye, but also possessed of the least properties—in fact, of none at all. The sky has created the continuing changes in the place by virtue of the action of what is in it—the flow of winds, the precipitation, the sun in its shifting positions with respect to the earth. "Yes, if a man stood by that spring and the rhythm of his life grew slow until it was like the rhythm of the redwood-tree, then he would see all things change" (271), but since this cosmic vision can never happen, this can become a parable, whose interpretation is "'Even as a man's hair grows gray, so everything changes, even the stars.'"

The family is leaving. Kathy wants Geoffrey to hurry "because there was a deep fear within her and a wish to be away from this place before anything happened" (272). He takes the half-reconstructed pitcher, intending to bring it along, but he realizes she doesn't want him to: it has become a symbol of his life and art, and both should begin again. So (unknowingly) like Gideon, he smashes it to pieces again against the bumper of the car. He goes back once more, looks at all the fragments (like those of the pitcher) of his uncompleted poem. They can never be made into a whole poem. He puts them in the stove, and sets a match to them. Out on the playa the family looks back and with "a wild joy of consummation and at the same time a deep guilt" (278) Geoffrey sees the house is on fire. He feels "fierce delight" that "by destruction . . .he had gained possession" (279), in that to no one else will the place ever be the same as it was to him. "So it was as if they were driving out of an enchantment, and coming back into their normal lives" (279).

So Geoffrey's story ends as they drive toward Hardin (Gerlach). But the frame has to be closed. In "How He Came Again to the Place," the tall man and the short are again driving through the hummocks. They find the house burned down, within the last year, probably. They find the pitcher fragments, and the taller one remembers seeing them before, but in a different location. They notice someone has tried to cement them together. "As they ate, they discussed who might have lived here in the years between their first coming and their second, and who would have been interested enough to reconstruct the broken pitcher" (282). We can see the truth of Geoffrey's sense that no one could again experience the place as he has, and also the sense in which he has become to the two what Jeff Morrow was to him—only the major artifacts left from his stay are ironic: the non-house, and the pitcher, broken just as it was before he came.

And here is where, as Stewart says, he pulls away the mask. "I, George Stewart, did this work." He was the tall one in the italicized passages. He names all his nonfictional companions, and, as himself, says that he told himself he'd know more about this place than any other one in the world. "But if you ask me, 'What is true, and what is not? Is there really such a place?' I can only say, 'It is all mingled! What does it matter? In the end, is what-is-seen any truer than what-is-imagined?. . .'" (284). Thus the author, in his own persona, draws attention to his work, which contrasted real space to the verbal construction of it, as entirely a verbal construction. But he also asserts that it doesn't matter whether it is or is not. "Yes, this is my little world, which godlike I created, and now abandon to uncaring time."

The last we read is of the two men waking up and seeing " a tall mountain-ram walk out from the hummocks, moving toward the spring" (285).

Sheep Rock was a little too actionless and thought-provoking to receive wide critical approval. Its rich ecological consciousness does not seem to have been appreciated in the year the Nature Conservancy was founded, maybe because of its very inclusivity. Some private people were moved by it, like Julie Anderson, for whom it brought back memories of driving west from New York in 1935 with her children: ". . .you seem to think my thoughts for me" (Anderson to Stewart 8 Sept. 1951).

The broken pitcher itself had an interesting afterlife. Stewart's friends Kenneth and Pat Carpenter of Reno, who had visited Black Rock many times with and without Stewart, were given custody of the pitcher. In 1969 Kenneth Carpenter wrote to him "I think it would be difficult, even for you, to realize the attachment the Black Rock has for myself and my wife. . ." (Carpenter to Stewart 16 Sept 1969). Later that year, Carpenter wrote "Last night I began once again reading *Sheep Rock* with the pitcher across the room from me atop a bookcase" (12 Dec. 1969). Three years later, in somewhat of a vindication, he says that he and Pat had again visited the rock. "Your two ravens of *Sheep Rock* were still there in 1963 and for a few years after." This time, they met a couple camped at the spring and shared a beer with them. The woman asked them if they knew *Sheep Rock*—she had a battered copy in her car (Carpenter to Stewart Nov. 3 1972).

*

We recall that Stewart took his photographs for *U.S. 40* in the late summer of 1950, on a coast-to-coast trip that we can imagine as a sort of escape from the pressure of the Oath situation. He had recently finished *Sheep Rock*. Stewart calls this literary practice, in an ecological figure, "superfetation [which]. . .is what a rabbit does. She starts one litter before she finishes the last" (*Little* 194). Respecting his next "litter," he says that he knew he was an "anachronism" in his attitude toward "picture books" that at the time "were just becoming popular." He thinks, as opposed to the coffee-table book mentality, that "a picture should tell a story," and his goal was to "tell the story of each picture," not just provide a "fine moment." "What I tried to work out in that book was just what everything was" (*Little* 194).

U.S. 40 was, he admits, and anachronism in another way, because "the new idea on freeways killed old U.S. 40" (when the Vales retraced and rephotographed Stewart's route in the early 1980's for *U.S. 40 Today*, they found a lot of vitality left on many parts of it, however). *U.S. 40* came exactly in the gap of time between the postwar rise in autotourism and the passage of the Federal Aid Highway Act (1956), whose results have overwhelmed the great traditional national highways—

an overlay somewhat like the jeep tracks on emigrant wagon tracks observed by Geoffrey Archer's family. On the other hand, it preserves brilliantly the "vernacular landscape" through the unposed, unembellished honesty and inclusiveness of the photographs.

There is a third element of environmental apprehension in this three-mode text: the brilliant route maps drawn by Erwin Raisz (who would also do the maps for *U.S. 40*'s sequel, *N.A. 1*). Raisz's maps complicate the relationship between Stewart's photographs and his text, as "cartographic discourse," since they are "cognitive" maps, with locations indicated by a minimum of neutral symbols and a maximum of pictographic detail. A question raised by Raisz's maps is—whose geographical cognition do they represent? The author's, the cartographer's, or a collaborative consciousness? As Mark Marmounier says, all maps must inherently lie (1), whereas the camera's latitude for lying is much less (although it still exists, as the Vales repeatedly point out the differences between their photos and Stewart's of the same places are not purely temporal, but often based on atmospheric conditions, such as cloud cover). Raisz himself does not present differences in cognition or the discursive possibilities of cartography. His own analogy to mapmaking is the survey of a Persian rug by a large team of ants who work to "reveal" a "wonderful design," that they did not know existed. "No verbal description of a region," he says, "can rival the impact and retention possibilities of a map" (1). This is the professional cartographer speaking. In Stewart's book, Raisz's maps, with their "drawn" features, spatial distortion, and deliberate omissions, have a much less objective, but much more interesting identity.

I think the Vales picked on a key dynamic underlying *U.S. 40*, and, in fact, much of Stewart's work. We have been repeatedly reminded of his real and fictional cross-America journeyings as somewhat of a life-motif, and his early ones as generative of his creativity. But this itinerancy is balanced by the fixity of his actual habitation and of the sites where his work takes place—regional, local spaces. The Vales suggest that a constant motif in American, and maybe western hemisphere, civilization is a "conflict between constancy and change," as inherent to the "human condition. "This conflict is an expression of the contrasting tendencies toward security and adventure, between what Daniel Luten has called the contrary personality traits of homesickness and wanderlust" (189). Similarly, John Brinckerhoff Jackson considers as twin impulses: footlooseness, and the desire to belong, which might make a highway a menace (27).

I'd suggest that Stewart's ecological consciousness is particularly shaped by this conflict, and that it manifests itself most strongly in his two road books, with their three forms of text interacting. Raisz's maps give a textural fixity to long sections of a route which we are asked to imagine ourselves adventuring over in motion and through time. Stewart's photographs give a similar sense of constancy to particular points *on* Raisz's maps, but his "stories" of the photographs more often than not move us explicatorily through time to the moment of the photograph, or speculatively, even, through time beyond it. And the photographs themselves, by way of their culture/nature inclusiveness, contain features that are fixed or caught at a point of time in motion.

Hence I would characterize *U.S. 40* as a study in the ecology of space and time, where the interdependence of the three media present in it harmonizes with that of the phenomena these media display. I would also suggest that in doing this, Stewart is creating a Sauerian artifact. The book's concern is precisely with the basic goal Michael Williams attributes to Sauer; the understanding of "the fashioning and modification of natural landscapes by human culture to produce cultural landscapes" (10). Similar to the artifacts that Geoffrey Archer and his friends find, *U.S. 40* is a "cultural expression of landscape" (*Land* 319), or, more generally, of place. It is interesting to compare this complex ecology with the one used as forced analogy in *Highways in our National Life: A Symposium* (1950). Here the highway is the circulatory system, a footpath society has "poor circulation," and "main Trunk" routes are like arteries and veins "leading directly from the smaller organic systems to the heart. Or, in another figure of speech, they are like the main valleys of great river systems, being fed by smaller river systems and facilitating the drainage functions of the whole river shed" (Zimmerman 123-30).

Crossing the nation can also be a memorial experience, in collective terms and in terms of the author's own life. ". . .[T]he reenactment of settlement by crossing the landscape often functions as a rite of passage into (or reaffirmation of) US citizenship" (Holmes 169). Stewart's mapped journey reenacts his primal one of 1919 and the collective crossings of the country by the settlers of the West.

U.S. 40 is fundamentally organized as a temporal sequence of spaces. Its endpapers, drawn by Raisz, present, at the top, three frescoesque panoramas: in a single space, we see a continuous scene beginning at the Atlantic coast and ending at the Pacific. On the right, soldiers are in formation near a New England village, presumably indicating the Revolution, while east of the Mississippi, log cabins are being built, and west of it Indians are chasing buffalo while covered wagons mount the Sierras and steamboats enter San Francisco Bay. This dominant fresco, in true classical tradition, spatializes the temporal. The middle fresco demonstrates the physical geography of the continent, but also goes underground—with tables indicating types of landforms and prehistoric eras. The bottom is a cross-section of the same continent, tracing sea level elevation and, through the heights of cloud formations, levels of annual rainfall.

After a brilliantly articulated "Background" section, the mainland of the book is divided into named stretches of U.S. 40, with Raisz's maps of each section, an introduction, and the photographs and text on facing pages. The sites of the photographs are flagged on Raisz's section maps, so the reader really has to go back to the road each time to locate them topographically.

In his "Background," Stewart has many interesting things to say about the relationship between roads and land. He distinguishes between a "highway" and a "route." A route is an abstraction, a highway a physical entity. You need machines to relocate a highway, but "to relocate a route one need only draw a line upon a map, or make a decision within a mind" (4). As a highway, U.S. 40 is as complex as a human body, or a human personality, always changing. " . . .[I]t cannot be weighed, or even defined clearly—though it is highly interesting, and can be talked about indefinitely." As a route, it cannot really be photographed; it has an "almost ineffable continuity, in time as well as in space" (5).

But the author argues that in the book, U.S. 40 is even more than a highway and a route. "It must be not only what can be seen, but also what can be felt and heard and smelled."

> We must concern ourselves with the land that lies beside it and the clouds that float above it and the streams that flow beneath its bridges. We must remember the people who pass along it, and those others who passed that way in the former years. We can forget neither the ancient trees that shadow it, nor the roadside weeds that grow upon its shoulders. We must not reject the wires that parallel it, or the billboards that flaunt themselves along its margins. . . We must not avert our eyes even from the effluvia of the highway itself—the broken tires, and rusting beer cans, and smashed jack rabbits. (5)

It is clear that U.S. 40 then is a locus for observing totalized environment; it is a cross section of America in time and in space.

Stewart also provides a rationale for choosing U.S. 40 as his environment. He emphasizes it as the most historically important of the transcontinental highways, but also says

> Perhaps the choice of U. S. 40 rests fundamentally upon the author's own whim. My destiny seems to have thrown me with that road. Once I wrote a book called *Ordeal by Hunger*, and found that to trace the course of the Donner Party I also had to follow long sections of U. S. 40. I found myself driving that same highway against and again when working on *Storm* and *Fire*. (8)

The next section of the introduction provides a history of U.S. highways, from color-coding, to naming, to numbering. Of particular interest is that many sections of current numbered highways preserve the routes of earlier, eccentric, unnumbered ones they were constructed over, as though the Persian rug pattern in Raisz's analogy covered up and partly followed earlier patterns at deeper levels. This brings up the question of the cultural evolution of road courses. Stewart mentions the popular 19th century idea, a perfect linkage of the cultural and the natural, as promoted by Benton and Fremont, that roadways followed the trails made by hunters following animal trails. He quotes his biographee, George Derby, "John Phoenix," ridiculing this idea of buffalo as the "pioneer engineers" (18). The evolution, he says, is more complex than this, but the superhighway of "today" may still curve eccentrically as its 1900 ancestor did—and as over time a river will deepen its impression on the land, but not suddenly change course in order to flow straighter.

Another highway-land distinction Stewart makes is between highways that are dominating, equal, or dominated. On the dominating highway, usually multi-laned, you are more conscious of the highway itself than of the land surrounding it. For example "The parkway by-passes towns, and therefore the motorist has no sense of actuality.. . .when you drive along the parkway, you are not seeing the real United States of America. The dominated highway ". . .is one which seems to be oppressed and lose its own identity because of the surroundings through which it is passing," as in the case of the city highway dominated by tall buildings. However, the equal highway " . . .seems to be an intimate and integral part of the country side through which it is passing" (22-23). We could say, I guess, that the equal highway best integrates nature and culture.

At this point, Stewart bewails the lack of good literature about motoring, and recalls his own childhood encounters with automobiles, as told in his autobiography. "The automobile and I are .. . .very close to being exact contemporaries" (24). He first saw a car when his father took him on the trip to Pittsburgh. The first car came to Indiana about 1903, when he was eight, and had his first ride in his uncle's car in 1904. He was of the generation of boys who sang "'In my merry Oldsmobile,' and shouted 'Get a horse!'" (25). He learned to drive in 1914, at 19, in an old Model-T. When his father got his first car, also a Model-T, in 1915, ". . .I taught both my father and mother to drive, something that very few children in the future will be able to say" (26). ". . .[O]nly the generation of which I am one will ever have grown up along with the automobile, and have experienced the miraculous unfolding" (29).

Stewart seems to be pretty accurate about the lack of books centered on motoring. Most "guided tours" of the U.S. were purely anthropocentric. *On the Road* and *Travels with Charlie* had not yet burst upon the scene. In 1940 Benjamin Appel had done a road book structured around city names and route numbers, but it was titled *The People Talk*, and all it contains are people talking. Two great World War II chroniclers published road books in 1947, Ernie Pyle, *Home Country*, and Bill Mauldin, *Back Home*, but, understandably, here too "home" is people, however wonderfully drawn. Ben Lucien Burman's *It's A Big Country: America off the Highways* (1956) is an early example of the "blue highways" subgenre. Burman talks with regional eccentrics, but his book is most revealing in suggesting that "real Americans," as it were, can be found only by leaving the highways. Australian Alan McCulloch wrote a book about crossing the U.S. actually called *Highway Forty* (1951), but most of it, like Burman's, is about eccentric people, and lots of it takes place off of U.S. 40. Some of McCulloch's observations are Stewartian, however, as when he describes crossing the California border into Nevada: "A tightness comes into the atmosphere; buildings assume a new and sinister appearance; and the laughter of the tourist develops a slightly hysterical note. Muscles are flexed; pockets are buttoned up; one sits up straight in one's seat, and eyes become watchful, alert . . . " (97). McCulloch's boundary experience perfectly illustrates David Sibley's view of the mingled anxiety and exhilaration produced by traversing a boundary between known and unknown territory (32).

Probably few Americans would have read even the English version of Japanese mining engineer Hidesaburu Kurushima's *U.S.A. Through Windows of Planes and Buses* (1953), although it is exactly what its title calls it, and more than many other native texts actually follows the road. Kurushima's professional purpose in traversing the U.S. was to visit chemical factories, and he celebrates the "Pioneer Spirit" of Americans, but his landscape descriptions have a quirky aptness. Here we are on U.S. 66:

> A plough was drawing its trace far away on the hill where silver colored wind mill turns, and somewhere the green of wheat makes patches in the red soil. Oh! Spring has come. A several days ago [sic.] I had passed Sierra

> Nevada in snow. In the desert, I could not say what season it was. It was very warm in day time like summer. Now really I was in the spring. (112)

John Gunther's massive *Inside U.S.A.*, which reached its second edition in 1951, does a circle tour of all the states, but is pictureless and featureless, even though it begins in California, ". . .so ripe, golden, yeasty. . .a whole great world of its own," and actually covers the Loyalty Oath controversy, with sympathy for the faculty (I, 48-9). Probably the most ecocentric road book before *U.S. 40* was Donald Culross Peattie's *The Road of a Naturalist* (1941). Peattie's book has a few drawings, but is not primarily pictorial. It does have a coast-to-coast aura: "To cross America . . .and then to recross it within ten days' time, is for me to experience nostalgia double the whole breadth. I long for the places I have left behind. . .Yet as I rush west, eagerness runs ahead of the wheels" (73). Peattie writes as a militant ecologist. 'It was from a hard first necessity that our young nation destroyed the balance of American Nature. . . .But we have wasted, we have robbed and slaughtered and made wanton ruin of our wealth" (155). But his text is paradoxical. It is not as much about what the author "sees" in nature, but about the author seeing himself seeing nature.

Stewart eschews such solipsism. His book's goal, he says, is for the reader to integrate text and picture as much as possible, constantly shifting from one to the other. His pictures were taken neither for "aesthetics" nor for "news value," and therefore are not to be seen as pure "wholes" but as, in contemporary terms, multi-dimensional, with a foreground, middle ground, and background. His aim is to be inclusive. "Like Walt Whitman, I reject nothing" (34). A friend complained that telephone wires ruined one picture; he had actually positioned himself so that the wires would be as prominent as possible. "Primarily, and always, my subject has been the highway" (35). His pictures seem based on the premise that "every place tells a story." As Patricia Limerick says in her essay on crossing the continent from West to East, "Never the simple, pristine, virgin place of the European imagination, the [U.S.] landscape is now knee-deep in stories, many of them forgotten and ready for rediscovery" ("Disorientation" 1034).

I hardly intend to burden the already overburdened reader with a detailed deconstruction of each of Stewart's pictures, but I do want to characterize each section of the road, and point out some of the meaningful ways in which the author tries to implement his plan of environmental inclusiveness. In "Jersey Prologue: Atlantic City to New Castle," he discusses the choice of following the road East to West, a choice ". . .based perhaps, pusillanimously, upon analogy and convention" (37)—although, as we have discussed earlier, he deliberately has Ish go west to east, "gradually piercing down through layer after layer of [his] history" (38).

A good, and representative example, of a "storied" picture is number three, a farmhouse by the road near Woodstown, in western New Jersey (Stewart has quoted the WPA guidebook as calling this route "bog to bog"). We turn to Raisz's map, and find the 3 beside the dots of houses representing Woodstown, and, as is a convention in all his maps, a centering church steeple. There is a picture of a cannon--"Old Cannon"-- and an arrow directed to the preceding town, Pittsgrove, although neither the cannon nor the town are mentioned in Stewart's text. Raisz's drawing faces us north, geographically, and New York is a tiny clump of tall buildings, while in the foreground is a great expanse of the Pine Barrens and empty land with its products named, from peas to poultry. The Delaware River is fully articulated, and the towns along it, while the Susquehanna is far in the distance on the left. On the one hand, the "important" features of a conventional road map are diminished in scale or absent, but on the other the "3" is a tiny and lonely figure in a great expanse.

The author says he's consulted Mrs. Annie Newell of the Salem County Historical Society, but no one knows the house's specific history. However, its details are revealing. It is constructed of homemade brick, cemented over more recently. The end windows show it was not built from the mindset of close-bordering houses in an urban space, but "its rigid compactness and lack of adjustment to outdoor living" suggest the "townmindedness" of its English colonist builders, who are coming from a village tradition (44-45). The double-hung windows are described in detail, the off-center front door as being typical of the middle colonies. Its lightning rods are "probably a contribution of the lightning-rod-salesmen era of the later nineteenth century" (45). Its lack of chimneys suggests the mildness of southern New Jersey winters. It is not adapted to summers; there are skimpy eaves, and only one large willow tree. Its barn has an overhang to allow hay to be lifted to the loft. It displays a typical Red Man tobacco sign. Banks show the passing highway has been cut down from the original one about five feet. A local phone line of ten wires is on the left of the highway, with a local power line at the right, supported by a push-strut. I cannot find a single detail in the picture that is not mentioned by the text, and things the text notices in the picture I did not pick up. This is the essence of rich detail in the "typical" which we will find throughout the text.

"Post Road: New Castle to Baltimore," provides a detailed history of the development of roads in this highly-settled region, and ends with a historical drawing of early colonial roads. One interesting photo, number 6, "Bush River," shows a four-lane with truck, filling up half the space, with, in the background, the "'drowned coastal plain'" of the Chesapeake near Aberdeen Proving Ground. The text details the condition of the highway and its drainage, but is most interested in the background. The topographical changes since prehistoric times which produced the plain are discussed—the water from the melting glaciers flowing back up streams valleys, turning them into bays. The vegetational history is also incorporated: it was all forest until white settlement; old trees have been stripped, and young elms are sprouting, since their seeds are more easily wind-borne than other deciduous ones (Dutch elm disease is not yet in the picture, presumably). Stewart also connects this estuary with a particular moment in Captain John Smith's exploration of the Chesapeake, telling how at Bush River his barge was full of sick colonists, and threatened by waterborne Indians, so he put the sick men's hats on sticks, and gave them the impression of a large force. Here we have, in one picture, the road, the historic and current plant life and aquatic conditions, and a cultural encounter event.

A notorious shot (11) in the next section, "Bank Road and Turnpike: Baltimore to Cumberland," follows one whose text describes the geography and agriculture of the Appalachian foothills. There we learn that since Maryland is east of the line where township-section boundaries were surveyed, the planted fields have irregular shapes. "The sky, as if attempting to match the landscape in delicacy, shows an overcast of strato-cumulus, thinner in some spots than others, producing an opalescent tone" (77). This picture's contrast to number eleven, titled "Horrible Example," is notable in Stewart's book. The "Horrible Example" gives a picture of the Antietam Creek bridge, and the road's role here in the Civil War. But beside it "The billboards ruin everything. The historical flavor, the old-time architecture, even the beauty of the wooded hillside—all are sacrificed" (79). To Stewart, utility lines and poles enfold themselves into the landscape, but despite how he tries, he can not get billboards to fit into his holistic vision. "They are an abomination!" (79). A comparison with the Vales' pictures is illuminating here. The "Maryland Countryside" of such pastoral beauty in Stewart is now (1980) totally subdivided, suburbanized, and to me, the beauty is destroyed. To the Vales, however, "in this case we find the sturdy white homes scattered in a pleasing pattern on the rolling countryside to be rather attractive" (35). However, the Vales' picture of the Antietam bridge shows even more billboards, and here they agree with him that they "distract our eyes from other features of the landscape" (37).

Stewart's "Mason Dixon Line" (16) exemplifies well his analysis of environmental change. He points out the "raw cut" where road straightening has been done as a symbol of "changing civilization," for ten years will reforest its slopes. In the middle distance, likewise, "The hardwood forest is encroaching upon what was once a farm" (101). This scene of abandonment and implacable reforestation is very reminiscent of what Ish experiences driving east (the Vales' picture [43] is even more revealing, since they note that a 1916 picture of this same scene showed completely open pastures, while their 1980 picture shows total forestation of Stewart's abandoned farm).

When *U.S. 40* reaches the Wheeling-to-St. Louis section, Stewart mentions its poor maintenance in the eastern midwest, explaining it as caused by its unimportance as a route between major cities. Then he remembers his first encounter with U.S. 40, thirty years before:

> In 1919, freshly discharged from the army, I hitchhiked westward from New York, and traveled along the National Old Trail, as it then was known, from Washington, Pennsylvania, to St. Louis. The old S-bridges were still in use. J As far as Terre Haute the road was, according t standards of the time, well paved and heavily traveled. But at the Illinois line the bottom dropped out of it. Only an occasional Model-T braved the morass, and the ruts, between towns. The redbud was in bloom and beautiful along the streams, but the road itself was unspeakable . . . (120)

A 1957 text on American highways, incidentally, considers that year, 1919, "was the beginning of the modern automobile age," the year when "people finally decided, once and for all, that automobiling was more than a recreation. It was a necessity" (Tyler 30-31).

Stewart's picture no. 23 is of one of those "S-bridges," off the main highway, which forms an S-shape as it veers to cross a stream directly at right angles. He (from an incision?) somehow knows that this bridge was built in 1828, and uses the occasion for folk-culture commentary on the S-bridges' origin: shaped like a Z for Ebenezer Zane, or designed by a drunken Englishman and a drunken Irishman. He follows an authority in concluding that the shape was purely economically-driven. It would take less material to cross a laterally-approached stream at right-angles. Here, the Vanes point out a midjudgement in Stewart's future-history of the bridge. He said saplings sprouting along the margins would soon crack the bridge's parapet; actually, in 1980, the whole space had been made into a park and cleared of wild growth---which illustrates Stewart's own maxim that unknown circumstances can change everything.

The picture of Thespian Hall, in Boonville, Missouri (36), allows us, by way of Craig Campbell's "In George R. Stewart's Footsteps," to experience three levels of time, since the Vales' photographed it in 1980, and Campbell did in 1992. "The oldest surviving theatre building west of the Alleghenies," Thespian Hall was, according to Stewart, a Civil War hospital and military prison. It was in 1950 a movie theater with a marquee, the "Lyric," and Stewart is unhappy with the "hideous and unnecessary modern sign" between the columns, although the building is fake-classical itself, with chiselled brick Corinthian columns, and wooden superstructure. Stewart also notes the Gothic revival house next to it, with a tourelle. He spends a good deal of interest in the telephone cable cutting the photo's corner, and gives a little psychological analysis of the shopping family at the left, seemingly upset by his presence.

In 1980, Stewart's hideous sign has been replaced by a discreet one, the paint has been scraped off the brick columns, the Gothic house has lost its tourelles and other features and is almost drowned from view by elms.

Campbell discovers, in 1992, massive restoration has been done, including blasting off nineteen layers of paint. There is now elegant lettering, "THESPIAN HALL" above the portico, vegetation has grown to surround it, and the original Gothic building is entirely gone. Three-ball lampposts, in Stewart's picture, gone in the Vales', have been reestablished (24).

Of the route from Kansas City to Denver, Stewart is particularly expressive, partly, perhaps, because we are crossing the last "terrain of security" of the emigrant trains he has studied so intensely. We witness with him—as they did—the "drama" of "the gradual drying up of the country, westward" (164). Trees shrink back to watercourses, cornfields yield to wheatfields and then to cattle ranges. "The fences also tell a story" (164). Wooden fences are the rule in the east; further west, where it is scarcer, osage-orange hedges are planted; in even more treeless areas, farmers made fence-posts of quarried stone. He also shows the interaction of landscape and technology by dividing this stretch into pre- and post-railroad, with the dividing point the town of Silver Lake, west of Topeka. In the eastern part, land was bought and divided before the railroad, so roads grew up as routes from town to town, "'section-line roads'," following property lines so as not to cross over private property (Stewart traces this development back to a Papal bull in 1493!). From Silver Lake on, with exceptions, the road parallels the railroad lines—there was little property to protect. Jackson makes such a distinction between a centrifugal, imposed, and centripetal "vernacular" road system; the former is based on a politically-defined landscape, the latter on a landscape defined by evolving inhabitance (J. B. Jackson 22-23, 42).

A picture from the Kansas City-Denver section is particularly interesting both for Stewart's analysis of it and for the changes in the Vales' photo. Stewart's number 48, "Routes Divide," is west of the intersection of routes 24 and 40. It is marked by dueling billboards advertising each as the shortest route. It is "short grass country," approaching desert, highly weeded as a result of disturbed land from highway construction, including lots of nonnative species. The signs are prominent indicators of the growing importance of the automobile, since their reason for being has no connection with any fixed population, only that one on wheels. In 1980 the intersection features on-ramps, an overpass, yet very little traffic, since the interstate has siphoned them away.

As sidebars to Raisz's map of "Berthoud's Road: Denver to Salt Lake City," there are geological sections as on the endpapers. The texture of the map is striking. The accidented terrain, shown in the usual 45 degree elevation, almost conceals the strong lines of the route itself. This is a good example of the non-dominant highway. I find that as the book, and the author, grow closer to the West Coast, the intensity and ecological concern of the photos and texts become more accentuated too. "Front Range and Hogback" (49) have a photo taken from a high ridge with the highway a tiny line below rocks. The text describes the geological upheaval producing the terrain to the neglect of the highway itself, just as the photograph does. The writer is more concerned with the tree growth relative to the rainfall runoff from the steep slope than with the highway itself.

In the next picture, "Two Species" (50), the camera observes a herd of tourists observing a herd of bison. "This picture shows five specimens of *Homo sapiens* observing thirty-six specimens of *Bison bison*" (197). In humorous mode, the speaker gives a Linnaen (as it were) description of the former: they are variant *Americanus*, sub-variant *touristicus*. The males are recognized by wearing "pants,"

". . .a tribal costume originally developed for ease in riding a horse, now grown useless in the automobile period, but retained for its symbolic value." The discussion continues with a mock-anthropological analysis of males and females worthy of Kroeber or Lowie. Picture 52, "Berthoud Pass—Eastern Approach," uses the conifer varieties shown to suggest the forest history and the effects of fire. The text also suggests that, although lightning is a primal fire source—as it is in *Fire*—humans produce many more fires ". . .—not to mention logging—so that the scales are tipped against the conifers. Only by the intelligent practice of forestry can the balance be restored" (201).

One of the richest pictures in its text-evoked content is a seemingly barren space, "Meadow Among Mountains" (57). The highway, with a moving truck, crosses the lower third of the picture, with a fence in the lower foreground, a seemingly desolate ranch above in the middle ground, and lightly-herbed knolls rising behind it. The text notes the stream to the right, completely hidden (from the viewer of the photograph) by willows and alders. The meadow above the road was historically the stream's flood plain. The knolls above it are "dry bench-lands or foothills," "thinly covered with sagebrush and bunch-grass." Higher on them is a "carpet-like growth of aspens," due to more moisture from deeper snows. "The adaptation of man to the scene is closely adjusted to its varying features," says the text, in a perfect evocation of cultural ecology. The ranch house is beside the treed stream, for shelter and water supply. It is September, so the hay has been cut and stacked, fenced from the cattle. The bench-lands provide open summer foraging grounds for the cattle. Since the stream, if too swollen, floods the meadow, the road has been adapted, making a great curve, slightly elevated, around it. The fence's wooden posts show we have "returned to a country where wood is obtainable as a local product." The earth in the foreground is "fluffy and puffed-up," suggesting it is inhabited by burrowing rodents (210-211). This text provides a mingling of multi-species' historical and present lives in a single place, and to me seems to exemplify the author's success in his quest to invest the picture verbally with the depth of story.

Obviously, in our survey of *U.S. 40*, the greatest interest attaches to the sections covering the Great Basin and California. Raisz's map of the former names details relating to Stewart's geographical concerns: a sidebar map of prehistoric Lake Bonneville's water levels, superimposed on Salt Lake City; the route of the disastrous Hastings cutoff, the shoreline of Lake Lahontan, the Black Rock Desert. The text gives a history of the routes crossing the Basin from the Donner Party to the Lincoln Highway, with the ghost of Lansford Hastings seemingly guiding the proceedings, since Utah refused to build a southwest-directed highway west of Salt Lake City, and insisted on a route crossing the salt flats to Wendover—approximating Hastings's route. "Both California and Utah largely ignored Nevada in the solution of this vexing question," says the official Lincoln Highway history (169), and that text's endpapers have a "map of strategic routes" from Salt Lake City to California that clearly shows how much more direct (though less picturesque) would have been the originally planned Lincoln Highway (now U.S. 50) across central Nevada than the ultimate one along the Humboldt River, that became U.S. 40, and thereby overlaid, to a great extent, the course of the original California Trail.

Many of Stewart's Nevada photos are of straight roads over barren landscapes, yet he always manages to find significant details, topographical and historical. At Emigrant Pass (75), he says "Why these people were always conceived as emigrants and not as immigrants is a problem to be referred to the folklorists, or perhaps to the psychiatrists." He also notes the shrubs marking two springs where the Donner party camped in 1846. "With their usual bad luck or bad management they almost lost three wagons in a grass fire, and during the night had a shirt and two oxen stolen by the local Paiutes. Not infrequently, even in these days, a traveler loses his shirt while crossing Nevada" [!] (254-55). The miner's "tie-house" in the next picture (76) while bleak, is full of telling detail. It has a tarpaper roof because of little snow, and a high stovepipe chimney because of the danger of fire, and faces east because of winter winds. It depends on an upslope spring, fenced to keep cattle out, resulting in rye-grass growth around it while the grass has been grazed off elsewhere. The sod-roofed horse sheds suggest that this was a pre-road dwelling site. This picture is very meaningful juxtaposed with the Vales', since Stewart's hunch about fire was right, and in 1980 it is a charred ruin, uninhabited, two of the original poplar trees also burned. The Vales also note that now, concealed by the remaining poplars, in the distance on the Humboldt River one can see the smokestack of the Valmy coal-powered thermoelectric plant (154-55).

The last Nevada picture in *U.S. 40* is of the Black Rock Desert, "Lahontan Story." Then the final Rasz map leads us over the part of the highway best known by Stewart, from Reno over the Sierras, down the Central Valley, to San Francisco. His text tells the story of the Stevens party as recorded in *The Opening of the California Trail*, and the winter survival of Moses Schallenberger. Of the several fine Sierra photos, the one of Donner Pass pleased Stewart the most. According to the Vales, "When we talked with Stewart a year before his death, he expressed particular fondness for, and pride in, this fine view overlooking the final eastern ascent to Donner Pass" (169). The Vales are surprised that, as in 1950, there are no signs, historical markers, or the like, at the pass, nor were there when I drove over it in 2005, although lower down, by Donner Lake, I could still see the old U.S. 40 shield signs. In Stewart's own text, he describes his inability, despite years of trekking the landscape, to find out where exactly the Donner Party crossed, and his continued amazement that wagons could ever have been pulled over the pass at any place.

Another telling picture is number 87, "Forest Primeval," showing "a very small area that may be claimed as the only bit of big forest still left along this particular highway from coast to coast. These trees should by all means be preserved, but on the contrary, in all probability, will soon fall before the loggers" (286-87). This view would seem, perhaps, contrary to that of Stewart's forest superintendent in *Fire* and his attitude in the "Demonstration Forests" essay, but not necessarily. As the superintendent would say, "From the point of view of forest management these trees are actually ripe, or overripe, for cutting," but they are "inherently much more valuable for scenic purposes than for lumber." It is too bad the Vales didn't include this site in their book, to see if Stewart's prophecy was right or not.

The final two pictures (91, 92) are a study in contrasts. The first is of the Bay Bridge, purposely emphasizing the bridge itself, its superstructure, with the "bold picturesqueness" of the San Francisco skyline reduced to a thin line. Stewart was able on an early Sunday morning to photograph the "most heavily traveled bridge in the world" (295) without a single car on it, whereas the Vales found it almost impossible to do so. They gloss their own picture with the lyrical verses at the end of *Earth Abides* concerning the endurance of the bridge as "a symbol of the unity and security of civilization" (179), and contrast Ish's belief in its permanence to the constant repair and upkeep needed on it since 1950. But what they note most is the changed skyline. In 1980 it rises much higher above the bridge's parapet, and high-rise buildings that were diverse in shape in 1950 are almost uniformly rectangular.

By contrast to the bridge, Stewart emphasizes the bathos of the highway's end, in a sort of desolate area of auto shops at the corner of Harrison and Tenth Streets in San Francisco. He meditates on where it might have ended (the site is not much changed in the Vales' picture) and decides that rather than a glorious view of the Pacific and the Golden Gate, this end is fitting, since it is not a plush boulevard, and whatever romance it has is that of the "modern world" (297).

In an afterward Stewart notes three changes occurring to U.S. 40: it is being four-laned, transformed into a limited-access freeway, and is bypassing cities and towns. A corollary of this accurate prediction, unfortunately in this case not accurate, is that as a freeway it will deter "'ribbon development;'" with the completed interstate, we have seen how just such development has been created, along with attendant urban sprawl, at almost every exit.

Another phenomenon he comments on is what is to him the destructive material exploitation of the U.S.'s natural heritage revealed by a cross-country trip: miles and miles of farmlands, oil fields, mines, manufacturing. "A jingo imperialist would be justified in feeling drunk with power" (299). Ironically he says "Only a supremely prosperous people could afford to waste so much—to let land revert to unproductiveness, to be careless of erosion, not even to practice forestry?" (300). The Vales, strangely, do not share this dark view of environmental destruction. Maybe because their book is a product of the "me decade," their closing view is much more sanguine, more like that of William Cronon. They use examples to show the subjectivity of perception "of what constituted that ideal, 'unadulterated' environment of the past" (188). They consider that the unmodified landscape of the U.S. is still much more extensive than that which has been developed. There is a ". . .dilemma inherent in assigning either positive or negative values to various landscape changes, particularly changes that involve development of wild or rural landscapes" (189). When Thomas Schlereth re-traced yet once more the Indiana section of U.S. 40, he accepted as a given the landscape changes. He ventures to explore the highway as a "physical artifact," an outdoor "museum exhibition," and an opportunity for "cultural research" (xi). Schlereth considers that the Indiana section of the highway was neglected even by Stewart's "pioneering book," which was a model for his own, but sees his objective as a "detailed, fieldwork-based community study of a transportation corridor's changing geographical, architectural, economic, and social history in a briefer compass" (xii).

Schlereth, unlike Stewart and the Vales, give prominence to commercial artifacts (gas stations, motels) and their evolution through the century, and devotes a good deal of space to the overlay effects of Interstate 70, using Stewart's terminology for it as a "dominating highway" (111), calling it a "linear palimpsest of the state's past" (142). In this respect he (unknowingly?) owes more to Ross Lockridge, Jr. than to George Stewart: the National Road literally and symbolically bisects Lockridge's map of Raintree County, and in such chapters as "The Great Road of the Republic," the "pull of the Great Road" (251) is felt, drawing Waycross (Straughn) Indiana into the linear movement of American history.

The contributors to the highway symposium referred to above share the optimism, or at least acceptance, of economic "progress," noting with pleasure that "dynamic physical and economic forces are constantly changing our environment" (Ross 289), and foreseeing hopefully that "The summer resort road of today may be the only outlet for an oil field discovered tomorrow" (Linzell 347). In another article, Theodore H. White complained of the "slaughter and waste forced on us by a road system no longer able to match the needs of a growing country" (45) in urging Interstate funding to replace highways like U.S. 40. White might not have agreed with one contributor to the highway symposium, who could say "It is reasonable to believe that roads cannot be designed to be safe for the general public to travel at speeds in excess of 65 miles per hour" (Clarke 304).

I say there may be a dilemma in so assigning values to particular landscapes, but, despite the Vales' protests, there is an inherent positive value in wild and rural landscapes, and, I believe, with Aldo Leopold, that the roadless, blank space on the map is a "site of vital biological life" (Van Noy 17).

Since Random House did not want to publish *U.S. 40*, it was taken up by Houghton Mifflin, which, with its interest in nature writing, liked the idea, and became Stewart's publisher for much of the rest of his career. There, his major editor was Paul Brooks, who was to become notable as editor of, and writer about, Rachel Carson, as well as a noted nature writer himself. Brooks was also to become the longsuffering object of Stewart's complaints, though they were much milder than those of another major client, Ross Lockridge, Jr., of *Raintree County* fame. Brooks has a lot to say about Lockridge in his autobiography, but nary a word about Stewart.

*

Of course, all during the fifties, Stewart remained active as a teacher. It was during this decade that, according to him, the Berkeley English Department grappled for its only time "with a really fundamental question, and it was my fault. . .I took a lot of personal punishment, created some ill-will, and won a hollow victory" (*Department* 42). This was over the issue of American literature's role in the curriculum, and how the word "English" in "English Department" should be defined. Stewart proposed that it be considered to refer to the language, not in "the insular sense." His proposal was approved by three-fifth of the Department, but it met three times to resolve the issue, with "a great deal of rancor, even venom." Stewart says he's thought a lot about it, and still can't decide why the issue upset so many people. But "I suggest, as a tentative hypothesis, that a considerable number of the members of the Department went into a panic at the idea of examining the bases of their orthodoxy. They had faith, but they lacked faith in their faith. They believed, but they dared not to consider why they believed" (43). This situation displays not only Stewart's willingness to be skeptical of received ideas, but also the persistent lower status of American literature in English Departments—an expression of the phenomenon Stewart described in his early article on Walt Whitman's greater acceptance in England than in his own country. In 1965 at Stewart's alma mater, the same situation persisted: the area concentrations from which we could choose as English graduate students were: Medieval, Renaissance, 18th Century, Victorian, and 20th Century British literature—and American literature.

Another scholarly-pedagogical disturbance Stewart caused created literally what its cause was titled: *The Sound and the Fury*. Stewart was fond of holding classes, and hosting gatherings, in his home. One such was based on a Faulkner project in his English 208 class in the spring of 1956. Stewart didn't really like Faulkner; in the traditional dichotomy, he didn't get much out of Faulkner's allegory and symbolism, his "quite impossible kind of melodrama," but liked Hemingway "tremendously," for his approach to writing, as opposed to the "hooey" of his ideas (*Little* 76). He asked for advice from Saxe Commins, since Random was Faulkner's publisher, particularly about the 1946 Appendix to the novel, which seemed to introduce inconsistencies with the original text (Stewart to Commins 7 Oct. 1956/*P).* In November, he hosted a gathering of students, professors, and interested lay folk at which the project's results were discussed. The governing idea, as I understand it, was to Hemingwayize the tortuous narrative line of *The Sound and The Fury*, to unravel the temporal sequence of the plot. He shared the results with C. S. Forester:

> 'I read their notes quite entranced. It makes perfect sense, and a quite consecutive narrative if it's worked on a damned sight harder than I was prepared to work on it when I read it—I've a much higher opinion of the book now, curiously. But I simply can't make up my mind if Faulkner wrote it that way or wrote it straight and then muddled it up afterwards. In either case he must have the hell of an all-embracing mind.' (Forester 2.614)

The difficulty was that, apparently as an appendage to the main explicatory purpose, Stewart contended that the (or a) secret of the novel was an incestuous relationship between Caddie and Benjy. The effect of this contention is reflected in a letter from Wallace Stegner, thanking Stewart for inviting him and four of his students to the gathering:

> They all enjoyed it immensely, and not by any means because some of your colleagues seem to have left their manners somewhere else, and their intelligence with them. My kids are all converts; I have already caught them instructing some of their less fortunate brethren on the true meaning of The Sound and the Fury, and I have distributed eight or ten copies of your chart [of the plot, unravelled] around as infection-points in the class. I think you really did something in this one. That probably explains the violence of the reaction in certain quarters. (Stegner to Stewart 15 Nov. 1956)

Henry Nash Smith was one who agreed on the incest in the novel (Smith to Stewart 13 Nov. 1956). By contrast, Stewart's colleague Tom Parkinson wrote a letter of apology for being "disagreeable" at the gathering, while still maintaining the novel is not a "puzzle" to be solved, but the story of the decay of a family (Parkinson to Stewart, n.d.). In January Stewart still couldn't "figure Faulkner out." "Is he playing a game or is he falsifying on purpose or is he just forgetful or had he been drinking?" (Stewart to Saxe Commins 11 Jan. 1957/*P*).

When Stewart, with his student Joe Backus as co-author, published the project's results in *American Literature*, they proclaimed that in the novel Faulkner was writing as a "playful opponent" ("Each" 441) of the reader. Their article includes two elaborate temporal charts of the "Benjy" episode and a map of the Compson property with the characters' routes through it lineated in the manner of

U.S. route 40. The complex charting does serve to enhance what Parkinson considered it to deny, "the theme of degradation and decay" (451). The article implies that the time sequence, understood, makes it necessary for Benjy to be sexually interested in Caddy, but doesn't go into any depth about the incest itself. The article concludes that Faulkner created the novel as a puzzle, and "in full consciousness *(a)* rendered it difficult and *(b)* rendered it solvable" (455).

From a scholarly and pedagogical point of view, Stewart and Backus were in the thick of things, to judge from contemporary criticism. Stewart had predicted "I wouldn't be surprised if it turned out to be the center of controversy. I imagine there will be plenty of attempts to 'flay' the authors . . .But I think there is basic truth in the article, and I am ready to stand by it" (Stewart to Saxe Commins 27 June 1957/*P*). Martha England, discussing how to teach *The Sound and the Fury* to college students, asserts that "The author did not intend that [the novel] should be read within . . .a rigid chronological framework," and that it is ". . .a violation of esthetic intent and artistic form to set a class to marking in margins the continuity of the separate events from a mimeographed table of dates and page-numbers" (221). But she does it anyway, deciding "in cold blood to ruin the Benjy section in the hope of making available the other three sections of the book." She finds that the result of having students do basically what Stewart and Backus had, gave them ". . .a deep respect for the author purely as a craftsman, a conscious and clever artisan who had adroitly placed the clues for reading a work that had seemed chaotic" (222). Another critic is concerned mainly with "Quentin's desire to convert Caddy's promiscuity into an act of incest . . ." (Vickery 1026), but this is an incest of wishfulness alone.

Stewart, in the manner of his more liberated Princeton professors, like Thomas Marc Parrott, held many such classes, particularly in creative writing, in his home. He was definitely trying to rouse interest in students whose passivity he regretted, if we can judge from a contribution he made to a *Nation* symposium, "The Careful Young Men: Tomorrow's Leaders Analyzed by Today's Teachers," in 1957. There, he seems to agree with his friend Karl Shapiro that "today's" students could be called the "Brain-Washed Generation." Stewart says "The present generation has no gods and heroes of its own," and doesn't like the kinds of writers admired by the "undergraduates-in-revolt" of Stewart's own generation (208). Stewart finds his students' admiration of Joyce, Faulkner and Eliot "very discouraging." Basically he considers the current generation of students as "timid, unadventurous, and conforming. . . there is far too little sense of excitement, of contemporaneousness, of eager and rebellious youth" (209). This sounds like the dictum of a seeker of the sixties. It seems that Stewart's own outward demeanor as a teacher didn't reflect these inner feelings, assuming they are sincerely expressed here. He did, however, inspire a number of undergraduates to become unconventional writers.

One, Hal Roth, who became a noted seafaring writer, remembered that in a 1952 writing class at his house, Stewart got his students to promise to tell him when they published their first book (Roth to Stewart 23 Nov. 1965). Dayton Hyde, environmental writer for children and adults, and proprietor of the Black Hills Wild Horse Sanctuary, says "I remember George Stewart well. He was a favorite professor of mine at Cal. I was an indifferent student, but got a bad novel off my chest in his class on novel writing. I found that we shared a great many interests and would spend hours talking to him in his office about running wild horses in northern Nevada . . ." Hyde says Stewart wrote a wonderful review of his second book, *Yamsi: A Year in the Life of a Wilderness Ranch*, and that when he coincidentally met him in San Francisco on Stewart's eightieth birthday Stewart regretted that "all too few of his students had become professional writers. . . .Looking back through the years and thinking back on twenty or so books I have written, I am well aware how much I learned from the man. As a lecturer he tended to be a little dry and studious, but on a one to one basis he was delightful with a twinkle in his eyes that I'll never forget" (Dayton O. Hyde, Email to the author 31 Aug. 2005).

Stewart's most hopeful protege, though, was Milton Lott. His first novel, *The Last Hunt* (1954) was begun in Stewart's writing class, published by Houghton

Mifflin, and became a film, directed by Richard Brooks, and starring Robert Taylor, Stewart Granger, and Debra Paget. Lott moved his family to a 67-acre ranch in the Bitterroot Valley soon after the book was published, and wrote to Stewart that according to Paul Brooks, the Pulitzer Prize judges awarded the Prize to *The Last Hunt*, but were overruled by their Advisory Board in favor of Faulkner (Lott to Stewart 29 Oct. 1955). A second novel, about the Ghost Dance, *Dance Back the Buffalo* (1959) was also well received, but somehow Lott lost his incentive. Lewis Gannett, a great correspondent of Stewart's and editor of the *New York Herald Tribune Book Review*, was very enthusiastic about the latter, and wrote to Stewart wondering if Lott would like to do an Indian book in Gannett's "Mainstream of America" series (Gannett to Stewart 27 Nov. 1959/*H*). Stewart felt the novel was something of a disappointment, and doubted he'd want to do a large nonfiction text (Stewart to Gannett 2 Dec. 1959/*H*).

It is a shame that Lott's inspiration seems to have faded soon after that, because his environmentalist fiction is so good, and upholds Stewart's tradition so well. *The Last Hunt* chronicles the near-extinction of the buffalo in the 1880's through the lives of two hunters, Charley Gilson and Sandy McKenzie. Sandy has become progressively more revolted by the hunting that has been his life, but Charley can't understand his feeling that mass killing of buffalo is a "waste." For Charley, if he doesn't kill a buffalo, someone else will. The best way to tame the Indians is to decimate their hunting grounds (103-4). Sandy looks at the empty plains, thinking ". . .[I]t was like looking backward in time, seeing the country as he had first known it with no litter of swollen, stinking carcasses and whitened bones, expecting beyond any hill to see the clean cones of leather tepees shining under the sun; herds of horses grazing on the sidehills and all the buses red with drying meat" (154). In a very satiric episode, he meets a "tenderfoot" zoological expedition ". . .out to study 'the monarch of the plains in his native habitat'" (169). The chief zoologist sketches a buffalo and then shoots it for the hide to mount in his museum.

On his last hunt, Charley is caught in snow, manages to kill a buffalo, skins it, shelters in its hide, and freezes to death there. It could be said of the book as of the film that it "not only condemns the senseless slaughter of the bison [sic.] but also raises question s about the Western myths of heroism and the pioneering spirit" ("Last Hunt").

Perhaps *The Last Hunt*, now as little known or respected as much of Stewart's own work, is the best novel inspired by him, but throughout the fifties his own energy for writing continued unabated. With the founding of the American Name Society, he returned to his interest in place names. He sought to define the field in its journal's second issue with "The Field of the American Name Society," which included a trial format for classifying place names. Elaborated in a subsequent article, "Classification of Place Names" it was to become the structuring format for his monumental *Names on the Globe*. Later in the 1950's he was to become president of the Society. As on some earlier occasions, he was able to combine onomatology and ecology in his article "*Leah, Woods*, and Deforestation as an Influence on Place-Names." The root "leah" in its different versions in many name situations is tied in with forest openings produced by deforestation. Thus we have the connection of "lea," as meadow, and "light." The opening as a small space in a larger forest slowly loses its identity as the forest is felled and everything becomes "open," yet it survives as a name. The irony is that while the name survives the place in deforestation, in *af*forestation, the people leave, and the name leaves with them (17). He also, in another article, provides an ecological metaphor for the study of names experienced as multidisciplinary:

> Names involve many fields of study. They must be considered as linguistic phenomena, involving particularly the problems of etymology. Names, particularly those of places, display a geographical background, and so are of interest to geographers. Personal names involve social habits and folk-customs. Titles and the names of fictitious characters display the creative mind at work. Considered therefore as a field of study, this is perhaps to be considered not so much a field as a tangled and luxuriant and almost pathless jungle awaiting the explorer's penetration. ("Names" 8)

Stewart was even up to doing a piece on the name-origin of the major contenders for the 1952 presidential nominations. Although he admits that the actual origin, as opposed to the attractiveness, of a candidate's name will have little effect on the voter, one can't help being intrigued that a Kefauver was originally "a maker of lance-points" or MacArthur the "son of a bear" ("Iron" 17).

One of Stewart's best "popular" essays appeared in 1960 as "Murder and Onomatology." It begins "That February morning I was thinking of an eleven o'clock class. As a professor of English, the last thing I expected was to get involved with a murder trial." Then he gets a call from Downieville, in gold rush country, a town that will figure importantly in his *Committee of Vigilance*. "The name brought memories. I had fought a forest fire near there; I had fished the streams; I had once kept the fire-lookout on Sierra Butte" (313). The caller, from the Attorney General's office, understands that Stewart is an authority on names. The murder accusee denies that he committed the crime, but says he knows who did, someone named "D'Avious." The accused, named Motherwell ironically, attached himself to a rich widow, rode across the country to California, registered in a Marysville motel, and the widow was never seen again until her bones were found a year later near Yuba Pass.

Stewart was being asked to do the impossible, to "prove a universal negative" (314), that there was no one in the world named "D'Avious." But he tries, using all the resources of the language teachers he knows at Berkeley. After consulting them without definite opinions that such a name could not exist, he goes to the university library, looking first through encyclopedias and next through phone books of U.S. cities. Finally, he finds one close match, a Steve Davios in Manhattan. He then has to go to the Downieville courthouse to testify.

As an "expert witness" he tells the story recounted above (the FBI had examined Steve Davios and decided he was not a possible suspect). The defense counsel tries to ridicule his credentials. "I had a good moment when he demanded, with the suggestion of a sneer, whether there was any particular term to designate the specialty which I presumed to profess. I replied, 'Onomatology.' What the court reporter made of it, I am still wonder. Afterwards one of the reporters asked me how to spell it" (316).

Motherwell received a life sentence. He "is, among other things, a man of creative, though sometimes macabre, imagination—witness his burying a baby's body in a pet cemetery" (316). So Stewart deduces how Motherwell started with "Davis" and altered the name to sound foreign; he also suggests that the name was a macabre joke, being one letter-shift removed from "devious."

As a final shorter essay of some interest from the 1950's we might mention Stewart's widely admired "The Two Moby-Dicks," to which he applied the same textual deconstruction he used in the Faulkner article. Stewart's goal was to show that there are really two entangled and complete texts represented in Melville's novel: an "original" story to chapter 15, the continued original story highly revised to chapter 22, and the rest of the novel "as it was written after Melville reconceived it" (417). Stewart uses many tangible and less tangible types of evidence—from textual inconsistencies to "atmosphere," to arrive at his conclusion, with a particular emphasis in the changes in types of names employed by different characters. He notably uses his own experience as a novelist as evidence. The emergence of Shakespearean allusion in *Moby Dick* is given an affective origin: "During weeks or months [Melville] has been turning the subject over in his mind. Then, in an instant, *he sees*! At such moments he is very likely to get the idea down on paper as rapidly as possible, in a kind of panic that he will forget something. (I am not now writing in theory or at second hand; I have done it myself)" (437). In his notes for a (undelivered?) lecture on how he writes, Stewart says that a novel happens with him as an "original flash" ("Notes").

"The Two *Moby-Dicks*" got at least two responses: John Parke wrote "Seven *Moby-Dicks,*" not directly criticizing Stewart, but, because his different *Moby-Dicks* are, as it were, "layers of deep meaning," he implies a shallowness in purely textual studies. Edward Stone's attack on Stewart's view of Shakespeare in the novel is much more direct. Stone argues that ". . . [Stewart's] theory finds less Shakespeare in UMD [chapters 1-15] than can actually be found there, and (2) conversely, the Insight Passage in Chapter XVI so important to the theory ["*he sees!*" above] does not contain the Shakespeare allusion that Professor Stewart finds in it" (445).

Even before these critiques came out, Stewart had sailed far beyond the reaches of Moby-Dick. In 1951, the Stewarts took a six-month trip to Europe, ending up in Greece. They returned to the U.S. in January, 1952, and in July Stewart got a call "from Washington" asking if he wanted to be a Fulbright scholar in Athens for the next academic year; he bargained for half a year, since, in his arrangement with Berkeley, he was allowed an annual half-year off from teaching (*Little* 193). Stewart doesn't know how he got offered this Fulbright, but he thinks it may have been through the influence of his predecessor in the position, Morris Bishop, professor at Cornell and writer of popular humor books—and a great friend, incidentally, of my parents. Bishop would later repeatedly urge Stewart "Why don't you ever come East?" (Bishop to Stewart 22 Mar. 1954). Stewart chose as the topic for his lectures to Greek students "American Ways of Life," and thus was generated his next book, of the same title, but addressed to Americans, and also, though he had thought about the story long before, his last novel, of Greek colonizing, *Years of the City*.

His *Harpers* article "Fulbrighting in Greece," gives an excellent insight into his experience there. "In Athens," he says, "I found a university valiantly struggling to recover from the ravages of war, and a program in American studies which had to be created rather than continued" ("Fulbrighting" 76). Since he discovered his students didn't know much literature, he decided to emphasize "civilization," and thus ". .. was put into the paradoxical position of trying to teach civilization to the Athenians." His students were garrulous, and although they knew English—gleaned from all sorts of sources—they would often break into cascades of speech unknown to him. "But they were in general eager, polite, and intelligent" (77). He initiated the "revolutionary procedure" (for the place) of inviting students to Sunday afternoons at his house—without informing the university authorities. "In Greece the continental tradition holds, and a professor is a thing apart from and above his students" (77), but these afternoons were great successes. Stewart's consular representative suggested that he expand his work and give a series of lectures in Greek provincial towns, so he worked out a talk called "The Influence of Greece Upon the United States," and, as a gesture, memorized by rote, with the help of a tutor, the first ten minutes of it in Greek.

He set out on the "Greek circuit," and describes his experience in Pyrgos, near Olympia, as typical. After a great feast, everyone went to the bare lecture-hall, full of people dressed in poverty. The regional governor, the nomarch, gave a long introduction about Stewart in Greek. Mrs. Stewart whispered to one person 'What's he saying?' The reply was 'He is telling what your husband has done.' "Ten minutes later my ever-loyal spouse whispered again: 'Well, he can't still be talking about my husband; George hasn't done that much!'" (79) However, he felt the lecture series was very successful, bringing the American presence where it wouldn't otherwise be seen. It also allowed him, although he doesn't say this, a close view of provincial Greece very helpful for the credibility of his novel *The Years of the City*.

In October, Stewart wrote to Saxe Commins "I have been writing hard, putting my Athens lectures into shape for a book. I am nearly through with them now" and inquiring if Commins had read his "Fulbrighting" article in *Harpers* (Stewart to Commins 7 Oct. 1953/*P*). Commins replied complimenting Stewart on the article; he handled with tact "the delicate matter of our presumption in bringing 'civilization' to Athens" (Commins to Stewart 16 Oct. 1953). Stewart says in his "Author's Note" to *American Ways of Life* that about half the chapters in the book were first presented as his Fulbright lectures in Greece, and, as a mode explaining its lack of specialization, says that "Seen from a foreign country, the differences between the various regions of one's own country tend to disappear, and the national unity to appear stronger" (299). True, but judging from some of his "politically incorrect" (for 1954) characterizations of America, one might question the "delicacy" of the original lectures, and wonder why the United States

Information Agency wanted to use some of the book's material in its Voice of America broadcasts (USIA to Stewart, July 1954).

*

One might consider *American Ways of Life* to be an idiosyncratic study in cultural anthropology, with a great emphasis on the physical environment's effects on culture. Stewart calls it ". . .the anthropology of a large American country" (*Little* 196). Its premise might be the riddling one expressed by Sterling Lamprecht: "Men could neither be, nor be what and as they are, were nature not what and as it is; but, just as truly, nature could not be what it is, were there not men within it" (7). Thus Stewart begins by using a "device of science fiction," a "'historical' event that never occurred: the Chinese discovery of America by a navigator named Ko Lum Bo, who was trying to reach Ireland in search of a mythical beverage named Wis Ki (11). I hope Patricia Limerick has read this passage, for it emphasizes the contingent source of American identity, based on the hereditary attributes of its colonizers and the environment, ". . . all the influences of the land itself—its size, continental nature, topography, soil, climate, native plants and animals" (13). Although Stewart says that the land influenced the inhabitants in "subtle ways" (14), he considers the environmental influence less important than the hereditary (16). Nonetheless, my discussion of the text will emphasize what he says about the former, both because the actual text seems to belie this premise, and because the presence of the environment in the discussion distinguishes Stewart's book from the many other mid-century ones of "cultural psychoanalysis," into whose group it generically fits. Most of these texts are socially, politically, and economically embedded, and torn between spoken and unspoken nuclear fear and economic pride. Stewart goes deeper.

In his chapter on language, he emphasizes the environmental effects on changes in English in America—new physical things demanded new words, while the absence of European topography, flora, and fauna, caused their names to die. There is an interesting commentary on the war of words between "buffalo" and "bison": "buffalo" was determined not to be scientifically accurate, but it was the word of the overwhelming majority, and continues to rule. The distinction serves ". . .to identify any man who says *bison* as the pedant he is likely to be" (41).

Compared with language, Stewart considers religion to have been powerfully affected by the environment. It manifests "extraordinary complexity." That the nation is predominantly Christian is one of those "self-evident" received ideas that historians never examine. He emphasizes the de-churching of the population as it spread westward and scattered, and therefore the degree of purely nominal church membership based on geography. In one telling footnote (did the Voice of America broadcast include this?) He says that "Atheists have had a bad break in the United States. . .Even though an American may quite readily say that he has 'nothing to do with churches,' he will rarely say that he is an atheist. The term 'religious preference' has come into use. . ." So that one would state "preference" for a certain sect without professing belief, ". . .much as if a man might state that he preferred drowning to hanging, although not really enamored of either" (54).

So there has arisen a myth of defection from an original majoritarian Christianity which never existed in the first place. "The ancestry of the unchurched may or may not be honorable, but is at least ancient" (58). Since the Revolution onward, the great Protestant sects have been strongly nationalistic, "so that an unreligious attitude can often be made to seem somewhat un-American," and an atheist seeking a turn to speak on the radio, in the name of freedom of religion, "is likely to meet frenzied resistance." "Similarly, when a letter in a correspondence column mildly points out that 'religious freedom' also means 'freedom to have no religion,' there is a great raising of hackles" (71). Perhaps Stewart's view here reflects that of Charles Camp.

This areligious emphasis was sort of dangerous in 1954—would it not be even more so today?—and suggests the Stewart of *Year of the Oath*, not to mention *Man*. But here he can defend his criticism of the American religious way of life on his original stance that religious freedom, or at least "indifference" in the Crevecoeurian sense, is an environmentally-determined primal attribute of the nation. Of course, Stewart was, privately, fairly satiric of religious belief in general. In some random notes he suggests the fictional discovery of a "Gospel of Thomas" which restates New Testament events in a "yes, but" mode:

> Yes, he changed water to wine, well enough, but all he could get was vin ordinaire.
> We, he could walk on water, but you notice he kept close to shore.
> Oh, he raised the dead all right, but he showed very poor judgment in selecting the ones he brought back to life.

Stewart spends a lot of space talking about food, because he sees food as of great importance to Americans; and here again, despite his premise, he sees the obvious dominance of the environment in determining the American diet. In his discussion of the success or failure of domesticated plants and animals as American food sources, he includes the literal and figurative regional identifications of certain particular foods. A good example is his coverage of corn. It is rural rather than urban in association, but is "protean" in its presence on the table. "Being thus ubiquitous and universal, corn has come to have a sentimental and symbolical value far exceeding that of wheat" (97). Its "bucolic suggestions" are everywhere, particularly in our literature. Stewart refers to Stephen Vincent Benet's *Western Star* as making the eating of corn "the symbolic act by which the colonists cease to be European" (97-98). He also discusses the nature/culture interactions involving food and environment. The "general environmental feature" of the country's size leads to high cost of labor, which in turn generates labor-saving cooking devices, and the development of prepared foods. He also considers American drinks, particularly alcoholic ones, to have been environmentally determined: the dominance of "hard" liquors in America, as opposed to Europe, originated with the slow development in the colonies of grain production sufficient for beer, and the swift westward mobility of the population into areas where it was hard initially to transport, or to grow, grain and hops. Stewart concludes his food and drink sections with a discussion of the tolerance of food varieties, and intolerance of certain drinks. "In general, the American is tolerant about what is eaten. Short of cannibalism, and perhaps hippophagy, he has no strong food aversions," and the extreme environmental conditions of the western frontier made even cannibalism justifiable by necessity (129).

As far as clothing goes, Stewart sees a disjunct between culture and environment; although clothing is becoming more informal (as of 1954), both Europeans and Native Americans seem to have dressed as a function of culture rather than comfort in—e.g.—differing temperatures. He provides a delightful personal comment in this regard:

> My father, who had been accustomed throughout his life to wear a vest, always appalled me with his willingness to wear a vest in hot weather. A Union officer at Gettysburg tells that he was hit by a spent bullet, but not badly injured because he was wearing three suits of underwear! If I had been wearing three suits of underwear on that hot July day, no one would have needed to shoot me. I would have been dead already. (142)

Another area where Stewart finds immunity from environmental causation is that of shelter. Despite the iconic role of the log cabin (only introduced in America by the Scandinavians), most rural housing was built on urban models—close together when there was no environmental necessity. We may recall the farmhouse in *U.S. 40* as an example of a structure ". . .foreign and imposed upon the land rather than something naturally connected with it" (160). Stewart describes the "new" house movement beginning around the 1870's, with freestanding, separate, wide-windowed, wooden houses, often with "balloon frames," as a development which both broke down the distinction between "outdoors" and "indoors," and aided in psychological individuation based on the environmental location of a person's house (164-65). In his book *Borderlands*, John Stilgoe gives great detail to this opening up of living space during the Gilded Age, but more specifically than Stewart ties it to the ironic development of mass transportation which permitted upper-middle-class city workers to commute from the "borderland good life" (168). Stewart describes his own house at 100 Codornices Road in Berkeley as being built on this model but still retaining the "structure of the original English framed houses" (166).

It is suggested that the book's section on Sex appropriately follows the one on Shelter, since the privacy provided by the "new" house allowed more ease in the practice of the former. As at several points in the text, Stewart "maps" the cultural phenomena he discusses on the plat of the United States. As a good example of this, and to illustrate the connection between sexual customs and geography, we can look at his map, based on the 1950 census, of the numbers of women in relation to men in the states: in the north central, far west, and west coastal states, and, all by itself, West Virginia, men exceed women. In all the other states, from Maine to Texas and Colorado to Florida (and, all by itself, California), women exceed men. Stewart contends that this still-persistent "rarity value" of women in the west strongly affected American sexual behavior. Much of it was governed by "a kind of economic and geographic determinism" (188), and the frontier condition, with little access to settlement and ceremony, lessened the importance of sanctioned sexual relationships.

In his Conclusion, Stewart sums up his view of the role of the environment in all the cultural activities he has chosen to discuss:

> Environment, whether acting directly or indirectly, seems to have been at its most potent, rather curiously, in establishing our drinking habits. . . .The environment has also exercised a strong influence upon food and upon religion. It has been of less importance in shelter, arts, language, sex, and play; upon clothing, strangely, it exercised scarcely any influence at all, until recently. Finally, environment may be said to have been of negligible influence upon personal names and holidays. (295)

He also, here, reverts back to his initial epigraph from Archibald MacLeish, one of his favorite poets, taken from MacLeish's "Land's End." He says one of MacLeish's lines is, in effect, refuted by the text he has written: "It is a strange thing—to be an American." Stewart suggests it would be acceptable if extended further: "It is a strange thing—to be a human being." Being one of a species that is "strangely unique" in the history of the world can be "somewhat terrifying" (297). He suggests it is "strange" to be of any nationality and that in fact "Strangeness . . .is nothing that any nation should be ashamed of, but should rather treasure" (298).

It is strange to think of Stewart treasuring his own strangeness. As suggested at the outset of this discussion, perhaps it is strange to see Stewart writing what might be considered a complacent book about America at mid-century, even though he is capable of discussing Alfred Kinsey casually. But I'm not sure that *American Ways of Life*—despite the atheism passages—is as complacent as it might seem. It almost appears to want to anchor the free-floating anxieties of its present in concrete reality. If we look at a few contemporary texts that are generically similar, it does seem strange. John Dos Passos writes of the ". . .abnormal times like our own, when institutions are changing rapidly in several directions at once and the traditional framework of society has broken down. . ." (9). Henry Steele Commager characterizes 20th century Americans who ". . .knew more about the mastery of their physical environment than ever before, about saving human lives and natural resources; yet never before had life been so precarious for those who survived infancy, and the resources of the nation vanished with terrifying rapidity" (407). Even beloved Ike evokes the dangers of civilization's destruction and the "condemnation of mankind to begin all over again the age-old struggle upward from savagery toward decency, right, and justice" [one wonders if he'd been reading *Earth Abides*] (Davie 135). A 1950 sociology textbook, *The American Way of Life* bewails the "social, economic, and political stupidity of mankind, which prevents us from increasing the food supply as rapidly as science and technology permit" (Barnes and Ruedi 165). Horace Kallen cynically and environmentally suggests that "every civilization seems one more wilderness requiring in its turn to be tamed by men pursuing happiness" (14-15).

*

Stewart, by contrast, chose to formulate his version of this apprehensive American prophecy in a typically contrarian way, by telling of the rise and fall of an ancient Greek city.

Stewart's city is not one particular city. If you spot its one historical reference, you may date its story as extending roughly from 700 to 500 B.C. He began it through fascination with "the tragedy of those Greek colonies. They started out so finely, so many of them, and they just seemed to grow old, and the situation changed." But again, their history isn't really tragic because "they lived their lives," shaped just like those of human beings (*Little* 198). He also admits to having made, in *Years of the City*, lots of analogies to the U.S. "They had many of the same problems." They had to contend with the natives, they developed military superiority through the phalanx as the American colonists did through gunpowder. Despite this implied topicality, Stewart in the 1970's was pessimistic about the novel. "Of course, it's never been a popular book and never will be. . .It doesn't in an obvious way touch the great ideas of the present time. Although in a more basic way I think it does. The question of civilization" (*Little* 199). He considers that it poses the question of whether a country gets old or not. This may have something to do with his view, discussed earlier, that his imagination was "flagging" when he began *Years of the City*, and had doubts about engaging on the project: "I had a definite feeling I was getting older" (*Little* 203). However, the idea of aging civilizations was much in the air at mid-century. "Where they are equally smooth and slow, the life of society is like the life of an animal, a continuous unconscious process of growing up and growing old, or perhaps *not* growing old but just growing" (Kallen 33-4).

Stewart, like us all, was certainly getting older, but he was always very much in tune with the events of his present. He was surely conscious of the spatial challenges facing baby-booming America in 1953. Suburbanization was reshaping the texture of population nationwide (a situation he addresses at the end of *U.S. 40*). "From Boston to Los Angeles, vast new subdivisions and virtually new towns sprawled where a generation earlier nature had held sway" (K. Jackson 243). The "single-family tract house," the "postwar automobile suburb" (Stilgoe 305), was the locus of American dreams, "a private haven in a heartless world." It was also, though, a dream "accompanied by the isolation of nuclear families, by the decline of public transportation, and by the deterioration of urban neighborhoods" (Jackson 244-45).

Suburbanization and urban deterioration established a "crisis of the city" as a subject of national concern. Sociological theories abounded to mourn, explain, and address this crisis, for which "urban ecology," the dominant pre-war urban sociological model of the "Chicago School," was considered inadequate by many, such as Julian Steward. Steward criticizes the consideration of urban zones ". . .as if each were a biological species in competition with one another for zones within the urban area," as culturally provincial. "For example, most of the cities of ancient civilizations [like Stewart's Phrax] were rather carefully planned by a central authority for defensive, administrative, and religious functions" (Steward, *Theory* 33).

There was a lot of urban pessimism connected with these analyses. "Some observers of the urban situation suggest that the physical city as it has existed for hundreds of years is not only undergoing a transformation but, like some factory buildings, is becoming obsolescent" (*Metropolis* 4). The tightly knit "urban fabric," woven and exported by the Greek model cities was, in its American manifestation, "loosening." This was both a liberating and threatening development, since, to many, "The modern city is, irrevocably, the fate of modern civilization as we know it. Human existence today is collective, not individual" (Riemer, 11-12, 29).

In the above mode, *Fortune* posed the question "'Are cities un-American?'' "The growth of the metropolis and the growth of the city are not necessarily complementary: quite the opposite; in this time of 'urbanization' there seems to be a growing alienation between the city and what most people conceive of as the American way of life" (Whyte 4). This is a way of life based on a belief in 'the beneficial effects of science and technology . . .in universal mobility, . . .the multicar family, . . .suburban sprawl" (Hall 35). Peter Drucker associated urbanization with industrialization which "uproots—quite literally—the individual from the social soil in which he has grown. It devaluates his traditional values, and parlyzes his traditional behavior" (7).

Stewart himself, as this study emphasizes, considers human communities from the cultural ecologist's point of view, in a mode of encompassment, not just analogy to nonhuman communities, as the Chicago School did. His responses to urbanization have been seen in *East of the Giants*, and to deurbanization in *Earth Abides*. In *The Years of the City*, although it draws on his own experience and historical research to chronicle a colonial city of *Magna Graecia* from founding to destruction, he is entering obliquely a heated national dialogue about the nature and future of contemporary U.S. cities.

Obviously, this debate still continues. Although slightly anachronistic to his novel, the sense of urban crisis is well expressed, from an ecological point of view, by Greenwood and Edwards: "The complexity and diversity of the world's great cities and of the urban civilization for which all mankind seems headed are so great that they constitute a kind of ecological climax," but not in the Clementsian sense of stability, but one in which stability can be maintained only by intensification of growth (63-65). The crisis raises the idea of survival as possible only in a "closed system" in which a city becomes "self-maintaining in a purely technological sense," cordoned from agricultural nature. Yet humans cannot survive without participating in the "Harmonious interpenetration of human environment and natural systems," despite the current human threats to this condition (66-7). Expressed differently, the city at mid-century faces two possible outcomes: it may "contain such deeply imbedded elements of decay or prove to be so at the mercy of new forms of energy" that "our time will be recorded in history as the finale to the age of great cities;" or, if we can "secure a more conscious control over the processes that determine and shape its development," we will be able "to obtain a sufficient control over the growth pattern of [our] cities to lay the foundation for an urban world culture" (Dunham 3).

Such a 20th century double-bind situation is present in *The Years of the City*, and is made explicit in Stewart's unpublished essay "Greek Colonies and the Thirteen Colonies." There, after presenting a complicated enumeration of likenesses and differences, many based on the contrasting physical environments the two colonial enterprises sited themselves in, he concludes that between the two "finally the parallelism breaks down. The Greek colonies were successfully founded, existed successfully, and even brilliantly through several centuries, and then went under. The English colonies developed into the United States of America. A few hundred years from now, that nation may, like the Greek colonies, have gone under—in one sense or another" (30). But the two major reasons for the Greeks' failure involve problems their colonial city-states share with the 20th century U.S. cities: they failed to connect and interact with an agrarian "hinterland," and they failed to remain united to their mother-cities and to "unite among themselves" in a common interest. Stewart's walled city, Phrax, can never let down its walls to allow a "harmonious interpenetration" of the urban and rural.

In using an archaic city as for his experiments in urban ecology, Stewart was going against the grain of the urban novels written in the 1950's. Most city fiction contemporary with *The Years of the City* is realistically "contemporary" or futuristically dystopian. Writers, not of these persuasions, says David Weimer, have either "an intimacy with the metropolis so complete as to deprive them of the capacity for saying anything much about it, or else 'get out of the city' altogether" (144, 146). Carlo Rotella's *October Cities* chronicles the topical novels expressing ". . .a spreading, deepening conviction that America's cities were in crisis" (6). Nelson Algren, Warren Miller, Evan Hunter, James T. Farrell, Paule Marshall, many others, are writers of this social realist persuasion. William Manchester's dismal *City of Anger* can well represent the topical immediacy of these narratives of ethnic strife, riot, crime, and physical decay. In his city "the alleys crowded upon one another like magpie tracks and the air lay mean and stagnant half the year and cold and dead the other half." The "borderlands" have been invaded and decayed. By the "'Elbow'. . . a hundred years ago when the foul and sagging brick barns there were new and the hills around were green with farmland. . .the gates had carried the names of gentlemen" (26-27).

The above "ecological regression" of an urban neighborhood can be paralleled in much city fiction. Stewart gives the complete curve of urban growth, prosperity, and decay to his fictional city of Phrax. By contrast, the changes in Manchester's city are local, and have occurred in a recent present. Nonetheless, "Set in specific neighborhoods, representing the urban dramas of the day, even the most narrowly 'literary' works. . .were received at the time as *socially* weighty prophecies or warnings" (Rotella 8).

Central to the inadequacy of topical fiction as weighty prophecy is, Rotella asserts, the inadequacy of the current urban "ecological model," which "with its natural succession and formalized competition among groups, seemed badly fitted to account for the postwar inner city's seemingly permanent black ghetto and the purposive city-shaping of agents like pro-growth coalitions" (60). The urban ecology Rotella evokes also resulted in ". . .the following implicit position: due to the natural character of the city, it would be unwise to meddle with the competitive forces for the purpose of correcting its physical obsolescence" (Dunham "City" 158).

Elizabeth Wheeler reinforces this perception of sociological inadequacy in her analysis of the literal and literary trope of "containment" in postwar fiction. "Postwar sense of place was highly contradictory, marked by new freedom of movement and new restrictions on movement. Paradoxically, containment culture emerged in an era of unprecedented mobility" (9). We could consider here Ish's ultimate rejection in *Earth Abides* permitted *by* the destruction of the city, and the progression toward "ghettoization" of Phrax in its decline, as it becomes both more estranged from its "hinterland" and more vulnerable to invaders. Wheeler says the "inner" city of immobility, post-war, underwent a "concrete quarantining" by race, class, and physical dissection. Through abandonment, demolition, "urban renewal," displacement, an "encapsulation of landscape" in fact and fiction produced "a dislocated sense of place that never takes belonging for granted" (14). This may be why an urban ecologist of the time who can say that "natural selection in the urban environment leads to the establishment of natural areas," as in plant communities, can complain about the failure of the urban novelist to retain "a semblance of meaningful relationship between social events and the individual life history," and contend that some "have moved the lack of meaning in individual existence into the very center of their plot" (Riemer 120, 291). To the traditional urban ecologist the very subject of contemporary urban fiction becomes the testimony of its "failure."

When we address the relationship of Stewart's novel to those analyzed by Rotella and Wheeler in the context of inadequate urban sociologies, we need to become involved with the different breeds of "urban ecology" flourishing at its time. That of the Chicago school had its genesis in 19th century discipline-formation based on the organization of the life sciences and the ideas of Georg Simmel and Oswald Spengler. This movement fused biological thought with a collective organicism represented in the urban human community by the rise and fall of the Roman Empire.

Although one could see Stewart's *Years of the City* as presenting the Spenglerian view of the organic failures of "Apollonian" civilization, I don't think Stewart's microcosmic city is so stylized. His intellectual friends were sceptical of such "big pictures," as the Chicago School was not. Carl Sauer called Spengler's theory of history both "brilliant" and "pretentious" ("Land" 327). Kroeber's Spengler is too totalistic, and does not, despite his pretensions, consider "culture growth an organic process in the modern biological sense of the word organic" (*Configurations* 827). Ruth Benedict didn't think it adequate to be applied to the complexity of 20th century civilization. Spengler (and his twentieth-century followers) wanted to have it both ways. "Man" is the builder of the city as machine, wanting to build a world himself, enslaving nature after "robbing Nature's treasures of metal and stone . . .managing her water in canals and well, . . .breaking her resistances with ships and roads, bridges and tunnels and dams" (84-5). But his "anti—urbanism and agrarian mysticism," as neatly characterized by Martindale, also imagined the city in the manner of an organism, ". . .as it grows from the primitive barter center to the city of culture, in the course of its majestic evolution flowering as civilization and wilting in a final destruction" (41).

The defining text of neo-Spenglerian urban ecology is *The City*, an assembly of essays by University of Chicago scholars, led by Robert Park, who begins his own essay with reference to Spengler (the volume was the product of papers presented at the 1925 American Sociological Society meeting devoted to "The City" [Gaziano 874]). Park's collaborator, Ernest Burgess, says urban growth can be thought of "as a resultant of organization and disorganization analogous to the anabolic and katabolic processes of metabolism in the body" (53). In the most ambitious of these essays, R.D. McKenzie directly evokes "the young sciences of plant and animal ecology" (63) to translate their processes and taxonomies into urban terms—types of communities, cyclic development and succession, adjustments to disturbances in equilibrium. He gives as example "the case of Greek cities, [where] the surplus population emigrated in groups to establish new colonies" (69). Thus the Chicago School ". . selectively appropriated ideas from one context and applied them in an innovative fashion to a different order of phenomena: the processes of *social* organization and change. In other words, sociologists used biological concepts as tropes" (Gaziano 875).

Park greatly elaborated on *The City* in *Human Communities* (1952). The city is a "super-organism," an interesting borrowing of the term coined by Kroeber in 1917 as a way of transcending the unresolvable dualism between the social and the organic. Kroeber says, as of mid-century, that his 1917 essay ". . .appears like an antireductionist proclamation of independence from the dominance of the biological explanation of sociocultural phenomena" (*Nature* 22). Park uses it in an opposite sense, as analogous to the "biotic community." (119). In Park, the "'web of life,' in which all living organisms, plants and animals alike, are bound together in a vast system of interlinked and interdependent lives" becomes the city's model (145).

The influence and independent adoption of this urban ecological model cannot be underestimated. An early exemplar is Niles Carpenter, who bifurcated the structure of the city into "morphology" (the total layout of a city) and "ecology," the "functional differentiation" (69) within the total layout, for which functions Carpenter adopts the phrase "areas of utilization" (83). These areas are distinct, yet their "intricate geography" (82) is always in transition. For Carpenter, the downside of this ecological model is Spenglerian: overexpansion of the city may degrade its standard of living, trade and industry will decay, ultimately creating "a regression back to a less urbanized type of society" (429-31). Many urban sociology texts of the 1950's, as well as Park's own, are, however, based on his ecological model. It may be expressed *via* "the Darwinian theory of the struggle for existence" (Lee 231). It may be used to characterize segregation: "The segregated areas are ecological representations of a cultural transition which immigrants experience before complete assimilation is achieved" (Bergel 90). The "Family-in-its Home" can be envisaged as the basic "human organism," a cell with nucleus and nucleoplasm (Williamson 30).

Today, one will find a "new" urban ecology with a very different, less totalistic, conceptual basis. The new urban ecology is much more instrumental. It does not take the city as a "given," and seek to analyze it in terms of an organic model. Rather it is considered as an entity in need of re-creation through transformation and introduction of nature-friendly material entities and institutions. ". . .[T]he city, in [the Parkian] approach, came to be a large system with many subsystems in a state of homeostatic fluctuation and balance." However, this analogical approach, while it might make logical sense, takes no account of the "widely divergent" empirical situations represented by different cities (Bennett 168-69). Andrew Ross links the old and new ecological urbanisms, pointing out the inadequacy of the socio/literary image of the city "as an immense biological organism" (17). The new ecological urbanism works to compensate for this model-centrism by modifying a city's material environment and social matrix. In literary terms this means reconceiving "nature and its cultural representations in ways that contribute to understanding the contemporary cityscape" (Bennett and Teague 10). "This view emphasizes that many of the issues that have historically concerned mainstream environmental groups—such as endangered species, wetlands and habitat protection, and wilderness and national parks issues—are intimately connected to patterns of urban development and growth" (Beatley and Manning 22).

But precursors of today's urban ecology were already articulate and active in the 1950's, and I believe it is from their viewpoint that Stewart's novel arises. These urbanists perceived the ". . .biological fallacy, that of ascribing to inorganic forms the biological sequence of growth, maturity and decay . . ."(Tunnard 44). Not surprisingly, one of the strongest advocates of a proto-"new" urban ecology was Frank Lloyd Wright. His delightfully polemical *The Living City* (1958) begins "The value of Earth as man's heritage, or of Man as earth's great heritage, is gone far from him now in any big city centralization has built . . ." (17). For cities, his advocacy is of a "New space-concept" (23)—"organic" architecture and the organic city. Wright was not an enemy of cities; he advocates not their destruction but their reconception. And he was optimistic: "Of all the underlying forces working toward emancipation of the city dweller, most important is the gradual reawakening of the primitive instincts of the agrarian" (62). Interestingly, in *Man*, Stewart's negative characterization of the Greek city is based precisely on this abandonment by its residents of their agrarian instincts: ". . .they considered 'work' to be beneath them," and lived off the products of conquest and slavery" (210).

The prolific Lewis Mumford in 1951 sounded absolutely Spenglerian: ". . .the actual effect of the contemporary effort to strip architecture down to building was to make the machine—the dynamic instrument of this change—itself an object of veneration. Feelings and emotions that had hitherto attached themselves to organisms and persons. . .were now canalized into the machine" ("Function" 157). But this did not, for him, imply a *laissez-faire* attitude. He says in 1956, "The needs of life . . .are much more subtle and complex than the needs of machines, and for this reason a good mechanical solution to a human problem can be only a part of an adequate organic solution which meets the needs of life in all its dimensions *(Urban* 209). The problem is not the use of the machine in itself but "the displacement of man as a responsible agent, who must control and direct its results for human purposes" (208). In terms of the planning of cities, a "third way" must be found between the plans of Protected Man in the walled city and those of the capitalist "Exploratory Man." This new type must be "devoted to the intensive but balanced cultivation of our natural and human resources" (179-80).

In his monumental *The City in History* Mumford begins with a dictum that could premise Stewart's novel: "If we would lay a new foundation for urban life, we must understand the historic nature of the city, and distinguish between its original functions, those that have emerged from it, and those that may still be called forth" (3). In fact, Mumford attributes the destruction of the ancient walled city to forces analogous to those creating the crisis of the modern city: forfeiting the "sense of limits," and "dynamic balance" characteristic of "natural ecologic communities" (52). In the Phragian (as it were) city, cooperative urban polity was undermined by "death-oriented myths which attended . . .the exorbitant expansion of physical power and technological adroitness" (53). The Polis becomes the Necropolis, "fire-scorched ruins, shattered buildings, empty workshops, heaps of meaningless refuse, the population massacred or driven into slavery" (53). This sentence summarizes the panorama which concludes *The Years of the City.* By analogy, the self-destructive megalopolis of the present is based on "a deep contempt for organic processes that involve maintaining the complex partnership of all organic forms, in an environment favorable to life in all its manifestations." The oldest and most fundamental of all human relations, which must be the basis of the city, is that of the human "to air, water, soil, and all his organic partners" (527).

Jane Jacobs became a celebrity urbanologist with her 1961 *The Death and Life of Great American Cities.* There, her crowning concept is an urban neoecology, where cities are perceived as "problems in organized complexity, like the life sciences" (433). But these problems had to be addressed in complex detail, not by holistic modeling. City planners' desire to create order out of urban chaos is based on a "long-established misconception about the relationship of cities. . .with the rest of nature" (443). The eighteenth century's "sentimentalization" of nature, she argues, led to an intellectual, moral separation of a benign nature from a malignant city, the "enemy" of nature (444), which both disenabled the study of cities as "part of nature" and enabled the destruction of nonurban nature by its lovers: ". . .each day, several thousand more acres of our countryside are eaten by the bulldozers, covered by pavement, dotted with suburbanites who have killed the thing they thought they came to find" (445).

Long before 1961 Jacobs had been a champion of the un-"renewed" *urbs* as a site of "the most intricate and unique order" (Jacobs, *Death* 447), rather than disorder. The true and vital complexity of the city is revealed, she said, by the pedestrian-eye view of it, not the mapmaker's eye. Decentralization and destruction for urban renewal "will not revitalize downtown; they will deaden it" (Jacobs, "Downtown" 157). The street, not the block, is the primary vital entity in a city, as are its nodes—the public squares, in which 'several currents of life" come together (170). "The remarkable intricacy and liveliness of downtown can never be created by the abstract logic of a few men" (183).

Thus we find Wright, Mumford, and Jacobs all basically agreeing, with different emphases, on a new ecological paradigm for urban study and action, one that emphasizes the importance of studying cities' individual and collective pasts, on recognizing cities as phenomena of nature, and of working to renew them "on the ground," enhancing, not replacing, the attributes they possess in common with other organic systems.

On the one hand, the Phrax of Stewart's *Years of the City* lives and dies far in the past as a rebuke to the limited vision of contemporary novelists' sociological realism. As such, it is a rebuke seemingly couched in the manner of the traditional urban ecologists—namely, that as organisms, cities live, die, and provide the seeds for other cities. In this guise, Stewart's biography of a city could constitute an "organic naturalism" more pessimistic even, though on a broader scale, than that of the urban realists. In *Earth Abides*, Ish discovers that he can't Frankensteinianly jolt life into a dead city through "urban renewal." The library remains abandoned, the survivors' lineage will have to start all over again at the tribal level. Similarly, Phrax, his Hellenic city, will die from "old age," to be supplanted by other cities being born elsewhere.

On the other hand, Phrax in its years of youth and maturity, though they be transient, exists as a dynamic form of the reconceived, habitant-friendly new urban ecology of Wright, Mumford, and Jacobs. Although walled, it has an internal dynamic allied with that of the cultivated and uncultivated space outside it. One might compare the life of Phrax, at the edge of the sea, with that of Rachel Carson's shoredwelling organisms in her 1955 book of that title.

> To understand the life of the shore, it is not enough to pick up an empty shell and say 'This is a murex' or 'That is an angel wing.' True understanding demands intuitive comprehension of the creature that once inhabited this empty shell: how it survived amid surf and storms, what were its enemies, how it found food and reproduced its kind, what were its relations to the particular sea world in which it lived. (Preface).

Such is Stewart's take on his city: to interpret its life, in Carson's words, 'in terms of that essential unity that binds life to the earth." This unity, in Stewart's city, combines the inevitability of its death as an organism with the flourishing ecology of human-nature interdependence in its daily life.

Stewart's Foreword to *The Years of the City* contains a warning: "It is Greek—yes. The names alone would show it. But do not turn to the atlas, hunting a hill behind a beach and a narrow plain with mountains beyond. Do not consider too deeply what century. Remember that many men have voyaged and founded cities and then grown older—and their cities too. It has happened, and may again, and the tale will be told." Well, I did consult the atlas---Kiepert's *Atlas Antiquus*—and on the Ionian shore of southeastern Italy, where Stewart says he imagined his city, found three major Greek colonial cities: Croton, Caulonia, and Locri, all of which could satisfy Stewart's geographical criteria. Phrax is however, a composite city, drawn from the attributes of these and from other primary and secondary sources. Thucydides describes Epidamnus, colonized from the "mother city" by a "multinational force" under the leadership of Phalius. As are many founders in the Greek historian's account, Phalius is a descendant of Hercules. Like Epidamnus Phrax faces its first collective marital challenge from "neighboring barbarians" (in Stewart, the "Horde"), and its embassy seeking outside help is rejected (161-7). He might have chosen the name Archais, the orphan founder of the lineage whose individual's lives are at the forefront of the narrative, because Thucydides names Archias ("of the Heraclidae") as founder of the Corinthian colony Syracuse in Sicily (410). In his "Greek Colonies and the Thirteen Colonies," Stewart refers to colonization accounts by Herodotus, Xenophon, and Thucydides, with the greatest emphasis on Syracuse and Cyrene, on the Black Sea. With its philosopher and obsession with the Olympic Games, Stewart's novel can also evoke Croton, site of Pythagoras's school. With its interurban rivalries, it can evoke the conflicts between Caulonia and Locri.

In twentieth-century historians, like Kitto and Glotz, many of the basic attributes of Greek colonial cities could be found, as well as in Chester Starr's *Origin of Greek Civilization*, cited by Stewart in "Greek Colonies." Kitto emphasized the noncommercial motivations of the great period of colonization (c. 750-550 B.C.), the time span of Stewart's novel. Kitto says "Land was what the colonists were looking for." "The impoverished peasant would give up his shrunken and mortgaged bit of land in the home-country for a share in the vacant land overseas---and the struggle could begin afresh: either he and his descendents would prosper and become the landed nobility of the new polis, or they would fail and be ready once more for colonization and revolution" (81-82). Except that many of Stewart's colonists are tribal leaders and warriors, not simply peasants, this preoccoupation with the allotment of extramural land dominates Phrax's early history and its early intermural conflicts. Similarly, in Glotz's account of Greek city-formation one finds many of the materials Stewart used in creating his city: the polis in general as a "work of nature" (2); three stages in the evolution and devolution of cities (5); and its central hill and citadel or acropolis (19). "A small tract of land shadowed by a mountain, watered by a stream and indented with bays—such was a State" (28), and such is Stewart's Phrax (or, may we dare suggest, Stewart's Berkeley, California).

The Years of the City is shaped through four Books: "How they Founded It," "How they Made it Strong," "How they Made it Great," and "How it was

Ended." Between each, in the structure he so often uses, is an "interbook," a narrative summary of longer stretches of time. These interbooks are titled "The Years of the City," and are reminiscent of the year-naming interludes in *Earth Abides*. The narrator, as elsewhere, often universalizes and distances events by adopting a "Homeric" tone and diction, suggesting a momentum of fatality: "So they all labored as they could;" "So a few days passed, though not many, for with every day a difference showed in the line of the wall and the palisade" (54). Each book has, as a lead character, first Archais and then an abecedary sequence of his descendents, whose importance in the life of the city is not as great as their importance in the consciousness of the reader. Stewart says his sequence of names, "which one reviewer spotted and did not like," was carefully chosen: Archais, as in archaic; Bion as "life" ("since Bion represents the strength of the city"); Callias as "beauty" ("aesthetic middle age" of the city); and "Diothemis" as the "judgment of God," since he "lives in the time of the city when it is approaching destruction, partly because of the sins of the fathers" (Backus 55-56).

Thus, the novel begins in intimacy with "Archais" (nameless at the outset), as an undetected stowaway on a ship from the mother city in sight of land. He takes in the coastal topography, and, found out as a thief, is brought before the Founder, Hippocleides. The Founder then takes the boy under his protection, although he is nameless and tribeless, and he himself is both aging and vulnerable. Hippocleides has contempt for his own settlers, not "'a people,'" but "'many persons'." Like many of the Plymouth or Jamestown colonists, they are "Dispossessed villagers and broken men, debtors and adventurers. . .fugitives from sacked cities. . .wastrels and drifters. . .And out of all of this I must found my city" (14). Thus the survivors of failed cities are the "seeds" from which a new city must spring. Important is the reference to "sacked cities," since Archais bears the childhood memory of being carried through the fires of a burning city by his father, who scarifies his forehead to identify him.

Confirmation of oracular prophecy is necessary to begin construction of the city. Its topographical location for defense and cultivation is approved by the leaders of the four main tribes among the colonizers. Every large ecosystemic detail is noticed. The "'farther mountains'," notes the Founder, "'. . .are dark green, shading into black, and so I know that they must have forests of oak, and chestnut, and pine, and—still higher—fir-trees. Swine will do well beneath the oaks and chestnuts, and fir-trees will give us timber for ships'" (26). But the decision to stay is made only when the oracular three eyes of the weeping mother are determined to be springs; since Archais has found the third spring, his position is elevated, and he partakes in the liberation of founding. (Carpenter quotes Pliny the Elder: "'Springs make towns . . .'" [39]).

Developmental stages in the young city are carefully dramatized by the narrator. The Founder, in Assembly, gains assent to the settlement, pronounces the basic roles of its constituents, and, at the behest of the soothsayer, finds out from captives slaves of the native "hill-people," their original name for the place which, transliterated, becomes "Phrax." In *Names on the Land*, Stewart emphasizes this technique for naming on the part of the American colonists. Among other notable preliminaries to the actual construction of the city walls are the landing of the domestic animals, sacrifice of some of them, transfer of the fire brought from the mother-city, and the unloading of goods, which are, initially, "the property of the city as a whole" (44). City planning is also a major activity. The soothsayer can recite from a how-to poem, "On the Founding of Cities," and the Founder draws with spearpoint on the earth a plat map of the perimeter he has paced. This astounds Archais, who finds the map "in some way the very spirit or shape of the city, as a god might know it" (47).

The mapping of the city on the very ground where it will be built is an important moment. Although Phrax will be a walled city, its civic space clearly separated from the extramural natural space, the Founder has outlined it such that its walls will partake of, or actually be constituted by, natural features already in place, like cliff and rockface. Phrax, as planned by Stewart, its literary Founder, is not a historical manifestation of the "neo-romantic dis-urbanism" (Tunnard, *City* 257) criticized by opponents of an ecologically-modelled city. Rather, it is a prototype of a city distinct from, yet in harmony with, the "non-city;" ". . .the forms of nature were used with the forms of architecture to create the plan . . ." (255). Or, in Charles Abrams's formulation, they are ". . . blending their new works with old vistas" (294).

The mapping and construction of the city relate directly to the crisis which occurs when an embassy of the hill-people, "Peoples of the Eagle," comes to demand by what right the Phragians have taken possession of land not their own. To the Founder, the land is "Empty;" to the natives (read "Native Americans") it is filled by their pasturage and burial sites. Such a debate's connections with European settlement in America are pretty obvious, and discussed at length in Stewart's "Greek Colonies." Despite his emphasis in the latter essay on the advanced social organization of the natives encountered by the Greeks (21), the hill-people are presented as martially inferior. Also, for Stewart's Greeks, possession and inhabitation create ownership. For the Peoples of the Eagle, ownership has more of the kind of spiritual identity that Archais has attributed to the map of Phrax. Perhaps here we can notice an encounter between holistic and instrumental urban ecology. In any case, the natives' curse on the city impels it to its first successful defensive war, in which the Founder in armor collapses through exhaustion. The war leads to an expected embassy from the hill-people, seeking a treaty. This embassy in turn leads to a debate among the citizens Assembled over whether a vote on the treaty will be by tribe, as in the mother city, or among all the citizens as one "people," despite the disparity, in the latter choice, between amounts contributed by each settler to the collective enterprise.

The construction of the semi-organic city and the questions both of its legitimacy as an entity and of its internal coherence, come together at this assembly. They will re-emerge in later stages of its growth. As the narrator sums it up, "Thus they talked with the hill-men, and fought their first battle, and made a treaty to establish themselves in the land, and then began to quarrel among themselves, as is to be expected after the founding of a city" (107).

A second phase in the city's early growth is characterized by the politics of agricultural space: ". . .unless the earth yields wheat and barley, how shall there be a city?" (112). And how shall the tillable soil be apportioned? The latter question is deferred due to the importance of the plowing and sowing of seed, and here the narrator again refers to the city's position in natural space. However it grows internally, the city is bound to the unwalled earth that surrounds it, ". . .soft. . .and black and steaming behind the plowshares" (113). Referring back to the urban dilemma defined by Greenwood and Edwards above, this urban-agricultural interface must exist for both realms to survive.

One could see the first plowing as the agrarian equivalent of building the city walls. Unlike the casual way plowing is presented in *Man*, here the plowing takes on the primacy of a defining act of humanity. "Fittingly, when a man plows the earth, he should walk [naked] as men first walked when they came from the earth" (113). This parity of furrow and wall is like Mumford's idea of a "commensal relationship" between city and "Mother Earth" akin to that between mother and child, unmediated by "life-hostile" technology and institutions (Mumford, *Urban* 16). In the Greek world, though, the relationship takes on a non-maternal, sexual form. Some of the plowers, reverting from the Founder's civic religion to their "natural" one, choose a woman to inseminate in the furrows. Archias, watching this scene, and disturbingly aroused, is reassured by his "foreigner" friend, the [probably Hebrew] Johanan, "'Like this city, you are growing older'' (117).

A sign of this growing is the first instance of a reflection that many citizens will entertain in later years. The Founder looks back to "'see what might have been done differently'" (121). This retrospect relates to the organic critics' stance toward the modern "exploding metropolis." It is also a sign of the stage in the life of the city when, like a young person, it has grown old enough to be self-conscious about having a personal history, and to be able to be revisited memorially. This civic memory is elaborated on by the surveyor who is laying out land boundaries and roadways. He tells his workers to be flexible to topography in their measurements, saying, in the Mumford manner, that "'. . .in dealing with the land. . . we must give or take little, because we are sprung of the earth and it is our mother and in dealings between mother and children, matters cannot be altogether of measurement and law'" (126). This is "new town" theory put in practice mellenia before its time. Even more poignantly, the surveyor, as a farmer endowed with foresight ("since at the time of the plowing they must consider the reaping"), reflects on the "years to come" when he will 'lie in the earth" and his progeny will "look from the wall of the city upon the land." He imagines them seeing fertile cropland, laid out as he surveyed it. "'My son and my grandson will see it, and thus I too will have done something in the founding of this city'" (127-8).

Once the land has been plowed and sown, though, a violent dispute breaks out between those who favor equal division for all, and those who feel the land should be divided proportionately to each settler's contributions to the expedition. This one of many negotiations between urban unity and tribal separation is resolved through the Founder's ingenious manipulation of his people's environmental perception. Here we see how dependent the city is on the existence of one "final arbiter," and how much its identity is composed not of walls and plows but of intangible collective emotion. The assembly asks "'My lord, tell us what is right!'" The Founder is silent, and then his moving finger guides their eyes around the cultivated fieldscape. "Then the Founder cried out at last in a loud and triumphant voice, 'Look, men of the Phragians, look upon our fields! Now, with the new sprouted seeds, they are green!'" Archais realizes the fields had not suddenly become green at that moment. "Yet at the moment it seemed to him, as doubtless it seemed to all in the crowd, that by his sudden commanding them, the Founder had caused them to see what they had not seen before, and had even caused the grain itself to appear." The resultant collective perception is "that in the growing of the grain rested the future of the city, and not in this jangling between men in the assembly" (143). Kevin Lynch says in his study of urban environmental perception, "The symbolic organization of the landscape may help to assuage fear, to establish an emotionally safe relationship between men and their total environment" (127). However, in the long view, this harmony is one of innocence; we will witness the slow reversal of these priorities, the breakdown of collective perception and thereby of security, and despite its growth in population, the city's recession from the "green," in the course of its slow dying.

The first "interbook" of the novel, as the subsequent ones, is built around a fatalistic metaphor: 'Once it had been founded, the years of that city began to run, as the wine flows when someone has struck the wineskin with a knife or a spear-point, unknowingly. For, as all men know, the years of a city are numbered, like those of a man" (153). The wineskin figure as repeated truism is provocative. It can be related to Mumford's recasting of Spengler's and Toynbee's urban ecology as expressed in the polis-to-necropolis schema of Patrick Geddes (*Culture* 284-295). Mumford insists on a vital *caveat* in his own ecological figure: "If the crown is blighted by disease, it may still put forth new shoots at the base, and in time these shoots may flourish ad provide anew trunk and crown." Non-figuratively, ". . .while there is life, there is the possibility of counter-movement, fresh growth. Only when the big city has finally become wasteland must the locus of life be elsewhere" (295). In Stewart's novel, there are a number of possibilities for count-movement; unfortunately, they all wither.

These first interbook years see the death of the Founder, and the arrival from the mother-city of a "lawgiver," Zenotor, whose reforms—legal codes, written laws, coinage, and others—tend to weaken tribal identity, undermine rituals, and create mediating systems between the walled city/plowed field interface. Through this social engineering is created, in Mumford's conception, the "machine." Also, as a result of population growth and war threats from without, Clearchus, the *de facto* military governor, orders the building of new walls, which "regularize" the previously terrain-friendly irregular shape of the city. The result of the expanded land area is the city's first geosocial regionalization. The original hilltop space becomes the "Upper Town," in effect a "slum," even though the major civic buildings are still located there. This discord is symbolic of impending disorder; the "ideal public square in the political landscape" (J. B. Jackson 18) has lost its centrality. The rich move to the more spacious "Lower Town." "The Harbor" becomes a separate commercial zone, including a "small street where the prostitutes lived." The narrator emphasizes that, despite these changes, "nearly all the Phragians were farmers . .. " Yet, ". . . as everyone agrees, the real life for a man is in the city . . ." (168). This comment suggests a new degree of perceived separation between city and country, the sort that Jacobs discusses as the origin of urban decay.

The second book of *The Years of the City* is centered on the second generation of citizens and of Archias's line, in the person of his son Bion. We meet Bion as a shipmaster, approaching the city from the sea, as his father did in the first book, and finding the city besieged by the barbarian "Horde." Safe within the walls, Bion becomes engaged with Clearchus in a discussion of whether a city itself can grow old, as individual humans do—a continuing question in the novel. Clearchus sees this idea as expressing an inherent disloyalty, when entertained in a city under siege. It is necessary to pretend the city is ageless and to hold out against the invaders since "'we have been part of the city since before we were born. She bred us, and has put her mark on us'" (226).

Clearchus sends Bion to seek aid from Echelos, the tyrant of a nearby city called "The Mount of the Doves." Perceived by Bion and his companion Ben-nekar, this city presents an ironic contrast to Phrax. On the one hand it is sterile, its populace cowed and silenced by a brutal oligarch on the model of Dionysius I of Syracuse. On the other it is dominated by a temple mount and its "doves"—sacred whores in the mode of *Gilgamesh.* If the Mount of Doves is dystopic, it certainly contradicts Mumford's view that in a civilization at its "mechanical apex," sex has no "central part" ("Development" 54-55). But Stewart's erotocentric tyranny makes precisely this point. On the Mount of Doves, sex has become mechanized by professionals, and transmuted alchemically into power. Thus the Queen of Doves seduces Bion, seeking to suborn him to murder the oligarch Echelos.

Fortunately, and gratefully, returned to his own still-besieged city, Bion walks its streets to his house in the old Upper Town as the appreciative pedestrian

Jane Jacobs urges all city planners to become. While walking Bion experiences with pride the city's "mixed use," both the poorer areas, where he smells "the heavy odors of people crowded together, mingled with the rankness of animals," and the awe-inducing Old Marketplace, "the sacred ground of the city" (288-89). Back at his own home, the same house Archias built, Bion observes the city laid out below him, as his father did, and the vastness of the view renews in him a "sense of dedication" to Phrax (292).

Bion is killed in the epic campaign to exterminate the Horde (a campaign mapped on the novel's endpapers), but he leaves his new wife pregnant with his son Callias, who will be the central figure in Book Three. The narrator ironically quotes from the account of this campaign in the *History of the Phragians* which will be written later in time by the adult Callias. This quotation is ironic because Callias's history is completed long before the history we are reading, *The Years of the City*, is, so it cannot tell us the whole history of how the city dies. Nor can Callias know that the scroll on which his history is written will fall to the floor and be lost in the dust of his sacked house, never to be read by posterity.

The years following this great military campaign of Sanaxis are considered by the narrator to be the most prosperous in the history of Phrax. Due to economic growth and a greater work force of slaves, the citizenry achieves the leisure necessary to develop a cultural life, including literacy, arts, and sports. These years are marked both by uneventfulness and revival of "ritual time" based on ceremonies and periods of celebration (what Stewart in *Man* calls an "ideology of stability" [180]). The narrator describes this cycle of ceremonies in the present tense, expressing a sense of the unchangeable. When the narrative returns to the past, it emphasizes the greater connection Phrax now has with the increasingly colonized Mediterranean world. This world is dominated by two tendencies. The cities "advanced upon the hill-folk, conquering their towns, enslaving their people or putting them to tribute, and making use of the hills for pastures" (358). Cities are also often falling "under the power of one man," a tyrant, who gains control by offering stability in a conflicted time.

"In any colonization the land itself is of primary importance," Stewart says in his essay on Greek and American colonies (23). Thus it is important to note that the narrator, while giving the reader a tour of the now almost entirely cultivated land outside the walls of Phrax, also allows the reader to talk with an older rural resident, and to ask him if things are going as well as at the time of the Sanaxis campaign. The reply is that things are not as good:

> 'This field, this one we see here, has gown old—even as I have grown old. It does not bring forth so much grain any more, even though we manure it. The olive-trees, it is true, produce more, but the river floods dangerously, and you can see that it has left a layer of unfertile sand over there on the field. Some say that the floods are caused by the cutting down of trees, or because the goats have eaten the bushes away, but it may be merely because of the will of the Gods.' (361)

The environmental degradation of agricultural land whose produce is the lifeblood of the city, foreshadows the consequent degradation of the urban space, as we will witness it through the perceptions of Callias.

The reader meets Callias in the same, much-enhanced, paternal house, as he hosts a visiting philosopher, Andron [Pythagoras?], who provides what might be considered the perspective of a visiting city planning consultant. Callias proudly shows Andron his literary collection, particularly the latest best-seller, *The Odyssey*[!]. Stewart had consulted with Sir Denys Page of Trinity College, Cambridge, about the date of *The Odyssey.* Page agreed with Stewart that since the epic doesn't deal with Greek colonization, it must have been created no later than 800 B.C., but offered the counter-argument that Greek epics consciously eschew topicality (Page to Stewart n.d.). Interestingly, this is precisely the topic Callias discusses with Andron, in terms of his own *History of the Phragians*: are past events particular or universal? "'When we read the story of the development of one city, as you may read the story of that of Phrax in my own humble work, do we not read the story of all cities. . .?'" (378). Their conversation is interrupted by the entry of his three-year-old son Diothemis (whom we will meet at death's door in Book Four with his own grandson running to him).

Callias holds a banquet "symposium" in honor of Andron, and is asked to include a guest of whom he is suspicious—Melas, who has been hired to construct a new temple. This is a fatal error, because Melas uses the banquet to introduce, under the guise of explaining the difficult economic growing pains and increasing class hostility in Phrax, the existence of a mysterious organization called the "Distributors." The Distributors, according to Melas, "enemies within," advocate a redistribution of land, and have put the city in great peril. Stewart's sociological anatomy of Melas's rise to power by manipulating public fear of this supposed subversive organization is clearly derived from his experiences with the Loyalty Oath, and more generally from McCarthyism as a whole. If an ecological analogy is appropriate here (which it may well not be), Melas could be considered a non-native invasive species in the habitat of the city . . .but then again, this is a bit too Parkian.

In any case, Melas's rise to power, though based on calculation, proceeds almost "organically" (although Raymond Williams stresses the "need for caution in using the word without immediate definition" [264]). Melas incites riots, which he then blames on the Distributors. He hires a professional agitator whom he then arrests, displaying to the crowd the wounds this agitator supposedly inflicted on him. As violence breeds violence, he forces the Assembly of Tribes to pass a law creating what Andron says already exists in many expanding cities, a police force, of which Melas, is, naturally, the chief. The force includes plainclothes enforcers nicknamed "ravens" by the populace. They arbitrarily arrest or drive into exile many powerful figures in the city, on the grounds of criminal activity or temple desecration. Throughout this period, and as Melas closes in on Callias himself, the scholar remains remarkably sanguine. Comparing the city to a tree, he tells Andron "'some leaves may be turning yellow and some branches may be diseased, but the trunk and the roots are healthy'" (455). But as they look over Callias's parapet at the city below, Andron expresses skepticism: "'We do not think of breathing until there is some restriction upon it'" (456).

Now under house arrest, Callias is in his courtyard at night when his elder son Clearchus and several others scale the cliff to his house. They are forming a group to overthrow Melas, following a "day of blood," a *kristalltag*, in which many of his opponents have been killed and Clearchus wounded. They seek Callias as their last hope to lead a rebellion, but he refuses. At this point Andron himself departs while it is expedient, leaving behind his thoughts on the life-spans of cities. "'The life and development of a city can perhaps be considered as natural an event as the lives of the individual men composing it'," he says, but there is in it a "progression" through many forms. Callias has been blinded to the present proliferation of tyrants by persistently looking backward at the history of his city. Andron's statement could be considered a meta-assertion about *The Years of the City* itself, whose premise is that looking backward can provide a perspective on the present. And Andron at least partially contradicts his own philosophy by explaining to Callias in great detail the political history of Melas's rise to power. Callias can only be plaintive: "'Is it my fault that I was born when the current of the times set in a certain direction?'" (499).

The eighteen-year rule of Melas turns Phrax into a version of The Mount of the Doves. The city becomes wealthy and renowned, with the construction of much monumental architecture, the "works of Melas." But there is little individual freedom, and Melas wields power through a personal army of "spearbearers." By now the separation of the civic and rural worlds is complete. Imports replace the diminished agricultural yields of the Phragians' lands. Despite its success, Phrax has essentially become a "machine" whose only knowledgeable operator is Melas. Like the 1950's metropolis viewed by the new urban ecology, Phrax is already "dead," a "prison-city" (Wright 58).

To an extent the death of Phrax is caused by a lack of organized governance. There is no sanctioned central authority following the death of the tyrant Melas, and the city's commercial prosperity declines through a series of *coups d'etat.* Another important factor is agricultural decline. ". . .[A]nyone now going about the countryside noticed the gullied fields that had once been fertile and were now producing little, and the farmhouses that had gone into decay, and the villages where people huddled together in poverty." Some say "the land [is] growing old." Dotheimis says "'A city is like an egg—once dropped, difficult to put together!'" (511). Eventually civil war rages in the city, with the Upper Town held by one force, and the rest by another. The fire from the mother-city goes out. The harbor becomes ensilted and abandoned. ". . .[T]he wine grew so low in the wine-skin, that it flowed only by dribbles, with now and then a little spurt" (518).

The final Book is played out from the viewpoint of the greatly aged Diothemis, great-grandson of Archias, still living in the now impoverished house Archias originally built. Diothemis looks down on the panorama of Phrax in the throes of its final siege from the same balcony where his precursors had observed its prosperous pride. In one of the devices of narrative symmetry derided by certain reviewers, Diothemis is approached by a shabby urchin (to whom he says "'we are both under sentence of death'" [528]), who turns out to be his grandson by one of his own illegitimate children. The urchin's father scarifies the grandson and flees from the city with him by boat. Diothemis, looking down at the sea front, can't be sure whether the boat has escaped the enemy archers in the harbor. This final view of the now ruined city from above, accompanied by the sounds of moaning and wailing, ". . .never quite dying out, as if in some way the city itself sent up a voice of distress" (548) is the final incarnation of the original map drawn by the Founder and observed through the wondering eyes of young Archias.

Lee Rozelle considers the works of many modernist authors to "outline an ethos of unsustainability that disconnects the urbanite from the pleasures and responsibilities of place" (102). *The Years of the City* anatomizes this ethos at work in an ancient city, while at the same time presenting the city itself as unsustainable in another sense—incapable of immortality. Stewart's double vision of the ecological city, how it can be made sustainable or unsustainable in one sense by human agency, but is in the long run mortal, partook of but challenged both versions of urban ecology dominant at mid-century.

"Stewart displays an amazingly rich imagination in this volume," Arthur Hakel exuded in the *Oakland Tribune*. "It is filled with a wonderland of minutiae which give life to person and scene but it is also such a perfection of organization that the junipers of detail do not obscure the ponderosas beyond" (Hakel). The *Time* reviewer derided this organization, the city's "neatly Spenglerian life cycle." Stewart's former pupil Milton Lott thought that this organization was precisely its virtue. It is a ". ..novel in the old tradition, large in scope, richly peopled, and above all, philosophical in import" (Lott to Stewart 29 Oct. 1955). The author himself seems to have been less upset by his reviewers than by his publisher and by his boss.

In the former case, Houghton Mifflin may well have said "We all drool a bit when we think about a Stewart novel" (Lovell Thompson to Stewart 15 Oct 1954), but Stewart replied with gall: "I spent $250 getting a good clean text of *The Years of the City* and the carelessness of your editor with another person's property is amazing." In fact, Stewart complains the editor treated him like a "schoolboy" (Stewart to Paul Brooks 21 Dec. 1954). Seeking to soothe his author (as he had to do with so many others), Brooks sent Stewart a telegram offering to compensate by "sweetening the pot" (Brooks to Stewart 2 Jan. 1955). Stewart expressed surprise, but, needless to say, accepted the "sweetening" (Stewart to Brooks 13 Jan 1955). Later, Brooks sent Stewart a more measured appreciation of the novel: "We were aware of the universal application of the story of the rise and fall of the city, and the unfortunate aptness with which much of this applies to the present day. Maybe we should have a subtitle—'The Years of the City—and of the Oath'" (Brooks to Stewart 18 Jan 1955).

The problem with the boss was more amusing. President Sproul denied Stewart's request to post ads for *The Years of the City* around the Berkeley campus (Sproul to Stewart 27 July 1955). Stewart had cited a poster for a student drama society play "Who is the Girl from Golden Gulch" as a precedent. Sproul says that if Stewart wants similarly to "desecrate the landscape with purple and gold signs," he'll have to get the drama society to present a staged version of his novel. To which Stewart replied (Stewart to Sproul 4 Aug. 1955), "Thank you for your recent letter which seems to grant me the privilege of posting the campus and destroying its beauty," revealing that his original request was a form of environmentalist satire. He continued to the effect that so few students buy serious books anyway that contemporary novelists are forced to teach in universities, "with some exceptions made for the fortunate few who, because of enlightened administrations, teach on a half-time schedule." This was of course a complement to Sproul, since Stewart was about to set out for a fall in Mexico and Central America to take photographs for his next book, *N.A. 1*.

Chapter VII
Various Excursions

Superfetation was the byword for Stewart's professional life in the mid-1950's—perhaps in a sense for his private life too. As *The Years of the City* was being written and published, he was travelling widely to create a sequel to *U.S. 40*, first on the Alaska Highway (with geologist Parker Trask), and then from the Mexican border south to Costa Rica with Ted and his friend Hal O'Flaherty. And in between these trips his first grandchild was born. He was also being pursued by publishers—which was maybe another reason for him to leave the country.

Although Stewart had a warm personal relationship with Alfred Knopf, he wasn't prepared to change publishers. But representatives of both Knopf and Harpers were wooing him passionately to do another book in the mode of *Storm* and *Fire*. Knopf apparently saw his cosmic takes on the earth more in the mode of Rachel Carson's *The Sea Around Us*. "Perhaps the time has come when a really fascinating general gook could be written about what the meteorologists call 'The Ocean of Air'," Knopf's Philip Vaudrin wrote him, including a pre-processed outline of the book with suggested chapter headings such as "War of the Winds" and "Planetary Air-Conditioning" (Vaudrin to Stewart 4 Mar. 1953/*R*). This suggestion was not pursued, but the representatives of Harper's, Simon Bessie and Evan Thomas, were much more persistent, pressing their attentions upon him with gift books, visits, and, as they appear to me, seductive familiarities. After one visit, Thomas sent Stewart a breathless telegram "to say that I have told [Cass] Canfield and other editorial colleagues here as well as sales department that I dare to hope you may give us a chance at book I call "Hurrican!" and all are tremendously keen and hopeful. . ." (Thomas to Stewart 27 Feb. 1956/*R*). Canfield followed up with more enthusiasm: "There is no question that you are the one person best fitted to write such a volume. ..," and, name-dropping, mentioned his conversation "the other day" with Rachel Carson about jet stream theory (Canfield to Stewart 28 Feb. 1956/*R*). Stewart, I suspect, may have been pulling the editorial legs by suggesting his real enthusiasm was for *New Yorker*-type cartoon anthologies (Stewart to Simon Bessie 31 Jan 1956/*R*), maybe a collection arranged around archetypal themes such as "the flying carpet, the cannibal-missionary situation, the African safari, the man figuratively undressing the girl . . ." (Stewart to Bessie 15 Jan 1956/*R*). By March, Stewart was writing "The flood of letters and telegrams from Harper's almost overwhelmed me. . .," but in a cross-up he says he mentioned the hurricane idea to Paul Brooks, Brooks had become interested himself, and "Since I offered the idea to him first and since he is publishing other books of mine, this puts me under some obligation" (Stewart to Evan Thomas 18 Mar. 1956/*R*). News from Carl Carmer that Stewart was doing more California books made that trail open up too; Bessie wrote him about that with a slightly plaintive P.S. :"As I am sure you know, I very much hope you will be doing that hurricane book for us" (Bessie to Stewart 28 Mar. 1956/*R*). In 1957 they were still after him. Thomas sent him a copy of Leonard Ormerod's *The Curving Shore: The Gulf Coast from Brownsville to Key West*, saying the author was inspired by *U.S. 40* (Thomas to Stewart 4 Feb. 1957/*R*). Perhaps Stewart was being a tease, though, too. In July 1956 he had written to Saxe Commins that "Partly on account of health and partly because I have felt that I have been working too fast of late, I have decided to take a kind of year off from writing" (Stewart to Commins 29 July 1956/*P*). Of course, at the same time, he says he's been revising *Names on the Land* to cover Alaska and Hawaii, and also revising *Ordeal by Hunger*.

Throughout all this period, though, Stewart was frying other fish too. In 1953 Paul Brooks wrote that Stegner had told him about Stewart's plans for an *N.A. 1* book (Brooks to Stewart 16 June 1953). Having already been to Alaska, Stewart wrote to Brooks in February, 1955 about his planned August trip to Mexico, suggesting he could have the entire book done by the next February

(Stewart to Brooks 13 Feb. 1955). He also wanted Erwin Raisz to do the drawings again, but with a different focus, saying that in *U.S. 40* they played *against* the photographs, whereas in the upcoming volume he wants them to show what could *not* be photographed. Stewart must have been behind deadline, for Brooks in May wrote anticipating the *N.A. 1* text. Stewart had suggested the hurricane book to him anyway, but Brooks thought maybe he should take a break (Brooks to Stewart 29 May 1956). He received the manuscript not long after, and was very impressed. The photographs are "really superb." Like *U.S. 40,* it is "an extended lesson in observation. "You give the reader a sense of immediacy, of being on the spot, which I think is almost unique" (Brooks to Stewart 19 July 1956). Stewart had also, through his agent Annie Laurie Williams, arranged for well known film historian and cinematographer Richard Dyer McCann to travel U.S. 40, with an eye to making a film based on Stewart's book. McCann had a complete script which he sent in 1955, along with the news that many major automakers and oil companies had been approached to sponsor the film, but none was willing; he was still hoping to interest Disney in the project (McCann to Stewart 26 April 1955). Likewise, General Motors refused Stewart's request for a car to use for publicity on his Alaska trip (G. D. Burns to Stewart 24 May 1954).

One could see the *N.A. 1* project as either an attempt to complement *U.S. 40* in a "totalized" view of the North American Continent, and/or an example of the "arrogance" that Stewart attributed to himself at times. To create an "X" cross-section upon the continent, cartographical, visual, and narrative, could be considered a figurative "colonization" of the space, and act of *virtual* possession, which covers its traces through the self-distancing of the creator. Peters describes the strategy of colonizing through cartography with reference to Champlain's *Carte de la Nouvelle France*. Champlain's interjection of maps into narration "facilitates and reifies the conceptual delimitation that poses [him] at/as the center of an apparently objective epistomology . . ." (94), revealing while concealing the creator's identity.

Another take on the map + text and personal identity is in Harley's famous "Map as Biography.""Personal identity," says Harley, "is always implicated in the maps [or, surely, photographs] we collect." As a map can be a "biography of the landscape it portrays," it provides ". . .a rich vein of personal history, and. . .gives a set of co-ordinates for the map of memory." We read such maps "as transcriptions of ourselves" (18).

If we consider *N.A 1* and *U.S. 40* as media-enhanced maps, they do both objectivize (through the unposed photographs) and personalize (through the text and Raisz's sylized maps). For Stewart himself, as in *Sheep Rock*, "I made this." The texts obviously reach out to the reader but they substantialize the continent-encompassing personal experience of their creator, so that he can look at them and see himself, virtually at least, at any point on that continent.

The ostensible purpose of *N.A. 1* is actually anti-colonial, in a historical sense. "N.A. 1" is Stewart's name for the conflation of the Alaska Highway and the Pan-American highway. These roads could of course be considered in themselves colonial enterprises, lines of possession drawn on "virgin land," like the map of Phrax drawn by the Founder. In the Alaska section of *N.A. 1*, Stewart presents the highways, and his work portraying them, as vehicles for de-politicizing national borders drawn on the North American continent. The continent's "true" identity is as a great "biome," geographically unified. The quadrants fixed by the white colonizers distorted this reality. A Martian looking down at pre-Columbian North America would think its main axis of population was North-South, not East-West, the assumption of the post-colonialist (6-7).

N.A. 1 is the first text to see the route from Circle, Alaska to San Isidro, Costa Rica, as a whole. "No one has driven these routes "with much sense of continental exploration" (12). Stewart imagines the writer's/reader's stance as at the center of the continent, looking equally in each compass direction. This is actually the opposite of Champlain's imagined map-viewer, the King of France, typical colonialist, looking from the East to all his new Western lands.

With this same anti-border stance, Stewart has omitted the U.S. link of the two highways altogether: he wants "us" to look beyond "our" borders.

The Alaska section, part I of *N.A. 1*, is sort of thrown into the cauldron of Alaska statehood in the same way that *Years of the City* was into that of "urban crisis." As it moved toward statehood in 1959, Alaska was the object of the lower 48's fascination—and emigration. It was also the object of environmentalists' concern, since the "postwar tourist invasion" (Allin 89) was synchronous with strong movements to preserve this "last American wilderness." Exemplifying this doubleness of invasion and preservation, you could find a writer of advice for "travelers to Alaska" touting Skagway, "set right down in the heart of the Tongass National Forest," as a "center for a lumbering industry," and more, ". . .a regular Alladin's lamp: if the Aluminum Company of America builds a four-hundred-million-dollar smelting plant in the Taiya Valley district, it would make her population shoot up to fifty thousand, and then lots of small industries would flourish" (Rossiter 77). In the same year, Bernard Ederer, canoeing down the Klondike River and then travelling by narrow-gauge railway to Skagway, found that the town which "had, in 1898, been a bustling little city of about fifteen thousand, but now contained only about three hundred," full of old sourdoughs and socked in by impenetrable weather (150).

Stewart's work isn't mentioned by the revisionist environmental historians who tend to see environmentalists like Robert Marshall, and Olaus Murie, as complicit in the destruction of the Alaskan "wilderness" they spent their lives ostensibly defending. Presumably Stewart, who throughout emphasizes the ease of traversing the Alaska highway if well-prepared, would fall into this school of hypocrites. However, I prefer to see him in his cultural ecologist role—not encouraging the invasion of Alaska but describing, in word and image, the nature of the human presence in nonhuman nature.

Donald Worster, in particular, has criticized iconic Alaska preservationists. He characterizes Olaus Murie, during his period with the

Bureau of Biological Survey, spending his time "blazing away at the animals he saw . . . Always on the lookout for good specimens, he shot the healthy, strong, and handsome, not the weak, or sickly animals" (166) For Worster, Murie's career was part of a "new economic organism" based on the consumption of non-renewable resources. Similarly, by the time of Bob Marshall's last Alaska visit, in 1937, "that other great infernal machine, the airplane, which had brought Marshall in so many times, had also become a regular presence," and his work in founding the Wilderness Society involved combatting "this noisy mechanical intrusion, which of course he himself had helped to promote to a degree" (169).

More recently, Susan Kollin has argued that "Alaska's status as a natural wilderness area might be best understood as a sign of its intense and even unrelenting cultural production" (17). Bob Marshall maintained a "position of innocence" and "never acknowledged the ways his experiences in Alaska contributed to the land's economic development" (45). "U.S. conservationism should be understood as part of a larger colonial environmental movement that often involved the management of other nations' natural resources" (54). In the voice of William Cronon, Kollin summarizes thus: "If environmental advocates want to forge changes in the ways nature should be conceived, then we must consider seriously an ecology that integrates human being into nature and that does not set up certain lands as sacred spaces while condemning others as sacrifice zones" (160).

The above false dichotomy I suggest would amuse Stewart, who was so much aware of the intermingling of human and nonhuman areas of activity, shown in the mixed landscapes of his Alaska pictures. Stewart does not set up the polarity of "sacred spaces" and "sacrifice zones" as straw men representing the environmentalist viewpoint in order to be able to refute it. Almost all his photographs, as he emphasizes, contain paved road itself, but that fact does not mean that he endorses building paved road everywhere.

Like Stewart, around mid-century, other pre-ideological writers had mixed viewpoints characteristic of the period between the conservationist orientations of the New Deal and the New Frontier, when capitalism ruled and population exploded. These mixed viewpoints belie the polarized assumptions of revisionists like Worster and Kollin.

In 1939, for example, Harry Franck glorified mining, and deplored "coyote and wolf depredations among caribou, mountain sheep, and moose . . ." (28-9). "Alaskans want to hunt wolves by airplane" (29), but on the other hand, the Natives' criticism of wolves for killing their reindeer is considered by white Alaskans "an alibi, to cover up their illegal killing of reindeer for dog meat, because they are too lazy to catch and dry fish for them" (253). Franck also characterizes Alaskans as unhappy with the autonomy granted in the Organic Act of 1912, but not enthusiastic about statehood, which would symbolize the end of Alaska as, "our last frontier, in the sense of a free land where any man (or woman) may carve out a future" (150).

Two good examples of pre-war relative enlightenment are the U.S. National Resources Planning Board's report on Alaska resources (1938), and the Alaska volume of the WPA's American Guide series, written by Merle Colby (1940). The Report supports limitation on the leasing of public lands, addressing the obvious but still-paradoxical question of how the territory can be both developed and conserved. After comparing different approaches to its resolution, the report concludes that "no policy of forced development for Alaska appears necessary" (22)—in effect endorsing a policy of benign neglect with respect to development. However, perhaps influenced by Marshall and his allies, it comes out strongly for wildlife preservation, by contrast to its "depletion" in the lower West (27). While supporting timber harvesting and forest industries, particularly in the Tongass, the report speaks with forked tongue, since it also emphasizes conservation-based planned use, to "avoid the mistakes that arose from hurried development in the West (137), such as deforestation and water pollution. Finally, it explicitly proposes the creation of wilderness and roadless areas; for example, recommending "that a number of tracts along the Alaska coast be set aside as areas to be kept so far as possible in the primitive state by closing them to roads, hotels, and private homes" (142).

Colby in the Guide also defends "wilderness," attacking "a group of anticonservationists who prefer to see Alaska serve solely as a source of raw materials for the United States" (12). Colby saw the need for constant vigilance in controlling and regulating the exploitation of natural resources, evoking the depletion of fur seals and salmon. There are some tendentious references in his work also: impercipiently he sees little future for oil exploration in Alaska (71), but prophetically considers "its front door opening on nations of the North Temperate Zone" (13-14), and foresees a proposed international highway from the mainland U.S. (97).

These last two visions converged with World War II, and the perception of Alaska as a space of both military vulnerability and opportunity. In 1944 Herbert Lanks got permission from the Army to traverse what had been completed of its new Alaska Highway, "America's northern life-line" (20), still under construction. On the way, he noticed the highway-building's effects: the massive clearcutting, the mountains of dead oil drums, the decline in river commerce. "As this book goes to press," he says, a branch highway is being built to "serve the pipe-line carrying oil to a great refinery at Whitehorse" (49). As well as a commercial transport and oil access route, the "Alcan" highway's prime purpose, says Lanks, is for "the ground servicing of the skyway to Alaska" (151). Apparently the confluence of trucks, pipelines, and airplanes couldn't keep the author from experiencing sublimity: "As the flood of lunar light poured down on the glistening white of the ice river directly before us, we experienced one of the rare movements [sic.] in which both body and spirit are sublimely uplifted' (139).

Stewart gives a very detailed history of the highway Lanks traversed, from its conception as a war route in 1940 to the final "meeting of the cats" (49). He defines the motivation for its construction partly in terms of national psychology, as a way of therapeutically redeeming Pearl Harbor. The builders' byword was "'The road must get there before the Japs!'" (41). But the highway experienced both boosters and detractors: it could be the main route of defense against Japanese invasion of the U.S. or it could promote southern invasion of Alaska by the nation's own people of the lower 48. One postwar writer foresaw that in Alaska "development of the type which has characterized the growth of America seems assured," and that "those who have lived in Alaska a long time realize that an end already has come to a phase in the history of the country, a phase which had a great deal of attraction to it, but one which had to go" (Sundborg 5). Although Alaska's separation "had to go," given the "thrilling" activity of salmon canning (120), and the great potential of coal and oil exploration, the highway itself, to an "opened up" Alaska (11), "is not scenic or direct, nor does it open up country as favorable from the development standpoint as that which would be tapped by other routes" (162).

As the highway was improved throughout the 1950's, it was viewed more favorably by all the above criteria. The Englishman Frank Illingworth traveled the highway with great enthusiasm, despite his contrast between humans' "engineering successes" and those times when [man's] "outlook slips back to that of the wild dog—a wild dog all the more dangerous because, while temporarily insane, he yet retains all his scientific ability" (128). Illingworth apparently didn't see the highway as related in any way to the latter outlook, or to the killing of wolves by cyanide bombs (234). He relates with glee capturing a porcupine and chasing it back and forth across the Alaska Highway (138). Stewart, writing a couple of years later, says "The building of the highway has not yet brought to the region as a whole anything like the development that its pre-war advocates declared it would" (140). Its solid surface, he observes, helps moose flee wolves, and forest fires to spread. The intrepid Japanese traveler whom we've met before, Hidesaburo Kurushima took the bus from Fairbanks to Anchorage in 1950. There were only four passengers and they passed by only ten houses on his route; the driver took them on a rough road, saying it was more "picturesque," through a "wild primeval forest" (357). Kurushima describes a generally depopulated landscape.

As we will see, Stewart's highway is not flooded with vehicles either—although he presents statistics from 1952 to show traffic is increasing--, a condition which contradicts that presented by much periodical writing. For example, back in 1949 one journalist had enthused that "by boat, plane, and car, hundreds of Americans were moving last week toward the last great U.S. frontier—Alaska. Up the Alaska Highway. . .through some of the world's most majestic mountains and some of the continent's most unpeopled wilderness, jogged twenty families a day" ("Promised" 26). Stewart evokes the "dangers" of the Alaska trip touted by much popular journalism. "Calling the trip to Alaska a hazardous journey is—in these days—silly"(21). Yet this image of danger is so ingrained that, he says, when people hear he's driven to Alaska, ". . .they look upon me as a kind of Arctic explorer, and I feel like Hearne or Mackenzie . . ." (22).

Both volumes of *N.A. 1* have the signature mapped endpapers, in this case, the entire continent viewed facing northeast, with the Canada/Alaska and Mexico/Central America routes outlined in bold. The visual result is a United States reduced in profile to interstitial space. This visual angle also reproduces what Stewart's imaginary "Martian astronomer," in his introduction to the Alaska volume, sees from outer space. To the Martian, North America "'appears to us, through our telescopes, as a large mass of land, shaped like a triangle, and standing upon one of its apices . . .'" (6-7). The Martian astronomer also sees the "'. . .essential part of the continent is that great axis of mountains and plateaus which may be said to form a western side to the triangle. . .'" (7). Stewart comments on the geographical and prehistoric accuracy of this observation, since both migration into the continent, and pre-Columbian centers of civilization followed this axis, whereas, before European conquest, the east-west extensions of it could be considered '"minor excrescences'" (7).

After discussing some of the aspects of his trips, covered above, Stewart says his trip was made in a "1954 four-door sedan, American-made, one of the 'medium-priced' models. I do not name its manufacturer. Automobiles do not advertise books, and I see no reason why books should advertise automobiles" (17), a disingenuous comment, since Stewart did try to get Ford to sponsor his excursions.

The general description of non-human nature on the Alaska highway is somewhat disillusioned. The road is "surprisingly monotonous," despite some spectacular scenes: ". . .the forest lacks majesty" (31). Rather than chasing porcupines on the highway, Stewart enjoys the memory ". . of a cross-fox gaily romping across the highway a hundred yards ahead" (31). He comments on the retreat (by 1954) of larger mammals from the highway's vicinity since his first trip on it in 1948—although no hunting is allowed within a mile of it. But "The country is most of all notable for its great emptiness—both of people and of their evidences" (31).

In my view, the sequence of maps and photographs somewhat contradicts this characterization. First, Erwin Raisz has definitely followed the directive referred to in the Stewart-Commins correspondence, and the route itself is de-emphasized in contrast to the complexity of the named terrain surrounding it; lakes, mountain ranges, and rivers overwhelm the tiny line of highway. Also, most of the maps are projected from an east-to-west perspective (east at the bottom, west at the top), so our conventional north-south viewpoint has been rotated 90 degrees, and the mapped highway, although "literally" heading north or northwest "reads" as though it is going from west to east. The affect of this movement, given the conventions of east-to-west mapping discussed by Limerick in the previous chapter, suggests a movement from "wild" west to "tame" east, when the literal progress on the highway is if anything in the opposite direction. This mapping is anti-monotony.

Also, the landscapes Stewart photographs are not at all "empty." In fact, rather than following the procedure I used in discussing *U.S. 40*, of describing in detail particular pictures, I am going to emphasize the environmental presences in the whole sequence of pictures. The very first pictures, of the Fraser River canyon, suggest an idea of "involved separation." The deep, rock-strewn canyon wall in the lower picture, with the walled roadway in the upper right snaking around an abutment, is fronted by three fir trees: "Just as the three gaunt trunks of Douglas firs, like bars across a window, present a view and yet restrict it, to the famous canyon has at once offered a passageway and yet made the passageway difficult, since the time of the first explorers" (73).

"Dry Belt" (2), is described with detailed climatic explanation of its "'park-like'" openness, but the most interesting feature, crossing the lower third of the photograph, is the "Russell fence," which Stewart says is a common feature of pastureland in this area of British Columbia: a sequence of wired tripods supporting several parallel horizontal timbers. The fence dominates the picture and also the only text, literary or non-literary, that I can find that discusses *N.A. 1*, "The Geography of the Russell Fence." Thomas Eley and Cherie Northon, self-described "geographers of the Berkeley School . . ." (114), became intrigued with this particular fence design, and studied its occurrence in Western Canada and Alaska, using as "baseline photographs" those from *N.A. 1*. They characterize Stewart as being at Berkeley when "such greats as Carl Sauer were shaping Berkeley's geographical tradition. In our opinion, Stewart was also very much a geographer" (114).

Eley and Northon begin their discussion with the Stewart photograph referred to above and, as in the Vanes' book, juxtapose it to their own picture taken at the same site in 2002. In Stewart's tradition of "cultural geography," they insisted on actual field travel, photography, and interviews to establish the presence of the Russell fence fifty years after Stewart chronicled it. Just as Stewart, they remain baffled by the origin of the name "Russell," although interviewees gave them many interesting theories of its origin. The fence itself, they say, probably originated some time after the 1859 Cariboo Gold Rush (117). But they interestingly chronicle the rise and fall of the fence, at one time being replaced by barbed wire, but, at the time of their writing, being widely re-adopted, for its ease in construction and as, it seems, as a sort of cultural symbol of resonance. I think Stewart would have appreciated this response to his text, since he was always more interested in material culture than in its verbal representation (except where names were concerned).

"Intimate Road" (3) is a beautifully greytoned photo of the tree-shaded road bending under trees near Soda Creek. "Intimate" is a strong word from Stewart. It is by contrast to modern highways which

> . . .become 'dominant' and one might even say 'arrogant' with respect to the country through which they pass. They slash the hills, fill the ravines, run the brooks through culverts, slice the forest back. That is why one should treasure the few bits of intimate road that are still left, but will not long remain" (76).

The highway north from Williams Lake to Prince George in 1954 "was stillwholly adapted to the country, not imposed upon it." Even the ill-constructed "lazy-man's fence" (77) beside it makes the road "a little more flavorful," evoking the old stage road that it was up into the 20th century. It is worth reflecting on Stewart's predilection for "intimate" and "flavorful" roads. The words suggest environmentally friendly passageways, and also a sensuous appreciation for the presence of human construction in harmony with nonhuman nature.

Picture 5, "Farm in a Clearing," brings up another aspect of cultural construction in environmental space. The author tells us that "The farm in the clearing goes back very deeply into North American history. . ." (89). Except for the wire fence in the foreground, this farm is in the position of an archetype. "The forest of conifers and white-trunked aspens presses close in, ready to return if vigilance is relaxed." The buildings are clustered right where the hill-slope begins, " . . .close-set, almost as if the settlers still were a little nervous about Indian attack." The house is of boards, even though logs are much more available, and log houses are "weatherproof, comfortable, long-lived, and easy to build." The author considers building a board house in log house country to be evidence of a form of "traditional snob-appeal." ". . .[T]he framed house bespeaks the town, civilization, and perhaps even running water and a bathroom." Thus the farm presents itself as a text to be read by its observer, with frontier past and urban present mingled therein. In *U.S. 40*, the urban-structured rural farmhouse in New Jersey expressed the same ambivalence.

At Summit Lake (6), "Take a good look at the pavement here" (91), since there will be almost no more until the traveler reaches Alaska. The lake gives the author reason to tell us about the whole terrain of Arctic drainage, of which it is at the southwestern corner. We are also given a paean to northern lakes in general:

> The lakes of the north rate book to themselves—like beads along the highway, blue and green and shining silver, placid and bright beneath the sun, angry and dark in the storm, ice-bound and snow-covered in their seasons. Even their names suggest the unknown and faraway—Kluane, Teslin, Muncho, Azouzetta, La Hache.

In his section on the stretch from Dawson to Whitehorse, Stewart discusses the near-desuetude of the Canadian section of the highway; the Canadian government was legally obligated to maintain it, but it served, from their point of view, very little purpose after the war, and its abandonment was urged. It is intriguing to follow his account of the re-opening of the road which many wanted to revert to "grass," as perhaps today's environmental*ist* would. But for Stewart it is sort of like a contemporary "opening of the West," like a time-reverse of Ish's travel experience. He uses "travelers' accounts" to chronicle its restoration. Mr. and Mrs. E. O. Goulet were some of the first postwar travelers; with many accidents which, given the technological differences, would fit very well into a story of the Donner party, they managed to drive from Fairbanks to the U.S. border in 1946 with their Persian cat, Pansy [!]—although at Dawson Creek Pansy eloped with an "attractive tom" (104).

He next tells of the late Senator Richard Neuberger's trip in 1947; Neuberger was required by the Canadian authorities to carry less survival gear than the Goulets were, but he still needed an RCMP permit. The third account is of his own trip in 1948. At that time all he had to do at the Canadian border was to demonstrate he had enough money to get to Alaska, but a lot of the road was still settling, and extremely bumpy. Stewart was much more of an explorer then than in 1954.

A significant picture for seeing the highway as a cultural construction is "Contact Creek" (17). This is where the southbound and northbound road builders made contact. The original bridge, now (1954) in ruins was called "Golden Spike bridge," by obvious analogy. In the picture of the current, slightly primitive, bridge and the original ruined one, Stewart finds "a rearward glance at the history of the highway (123), emphasizing the contrasting structure of the two bridges and the surviving piles of rotting, downed trees from the original construction. A similar archaeology can be found at Watson Lake ("Folk-Custom" 18). It shows the accretion of (often facetious) directional signposts with legends such as "New York, 3600." To the original signpost with nine direction-pointers, Stewart found two more posts covered with pointers in 1948. In 1954, a wonderful stratification of pointers on barren terrain numbers about 250. You can trace the history of their construction through levels of decay of older signs. Stewart discusses like an archaeologist the changes in the signs, and concludes ". . .that the human male, like his best friend, has an urge to leave some posted record of having passed by" (125).

At "Mid-Point" (19), Stewart is able to bring in some of his observation on forest fires. The road clearance allowed abundant second-growth spruces, "thick as grass," leading to inevitable fires in dry summers. No one is present to control them. To him, the fires in this location do little harm. Fires are bad for caribou and good for moose, since brush and aspens, good food for the latter, spring up after the spruces have been burned. A contrast to this desolation is what Stewart (ironically?) labels "Bit of the New North" (21),

Whitehorse, seen from above. He repeats the source of the town's name—the rapids looked like white horses, a white horse hauled freight around them, or "some other reason" (130). The town died slowly after the gold rush, but was reborn with the highway and became Yukon Territory's capital. "Like any new American town Whitehorse shows the scattering that goes along with automobile transportation" (131).

Stewart recounts the complex history of the routing of the highway from Whitehorse to Fairbanks, with particular emphasis on "the effect of the construction of the highway upon the country through which it passes" (139). Here again, the effect is, as it were, "empty." No Indian settlements were displaced, there has been very little commercial development, except for Fort Nelson, the one example of "ribbon development." In fact, Stewart says, the pre-war prophecy of great development potential (as in some of the material quoted above) has simply not been realized. Agricultural development has been "microscopic." Lumbering is only local. There is little mining. All one finds are the "parasitic growths" (140) of tourist facilities. There seems to have been little effect on animal life. "Wild animals, in fact, are quick to make use of the works of civilization for their own ends." For example, mountain lions moved into culverts for winter quarters, and beavers dam culvert outflows (as shown in "Beaver," 28). Moose can outrun wolves on the harder surface of the highway. The only really negative environmental effect of the highway, at the time of writing, is based on the truism "Fire follows man," and he notes how much of the forest has been burned between 1948 and 1954.

The final section mapped by Raisz and summarized by Stewart is the Steese Highway, north from Fairbanks to its terminus at Circle. Named for James Gordon Steese, Colonel of U. S. Engineers, it brings the traveler for the first time "into what might be described as a fully arctic environment" (163), dead-ending at the banks of the Yukon River. For his discussion of the highway, Stewart corresponded with Steese himself. "We may consider it somewhat remarkable that as of the time of writing this road has maintained itself for many years as the most northern point of the continent to be reached by automobile" (164), and, according to Steese, there are no plans to extend it further.

The last picture in the text, "The End" (34), is the one which most accurately portrays the emptiness Stewart began with. The Yukon River stretches across the center, above and beyond it desolate flats under dark cloud-cover. The lower two-thirds of the picture are of the scrappy house and property of an Indian who works the sawmills, "typical of the down-at-heel and ill-kept premises that are to be found in the farther reaches of the north." There is a sled-dog pen, and oil drums block the road to keep off tourists. Here ". . there is nothing to do but touch the bumper to the oil cans, backup, turn around, and start south.

"You are safer driving south of the border than driving the same distance on one of our highways in the United States," says Stewart, "because you are not exposed to the dangers of heavy traffic" (*N.A. 1 Looking South* 4). Of course, there are "certain special hazards," particularly things *on* the road: *piedras* (stones) and *ganado* (livestock), and, the most dangerous of all, *gente* (people), since Latin Americans consider the road the place you are supposed to walk (5-6). Speaking as one who has travelled by car in Latin America since the 1930's, Stewart has much more negative things to say about the *Americanos* of the north than of the south. Roads in Central America and Mexico will continue to improve because of *el turismo*, but the latter is "a great corrupter, and even is likely to kill the thing it loves" (11). Stewart compares the effect of tourists on the countryside and towns as analogous to that of the highways "scarring the hillsides, impos[ing] themselves upon a landscape and mak[ing] it something different . . ." (11). He describes driving the incomplete Central Highway of Mexico in 1949, where people lived in what might be called "'pastoral simplicity;'" whereas "In 1955 the region had become something else, very conscious of tourists. Children had become corrupted into being beggars . . ." (12). And attitudes have changed. The Indians of Guatemala, once friendly, have become sullen. "Certainly the untactful use of the camera has something to do with it." He calls for "education on both sides," particularly on the part of the tourists who need to stop considering "the local inhabitants as exhibits of a zoo."

Stewart considers the Pan-American Highway the more striking achievement, compared with the Alaska Highway—because it was a peaceful, international collaboration. He provides a history of the highway from President Harding's initial interest, to the Hoover bill of 1930 providing funding for a survey, through the stages of construction. The 1920's and 1930's were characterized by "stunt" journeys—real car trips through unfathomable terrain, or vehicular travelers who pretended to have gone from Panama to Washington, D.C. on foot. Two names we will remember from the Alaska Highway, Harry Franck and Herbert Lanks, published a photo book *The Pan American Highway* (1940). In his front-page review of *N.A. 1*, Lewis Gannett contrasts Stewart's "sensible" yet "dramatic" and "original" book to Franck and Lanks, who seem more concerned with pictures of "lovely Indian girls, many of them bathing in the semi-nude" (Gannett 1). Presumably these girls were real, yet it is surprising that ". . . to 1940, no overland trip between Panama and the United States can be fully authenticated" (26).

Raisz's maps of the Pan American Highway are interesting because they reverse the point of view of the first volume. Here we are looking from west to east, on the map, and, in terms of our habitual stance, we feel that we are moving east as we move south toward Costa Rica. In his introduction to the first segment, Ciudad Juarez to Mexico City, Stewart recalls his trip with his wife on this route in March, 1949. After some pleasant travel, darkness fell, the gas gauge read empty. "We drove on, through detours with dust six inches deep, not knowing where we were half the time, expecting any moment to have the engine cough and die" (57). In a tiny village an itinerant peddler sold them two gallons of gas. They were directed off the road to Durango along a "twisting and dusty trail" to another small village, with only one light in a house. He went to the door, in search of a guide and was met by a man wearing a pistol three feet long. Surprisingly, this gentleman was friendly and indicated the Stewarts could follow another car that was going their direction. "In this car were four Mexican with handkerchiefs tied round the lower parts of their faces. Having seen plenty of people like that in Westerns, I knew that these were bandits. But . . .I thought that I might as well be robbed in the desert as robbed in the village, and I followed" (57). It turned out that they were masked just to keep out the dust.

The texture of the southern volume is much different from that of the northern one, since the terrain bears so much history of occupation. Thus there is as much human as nonhuman architecture in the photographs. They do start out dramatically with "Sand Dunes" (1), portraying a scene of primeval conflict between plants and sand, a ". . .battle, throughout the centuries, between plants and wind, with the sand passive between them. The plants are conservative; the wind, destructive. The plants try to hold what they have gained, and in good years to extend themselves. The wind tries either to bury the plants or to blow the sand away from their roots" (61). Many of the photographs, though, emphasize the deep engagement between the artifacts of material culture and the natural landscape. An excellent example is the photograph of Zacatecas (8), which is dominated by two opposite-bending curves. One is the skyline of the mountain La Bufa, at its summit a "great outcropping of gray rock," rising from it a church dedicated to the Virgin and a weather-observatory. The other is the late-18th century aqueduct, whose dark arches, at points buttressed to withstand the vibrations produced by auto traffic, appear to end in the farthest perspective at the equestrian statue of General Gonzales Ortega, commander of Mexican forces against both the U.S. and the French (75). Through the dark arches can be seen the four lanes of the highway. In this sinuous symmetry of natural and artificial forms is a sort of balance of inhabitance which may be belied by the actual behaviors of humans, absent in the picture itself.

The "Way" from Mexico City to the Guatemala border is characterized by a culture shift in architecture, agriculture, herd animals, and clothing styles. Stewart describes his own trip from Puebla to Cuernevaca by way of Matamoros in 1938. The road was unspeakably rough and only later, apparently, did he discover that on a contemporary map there was no road at all after Matamoros. . .so he had in effect been traversing a roadless area. Only in 1950 was the "Way" completed to the Guatemalan border. One picture from this section, north of Oaxaca ("Ridge Road," 17), provides an example of a terrain-friendly road, windingly following the pattern of mountain ridges. Stewart notes that in the 1920's U.S. 99 north from Los Angeles looked very much like this. By implication terrain distortion and road straightening will come. He also points out the erosion along the highway due to deforestation for charcoal. ". . .[U]nless something is done quickly, such a region as this seems destined soon to become a maze of treeless and grassless gullies" (109).

A number of the photos taken south of Oaxaca show the presence of the "certain special hazards on the road." "Cuidado con el Ganado" (26) pictures a flock of goats, wandering happily without a herdsman; "Highway Utilization" (29) portrays a Mexican Indian drying his corn on the road, in his hand the peso note he's just been given for allowing his picture to be taken. In "Waiting for the Bus—Hot Country" (27), the humans in the road dominate the scene, and Stewart describes in detail their individual diversity, based on their costume. The total contrast is "Highway Disappearing" (33), near the Guatemala border. "This might be called a science-fiction pre-view of what our highways would be like in a year or two if man were quietly removed from the earth" (141). This unmaintained section is pressured by vegetation on each side, and some sprouting in the middle. ". . .[I]n a few more years the highway might well be entirely overrun with vines, with reaching branches, and with more bushes sprouting up from cracks in the asphalt" (141)—an imagined scene straight out of *Earth Abides.* Further south, in El Salvador, Stewart photographed an imposing sculpture base, inscribed "Asi Termina El Imprudente" ("'This ends the rash man'") supporting "the badly-smashed wreck of an American car" on a simulated roadway of large stones (179). Beside it a real man standing in an oxcart seems to be looking reproachfully at the photographer. Further south, in Honduras, the photographer finds a dead pig, probably hit by a car, surrounded by crows and vultures. He titles the scene "'Dogs and vultures,'" evoking the opening of the *Iliad*. The scene ". . .gives some indication of what the reality must have been at the Achaean beachhead, after Chryses had incited Apollo's vengeance against the captors of his daughter" (191).

One feature that dominates many of Stewart's Guatemalan pictures is human work, or the products thereof. Work itself has two modes, for in one instance we see works meant to open the mountainous landscape and in the other immemorial work being carried out in the very modified topography produced by the former work. Right over the border, picture 34 shows roadbuilding work in the very difficult Seleguar River gorge, where cliffs have been blasted away, and, almost symbolically, according to the road workers, whole agricultural fields have slid as a result down into the gorge (161). Stewart's three pictures of "Burden Bearers" (36) are striking because of the heaviness of the burdens—two people bent under charcoal, three with tremendous loads of pots. The charcoal bearers' stances betray ". . .an effect of poverty, over-work, oppression, even fear." The pot-bearers are headed on a three-day trek to Guatemala City, on a hard road under electric wires. Their role is ancestral, its setting recent. "Road Work" (41) shows two different road crews clearing the highway with oxen and wheelbarrows. A telling evidence of agricultural work is "Land Use" (39). Here, an erosive hillside has been planted with hills of corn in contoured furrows, throughout a pine forest. The trees' branches have all been gathered for firewood or charcoal, so only tufts of needles at the top remain. This scene contrasts to the agrarian landscape in El Salvador (45), where land has been wisely used, with fields laid in contour between hillside streambeds, giving the water-retention benefits of terracing.

In Nicaragua, Stewart and his companions had the interesting experience of pausing by a "primitive-looking house," which suddenly disgorged a whole village-worth of curious people, whom Stewart lined up for a photograph. "Though I am no anthropologist," he tried to figure out what the social structure of this strange group was. He noticed a matriarch, three mothers, and thirteen children, but no men. "Apparently, these people all live in the same house, and would seem, from their smiles and interest in life, to live there happily" (201). Near Lake Nicaragua, in more tropical setting, he photographed two girls only who ran up from a group of huts to be photographed. "In such lush tropical surroundings living is likely to come easily, and high infant-mortality keeps the population within the limits of the food supply" (209). He equals this cynical Darwinian comment by saying "Some commentators upon Nicaragua would suggest that the lighter complexion of the smaller girl may have some linkage with the occupation of this country by our marines during the nineteen-twenties . . ."

The end of the Pan-American highway—in 1955—is very similar in composition, if not climate, to that of the Alaska Highway at Circle. "The only creatures of which you will commonly be conscious at both ends of the highway and along it are, man, the dog, and the mosquito" (*N.A. 1—Looking North* 11). At San Isidro in Costa Rica "the road sinks back into the primitive." In is 130 miles from this point to the head of the road crossing the Panamanian border.

At the end of this second volume, Stewart reflects on "Looking Both Ways." He has two significant points to make. The greatest cultural contrast on the continent is between English- and Spanish-speaking America. The greatest natural contrast is between "civilized and primitive country, or between thickly inhabited and largely uninhabited country" (226). There is lots of uninhabited country. "Man in his millions concentrates himself in small patches." He predicts great development in extending and improving the highway. "If we accept the premises of civilization, everything that has just been stated may be considered optimistic" (226). But, tellingly, "The highway. . .is to some extent a destructive agent" (226-227). It brings fire to the north, and everywhere "opens up the country to ruthless exploitation." This is inevitable. "But we should exercise some foresight, lest the country along the highway should be degraded into a kind of continental slum."

Which might be one way of describing the "crazy American night" (100) of another great 1957 road book, the generic antithesis of *N.A. 1*, Jack Kerouac's *On the Road*—although much of Kerouac's experiences therein happened ten years earlier. It is fascinating to juxtapose these texts, so absolutely different, and yet both so consumed with continental identity and mobility. Despite the differences in form, I don't think Stewart and Kerouac are that different in their "visionary" sense of America. In *On the Road* the narrator crosses and recrosses the continent in consciousness of its cumulative historical heritage. Looking at the Mississippi, he meditates on the ". . .grand Odyssean logs of our continental dream" (103). "'Whither goest thou, America, in thy shiny car in the night?'" (119). Stewart would also have been with Kerouac in his praise of "the fabulous white city of San Francisco on her eleven mystic hills. . ." (169), and Kerouac's obsessive returns to San Francisco, his immersion in it. When Jack and Dean go to Mexico, late in the novel, their observations are not much different than Stewart's: "Across the fields an old man plodded with a burro in front of his switch stick. The sun rose pure on pure and ancient activities of human life" (178). I suggest that despite the "geomysticism" of Kerouac, that could be considered proto-deep-ecological ("The. . .earth is an Indian thing. As essential as rocks in the desert are they in the desert of 'history'" [281]), he is, compared with Stewart, essentially an addict of culture. His intense empathy and ego(not eco)centrism are enmeshed in webs of human relationships. A reader of *On the Road* will find lots of topography, but not much non-human nature. The speaker assumes the power to see inside the emotional lives of others, individual and collective. Stewart, as writer, experiences other humans as participants in a larger environment, but does not presume to do more than speculate about what entrances Kerouac. On the other hand, you can imagine a combination of the sensibilities of *Earth Abides* and *N.A. 1* in this striking evocation by Kerouac of the Mexican Indians:

> They had come down from the back mountains and higher places to hold forth their hands for something they thought civilization could offer, and they never dreamed the sadness and the poor broken delusion of it. They didn't know that a bomb had come that could crack all our bridges and roads and reduce them to jumbles, and we would b e as poor as they someday, and stretching out our hands in the same, same way. Our broken Ford, old thirties upgoing America Ford, rattled through them and vanished in dust. (199).

Of Kerouac, Harold Davis wrote "I understand Jack Kerouac has been taken up as a promotion by some firm of commercial bigshots in New York and he is required to make an ass of himself at regular intervals to keep the market up" (Davis to Stewart 12 Oct. 1959).

Stewart's "road" books definitely had an influence on his expanded edition of *Names on the Land* (1958). He did a good detail of specific revision, but thinks most of the text is good as it stands. "I have seen it noted in print so often as a 'classic' that I am beginning to believe what I read. That is one reason why I am willing to let the text stand almost as it was originally written" (vii). As it was the result of a "single impulse," it should retain the integrity of that impulse, particularly since Stewart does not subscribe to the idea that a writer grows wiser with age (viii). What he did do significantly was to add chapters on Alaska and Hawaii, the new states, and, most interestingly, a general update titled "Current affairs—1944-1958." He finds that none of the world circumstances of this period—World War II, the Cold War, the Atomic Age—have left much of a mark on American nomenclature. Main changes seem to be the "filling-in" of newly-mapped spaces, particularly with commemorative names. He finds the hot-spot for *renaming* in the Appalachian states, noting the "West Virginia community which has made Mountain out of Mole Hill" (429).

*

The late 1950's and early 1960's was a period of intense intersocial life for Stewart, and also a time of reflection on his future. His manic writing activity continued, but he was thinking about whether his teaching career would continue. During this time one might say he had a plateau of importance as a major writer. He became pretty close with both Carl Sandburg and Robert Frost. Joe Backus, thanking Stewart for an opportunity to meet Frost, transcribes a conversation between the latter and Terrence O'Flaherty, Berkeley graduate and famous *San Francisco Chronicle* columnist. This presumably occurred at Stewart's house on Codornices Road:

> Frost: "They didn't like [Dylan Thomas] over here: he was against the schools, and there was the drinking and women. They didn't mind the women and drinking so much. That was to be expected. That was all right. But he cried all the time. They didn't like him to cry."
> O'Flaherty: "He was a good drinker but a poor crier."
> O'Flaherty: "He couldn't hold his tears."
> Frost: "Yes, that's right." (Backus to Stewart 13 May 1958)

Frost and Sandburg often could be found at Stewart's house, but never at the same time since "they hated each other. It wouldn't have been a good idea to have them together, though it might have been fun." Sandburg "became quite a good friend towards the end of his life." But the last time he stayed with the Stewarts to give a reading and sing, "He was senile. He shouldn't possibly have been trying to put on a show. He couldn't remember the words of his own songs" (*Little* 89).

Stewart sees Frost as a great actor. 'I think Robert always rather liked me, because he realized I saw though his part." Frost was very conservative, Sandburg very liberal. Stewart remembers Sandburg staying with them when Frost gave his famous reading at Kennedy's inaugural. "He was delighted when Robert forgot his part." Stewart's view of this famous moment is revisionist to the core. "I'm a complete cynic. That was a beautiful piece of acting. One of the best things he ever did." Not only did Frost not support Kennedy, he didn't like him; it would have been better if Sandburg had written the inaugural poem. Stewart's analysis of the scene is that Frost couldn't write a good poem for Kennedy because his heart wasn't in it. So he pretended not to be able to see his text. Stewart's Frost "had never been a patriot." He never supported the New Deal. He was a reactionary (90).

Stewart had also become active in "The Club," a perdurable group of intellectual males who met monthly to hear and discuss a paper written by one of them. "The Club" has gone under different names at different times. In 1961 they called themselves "The Anonymous Group," when, in November, they met to hear Stewart's paper "Random Thoughts on Doom." The minutes of that meeting say "The perennial question of a name for the group yielded only the usual obfuscation and no decision" (Minutes 10 Nov. 1961). Clearly, Stewart in his paper is wryly playing on both his literary reputation as a doom-meister, and the nuclear anxiety of the time. He identifies four levels of collective doom. The "really root-and-branch doomsters" seem to envisage "the actual destruction of the earth" (1). Next come those who see the earth surviving, but devoid of life. Thirdly, the "moderate doomsters" "merely suggest the wiping out of all higher life, including the human race." Finally, and apparently most interesting, are the "half-hearted" group who "think in terms of the doom of 'our way of life.' Just what they mean by this is a little hard to make out, and sometimes 'our way of life seems to be confused with the ideas presented in the platform of the Republican Party" (2). He goes on to discuss at length what he says is not the subject of his presentation, that is, as opposed to collective doom, the taboo subject of "personal doom," that is, death.

What mechanisms of doom do collective doomsters "regard, if we may so put it, with most favor" (5). He identifies five: atomic energy, war, overpopulation, race, and "conflicting political ideologies, or we might say, political intolerance" (5). But he places himself outside the category of doomsters, whatever the cause, since his lifelong study of mankind has led him to conclude that "Mankind. . .has always been in a terrible state, and has always in some way or other come through" (6-7). What I find interesting is the emphasis Stewart places, despite his satiric tone, on race as "a critical difficulty of our time" (11). He traces the evolution of racism from classical times to the present, and delves into the multiple meanings of "race" and "superior."

> Painstaking research might establish beyond cavil that white males of the age group twenty-thirty years were superior to their black counterparts by ratio of 1.323 in distinguishing the differences in taste between three varieties of cucumbers. Or do we mean "superior" at inventing an improved atom bomb, or "superior" at surviving the radiation and accumulated mess subsequent to its explosion? (21)

Ultimately, doom has morphed into race, as his main subject, and as well as politically incorrectly discussing the issue of racism at Berkeley, he also uses a personal example of unnecessary reticence respecting the naming of races. This is "One of the few differences I ever had with my beloved and now-lamented editor at Random House, Saxe Commins" (27). This is the case of (unnamed in this talk) Milt Abrahms, the New York survivor in *Earth Abides*, and Commins's request, to which he acceded, not to call him "Jewish," although he was a minor character, very likeable, and "I was describing him as he appeared to another character [Ish] in the book, and surely this other character, an ordinary enough American, would have been likely to think in terms of such a word." Needless to say, for a talk by Stewart, "the paper proved to be provocative and all joined in the ensuing discussion. . ." (Minutes).

One opportunity for such socializing he chose not to take was going to his 45th Princeton class reunion. He wrote a poem "On the occasion of not attending my forty-fifth reunion" (in June, 1962). The poem humorously evokes the wartime experiences of the class. Here is the first stanza:

> Gentlemen, Class of Seventeen,
> Gentlemen—those that are here, I mean—
> Gentlemen, we were young together,
> Strong on the wing and fit of feather,
> In that excellent time when every stripling
> Had read his Alger and Henty and Kipling,
> And the British *raj* was strong, like fate,
> And few of us knew how to fear, and hate.

Stewart, a tolerant man, cultivated numerous literary acquaintances during these years. He did lose one to mortality, Harold Davis, a voluminous correspondent and friend who in Stewart's view "did one wonderful book, *Honey in the Horn.*" Stewart remembers him in one of many incarnations as a "hillbilly singer," on "one of the great evenings of my life" jamming on guitar on San Luis Road with Carl Sandburg and Bertrand Bronson (*Little* 86). When he died, in 1960, everyone worried about his wife Bettie, but she ended up marrying a millionaire—his publisher. "I always said she was a professional wife" (*Little* 88). Humorously, that very same millionaire, Thayer Hobson of Morrow, wrote to Stewart right after Davis's death, soliciting Davis's letters to Stewart for a collection which Harry Ransom wanted to buy from Bettie for an H.L. Davis Collection at the University of Texas (Hobson to Stewart 9 Nov. 1960/*R*). Stewart replied that he didn't think Texas was a good fit for Davis's papers and that "there ought to be some game laws established as to how long you decently wait before approaching the widow. As it stands now, the man with the least sense of good taste is likely to be the winner"[ouch!] (Stewart to Hobson 13 Nov. 1960/*R*). "As far as my letters are concerned, I have decided that they are part of my own papers, and I shall keep them in that way." "Bettie is here with me now," Hobson responded, "I can understand your feeling about the University of Texas but the fact remains that Harold left Bettie with just about enough money to pay the funeral expenses and her total resources are the house in Oaxaca and a Volkswagon" (Hobson to Stewart 15 Nov. 1960/*R*). I don't know if Texas got a Davis collection, but obviously Hobson soon got Bettie; they were married before the year was up.

He had become friends with British Poet Laureate Robert Bridges in the 1930's. Joyce Cary had written him in 1953 "I had such grateful memories of your and your wife's kindness during my last visit . . ." (Cary to Stewart 18 Oct. 1953). In 1960 C.P. (Sir Charles) Snow spent the fall semester in Berkeley and got to know the Stewarts very well. Snow had just published his famous lecture on *The Two Cultures,* and he had lots in common with Stewart thereat, since Stewart was if anything a monoculturalist. I would have enjoyed listening in to their conversations. Snow wrote "The non-scientists have a rooted impression that the scientists are shallowly optimistic, unaware of man's condition. On the other hand, the scientists believe that the literary intellectuals are totally lacking in foresight, peculiarly unconcerned with their brother men, in a deep sense anti-intellectual, anxious to restrict both art and thought to the existential moment" (*Cultures*).

In Stewart, Snow met a literary intellectual who had steeped himself in, and had great respect for, scientific disciplines, and whose works brought the cultures together. Perhaps that is one reason why Stewart's works were not highly regarded by the "literary intelligentsia" as a whole. Perhaps that is why I myself was so attracted to Stewart's works at exactly this time, since my reaction to Snow's essay was so strong, and I argued it passionately with others.

When Snow had returned to Britain, Stewart sent him a copy of his pamphlet "On University Government," published by the Berkeley AAUP. Snow replied:

> Dear George,
>
> It was a great pleasure to get your fighting speech on University Government. It reminded me of the good times we had with you and Ted. Give her my love. We think and talk of you very often. (Snow to Stewart 17 Jan. 1961/*R*).

Snow is referring to Stewart's statement presenting a resolution to the Academic Senate respecting a case where an exam question was ruled "improper" by the Board of Regents over the heads of the faculty and the university administration. Stewart regarded the "intrusion" of the Regents into the realm of instruction an ultimately even greater threat to academic freedom than the Loyalty Oath issue. "If the Regents can declare one examination question to be improper, they can declare any examination question to be improper. The next one to be so declared may be mine, or it may be yours" ("University").

During this period, Stewart corresponded a lot with the noted American academic and literary figures with whom he was associated. His cousin Alfred Barr, now the eminent director of the Museum of Modern Art wrote "I feel so proud of your versatile talents as a teacher of English, novelist, and historian" (Barr to Stewart 6 Feb. 1963). In his correspondence with fellow Western historian Dale Morgan, Stewart made the statement I see as his life-motif "I've been climbing out on limbs all my life and remarkably few of them have been cut off behind me" (Stewart to Morgan 1 Nov. 1960). "Both my wife and I are great admirers of your books," wrote noted nature writer Roderick Haig-Brown (Haig-Brown to Stewart 30 July 1963). Karl Shapiro remembers flying over the Codornices house on his way out of Berkeley "I'm sure I saw the reservoir and the rose garden" (Shapiro to Stewart 14 Mar. 1963).

*

Several of Stewart's notable correspondents of this period, including Dale Morgan, were communicating about his next book, *Pickett's Charge* (1959). He told Philip Van Doren Stern about his first visit to Gettysburg, when he was in the Ambulance Corps camp in Allentown. They were mobile in Eastern Pennsylvania a good deal of the time, and camped in pup tents beside the Emmetsburg road, "about where Archer's brigade went over the fence;" later, he went through Gettysburg on his hitchhike to California in 1919 (Stewart to Stern 8 Nov. 1962). He exchanged letters about Gettysburg with the pre-eminent public historian of the battle, Bruce Catton, who told him "You have gone more deeply into the details of regimental movements at and around the angle than I ever did" (Catton to Stewart 24 Apr. 1958). Allen Tate called *Pickett's Charge* "a masterpiece. . .I thought I knew something about Gettysburg . . .but my knowledge was as a grain of sand to a boulder." Tate, whose maternal grandmother's cousin was Confederate General Armistead particularly struck with " . . .admiration of your technique of the time element" (Tate to Stewart 12 Feb. 1961). "I appreciate your critical acumen in picking out the handling of the time-element for comment. It was quite a job all right!"

(Stewart to Tate 19 Feb. 1961/*P*). After its publication, Wallace Stegner wrote "Last weekend, passing through Gettysburg, we murmured your name reverently" (Stegner to Stewart 1 Nov. 1961).

With *Pickett*, Stewart had again chosen his time well. Contemporaries may not be aware of the intense public interest in the Civil War as the time of its centennial approached, and the massive number of publications, memorials, and ceremonies that surrounded it. Bruce Catton was the star historian of the time. I know my family had, and I read, all his Civil War volumes, such as *Banners at Shenandoah* (1955) and *This Hallowed Ground* (1956). Then there was MacKinlay Kantor's *Gettysburg* (1952), Evan Kushner's *Campaign at Gettysburg* (1958), Fairfax Downey's *Guns at Gettysburg* (1958), and Holt's rival to Stewart, Alan Hollingsworth's and James Cox's *The Third Day at Gettysburg: Pickett's Charge* (1959). Right now I am looking at an old photo album full of boring black and white pictures I took of all the statues of generals, of Spangler's Spring and the Devil's Den in 1954. Stewart himself said "I hope all this flood of writing for the centennial really accomplishes something here and there. So much of it seems to be merely copying from books already written and re-telling stories already often-told" (Stewart to Allen Tate 19 Feb. 1961/*P*).

Stewart's enterprise was much less grandiose than so many other Civil War battle histories of the 1950's. It might be called, for want of a better term, archeo-journalism. He himself invented a term in his subtitle: "A *Microhistory* of the Final Attack at Gettysburg, July 3, 1863." Insidiously antiheroic, it conveys the minutiae of the day through a complex weaving of events, in which the famous and the infamous are equally significant and equally vulnerable to the almost autonomous collective entity they have created. *Pickett's Charge* is also a work of cultural geography. The human actions at Gettysburg are half-created by the topography and vegetation of the space where they occur. And these actions half-create "Gettysburg" as a mapped and named place of battle which before the battle existed in a completely different form. As dramatized in

Robert Penn Warren's Civil War novel *Wilderness,* the battlefield becomes almost immediately after it ceases to exist as a living field of battle, a site of repair, for those who would observe its landmarks—like Devil's Den—unnamed before, and the new-minted icons strewing it.

Charles Morrissey, reviewing *Pickett's Charge* in the *Oakland Tribune,* says that Stewart's initial claim, that the charge was "the central moment of our history" (ix) is overstated. But Stewart clearly states that a different result "there by the clump of trees and the angle of the stone wall" might not have "decisively altered history" all by itself. His point is that it was a *symbolic* moment in our history—if I may extrapolate, *representing* the preservation of national unity.

Another premise of the microhistory, based on what Stewart says is an innovative reading of all the battle's records from both sides of the conflict, is that it was no "shining moment." In fact, its seeming simplicity, in tune with a viewpoint we have seen him hold throughout his life, becomes increasingly complex the more it is examined. ". . .[I]ts key-note was confusion—of smoke, fear, excitement, and broken ranks" (x). And therefore, since the whole war was indescribably complex, ". . .[W]e may be able to see the war as clearly by looking minutely and carefully at a period of a few [15] hours as by looking extensively and dimly throughout four years" (xii).

Thus he begins in the relative silence of the night, with the men on both sides sleeping or resting. As artillery begins to be moved into position, we are allowed to observe Lee observing the field from the "point of woods" (one of the many place-names created by the battle). The morning mist is imagined half-concealing his figure, and "we may take that as a symbol; for even yet the man, whatever he was, is blurred by the shifting mists of his legend" (8). The question his presence provokes is "'Why did Lee order Pickett's Charge?'"

"As he stood there, Lee could reflect upon two days of fighting throughout which, as reckoned in the dark ledgers of war where all the entries are in red, he had operated at a profit" (8). Stewart allows us to look at the details of terrain and human dispersal through Lee's eyes, from his point of elevation, and to be "in" his mind as he examines the specific terrain of the jagged stone walls on Cemetery Ridge, where the Union line was emplaced. Paradoxically, Lee is imagined "weary of victories. He might well, he realized, victory the Confederacy to death" (14). Stewart gives us Lee's (legendary?) statement at this moment: "'The enemy is there, and I am going to strike him'" (20). We are also allowed, in this uncollapsed moment of time, to see General Longstreet beside Lee ". . .in the brightness of the newly risen sun" (21). Behind Lee loom, "in spirit the romantic warriors of the past. . ." Behind Longstreet " . . .mustered the warriors of the future—men with repeating rifles, machine guns, and electronic computers," as he opposes Lee's resolve. Thus Pickett's Charge can also be seen retrospectively as a choice between two modes of war, and even two philosophies of life; or as the last pretechnological encounter.

As Lee and Longstreet survey the field, deciding, based on the topography of ridges and hollows, where to move troops and station artillery, we are allowed to view them through the eyes of other soldiers, and view those soldiers themselves. We also get to know the names, appearances, and capacities of the different arms in the Confederate arsenal. We follow Colonel E. P. Alexander, of the Confederate artillery, as he places his batteries at different positions amid treeclumps and fields. The colorless Alexander is contrasted to his Chief of Artillery, pastor and Brigadier General William Pendleton, "Parson Pendleton," who preached with a surplice over his uniform. "Still, one must respectfully point out that on this particular morning it was a question of salvos, not of salvation; of a cannonade, not of a canonization" (46).

Throughout his narrative, Stewart clearly locates the troops in physical space. For example, when Pickett's brigades have been advanced over Seminary Ridge, we see them where they are, and we see what they see:

> A hundred-fifty yards ahead up an easy slope, sharp against the bright sky, the men saw the crest of a low rise. Where they stood, in the swale, they were concealed from the enemy, even from the lookouts on the

> tops of the hills. A little to their left a rail fence zig-zagged up the slope. In front of their center they saw a farmhouse and a barn against the skyline. Just under the shelter of this low crest a line of guns was in position . . .(47)

Again, when describing the complex location of the Union divisions, brigades, and batteries on Cemetery Ridge, the author places them in a landscape shaped by geology and inhabitance:

> As for the low ridge from which you are conceived as looking, in some geological age, along a narrow crevice, molten rock had pushed toward the surface and then solidified. In later millenia, as the surface eroded, this rock was left as a gentle, forested rise. Now for a hundred years the hand of man had lain heavily upon this land; the once-wooded slopes and the swales were now all plowland, treeless. Even the ridge was mostly in pasture, and so it stood out clearly, emphasized a little by the growth of trees and buses that still crowned it here and there (52).

Most importantly, "The hand of man had done more than cut the trees." Weathered rock broke off in chunks, gathered by cultivators into loose walls but some left strewn on the ground. To Stewart, the events of the day were determined, at least in part, by the acts of nature in the geological past and of humans in past centuries. Pickett's Charge is a moment in the deep ecological history of one particular place on the globe.

Both the successes and failures of the Union defensive line and Pickett's advancing troops were influenced by "the necessities of terrain and cover" (89). Pickett's own brigade, unlike the other two in the attack, did not advance directly to meet the Union line straight on, not because Pickett was confused or incompetent, but because he had surveyed the terrain from advance and found a thicket which his troops had to bypass to avoid being entangled (89-90).

Here we might bring up the sense of time that Allen Tate so much admired in the book—Stewart's "novelistic" sense of pacing. Time is first evoked when the author questions a phrase he's just written down: "By this time. . ." (48)

> But what time? Nine o'clock at least. Perhaps, ten. What, even, does this mean? Whose time are we using? There is time as marked off by

> the sun, and as struck by the courthouse clock. There is time as it is ticked away by the watches in the pockets of thousands of officers, and of a few privates, in each army. Most of all, there is time as it appears to the men themselves, so that to one it lingers and to another it speeds. Then, after the battle, if two men, equally qualified, write down the minute of some particular event, their opinions differ by as much as five hours! (48)

According to Stewart, added to this Faulknerian subjectivity of perception is the literal difference. "Some evidence suggests that time in Lee's army was about twenty minutes faster than in Meade's army."

Another temporality is the opposite of this one, the mutually experienced "noon-day lull" under the blazing sun. The author fills this lull with descriptions of pre-battle arrangements, but also makes its presence vivid: 'At noon the heat and the stillness lay heavy" (93). "To one private, the mere absence of noise became something positive, and he testified, 'while the stillness was going on'" (100-101). For the Union troops "By noon it was so hot that the sun seemed for the moment, more than the Confederates, to be the enemy" (101). He paraphrases Haskell's famous account of the battle in describing the bizarre Union generals' picnic, in the stillness, made of a few chickens, some butter, and a huge loaf of bread already half-eaten by a hog, after which the generals leaned back and lit cigars "under the shade of a very small tree" (105). In this stillness, there is a wondrous sequence of excursions: the complex deconstruction of note texts exchanged by Longstreet and Alexander (110-112) prevaricating on necessary conditions for a charge; Professor Jacobs of Gettysburg College observing that the courthouse clock was about to strike one (120); a single section which reads "About this time, an immense flock of wild pigeons flew overhead darkening the sky. The men watched idly. No one has recorded in which direction the pigeons were flying, or what seemed to be their purpose" (121). "On Cemetery Hill an artilleryman heard the hum of bees" (121).

At 1:30 the Confederates fired the signal shots indicating the beginning of the charge. In keeping with his view of the subjectivity of perception, Stewart provides a list of five different views of where the first shot hit, and an almost humorous anecdote of a Union soldier thrown in the air by a cannon shot passing through the ground beneath him. The soldier flew through the air and landed behind the rear lines, dead from impact, without a scratch on him. An officer went back to observe him and remarked "'He has passed over'"[!] (138).

As the Confederate cannonade continued, Stewart describes the scene: "Even nature was disturbed, one soldier noting that the small birds flew about in confusion. Over much of the field the rising smoke obscured the sun, which undoubtedly appeared like a pasted red wafer, though no Kipling or Crane was there to use the words" (150). At 3:00 Pickett's brigades rose and assembled; at this same time, the New York Stock Exchange closed on a bullish note (172).

One could see the time-span of the cannonade, and more largely, that of the entire day, as an example of "cultural adaptation" to a dangerous environment (Hardesty 28-31). Stewart remarks that many of the Union soldiers got used to the cannonade and found it boring. David Passmore discusses battlefields as landscapes "that have hosted the extremes of human experience," in the context of cultural/ecological history (96-97). But he also says that, through the growing movement of military archaeology, we are achieving a ". . .deeper understanding of the relationship between warriors and landscape, recognizing here that battlefields are places that are encultured by the act of war . . ." (98). But I see Stewart as presenting the day culminating in Pickett's Charge in the way he did the temporal duration of fire and storm, as an encultured place in the present of battle, not retrospectively (although his book is itself a retrospective attempt to, as it were, enculture his reader in the present of the battle). His sense of battle corresponds to that of Keegan, a "moral conflict," consisting of "a mutual and sustained act of will by two contending parties, and if it is to result in a decision, the moral collapse of one of them" (302). The battlefield is a separate place, a "hostile environment" (314) in which the moral conflict is enacted, and where it is resolved—if resolved—through adaptational strategies unique to the "cultural ecology" of the time and space that define it (Bennett 23).

In the case of Pickett's Charge, the collective action constituting the charge disturbed the adaptational stasis of the battlefield. The chargers and defenders themselves, after following an anticipated ritual plan, became, as former closed in on latter, entangled in chaos: "'everything was a wild kaleidoscopic whirl'" (198). There was a breakdown even of requisite urgency: ". . .when one would expect only excitement and hurry, sometimes there appeared a curious calm and almost a sense of leisure. . ." (203).

Once the charge has reached the infamous "angle" of the wall, Stewart subjectivizes time once again. "Not more than fifteen minutes had probably elapsed since that great moment," and though battle is still fiercely joined ". . .so much had the situation altered, so many things had shifted, that the memory of that event was as of something that had happened to them at Chancellorsville or Sharpsburg"(235). And at virtually the same moment, 900 miles away, "Pemberton was arranging with Grant the terms of the surrender at Vicksburg" (242).

After the microhistory is thus internally and externally opened out in time and space, both are condensed immediately to a pinpoint, as Haskell sends a sergeant forward with the Union colors, speaking "with the words of melodrama that came naturally to the men of that war, 'Let the Rebels see it close to their eyes once before they die'" (244). When the sergeant falls with his flag all the troops behind him react almost epiphanically, in a countersurge, "'a strange resistless impulse'" which deals the attackers a final blow.

In his last chapter, "The Story of the Story," Stewart returns the fifteen hours he has recounted, as a durational entity in a present time, to what it was for the reader before entering the story, the "High-water Mark," something "symbolically decisive" (281). The accreted "legend" of Pickett's Charge contains many "alternative stories" of what might have happened if things might have been done differently. The contrast between these stories and the "real" story only emphasizes the contingency of cause and effect, involving humans and geography, that created the "real" story. That Stewart saw the event in the mode of an ecosystem is supported by his treatment, in one of the appendices, of the battlefield itself as an "important document since it enables us to determine cover, distances, and therefore, on occasion, such other matters as time and numbers of troops" (302). Like Keegan and Passmore, quoted above, Stewart presents the battlefield as a defined geographical space which participated in shaping the cultural event that gave it its identity. He examines the terrain, buildings, fences, fields and crops, and tree-growth. The last is the most important, since most altered since 1863, needing to be extrapolated back, and also because of all the geographical features of the terrain it was probably the most decisive environmental influence on the course of action.

It is useful to compare Stewart's account with contemporary and subsequent ones, "[a]s the flood tide of books on the American Civil War rushes on," in the words of the *Military Affairs* review of his book (Hassler 218). Glenn Tucker's smoothly-written *High Tide at Gettysburg* (1958) elides the charge into the flow of battle action gracefully, but does not use Stewart's devices of time-manipulation, and his seemingly "irrelevant" details that add texture to the lives involved. In some contrast, Fairfax Downey's *The Guns at Gettysburg* of the same year is more aestheticized, with the third day of battle divided into three chapters, "Mustering of the Cannon," "The Cannonade," and "Charge," its text interspersed with bars from battle-songs. But, like Tucker, Downey is more interested in the high profile events and people of the day. His coverage is generalized and strategic.

With the advantage of time and accumulated sources, more copious accounts than Stewart's have been written about the charge itself. Probably the one that comes closest, of those I've seen, to the "microhistory" in its detail is Jeffry Wert's *Gettysburg: Day Three* (2001), which quotes from numerous common soldiers' accounts. Earl J. Hess's *Pickett's Charge—The Last Attack at Gettysburg*, also published in 2001, is a massive tome but seems to me to recur to the strategic level of the 1950's histories. The diversity of articles collected by Gary Gallagher in *The Third Day at Gettysburg & Beyond* (1994) gives it a liveliness the other volumes lack. Especially interesting in this collection is Carol Reardon's essay, a run-up to her great expansion on Stewart's "Story of the Story," *Pickett's Charge in History and Memory* (1997). She includes a paraphrase from Faulkner's *Intruder in the Dust* which Stewart should have used: ". . .[F]or every southern boy there comes a time when it is still just before one o'clock on July 3, the cannonade has not yet begun, and once it does, life will never be the same. . ." (84). I don't think Reardon is really fair to *Pickett's Charge* in her full-length book. While she interestingly sees Stewart in the lineage of pro-Longstreet revisionist Glenn Tucker (a Stewart correspondent), she trivializes his insight and literary treatment: "Mostly Stewart had an eye for catchy vignettes. Unfortunately, it seems he treated all those disconnected threads as equally valid historical sources; readers never learned that it mattered a great deal who told the original story, when he told it, and why" (*Pickett's* 207). This is a total misreading of Stewart's text. He clearly states the reliability of different sources, but he doesn't refuse to articulate them, simply because they may be unreliable.

In these recent studies, Stewart is referred to only briefly, but President Eisenhower's press secretary James Hagerty thanked Stewart for sending *Pickett's Charge*, and said "I know the President will enjoy his copy" (Hagerty to Stewart 22 Sept. 1959).

*

As his *Ordeal by Hunger* was about to be published in 1936, Stewart sent his editor at Holt another book manuscript, written in 1932 and entitled *Great Excitement*. According to him it was accepted by the Press of the Pioneers, but publication was constantly delayed. Stewart says he thinks he has "done something original in developing the story entirely from newspaper clippings and thus keeping the amazing local atmosphere of early San Francisco" (Stewart to Richard Thornton 6 Mar. 1936/*P*). Unfortunately, the press felt that its market would be limited to the West Coast, "and the book would require special promotional effort of a kind that we cannot well give it" ([Thornton] to Stewart 9 Apr 1936/*P*). In his acknowledgements at the end of *Committee of Vigilance* (1964), Stewart says

> My interest in the Committee began in 1920, when I first read the newspaper accounts and prepared a report in a class at the University of California under Professor C. W. Wells. In the early thirties I attempted to tell the story by means of newspaper clippings. The present book thus represents a return . . .

Chapter ten of *Committee of Vigilance* is entitled (from a newspaper headline, as all the chapter titles are) "Great Excitement," and this is clearly the text he offered to Holt in 1936, as he implies in *A Little of Myself* (189).

Committee of Vigilance can well be considered a companion history to *Pickett's Charge*, an urban version, as it were, of the latter. Both deal with cultural adaptation to a closed environment disturbed by violence, although the former is more "dangerous," with respect to its topicality in 1964. As an example, history professor Joseph Boskin of USC, replied to Stewart's 1968 queries on urban racial riots, presumably for his paper on this topic (see below), seemingly agreeing that the riots of the 1960's were similarly a consequence of "historical and ecological factors" (Boskin to Stewart 26 May 1968). And even before its publication, Stewart was assuring an ACLU friend that James D. Hart and C.S. Forester had read the manuscript "without being disturbed over its being an incitement to lawlessness" (Stewart to "Walt" 21 Aug. 1963). Stewart himself was to all my knowledge completely law-abiding. I leave it to the reader to explore why in 1955 J.D. Holstrum sent Stewart a statement: "This is to certify that George R. Stewart has not been arrested here on any charge" (Holstrum to Stewart 13 July 1955).

Committee of Vigilance revisits a number of issues addressed in his earlier books: the flourishing social instability of pre-statehood San Francisco of *East of the Giants*, the defiance of established "law" for the sake of a higher value in *Year of the Oath*; the subversion of urban social order by organized "revolution from within" in *Years of the City*. Stewart's long subtitle defines the particularity of the situation he is addressing: "An account of The Hundred Days when certain citizens undertook the suppression of the criminal activities of the Sydney ducks." A narrative created from documentary evidence, this is a case study of a phenomenon widely associated with the West in folklore, popular culture, and myth. But, more generally, it tightly focuses a question basic to U.S. national identity, and persistently relevant: the justification for rebellion against established authority.

Seen in the light of environmental concern, it draws from the often contrary thinking of Julian Steward and Robert Lowie. Steward readily concedes that as it gains complexity, "Culture increasingly creates its own environment" (*Evolution* 52). It also contains in microcosm an example of Steward's multilinear evolution concept, "applicable to changes occurring today . . .," "an ecological approach—an attempt to learn how the factors in each given type of situation shaped the development of a particular type of society" (*Evolution* 62-3). In the case of 1851 San Francisco, the parallel evolutions of different ethnic, commercial, and political subcultures caused, in unintended concert, the temporary creation of a "voluntary association" (Lowie's term), an *uberkultur*, which evolved to a point where it became too ill-adapted to its own environment to maintain its dominance. In Lowie's terms, the committees of vigilance intruded the "customary law" of "simpler societies" into a space of urban complexity. Lowie uses the example of the Yurok indians to demonstrate that "Public opinion can create a definite code," and that "even in the absence of constituted authority. . .[they]. . .have organized complex system of law" (*Introduction* 285-6).

In fact, the committee of vigilance could be considered, in his terms, the efflorence of primitive law into a modern system of law, based on the perception by its initiators that "constituted authority" for all practical purposes did not exist. Lowie characterizes the primary differences between primitive and modern law as follows: "Early law is conceived largely in kinship rather than in territorial terms; it coincides more closely with the ethical notions, hence the public opinion, of the peoples in question; it fails to discriminate public and private wrongs, the 'crimes' and the 'torts' of our jurisprudence" (*Social* 158-9). All three of the "early law" attributes characterize the 1851 Committee. Identification codes created a numerological kinship and hierarchy among its members: the lower your number, the earlier you joined the Committee, the higher your prestige. The offenders apprehended—and in some cases, executed—had not necessarily committed high crimes and misdemeanors against the state, but rather offended the moral sensibilities of the Committee through private acts. The Committee also validated itself, to a certain unspoken extent, as the moral agent for punishing the "constituted authority" for its perceived failure to do its duty.

Stewart sets 1851 as the time ". . .when the city was just leaving the simple crudities of the frontier behind, and was entering for good and for bad, into the full complexities of civilization" (1). Writ large, it was on the cusp between "early" and "modern." The precipitating event in the creation of the Committee was the simple breaking-and-entering of C. J. Janson & Co.'s dry goods story on Montgomery Street, on February 19, 1851. The suspected perpetrators were Australian ex-convict sailors, collectively known as the "Sydney ducks," who inhabited their own "Sydneytown" ghetto, ". . .a slum of disreputable rooming-houses, dubious gambling-joints and cheap groggeries" (2). The robbery and beating of Janson himself created a good example of media-driven public opinion. San Francisco's newspapers editorialized against the crime disproportionately to its actual severity, ". . .in their moral enthusiasm. . .neglecting the details that guilt should be properly established and that nothing would be gained a much lost by hanging the wrong men" (8). Stewart emphasizes that the "lynch law" calls were not expected in San Francisco, which had a well-organized police force. He contrasts law enforcement in organized and disorganized communities along the advancing frontier, with his typical demystificatory view of the latter.

> In a curious way Americans are proud of [the Wild West], and there are, indeed, certain phases of it which are both heroic and even morally admirable. But most of it should be written off as a national disgrace, and in a hundred years more we may get around to doing so.
>
> It was essentially a rule of violence and of the exploitation of natural resources and of weaker individuals and peoples. The genocide of the Indians (in some instances tribes were annihilated) was its worst feature. (14)

The Committee of Vigilance represented, thus, an eruption of "Wild West" lawmaking into a large city, but Stewart doesn't carry over his above characterization of it to the Committee itself. His discussion is more subtle and detailed. For one thing, the 1851 Committee was acting on precedent—in the Gold Rush chaos of 1849, citizens banded together for self-protection as the "Hounds," later the "Regulators" (interestingly echoing the "Distributors" of *Years of the City*), and actually forced the establishment of a constituted police authority to halt their activities (15-16). Thus the Committee had the weight of urban, not just mining camp, tradition behind it.

Ultimately the 1851 Committee was formed through the confrontation of city authorities and an outraged populace, holding the accused perpetrators of the crime in defiance of them, and urged by anonymous handbills to hold a public meeting. At the meeting, after much speechifying and maneuvering by Mayor Geary and other elected officials to co-opt it, the crowd unanimously votes for a proposal offered by William Tell Coleman, a completely unknown citizen, of a 12-person "extra-legal" court to try the offenders. Stewart provides a verbal portrait of Coleman which evokes civilized menace: "His handsome and classically regular face was distinguished by a tight lipline, which might be taken to indicate strength and self-control. Though his hair was dark, his eyes were of that pale blue which the early West often associated with men who were extremely dangerous. . ." (28)

The extra-legal jury returns a split verdict, and the meeting disbands. But Stewart comments on the self-righteousness of newspapers and "public opinion." The "man in the street" ".. . .felt virtuous because he had restrained his passions and kept from deeds of blood. But also, he had proved himself a dangerous fellow who would stand for non nonsense. Let those people at the city hall see to it that the Sydney ducks were got under control!" (42). Stewart however, sees this self-righteousness as totally unjustified. "The law had been overthrown" (42). He does contrast a separate incident the day after the "trial," when a mob captured a thief, put a rope around his neck, basically tortured him, and threw him into the bay without killing him. This incident ". . .may also be referred for consideration to those who maintain that the men who organize an extra-legal court and give as fair a trial as they can are really behaving worse than a mob, since they are acting with premeditation" (47). The implication here is that organized extra-legal action is preferable to disorganized.

Stewart offers much background to criminality in San Francisco. In 1851 it was defined, like Venice, by its sea-access, and its main reason for being was as a supply *entrepot* for inland mines. In his view, criminals of that San Francisco were actually just one group of specialized capitalists, professionals "who supported themselves by robbery because they found it easier, more profitable, and more exciting, than ordinary labor" (55). Professional criminals were organized as gangs; they had their own lawyers to protect them through bail, trial delays, and false witness (51-56).

A lull in extra-legal action ended in April, when a major fire destroyed 18 blocks of the city. The most prevalent rumor was that it was arson as revenge for imprisoned Sydney ducks. In June an anonymous article in the *Alta California* proposed the organization of a "committee of safety" to board all Aussie-origined arriving ships to look for potential criminals. After the synchronous temporary dissolution of the city's Grand Jury, a nameless group of a hundred met in the storeroom of a local firebrand, Samuel Brannan, established itself as a committee, and wrote a constitution (91). As Stewart notes, the constitution required its signatories to "pledge their honor" to defend each other in carrying out their duties; as only "gentlemen" had honor to pledge, and those present were all invitees, they all saw themselves as "gentlemen," with the accompanying attributes of respectability 93-94).

The chapter describing the first action of the new Committee bears Stewart's original title for his book, "Great Excitement." A Sydney thief named Simpton stole a safe, cornered on a dock, tried to row off with it, cornered again, threw it in the bay, was captured, and taken to the Committee's meeting rooms where he gave the alias of John Jenkins—which he would bear into history. Defiant throughout, "arrogant, profane, foul-mouthed, and abusive" (110), Jenkins was tried, convicted, escorted to the old city Plaza.
The Committee forces were attacked by the police and other rescuers, and Stewart describes a scene of total chaos and mayhem, through which Jenkins's captors managed to drag him, and get him swinging in the noose from a beam (111-113).

Stewart considers that

> Yet he too was one of us, and there is even a little that we can admire. He died in the best traditions of crime. He cursed his captors and asked for no pity. Instead, he asked for brandy (a gentleman's drink), and tossed it off. He asked for a cigar too. Then he tipped his chair back against the wall, and coolly puffed away. As they took him through the streets, he was still smoking it (115)

David Johnson has an insightful perspective on the ritually repeated hangings, such as Jenkins's. He is describing a "gold rush lynch court" open to public access, unlike the Committee's closet tribunals, but the psychology is the same with respect to the public hangings themselves. Popular tribunals "*transcended* rather than *obstructed* the law" (565). The "rage and excitement" surrounding the executions was "not described as the rage of an individual, but as that of the people taken as a single sovereign, and in this respect rage and excitement served as an unerring sign that society's moral sensibility had been violated. Such outrage spoke to an inherent, natural understanding of justice, unreachable through the procedures of due process" (564). James Shields and Leonard Weinberg have a less sanguine (if the word is appropriate here) view of what they call "reactive violence," studied in contemporary attitudes as a frontier value survival. To them, the urge to vigilantism expresses ". . .anomia, that is. . .a sense of personal disorganization and lack of control over one's environment" (99)—presumably whether or not this "sense" corresponds to reality.

What Stewart does establish is that *outwardly* the supporters of the Committee were normal, average, peaceful people who nonetheless openly endorsed the hanging and were supported by the newspapers, who said that Jenkins was judge "with calmness and deliberation" (122). With this endorsement, the Committee was emboldened to announce its identity and a membership consisting of the "best people:" "By openly announcing themselves, they transformed their organization from a secret cabal or a possibly sinister conspiracy into a large public group, partaking—as the *Alta* once pointed out—of the nature of a revolutionary party" (129).

Stewart will show how—unlike Melas's organization in *Years of the City*—the constitution of itself as a public, political entity, eventually led to the "aging" and death of the Committee. It could maintain its efficacious legitimacy only by being illegitimate. In this way it differed from the popular tribunals Johnson analyses, since they lacked the organizational continuity necessary to become dis-organized. However, for a while the Committee was very successful in its goals; it became in effect a "bureau of investigation" of crimes (131), since the Jenkins hanging had such a deterrent effect on the kind of open robbery he had committed. At the beginning of July the Committee arrested one "William Stephens" on suspicion of robbery. A great debate ensued as to whether Stephens was actually one Stuart, who had escaped hanging in Downieville, in gold country, when the rope broke.

Our author interrupts the developing Stephens-Stuart case to tell of another public lynching in Downieville, which occurred while the multinamed "Stephens" was incarcerated in the town's jail. On the 4th of July a Scot, named Cannon, drunk, got into conflict with a fiery Hispanic *puta,* Juanita. On the next morning he came to her house and threatened her, at which she stabbed him in the heart. "The hunt was up! Men nursing hangovers staggered out into the blinding sunlight of that July morning. *She stabbed him!* Men dropped their shovels by sluice-boxes and hurried to town. *That Spanish bitch!* Men in the second day of drunkenness came reeling out of the saloons. *Hang her!"* (157).

This case is the direct opposite of the Stephens one, and more truly representative of "gold rush justice." But Stewart makes the meaningful point that the Downieville men were "driven into madness . . .by the sight of this woman whom they held captive but could not possess, and could not humble" (158)[.] The crowd rejected a judge and jury. A courageous doctor in the town, Dr. Cyrus Aiken, declared she was pregnant; she was "examined," found not to be, and Dr. Aiken was given 24 hours to get out of town. Juanita's hanging was arranged from the bridge (as I drove over that bridge in 2005 the scene came to mind). Stewart brings up the strange collaboration, somewhat evident in the case of Jenkins, between the mob and its victim—as though they are all collaborators in a ritual: "Then, strangely, the spirit of that mob was so strong that it seemed to sweep Juanita along with it, so that she became a part of it. No longer did she seem its victim, but rather its spirit, as if the votaries were bearing some priestess to the sacrifice. . . " (160). Juanita embraced her sacrificial role, waved, and cried "adios, amigos!" before she swung (161). Elsewhere Stewart remarks on the public acceptability of such sacrifice: "The New Testament, in spite of its horror of the Crucifixion, accepted the idea of crucifixion" (120)

Meanwhile, "Stephens" (Stewart calls him "Stuart" so I will henceforth) was taken to San Francisco and interrogated by the Committee. Stuart was very forthcoming, even showing maps of how his gang had planned to rob the

Customs House. His last examination by them was at 10:30 PM on July 7. "Just four weeks had passed since the hanging of Jenkins, and again the moon rode high. Inside the room the lamplight illuminated the faces of the prisoner and of the thirteen men. . ." (175). Stuart actually became enamored of telling stories of his crimes, for example, of visiting Missions to try to steal their gold and silver. He "'could not find any golden images though I attended mass regularly'"(183)[!]. On July 11, bells were rung for a public meeting of the Committee to discuss Stuart's case. It had been determined that if he confessed enough, he would be handed over to the legitimate courts for trial, but the meeting decided he had not fulfilled this agreement. He was paraded through the streets and hung from a derrick in the harbor (200). Public condemnation of this act spread, but the Committee didn't care: "Only a strong government can permit open criticism" (207); also, many members of condemning entities were themselves members of the Committee.

We could trace the beginning of the end for the Committee's power to this hanging and the subsequent visit of the lame-duck California Governor, John McDougal, "His Accidency," to San Francisco and to the chambers of the Committee itself. Apparently the latter thought it had the favor of the Governor, but the result was that it itself split into two factions, conservative and radical. The former wanted to cooperate to some degree with the Governor, the latter wanted to organize a full-scale revolutionary overthrow of the city government. Stewart calls this period, early August, the late middle-age of the Committee, its activities having taken on an "autumnal atmosphere" (236)—similar, in a way, to the minutes after the High-Water Mark at Gettysburg when it already seemed a defeat distanced in the past.

The crisis of age came with the arrival by steamer, with Sheriff escort, of a much-wanted criminal, Sam Whittaker (August 11). The Committee wanted to take custody of him, and planned to hang him from the yardarm of a vessel (257). Meanwhile, John McDougal had made a risky visit to San Francisco. He became a man of action, determined to preserve Whittaker for established justice. At the Union Tavern (he was a notorious drunk) the governor found out what the Committee planned. He waked the county sheriff at 2:00 A.M. to get a habeas corpus writ, and a judge at 3:00 A.M. to issue a warrant. Whittaker and his colleague McKenzie were then spirited off to jail. On the evening of August 20 McDougal issued a famous proclamation, a strongly-termed condemnation of armed and organized bodies of citizens, whose actions might result in "all the horrors of the Civil War" (269).

The rescue and the proclamation enraged radicals. McDougal ". . .had brought the city and the state to the verge of civil war and revolution" (270). "When men face such times of uncertainty and suspicion, in a nation or in a Committee of Vigilance, the moderates go under"(275). What happened was a stealth attack on a church service in the jail attended by Whittaker and McKenzie. Committee squads smashed open the chapel, rushed the two prisoners into a carriage, and to the Committee headquarters, where they were both hung from beams. The whole operation took twenty minutes. Stewart says "Like an aging fighter, the Committee had pulled itself together and scored another knockout. But its days of vigor had passed" (287). "Two miserable lives had been, somehow, at stake, and the swinging bodies had demonstrated, in people's minds, not so much the triumph of justice over crime, as the triumph of the Committee over the governor" (287).

A sure sign of the Committee's end was its entry of slates of candidates in the September 1 election. Though they won, in effect it was an acknowledgement of absorption into the legitimate process, and the Committee effectively disbanded on September 16 (298).

Stewart's reflections on the impact of the Committee give it a sustained importance. Linguistically it made "vigilante" a common word, as well as "vigilantism," although time has distorted the terms into near synonymity with "mob action." But it also highlighted the political issue of the relation between the individual and the state ". . .and this problem is perpetual, complicated, difficult, and not wholly soluble" (308). This is the problem so deeply meditated on by Ish, particularly in connection with the execution of Charlie. Is there any distinction between different kinds of illegality: actual crime, conscientious objection, collective disobedience—revolution, insurrection? Stewart says that "Most people would attempt to make some distinction on the basis of such standards as those of motivation and individual conscience" (309). Most of the Committee would have felt "self-defense" a sufficient justification for the illegality of their actions. But, as "conscientious objection" to performing a certain act gains legitimacy, is the positive performance of an act on the same grounds of conscience—as the Committee did—no less legitimate (310)? "Just as a man may refuse to bear arms because his conscience so forbids him, similarly a man, we might think, may go out and hang someone because his conscience so commands him" (310). Ultimately, Stewart gives a half-defense of the Committee. It was reacting to true failures in the justice system; it could have taken the road to revolution, but voluntarily disbanded instead; it was "moderate" for the time—no mass executions, no interrogation by torture.

This partial endorsement of vigilante justice (in its original sense) gives his paper "American Riots—Before Watts" a particular salience. Written in 1968, for presentation at a meeting of "The Club," it draws on the history of riots in the U. S.—in which he includes the Vigilance incidents of 1851—as a vehicle for gaining "perspective and courage" in the face of the frightening present (1). This "mass-violence in our cities is not new," he says, but riots have not been adequately discussed by U.S. historians. The word itself, as deriving from the English Riot Act of 1714, was applied by the British to the American actions at Lexington and Concord. "Actually, there can be no argument about it, the whole glorious affair of that day of April 19, 1775, was a riot. So, for that matter, we can consider the Boston Tea Party and even the whole Revolution" (2). The actions of the Committee of Vigilance are not considered "riots" by historians only because they were so well planned. The tendency of Stewart's paper is to suggest that riots are "as American as apple pie," to quote a famous revolutionary. He suggests that most historical riots did not occur on the basis of ideology (3), and his own discussion of them is not ideological.

Seen in tandem through the window of the neo-social Darwinian, *Pickett's Charge* and *Committee of Vigilance* could both be considered narratives of adaptational conflict between culture-defined species. There is a crucial difference, however, between Confederates versus Yankees and Vigilantes versus "Established Authority." Both conflicts were, literally, for control of a limited physical space and symbolically for control of what that space symbolized. But, unlike the Civil War, the war in San Francisco was complex and internecine. There was no Cemetery Ridge. The two forces invested the same terrain. And there was no *programme* for ecosystemic-cultural change in the latter case. The Committee and its opponents were opposed with respect to the law-enforcement process, but not with respect to a clearly-defined terminal goal or goals. On the other hand, both situations involved a question of the role of culture in nature. You could say that all parties in these conflicts were ultimately fighting over issues of morality. Is it morally justified to kill white Southerners in order to free Southerners' black slaves? Is it morally justified to hang San Francisco thieves to deter San Francisco thievery? As Joseph Carroll points out, the responses to moral dilemmas cannot be made or adjudicated based on an assumption of cultural autonomy. You cannot "segregate morality from biology" (365). "Morality is *distinct* from simpler forms of biological activity, but it is not antagonistic to them" (365). Hence neither conflict is qualitatively separable from the physical environment where it was played out or the noncognitive biology of the players.

*

In order to show the connections between *Pickett's Charge* and *Committee of Vigilance*, I have slightly distorted the chronology of Stewart's literary career. Between these two works, he was engaged in what might be considered the final phase of the descriptive environmental writing initiated by

Ordeal by Hunger. One project in this period proved to be (probably with justification) abortive. In 1963 he wrote to Paul Brooks "Though I am sixty-eight years old now, and though the future is never sure, I have some expectation of having ten more years of good work in me," and describes his current project: a sequel to *Earth Abides* named *If*, whose theme is the consequences to humanity if certain basic changes in the earth occurred—such as the loss of gravitation (Stewart to Brooks 5 Oct. 1963). A few months later, having apparently seen parts of the manuscript of *If*, Brooks provided substantial criticism of it, particularly on the grounds that it lacked novelistic content—Stewart wasn't "showing" what happened in these cases. There was a lack of basic novelistic features—plot and character development (Brooks to Stewart 16 Jan. 1964).

A dispassionate reader cannot help but agree with Brooks. Although more explicitly topical than *Earth Abides*, *If* is, in a word, boring. It would have been much more provocative if worked out in an explicitly predictive nonfiction form, as in the works of Alvin Toffler. Stewart introduces his text by saying "Each 'if' supposes a single and particular alteration in a very large and complicated system. The system may be the world or even the universe, and in every instance it is in some way the environment of the human race" (1). In a way, then, *If* is a work of speculative cultural ecology, for every particular alteration produces effects "all through the system," conceived of as integrating human and nonhuman phenomena. Stewart toys with the generic issue, arguing that the book has no precedent. It could be considered science fiction without the "fiction," but it is not a work of science. However, it "might be considered science-fiction without the story-element and the characters" (2). In fact, with the exception of some scenes, there are no characters at all, and Stewart expresses satisfaction with this situation, since it is what happens, not what happens *to* individuals, which is the center of interest. The weakness of science fiction is that there are too many characters in it whom no one really cares about (3). The two important factors in the scenarios of "disaster" he outlines are change, and the "rapidity" of change, for which humans don't "have time to adjust by cultural change and by biological evolution" (4).

A good example of what Stewart is doing here is provided by his sixth chapter "Perhaps, by Ice" and his seventh "Perhaps, by Fire." In each case he was inspired by Robert Frost's famous poem "Fire and Ice," although, "as I once pointed out to Frost in a discussion," these terms wouldn't have the weight they bear for a reader who lived in a physical environment from which one or the other was absent. For the "ice" chapter Stewart provides as narrator his one recurrent character, George Oxley, a "retired lawyer (lawyers are always with us)," writing retrospectively at age 80 in the year 2075. Unfortunately, Brooks was all too right: the narrator has no identity, he is purely an expositor, and Stewart might as well have written the story of this "big chill" in his own persona. The "Fire" chapter does away with Oxley altogether, and its interest is purely circumstantial, since it chronicles the effects of an actual named phenomenon happening in the present—global warming. In this regard Stewart is particularly prescient, and the one redeeming trait of the whole volume is his willingness to "go out on a limb" with topical commentary. Here, he suggests that considering the effects of rising oceans "may do something to prevent the irresponsible suggestion of some H-bomb enthusiasts, that their new plaything should be used to melt the Antarctic ice."

In forwarding his partial text to Brooks, Stewart offers suggestions for "the rest of the book," which include an expansion on the "'Earth Abides' hypothesis, i. e. the assumption that about 99% of the population is suddenly removed by a new virus, and "If there is atomic warfare to a degree short of annihilation, how do we reconstruct?" One amusing idea is that "The irresponsible, ignorant, and some of the religiously fanatic reproduce themselves heavily over a period of some centuries, while other people have small families." The final one is what would happen "If things keep on as they are now going. (But this is perhaps too horrible to contemplate."

The early sixties are a time when Stewart's life was changing. Most prominently, in 1961 he made the decision to retire. The current English Department chair, Mark Schorer, asked him not to. His reply was cogent. "I have taught long enough," he says. He estimates that since 1920 he's taught 215 courses, 8,500 students, and uttered 22,000,000 words in class. "Although few of these can have been golden, they have all, so far, I think, made sense. Probably, therefore, I had better quit while I'm ahead. I hope now to devote myself to writing and fishing" (Stewart to Schorer 22 Nov. 1961). To another correspondent he wrote of retirement, "The occasion seems to me one of the greatest ones of anyone's life, comparable to marriage and passing the doctor's oral, even if no[t] quite equaling birth" (Stewart to "Howard" 27 May 1962). In a letter to Benjamin Lehman, following his retirement dinner, he said "Retirement, I think, may be considered the symbolic time of entrance into old age. And that stage of life seems to call for more conscious adjustment and planning than does any other. I have been working on the adjustment all year" (Stewart to Lehman, 27 May 1962/*L*). At his retirement he was awarded an honorary Doctorate of Humane Letters.

Tied in with his retirement was the much-celebrated centennial of the University of California. To the proposal that he write the centennial history of the university he considers himself a "natural" for it, but "I have bucked the Regents a couple of times, and I have had a run-in or two with Clark Kerr also." However he offers to write it for $50,000 [!] (Stewart to Robert Gutwillig 3 Feb. 1963). Although this never happened, he was asked in 1964 by Mark Schorer to write a centennial history of the Berkeley English Department, and agreed, despite, as he admits in the Foreword, having "often been in the opposition" (*History* 1). By March, he could write to Lehman "I think that I have done a pretty good disappearing act at the department. . ." (Stewart to Benjamin Lehman, 3 Mar. 1963/*L*). In the summer the Stewarts took a vacation at Packer Lake, under the Sierra Buttes where he had been fire lookout in the 1940's (Stewart to Benjamin Lehman, 15 July 1963/*L*). In 1964 Stewart and his wife took a five-month cruise in the south Pacific, and in 1965 he became president of the Berkeley Faculty Club, so however retired he was, he remained very active in personal, social, and writerly terms.

*

The California Trail is "The only book I ever did for a publisher"—the American Trails series, issued by McGraw-Hill—but his longtime publishing associate Howard Cady persuaded him to do it on the grounds that otherwise someone else would do it badly (*Little* 209-10). However "I had actually been working on the Trail ever since the time of *Ordeal by Hunger*, piecing it out here and there." Joe Backus went with Stewart as far as Scott's Bluff, NB, to observe parts of the trail he'd not previously seen. Reminiscing, Stewart recalls his near-fatal illness in 1958 while writing *Pickett's Charge*, and the cusp of time when *The California Trail* was written. When he finished it, "I knew I was getting old" (*Little* 214). The book doesn't show it. In fact it is one of his most consistently praised and reprinted works.

Stewart takes on his "epic voice" to set the tone of the book. He considers it literally as "one of the great epic tales" of America (5). As a classical epic does, it begins with a "proem," but as an epic of heroic collectivity, a "democratic epic" (6), it is told through chapters defined by the chronology of traverse, from 1841 to 1859, with a couple of his patented "interchapters." That this epic journey is also a personal one for the author, the last of many literary cross-America voyages, is revealed in a telling footnote about the 1841 emigrant J. B. Chiles:

> My authority for this detail [that Chiles quit the party after Fremont expropriated the hindquarters of a deer Chiles had shot] is Chiles's' son William, about seventy years old when I talked with him, late in 1919 on a rainy morning before breakfast in his cabin at the old toll gate on the Mt. St. Helena road. I got hungry and went to breakfast before I had got all that I might have out of him, not then knowing that I would be writing this book. But I wrote some of it down for a class exercise and Professor Herbert E. Bolton asked me to give it to the Bancroft Library. So, the other day, in 1961, I was able to read it again. (41)

In his acknowledgements, he mentions the many later times when he followed parts of the trail: following the Truckee part with Wendell Robie in 1936, the Black Rock visits in 1941, 1947 and 1953, flying low over the 40-mile desert with Lowell Sumner in 1950, exploring Goose Creek and City of Rocks with James D. Hart in 1952, and the extensive trips over the route with Backus and David Lavender in 1960 (331). So, in effect, the book is a collective epic of Stewart's and his closest associates' experience of the trail as well.

As in *Ordeal by Hunger*, but more explicitly, the trail is imagined to be environmental space interacting with the mobile cultures of the groups which followed it. In the procession of years, different epic encounters occurred which reciprocally affected both the emigrant culture and the nature traversed by the trail. The first such encounter was that of the Bidwell party and a trapper encampment in 1841. "This meeting on Green River, in the very heart of the mountain country, may be viewed as symbolic" (17). It represented the end of trapper *rendezvous* and the beginning of emigrant passage as the centering ritual of cultural presence in the land. "As one era ended, another was beginning" (17). Then, "Like the meeting of the trappers and emigrants at Green River in '41, [the] establishment of Fort Bridger in '43 may be considered symbolic of new conditions" (43). Bridger purposely established it between Fort Laramie and Fort Hall as a supply point for the emigrant trains, accepting them as the new reality of human presence on the land. But the fort also established a space of permanent white habitation where there had been none before.

The failed expeditions of 1841 and 1843 had revealed what routes *not* to follow to reach California, so the departure south from Fort Hall of the Stevens party, the first successful one was "a critical moment in an epic story" (62), and, as is appropriate to an epic, Stewart enumerates the "personnel" (in an epic it would be the warriors) of the party. But the critical moment in the specific story of the Stevens party is November 25, 1844, which may be "considered the date of the opening of the California Trail" (72-73), since it is the date when

Donner Pass was crossed for the first time, by the chain-raising and lowering of wagons. "Like the ancient Israelites, whose Scriptures many of them read so earnestly, some emigrants were quick to see divine intervention" (72) in this remarkable traverse.

With Caleb Greenwood's west-to-east traverse in 1845, the story was again altered "in a more subtle way" than the multiplication of wagons such that records of wagon-train members are no longer kept. This subtle change is from the crossing being "almost wholly the struggle of man against the forces of nature," to "the competitive struggle of man against man. For, it would seem, once men have overcome nature, they inevitably begin to fight one against another" (83). This is a profound change in the relation of "culture" and "nature," when the former's adaptation to the latter has become so successful that social organization at least partially takes the place of nonhuman nature. Another aspect of this transformation, discussed in *Man*, is in the relationships between whites and Indians. That the primary inhabitance of the land has passed from the latter to the former is represented by Sam Kinney's enslavement and "breaking" of a Digger Indian he named sarcastically "my man Friday" (95). Although Friday managed to escape into the desert, another member of Kinney's party fulfilled his longtime desire to kill an Indian. These events initiated another persistent feature of the emigrant trains' cultural transformation. The formerly peaceful and poverty-stricken desert Indians became predators of the wagons-trains.

The other side of this picture is that, increasingly well-organized and supplied, the wagon trains by 1846 had become, in cultural terms, migratory villages, but much changed in "folk habits" (123) from their stationary agrarian villages of origin. As villages with special adaptational needs, there were many different experimental forms of governance involving the relations of the individual to the collective, but no permanent form. "The company may thus be compared to an alliance or confederation of sovereign powers, not to a unified nation" (125). Since the individual was the ultimate sovereign power, Stewart says, retrospective to *Committee of Vigilance*, that crime was one of the most difficult circumstances, since, as there, there was a vacuum of civil authority, and often enough the Old Testament's sanction of retributive punishment took on the force of law (125).

With the Bear Flag Rebellion in 1846, and accompanying political chaos, Stewart considers the emigrant trains to have taken on a political identity involving them in events far beyond their own "village limits," since anyone going West had to think, as not before, about what conditions would be encountered at the end of the trail. Nonetheless, symbols of an expanding "human domain" were present on the trail. Stewart notes the appearance, at Deer Creek, of the trail's first billboard. "Of course, it was a poor thing," he notes ironically, "compared to those magnificent ones now lining our highways over the mountains and across the deserts, giving our city-dwelling drivers a feeling of comfort and security" (187). The billboard reads

> NOTICE
> To the ferry 28 ms the ferry
> good and safe, maned by experienced
> men, black smithing, horse and ox
> shoing done all so a wheel right (187)

With the discovery of gold came another symbolic change in the emigrants and the trail. Stewart says 1849 could be called "The Year of the Madness" but also "The Year of the Greenhorn," when for the first time the overwhelming majority of migrants had no extraurban experience whatever. The thousands of would-be migrants piled up at St. Joseph, Missouri, reading guidebooks to take up the time until the May grass was tall enough for the cattle to graze. Stewart's main point in describing the 1849 season seems to be the environmental impact of the excessive number of people and animals on the trail. As, several years earlier, Man versus Nature had transformed into Man versus Man, the situation had returned to its former state. There was what he calls a "breakdown of free enterprise" (226), since there was no centralized organization to use the assembled manpower for building bridges, ferries, and any other traffic facilitations. The wet spring made trail routes mudholes, the buildups of wagons waiting to cross rivers caused population concentration, spreading cholera, and overgrazing of pastureland, the disposal of used and unneeded items created polluted sites. The Fort Kearny region "became a vast dump" (229). "Scattered along the trail were more than twenty thousand people, the equivalent of an important city by American standards of the time. They were totally severed from the effective authority of any government" (240).

It is amazing that this anarchic "ribbon development" (as Stewart might have called it) did not lead to more crime and violence than it did. "There was no mass violence, no breakdown of the general standards of decent conduct, no connivance with the Indians, no banditry" (243). Ironically, it was the permanent residents of the desert West, the Indians themselves, who suffered most, from depredation of their food supplies, game and grain. As a result, the Paiutes in particular waged incessant reciprocal depredations on the wagon trains. Fundamentally, there is no cultural term to characterize or analogize the 1849 migration. Stewart ends up with a "folk movement without leaders" (294).

The author summarizes the 1850's travel briefly, since most of the significant stages in the epic had been passed. In fact, he sees the decline in epicality characterizing these years. "In '49 there was always a touch of the heroic, but in '50 there was more than a touch of the sordid" (299), with more man-to-man violence and more suffering of greater numbers of unprepared migrants. Nonetheless, each year an increasing number emigrated. In 1851, "This was really the New West—of the businessman, and the chamber of commerce, and the subdivider" (303). New routes were opened, and, as in *U.S. 40*, competed for travelers. Indians were as likely to charge fees for river crossings, or for pasturage, as to steal cattle. With the first organized trail-breaking by Frederick Lander, a professional engineer, in 1858, Stewart sees the end of the trail as a privileged environment. "A trail is a fragile and delicate thing—like some kids of plants and animals, unable to withstand the advances of civilization. Do enough work on a trail and send enough traffic over it, and it necessarily becomes a road" (318).

As with *Pickett's Charge*, Stewart concludes by chronicling the later history of the trail, after it had been superseded as a passable route by the railroad in 1869. "The railroad dominated for a generation, and then came the highways, which we still sentimentally call trails" (320). Palimpsestically, many current roads closely correspond to the original trail, showing that the pioneers had chosen the best routes, but, as he writes, much of the original trail is obliterated or impassible.

An interesting supplement to *The California Trail* is Stewart's *Donner Pass and Those Who Crossed It*, first published in 1959. With copious photos and illustrations, he chronicles a central space in his own life as an explorer of terrains, and in the life of the West itself. The illustrations effectively mingle present and past, showing survival and change of topography and inhabitance. What gives the book its environmental impact is Stewart's discussion of the pass's post-migration history, in particular the destruction of natural phenomena by mining and logging. He chronicles the topographical changes produced by hydraulic mining, the siltation resulting from the tailings, and the resultant threats to valley agriculture. Also important is the building of the rail line through the pass. "The magnificent forest along the right of way was cut down ruthlessly to supply ties, timber for trestles, and fuel for the wood-burning locomotives" (51). The Donner Pass section of route 40 and the railroad, as dramatized in *Storm* are presented in numerous photographs—for example of the rotary plows—so the reader can form a good visual sense of the setting of that part of the novel. With these two books Stewart effectively says farewell to his career-long following of trails.

Chapter VIII
Trail's End

"In a sense," says Stewart, "*Good Lives* was an attempt to sum up my life. ..and see whether I had been able to do anything that way, or what was it that the good life was?" (*Little* 215). "I tried to rescue two or three people from oblivion that should have been rescued. I don't think I succeeded very well in rescuing them from oblivion, because nobody ever reads the book, but there they are anyway."

Good Lives was published in 1967, when Stewart was 72. It consists of a series of short, reflective biographies of a diverse group of humans—all male—in whose lives he had become interested over the course of his career: William the Marshal, Heinrich Schliemann, Joab Ben-Zeruiah, Francisco Eduardo Tresguerras, Henry of Portugal, and John Bidwell. A Foreword and Afterword seek to bring these historically diverse individuals' lives into a definition of what a "good life" is. Obviously they are monitory surrogates for the author's own self-examination, in the great tradition of *nosce te ipsum* as a prelude to death. Obviously, with Schliemann and King Henry, the author is not dealing only with people lost in oblivion. Clearly, also, it would be a distortion to try to twist this text into an "environmental" reading.

Superficially, *Good Lives* follows the model of Kroeber's *Configurations of Culture Growth*, in seeking to trace at the individual level what he there traces at the collective cultural level, the "clusterings or spurts of higher cultural productivity" (5) at particular historical times, the "clustering of genius" (16). But Stewart isn't interested, here, in collective cultural achievement, or in high productivity or genius. He is interested in less overt attributes than cultural production. The whole point is that, with the mentioned exceptions, his characters led, in some senses of the word, "good" lives while not gaining lasting acclaim from their culture or subsequent ones. Kroeber defines achievement causation in almost purely cultural terms, while Stewart, because he is dealing with deeper attributes of character, is concerned with causations of "goodness" in a way that includes environmental factors.

He initiates the discussion by considering what the "good life," as a 20th century phrase of currency, does *not* mean. In his book, it is not defined in religious, moral, or hedonistic terms (xi). With these excluded, he proposes to derive inductively, from the contemplation of these lives, a definition in other than the above realms of meaning (xii). He facilitates this inductive method by the use of his "interchapter" technique to look back on each life he has chronicled individually, in terms of why he attributes a "good life" to that individual. For example, his first personage, William, hereditarily the "King's Marshal" in 12th century Britain, maintained the values of "justice and order" in "an age which was always close to anarchy and violence" (53). However, the social values maintained by William could well be argued to have been predetermined by heredity and position, and not attributes forged and held by him. Thus Stewart leads in to the man he clearly is most interested in, Heinrich Schliemann, the "discoverer" of Troy. The idea is that Schliemann, we might say, began with nothing and "invented himself" from his own inner resources and Stewart's much-prized "luck."

In a postmodern moment, he begins his narrative of Schliemann by identifying the novelistic technique of introducing a character as initially "in a state of nudity," in order to show that the hero "begins with nothing, stripped naked before the world" (55). He seizes the opportunity to do this with Schliemann, presenting him as a half-dead, stripped castaway on Texel, an island off the coast of Holland, in 1841 (age 19). As he describes his hero's boyhood (acknowledging the untrustworthiness of Schliemann's own autobiographical statements), Stewart emphasizes that he was "religious without being of any particular religion," and what he believed in was "Fortune, or Luck" (66). "This belief in luck is a rather attractive part of his character, for it takes away from his egotism. After a great success he can quite simply maintain that it was merely his good luck" (66). Stewart gets great pleasure from recounting how Schliemann, "badly adjusted" and "sex-starved," arrived in San Francisco in the signal year 1851, and established a bank in Sacramento, becoming prosperous partly because he knew so many foreign languages.

But his California days were brief. As Stewart mentions, in what I see as self-reference, Schliemann was an "eternal tourist . . .seeing everything, always from the outside," but always returning to his beloved St. Petersburg in Russia. Finally however, "he did not come back at all. He kept on going, and eventually the curved surface of the earth returned him" (79). Stewart's Schliemann, in his determination to find Homer's Troy, is perhaps naive, but intelligent and persistent. "The Achaeans besieged Troy for ten years; Agamemnon, in the end, captured Troy; Troy, we may say, captured Schliemann. He amassed great spoil at Troy and won high fame, but Troy took him as an active man of forty-six and cast him out as a dying man of sixty-eight" (93).

Stewart's interchapter on Schliemann is perhaps the most significant one for the book as a whole. "The individual cannot, generally speaking, affect his own environment to a significant degree," he says. "Even if he attempts to escape from it, he merely escapes into some other one. Therefore, any life—good, bad, or indifferent—must be seen and judged against the background of environment" (106). And for Stewart, as I read it, "environment" as used here is the totality of the cultural and natural. Thus William the Marshal's environment was feudalism, Schliemann's, 19th century capitalism. "It surrounded him as water surrounds a trout, and he assumed it as the trout assumes buoyancy and dissolved oxygen" (106). The point is not environmental determinism, but, shall we say, environmental immersion. There is no way of gaining any true knowledge of the individual without accepting, provisionally, the total environment in which the person lived. The person did not, and cannot, have an identity outside of the environment, in this sense, of h/her life. Thus to understand his next "hero," the Old Testament Joab, "we must enter imaginatively into the life of a primitive and aggressively warlike tribe. We must consider manslaughter as an everyday matter. We must accept the idea of the blood-feud" (106).

I would refer this idea of "environmental immersion" to Stewart's great intellectual comrade, Carl Sauer. In *Good Lives* Stewart attaches the specifics of individual personality to Sauer's theory of the historical nature of culture. Sauer says that "An environmental response . . .. .is nothing more than a specific cultural option with regard to habitat at a particular time." He relates culture to environment by redefining the relation of "habit" and "habitat:" habit is the activated learning common to a group . . .that. . .may be endlessly subject to change" (*Land* 359). In Stewart's individuals we find "activated learning" which in each individual is partly, at least, the product of a union of habit and habitat. The great variety of individuals, habits, and habitats that his biographies reveal is a manifestation of the incessant changes in both as "culture traits or complexes" encounter other cultures, habitat change, or enhanced "energy of invention" (360).

Thus Joab Ben-Zeruiah's habitat was Bethlehem, "a large village of the early Iron Age," and his "habits" were those of his agrarian tribal culture (111). The conflict which defined his life was between two cultures, that of his "rural" tribe and that of his "urbanized" former intimate David, who had, as it were, gone to the "big city," Jerusalem, to make his fortune. It is interesting that, after recounting the bloody tribal warfare that enmeshed Joab for much of his life, Stewart characterizes his "goodness" in terms of personal stability and consistency. He "lived simply by his code of life, and fulfilled himself. He did that work that must be done. He was staunch in his loyalty" (149).

Stewart discovered his next subject, Francisco Eduardo Tresguerras, during his times in Mexico, and in *N.A. 1* describes the churches and bridges he built. Here, Stewart describes his magnificent church at Celaya, finished in 1807, not as architecture but as "biography," since every detail expresses his personality, and since he was partly a practitioner of the baroque "habit" dominant at the time, although, in many details, a rebel against it. Stewart has a great picture of Tresguerras, elderly, sitting in his fields across the river from

Celaya, contemplating the dome of his church, and asking passers-by if they know the name of the architect. In his interchapter, he suggests that all the figures portrayed so far, even William the Marshal, a younger son of a minor baron, were to some degree "self-made" and not at the top of society. With Henry the Navigator, there is a different challenge: how can you actively live the good life if you "have it all" at the moment of birth? "Where would the challenge be?" (195).

Stewart, as I understand it, sees Henry's achievement that of seeking geographical knowledge for its own sake, regardless of his social position. He, more than any of the others, actually lived the legend that his life became. Henry is in direct contrast to the book's final figure, in almost every respect. John Bidwell, not only "obscure" to posterity, was born "in all the economic and cultural poverty of the American frontier." Yet he lived a life that "might be taken as a textbook demonstration of the American dream. Fill the portrait out, here and there, with some imaginative touches, and we might well have The Great American Novel" (243).

Stewart introduces Bidwell as a young man in 1843 California, riding north from Sutter's Fort. Bidwell and his companions come upon a beautiful place "where a little stream. . .flowed along, embowered among sycamores" (245). This vividly described natural space would become Bidwell's "kingdom," a place on the earth that was to center all his future life. He became a Mexican citizen to qualify for a land grant, and then fought the Mexicans in the Bear Flag Rebellion and as a U.S. citizen in the Mexican War. In 1849 he bought part of his "kingdom," the Rancho del Arroyo Chico—and later, the rest. He built his own cabin, began sowing wheat, scythed it himself, and began to accumulate money and goods in the 1850's. He propagated multiple species of trees and plants and "developed into an experiment, a man with a deep love of the land and of all that it could produce" (268). He allowed Indians to live n his land: "almost alone among early Californians, [he] treated the Indians with humanity, and gave them protection" (269). Bidwell founded the city of Chico, became a Union general in the Civil War and a congressman. Because of his gardens, he was visited by many naturalists, including Asa Gray and John Muir. He became something of a political "rebel," and "an early liberal and progressive" (279), opposed to trusts and to anti-Chinese agitation.

Clearly, to this reader anyway, Bidwell is Stewart's favorite among the figures he profiles, and the one whose values he felt most kinship with: environmental concern, anti-racism, social progressivism, a radical streak. But in his "Afterword" he points out the validity of the writer's maxim "'Don't state; demonstrate,'" (289), as applied to his character. So the lives themselves, rather than conclusions drawn from them, are best guides to understanding the "good life." However, he says he will venture further, partly because people have attributed autobiographical motives to him. He needs to get beyond the dilemma of accepting (egotistically) or refuting (ungratefully) the statement made by one of his friends, "'Why, George, you have lived the good life yourself'" (289).

He admits the flaws in his book: his six characters were not perfect, they include no women, they are not ethnically diverse. They were also all men of action, and, looking back, he sees someone being justified in asking "'is there no place in the good life for contemplation'?" (291). He is also struck by the lack of humor in their lives, but blames it on their sources: "The Bible, for instance, is notoriously a humorless book, and its writers would not have recorded Joab's witticisms, if he made any" (292).

The common positive traits he sees in the six are, first, "a sense of goal," but not one implying narrow-minded ambition. ". . .[T]hey were men of breadth, and enjoyed many contacts with life" (292). "They were deeply committed. They lived hard; they gave themselves, day by day, year by year. They were not half-hearted. In old age, not one of them had to look back and think that life had passed him by" (293). Their lives were distinguished by responsibility, loyalty, and courage. "They kept a larger view of life. . .They were not content with eating and drinking day by day; they looked before and after" (295). They also attained, as old age approached, "an integration of character," and an acceptance of "the finitude of man's years. There is no suggestion that they fought hopelessly to be young. Rather, they matured and aged, until the end came" (296).

The reader might well see, in all these qualities, not necessarily ones that Stewart believed he possessed, but ones that he wished he had possessed, or even aspired to possess in the (ultimately) thirteen years that were left to him.

*

Our author was still involved with his favorite concerns. He wrote an article on stagecoaching, focusing on four "classic" journeys to California made by Horace Greeley, Sir Richard Burton, Mark Twain, and Samuel Bowles and Schuyler Colfax. Greeley's stage trail was "wholly 'natural.' Laid out only a few weeks before, it had little past and even less future," before it was superseded by another (6). Stewart traces the ascent of stage travel from this lowly state to the VIP trip of Colfax and Bowles in a coach pulled by four matched blacks. In terms of onomatology, one of the many papers he presented at meetings of the renowned and, actually still-alive institution known only as "The Club") was "The Four-Letter Words" (September, 1969). The words themselves are not fit to print in this text, but Stewart speaks about them while pretending to maintain the strictest scholarly standards. "I regret [the] general dearth of knowledge in this field. . .This is not an essay in pornography. My raw data may be of the sort usually termed raw, but my methodology and treat[ment] are such, I hope, that my study might meet the standards of a learned journal."

*

The full-length book Stewart wrote next, I suspect, was both a way of "giving himself," in the manner of his models above, and also of responding to an immediate and personal environmental crisis, during the time of which it was written. Although she doesn't mention him in her pantheon, Stewart, with his next book, clearly became one of Sylvia Tesch's

> . . .handful of new visionaries and their supporters. . .[who]. . .began promoting the idea we know today as environmentalism. They took the ecological principle that people should not interfere in the balance of

> nature and the ethical principle that nature should be exalted and added a political principle. They argued that all of nature is seriously endangered, and that we must change our values and our institutions in order to save it. (43)

I suggest that Stewart would consider he was an "environmentalist" long before the sixties, but that his "environmentalism" was also more personal and immediate. The Stewarts' house at 100 Codornices Road in Berkeley, built in 1950, is at the end of a short, steeply rising and leftward curving street. When it was built it directly overlooked a city reservoir, Berryman Reservoir, which apparently at that time was "naturally" bordered by vegetation. The reservoir was built in 1884 "by a private water company to capture runoff from Codornices Creek and local springs" (John Hurlburt, Email to the author 12 July 2005). It bordered Codornices Park, one of the first parks in Berkeley, which opened in 1915 "with a splendid field house, a fine tennis court, and many other play features" ("Parks"). The reservoir was contained by an earth dam, and its potential instability caused it to be covered temporarily in 1918, and reduced in size and recovered in the early 1930's. The East Bay Municipal Utility District (EMBUD), which owns the property, and its engineering studies (in the present) "indicate that a major seismic event could seriously damage the dam," so it was scheduled for drainage in late 2005, to be replaced by a "small. . .seismically safe water storage tank" ("Berryman"). However, because of water quality concerns, it had been covered again, more securely, in 1969. It was this planned capping which led Stewart to participate in the one environmental protest action I know of in his life, and which, I think, impelled him to write his most controversial book, *Not So Rich As You Think*. Also, although he nowhere says this, I suspect the reservoir capping led him to sell his house and move, with Ted, to the Sequoias, a retirement residence in San Francisco. The move, he told Benjamin Lehman, "was a big shock to both of us" (Stewart to Lehman, 22 Aug. 1971).

John Hurlburt says "It would have been a beautiful view from Mr. Stewart's residence. . .I can understand why the residents were protesting"

(Hurburt, Email to the author 12 July 2005). In May, 2005, one could see the truth of this. Stewart's house looks down on a desolate desert of gravel, punctuated by planters containing dead plants. I don't know to what extent Stewart was cognizant of the rationale for the capping, since the pollution from pesticides and fertilizers, etc., which led to it is precisely what Stewart condemns in *Not So Rich As You Think*. Nonetheless, he did enmesh himself in a no-win conflict between aesthetics and pollution.

In January, 1967, the City of Berkeley was considering a bond vote for "improvements" at many city parks, including Codornices ("Berkeley"). The history of the community protest of these "improvements," in which Stewart was involved, provides an excellent microcosm of grassroots environmental activism on the threshold of Earth Day.

In April, 1967, area citizens formed an organization named "Urban Care," under the direction of Dale Tillery, a Codornices Road resident. At this point, the draining of Berryman Reservoir was a *fait accompli*, and the roofing of it prior to refilling was in process. Bids for initial excavation were due to be opened on April 27. Tillery accepted the roof, but wanted it redesigned; he sought revival of an original idea, dismissed as too expensive, for fountains and a reflecting pool on the roof. However, says the Customer Relations director for the East Bay Municipal Utility District, "we stated quite bluntly that the Berryman project would proceed as planned (J. H. Plumb to J.W. McFarland, 21 Apr. 1967/*D*). It may be in the face of this bluntness that Stewart's neighbor Florence Dickens Gray wrote to him in sadness at the felling of 79 trees and suggesting that a letter from him might help (Gray to Stewart, n.d.).

Perhaps as a result of such urging, Stewart on May 5, 1967 sent a statement to EMBUD--one which must have received wide currency. Geoffrey W. Fairfax of Honolulu, author of *The Architecture of Honolulu* and quite possibly an associate from Stewart's World War II Navy days there, sent him a copy of his own letter to the editor of the *Honolulu Advertiser* which referred to Berkeley citizens banding together "in an effort to preserve a small and very beautiful hillside lake," and quoting extensively from Stewart's statement. Fairfax says that this effort inspired Hawaii citizens to organize opposition to high-rises on Diamond Head (Fairfax to Stewart, ? Dec. 1967). Stewart's first paragraph reads:

> The destruction of beauty under the alleged necessity of saving dollars has been a continuing, but evil, practice of American civilization. Beauty is not easily appraised in dollars, but to more and more Americans, such operations seem to be proceeding at a loss since the dollars saved do not equal the beauty destroyed.
>
> Moreover, the parsimony is evident only in one year's budget, but the loss of beauty continues through the indefinite future into the lives of our children and grandchildren. Our generation will be judge in the years to come by what we did, and often it has been irreplaceable harm—to our countryside and our cities.
>
> (Stewart to East Bay Municipal Utility District, 5 May 1967/*D*).

He goes on to say that "Several years ago," citizens set out to save Berryman reservoir, "which in an almost unique manner, in the midst of a large city, offers vistas worthy of a forest-surrounded Sierra lake." Stewart also describes a "'region' of beauty," in effect an organic ecosystem, of which the reservoir is only one part. This includes the Rose Walk, to the west, and to the north Codornices Park itself with its "tree-crowned, bird-haunted canyon, where during most of the ear a little brook goes brawling over its stones." He is indignant that in the name of economy, the water surface of the reservoir will be sacrificed, "when we should be developing it and integrating it with the other features." He concludes by urging the Utility District at least to consider modifying its plan for a cap on the reservoir. (Ironically, in 1962 the Utility District had solicited him to endorse in an advertisement their water development program: "you would be the ideal person to be featured in this ad" [Charles Wilmarth to Stewart 10 Oct. 1962]).

I can find no specific response to his statement. Urban Care continued to oppose the "'concrete and crushed aggregate, pastel colored asbestos-cement panels'" planned for the capping surface as not fitting the "lovely natural complex" of the area defined by Stewart (Dale Tillery to John W. McFarland, 12 May 1967/*D*). Urban Care's continual propaganda drove the District to plan a meeting with their representatives, the city's, and Urban Care's, on site at the reservoir (John W. McFarland to Dale Tillery 22 May 1967/*D*). Following this meeting, the District agreed to find out cost and logistics information on a reflecting pool topping a capped reservoir in Cincinnati, used by the organization as an example of what could be done to render the project aesthetic.

As a result of researching the project, the Utility District determined that, although Cincinnati could not provide specific cost estimates, since pool maintenance proved to be more expensive than they had thought, a pool at the Berryman site would add $200,000 to $300,000 to its cost. "The primary reason for these added costs is the complex geology and foundation condition existing at Berryman and the resulting necessity to design adequately for seismic factors." Since the Utility District "firmly believes that the project as now designed represents the optimum solution . . . [,] we again affirm our view that no change should be made in this project" (J.S. Harnett to Dale Tillery, 29 June, 1967/*D*).

Individual private citizens, such as Stewart, also wrote in. Mrs. C. R. Nicewonger "A Bekeleyan since 1907!") chastised Berkeley's mayor. The "good will" of EBMUD was not enough. "It has not prevented tree-cutting and the alteration of our landscape beyond repair," and recounts a clump of trees saved from the saws accidentally by a Parks Department intervener (Nicewonger to Wallace Johnson, 21 June 1967/*R*). Interestingly, Ms. Nicewonger later recanted, having been told by Florence Gray that EBMUD was landscaping Euclid Avenue. "There are those who blame the E..B.M.U.D. for the loss of beauty at Berryman Reservoir. We however, are aware of the true causes . . ." (Nicewonger To Paul Fletcher, 25 Aug. 1969/*D*). One might wonder what the true causes were.

The protests by citizens and stonewalling by public entities continued. Almost a year later, Adele Smith of San Francisco, Assistant Director of the Institute for International Education, sought to emphasize the negative impression the Codornices alterations had made on the many foreign visitors hosted by her organization. "I am at a loss to explain or justify the reasons for the destruction of an incomparably beautiful natural area in favor of –of all things—a ball park!"

She points out that the oleanders planned for the urns on the roof are a poisonous plant, and recounts an incident visiting the park on Sunday with her grandchildren, as she often did, and the children's desire to share with a couple of "little Negro girls" they met, "the secrets of a very special 'super tree'." But when they get there, they

> . . .found the tree was no longer there; it had been cut down along with others to make way for the encroaching ball field. The children were inconsolable, and the 8-year old grandchild cried out, 'When the ball park is finished, it won't be any fun to come here any more.' On being asked why, the child replied, 'It won't be wild and quiet any longer, and it won't be secret or private.' (Smith to Berkeley Civic Arts Commission, 10 June 1968/*D)*

The Utility District's representatives, for two years, monotonously repeated that their decision on the roof was final, and there was no turning back. This unmoving stance actually seemed to inspire greater efforts on the part of Urban Care and other individuals. It is interesting to see this developing grassroots ingenuity in the context of Stewart's book. On the one hand, the protesters were taking kind of action he implies—but never specifically advocates-- in *Not So Rich As You Think*, as necessary to avoid catastrophic effects of pollution. On the other hand, the driving issue for the protesters was the preservation of "urban wilderness" space and landscape aesthetics. The main cause given by the EBMUD of today for dismantling the reservoir is exactly the water pollution that Stewart bewails in his book; but pollution is not mentioned in any context in the correspondence of either party to the 1960's disputes.

Urban Care enlisted "big guns" to endorse its position. The biggest was probably James Biddle, President of the National Trust for Historic Preservation (Biddle to Board of Directors, EBMUD, 28 May, 1968/*D*). One of EBMUD's own landscape designing firms opposed the roof, saying even if the reflecting pool was impracticable, there were plenty of other environment-friendly alternatives, turfing, a dry meadow, or a less obtrusive completely flat cover (Walter Thomas Brooks to Berkeley Civic Arts Commission, 29 Mar. 1968/*D*).

The Regional Parks Association's board unanimously voted to urge suspension of development plans until the area's "distinctive woodland character" could be safeguarded. "The Codornices-Berryman area is one of the last natural glade and creek areas left in Berkeley," and there are plenty of ballpark facilities nearby (Regional Parks Association to Berkeley Civic Arts Commission, n.d./*D*). Jerry Jackson, a self-described urbanologist and member of the Urban Land Institute said that the Institute had selected Codornices Park "as one of three parks in the Nation to exemplify exceptionally well planned community open space. . . .If the EBMUD and City elects to continue on their present course, they are dissecting one of the few historically and esthetically significant landmarks in the East Bay" (Jackson to Wallace Johnson [*et. al.*], 20 July, 1968/*D).*

The final move by Urban Care preserved in correspondence shows the evolution of the group from reaction to proaction. In June, 1969, Urban Care "applied to the America the Beautiful Fund for a grant to develop a coordinated and comprehensive plan for the restoration of Codornices Park (J. Laurence Mintier to Board of Directors, EBMUD, 15 Sept. 1969/*D).* They received the grant, and Berkeley Environmental Design graduate student B. K. Gosain developed an alternative plan which was presented at an open house on the campus (Marion A. Corten to John S. Harnett, 1 Feb. 1970/*D*). Harnett replied, after the EBMUD representative attended the open house (and as he had said to Urban Care before), that they wanted further recommendations for improvement to wait until the currently designed roof had been installed. "As we have previously indicated, we believe approval would be given to additional landscaping around the perimeter of our property or other minor planting changes. However, major changes involving roof loads or drainage on the roof can not be considered" (Harnett to Corten, 6 Feb. 1970/*D*).

Thus, for all practical purposes, ended the saga of EBMUD versus The People. In some senses it may be considered a tempest in a teapot, and not germane to the literary career of George R. Stewart. I myself do not agree. Stewart Udall wrote in 1963 "Our mastery over our environment is now so great that the conservation of a region, a metropolitan area, or a valley is more important, in most cases, than the conservation of any single resource" (196). In contrast to such localism Justice William O. Douglas's 1969 *Points of Rebellion* points nationally to the same issues that evoked rebellious stances in the residents of Euclid Avenue: "Virgin stands of timber are virtually gone. Only remnants of the once immortal redwoods remain. . .Hundreds of trout streams have been destroyed by highway engineers and their faulty plans." "Youthful dissenters," says Douglas, "are not experts in these matters. But when they see all the wonders of nature being ruined they ask, 'What natural law give the Establishment the right to ruin the rivers, the lakes, the ocean, the beaches, and even the air?'"(50-51). In other words, local and national environmental action, youth and adult concerns therewith (*malgre* the generation gap) and environmentalist muckraking (such as Stewart's) were dovetailing into the making of Earth Day and its heritage.

In view of the above history, I think Stewart is slightly disingenuous when he says that *Not So Rich As You Think* was inspired by two engineering professors, L.M.K. Boelter of UCLA, and George Maslach at Berkeley, who urged him to write it. (He says Boelter originally suggested it as a sequel to *Storm* [*Not So Rich As You Think* 241]) Much of his discussion of it in *A Little of Myself* is on the theme that he "jumped the gun" on the subject. "I came out with that before people were really interested in the subject.. . .I apparently saw the crisis a little bit ahead of other people in general," although he thinks it's a very good thing that environmentalism has come "to be an emotional campaign, particularly among the young" (*Little* 237). Actually, it was an emotional issue to him in 1967. He doesn't attribute the book to personal experience such as the Berryman affair, nor to a forced move to the Sequoias, which he told his alumni secretary was "not . . .a withdrawal from the world but . . .the establishment of a firm base from which to operate" ("Class Notes" 10 Feb. 1970).

There is certainly no "withdrawal" in *Not So Rich As You Think*, which won the Sidney Hillman Foundation award in mass communications. Despite Stewart's deprecations, its importance can be judged from the emphatic praise of Stewart Udall, Secretary of the Interior, in the *New York Times Book Review.* Udall relates Stewart's reputation as a "respecter of nature" to *Storm, Names on the Land* and *Earth Abides.* "The value of this book transcends its scientific insights, provocative as they are. . . Seldom has it been so clearly stated that we must accompany our wealth with wisdom, and anticipate our speed with sanity" (Udall 6). "Stewart ultimately places the blame, as men must in the 1960's, on warped notions of national 'progress' and an indifference to what Kenneth Galbraith has called 'the economics of beauty.'" Ann Ford of Houghton Mifflin sent Stewart Hal Borland's equally positive comments. The book is "A magnificently grisly presentation of the situation. . ." and ". . .the best answer I have yet found to those who say they can't afford to stop polluting the rivers, the air, and the very earth" (Ford to Stewart ll Dec. 1967).

These comments imply an existing awareness of the problems Stewart discusses; his book's importance lies not in any uniquely prophetic awareness, but in that he more cogently than many "muckraking" predecessors brought together into a single, forceful condemnation the different modes of environmental destruction being practiced in the name of prosperity. He also did so in a most symbolic year (1968), when cultural issues such as racism and Vietnam tended to be at the forefront of public concern.

In his concluding note, Stewart expresses the view that *Not So Rich As You Think* "is a natural development out of much of my earlier interests and work," since in so many of them "I had considered environment and the complex system of human ecology" (241). As a culminating environmental statement, it is also an expression of politically incorrect urgency: "The crisis is not about to arise; the crisis is here" (2). The "future historian" Stewart often uses, summarizing what the present American generation has accomplished, will probably write "'Of the waters, they made a cesspool; of the air, a depository for poisons; and of the good earth itself, a dump where rats nuzzled in piles of refuse'"(1). The future historian does not hesitate to condemn the ethic of "production;" "Thus to arrive, we have allowed every year in our accounting a hidden and unnoted, though sizeable, item—the added degradation of the environment" (3). He considers the current title too low-toned for the urgency of the problem; rather, the first chapter's title, "Horror Story," would be more appropriate. But "Let the fact themselves do the screaming . . ." (4).

The most important initial point Stewart makes is that, because matter is conserved, the principle of all waste disposal is really one problem. Burning garbage produces smog. "No matter where or from what the materials originate, they must be passed on into the same earth, water, and air" (5). He is struck by the "failure to grasp this unity." And here Stewart uses his expertise in "naming;" evidence of the failure to grasp it is that there is no one single collective word in English for the whole conception. The closest he can come is the World War II term "Crud."

He recurs to the ideas of *Man* in his second chapter, "Down from the Trees." "The trees offered a built-in sanitation and refuse system" (9); even the dead simply fell upon the earth, and in decay returned to the soil. The downfall of natural sanitation was the development of fixed dwelling sites and centralized waste disposal. Even with the development of neolithic cities, the arboreal principle of dropping waste where you were was preserved. Any sanitation regulations were based on animistic religion. "Hesiod warned his readers against urinating in streams. Probably, however . . .he. . .was considering that such an act would be an insult to the river-god. . ." (14).

As he follows the course of "sanitation history," Stewart reaches the agrarian spaces and rural villages of Jeffersonian America, where still most waste disposal was earth-friendly. Given this history of non-destructive waste disposal, now, "Why these mountainous dumps, fouling both land and earth and air? Whence this green algae clogging the lakes? From what curse on the people have come these putrid streams? Even what was once the clean air itself—why does it now bring tears to the eyes?" (23).

The answer is that the enormous disposal problem since the 1870's has clear sources: population growth, urbanization, the development of the products and waste products of an "affluent society," and the invention of synthetic technology (25). "The people have increased but the environment has not" (25). Each person has less space wherein to discard waste. "The city-dweller has no way of disposing of his own waste. His dog has no place to bury a bone, and the very dog-droppings become a matter of city ordinance" (27). And waste-disposal is not a priority anyway. "Americans have developed a psychological state of mind in which anything to do with saving or re-use is opprobrious." It is almost "unpatriotic" to use anything fully (29). "Our civilization is going to have to come to a working agreement with the environment . . ." (30).

In this connection, Stewart presents a moral tale. Driving south through the Imperial Valley in cotton-picking season, he saw countless cotton-boles strewing the land and roadside, blown from trucks that were driving from field to gin. No one was trying to recover them. Across the border in Mexico, boys were walking behind the trucks, gathering every boll (31). There is a clear moral here, although Stewart does not fully develop it: full use can come only with a certain level of need and maybe a large enough population to use fully what is produced.

Stewart also anticipates another basic problem that has steadily become more serious since 1968—the disposal of nonbiodegradable materials. "Unless we accept a conscious planning of the universe," there is no organism adapted to consuming and breaking down all the synthetics not found in nature. ". . .[T]he whole situation of disposal seems so closely involved with civilization itself as to be automatically produced and essentially unsolvable. The crisis appears to be desperate, and it may well be so" (33). We don't even know if "civilization has already passed some point of no return," in terms of the future effects of pollutants in the earth and atmosphere, and the psychological effects of this presence.

Sewage disposal is tied in to a theme in much of Stewart's Western writing---the centrality of rivers to civilization: ". . .rivers have always been closely entwined with the life of man" (35). The pollution of water by human excreta is wryly discussed. In a reverse process of social evolution, the 20th century has seen taboo development with respect to excreta. "Before 1900 young couples went out courting behind some old gray mare, and they learned, literally, to face the problem" (39). Increasingly, however ". . .the excretory process became . . .cloaked in secrecy" (40), while, paradoxically, sexual demonstration has become increasingly public. Such an attitude carries over into neglect of sewage disposal systems, many of which, in the U.S., were constructed ". . .when cities were much smaller, and when affluence had not yet established the joyousness of being wasteful" (41). "We can transform sewage, but we cannot destroy it," Stewart says, in recounting the effects of untreated waste, such as deoxygenation of water (49). He spends a good deal of time seeking to combat the "almost religious fixation against the use of human fertilizer," (50), by demonstrating various ways of recycling human waste by way of algae, in diagrammatic form as oriental agriculture does, as opposed to the Western idea of a straight line from crop to ocean.

Stewart becomes more vehement in his condemnation of pollution by factory effluents. He lists the famous rivers of America, all of which are so polluted, from the Mississippi, "colon of the Middle West," to the Androscoggin, the "Miss America of Pollution." ". . .[T]he problem of factory-effluents shows the new relationship of man to his environment. . . .Two centuries ago, man's activities seemed small in comparison with the river. He could safely, it seemed, pour into it whatever overflow of odds and ends he happened to accumulate. That era has ended" (63). As with the ethic of prudery about excreta, a cultural value underlies the tolerance of factory waste pollution. "In our civilization factories are 'good'" (64). They mean jobs. The greater the effluent per year, the greater the prosperity of the enterprise. Surprisingly, though, Stewart lists lots of hopeful signs for controlling factory effluents, signs which seem somewhat dated in 2005—like a minimal number of point sources of pollution. It is this optimism that intersperses the basically dark pessimism of the text that made Stewart's editor, Paul Brooks, question some of his passages, especially those relating to pesticides. "As perhaps you know, I worked very closely with Rachel Carson on SILENT SPRING, and inevitably became somewhat familiar with the subject" (Brooks to Stewart 5 Apr. 1967).

Stewart has a strangely benign view of major corporations. He considers many of their leaders, like the characters in *Good Lives*, to have the "long view" of their enterprises, and to be committed to taking measures to ensure their 'immortality" (67). He considers that they "live in fear of government regulation," even though some have been nominated by Stewart Udall as the nation's dirtiest industries (68). He does admit possible flaws in his basic premise of this chapter, that affluence provides a built-in resistance to effluence: we don't want to compromise our good life by letting effluents destroy our places of leisure. Our civilization will still have to pay for its cleanup: "'Clean up or perish!'" (75).

Land disposal of wastes—garbage—is the next subject of Stewart's concern. Compared with waterborne waste, there is ". . .a surprising lack of concern about the pollution of the American land" (78). Stewart's history of garbage as a word is telling: there is no Romance language equivalent, since it developed so recently in history as a phenomenon. Particularly in the U.S., no consistent garbage disposal system has developed. There has been ". . . no technical breakthrough since the invention of the garbage pail. . ." (82). Incineration just puts the dump in the air. Urban sprawl diminishes the space for land disposal of garbage. Stewart concludes his pessimistic view of garbage with the suggestion that the elevations of the flat midwest be diversified through the creation of artificial mountains from garbage.

As opposed to garbage, "junk" is very new, and a typically U.S. creation. It is "something new and characteristic of our own time" (97). In fact, the later 19th century might be considered "the early junk period," as recalled by Wallace Stegner in *Wolf Willow*. Stewart himself recalls that "his own first self-employment was in the junk business. (If he had stayed with it he might be richer than he is now)" (98). In Indiana, water-pipes were being laid, and their deep trenches were "romantic places to wander." He found he could gather the tailings from their molten-lead joints, melt the lead on the stove, pour it into a baking-powder can, and sell it to the junkman—for a dollar, big money in those days.

The problem of junk is particularly serious with complex technological objects, like television sets, which contain nonbiodegradable components and can't be realistically separated into them when discarded. He emphasizes paper, which is often considered benign, but is really an "unnatural substance," extremely resistant to organic decay. "'Book-burning' is a term of anathema. But did you ever try to burn a book? Any one who does so try might well be considered, in the words of the old song, more to be pitied than censured" (105).

Stewart has the unpopular (particularly at the time) view that recycling will not solve the problem, since recycling of complex materials is not economically profitable. He suggests a "design for recycling." Even though we have an "essentially unplanned economy," it would be possible to create products—at least packaging materials—in manners that anticipated ease of recycling. He suggests automobile design which excludes metals hard to recycle, although it might not be worth the trouble to redesign cars since "the automobile itself—or, at least, the internal-combustion engine—will apparently have to be given up because of its production of poisonous smog . . ." (110). His postlude to the junk issue somewhat reverts to the famous image of the abandoned car in *Earth Abides*. The abandoned car brings to the American male "an image of death.. . .Certainly he is deeply identified with it. In that heap of dead cars, he sees, unconsciously, a heap of corpses. He even views himself—old, impotent, dead. He sees the end-point" (111).

When dealing with agricultural refuse, Stewart, with appropriate scholarship, retells the Heraclean story of the Augean stables. "Many places in the United States are rapidly coming to rival the Augean Stables . . ." (134); their content can be divided into field-refuse, pesticides, and manure. When Stewart discusses pesticides, he seems to manifest a little jealousy of Rachel Carson; they seem to be her "personal property." In his second foray into unwonted optimism, Stewart suggests that pesticide cleanup was already occurring as she wrote, and soil contamination from pesticides is not as bad as she said. This is the section of the book that Paul Brooks really objected to. Stewart says "If common practice could have kept up with common sense, Miss Carson would really have been belaboring a dead horse" (135). For Brooks, it is no dead horse.

> On the contrary, while you are quite right in saying that these chemical controls are a self-defeating approach to the problem, most well-informed conservationists feel that the fight to control these chemicals is going to continue for at least another decade. I haven't seen the recent figures, but I wouldn't be surprised to learn that large-scale industrial use of pesticides is greater than ever before.
> (Brooks to Stewart 5 April 1967)

One might second Brooks by considering that because *Silent Spring* swiftly ". . .precipitated significant political action and inspired reappraisal of the role of chemical pesticides in damaging the environment" (Payne 149), the progress Stewart notes, if real, was not contemporary with, but was caused by, public response to her book.

It must be admitted that Stewart gives full credit to the danger of DDT, and the ability of insects to adapt genetically to it, its chemical stability, and ability to accrete in the bodies that ingest it (138). "*Silent Spring* takes its title from the idea, and it is largely fact, that the singing birds have died off where the pesticides are used, or where their food is affected by the drugs" (141), but even greater damage is done to pollinating insects and biodegrading microorganisms. Nonetheless, "The whole idea of pesticides is yielding to what are known as bioenvironmental methods of control" (141). From the point of view of 2006, this is an overoptimistic observation; despite the widespread use of the latter methods, they are not practicable in large-scale industrial agriculture.

Closer to home and direct observation is Stewart's chapter on "Mineral Refuse," since it is a basic feature of the Sierra foothills he traipsed for decades. His discussion of environmental damage here is more subtle than of earlier issues, since he asks the question of whether landscape disturbance, as by mining operations, can be considered an environmental health danger. "The almost brutal dislocations of inanimate nature—do these have also their effects upon the human adjustment? Is such a phrase as 'the rape of the land' a phrase only, or does it have psychological implications?" (151). His idea is that damage to nature is damage to culture. "Alienation from the land may have its analogies in alienation from society. In the long run any degradation of the environment, any brutal and irreversible dislocation of the processes of nature, may not be free of health and hazard problems" (152).

Stewart's breadth of coverage of landscape disruption may be partly owed to Carl Sauer's influence. Not only does he decry the destruction of forest cover by mining, but he covers in detail the effects of strip-mining, and, most originally, the "demolition debris" produced by "urban renewal." Renewed areas are well and good, "But, to be reconstructed, they must first be laid waste" (159). He evokes Schliemann's "embarrassing" discovery of layers of demolished cities where he expected to find only one. "In addition to slum clearance, the construction of freeways has resulted in square miles of devastation" (161). This is a very far-sighted view of urban change, and may relate to Stewart's urban studies for *The Years of the City* and *Committee of Vigilance*. I know from my own study of urban renewal in Johnson City, TN, that the idea of renewal causing more harm than good—culturally and socially—had a while to go after 1968 before being legitimized.

Another act of demolition which Stewart attacks is its inverse—the destruction of estuarial areas by fill from demolition. ". . .[M]ore and more, a case is being made for swamps and tidal flats in the general ecology" (162). City planners should consider where demolition materials. "For instance, instead of mere filling-in of bodies of water, there might be use of fill to increase the complexity of shorelines, with resulting improvement of boating, fishing, and other recreation" (163).

Stewart begins his sections on air pollution with a quote from "a literary work entitled *Storm*, now almost old enough to be termed a classic" (165): "As a crab moves on the ocean-bottom but is of the water, so man rests his feet upon the earth—but lives in the air." The passage continues in words that might be considered, as of the time of writing, prophetic, "As water environs the crab, so air surrounds, permeates, and vivifies the body of man. If traces of noxious gas mingle with it, he coughs and his complexion turns deathly gray." (165) He points out that the passage, written in 1940, had in mind only military gas-warfare or some extremely unusual event. "Now, a quarter of a century later, though universal peace still seems as far away as ever, war is quite possibly a less critical problem than air pollution" (166). Since air pollution is necessary to industrial civilization, "The situation has quite possibly become irreversible, that is, the system, perhaps, cannot now be changed without the destruction, or serious crippling, of the civilization that depends upon the system . . ." (166).

Scott Dewey's excellent history of air pollution tells us that

> The shift in the popular mood toward more anti-corporate sentiments during the late 1960s and early 1970s gave promise that the old notion of leaving the problem to the experts in industry to fix voluntarily would henceforth be banished; from that time on the industries would have a powerful and persistent governmental and public presence policing their pollution and helping to keep them on the straight and narrow" (250-51).

However, as he admits, this "promise" was not, as the result of conservative, anti-environmental policies, aggressive industrial responses, and a globalized industrial economy, realized. From the perspective of today, Stewart's pessimism seems vindicated.

Such appears particularly true when we consider how many air pollution sources described by Stewart flourish today. He discusses atmospheric particulates (171-3); ozone, fluorides, and other airborne chemicals, the "monstrous progeny of urban concentrations" (180); auto, and all internal combustion engine emissions (". . .the capacity of the internal combustion engine to produce poisons seems to have destroyed its usefulness for civilization" [191]); power-plant emissions concentrated by topography, as in the Appalachians (193); and the "Ultimates," CO2 and atomic wastes (199 ff).

The CO2 is particularly serious: ". . .it traps heat by the process known in the archaic language of scientists as 'greenhouse effect'" (200). Prophetically, he ridicules what you can find in articles today—commercial advantages associated with global warming—and suggests the greenhouse effect's potential to disrupt climate, human habitation, melt polar ice, raise ocean levels. Of course, Stewart's concern with global warming did not originate with him. According to one of his sources, the 1965 *Report of the Environmental Pollution Panel* of the "President's Science Advisory Committee" "The possibility of climatic change resulting from changes in the quantity of atmospheric carbon dioxide" (113) was proposed as far back as 1899, and the report uses much statistical evidence to indicate an increase in atmospheric CO2 in the 20th century, including the polar ice melt (123). This CO2 study was directed by Stewart's oceanographic friend, Roger Revelle, and is also used as a source by Henry Still, whose *The Dirty Animal* (1967) is the nearest prototype of Stewart's book: ". . .[M]an's artificial production of this gas is overwhelming the delicate balance established and held by nature through countless centuries. The result may be a drastic change in the entire earth's atmosphere with disastrous consequences for the dirty animal who has brought the condition upon himself" (155).

The *Report* gives but slight attention to other forms of pollution that Stewart, perhaps thinking like a writer, considers very significant; one is noise.

> One of the greatest contrasts that we would notice, if transported in time to a city of some centuries ago, would be the unaccustomed, and therefore almost terrifying, silence. Shakespeare, working at a manuscript, would have had as disturbances only the minute scratching of his pen, occasional human voices, the clunk of a horse's hoof on a cobblestone, the yelp of a dog, perhaps a distant sound of trumpets. (211)

Another is visually perceived "ugliness" as a "problem of refuse." He does not see "beautification" in Lady Bird style, as a high priority. Beauty is in the eye of the beholder. But visual ugliness creates a psychological disturbance in that it suggests "disorder and impermanency" (213). "What we may call the ugliness of disorder and impermanency seems to be the psychological refuse-product of modern civilization" (215). This condition is not an attribute of human detritus on the earth alone. "Now in what can only be called an unnatural state of disorder, we live upon a largely 'skinned' earth" (214), whose bare surface is exposed. Even if the "average citizen" appears to accept this disorder, the apparent acceptance ". . .as a part of his civilization leads him to accept disorder as a natural state of affairs in his own life and in his relations to society" (215). This is what Deborah Winter, more contemporarily, calls the "psychology of overconsumption." "From my perspective, much of the abuse of our environment comes from the attempt to fulfill emotional and spiritual needs with material possessions, an attempt that results in both ecological and psychological deterioration" (262).

Stewart's take on this emphasizes less the overconsumption itself, and more the psychological dislocation produced by the effects, or the by-products, of overconsumption. "As a mere 'normal' by-product, however, our civilization subjects its people to destruction and destruction again, such as not even the hordes of Tamerlane could accomplish" (215). In *Man*, Stewart considered "conservatives," who "keep things from flying to pieces," complementary to "progressives" who keep the world from settling into "dull monotony" (275). Here, he says that "like any other species, man is necessarily conservative, needing a base of ordered solidity" (215). Hence, politically, the difference between "radical" and "conservative" is superficial: "Actually, they both cling about equally to building the futures of their lives upon the established habits of their already-experienced years" (216). The consequence is that the psychological effects of disorder and impermanence, of frantic mobility or landmark-destruction are very similar to those produced physically by pollution, and their joint victim is the individual.

> It is all part of a system which has its economic ends in view, and must subordinate to those ends the comfort and mental adjustment of the individual. By moving him to a new job the corporation, in fact, usually pays him more money. As in polluting the stream and poisoning the air, the basic action is normal and even laudable. No one considers the effect of the wastage. Finally perhaps, it may force itself on society by such

> mechanisms as juvenile delinquency, and 'nervous breakdown.' So also, no one paid attention to what was run into the streams until they became foul. (217)

Because there are so many such ramifications of refuse disposal problems, it "should therefore move to a high place among the concerns of civilized man" (220). As projected into the future, although "prophecy is a tricky trade," two aspects of this problem seem "most dangerous:" the "mass production of some violent poison," or the slow, accumulative disruption of civilization "pecked to death by ducks" (222). "Civilization, therefore, may meet its end, not from the increase of carbon monoxide or some pesticide, but from the decrease of honest, responsibility, and decency" (222).

In shadowing here an environmental ethics of moral self-interest, Stewart is somewhat of a John the Baptist. Roderick Nash has persuasively outlined how the "moral circle" was widened through the 1970's toward holism. In the early 70s, "Much of the [ethical] controversy turned on the question of whether environmental ethics were utilitarian and instrumental—derived from human self-interest—or whether nature possessed interests, value, or, perhaps, right which people ought to respect even at considerable personal sacrifice" (Nash 124). Stewart only by implication attaches "rights" to nature. However, he asserts a human moral self-destruction inherent in habituation to environmental destruction. And to prevent the former, it is suggested, the right of the latter *not* to be destroyed must be granted. ". . .Contractors eagerly seize upon the opportunity to fill a marsh, without any consideration of whether the marsh—as a needed link in a biological chain—should be preserved for its wildlife" (230). Whether "needed link" implies an ultimate beneficiary—humans—or whether the wildlife themselves are inherent beneficiaries is a distinction perhaps too subtle to be worth parsing.

One way in which the author widens the circle of his environmental concern is in his final emphasis on religion. He maintains that Judaism and Christianity "present a philosophy of production" (238), in harmony with the goals of "western Civilization." But he calls our attention to eschatology, and the tradition of Jehovah as Destroyer, about which "theologians appear to be a little shamefaced." In imagining a theology encompassing both creation and destruction, the author calls on us to offer praise to Shiva (239):

> In Hinduism equal share is given to the principle of getting rid of things. Of the great triad, if Brahma is the creator and Vishnu the preserver, Shiva is the destroyer, and his work is held equally essential. In fact, his worshipers assign him first place, pointing out that, being the destroyer, he is also creator. The new can burgeon forth and be young—only after the old has ceased to be.

The reactions to *Not So Rich As You Think* were diverse. Mariel S. Wellington advised Herb Caen, who, as a longtime friend of Stewart you would think to have known better, that the book was not by some Stewart of Davis, but by her neighbor and good friend George R. Stewart (Wellington to Caen 28 Sept. 1969). Charles Camp, maybe already feeling the risings of faith, said "You evidently don't feel that there is any particular plan for man's future here on earth. Get rid of that superstition and we may make things work better" (Camp to Stewart 22 Sept. 1969). James Fowler, Director of Public Relations for the Institute of Scrap Iron and Steel was dismayed by his chapter on junk (Fowler to Stewart 23 Sept. 1970). Whereas John C. Ledbetter, president of the "Whole Earth Corporation," apparently a pollution engineering company, praised Stewart's insight into pollution problems (Ledbetter to Stewart 15 Oct. 1970). And Robert Kennedy thanked him for the book (Kennedy to Stewart 22 Nov. 1967).

Stewart's book is also an early entry into the field of what Lawrence Buell has entitled "toxic discourse." Buell sees toxic discourse as manifesting itself most in figurative toxicity, but lots of Stewart's coverage of intangible waste, as in psychology and religion, is inherently figurative; he also, before it was "widely-shared," considers the toxicity of waste to be a "paradigm of cultural self-identification" (Buell *Writing* 53), and hence his urgency about its dangers.

*

Not So Rich As You Think may be considered, as Stewart himself appears to have considered it, his final and culminating environmental statement, but that does not mean his activity as a writer dwindled down after its publication. In fact, the very opposite was the case, for he was already launched on three projects which ultimately would fulfill his career in the realm of name studies. He was also writing shorter pieces and presenting papers related to his environmental concerns.

The most topical of the latter is a paper presented to the Friends of the Bancroft Library, "Historical Attitudes Toward the California Environment." He introduces it apologizing for his grandiose title with an anecdote about a professor whose friends determined that the three most popular current subjects were India, elephants, and sex-life. So he announced his (dull) subject's title as "The Sex-life of the Indian Elephant, and drew an immense audience" ("Historical").

Stewart's views are a bit more "radical" in this paper than in his book. He begins by asserting that most people's attitude toward any environment ". . .is to be unconsciously oblivious to it as an objective reality and to exploit it for short-term profit." However he extends this attitude to nonhuman organisms as well, using "California" examples of fermentational microorganisms in wine which poison themselves with their own alcohol, and beavers who level their own aspen groves. Humans, with higher intelligence, should presumably know better, but from the first Californian to today's the "attitude toward the environment was. . .the unconsciously ignoring of the environment as anything in itself."

Subsequently, Stewart presents four "organized attitudes" toward the environment in California. "Preservation" was the first, symbolized by Yosemite, but, as he says, the act establishing Yosemite as preserved space also insisted on "improvement," which meant "you cleared access roads, dug out trails, established campgrounds, and built a hotel." For 19th century preservationists, creating a "park" meant creating what a "park" meant in the 19th century—the equivalent of "an English gentleman's well-kept estate. . ." The second attitude, tied to the establishment of National Forests is "reservation," as they were designated initially "forest reserves." Reservation implies public access to public lands but also "ultimate change and expenditure." Thirdly, a term about which Stewart expresses ambivalence, is "conservation," as the designation of use for a movement flourishing roughly between 1920 and 1965, and represented by the Sierra Club. He sees it as in many ways a return to "preservation," and although successful in many cases, were stigmatized as "elite," thus alienating both their opponents, the business world, and potential allies, the average citizens.

Most importantly for his taxonomy here is the "fourth conscious attitude" of only the "last few years," which he names "restoration," eschewing the overused and misused term "ecology." "The tenets of this new movement differ strikingly from all of the preceding three. . .," in having no spatial limits, in attacking rather than defending, and not just in seeking to preserve but in ". . .taking something that now exists and changing it into something better." This latter goal really means returning things to a prior condition, so that we have something rare in America, "a massive movement that is philosophically reactionary," and one, which for the first time, involves large numbers of people.

Stewart goes on to apply these categories specifically to the signal event of California history. He presents the Gold Rush as an environmental phenomenon, creating an ecological catastrophe: razed forests, Indian genocide, polluted streams. "It is all one story. . . of what you do with something . . .after we get through with it, whether it is yesterday's newspaper, or a thousand cubic yards of hydraulic tailings, or the exhaust from your automobile." As in *Not So Rich*, he also connects waste intimately with "all our other pressing problems, such as increase of population, excessive urbanization, alienation of the individual from society, and eventually even with war, drugs, pestilence, racism, and starvation." He concludes with a declaration in which the "real Stewart," you might say, a man in the neighborhood of eighty years old, truly, and the only time I know of, comes out of the closet: "We should end the Vietnam War and the space-program, and not, then, cut taxes and return man-power to private industry. No, we should re-channel that energy to combat our many unescapable crises, of which one is the problem of the environment—in California and elsewhere."

Stewart also took his ecological concerns to another extreme. He was perhaps inspired by the illustrations to *Not So Rich* by popular cartoonist Robert Osborn, many of which are disturbingly comedic. He might also have seen parts of Joseph Meeker's *The Comedy of Survival: Studies in Literary Ecology*, the first text to use that term, published as a whole in 1974. To Meeker, "Literary comedy depicts the loss of equilibrium and its recovery" (25), the "loss of equilibrium" being cognate to the "disorder and impermanence" discussed in Stewart's book. "In the world as revealed by comedy," says Meeker, "the important thing is to live and to encourage life even though it is probably meaningless to do so" (26). Similarly, as Meeker elaborates it, based on somewhat *passe* climax ecology, "biology is also comic:" humor deters aggression, and is essential to interspecies bonds. It also follows principles of organization found in natural structures (27). One of Meeker's later commentators connects comedy with, in effect, cultural ecology: "Comic humanity is not free to manipulate or change is environment for its own benefit; with it is free to do is to use the laws of that environment to its own advantage, knowing that in doing so the chances of survival are increased" (Elgin 19).

Whether or not these connections between ecology and humor influenced him, Stewart wrote a series of "seriocomic verses on endangered species," which he entitled collectively *Ecological Eclogues,* and which he submitted to *The New Yorker.* Needless to say, the "Eclogues" have a professorial preface in which he defines the form, classically: "short poems on pastoral themes, graceful and pretty, with occasional mentions of only a few animals, chiefly sheep." Immediately he declares that his poems don't follow this formula, but that the words "ecology" and "eclogue" sound nice together. The poems are "Edwardian (or old fashioned)" in style. He isn't sure whether they are serious or humorous, since every thing seems "to mix tears and laughter inextricably." There is a "great sadness" about extinction, but extinction is in many ways natural, and "some creatures seem to be essentially comic in their very natures." "Besides, comedy—even if it provokes a laughter that is rather grim—is more social than tragedy" and who is going to read a series of dirges? All the creatures have been chosen from actual lists of endangered species.

Stewart is a little disingenuous here. He's being truly "politically incorrect" at the historical moment, and I can hardly believe he wasn't aware of the disturbing dissonance between tone and content in these poems. But in all his incidental poetry—maybe even in the comically overserious poems of *Sheep Rock*—Stewart writes with humor; it is his natural vein. And one could gloss Meeker in regard to the "cognitive dissonance" produced by these verses, since their tone forces you to laugh through your tears, if you will, in the interests of survival:

The Crocodile

I cannot love a crocodile;
I do not trust his toothy smile.

But I must hail him, "Welcome, stranger!"
Because the species is in danger.

The Leopard

The question is, "Why should we jeopard
The race of the Siberian leopard

To win our ladies cozy coat-skins?"
We might as well make use of goat-skins!

The goats, to date, show no elation
At this suggested surrogation.

Gorilla/Man

A scientific treatise states
The great ape rarely copulates.

His fate, therefore, cannot be blinked—
Gorillas will be soon extinct.

So too will man be in his season,
But for, I trust, another reason.

The New Yorker rejected *Ecological Eclogues.* But Stewart was understanding: "Having begun my profession[al] life as a writer of light verse for *Judge* and the old *Life*, I deserted that field for prose during a period of some fifty years. There may be a certain odor of Edwardianism about my present efforts (Stewart to Mary Phelps 21 Jan. 1974).

*

Stewart had earlier received another rejection, very tastefully made by Paul Brooks of his "Autobiography" (extensively quoted above) based on the first seven chapters. Brooks said it would be more appropriate as a family document (Brooks to Stewart 2 Mar. 1971). However, Stewart had little time to worry about these matters. He was deeply engaged throughout the 1970's on his three books for Oxford University Press, *American Place-Names,* the epic-length *Names on the Globe*, and *American Given Names.* The first, published in 1970, and the third, in 1978, remain standard reference texts in libraries everywhere. The second, a much more complicated book, was published in the year of his eightieth birthday (1975). By the time of *American Given Names* he had been deeply compromised by Parkinson's disease. "Of all my books, this is the one which was done under the greatest difficulty," he wrote his editor (Stewart to Caroline Taylor 21 Mar. 1978), although he was still capable of his usual wit, in discussing the new order of female given names in the American colonies: "No longer—and the Wife of Bath would have approved—was the prize set up for virginity" (15).

In 1972 Stewart had written to Paul Brooks about a new (never-to-be-published) novel *The Shakespeare Crisis*, which he "tore through . . . with spirit (in spite of my 77 years). It was to be set in the same university as *Doctor's Oral*, but with new problems (actually a faculty conflict over the authorship of

Shakespeare's plays) (Stewart to Brooks 11 July 1972). Apparently, the project never went further, since in 1973 he told Brooks he was already 2/3 of the way through *Names on the Globe* (Stewart to Brooks 20 May 1973).

As is usually the case, Stewart's "Author's Note" at the end of the text is a familiarly-written source for background information. For *Names on the Globe*, he explicitly states that his author's notes have been meant as personal and anti-scholarly. He says "Now in my eightieth year, having written for about thirty books those eloquent words 'The End,' I somewhat reluctantly turn my thought once more to composing something which is, anomalously, post-terminal" (393). Here, he describes his childhood fascination with names, and his adolescent inspiration from Isaac Taylor's *Words and Places*. He tells of the evolution of his work on names from his first research for *Names on the Land* in 1940. From 1945 on, he maintained a running file of world place-names, "Gradually. . .some conception of the present work began to take shape in my mind," and he was thinking of its title as early as 1950 (394). For the next two decades the work stood "somewhere in the tail of a lengthy waiting line of projects to be accomplished.. ."

When *American Place-names* was published in 1970, he realized that *Names on the Globe* had reached the head of the line. In December 1974, he wrote to Benjamin Lehman "I have finished a book . . . called Names on the Globe. I may wreck what reputation I may have by keeping on writing after I am too old. Oxford Press, however, likes this one very much. And, as usual, I am started on another" (Stewart to Lehman, 16 Dec. 1974/*L*).

The first two "Books" of *Names on the Globe* are extensions of an original project. Book I, "a kind of philosophy of place-naming," was initiated by his 1940 article "What is Named?" Book II elaborates his structure in "A Classification of Place-names" from *Names* (396). His final tribute in his "Notes" is to Theodosia "who might well be given the title Encourager of Books" (400).

Like *Names on the Land*, *Names on the Globe*, as well as a study in "onomatology," is one in cultural ecology. It explores, on a world scale, how humans create and relate to the identity of places. In the 1976 *Names* festschrift for Stewart, Madison Beeler characterizes this view of place; Stewart's works "manifest both a sense of place and a concern for the historical background which explain[s] the present" (77). Stewart says at the outset, "A sense of place is older than man. What is a 'haunt' or a 'lair' but a place known and remembered—known, remembered, and set apart from other places?" (3). He defines "place" as "any area which an observing consciousness, whether human or animal, distinguishes and separates, by whatever means, from other areas" (4). As to what is chosen to bear a name, Stewart uses his earlier formulated "Principle of Entity and Use." Entity is the recognition of the separateness of the place from others; use refers not only to the usefulness of the place, but also to the usefulness of the name of the place, since it may well be valuable to humans to identify by name places that are, for example, useless or dangerous (10-11).

Stewart's idea of the "what" in "what is named?" is subjective and multivalent, since one name can refer to differently-defined entities, depending on the namer. This is particularly true of human-created structures, for example, the name of a town, which could refer to its legal entity, its physical extent, or its inhabitants (11). "What is named" can also be divided into "feature-names" and "habitation-names," the former generally "hydronymous,' referring to water-featured, or "oronymous" referring to prominent land-features (13).

The next issue relates strongly to the name-history in *Names on the Land*, to wit, place-name density: the number of names for any defined unit of space. The number of named places is "appallingly large;" in 1945 the U.S. Board of Geographic Names estimated there were 31/2 billion names in the world (16). Throughout the world, however, most place-names follow a specific + generic pattern, as in "Thunder + mountain" (21). They also play on a culture/nature interface. One side of this is the survival, alteration, or extinction of names when one namer culture replaces another; the other is the survival, alteration, or extinction of names when the place named ceases to exist. In another mode is the transmission of "tribal" names to places, or places to tribes.

Stewart identifies numerous other "habits of thought" which seemingly apply to all human namers. These are notable for being often "habits" that apply to intra-cultural uses of language, as well as cultural naming of places. For example, the "Principle of Point of View," refers to the directional naming of places based on the position of the namer relative to the place. Stewart's example is the North Sea, which, logically, should be called by Britons the East Sea (79). Another form of cultural imposition is in the different types of "descriptive names." The namer chooses a particular feature of a place as the prominent one, and although there are other features present, obviously, the name is derived from the one chosen as prominent. The modes of descriptive naming he enumerates range from the literal to the figurative—from a sense perception to a likeness perception, as, in the latter case, when a mountain looks like a camel's hump it becomes Camel Mountain (93).

A cultural naming system we have seen Stewart refer to earlier with respect to the American West is "incident names." A "cultural event" of any type—from a powwow to a murder—that takes place in a particular locale may be incorporated as the name of that locale. As Stewart has pointed out in other writings, the incident itself may be totally forgotten, but the name remains. "Possessive" names involve an even greater imposition of cultural phenomena on natural; the famous one Stewart discusses in *Names on the Land* is "Bronx" from "Bronk's" farm. I think there is a great difference between incident-names and possessive names, since the incident is time-limited but the possession is, in theory if not in fact, forever, and therefore implies that the place is somehow inseparable from its possessor. Stewart considers that "With habitation-names the tendency of survival for possessives is especially strong" (113). Stewart was not to live to see his own name figure in one of his categories of name-types, "commendatory names," since Stewart Peak near Donner Pass did not receive its name until 1984.

The latter half of *Names on the Globe* provides a historical overview of naming cultures, from the Egyptians to the present. Stewart's discussion of the current status of naming is particularly significant, since it is his last official word on the subject. He considers that the U.S. in the later 20th century is still "highly primitive in its name-pattern," and that the density of U.S. names is bound to increase. But some specific tendencies are notable in contemporary naming. Increasing nationalism increases official methods of naming, and therefore moves naming away from the descriptive and more towards commemoration or commendation. Also, new terrains for naming have emerged following World War II. Stewart specifically mentions ocean-bottom features and the independent status of new nations.

*

Despite his physical disabilities, Stewart was mentally and socially active to the end of his life. While at the Sequoias he belonged to numerous clubs, including "The Club," to whose members he and Charles Camp presented numerous papers. His eightieth birthday was highly recognized and commemorated. Josephine Miles sent him a poem:

> I admire greatly
> Even though belately
> That you are eightly
> Grand and Stately

(Miles to Stewart 1975?)

Old friends did not forget him. Malcolm Cowley was born and grew up near Stewart's Indiana, served in World War I, and was a lifelong intellectual friend. His wife Muriel wrote an affectionate Christmas letter in 1975, since her husband was too busy writing book reviews. She congratulated him on the nature trail that had been named for him at Thornton Beach State Park. "Over Thanksgiving, when we had overnight guests for four nights, I took a Valium each night." She was aghast that the next president might be "Hubert Humperdinck" or Ronald Reagan. "Lord have mercy on us. The thought makes me feel tangled in chicken wire, tar, and feathers" (Muriel Cowley to George and Theodosia Stewart, 14 Dec. 1975). He was consulted as a sage. "I wonder if you would be so kind as to write me your answer to the question 'Will Civilization, as we know it, survive the century?'" (George Hassler to Stewart 27 Feb. 1979).

One amusing activist campaign he waged at the Sequoias was for the permission to drink wine in the dining room. He demanded it as a "personal freedom" issue; freedom being a right even of the elderly (Stewart to "Mr. Irvin" 25 Mar. 1971). When he got no satisfaction he wrote to his Representative, Leo McCarthy, of the House Committee on Aging, urging the rights of the elderly and that they be given representation on the boards of directors of nursing homes (Stewart to McCarthy 10 June 1974). He collaborated with John Caldwell's pamphlet on him for Boise State University's Writers of the West series. "As a general principle, don't put off anything that you want to do with a man who has just passed [his] 84th birthday" (Stewart to Caldwell 19 October 1978).

And many of his former students wrote to him about the impact he had had on their lives as writer and teacher. San Francisco lawyer Daniel T. Goldberg was happy to read in Herb Caen's column that he was alive and well "I was a student in your first-year English class at U.C. in 1932 or 33" (Goldberg to Stewart 20 Sept. 1979). Florence Little had owed him an apology since 1929: she was the first of his Middle English students to take the M.A. oral and did badly (Little to Stewart 16 Sept. 1979). "I was at UC as a student from 1950-52 and I remember your courageous opposition to the Loyalty Oath. Through your works, I feel as if I had known you for 30 years" (Maury and Jenny Dunbar to Stewart 19 Apr. 1979). Alan McGregor, a current graduate student at Berkeley, told him he'd become addicted to his writing, and that *Earth Abides* was being taught in two courses that year (McGregor to Stewart 11 Jan. 1979). Willard B. Moore wanted to talk with him about *Earth Abides,* calling it a novel ahead of its time, and a forerunner of the "ethnographic novel" [whatever that might be]. A note from Stewart says "I wondered what became of you" (Moore to Stewart 10 May 1975). Three months before his death, Frank Craig of Edinburgh, identifying himself as a 54-year-old deck officer on Chevron tankers wrote a fan letter about *Storm,* which he had read many times (Craig to Stewart 31 May 1980).

One student was just too late. David Livingstone, a high school senior wrote "I, like many before me and probably many after, want to make a profound change in my environment. Basically, I would like to change the world" (Livingstone to Stewart 13 August 1980). Two weeks later he had to send a letter of apology: "I never met your husband but of all the people in the world who have ever lived, I would like to have talked with him and Socrates" (Livingstone to Theodosia Stewart, n.d.).

It might be most in Stewart's spirit, though, to close this work not elegaically, but with what may be his last published writing, a work of witty nostalgia entitled "Fireside Chat." Here he recalls the 1920's English Department at Berkeley, and the hope of every lecturer and doctoral student then to climb the ladder to tenure. Unfortunately, the system of advancement "gave an opportunity for personal favoritism, as natural friendships over the course of several years developed between professors and graduate students." In order to create a more merit-rewarding system, around 1927, chair Willard Durham arranged to publish through the university press an annual English Department volume on a broad literary subject. 'Then, during the year we would meet in each others' houses and one of us (regularly the host) would read a paper as his contribution to the volume. The gathered scholars would then discuss and criticize the essay. To conclude a pleasant evening, there would be an offering of cookies and coffee (These were Volstead times, and a professor, whatever his opinion, rarely had any money for even bootleg gin)."

At this point, he introduces the idea of fire—in terms of fires he's experienced in his 60 years in the Bay Area, and as in the phrase "to dismiss from a job." Then we meet the "new face" in the Department, "a very young instructor whom I shall call Harold Robertson." Robertson was not married, but he did have a mother. "Naturally, she was much devoted to her brilliant son. They lived in a modest little cottage to the south of the campus, a quiet and rather lovely place to live in those days. . ." When Harold's turn to read a paper came, they met at the cottage; the mother would fix the refreshments. It was a mild spring evening.

Unfortunately "the room was oven-like. . .The chimney was drawing excellently, and the flames rushed upward." The attendees opened windows, which made the fire even hotter. A second phenomenon was, on a side table, "a superb display of cookies, sweet cakes, and scones." These things told the same story: Mrs. Robertson, "seeing to it to give Harold a worthy introduction, . . .had possibly overstepped a little."

"Then, Macbeth-like, came the knocking at the door." Harold, displeased, answered it. The visitor said. "'I'm sorry . . .to disturb you, I know you're having company this evening.' Then, with just a shade more emphasis, "'But your house is on fire!'"

"Never have I heard a better line," says Stewart, "or one more fittingly delivered. . .During a long moment I had a horrible idea that we were going to perish, but with honor." Stewart went outside, and, for the only time in his life, he says, the whole department followed him. The fire department arrived, extinguished the fire, but great clouds of soot poured out on everything including thc Scottish pastry.

*

George Rippey Stewart died on August 22, 1980 at the age of 85. On the day of his birth, the big news was the dedication of a funerary monument in a Chicago cemetery to the Confederates who died in Chicago prisons during the Civil War. Veterans from both sides were present, and there were "many patriotic utterances" ("Blue's"). On the day of his death, Islamic militants were demanding freedom for Kashmir, Billy Carter was denying he had lobbied for Libya, and the ACLU accused the Justice Department of illegally jailing foreign nationals. Stewart's *New York Times* obituary characterized him as "a prolific novelist and scholar whose interests embraced literature, the sciences and the humanities" ("Scholar"). He was remember in a memorial service attended by 300, after which the Berkeley carillon played his favorite songs, such as "Sweet Betsy from Pike" and "On Top of Old Smokey" ("Class Notes" 17 Nov. 1980).

For a while in the early 1980's, Bob Lyon tried to establish a George R. Stewart section at the Western Literature Association Conference. He planned elaborate conference activities for the Friends of George R. Stewart, particularly a week of events at the 1984 Reno WLA meeting. A newsletter and membership lists (presumably sent to Theodosia Stewart, includes Ken and Pat Carpenter, Victor Moiterot, and the Vales as members; one has as a letterhead "The George R. Stewart Fan Club of Silver City" (16 Feb. 1983; 24 Apr. 1984).

In October 1984 the United States Board of Geographic Names designated a 7,389-foot mountain a half-mile from Donner Pass, in Nevada County, CA as George R. Stewart Peak ("George R. Stewart Peak; "Class Notes" 21 Nov. 1984). In 2005, Jonathan Yardley, *Washington Post* book critic, wrote an excellent article on the Horatio Hornblower novels by Stewart's great friend, C. S. Forester, in a series where he "reconsiders notable and/or neglected books." I Emailed Mr. Yardley, suggesting that Stewart would be a good subject for his series. He graciously replied that he didn't know Stewart's work, but would keep an eye out for it (Email to the author 28 Dec. 2005).

The words Yardley uses to characterize the Hornblower saga could characterize Stewart's work as well: "elegantly written, profoundly intelligent, historically and factually accurate, and deeply humane. It is that rare and precious thing that entertains while it enriches." To which we might add Wallace Stegner's valediction:

> As historian or novelist, anthropologist or pundit of place-naming, he is consistently an expositor and defender of the human capacity for cooperation and organization and long memory which flowers as civilization. His books teach us who we are, and how we got to be who we are. (Stegner *Where* 171)

Bibliography

Primary Sources in the Bancroft Library, University of California, Berkeley

A. George R. Stewart Collection, MSS. C-H 13, 70/88 (excluding correspondence)

"American Riots—Before Watts." Typescript.
"Autobiography." Typescript and Handwritten MS.
"Greek Colonies and the Thirteen Colonies." Typescript
"Ecological Eclogues." Typescript.
"Historical Attitudes Toward the California Environment." Typescript.
"If." Typescript.
"Rereading Notes." Typescript and Handwritten MS.
"Travel Diary." Handwritten MS.

B. "The Club" Collection

"Random Thoughts on Doom." Typescript.

C. Regional Oral History Office

A Little Of Myself. Typescript Oral History. "Diverse Memoirs" series. Suzanne B. Riess, interviewer. Intro. James D. Hart. University of California: Regional Oral History Office, 1972.

Other Primary Sources

A. Princeton University, Seeley G. Mudd Manuscript Library

George R. Stewart Alumni File

B. East Bay Municipal Utility District

Berryman Reservoir correspondence

Published Materials
Books

American Given Names: Their Origin and History in the Context of the English Language. New York: Oxford U P, 1979.

American Place-names: A Concise and Selective Dictionary for the Continental United States of America. New York: Oxford U P, 1970.
American Ways of Life. Garden City NY: Doubleday, 1954.
Bret Harte: Argonaut and Exile. [1935]. New York: Kennicott, 1959.
The California Trail. New York: McGraw-Hill, 1962.
Committee of Vigilance: Revolution in San Francisco, 1851. Boston: Houghton, Mifflin, 1964.
Doctor's Oral. New York: Random, 1939.
Donner Pass, and Those Who Crossed It. Menlo Park, CA: Lane, 1964.
Earth Abides. [1949]. New York: Fawcett, 1976.
East of the Giants. [1938]. New York: Ballantine 1971.
English Composition: A Laboratory Course. 2 vols. New York: Holt, 1936.
The English Department of the University of California at Berkeley. Berkeley: U of California P, 1968.
Fire. New York: Random, 1948.
Good Lives. Boston: Houghton, Mifflin, 1967.
John Phoenix, Esq. The Veritable Squibob: A Life of Captain George H. Derby, U.S.A. New York: Holt, 1937.
Modern Metrical Technique as Illustrated in Ballad Meter (1700-1920). New York: n.p., 1922.
Man: An Autobiography. New York: Random, 1946.
Map of the Emigrant Road from Independence, Mo. To San Francisco, California, by T. H. Jefferson. Ed. George R. Stewart. San Francisco: California Historical Society, 1945.
N.A. 1—Looking North. Boston: Houghton, Mifflin, 1957.
N.A. 1—Looking South. Boston: Houghton, Mifflin, 1957.
Names on the Globe. New York: Oxford U P, 1975.
Names on the Land: A Historical Account of Place-Naming in the United States. New York: Random, 1943.
- - -. n.p.: Editions for the Armed Services, Inc., 1945
- - -. Rev. Ed. Boston: Houghton, Mifflin, 1958.
Not So Rich As You Think. Boston: Houghton, Mifflin, 1968.
The Opening of the California Trail. Berkeley: U of California P, 1953.
Ordeal By Hunger. New York: Holt, 1936.
- - -. Rev. Ed. New York: Ace, 1960.
Pickett's Charge: A Microhistory of the Final Attack at Gettysburg, July 3, 1863. Boston: Houghton, Mifflin, 1959.
Recollections of old Times in California or, California Life in 1843, by William Henry Thomes. Ed. George R. Stewart. U of California: Friends of the Bancroft Library, 1974.
"Stevenson in California: A Critical Study." Thesis U of California, 1920.
Storm. New York: Random, 1941.
- - -. New York: Random, 1947 (Modern Library edition).
Take Your Bible in One Hand: The Life of William Henry Thomes. . .

San Francisco: Colt P, 1939.
The Technique of English Verse. [1930]. Port Washington, NY: Kennicott, 1966.
U.S. 40: Cross Section of the United States of America. Boston: Houghton, Mifflin, 1953.
The Year of the Oath: The Fight for Academic Freedom at the University of California. Garden City, NY: Doubleday, 1950.
The Years of the City. Boston: Houghton, Mifflin, 1955.
This California. (photographs by Michael Bry) San Francisco: Diablo P, 1965.

Periodical and Anthology Publications

"The All-American Season." *New York Times Magazine* 24 Sept. 1944: 18, 35.
"The Bad Old Summer Time." *New York Times Magazine* 25 June 1944: 20-42.
"A Ballade of Railroad Folders." *Life* 19 Feb. 1920: 307.
"The Basin and Desert." *The American Heritage Book of Natural Wonders.* Ed. Alvin M. Josephy, Jr. New York: Simon and Schuster, 1963. 305-352.
"The Beleaguered Wagon Train." *The Pacific Spectator* 4.3 (1950). 320-322.
"A Biography of Scott Fitzgerald and the Age He Exemplified." Review of Arthur Mizener, *The Far Side of Paradise: A Biography of F. Scott Fitzgerald. San Francisco Chronicle: This World* 28 Jan. 1951: 16-17.
"Blood Against Water." *The High School Item* Mar. 1913: 5-8.
"Bret Harte on the Frontier: A New Chapter of Biography." *Southwest Review* 11.3 (1926). 265-272.
"California." "The Careful Young Men: Tomorrow's Leaders Analyzed by Today's Teachers." *Nation* 9 Mar. 1957: 208-9.
"A Classification of Place Names." *Names* 2.1 (1954). 1-13.
"Color in Science and Poetry." *The Scientific Monthly* Jan. 1930: 71-78.
"The Field of the American Name Society." *Names* 1.2 (1953). 73-78.
"The Drama in a Frontier Theater." *The Parrott Presentation Volume.* 1935. New York: Russell and Russell, 1967. 183-204.
"Fireside Chat." *California Monthly* Oct. 1978: 2, 10.
"Fulbrighting in Greece." *Harpers* Oct. 1953: 75-80.
"Gunfire to Westward: The Pacific Coast in Wartime." *Mademoiselle* June 1942: 37, 80-82.
"How Cities Get Those Funny Names." *Science Digest* 19-5 (1946). 26-28.
"The Iambic-Trochaic Theory in Relation to Musical Notation of Verse." *JEGP* 24 (1925). 61-71.
"'Iron-Hewer' or 'Man of Toft'?". *New York Times Magazine* 4 Apr. 1952: 17.
"The Knights at Rhodes." *The Nassau Literary Magazine* 70.2 (1914). 128
"The Moral Chaucer." *Essays in Criticism by Members of the Department of English, University of California.* Berkeley: U of California P, 1929. 91-109.
"In Memoriam C.S. Forester 1899-1966. *Names* 14.4 (1966). 249-50.
"It Pays to Watch the Sky." *Nation's Business* 34.11 (1946). 50-52.

"Popular Names for the Mountain Sheep." *American Speech* 10.4 (1935). 283-288.
"*Leah, Woods,* and Deforestation as an Influence on Place-Names." *Names* 19.1 (1962). 11-20.
"McGinnity's Rock." *Esquire* Jan. 1947: 102-104.
"The Meter of *Piers Plowman.*" *PMLA* 42 (1927). 113-128.
"Mexico by Ear." *California Monthly* Apr. 1938: 8-10, 24-25.
"Mountains of the West 3—South Central Panorama." *Ford Times* Mar. 1949: 31-36.
"Murder and Onomatology." *The Nation* 9 Apr. 1960: 313-316.
"Names." *Idea and Experiment* 4.7 (1954). 7-9.
"Names on the Land." *Life* 2 July 1945: 47-55.
"Naming of Towns, Rivers, and Mountains." *Esquire* July 1945: 100-104.
"Nomenclature of Stream-Forks on the West Slope of the Sierra Nevada." *American Speech* 14.3 (1939). 191-7.
"The Novelists Take Over Poetry." *Saturday Review* 8 Feb. 1941: 3-4, 18-19.
"On University Government." Berkeley Chapter, American Association of University Professors Oct. 1960.
"One of 120,000. *Holiday* Nov. 1947: 66-70, 130-131.
"A Proposal for Forest Demonstration Areas Along Highways." *Journal of Forestry* 48.5 (1950). 356-359.
"The Regional Approach to Literature." *College English* 9.7 (1948). 370-375.
"Report on the Nation." *New York Times Magazine* 8 Aug. 1943: 14-15, 27.
"The Rivers of America." *Saturday Review* 30 Dec. 1939: 12-13.
"San Carlos Day." *Scribner's Magazine* 68.2 (1920). 209-211.
"Sonnet." *The Nassau Literary Magazine* 73.2 (1917). 84.
"Time's Petty Pace." *Esquire* Nov. 1946: 105-107.
"Travelers by 'Overland'." *The American West* 5.4 (1968). 4-12.
"The Two Moby-Dicks." *American Literature* 25.4 (1954). 417-448.
"The United States Army Ambulance Corps." *The Princeton Pictorial Review* 6.3 (1918). 64-67.
"Twilight of the Printed Book." *The Pacific Spectator*. 3.1 (1949). 36-39.
"The West as Seen from the East." *A Literary History of the United States.* Ed. Robert E. Spiller, *et. al.* Rev. Ed. New York: Macmillan, 1960. 771-777.
"What's In a Name?" *Children* Dec. 1927: 22-23, 62.
- - - and Joe Backus. "'Each in its Ordered Place:' Structure and Narrative in 'Benjy's Section' of *The Sound and the Fury.*" *American Literature* 29.4 (1958). 440-454.

Secondary Sources

Abrams, Charles. *The City is the Frontier.* New York: Harper, 1965.
Adam, Barbara. "Time and the Environment." Redclift, Michael, and Graham Woodgate, eds. *The International Handbook of Environmental Sociology.*

Northampton, MA: Edward Elgar, 19997. 169-78.

Adams, Ansel. "Authentic Account of the Donner Party." Review of George R. Stewart, *Ordeal by Hunger. Sierra Club Bulletin* Feb. 1936: 114-115.

Adams, Rachel. "Ishi's Two Bodies: Anthropology and Popular Culture." *Ishi in Three Centuries.* Ed. Karl Kroeber and Clifton Kroeber. Lincoln: U of Nebraska P, 2003. 18-34.

Allen, Brooke. "G. A. Henty and the Vision of Empire." *The New Criterion* 20.8 (2002). 20-24.

"Alumni Plea for UC." *Oakland Tribune* 23 May 1969: 1, F7.

Amazon.com."Books: Earth Abides." 24 Oct. 2005 <http://www.amazon.com/Gp/product/1417617861/103-4149821 5696639?v=glance&N=2. . .>.

American Forestry Association. *Proceedings of the Fourth American Forestry Congress.* Washington: American Forestry Association, 1953.

An American Soldier. *Before I Die.* Los Angeles: Circle-V P, 1942.

Appel, Benjamin. *The People Talk.* New York: Dutton, 1940.

Arnold, Guy. *Held Fast for England: G. A. Henty, Imperialist Boys' Writer.* London: Hamish Hamilton, 1980.

Ashley, Leonard R. N. *George Alfred Henty and the Victorian Mind.* San Francisco: International Scholars, 1999.

Atherton, Gertrude. 1902. *The Splendid Idle Forties: Stories of Old California.* Ridgewood, NJ: Gregg P, 1968.

Backus, Joe. "George R. Stewart on Names of His Characters." *Names* 9.1 (1961). 53-57.

Bancroft, Hubert Howe. *California Pastoral, 1769-1848. The Works of Hubert Howe Bancroft.* 35. San Francisco: The History Company, 1888.

Barbour, Michael G. "Ecological Fragmentation in the Fifties." *UncommoGround: Rethinking the Human Place in Nature.* Ed. William Cronon. New York: Norton,1996. 233-255.

Barnes, Harry Elmer and Oreen M. Ruedi. *The American Way of Life: An Introduction to the Study of Contemporary Society.* 2nd ed. New York: Prentice-Hall, 1950.

Bates, Marston. "Man as an Agent in the Spread of Organisms." *Man's Role in Changing the Face of the Earth.* Ed. William L. Thomas. Chicago: U of Chicago P,1956. 788-806.

Beatley, Timothy and Kristy Manning. *The Ecology of Place: Planning for Environment, Economy, and Community.* Washington: Island P, 1997.

Bedichek, Roy. *Adventures with a Texas Naturalist.* Garden City, NY: Doubleday, 1950.

Beeler, Madison S. "George R. Stewart, Toponymist." *Names* 24.2 (1976). 77-85.

Begeman, Jean. "Loyalty Oaths for Teachers." *New Republic* 10 Oct. 1949: 15-16.

Bell, Ian. *Dreams of Exile: Robert Louis Stevenson: A Biography.* New York: Holt, 1993.

Benedict, Ruth. 1934. *Patterns of Culture*. New York: Penguin, 1946.
Bennett, John W. *The Ecological Transition: Cultural Anthropology and Human Adaptation.* New York: Pergamon, 1976.
"Berkeley Will Study Bond Vote." *Oakland Tribune* 24 Jan. 1967: n. pag.
Bishop, John Peale. *Green Fruit*. Boston: Sherman, French, 1917.
---."Princeton." Wilson, Edmund, ed. *The Collected Essays of John Peale Bishop*. 1948. New York: Octagon, 1975. 391-400.
"Blue's Tribute to Gray." *New York Times* 31 May 1895: 1.
Bookchin, Murray. *The Philosophy of Social Ecology: Essays on Dialectical Naturalism.* 2nd. ed. Montreal: Black Rose Books, 1995.
Boyer, Paul. *By the Bomb's Early Light: American Thought and Culture at the Dawn of the Atomic Age.* New York: Pantheon, 1985.
Bradley, David. *No Place To Hide.* Boston: Little, Brown, 1948.
Branch, E. Douglas. Review of George R. Stewart, *Bret Harte: Argonaut and Exile. Mississippi Valley Historical Review* 19.1 (1932). 132-133.
Brisbane, Albert. 1840. *The Social Destiny of Man, or, The Association and Reorganization of Industry.* New York: Burt Franklin, 1968.
Brooks, C. E. P. *Climate Through the Ages: A Study of the Climatic Factors and their Variations.* 2nd ed. London: Ernest Benn, 1949.
Bruccoli, Matthew J. and Jackson R. Breyer, eds. *F. Scott Fitzgerald in His Own Time. A Miscellany.* Kent, OH: Kent State U P, 1971.
- - -. *Some Sort of Epic Grandeur: The Life of F. Scott Fitzgerald.* New York: Harcourt, Brace, Jovanovich, 1981.
Bryan, Richard. "Testimony." *Wild Nevada: Testimonies on Behalf of the Desert.* Ed. Roberta Moore and Scott Slovic. Reno: U of Nevada P, 2005. 90-94.
Bryson, Christopher. *The Fluoride Deception.* New York: Seven Stories P, 2004.
Bryson, Michael A. *Visions of the Land: Science, Literature, and the American Environment from the Era of Exploration to the Age of Ecology.* Charlottesville: U P of Virginia, 2002.
Buell, Lawrence. *The Future of Environmental Criticism: Environmental Crisis and the Literary Imagination.* Oxford: Blackwell, 2005.
- - -. *Writing for an Endangered World: Literature, Culture, and Environment in the United States and Beyond.* Reno: U of Nevada P, 2005.
Bunting, Robert. "The Environment and Settler Society in Western Oregon." *The American West: Interactions, Intersections, and Injunctions.* Ed. Gordon M. Bakken and Brenda Farrington. New York: Garland, 2000. 109-128.
Burgess, Ernest W. 1925. "The Growth of the City: An Introduction to a Research Project." *The City*. Ed. Robert E. Park *et. al.* Chicago: U of Chicago P, 1967. 47-62.
Burman, Ben Lucien. *It's a Big Country: America off the Highways.* New York:

Reynal, 1956.

Buscovici, John F. *Indiana County*. Charleston, SC: Arcadia, 2003.

Caldwell, John. *George R. Stewart.* Boise: Boise State U P, 1981.

California Forestry Study Committee. *The Forest Situation in California*. Vol. 2 (1947). 19 Oct. 2005. <http://www.dharmacould.com/jackson/histdocs/FORSIT.html>.

Callenbach, Ernest. "Foreword." Stewart, George R. 1941. *Storm.* Berkeley: Heyday Books, 2003. vii-xv.

"Camp Upton." Brookhaven National Laboratory: Brookhaven History. 10 Sept. 2005. http://www.bnl.gov/bnlweb/histoy/camp_upton1.asp.

Campbell, Craig. "In George R. Stewart's Footsteps: Revisiting U. S. 40 in Missouri and Kansas." *Focus* 46.1 (2000). 23-31.

Canby, Henry Seidel. "Storm by George R. Stewart." Review of George R. Stewart, *Storm. Book-of-the-Month Club News* Nov. 1941: n. p.

Carpenter, Niles. *The Sociology of City Life.* New York: Longmans, Green, 1932.

Carroll, Joseph. *Evolution and Literary Theory.* Columbia: U of Missouri P, 1995.

Carson, Rachel. *Always, Rachel: The Letters of Rachel Carson and Dorothy Freeman, 1952-1964.* Ed. Martha Freeman. Boston: Beacon, 1995.

- - -. 1955. *The Edge of the Sea.* New York: Signet, 1963.

Castro, Adam-Troy. Review of George R. Stewart, *Earth Abides.* Classic Sci-Fi. 24 Oct. 2005. http://www.scifi.com/sfw/issue240/Classic.html.

Chesson, Peter L. 'Environmental Variation and the Coexistence of Species." *Community Ecology.* Ed Jared Diamond and Ted. J. Case. New York: Harper, 1986. 240-256.

"City that Never Was." Review of George R. Stewart, *The Years of the City. Time* 29 Aug. 1955: 90-91.

Clark, Ella E. "Forest Lookout." *National Geographic Magazine* July 1946: 73-96.

Clark, Michael. "Bret Harte's 'The Outcasts of Poker Flat' and the Donner Pass Tragedy." *Short Story* 1.2 (1993), 49-56.

Clarke, Gilmore D. "The Design of Motorways." *Highways in our National Life: A Symposium,* Ed. Jean Labatut and Wheaton J. Lane. Princeton: Princeton U P, 1950. 299-308.

"Class Notes." *Princeton Alumni Weekly.* 24 Apr. 1931: n. pag.

- - -. *Princeton Alumni Weekly.* 11 Nov. 1938: n. pag.

- - -. *Princeton Alumni Weekly.* 8 July 1949: n. pag.

- - -. *Princeton Alumni Weekly* 10 Feb. 1970: n. pag.

- - -. *Princeton Alumni Weekly* 17 Nov. 1980: n. pag.

- - -. *Princeton Alumni Weekly* 21 Nov. 1984: n. pag.

Collier, Richard. *The Plague of the Spanish Lady: The Influenza Pandemic of 1918-19.* New York: Atheneum, 1974.

Commager, Henry Steele. *The American Mind: An Interpretation of American*

Thought and Character Since the 1880's. New Haven: Yale U P, 1950.
Coppel, Alfred. *Dark December*. Greenwich, CT: Fawcett, 1960.
Crane, Clarkson. 1925. *The Western Shore.* Salt Lake City: Peregrine Smith, 1985.
Croker, Robert A. *Stephen Forbes and the Rise of American Ecology.* Washington: Smithsonian Institution P, 2001.
Crosby, Alfred W. *Epidemic and Peace, 1918.* Westport, CT: Greenwood, 1976.
"Current Poetry." *The Literary Digest*. 24 June 1916, n. pag.
Dague, Charles I. "The Weather of the Great Tillamook, Oregon, Fire of August 1933."*Monthly Weather Review* July 1934: 227-231.
Daiches, David. *Robert Louis Stevenson and His World.* London: Thames and Hudson, 1973.
Davis, Mike. *Ecology of Fear: Los Angeles and the Imagination of Disaster*. New York: Random, 1998.
Dewey, Donald. *James Stewart: A Biography.* Atlanta: Turner, 1996.
Dewey, Scott Hamilton. *Don't Breathe the Air: Air Pollution and U.S. Environmental Politics, 1945-70.* College Station: Texas A & M U P, 2000.
Dirks, Tom. Review of *It's a Gift.* http://www.filmsite.org/itsag3.html.
Dodd, Chuck. *Chuck Dodd's Guide to Getting Around in the Black Rock Desert and High Rock Canyon.* Chilcoot, CA: 19th Century Publications, 2004.
Dodds, George T. Review of George R. Stewart, *Earth Abides*. SF Site. 24 Oct 2005. http://www.sfsite.com/lla/ea92.htnm.
Dos Passos, John. *The Prospect Before Us.* London: Lehmann, 1951.
Douglass, William O. *Points of Rebellion*. New York: Vintage, 1970.
Dowling, David. *Fictions of Nuclear Disaster.* Iowa City: U of Iowa P, 1987.
Downey, Fairfax. *The Guns at Gettysburg.* New York; McKay, 1958.
Drucker, Peter F. *The New Society: An Analysis of the Industrial Order*. New York: Harper, 1950.
Duffus, R. L. "As the Wheel Turns: 3,091 Miles of America." Review of George R. Stewart, *U.S. 40. New York Times Book Review* 15 Mar. 1953: 3.
Dunham, H. Warren. *The City in Mid-Century: Prospects for Human Relations in the Urban Environment.* Detroit: Wayne State U P, 1957.
"The Earth Abides." *Escape*. 5 Nov. 1950; 11 Nov. 1950.
EBMUD Reservoir Replacement Project. "Berryman Reservoir Replacement." 12 July2005. <http://www.ebmud.com/water_&_environment/water_supply/current/_projects/berryman/htm>.
Egan, Timothy. "Era of the Big Fire is Kindled at West's Doors." *New York Times* 22 July 2005. http://nytimes.com/2002/06/23/national/23FIRE.html.

Eisenhower, Dwight D. "To Help Solve the Fearful Atomic Dilemma." *Profile of America: An Autobiography of the USA.* 4th ed. Comp. Emily Davie. New York: Grosset and Dunlap, 1960. 133-135.

Eley, Thomas and Cherie Northon. "The Geography of the Russell Fence." *The Geographical Review* (2003). 114-124.

Elgin, Don D. *The Comedy of the Fantastic: Ecological Perspectives on the Fantasy Novel.* Westport, CT: Greenwood P, 1985.

Ellis, Agnes L. *Lights and Shadows of Sewickley Life, or Memories of Sweet Valley.* Philadelphia: Lippincott, 1893.

England, Martha W. "Teaching *The Sound and the Fury.*" *College English* 18.4 (1957). 221-224.

English, Paul W. and Robert C. Mayfield. "Ecological Perspectives." *Man, Space, and Environment: Concepts in Contemporary Human Geography.* Ed. Paul W. English and Robert C. Mayfield. New York: Oxford U P, 1972. 115-119.

Fenn, G[eorge] Manville. *George Alfred Henty: The Story of an Active Life.* London: Blackie, 1907.

"The '59ers Find Promised Land." *Life* 30 Nov. 1959: 49-52.

Fisher, Vardis. *The Mothers: An American Saga of Courage.* New York: Vanguard,1943.

Fishgall, Gary. *Pieces of Time: The Life of James Stewart.* New York: Scribner, 1997.

"The Forest Situation in California." California Forestry Study Committee. 19 Oct. 2005. http://www.dharmacloud.com/jackson/histdocs/FORSIT.html.

Foster, Daniel G. and John Betts. *History of the CDF Archaeology Program 1970-2004.*
Section 8: "Voices." 19 Oct. 2005. <http://72.14.207.104/search?q=cache. VkC31UDHxA4J.www.indiana.edu/e472/cdf/history>.

"The Founding of a Robert Louis Stevenson Museum in St. Helena." *The Book Club of California Quarterly News-Letter* Sept. 1969: 84-88.

Fox, William L. and Mark Klett. *The Black Rock Desert.* Tucson: U of Arizona P, 2002.

Friesen, John W. and Virginia Lyons Friesen. *The Palgrave Companion to North American Utopias.* New York: Palgrave Macmillan, 2004.

Fulbright, Leslie and Meredith May. "Spreading the Flames." *San Francisco Chronicle* 29 May 2005: A1, A12-14.

Fussell, Paul. *Doing Battle: The Making of a Skeptic.* Boston: Little, Brown, 1996.

Gabrielson, Ira N. *Wildlife Conservation.* New York: Macmillan, 1941.

Gannett, Lewis. "Dramatic Roads to Far Places." Review of George R. Stewart, *N. A. 1. New York Herald Tribune Book Review* 22 Sept. 1957: 1.

Gardner, David P. *The California Oath Controversy.* Berkeley: U of California P, 1967.

Garrard, Greg. *Ecocriticism.* London: Routledge, 2004.

Gaziano, Emanuel. “Ecological Metaphors as Scientific Boundary Work: Innovation and Authority in Interwar Sociology and Biology.” *American Journal of Sociology* 101.4 (1996). 874-907.

“George R. Stewart Peak.” USGS GNIS (GNIS). 28 Dec. 2005. <http://geonames.usgs,Gov/pls/gnis/web_query.GetDetail?tab= Y&id=274661>.

Gilmore, George Gordon. Letter. *New York Times.* 8 Oct. 1944, 101.

Glacken, Clarence J. “Changing Ideas of the Habitable World.” *Man's Role in Changing the Face of the Earth.* Ed. William L. Thomas. Chicago: U of Chicago P, 1956. 70-92.

Glotz, G. *The Greek City and its Institutions.* New York: Knopf, 1930.

Gray, William. *Robert Louis Stevenson: A Literary Life.* London: Palgrave Macmillan, 2004.

Greeley, William B. *Forests and Men.* Garden City, NY: Doubleday, 1951.

Gross, Matthias. “Human Geography and Ecological Sociology: The Unfolding of a Human Ecology, 1890 to 1930—and Beyond.” *Social Science History* 28.4 (2004). 575-605.

Gummere, Francis. 1907. *The Popular Ballad.* New York: Dover, 1959.

Gunther, John. *Inside U. S. A.* Revised ed. New York: Harper, 1951.

Hamilton, Clayton. *On the Trail of Stevenson.* Garden City, NY: Doubleday, Page, 1915.

Hanson, John Wesley. *The American Italy: The Scenic Wonderland of Perfect Climate, Good Sunshine, Ever-blooming Flowers, and Always-ripening Fruits.* Chicago: W. B. Conkey, 1896.

Hagen, Joel B. *An Entangled Bank: The Origins of Ecosystem Ecology.* New Brunswick: Rutgers U P, 1992.

Hakel, Arthur. “Rise and Fall of a Greek City.” Review of George R. Stewart, *The Years of the City. Oakland Tribune* 4 Sept. 1955: n. pag.

Hardesty, Donald L. *et. al. The Archaeology of the Donner Party.* Reno: U of Nevada P, 1997.

- - -. *Ecological Anthropology.* New York: Wiley, 1977.

Hardie, Frances C. *Sewickley: A History of a Valley Community.* Pittsburgh: R. R. Donnelley Financial, 1998.

Harley, J. B. “The Map as Biography: Thoughts on Ordnance Survey Map, Six-inch Sheet Devonshire CIX, SE, Newton Abbot.” *The Map Collector* 41 (1987), 18-20.

Hawley, Ralph C. and Paul W. Stickel. *Forest Protection.* 2nd ed. New York: Wiley, 1948.

Hayden, Dolores. “What is Suburbia? Naming the Layers in the Landscape, 1820-2000.” *Taking Up Space: New Approaches to American History.* Ed. Anke Ortlepp and Christoph Ribbat. Trier: Wissenschafter Verlag, 2004. 1-20.

Heckman, Marlin. *Pasadena in Vintage Postcards.* Charleston, SC: Arcadia, 2001.

Hellman, George S. *The True Stevenson: A Study in Clarification.* 1925. New York: Haskell House, 1972.

Henty, G[eorge] A[lfred]. *Captain Bayley's Heir: A Tale of the Gold Fields of California.* London: Blackie, 1905 [?].

- - -, ed. *Famous Travels.* Boston: Hall and Locke, 1902.

- - -.*True to the Old Flag: A Tale of the American War of Independence.* New York: A. L. Burt, 1896.

- - -. *With Lee in Virginia: A Story of the American Civil War.* New York: A. L. Burt, N.D.

Hess, Earl J. *Pickett's Charge—the Last Attack at Gettysburg.* Chapel Hill: U of North Carolina P, 2001.

Hicks, Granville. "Civilization Destroyed." Review of George R. Stewart, *Earth Abides. New York Times Book Review* 23 Oct. 1949: 4.

Hinds, William Alfred. 1908. *American Communities and Cooperative Colonies.* 3rd ed. Philadelphia: Porcupine P, 1975.

Hine, Robert V. 1953. *California's Utopian Colonies.* New Haven: Yale U P, 1966.

Holder, Charles Frederick. *A Climatic Miracle in California.* Chicago: Passenger Department, Santa Fe Railroad, 1902.

Holmes, Rachel. "Reading Route Maps in United States Road Trip Books." *Studies in Travel Writing* 4 (2000). 165-183.

IMDb. "Red Skies of Montana." 18 Oct. 2005. <http://www.imdb.com/title/tt0045074/>

Ingerson, Alice E. "Tracking and Testing the Nature/Culture Dichotomy in Practice." *Historical Ecology: Cultural Knowledge and Changing Landscapes.* Ed. Carole L. Crumley. Santa Fe: School of American Research P, 1994. 43-66.

The Item Annual 18. Pasadena: Pasadena High School, 1913.

Jackson, John Brinckerhoff. *Discovering the Vernacular Landscape.* New Haven: Yale U P, 1984.

Jackson, Joseph Henry. 'Between the Lines." *San Francisco Chronicle—This World* 12 Mar. 1939: 20.

Jackson, Kenneth T. *Crabgrass Frontier: The Suburbanization of the United States.* New York: Oxford U P, 1985.

Jacobs, Jane. *The Death and Life of Great American Cities.* New York: Random, 1961.

- - -. "Downtown is for People." *The Exploding Metropolis.* Ed. The Editors of Fortune. Garden City, NY: Doubleday, 1957. 157-8.

Johnson, David A. "Vigilance and the Law: The Moral Authority of Popular Justice in the Far West." *American Quarterly* 33.5 (1981). 558-586.

K., I. L. "What Purpose Will Loyalty Oaths Serve?" *School and Society* 29 Oct. 1949: 283.

Kallen, Horace M. *Patterns of Progress.* New York: Columbia U P, 1950.

Kandel, I. L. "What Purpose Will Loyalty Oaths Serve?" *School and Society*

29 Oct. 1949: 283.
Kantor, Sybil Gordon. *Alfred H. Barr, Jr. and the Intellectual Origins of the Museum of Modern Art.* Cambridge: MIT P, 2002.
Keegan, John. *The Face of Battle.* New York: Penguin, 1976.
Kelly, Florence Finch. "The Tragic and Gruesome Story of the Donner Party." Review of George R. Stewart, *Ordeal by Hunger.* *New York Times Book Review* 26 Apr. 1936: 11.
Kerouac, Jack. 1957. *On the Road.* New York: Penguin, 1976.
Kerr, Clark. *The Gold and the Blue: A Personal Memoir of the University of California, 1949-1967.* 2 vols. Berkeley: U of California P, 2001.
Kiepert, Heinrich. *Atlas Antiquus.* Berlin: Dietrich Reimer, n.d.
King, Joseph A. *Winter of Entrapment: A New Look at the Donner Party.* 3rd ed. Lafayette, CA: K and K, 1998.
Kingsland, Sharon. *The Evolution of American Ecology, 1890-2000.* Baltimore: Johns Hopkins U P, 2005.
Kipling, Rudyard. "The Knife and the Naked Chalk." 1 Sept. 2005. <http://whitewolf.newcastle.edu.au/words/authors/K/KiplingRudyard/prose/RewardsFaries/. . .>.
Kittler, Friedrich A. "The City is a Medium." *New Literary History* 27.4 (1996). 717-29.
Kitto, H. D. F. *The Greeks.* London: Penguin, 1955.
Kolata, Gina. *Flu: The Story of the Great Influenza Pandemic of 1918 and the Search for the Virus that Caused It.* New York: Farrar, Straus, and Giroux, 1999.
Kovel, Joel. *The Enem y of Nature: The End o f Capitalism or the End of the World?* London; Zed, 2002.
Kroeber, Alfred L. *An Anthropologist Looks at History.* Ed. Theodora Kroeber. Berkeley: U of California P, 1963.
- - -. *Configurations of Culture Change.* Berkeley: U of California P, 1944.
- - -. *The Nature of Culture.* Chicago: U of Chicago P, 1952.
Kroeber, Karl. *Ecological Literary Criticism: Romantic Imagining and the Biology of Mind.* New York: Columbia U P, 1994.
- - - and Clifton Kroeber, eds. *Ishi in Three Centuries.* Lincoln: U of Nebraska P, 2003.
Kurushima, Hidesaburo. *U.S.A. Through Window s of Planes and Buses.* n.p. Japan: n.p., 1953.
Lamprecht, Sterling P. *Nature and History.* New York: Columbia U P, 1950.
Langellier, John P. "Introduction." McGlashan, C. F. 1880. *History of the Donner Party: A Tragedy of the Sierra.* New York: Barnes and Noble, 2004. ix-xiv.
Lattimore, Owen. *Ordeal by Slander.* Boston: Little, Brown, 1950.
Laxalt, Robert. *Dust Devils.* Reno: U of Nevada P, 1997.
Leake, Chauncey B. and Patrick Romanell. *Can We Agree?: A Scientist and a Philosopher Argue About Ethics.* Austin: U of Texas P, 1950.

Lear, Linda. *Rachel Carson: Witness for Nature*. New York: Holt, 1997.

Lee, Rose Hum. *The City: Urbanism and Urbanization in Major World Regions*. Philadelphia: Lippincott, 1955.

Lehman, Benjamin. *Wild Marriage*. New York: Harper, 1925.

Leider, Emily Wortis. *California's Daughter: Gertrude Atherton and Her Times.* Stanford: Stanford U P, 1991.

Leopold, Aldo. *For the Health of the Land: Previously Unpublished Essays and Other Writings.* Ed. J. Baird Callicott and Eric T. Freyfogle. Washington: Island P, 1999.

- - -. 1948. *A Sand County Almanac.* New York: Ballantine, 1978.

Leopold, A[ldo] Starker and the Editors of Time-Life Books. *The Desert.* Revised ed. New York: Time-Life Books, 1969.

Leopold, Luna B. "Land Use and Sediment Yield." *Man's Role in Changing the Face of the Earth.* Ed. William L. Thomas. Chicago: U of Chicago P, 1956. 639-647.

Levin, David R. "The Highway and Land Use." *Highways in Our National Life: A Symposium.* Ed. Jean Labatut and Wheaton J. Lane. Princeton: Princeton U. P., 1950. 268-276.

Lewis, Corey Lee. *Reading the Trail: Exploring the Literary and Natural History of the California Crest.* Reno: U of Nevada P, 2005.

Lillard, Richard G. *Desert Challenge: An Interpretation of Nevada.* New York: Knopf, 1949.

Limerick, Patricia. "Disorientation and Reorientation: The American Landscape Discovered from the West." *Journal of American History* 79.3 (1992). 1021-1049.

- - -. "Making the Most of Words: Verbal Activity and Western America." *Under an Open Sky: Rethinking America's Western Past.* Ed. William Cronon *et. al.* New York: Norton, 1992. 167-184.

- - -. *Something in the Soil: Legacies and Reckonings in the New West.* New York: Norton, 2000.

Lincoln Highway Association. *The Lincoln Highway: The Story of a Crusade that Made Transportation History.* New York: Dodd, Mead, 1935.

Linzell, S. O. and H. D. Metcalf. "Maintenance of the Highway." *Highways in our National Life: A Symposium,* Ed. Jean Labatut and Wheaton J. Lane. Princeton: Princeton U. P., 1950. 347-355.

Lofts, Norah. *Winter Harvest.* Garden City, NY: Doubleday, 1955.

Lott, Milton. *The Last Hunt.* Boston: Houghton, Mifflin, 1955.

Love, Glen A. *Practical Ecocriticism: Literature, Biology, and the Environment.* Charlottesville: U P of Virginia, 2003.

Lowie, Robert H. *Culture and Ethnology.* New York: Peter Smith, 1929.

- - -. *An Introduction to Cultural Anthropology.* New York: Farrar and Rinehart, 1934.

- - -.1927. *The Origin of the State.* New York: Russell and Russell, 1962.

Lynch, Kevin. *The Image of the City.* Cambridge: MIT P, 1960.

Lyons, John O. *The College Novel in America.* Carbondale: Southern Illinois U P, 1962.

M., N. B. "Cataclysm as Symbol." Rev. of *Fire,* by George R. Stewart. *Oakland Tribune.* 11 Apr. 1948. n. pag.

MacBridge, Roger Lea. *West From Home: Letters of Laura Ingalls Wilder to Almanzo Wilder, San Francisco 1915.* New York: Harper & Row, 1974.

MacDonald, Francis C. "Doctor's Oral." Review of George R. Stewart, *Doctor's Oral. Princeton Alumni Weekly* 10 Nov. 1939: 157.

McGlashan, Charles F. 1879. *History of the Donner Party: A Tragedy of the Sierra.* New York: Barnes and Noble, 2004.

Manchester, William. *The City of Anger.* Boston: Little, Brown, 1953.

Marks, Percy. *Which Way Parnassus?* New York: Harcourt Brace, 1926.

Marmounier, Mark. *How to Lie With Maps.* Chicago: U of Chicago P, 1991.

Marshall, Robert. "The Problem of Wilderness." *Scientific Monthly* Feb. 1930: 141-48.

Martin, Thomas S. *Greening the Past: Towards a Social-Ecological Analysis of History.* San Francisco: International Scholars, 1998.

Martindale, Don. "Prefatory Remarks: *The Theory of the City.*" Weber, Max. 1925. *The City.* Ed. Robert Park *et. al.* Chicago: U of Chicago P, 1968. 63-79.

Mavity, Nancy Barr. "Best-Selling U. C. Professor Strays from Cloistered Path." *Oakland Tribune* 11 Apr. 1948: n. pag.

McCabe, W. Michael. "Donora Disaster was Crucible for Clean Air." Pennsylvania Department of Environmental Protection. 14 Jan. 2005. <http://www.dep.state.pa.us/dep/Rachel_Carson/crucible.htm>

McCulloch, Alan. *Highway Forty.* Melbourne: F. W. Cheshire, 1951.

Meeker, Joseph. *The Comedy of Survival: Studies in Literary Ecology.* New York: Scribner, 1974.

Meine, Curt. *Aldo Leopold: His Life and Work.* Madison: U of Wisconsin P, 1988.

Merchant, Carolyn. *The Death of Nature: Women, Ecology, and the Scientifi c Revolution.* San Francisco: Harper, 1980.

Metropolis. New York: Ford Foundation, 1957.

Miles, Alfred H. *Natural History in Anecdote . . .* New York: Dodd, Mead, 1895.

Mizener, Arthur. *The Far Side of Paradise: A Biography of F. Scott Fitzgerald.* Boston: Houghton Mifflin, 1951.

Moore, Jerry D. *Visions of Culture: An Introduction to Anthropological Theories and Theorists.* 2nd ed. Walnut Creek, CA: AltaMira P, 2004.

Morrissey, Charles T. "An Examination of Pickett's Historic Infantry Charge." Review of George R. Stewart, *Pickett's Charge. Oakland Tribune* 25 Oct. 1959: n.p.

Mumford, Lewis. *The City in History: Its Origins, Its Transformations, and Its Prospects.* New York: Harcourt, Brace, and World, 1961.

- - -. *The Condition of Man.* 2nd ed. New York: Harcourt Brace Jovano-

vich, 1973.
- - -. *The Culture of Cities*. New York: Harcourt, Brace, 1938.
- - -. "The Human Prospect and Architecture." Mumford, Lewis. *Architecture as a Home for Man: Essays for Architectural Record.* Ed. Jeanne M. Davon. New York: Architectural Record Books, 1975. 207-209.
- - -. "The Natural History of Urbanization." *Man's Role in Changing the Face of the Earth.* Ed. William L. Thomas. Chicago: U of Chicago P, 1956. 382-400.
- - -. *The Urban Prospect.* New York: Harcourt, Brace, and World, 1968.
Murphy, Robert F. "Introduction: The Anthropological Theories of Julian H. Steward." *Evolution and Ecology: Essays on Social Transformation by Julian H. Steward.* Ed. Jane C. Steward and Robert F. Murphy. Urbana: U of Illinois P, 1977. 1-40.
"Names on the Land by George R.Stewart." Stewart, George R. *Names on the Land.* n.p.: Editions for the Armed Services, Inc., 1945.
Nash, Roderick. *The Rights of Nature: A History of Environmental Ethics.* Madison: U of Wisconsin P, 1989.
Neimark, Peninah and Peter R. Mott, eds. *The Environmental Debate: A Documentary History.* Westport CT: Greenwood, 1999.
Neuberger, Richard L. "Lone Women of the Mountains." *New York Times Magazine* 15 June 1947: 26.
Nisbet, Robert. *Teachers and Scholars: A Memoir of Berkeley in Depression and War.* New Brunswick, NJ: Transaction, 1992.
"Now Come On With Your Street Cars." *Indiana Gazette* 20 Feb. 1906: 1.

"1938: Literature, American." 12 June 2005. <http://encart.msn.com/sidebar_461500035/1938_Literature_American. html>.
Nissen, Axel. *Bret Harte: Prince and Pauper.* Oxford: U of Mississippi P, 2000.
Norgaard, Richard B. "A Coevolutionary Environmental Sociology." Redcliffe, Michael and Graham Woodgate, eds. *The International Handbook of Environmental Sociology.* Northampton MA: Edward Elgar, 12997. 158-68.
Norris, Frank. *The Octopus*. 1901. New York: Airmont, 1969.
Norton, William. *Explorations in the Understanding of Landscape: A Cultural Geography.* Westport, CT: Greenwood P, 1989.
"Old Aurora Colony." 2 Oct. 2005. http://www.robinwill.com/aur.html.
Paradise Ridge: Byck Family Estate. "Nagasawa Historical Exhibit." 2 Oct. 2005. http://www.paradiseridgewinery.com/nagasawa.html.
"Paint Your Wagon." 17 July 2005. http://wikipedia.org/wiki/Paint_Your_Wagon.
Park, Robert E. *Human Communities: The City and human Ecology.* Glencoe, IL: Free P, 1952.
Parke, John. "Seven Moby-Dicks." *New England Quarterly* 28.3 (1955). 319-338.

"Parks, Recreation, and Waterfront." 7 Nov. 2005. <http://www.ci.berkeley.ca.us/parks/parkspages/Codornices.html>.

Passmore, David. G. "Battlefields." *Patterned Ground: Entanglements of Nature And Culture.* Ed Stephan Harrison *et. al.* London: Reaktion Books, 2004. 96-98.

Pattee, Fred Lewis. Review of George R. Stewart, *Bret Harte: Argonaut and Exile. American Literature* 4.2 (1932). 223-224.

Patterson, Thomas C. "Toward a Properly Historical Ecology." *Historical Ecology: Cultural Knowledge and Changing Landscapes.* Ed. Carole L. Crumley. Santa Fe: School of American Research P, 1994. 223-238.

Paulson, William. "Literature, Knowledge, and Cultural Ecology." *Sub-stance* 22.2-3 (1993). 27-37.

Payne, Daniel G. *Voices in the Wilderness: American Nature Writing and Environmental Politics.* Hanover: U P of New England, 1996.

Peace, William J. *Leslie A. White: Evolution and Revolution in Anthropology.* Lincoln: U of Nebraska P, 2004.

Peattie, Donald Culross. *The Road of a Naturalist.* Boston: Houghton Mifflin, 1941.

"Port Huron Statement." 24 Nov. 2005. http://lists.village.virginia.edu/sixties/HTML.

Peters, Jeffrey N. "The Cartographic Eye/I: Champlain and the Uses of Early Modern Geographic Discourse." *Genre* 30 (1997). 79-104.

Phillips, Dana. *The Truth of Ecology: Nature, Culture, and Literature in America.* New York: Oxford, 2003.

Pound, Louise. *Poetic Origins and the Ballad.* 1921. New York: Russell and Russell, 1962.

Powell, Marian. "Apocalypse Then: Earth Abides by George R. Stewart." Strange Horizons. 24 Oct. 2005. <http://www.strangehorizons.com/2004/20041018/earthabides-r.shtml>.

Prescott, Orville. "Books of the Times." Review of George R. Stewart, *Earth Abides. New York Times* 16 Dec. 1949: 29.

"Princeton During World War I." Seeley G. Mudd Library. 26 July 2005. <http://www.Princeton.edu/mudd/news/faq/topics/WW1.shtml>.

Pyne, Stephen J. "Green Skies of Montana." *Forest History Today.* Spring, 2000. 37-8.

Raisz, Erwin. *Principles of Cartography.* New York: McGraw-Hill, 1962.

Reardon, Carol. "Pickett's Charge: the Convergence of History and Myth in the Southern Past." *The Third Day at Gettysburg and Beyond.* Ed. Gary Gallagher. Chapel Hill: U of North Carolina P, 1994. 56-92.

- - -. *Pickett's Charge in History and Memory.* Chapel Hill: U of North Carolina P, 1997.

Reck, Franklin M. "The Great Transformation." *American Highways Today.* Ed. Poyntz Tyler. New York: H. W. Wilson, 1957. 20-42.

Redman, Ben Ray. "'Of Major Stature. . .'" Review of George R. Stewart, *East*

of the Giants. Saturday Review 1 Oct. 1938: 5.
Resources for the Future, Inc. *The Nation Looks at its Resources: Report of the Mid-Century Conference on Resources for the Future.* Washington: G PO, 1953.
Restoring the Quality of Our Environment: Report of the Environmental Pollution Panel, President's Science Advisory Committee. Washington: GPO, 1965.
Reynolds, Horace. "The Naming of a Land." Review of George R. Stewart, *Names on the Land. Saturday Review* 6 June 1945: 10.
Riemer, Svend. *The Modern City: An Introduction to Urban Sociology.* New York: Prentice-Hall, 1952.
Robbins, Jhan. *Everybody's Man: A Biography of Jimmy Stewart.* New York: Putnam, 1985.
Rosendale, Steven. "Introduction: Extending Ecocriticism." *The Greening of Literary Scholarship: Literature, Theory, and the Environment.* Ed. Steven Rosendale. Iowa City: U of Iowa P, 2002. xv-xxix.
Ross, Andrew. "The Social Claim on Urban Ecology." *The Nature of Cities: Ecocriticism and Urban Environments.* Ed. Michael Bennett and David Teague. Tucson: U of Arizona P, 1999. 15-32.
Roszak, Theodore. *The Voice of the Earth: An Exploration of Ecopsychology.* New York: Simon and Schuster, 1992.
Rotella, Carlo. *October Cities: The Redevelopment of Urban Literature.* Berkeley: U of California P, 1998.
Rozelle, Lee. "Ecocritical City: Modernist Reactions to Urban Environments in *Miss Lonelyhearts* and *Paterson.*" *Twentieth-Century Literature* 48.1 (2002). 100-115.
"Ryan." Posting 17 Mar. 2002 [Charles Camp]. 14 Oct. 2005. <http://2thinkforms.org/anyboard/archive/4672.html>.
Sale, Kirkpatrick. *The Green Revolution: The American Environmental Movement, 1962-92.* New York: Hill and Wang, 1993.
Sallis, James. "Stewart's Dark Eulogy for Humankind." *Boston Globe* 16 Feb. 2003: E9.24 Oct. 2005. http://nl.newsbank.com/nl-search/we/Archives?p_action=print.
Saposnik, Irving S. *Robert Louis Stevenson.* New York: Twayne, 1974.
Sauer, Carl O. 1952. *Agricultural Origins and Dispersals: The Domestication of Animals and Foodstuffs.* Cambridge: MIT P, 1969.
- - -. *Land and Life: A Selection from the Writings of Carl Ortwin Sauer.* Ed. John Leighley. Berkeley: U of California P, 1963.
- - -. "Retrospect." *Man's Role in Changing the Face of the Earth.* Ed. William L. Thomas. Chicago: U of Chicago P, 1956. 1131-1135.
Scharnhorst, Gary. *Bret Harte: Opening the American Literary West.* Norman: U of Oklahoma P, 2000.
Schlereth, Thomas J. *Reading the Road: U.S. 40 and the American Landscape.* Knoxville: U of Tennessee P, 1997.

Schnore, Leo F. "Geography and Human Ecology." *Economic Geography* 37.3 (1961). 207-217.
Schrecker, Ellen W. *No Ivory Tower: McCarthyism and the Universities.* New York: Oxford, 1986.
Science Fiction Creators. "Escape Radio Log." 12 Dec. 2005. <http://ubots.com/radio/otr_escape.shtml>.
Sellars, Richard West. *Preserving Nature in the National Parks: A History.* New Haven: Yale U P, 1997.
Shade, D. D. Review of George R. Stewart, *Earth Abides.* "Lost Books." 24 Oct. 2005. http://lostbooks.org/reviews/1998-06-11.html.
Shafer, Robert. *The Conquered Place.* New York: Putnam, 1954.
Sheibach, Michael. *Atomic Narratives and American Youth: Coming of Age with the Atom, 1945-55.* Jefferson, NC: McFarland, 2003.
Shiel, M. P. Review of George R. Stewart, *Earth Abides.* SF Site. 24 Oct. 2005. <http://www.sfsite.com/11a/ea92.htm>
Shields, James and Leonard Weinberg. "Reactive Violence and the American Frontier: A Contemporary Evaluation." *Western Political Quarterly* 29.1 (1976). 86-101.
Showalter, Elaine. *Faculty Towers: The Academic Novel and its Discontents.* Philadelphia: U of Pennsylvania P, 2005.
Sibley, David. *Geographies of Exclusion: Society and Difference in the West.* New York: Routledge, 1995.
Sinclair, Upton. *The Goose-Step: A Study in American Education.* Pasadena, CA: Upton Sinclair, 1923.
Smith, Henry Nash. *Virgin Land: The American West as Symbol and Myth.* Cambridge: Harvard U P, 1950.
Smucker, John. "The History of the United States Army Ambulance Service 1917-19."10 Sep. 2005. <http://www.ku.edu/carrie/specoll/AFS/library/2-ww1/Smucker/isasc01/htm>.
Snow, C. P. "The Two Cultures." Current Issues in Biological Science. 15 Nov. 2005. http://info.med.yale.edu/therearad/summers/snow.htm.
Snyder, Gary. "Finding the place in the Heart." *Wild Nevada: Testimonies on Behalf of the Desert.* Ed. Roberta Moore and Scott Slovic. Reno: U of Nevada P, 2005. 20-24.
Southworth, Samuel Seaman. *California for Fruit-growers and Consumptives: Health, Profits, and Drawbacks.* Sacramento: S. S. Southworth, 1883.
Spaeth, J. Duncan. "Biography of Bret Harte." Review of George R. Stewart, *Bret Harte: Argonaut and Exile. Princeton Alumni Weekly* 5 Feb. 1932: n. pag.
Spengler, Oswald. 1932. *Man and Technics: A Contribution to a Philosophy of Life.* Trans. Charles Francis Atkinson. Westport, CT: Greenwood, 1976.
Spoehr, Alexander. "Cultural Differences in the Interpretation of Natural Resources." *Man's Role in Changing the Face of the Earth.* Ed. William

L. Thomas. Chicago: U of Chicago P, 1956. 93-102.
Springer, Thomas Grant. *The Californian: A Romance of the Last Frontier.* New York: Blue Ribbon Books, 1936.
Starr, Kevin. *Americans and the California Dream, 1850-1915.* New York: Oxford U P, 1973.
Stegner, Wallace and the editors of *Look. One Nation.* Boston: Houghton Mifflin, 1945.
Stegner, Wallace. *Beyond the Hundredth Meridian: John Wesley Powell and the Second Opening of the West.* Boston: Houghton, Mifflin
- - -. "Foreword." Stewart, George R. 1941. *Storm.* Lincoln: U of Nebraska P, 1983. vii-x.
- - -. *Where the Bluebird Sings to the Lemonade Springs: Living and Writing in the West.* New York: Random, 1992.
Steinbeck, John. *The Grapes of Wrath.* 1940. New York: Penguin, 2002.
Steward, Julian H. *Evolution and Ecology.* Urbana: U of Illinois P, 1977.
- - -. "The Foundations of Basin-Plateau Shoshonean Society." *Evolution and Ecology: Essays on Social Transformation by Julian H. Steward.* Ed. Jane C. Steward and Robert F. Murphy. Urbana: U of Illinois P, 1977. 366-406.
- - -. *Theory of Culture Change: The Methodolgy of Multilinear Evolution.* Urbana: U of Illinois P, 1963.
Stewart, Bob. "Desert Tested Resources, Endurance of Emigrants." *Nevada Sage* May 2001: 1, 8-9.
Stilgoe, John R. *Borderland: Origins of the American Suburb, 1820-1939.* New Haven: Yale U P, 1988.
Still, Henry. *The Dirty Animal.* New York: Hawthorne Books, 1967.
Smucker, John. "The History of the United States Army Ambulance Service." 10 Sept. 2005. <http://www.ku.edu/carrie/specoll/AFS/library/2-wwl/Smucker/usaac01.html>.
Stone, Edward. "Moby Dick and Shakespeare: A Remonstrance." *Shakespeare Quarterly* 7.4 (1956). 445-448.
Stone, Irving. *Pageant of Youth.* New York: Alfred H. King, 1933.
- - -,ed. *There was Light: Autobiography of a University: Berkeley, 1868-1968.* Garden City, NY: Doubleday, 1970.
- - -. "Twisted Arms Among the Ivy." Review of George R. Stewart, *The Year of the Oath. Saturday Review* 30 Sept. 1950: +12.
Strankman, Gary. "The Power of Names." *Ishi in Three Centuries.* Ed. Karl Kroeber and Clifton Kroeber. Lincoln: U of Nebraska P, 2003. 359-362.
Strohmaier, David. "Threescore and Ten; Fire, Place, and Loss in theWest." *Ethics and Environment* 8.2 (2003). 31-41.
Swados, Harvey, ed. *The American Writer and the Great Depression.* New York: Bobbs-Merrill, 1966.
T., H. H. "The Screen in Review." *New York Times,* 22 May 1952. 9.

Tansley, Arthur. "International Phytogeographical Excursion (I.P.E.) in America, 1913." *The New Phytologist* 12. 9-10 (1913): 322-26; 13 (1914): 30-41.

Taylor, Benjamin F. *Between the Gates.* 5th ed. Chicago: S.C. Griggs, 1879.

Taylor, Robert Lewis. *Adrift in a Boneyard.* Garden City, NY: Doubleday, 1947.

Tesh, Sylvia. *Uncertain Hazards: Environmental Activists and Scientific Proof.* Ithaca: Cornell U P, 2000.

Thomas, John L. *A Country in the Mind: Wallace, Stegner, Bernard DeVoto, History, and the American Land.* New York: Routledge, 2000.

Thomas, William L. "Introductory." *Man's Role in Changing the Face of the Earth.* Ed. William L. Thomas. Chicago: U of Chicago P, 1956. xxii-xxxvii.

Thucydides. Trans. Benjamin Jowett. Boston: Lothrop, 1883.

Truman, Benjamin Cummings. *Homes and Happiness in the Golden State of California. . .* 3rd ed. San Francisco: H. S. Crocker, 1885.

Tuan, Yi-Fu. "Home." *Patterned Ground: Entanglements of Nature and Culture.* Ed. Stephan Harrison *et. al.* London: Reaktion Books, 2004. 164-166.

Tucker, Glenn. *High Tide at Gettysburg.* Indianapolis: Bobbs-Merrill, 1958.

Tucker, Wilson. *The Long Loud Silence.* New York: Rinehart, 1952.

Tunnard, Christopher. *The City of Man.* New York: Scribner, 1953.

Udall, Stewart. "Pollution and Blight." Review of George R. Stewart, *Not So Rich As You Think. New York Times Book Review* 4 Feb. 1968: 10.

- - -. *The Quiet Crisis.* New York: Avon, 1964.

University of California, Berkeley. *General Catalogue, 1934-35.* Berkeley: U of California, 1934.

"The University Loyalty Oath: a 50th Anniversary Retrospective." 12 June 2005. <http://sunsite.berkeley.edu/uchistory/archives_exhibits /loyltyoath/symposium/timeline/>

Proceedings of the Board of Regents (1837-2000). University of Michigan. 14 June 2005.<http://www.hti.umich.edu/cgi/t/text/pagevieweridx? sid=b690991f57dbe3bdd874ac415da9 . . .>

Vale, Thomas R. and Geraldine R. Vale. *U.S. 40 Today: Thirty Years of Landscape Change in America.* Madison: U of Wisconsin P, 1983.

van Gelder, Robert. "An Interview with George R. Stewart." *New York Times Book Review* 14 Dec. 1941: 2, 31.

Van Noy, Rick. *Surveying the Interior: Literary cartography and the Sense of Place.* Reno: U of Nevada P, 2003.

Vickery, Olga. "*The Sound and the Fury*: A Study in Perspective." *PMLA* 69.5 (1954). 1017-1037.

Vizenor, Gerald. "Mister Ishi: Analogies of Exile, Deliverance, and Liberty." *Ishi in Three Centuries.* Ed. Karl Kroeber and Clifton Kroeber. Lincoln: U of Nebraska P, 2003. 363-72.

Vogt, William. *Road to Survival.* New York: William Sloane, 1948.

Waage, Melissa. Interview with the author. 24 Dec. 2005.

Wallis, W. D. "Geographical Environment and Culture. *Social Forces* 4.4 (1926). 702-708.

Warner, Charles Dudley. *Our Italy*. New York: Harper, 1891.

Watson, Matthew A. "The Argonauts of '49: Class, Gender, and Partnership in Bret Harte's West." *Western American Literature* 40.1 (2005), 33-54.

Waugh, John C. *The Class of 1846: From West Point to Appomattox: Stonewall Jackson and their Brothers*. New York: Random, 1994.

Wecter, Dixon. "Commissars of Loyalty." *Saturday Review* 13 May 1950: 8-11.

Weiler, A. H. "Trail of Trial." *New York Times* 29 Nov. 1964: X11.

Weimer, David. *The City as Metaphor*. New York: Random, 1966.

Wells, A. J. *California for the Settler: The Natural Advantages of the Golden State for the Present-day Farmer*. San Francisco: Southern Pacific Company, 1914.

Wert, Jeffry. *Gettysburg: Day Three*. New York: Simon and Schuster, 2001.

Wheeler, Elizabeth A. *Uncontained: Urban Fiction in Postwar America*. New Brunswick: Rutgers U P, 2001.

Wheeler, Sessions S. *The Nevada Desert*. Caldwell, ID: Caxton, 1971.

White, Theodore H. "Where Are Those New Roads?" *Colliers* 6 Jan. 1956: 45-51.

Williams, James Thaxter. *The History of Weather*. Commack, NY: Nova Science, 1999.

Williams, Michael. "The Relations of Environmental History and Historical Geography." *Journal of Historical Geography* 20.1 (1994). 3-21.

Williams, Raymond. 1958. *Culture and Society, 1780-1950*. New York: Harper, 1966.

Winter, Deborah DuNann. *Ecological Psychology: Healing the Split Between Planet and Self*. New York: HarperCollins, 1996.

Wolfe, Gary K. "The Remaking of Zero: Beginning at the End." *The End of the World*. Ed. Gary S. Rabkin *et. al.* Carbondale: Southern Illinois U P, 1983: 1-19.

Wood, Karen and Doug McGregor. *Indiana, Pennsylvania*. Charleston, SC: Arcadia, 2002.

Worster, Donald. "Appendix: Doing Environmental History." *The Ends of the Earth: Perspectives on Modern Envrionmental History*. Ed. Donald Worster. New York: Cambridge U P, 1988. 289-308.

- - -. *Nature's Economy: The Roots of Ecology*. San Francisco: Sierra Club Books, 1977.

- - -. "The Vulnerable Earth: A Planetary History." *The Ends of the Earth: Perspectives on Modern Environmental History*. Ed. Donald Worster. New York: Cambridge U P, 1988. 3-22.

Wright, Corinne King. *Cold Embers: A Romance of Old California*. Los Angeles: Wetzel, 1931.

Wright, Frank Lloyd. *The Living City*. New York: Horizon, 1958.

Yardley, Jonathan. "Hornblower, Still Under Full Sail. *Washington Post*. 26

Dec. 2005. http://www.washigtonpost.com/wpdyn/content/article/2005 /12/25/AR2005122500712_. . .>.

Zapf, Hubert. "Literature as Cultural Ecology: Notes Towards a Functional Theory of Imaginative Texts with Examples from American Literature." *Yearbook of Research in English and American Literature* 17 (2001). 85-100.

Zimmerer, Karl S. "Human Geography and the 'New Ecology:' The Prospect and Promise of Integration." *Annals of the Association of American Geographers* 84.1 (1994). 108-125.

Zimmerman, Carle C. "The Highway from the Point of View of a Sociologist." *Highways in Our National Life: A Symposium*. Ed. Jean Labatut and Wheaton J. Lane. Princeton: Princeton U P, 1950. 123-134.

Index

O